Daring to be Free

SUDHIR HAZAREESINGH

Daring to be Free

Rebellion and Resistance of the
Enslaved in the Atlantic World

ALLEN LANE
an imprint of
PENGUIN BOOKS

ALLEN LANE

UK | USA | Canada | Ireland | Australia
India | New Zealand | South Africa

Allen Lane is part of the Penguin Random House group of companies
whose addresses can be found at global.penguinrandomhouse.com

Penguin Random House UK
One Embassy Gardens, 8 Viaduct Gardens, London SW11 7BW

penguin.co.uk

Penguin
Random House
UK

First published 2025
001

Set in 10.2/13.5 pt Sabon LT Std
Typeset by Jouve (UK), Milton Keynes
Printed and bound in Great Britain by Clays Ltd, Elcograf S.p.A.

The authorized representative in the EEA is Penguin Random House Ireland,
Morrison Chambers, 32 Nassau Street, Dublin D02 YH68

A CIP catalogue record for this book is available from the British Library

ISBN: 978-0-241-60650-6

Penguin Random House is committed to a sustainable future
for our business, our readers and our planet. This book is made from
Forest Stewardship Council® certified paper.

MIX
Paper | Supporting
responsible forestry
FSC® C018179

For Karma

who always lives free

Freedom does not fall from the sky, and it is never completely granted, but taken and conquered.

Aimé Césaire

Contents

List of Illustrations

A Note on Terminology

Linguistic conventions on the subject of slavery have been evolving in recent times, and it will be helpful to set out the approach I have adopted in this book. The most important is the consistent use of the word 'enslaved' rather than 'slave'. This is in line with the emerging consensus that 'slave' is now understood as a derogatory term. The legitimacy of enslavement was not accepted by those upon whom it was inflicted. The term 'slave' was used by those who upheld and profited from the system. Moreover, enslavement was not a choice, and therefore cannot be implicitly likened to an occupation, such as being a labourer or carpenter. It was a coercive condition, forced upon men, women and children from the moment they were seized and traded in their African homelands. This bodily subjugation, maintained by a violent system of repression, is better reflected by the term 'enslaved'.

Incarceration was another significant dimension of the experience of enslavement, which I have tried to reflect in the use of 'captive' as a synonym for 'enslaved'. I sometimes use the terms 'human bondage' and 'bonded labour' (we could also say 'kidnapped Africans' or 'victims of forced migration'). However, no concept is perfect. While all these terms rightly shift the focus from the victims to the perpetrators, none truly capture another key aspect of Atlantic slavery, namely that the enslaved were considered property. This legal fiction, which turned the enslaved into commodities, was at the heart of the system of Atlantic chattel slavery. It enabled human beings to be bought and sold, denied any civil or political rights, and listed in legal and administrative records alongside buildings, valuable objects and animals – often without even mentioning their names. This dehumanization continued through the formal abolitions of the nineteenth century, when slavers received substantial financial compensation for their property losses. Hence my avoidance of the term 'slave-owner', which implicitly legitimizes this property relationship. I have chosen instead to refer to such people as 'slavers' or 'enslavers'.

Equally pejorative are the notions of 'witchcraft' and 'sorcery', which were the standard expressions used to refer to the captives' healing and spiritual activities. These terms were produced against a cultural and religious backdrop that represented Christianity as the civilized norm, and all other forms of religious belief (particularly originating from Africa) as barbaric. I have retained the terms 'witchcraft' and 'sorcery' when quoting from historical sources. But although they are still sometimes used in contemporary scholarship, I have concluded that they are debased. So when referring to these activities in my own analyses I have preferred to describe them positively, for what they were: expressions of African (and African-originating) religious and spiritual beliefs and practices. Those who carried them out were priests and priestesses. These men and women had often undergone years of training in a range of specialized skills. These could include the invocation of gods and spirits through prayer and bodily possession, and acts of curing, healing and divination, as well as casting spells, and providing protection from harm. As we shall see throughout this book, these spiritual intermediaries were frequently involved in the organization of revolts and insurrections.

The basic point arising from all these considerations is that the language of slavery was itself a form of power, which sought to dispossess the captives of their dignity and self-worth. Its terms, codes, and conventions expressed a racialized vision of society shaped by colonial and imperial prejudices about non-white people. In the twenty-first century such racist assumptions are no longer acceptable, and so our language needs to readjust. This is particularly the case with racial terminology. I do not use words such as 'negro' (except when quoting historical sources) and have replaced 'mulatto' and all similarly derogatory expressions about mixed-race people with the term 'people of colour', adapted from the United States (where it has a somewhat wider meaning).

At the same time a sensible balance should be struck to maintain the narrative's historical authenticity. For this reason I have kept 'slave' when quoting from original sources, and held on to such well-known terms as 'slave trade' and 'slave ship', as well as more specific repressive functions within the system, such as 'slave driver', 'slave raider', 'slave breaker', and 'slave hunter'. This is partly because there are no obvious alternatives, and partly because such terms more effectively convey the brutality of enslavement. 'Slave narrative' is more complicated but I have ended up keeping it, mainly because it is a recognized literary genre, at least in the Anglo-American world, and there is no elegant alternative.

In some instances, all available terms come with disadvantages, or there is not yet a consensus about their usage – so I have used them interchangeably. This is the case with 'maroon', 'runaway', and 'fugitive'. 'Maroon' is a word derived from a widely used pejorative Spanish term that likened escaped captives to stray cattle. But despite these origins it acquired positive connotations and was used by the enslaved as a badge of honour. The term continues to be deployed across the contemporary Atlantic by descendants of the enslaved to celebrate figures who resisted their captivity.

Both 'runaway' and 'fugitive' implicitly ascribe a sense of impropriety to the act of escaping. In reality it was the laws sanctioning enslavement that were illegitimate. For this reason, some believe we should embrace the term 'fugitive', as it draws attention to the carceral dimension of enslavement, and the wider disconnection between law and morality in the period of slavery. Others distinguish between fugitivity as a more individualistic form of flight, and marronage as an embrace of general freedom, in which the enslaved escaped to form independent groups and communities.

While captives acquired fluency in European languages, they spoke to each other for the most part in African languages and *kreyol* dialects, which have left few traces in the archive. This again highlights that the way in which the enslaved imagined and ordered their universe was different from that of their oppressors. I have managed to reflect this contrast in one important respect. Escaped captives who organized to defend themselves against slavers, and carried out attacks against their material interests, often described themselves as warriors, generals, captains, chiefs, soldiers, and combatants. I have used this military terminology in many places, in particular in the frequent instances where the authorities themselves referred to their conflicts with the captives as a 'war'. However, I do not think we should describe all forms of resistance as acts of war; that would stretch the concept too far. Resistance was a spectrum, in which military and insurgent action was a significant component. But this opposition could appear in a host of other social, cultural, religious, and intellectual ways.

In the ongoing search for precise terminology, one issue centres around the term 'abolitionism'. In conventional usage, white campaigners against slavery in Europe and the United States are described as abolitionists, even though for many of them the primary objective in the eighteenth and nineteenth century was the abolition of the slave trade, and not slavery itself. Indeed, many were adamantly opposed to the immediate ending of human bondage. We still call these figures 'abolitionists', and I have followed this convention. The true abolitionists were the enslaved men and women in Africa and the Americas who refused their domination and fought for their freedom. While referring to them as revolutionaries, rebels, insurgents, and conspirators, I have ended up identifying them as 'black abolitionists'. This serves to reinforce one of the book's principal goals: to recover and foreground long-erased black voices and perspectives from the story of enslaved resistance.

S. H.

December 2024

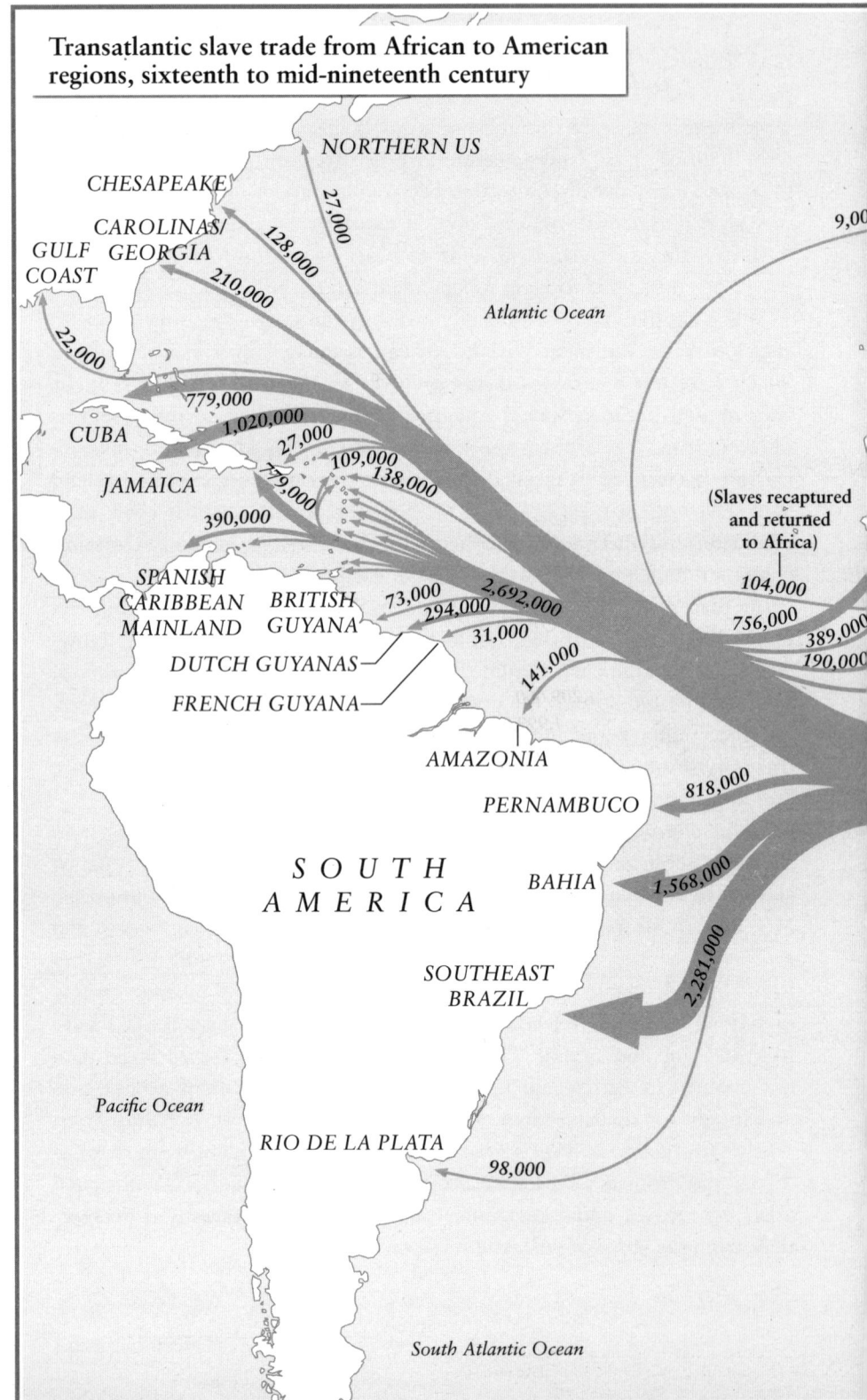

Transatlantic slave trade from African to American regions, sixteenth to mid-nineteenth century

NORTHERN US

CHESAPEAKE

CAROLINAS/
GULF   GEORGIA
COAST

Atlantic Ocean

27,000

128,000

210,000

22,000

9,00[0]

779,000

1,020,000

CUBA

27,000

109,000

JAMAICA

138,000

779,000

390,000

(Slaves recaptured
and returned
to Africa)

104,000

756,000

389,000

190,000

SPANISH
CARIBBEAN   BRITISH
MAINLAND   GUYANA

73,000

294,000

2,692,000

31,000

DUTCH GUYANAS

FRENCH GUYANA

141,000

AMAZONIA

PERNAMBUCO

818,000

S O U T H
A M E R I C A

BAHIA

1,568,000

SOUTHEAST
BRAZIL

2,281,000

Pacific Ocean

RIO DE LA PLATA

98,000

South Atlantic Ocean

Adapted from David Eltis and David Richardson, *Atlas of the Transatlantic Slave Trade* (Yale University Press, 2010)

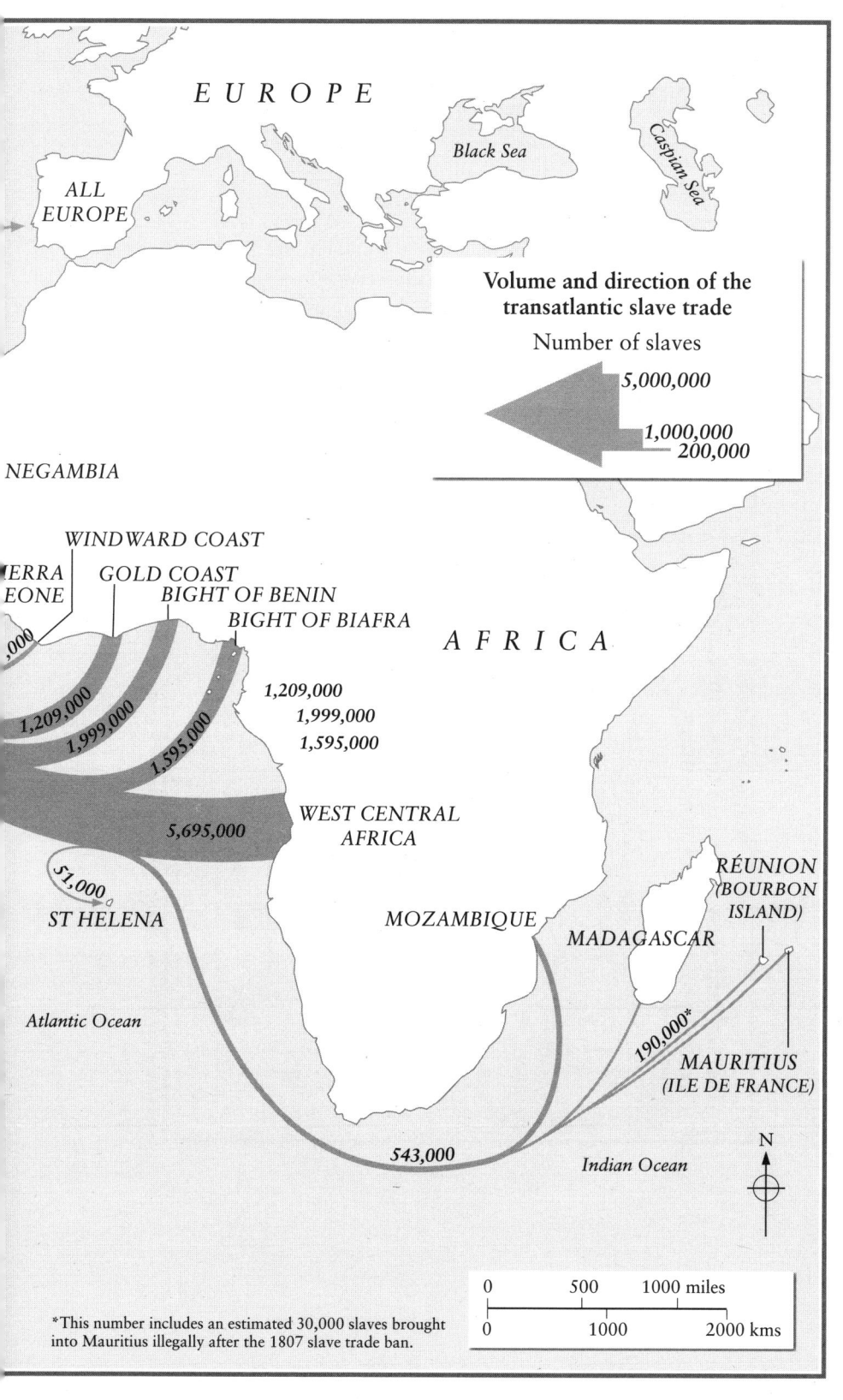

EUROPE

Black Sea

Caspian Sea

ALL
EUROPE

**Volume and direction of the
transatlantic slave trade**

Number of slaves

5,000,000

1,000,000
200,000

NEGAMBIA

WINDWARD COAST

'ERRA
EONE

GOLD COAST

BIGHT OF BENIN

BIGHT OF BIAFRA

AFRICA

000

1,209,000

1,999,000

1,595,000

1,209,000
1,999,000
1,595,000

WEST CENTRAL
AFRICA

5,695,000

51,000

ST HELENA

RÉUNION
(BOURBON
ISLAND)

MOZAMBIQUE

MADAGASCAR

190,000*

MAURITIUS
(ILE DE FRANCE)

Atlantic Ocean

543,000

Indian Ocean

N

0   500   1000 miles

0   1000   2000 kms

*This number includes an estimated 30,000 slaves brought
into Mauritius illegally after the 1807 slave trade ban.

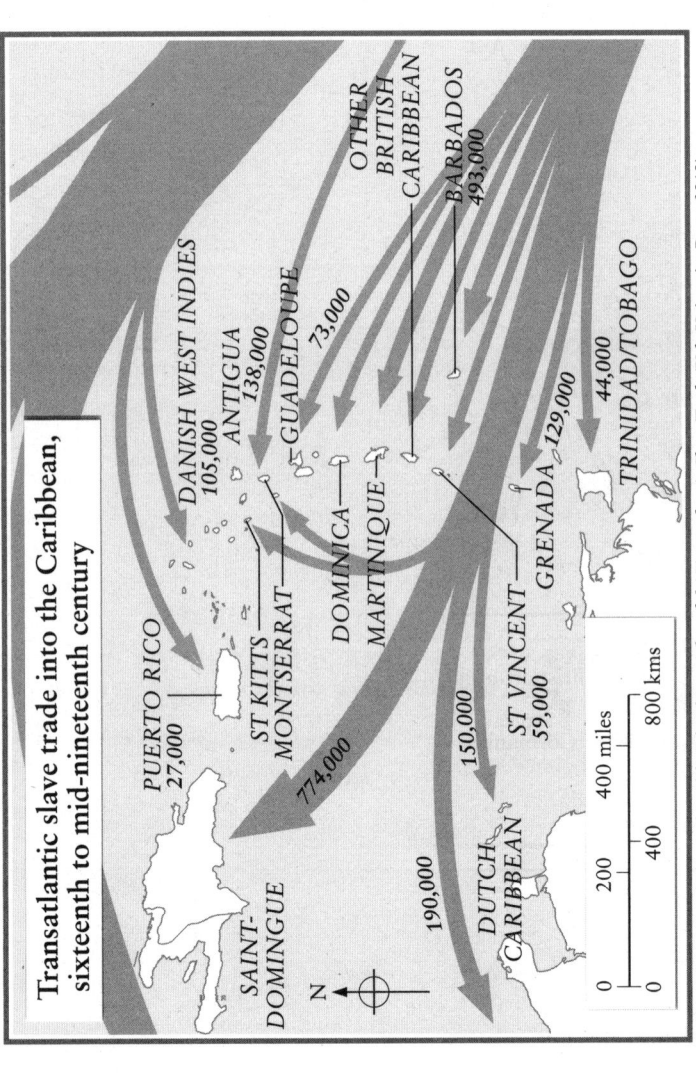

Transatlantic slave trade into the Caribbean, sixteenth to mid-nineteenth century

SAINT-DOMINGUE

PUERTO RICO
27,000

DANISH WEST INDIES
105,000

ANTIGUA
138,000

GUADELOUPE
73,000

OTHER BRITISH CARIBBEAN

BARBADOS
493,000

ST KITTS
MONTSERRAT

DOMINICA

MARTINIQUE

774,000

150,000

ST VINCENT
59,000

GRENADA
129,000

TRINIDAD/TOBAGO
44,000

DUTCH CARIBBEAN

190,000

N

0   200   400   800 kms
0   400 miles

Adapted from David Eltis and David Richardson, Atlas of the Transatlantic Slave Trade (Yale University Press, 2010)

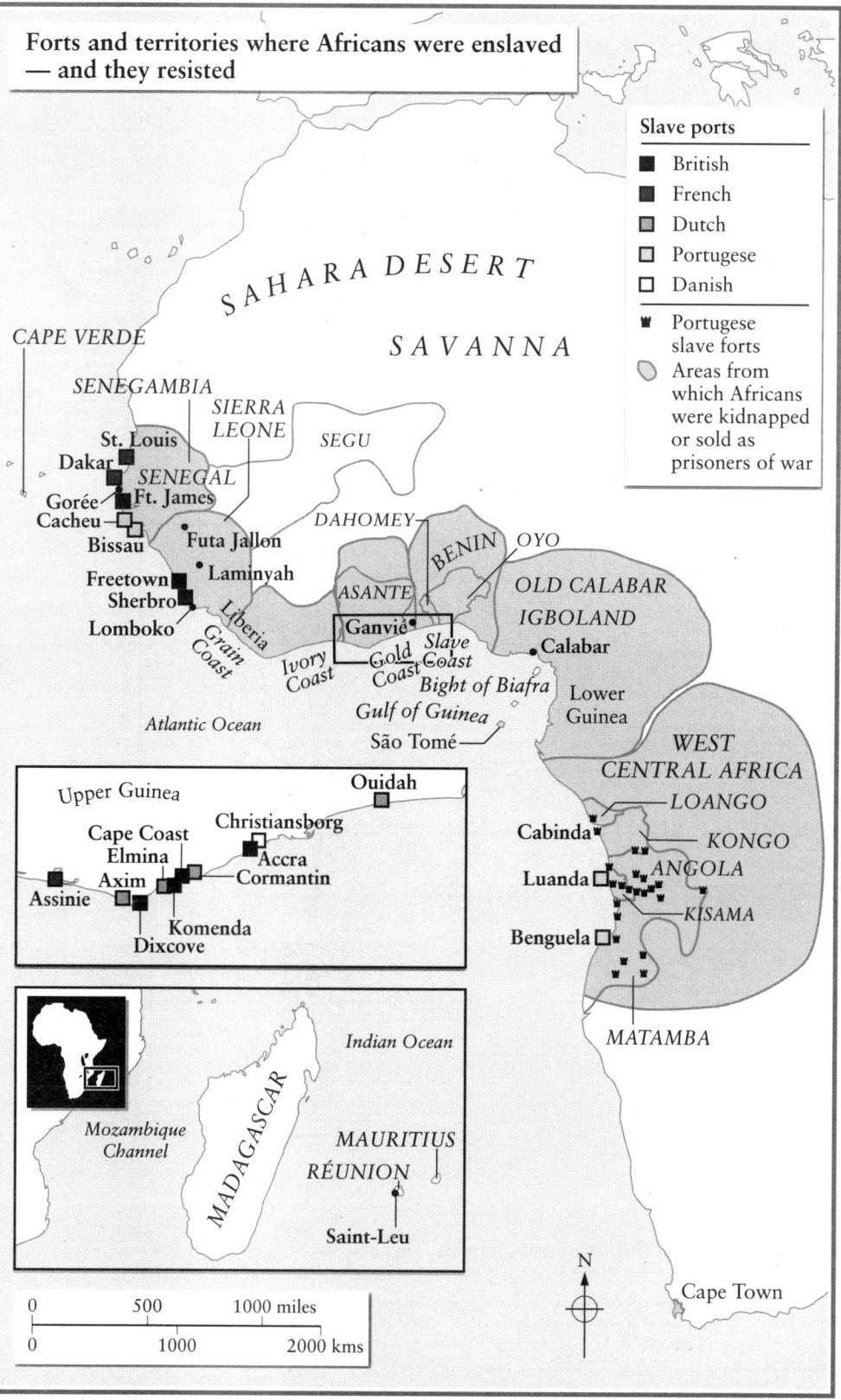

Forts and territories where Africans were enslaved — and they resisted

Slave ports

- ■ British
- ■ French
- ◨ Dutch
- ◻ Portugese
- ◻ Danish
- ⚶ Portugese slave forts
- Areas from which Africans were kidnapped or sold as prisoners of war

SAHARA DESERT

SAVANNA

CAPE VERDE

SENEGAMBIA

SIERRA LEONE

SEGU

St. Louis

Dakar

SENEGAL

Gorée · Ft. James

Cacheu

Bissau

Futa Jallon

DAHOMEY

BENIN

OYO

Freetown

Sherbro

Lomboko

Laminyah

ASANTE

OLD CALABAR

IGBOLAND

Liberia

Ganvié·

Calabar

Grain Coast

Ivory Coast

Gold Coast

Slave Coast

Bight of Biafra

Lower Guinea

Gulf of Guinea

Atlantic Ocean

São Tomé

WEST CENTRAL AFRICA

LOANGO

Ouidah

KONGO

Upper Guinea

Cape Coast

Christiansborg

Cabinda

Elmina

Accra

ANGOLA

Axim

Cormantin

Luanda

KISAMA

Assinie

Komenda

Benguela

Dixcove

MATAMBA

Indian Ocean

Mozambique Channel

MADAGASCAR

MAURITIUS

RÉUNION

Saint-Leu

N

Cape Town

| 0 | 500 | 1000 miles |
| 0 | 1000 | 2000 kms |

CANADA

OHIO   PENNSYLVANIA
NEW YORK
STATE

Chicago   Detroit   New   Boston
York   New Bedford
Harpers Ferry   Philadelphia
WESTERN ILLINOIS   DISTRICT OF COLUMBIA
VIRGINIA   Richmond
LOUISIANA   Great Dismal Swamp
Columbia   NORTH CAROLINA
SOUTH CAROLINA   North
Atlantic Ocean
New Orleans   Charleston
GEORGIA   BERMUDA

MEXICO   CUBA

Mexico City
San Lorenzo   Caribbean Sea
Yanga

Cartagena   Coro
Santa Cruz la Real   Demerara
Berbice
PANAMA   VENEZUELA
NEW   Cayenne
GRANADA
SURINAM
GUYANA

■ Principal centres
of the Underground
Railroad

Free states
and territories

PALMARES

BRAZIL

PERU   BAHIA
Salvador

MINAS GERAIS
PROVINCE

Pacific Ocean

N

Slave revolts and marronage in the Americas

0	500	1000 miles
0	1000	2000 kms

South Atlantic Ocean

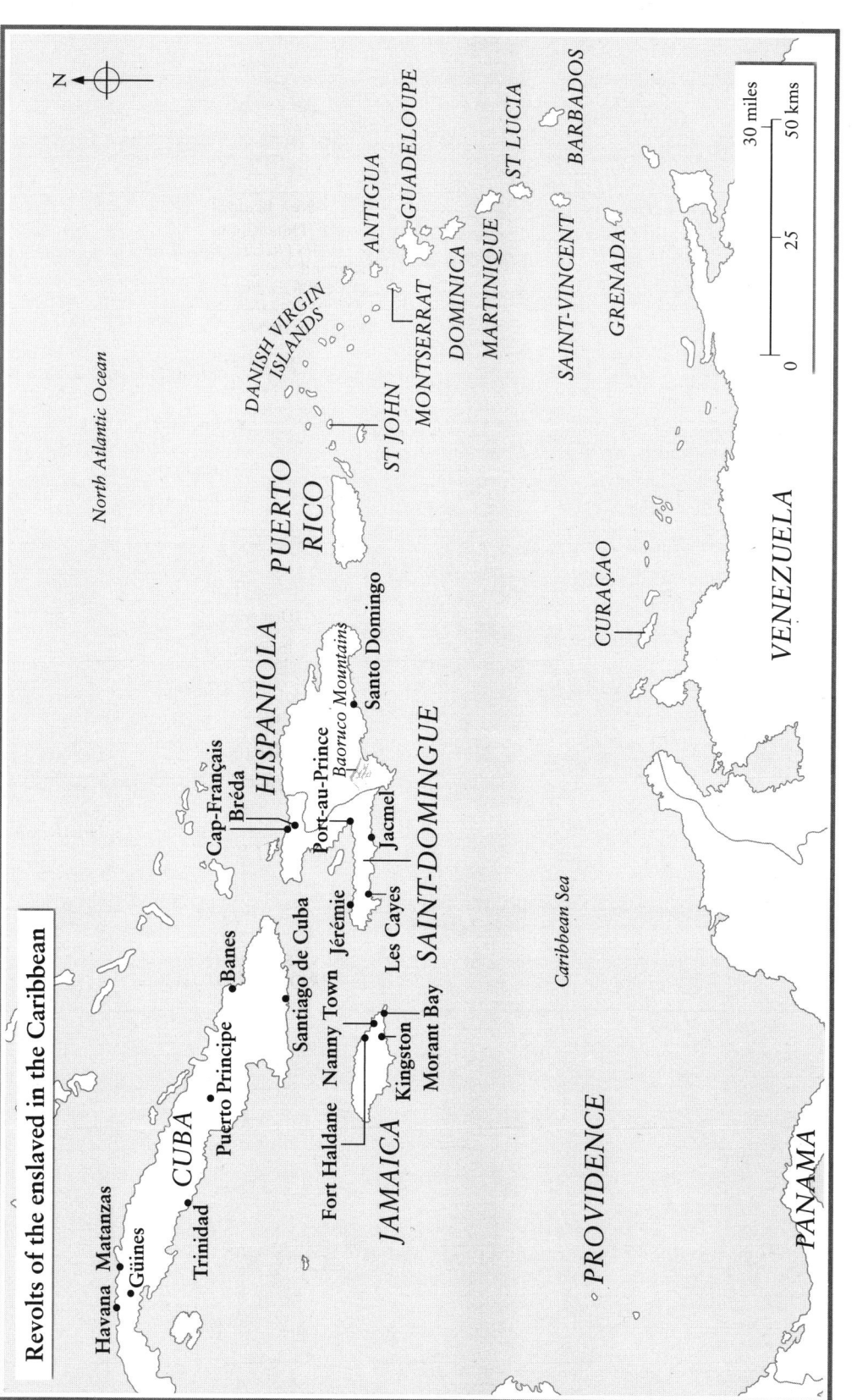

Revolts of the enslaved in the Caribbean

Introduction

Recovering a Vast Tradition

In May 2022 a statue honouring the memory of a black woman named Solitude was inaugurated in a public garden in Paris. Born in the French Caribbean colony of Guadeloupe to an enslaved mother who was raped by a sailor during her journey across the Atlantic, Solitude grew up as a house domestic. Around the time of the first French abolition of human bondage in 1794 she is thought to have joined a community of formerly enslaved people, among whom she lived until the early nineteenth century. Her life as a free citizen was short-lived: in 1802 Napoleon Bonaparte sent an army to restore slavery in the French colony. Solitude refused to give up her liberty and rallied the band of revolutionary military officers, soldiers, and labourers who opposed the invaders. Despite being pregnant at the time, she took up arms and fought alongside them.

When this rebellion was defeated in late May, Solitude was captured by French forces and sentenced to death. Her execution is believed to have taken place in November 1802, the day after she gave birth to her child. Her statue in Paris depicts her in a strong position, with her head held high, her hair flowing, and her eyes gazing upward. Her motherhood is symbolized by her left hand, delicately touching her swollen stomach. Her right hand holds up a copy of the fiery proclamation issued by Louis Delgrès, one of the leaders of the Guadeloupe anti-slavery insurgency, in which he reaffirmed the principle shared by Solitude and their fellow combatants: 'resistance to oppression is a natural right' (see Plate 1).[1]

Solitude's past life and contemporary commemoration are symbols that reflect this book's protagonists: men and women whose lives in Africa and the Americas were scarred by Atlantic slavery. This book will reconstruct their extraordinary resistance to this subjugation. Like most anonymous figures who stood up to human bondage, Solitude led a difficult existence. She was surrounded by violence from her birth, during her life, and at her death. As with the overwhelming majority of enslaved women and men, little is known for certain about her. No document bearing her name has been found in the French colonial archives. The only specific reference to her revolutionary days comes from Auguste Lacour, a nineteenth-century white creole (locally born) historian of Guadeloupe who wrote a few disparaging sentences about her 'explosive' role as an 'evil genius' of the 1802 anti-slavery rebellion.[2] Lacour was possibly drawing on oral sources, or quoting an official report which, like many such papers, has since disappeared. So we do not know when Solitude was born, what her mother's name was, how she made a living during her years of emancipation, or what happened to her child after its birth in November 1802 – although it is most likely they were enslaved.

But Solitude was plainly an exceptional figure. She refused to accept injustice and found ways of protecting herself: first by building an autonomous existence, and then confronting the forces sent by the French authorities to re-enslave her people. Moreover, despite her name, she was not alone, but was able to share her passion for freedom with like-minded people who resisted enslavement. As we shall see throughout this book, such networks of co-operation, friendship, and solidarity were a key feature of the lives of the enslaved, and a crucial factor in making their resistance possible. Yet Solitude's name was fitting considering the historical erasure she experienced after her death. Her official story, as that of her fellow anti-slavery combatants in Guadeloupe, was long buried officially. All traces of their activities disappeared in the colony after 1802. When slavery was finally abolished in 1848 by the French Second Republic (1848–52), the new authorities in Paris gave themselves all the credit. Solitude's intervention was lost, along with that of the countless women and men in the Americas who drove the collective fight for emancipation.

Her popular memory and spirit, along with the struggles of her companions-in-arms, survived through storytelling and folklore. These tales were picked up in later literary works such as Maryse Condé's story of the healer Tituba, whose song could be heard 'in the crackling of a fire between four stones, the rainbow-hued babbling of the river, and the sound of the wind as it whistles through the great trees on the hills'.[3] From the later twentieth century, Solitude's life was recalled in writings published in Guadeloupe and France, and in 1999 a statue in her honour was erected on her native island, in the district of Abymes.[4] Her Parisian monument – the first ever dedicated to a black woman in the French capital – marks a further step in this restoration and the slow but inexorable recovery of the vast tradition of black Atlantic resistance.

The era of Atlantic slavery began a decade after the arrival of the Spanish in the Caribbean in 1492, with the introduction of enslaved Africans into the island of Hispaniola – the territory today shared by the Dominican Republic and Haiti. It finally came to an end with the abolitions of slavery in the United States, Cuba, and Brazil in the second half of the nineteenth century. Across these four centuries, which accompanied and sustained the rise of European colonial empires, over 12.5 million men and women were kidnapped in Africa, enslaved, and transported to the continent's western shores, before being forcibly loaded onto slave ships. Around 10 million people survived the terrible ordeal of the Atlantic crossing – the Middle Passage, as it is known – and became the backbone of the slave plantation system in the Americas. Their labour was exploited in a triangular trade that then generated colossal wealth for the West, based on the production of key commodities such as sugar, cotton, indigo, rice, and coffee. It is estimated that between 1501 and 1875, Portuguese ships carried the largest contingent of enslaved Africans (just under 5.8 million), followed by Britain (3.2 million), France (1.3 million), Spain (1 million), the Netherlands (half a million), the United States (300,000), and Denmark (100,000).[5]

The enslaved challenged their captivity throughout the entire period. Their opposition began in Africa, as we shall see in chapter 1. The most renowned insurrection against Atlantic slavery unfolded in the French colony of Saint-Domingue, known as the 'Pearl of the Antilles' for its rich commodity-producing capacities based on enslaved labour. Just a year after the execution of Solitude by the French, revolutionaries in Saint-Domingue faced off Napoleon's enslaving legions, and defeated the French at the battle of Vertières; on 1 January 1804 the new sovereign black state of Haiti was born. Its first leader, Jean-Jacques Dessalines, a former enslaved labourer turned revolutionary commander, hailed the triumph of the new nation in the Haitian Declaration of Independence: 'We have dared to be free, let us have the audacity to remain so by ourselves and for ourselves.'[6] In his striking formula, Dessalines captured the political awareness of generations of enslaved men and women, the myriad ways in which they imagined their liberty, as well as the active roles they played in championing and fighting for their emancipation.

The central argument of this book is that resistance was integral to the practice of Atlantic slavery, and an inescapable part of it. This resistance defined how the captives saw themselves, their thoughts, beliefs and values, their actions, and their visions. I attempt wherever possible to transcribe their voices and conversations, trace their visible and covert patterns of co-operation, identify their forms of communication, reconstruct their ways of thinking and their religious and spiritual beliefs, and chart the individual and collective ways in which they stood up to their

predicament. In this sense *Daring to be Free* will adopt a broad definition of resistance, across all the areas that are generally seen to constitute
the phenomenon. These include verbal expressions of dissent, linguistic
manipulations, and myth-making; acts of self-harm, infanticide, poison,
and sabotage; narratives and memoirs; different forms of escape and
flight (marronage); cultural and religious beliefs and practices; and acts
of military rebellion, insurgency, and warfare. These dimensions will be
explored in their own terms and their multiple interconnections, and I will
emphasize the importance of notions of autonomy, self-rule, dignity, and
honour, as highlighted by James C. Scott in his classic studies of resistance
by marginalized and oppressed groups.[7]

For a long time, these forms of enslaved resistance did not feature in
national narratives about how slavery came to an end in Britain, France,
and the United States in the nineteenth century. Instead, the end of human
bondage was credited to the campaigns of enlightened white abolitionists
such as William Wilberforce, Victor Schoelcher, and Abraham Lincoln.
These men and the wider movements that campaigned against human
bondage undoubtedly played important roles in confronting and eventually overcoming slavery. However, abolitionists tended to believe that
enslavement engendered a sense of servitude among the captives, thus
inhibiting the full exercise of their human capacities.[8] The figure of the
kneeling captive was a standard feature of abolitionist propaganda from
the late eighteenth century onwards. Hence the liberal myth of abolition,
in which freedom was typically portrayed as an altruistic gift received by
largely passive captives. This hierarchical vision was encapsulated in the
Emancipation Memorial erected in Washington D.C. in 1876, depicting
Lincoln stretching his hand over a crouching black person with freshly
broken shackles. For much of the modern era, this paternalistic tale and
imagery dominated historic portrayals of the end of slavery, with the protests and revolts of the captives relegated to a secondary position – if
mentioned at all.[9]

While acknowledging that it was 'an important chapter' in its history,
the French historian Gabriel Debien's monumental work on slavery in the
French Caribbean avoided the subject of resistance altogether, claiming
that the relevant documentation had 'yet to be gathered'.[10] In the United
States initial attempts to study captive resistance faced entrenched claims
about the apathy and submissiveness of enslaved people in the South.
Pioneering American historians on this subject such as W. E. B. Du Bois,
Herbert Aptheker, and John Blassingame further had to overturn ten-
aciously held views about the ruinous moral effects of emancipation
on black people, and the allegedly benign character of the antebellum

Southern plantation system, as depicted in Margaret Mitchell's best-selling novel *Gone with the Wind*.[11] This retrieval of enslaved resistance was further galvanized by Ples Sterling Stuckey's ground-breaking recovery of the dynamism of African-American folklore, which pulled together the wide repertoire of captive stories, dances, and songs (notably Spirituals) to highlight the west African inspirations within slave culture.[12]

Thanks to the research of these early revisionist historians, and the works of later scholars such as Robin Blackburn and Eugene Genovese, resistance became an integral part of the field in the later decades of the twentieth century. It produced a corpus that was often inspired by Marxist theory. It applied its grand theories of social conflict, organized struggle, and hegemonic domination to the world of slavery, therefore equating resistance with collective action and larger-scale, violent conflicts. Herbert Aptheker uncovered 250 revolts in his research on American slavery, concluding that 'discontent and rebelliousness were not only exceedingly common, but, indeed, characteristic of American Negro slaves'.[13] Moreover, one of the most emblematic historical cases of colonial plantation slavery, eighteenth-century French Saint-Domingue, also proved to be the most comprehensive exemplar of resistance, with the enslaved there overthrowing their bondage and proclaiming Haitian independence in 1804, as just noted. It was no coincidence that C. L. R. James and Aimé Césaire, the authors of the two classic and still unsurpassed studies of the Haitian revolution, were strongly influenced by Marxism.[14]

This early research destroyed what Genovese called 'the myth of slave docility and quiescence',[15] clearing the ground for a significant growth of the subject over the past three decades. This renaissance was abetted by the geographical expansion of studies of slavery across the Caribbean and Atlantic worlds, the recovery of new archival sources, and fresh insights drawn from cultural and gender studies, anthropology, archaeological studies, and oral history.[16] At its best, this scholarship has produced work of high quality that overturned old certainties, brought back glimpses of lost histories – particularly in Africa – and widened the range of actors under consideration, while shedding revealing light on the practices and impacts of Atlantic slavery more generally. A particularly noteworthy bonus has been the growing acknowledgement that human bondage needs to be integrated into the study of broader historical events and political and economic processes in Europe and the United States. In some areas, this is now accepted as a given. For example, it is no longer possible to write credibly about the French and American Revolutions without engaging with their complex relationships around slavery and race, or by confining the analysis to conversations and interactions among white citizens only – many of whom owned enslaved people. Likewise, historians now appreciate the many ways in which Britain's Industrial Revolution was enabled by the huge contributions of slavery to the national economy.[17] In a similar vein, Robin Blackburn's most recent study has highlighted the distinct economic and technological strengths of the 'second slavery' in the United States, Brazil, and Cuba in the early and middle decades of the nineteenth century, thanks to its empowered connections with global capitalism.[18]

There has been a discernible shift in approach, too. The early literature on resistance was heroic and celebratory in nature, often focusing on the unifying role of charismatic figures and directly connecting past anti-slavery struggles with battles for social justice in the second half of the twentieth century. Aptheker campaigned in the United States for Civil Rights and against the Vietnam War, while C. L. R. James and Césaire were strongly engaged in the fight against colonialism. In former slaver colonies such as Jamaica, rebel leaders like Queen Nanny, Paul Bogle, and Samuel Sharpe were made into official national heroes, while Fidel Castro named the Cuban anti-imperialist military intervention in Angola in 1975 'Operation Carlota' after the most famous nineteenth-century Cuban enslaved woman rebel.

More recent scholars have been less directly aligned with such wider political movements and have moved away from the focus on particular individuals, concentrating instead on the actions and beliefs of the rank and file. This approach 'from below', typified by Carolyn Fick's *Making of Haiti*, and works such as Manuel Barcia's *West African Warfare in Bahia and Cuba*, Vincent Brown's *Tacky's Revolt*, and Marjoleine Kars' *Blood on the River*, has uncovered more complex forms of inspiration, experience, and mobilization. It has, moreover, flagged elements of political and cultural dissonance among rebels.[19] For example, some writings about the Haitian revolution have emphasized the long-term fractures between revolutionary leaders and peasant masses. This has opened up valuable insights into the plurality of visions of the future among the enslaved, who are no longer assumed to constitute a homogeneous political entity or necessarily to have shared common objective interests.[20]

In accommodating this greater plurality of voices and perspectives, the story of resistance to slavery has thus become more complex. Eurocentric accounts of anti-slavery thought and practice have been challenged, enabling a fuller understanding of the ways in which ideas about emancipation originated, combined, and travelled across the world, particularly in the Age of Revolutions.[21] The emergence of the field of Atlantic studies since the early twenty-first century has added to this geographical and intellectual diversity, particularly with respect to the military aspects of captive resistance and rebellion, and the African origins of the enslaved. This scholarship has sought to establish commonalities across French, British, Spanish, Dutch, and Portuguese experiences, and to draw comparisons across geographical areas; this in turn has highlighted the fact that the Atlantic was an interconnected realm. Yet this Atlantic-focused scholarship has also at times been marred by Eurocentrism, a tendency often to rely on English-language sources, and insufficient engagement with some of the excellent work produced by researchers from west Africa and the former Caribbean colonies.[22]

This book's principal geographical focus will be on the Atlantic world, but its inquiry will include references to enslaved resistance in the Indian Ocean territories of Madagascar, Bourbon Island (Réunion), and Ile de France (Mauritius), where I was born. Aside from a personal interest in my native country's history, examining these areas helps to underscore the global impacts of chattel slavery. Captives from Madagascar were enslaved and shipped to the New World, from Argentina to Canada. This trade lasted from the seventeenth to the mid-nineteenth century, with thousands of men and women ending up in the Commonwealth of Virginia.[23] Despite their distance from Europe and the Americas, these Indian Ocean islands were affected by radical Atlantic intellectual currents, especially during the eras of the French and Haitian revolutions. The islands witnessed intrinsically important manifestations of opposition by the enslaved, with revolts and acts of arson and poisoning against settlers, various and enduring forms of flight from captivity, and confrontations with the Dutch, French, and British colonial systems. Madagascar had a powerful tradition of female warriors, one of whom, a Malagasy fugitive named Madame Françoise, was a feared maroon leader in eighteenth-century Mauritius.[24] After the British abolition of the slave trade in 1807, Mauritius became a major site of illegal slave trafficking from Madagascar and east Africa in the early decades of the nineteenth century.[25]

These broader perspectives are relevant for another reason. Even though only a very small fraction of Atlantic captives were enslaved and transported to America,[26] the United States remains the epicentre of the academic study of enslavement. This has meant that the literature on slavery in general, and resistance specifically, has at times been overly shaped by questions, trends, and preoccupations originating from the American academic milieu – an ironic twist to the notion of American exceptionalism.[27] It is largely in this American context that more sceptical and pessimistic interpretations of the captives' experiences have gained traction. Drawing on Orlando Patterson's formulation of slavery as 'social death', Saidiya Hartman charted the terror of the experience of enslavement, and the continuation of black oppression after the formal end of slavery in the nineteenth century: 'emancipation appears less the grand event of liberation than a point of transition between modes of servitude and racial subjection'.[28]

Moreover, the closer focus on primary sources has prompted challenges to the veracity of major documents, such as the memoirs of the abolitionist Olaudah Equiano. Questions have been raised about the revolutionary character of landmark revolts, such as the Makandal conspiracy in Saint-Domingue and the Denmark Vesey conspiracy in the United States.[29] Indeed, doubts have been expressed about the very utility of resistance as a concept, for its over-sentimental view of heroic agency, and its problematic assumption that the enslaved formed cohesive communities.[30] The French scholar Frédéric Régent has concluded that resistance has now lost its core meaning, given the breadth of the phenomena it encompasses. In his view the term should be limited to actions with tangible material impacts on the slavery production system, such as strikes, sabotage, and marronage.[31]

The rise of postmodern, feminist, and postcolonial studies has further unsettled the grand narratives of resistance. In his revisitation of C. L. R. James's *Black Jacobins*, David Scott argues that from the perspective of the postcolonial present, revolution is not a heroic but a tragic enterprise, in which liberation remains at best an unfulfilled aspiration.[32] Noting the general silencing of women's voices in the archives, Marisa Fuentes confronts the dominant representation of resistance as 'armed, militaristic, physical, and triumphant', and the dehumanization of violence against enslaved women in male-dominated accounts.[33] In her study of the Cuban insurrections of the 1840s, Aisha Finch likewise states that 'it is important to observe how deeply masculinity and male embodiment have structured the way we think about black opposition'.[34] In a review of recent literature on slavery, Vincent Brown has accordingly identified a growing dichotomy between 'hopeful stories of heroic subalterns versus anatomies of doom', before concluding that 'the pendulum seems to have swung decidedly towards despair'.[35]

This pessimism is in part an expression of the American dominance in the field of slavery studies. More generally, this bleakness is connected to intellectual trends such as the singularly American construct of 'Afropessimism'. In its most radical expression, this approach identifies insuperable obstacles to the full inclusion of black people into American society, and it equates the experience of blackness in the West with a permanent condition of enslavement. Taking the 'social death' paradigm to its conclusion,

Frank Wilderson III thus asserts that 'human life depends on the death of Blacks for its existence and cohesion'.[36] This black exceptionalism has been vigorously contested, including by many African-American scholars and intellectuals. But its presence in the debate bears witness to the long shadow of enslavement and the ongoing sentiments of alienation and historical dispossession among black communities in the United States.[37]

Daring to be Free aims to offer as comprehensive an account as possible of Atlantic captives' resistance. It is not a fully inclusive history of Atlantic slavery, because our subject matter does not include much material about slavery's defenders, upholders, and beneficiaries, except where necessary to explain the actions and beliefs of those who challenged that system. Nor is this a general narrative about the history of abolitionism and abolition movements in Europe and the United States. It is interested in them only in so far as they draw out the (generally wide) gap between white reformers and enslaved advocates of their own emancipation. This is not a history of emancipation either, as the latter includes subjects such as military service and manumission (the legal freeing of the enslaved from bondage), which are excellently treated in Aline Helg's recently translated *Slave No More*.[38]

Nor indeed is the book a history of all forms of captive empowerment. Our focus here is on its critical dimensions, namely the political and intellectual ways in which the enslaved took their fate into their own hands, and struggled for their freedom through what the historian and social-justice campaigner Hilary Beckles aptly defines as an 'ethos of self-emancipation'.[39] In approaching the subject in this way, my aim is to avoid stretching the definition of resistance, and to home in specifically on the 'internal politics of the slave community'.[40] This perspective highlights the reflective actions and thoughts of the enslaved, in both the material and the spiritual realms, as well as their formal and informal networks of organization, which played a vital role in their capacities for resistance. It pays particular attention to their general and collective understandings of themselves and the world, mapping out the ways in which captives sought to contain, subvert, and destroy the power of their enslavers.

I will begin by exploring the experiences and formative influences of enslaved men and women on the African continent, before their capture and forcible transfer across the Atlantic. This essential part of the story continues to be overlooked in studies of slavery.[41] While there have been considerable advances in our understanding of the African dimensions of enslavement, for the most part this literature ends up focusing on the diaspora: what happened to the enslaved once they reached the New World.

Thanks in large part to the development of research based on oral traditions, information about various forms of African resistance to capture
and enslavement is now growing. We can trace back the origins of many
acts of opposition and rebellion in the New World to the skills, ideas,
and values that African men and women brought with them across the
Atlantic. One of the most extraordinary sources of this kind is a database
of over 7,000 African captives generated through interviews of elders and
priests in Benin in the early twenty-first century. Largely based on the
collective memory held by priests in the traditional west African *vodun*
religion, the information recovered about the kidnapped Africans includes
not only the captives' names but in many instances their occupations.
We find warriors (both male and female), hunters, artisans, peasants, and
priestly figures, healers, esoteric courtiers, astrologers, religious sculptors,
and cult leaders, reflecting the key significance of spirituality in the resistance traditions that developed in the New World.[42]

Extensive coverage will be given to enslaved women, too long marginalized in the literature on enslaved resistance. There is now overwhelming
evidence that women played major roles in opposing slavery, right from
the moment they were captured and ferried across the oceans.[43] Their
relative freedom of movement on board ship exposed them to sexual violence by European crewmen, as we saw with Solitude's mother earlier. But
it allowed these women to provide information and weapons to the lower
decks, where the enslaved men were kept in chains. The interventions of
women were often decisive in enabling revolts to occur. *Daring to be Free*
will show that women contributed significantly to the survival of runaway settlements, and they were often the main providers of religious and
medical support to enslaved communities. Moreover, women were active
in rebellions in Africa and in the New World, right from the outset. This
was highlighted by such imposing figures as the priestess Leonor, whose
determined peroration about the 'hundred blacks of all nations' who were
out to 'kill, maim, and dismember' the Spanish settler slaver population
terrified the Inquisition tribunal in Cartagena de Indias in 1620.[44]

Many such powerful female anti-slavery figures will be encountered
across this narrative, including the Quaker anti-slavery campaigner Elizabeth Heyrick from Britain, the runaway fighter Zeferina from Brazil,
the rebel leader Fermina Lucumi from Cuba, and the abolitionist and
civic activist Harriet Tubman from the United States. Their defiant spirit
was symbolized by two less well known enslaved figures. The first was
a domestic named Sarah Ann in British Guyana who responded to the
verbal abuse inflicted by her mistress Mrs Smith by organizing a group
of women captives to compose a song in which Smith's name was 'often

repeated for the express purpose of turning her into ridicule'.[45] The second was Roseline, an enslaved woman from Mauritius. She ran away from her enslaver in Port Louis in 1813, and when apprehended was found to be eight months pregnant. She was sent to the Bagne prison, where she gave birth to her child. Three days later she climbed out of the window of her cell and escaped again, this time with her newborn. No doubt with the assistance of other prisoners, Roseline managed to jump over the external prison walls with her baby, even though the barriers were more than three metres high.[46] We can infer again that in both of these instances the acts of defiance were enabled by group solidarities, the first resting on close bonds among domestics and the second on the co-operation and mutual support that existed among the prisoners.

The Haitian revolution is one of the other major themes. Moving beyond my previous focus on Saint-Domingue's principal leader Toussaint Louverture, this book explores the dynamic interventions of the enslaved, epitomized by the series of events beginning with the 1791 insurrection. Haitian revolutionary republicanism was centred around the struggle for emancipation and, once achieved in 1793, its preservation against vengeful white settlers and their foreign imperialist allies. The revolution's richness captured all the dimensions of effective resistance: its historical depth, the vibrant forms of organization, its incorporation of religious and spiritual motifs, and the capacity to spawn a plurality of emancipatory political traditions, all of which contributed to the Haitians' final victory in their war of national liberation. This was an inclusive revolution in which women made major intellectual, spiritual, and military contributions, as symbolized by the priestess Cécile Fatiman and the warriors Sanité Belair and Marie-Jeanne Lamartinière.

Haiti's ultimate force lay in its capacity to inspire enslaved resistance elsewhere, without offering a rigid model or fixed blueprint for anti-slavery mobilizations. Its success in this respect rested on its hybrid quality. It adapted the emancipatory message of the French Revolution to its own requirements, while drawing strength from wider geographical and historical sources – African traditions of resistance, struggles against enslavement in Saint-Domingue from earlier in the eighteenth century, and even from the period of Spanish occupation, and anticolonial revolts elsewhere in the Caribbean region. Speaking of his ancestors, the Haitian historian Jean Casimir observed that, 'as individuals and as a group, [they] never stopped resisting slavery and domination'.[47] Haiti's role in the history of resistance was further magnified in the aftermath of its declaration of independence, when the new postcolonial state became a symbol of black power: a source of unmitigated terror to white slavers, uncomfortable ambivalence for white abolitionists, and a beacon of hope for the millions of enslaved people still seeking emancipation across the Atlantic.[48]

The Haitian case underscores the value of seeing Atlantic enslaved resistance through a wide geographical lens. As in colonial Saint-Domingue, challenges to slavery occurred repeatedly within specific physical boundaries. This was the case with early rebellion patterns, which saw numerous revolts and conspiracies in single areas. For example, in Spanish Mexico, there were around a hundred uprisings between 1523 and 1821; among the most significant was the 1612 plot in Mexico City, which enlisted the support of black priests and planned to poison the Spaniards' food and water. Similarly in the United States, the Long Island revolt in 1708 was followed by rebellions in New York in 1712, Stono in South Carolina in 1739, and New York again in 1741. These uprisings often had numerous African material and spiritual dimensions, especially the military tactics deployed by the combatants.[49] Likewise in Brazil a series of revolts unfolded in the Bahia region between 1806 and 1835, a period that coincided with a massive influx of African-born slaves. These forms of protest were sometimes organized along ethnic or religious lines but they often brought together a composite array of enslaved groups, who set aside their differences to challenge their slaver enemies. Thus in May 1814 a conspiracy was uncovered in Bahia involving co-operation between urban captives and those from runaway settlements, as well as free black people and Muslim clerics. African cultural associations were mobilized as well, and the fighters planned to co-ordinate their actions by using conch-shell trumpets. Examples such as these demonstrated the sophisticated material and intellectual networks of co-operation that could lie behind many plans for liberation.[50]

Indeed, resistance was not confined to specific geographical spaces or ethnic groups. The captives involved in rebellions had often recently been forcibly transported from Africa, developing affinities with each other during this process. These connections were nurtured at the time of their incarceration on the African coasts and during the Middle Passage itself, which led to enduring links among the enslaved. This bond was so strong that many of those who shared this experience referred to each other as 'shipmates'. In this sense, and despite the atrociousness of the experience of human bondage, the Atlantic crossing was as much a connection as a separation.[51] Resistance was thus constantly creating links and synergies among enslaved individuals and groups – in the revolts on Middle Passage ships carried out by captives taken from the hinterlands of Africa, in the military skills and technologies brought by African captives to the

Americas, in the radical ideas, values, and practices that moved with them from Africa to the Americas, from one part of the Americas to another, and, starting with the later eighteenth century, from revolutionary and abolitionist Europe to the Americas.

A strong symbol of the fluidity of enslaved resistance was the phenomenon of maritime marronage. Across the Americas tens of thousands of individuals and groups banded together to flee enslavement across the seas at various points, finding refuge in Spanish, French, and British colonies, and later in independent Haiti. These maroons brought empowering ideas about freedom and racial equality with them. This trend was still being observed in French colonies in the 1840s, as detailed in a report from Guadeloupe that deplored the escape of over forty captives by sea, after taking a vessel from the Sainte-Rose region. The authorities despatched a patrol boat in pursuit but failed to catch the fugitives, who were never found.[52] Maritime connections also underpinned the alliances that captives forged with non-enslaved free black communities and people of colour, as well as sections of the white underclass. This nexus has been portrayed in Julius Scott's seminal book *Common Wind*, which connects the intellectual and social interactions of rebellious enslaved people in the Atlantic with the colonial populations of sailors, soldiers, market vendors, and escaped convicts.[53]

A related large-scale question is how to understand the transformations of enslaved resistance across the four centuries of Atlantic slavery. One approach has been to view evolving captive struggles as a function of the historical phases of plantation slavery. In this perspective, the early construction period (1500 to around 1750) saw an instinctive, more individualistic type of opposition, which became more purposeful and organized during the system's mature period (1750 to 1800), with its multiple, small-scale revolts and plots. This phase in turn gave way to the more structured rebellions of the late eighteenth century and first half of the nineteenth century. During this period, plantation slavery mutated again after the Haitian revolution and the British and American abolitions of the slave trade, experiencing an upsurge in the United States, Brazil, and Cuba. This 'second wave' of Atlantic slavery provoked further widespread resistance.

Viewing the history of rebellions in their entirety, Eugene Genovese offered another distinction: between early 'restorationist' revolts, driven by African ethnic and royalist traditions, and the universalist national and international movements inspired by the Age of Revolutions as from the later decades of the eighteenth century.[54] This amounts to seeing these earlier revolts as quests by the enslaved to return to the past, in order to reconstruct their former African ways of life. This division is sometimes presented in terms of a contrast between combative African-born captives and their more conciliatory 'creole' counterparts; the meaning and implications of the term 'creolization' and how it operated have been hotly debated among scholars of slavery.[55]

While helpful, these distinctions and demarcations are at times overly restrictive. As we will see throughout this narrative, those early revolts were driven by universal considerations, while later nineteenth-century conflicts (in Cuba, Brazil, and the United States) incorporated several African motifs. Furthermore, the preponderance of creole captives in early nineteenth-century Barbados did not prevent the 1816 rebellion. More fundamentally, it will become clear that these 'African' political, military, and spiritual components of resistance were dynamic and forward-looking, not merely a retention or reconstitution of traditional patterns of existence. In all these respects *Daring to be Free* thus takes a *longue durée* approach, viewing the genesis, performance, and impacts of resistance in cumulative rather than cyclical terms. Put simply, the enslaved developed cultures of self-empowerment that they transmitted across time, in their own areas and across the Atlantic region. These ranged from the methods of successful escape, hidden encampment-building, agricultural and guerrilla skills of runaways, to the religious rituals and spiritual systems that they crafted and drew upon, along with the multitude of anti-slavery visions which inspired their attempts at emancipation once they had been forcibly taken to the New World.

One of my aims in *Daring to be Free* is to draw on these rich experiences of resistance to map out the political and spiritual ideals of the enslaved. This exercise in recovery is fraught with complexities. The biggest obstacle is the nature of the slavery archive, almost entirely produced by those who upheld, advanced, and profited from the system of human bondage. Traders and insurers, slave-ship navigators and crew members, metropolitan elites and colonial administrators, pro-slavery journalists and pamphleteers, plantation owners and slave hunters, military officials and prosecutors all left copious records of the history of slavery and its captives. Yet the actions and thoughts of those who resisted were barely acknowledged in these documents, and indeed were often deliberately erased.

For instance, we now have much information about slave-ship rebellions, thanks to the material gathered from slaver sources and collated in the SlaveVoyages database.[56] Yet these documents only very rarely recorded the names of the men and women who fought for their freedom during the Middle Passage. Despite this deliberate and systematic erasure, these resources remain vital, as they often provide the only information available about these types of resistance. Reading these records – particularly those relating to runaway escapes, plots and conspiracies, and insurrections – against the grain can filter out the biases of their authors, interrogate the silences, and restore the critical agency of the enslaved, beyond the approximations and derogatory evocations of the slavers, and mindful that women have been written out of the archive.[57]

Not all contemporary sources were supportive of slavery. Accounts by white abolitionists, visiting travellers, and missionaries highlighted the violence of the slave trade as well as the brutal and degrading conditions in which men, women, and children were forced to work under the system of enslavement. A decade after Haitian independence, Pompée Valentin Vastey published an excoriating summary of some of the worst atrocities committed by Saint-Domingue's white slaver settlers.[58] Vastey's remarkable *oeuvre*, which inspired anti-slavery and anticolonial writings in the United States and Europe in the nineteenth century and beyond, has recently been rediscovered.[59] However, abolitionist literature in general terms brings little to our table, as it tended to dwell on suffering rather than resistance. Indeed, except for Vastey, the authors of these writings were all men and women who had little direct contact with Atlantic networks of captive opposition and rebellion, which by their nature were highly secretive. Likewise, court records and complaint procedures have more recently emerged as an important set of sources for captives' testimonies.[60] Again they generally provide overwhelming evidence of the brutality of slavery.[61] Sometimes, however, this material offers fleeting impressions of individual strategies of resistance, and of the subjectivity and humanity of the defendants, as with Sophie White's reconstruction of enslaved lives in eighteenth-century colonial Louisiana and Ile de France (Mauritius) through four dramatic court cases.[62]

By far the most significant single surviving source of captive testimony is autobiographical texts. These have created a huge repository of life experiences, especially in the United States, where just over 6,000 slave narratives of various sorts were catalogued between the early eighteenth and the mid-twentieth century. These writings are supplemented by oral interviews carried out by the Works Progress Administration (WPA) in the 1930s.[63] This material sheds useful light on the family, kinship, culture, and economic activities of the enslaved. It engages with individual and group resistance in some important ways: through accounts of education and escape, and the retention of African cultures, religious practices, and ideals.[64] Writings by African-American women have also helped broaden our understanding of resistance. At the same time, such texts generally avoid discussing militant enslaved action against slavers – a silence that can be explained by two reasons. Most of these texts, and particularly the larger-scale literary works, were produced for white audiences for abolitionist purposes. Their authors did not wish to unsettle the sensibilities of their readership by dwelling on violent forms of resistance to the captives' predicament. Moreover, most of the WPA interviews were carried out by white Southerners, who often had a limited view of the horrors of American slavery. In any event, as we saw earlier, black self-emancipation remained a problematic concept for European and North American abolitionists during the nineteenth century.[65]

Conversely, rebel commanders and foot soldiers such as Solitude left no written memoirs, as they were generally not literate and very few survived of those who played leading roles in plots, insurrections, and acts of war. Nat Turner's *Confessions*, based on interviews he gave before his execution, is the only such account we possess. Even Toussaint Louverture's posthumously published 'memoir', written in captivity in the Fort de Joux, is not an exception to this proposition, as this text was really a justification of his record in office in the 1790s, and a protest against the French military invasion of Saint-Domingue. His former life as an enslaved person only features allusively in the text.[66] While mentioning this literary erasure of resistance voices, we should point out that, unlike in Britain and the United States, there was no formal tradition of autobiographical slave narrative in France, even though texts produced by Haitian revolutionaries before and after independence circulated across the Atlantic and contributed to significant anticolonial interventions.[67] There were very few memoirs written by those who resisted enslavement in the Spanish and Portuguese empires. One rare exception is Esteban Montejo's autobiography, which covered his life as a teenage runaway captive in the 1870s all the way through to the Cuban war of liberation (1895–9). Montejo was still alive at the time of the Cuban revolution in 1959 – a reminder, as with the African oral sources, of the proximity of the world of Atlantic slavery to our contemporary epoch.[68]

If silence is one major problem in reconstructing the voices of resistance, distortion is another. Even those who wrote sympathetically about the plight of the enslaved before the nineteenth-century abolitions, such as radical Enlightenment pamphleteers and local Christian missionaries, typically approached the issue from a position of intellectual and moral superiority. When read carefully, the *philosophe* Denis Diderot's denunciation of slavery was not framed around a universalist vision of racial equality. As pointed out by one commentator, '[Diderot's] black person is unable to move beyond a literary existence.'[69] These writings could rarely imagine the enslaved taking charge of their existence and acting collectively to pursue specific or general emancipatory goals. Moreover, these texts had little to say about the features of the lives of the enslaved that allowed them to retain some sense of selfhood and dignity: their technical and linguistic skills, their forms of scientific and medicinal knowledge, their military experience, and their African-inspired religious practices and beliefs. Indeed, these writings tended to be contemptuous of the spirituality of the captives, which they dismissed as 'superstitions'.

A further issue was that later European commentators who wrote about enslaved resistance in the Age of Revolutions tended to represent the thoughts and actions of the rebels through radical Enlightenment frameworks such as republicanism, or the abolitionist language of individual liberty and rights associated with Western liberal traditions. This one-dimensional view continues to inform some of the scholarship on emancipation. However, as we will see, white abolitionists in Britain, France, and the United States had considerably more limited conceptions of black intellectual and practical capacities than those driving the men and women fighting for their own emancipation. This gap was apparent in the contrasting representations of the Haitian revolution, which was systematically avoided, belittled, or exceptionalized by white abolitionists. For a long time, this was the case with Western historical writings about that revolution, typically portrayed as a local echo of its American and French predecessors. Even now that the power and singularity of the Haitian revolution are more widely accepted, the ideological distinctiveness of its emancipatory vision of black internationalism remains to be fully explored.[70]

Daring to be Free will sketch a fuller picture of this black anti-slavery internationalism by focusing on its central ideal of autonomy. Forged by the enslaved in their struggles against their oppressors, this emancipatory vision was not based on a single philosophical or theoretical framework. It drew on a dynamic set of ideals that evolved through collective practices of resistance to enslavement in Africa, during the Middle Passage, and in the Americas. The Atlantic was in this sense an integrated space not just physically but intellectually as well, in which European emancipatory ideals of liberty and equality played a part. However, their role was not a preponderant one, especially if we think of the entire four-century duration of chattel slavery and not just the late eighteenth and early nineteenth centuries. It should be self-evident but let us make the point anyway: the enslaved did not begin to think about their emancipation only when European philosophers happened to start expressing unease about the morality of human bondage in the *salons* of the Enlightenment.

As Louis Sala-Molins wrote: 'the black person, always a slave and still always standing, truly invented his liberty'.[71]

Particularly in respect of its more belligerent forms, enslaved resistance was typically the work of minorities. This vanguard quality is typical of social, civic, and political movements that have challenged asymmetric power structures in modern times. To take a more recent historical example, only very small numbers of men and women took part in the Resistance during the Second World War. This does not diminish its political and moral importance. The underground movements of 1940–45 may not have defeated Nazi Germany militarily, but they performed important functions such as sabotage, intelligence-gathering, delegitimizing collaborators, and maintaining national dignity.[72]

Likewise – and this is my response to the more pessimistic analytical turn in the historiography – enslaved resistance must be evaluated beyond the single criterion of whether it led to the direct overthrow of the institution of slavery. In its different manifestations, this resistance had measurable impacts on the material and psychological foundations of the slave order, as well as promoting notions of black empowerment, dignity, and autonomy. These qualities were exemplified, among others, by the African-American abolitionist Frederick Douglass, who called for 'the storm, the whirlwind and the earthquake' to be unleashed so that slavery would be ended in the United States.[73] Resistance furthermore set substantive practical limits on the slavers' ability to pursue their economic objectives. During the early centuries of the plantation system, for example, maroon groups of escaped captives challenged the territorial dominion of European colonial powers and in many instances forced them to abandon the cultivation of large settlement areas. Hence the value of more sophisticated ways of thinking about 'success' when it comes to the resistance of the enslaved.

The chronological breadth of this book, combined with its particular focus on enslaved political consciousness, will I hope enable resistance to be understood not just as a set of isolated actions, but as a frame of thinking produced by determined and self-conscious political agents. Despite the overwhelming constraints they faced, the enslaved sought to transcend the 'social death' of human bondage to reflect upon their surroundings. They elaborated complex notions of freedom, honour, dignity, sovereignty, and internationalism that included visions of a future in which slavery had been contained or eliminated. It was a practical and oral rather than written tradition, embedded in action and verbal exchanges. It was grounded in stories, symbols, and myths about freedom, many of which later crytallized around the Haitian revolution.

Resistance thinking was often centred around individual figures, but one of the themes of this book will be identifying the networks of community and solidarity that made such leadership possible. Most plots and insurrections were preceded by lengthy discussions and secret planning meetings. Moreover, the enslaved developed forms of self-governance that combined humane behaviour with efficient forms of organization. Antislavery thinking was grounded in a resolutely martial culture. It associated the use of acquired military skills with the training of captives in fugitive settlements for defensive and offensive combat, and the celebration of African (and later Haitian) military achievements. Enslaved combatants practised techniques of guerrilla warfare long before the term was formally introduced into European languages during the early nineteenth-century Napoleonic Wars. Indeed, it is now understood that many of the enslaved saw their resistance as acts of war. This was clear from the very first captive insurrections against the Spaniards in the early sixteenth century, all the way through to the uprisings in nineteenth-century Brazil and Cuba, when the enslaved consciously described their actions – even small-scale ones – as acts of war.[74]

Above all, resisting captives fought to liberate themselves from white slaver domination. They celebrated their African qualities, and they rejected the slaver axiom that human bondage was a natural condition which could not be transcended. They challenged the slavers' association of blackness with savagery and affirmed their capacity and self-worth. They engaged in religious and spiritual pursuits of their own, and whenever possible separated themselves physically from colonial control. And despite their material disadvantage they came together to overthrow the slaver order so as to create free and self-governing communities. They alluded to their desire for liberty in songs and poems that they improvised in the holds of ships, in work gangs on plantations or waterfronts, or during nocturnal festivities which they secretly organized on plantations.[75] When they were punished for daring to be free, they met their fate with courage and stoicism, even if it entailed the ultimate sacrifice of their lives. In his novel about Solitude, which ends with a fictionalized account of her death, André Schwarz-Bart depicts her defiantly facing her executioner, and 'bursting into a throaty laugh'.[76]

The African Foundations
of Resistance

In the coastal town of Ouidah, in southern Benin, west Africa, a monument marks the location of the Tree of Forgetfulness. Established by the French, Ouidah was a major slave-trading post during the period of Atlantic slavery, with a population of around 20,000 at the height of its power. An estimated two million people were forcibly transported from there to the New World between the seventeenth and nineteenth centuries. Enslaved men and women were marched to the tree in chains from the fort where they were held, on the way to the coast where they would be embarked on ships and sent across the Atlantic. Women were made to walk around the tree seven times, and men nine. The symbolic aim was to make them forget everything about their way of life before their enslavement – their families, their occupations, their villages, and their cultures. The inscription on the monument indicates that the ritual had a further purpose: to turn the captives into 'beings without any will to react or to rebel'.[1]

Breaking the spirit of the enslaved was a central part of the system of chattel slavery. Yet as we will see throughout this book they refused to be crushed, and they fought back in a multitude of ways, beginning first in African lands themselves. The scale of these African struggles is still largely under-estimated, even among historians of the Atlantic slave trade, for many reasons. Most resistance took place in local settings, by individuals and groups not typically associated with powerful institutions and social and religious forces, and it left few direct traces in the archives. Narratives about African enslavement also bought into the myth of the slavers' invincibility, and the alleged docility of those they preyed upon. In any event, as we saw in the Introduction, most scholarly research has focused on what happened to these men and women once they reached the New World. Furthermore, slavery remains a difficult subject among west Africans, associated with family traumas, and feelings of collective guilt and shame. This was especially the case as the Atlantic trade overlapped with an indigenous system of bondage, which (even though it did not treat captives only as a commodity) came to be sustained by powerful local African states.[2] In the postcolonial era of independence, new African leaders preferred to emphasize national unity rather than hark back to these painful times. It is only relatively recently that scholars have begun to explore the rich traditions of localized memory and oral cultures of slavery in Africa.[3]

African resistance to slavery has been occluded because Western historians long maintained that precolonial Africans lacked a 'modern' conception of freedom, and that such ideals of autonomy and self-determination were only brought to the continent by enlightened European abolitionists and by the impacts of revolutions in the New World. Recent research has demonstrated the existence of powerful abolitionist currents in the seventeenth-century Black Atlantic, for example in the movement around Lourenço da Silva Mendonça, an exiled black Christian intellectual from the kingdom of Kongo who objected to the Portuguese coercive imposition of the slave system in west-central Africa. Mendonça took his case against the international slave trade to the Vatican, with the support of Black Christians from Angola, Brazil, the Caribbean, Portugal, and Spain. Well over a century before the emergence of abolitionism in Western Europe, this pioneering project was rooted in the refusal to accept chattel slavery in Africa, and it was underpinned by a sense of international solidarity and a comprehensive vision of freedom. In his closing statement Mendonça argued that slavery was contrary to divine, civil, and natural law, and was therefore an 'unnatural' phenomenon.[4]

Indeed, from its very beginnings, and at all stages of the process, slavery was vigorously opposed by local populations in Africa. It was a defensive battle fought by ordinary people against their own monarchs, aristocrats, and clerics, by spiritual communities standing up for their values against European merchants and slave traders, by decentralized societies trying to uphold their ways of life against powerful regional rulers and the warriors and mercenaries they employed, and in the final stages by enslaved men, women, and children who rebelled against the crews of the ships ferrying them across the Atlantic. In rejecting servitude, African peoples protected themselves from predators by both material and spiritual means. They radically separated themselves from slaveholding societies and sought to live freely in communities that embodied the values of respect, dignity, and honour. In doing so they often relied on traditions of war that mobilized vigorous conceptions of martial valour, as well as principles of communal unity and natural liberty. These oral traditions were often incorporated into the founding myths of collective groups, as with the inhabitants of the Sereer village of Fatick in Senegambia. They traced their origins to a warrior named Waal Paal, who had escaped from slavery and set fire to the forest in the area so as to stake his claim to the land of Fatick.[5] Such stories of resistance can still be heard in west African anecdotes, recollections, folklore, religious rituals, and fragments of narrative, and continue to be disseminated in African communities to this day.[6]

The transatlantic trade in captives was supported, financed, and under-written in Europe by governments, chartered companies, and private financial institutions such as the insurer Lloyd's of London. It relied on a steady supply of men, women, and children from Africa, procured by powerful states whose rulers developed significant stakes in the system, trading these captives in exchange for wealth, commodities, and weapons. Slavery existed in Africa, however, long before the advent of the transat-lantic trade and European colonialism. Between roughly 500 and 1600, ambitious rulers developed a system of internal bondage that contributed to state consolidation and the production of goods, and African traders were involved in the sale of humans across the Sahara and the Indian Ocean. After 1600, however, European commerce and credit transformed African slavery, leading to a further militarization of the continent and the creation of strong trade networks across the Atlantic.[7] This period saw the consolidation of powerful predatory kingdoms such as Oyo, Ouidah, Asanta, Loango, Segu, and Dahomey. These empires prospered by turn-ing their weaker neighbours into tributary states, forcing them to supply the kingdoms with captives. At times they waged wars of conquest and expansion against the tributary states, selling many of their prisoners into slavery. The forces at the disposal of these African empires could be con-siderable: at its height in the second half of the eighteenth century the Oyo army was around 100,000 strong.[8] By the mid-eighteenth century slave ports had been created across the west African coast, from St Louis and Gorée in Senegambia, Freetown and Sherbro in Sierra Leone, through Elmina, Cape Coast and Ouidah on the Gold Coast and Slave Coast in Ghana and Benin, all the way down to Luanda and Benguela in Angola. Dutch, English, French, Spanish, Portuguese, and Danish slave traders established themselves in these places, forging alliances with local rulers and brokers, and actively promoting wars of expansion by these states and kidnapping raids in the hinterlands.[9]

The single largest group of enslaved people in west Africa were prison-ers of war; in many places, such as Angola in the seventeenth century, and among the Bambara of Segu in present-day Mali, there was no specific word for slaves, they were just described as 'captives'. Those traded across the Atlantic were thus outsiders. Although they shared some features (enslaved people were produced through violence and initially treated as aliens), there were major differences between the African and Atlantic systems of slavery, practically and in principle. In the Atlantic trade, men fetched a higher price than women because of the ever-growing demand for forced labour in the New World. In the internal African slave system, it was the other way round: women were valued more highly than men.[10] Slavery in Africa was not based on race, and it was seldom an exclusively economic phenomenon. Its development was geographically uneven, and in many regions it was not a major feature of social life. Some African slaves found ways of becoming integrated into families and local communities, while others were able to achieve prominence and even rise to positions of power.[11]

In Africa there were some customary, legal, or religious injunctions against selling members of one's own community into slavery: thus the kingdom of Benin was largely successful in protecting its own citizens from Atlantic bondage.[12] In the eighteenth century the rulers of Futa Jallon (in modern-day Guinea) launched a holy war (*jihad*) and converted the populations under their control to Islam. As they spread the teaching of the Qur'an these rulers adopted the custom of not selling any member of their faith into slavery – even as they traded huge numbers of war captives to Europeans.[13] In many places, however, such moral protections did not endure: in Kongo, for instance, because of the rising demand for captive labour across the Atlantic, the distinction between freeborn people and foreigners who could be sold into slavery eventually disappeared.[14] Chattel slavery thus fuelled, and was enmeshed in, ever-growing cycles of warfare in Africa.[15] The presence of large contingents of warriors among the enslaved would have important consequences for New World resistance more generally, as we shall see in later chapters.

Atlantic slavery thus had a profoundly corrosive effect on African societies, for it spread to encompass people in diverse situations of misfortune, such as debtors, criminals, dissenters, family members who had fallen out of favour, and people sentenced by oracular judgements, such as priests and diviners. The most likely targets for slave raiders were dispersed and remote communities whose members were often the victims of kidnapping. These populations sometimes lived near the coast, but mostly in the hinterlands. It has been estimated that at least a third of transatlantic captives were taken by slave raiders in this way.[16] People could be seized in large groups, after frontal attacks by African imperial armed forces or mercenaries, or snatched by opportunist bands exploiting favourable circumstances, such as encounters with isolated travellers, attacks on herders and crop workers, or taking advantage of the temporary absence of adults. In his memoir the abolitionist writer and campaigner Ottobah Cugoano recalled how he was captured in his native village of Ajumako in the Gold Coast by 'several great ruffians' along with a group of young boys and girls as they were playing in a nearby field.[17]

Precolonial state institutions offered only limited protections to African populations against transatlantic enslavement. There are recorded instances of rulers protesting against the trade in captives. Nzinga Mbemba, a Bakongo king of Kongo (also known by his baptized name Afonso I), wrote to the Portuguese ruler John III in 1526. He complained that Portuguese slave raiders were causing immense damage to his country, and asked that they be recalled 'because it is our will that in these kingdoms, there should not be any trade in slaves nor any market for slaves'; there was no local tradition of enslavement.[18] The plea fell on deaf ears, as the Portuguese king was himself actively involved in the trade in bonded men and women, as were and would be so many other European monarchs. Nzinga Mbemba was eventually forced to compromise with the Portuguese and assist in procuring enslaved people for them; local white settlers later tried to assassinate him because he was not seen as a sufficiently reliable ally.[19]

This coercive relationship became a general pattern. African rulers who took a stance against the transatlantic trade risked being overthrown, often with the active complicity of European powers and the intrigues of locally based slave traders. Such was the fate of the Baga chief Tomba, a fearless local ruler (from present-day Guinea Bissau, west Africa) who led a vigorous opposition to slavery among villages in the Rio Nuñez area; European slavers joined forces with Tomba's rivals to have him kidnapped and enslaved in 1721.[20] Likewise, the ruler of Futa Jallon, Abdulkadur, who decreed in 1818 that the transatlantic slave trade was incompatible with Islamic teaching, was toppled a few years later by his rival Bubakar with the political and material support of local slave traders.[21]

Compelling evidence of massive African resistance to Atlantic slavery can be found from the very onset of the European colonial arrival on the continent. When the Portuguese gained control of the equatorial island of São Tomé in 1486 they attempted to turn it into a sugar-producing colony, with the intensive use of African captive labour. The island served as a base for the re-export of captured African men and women to the Americas. The sugar-production system was disrupted by repeated conflicts among slave merchants, white and mixed-race planters, and by the significant pattern of flight among black captives. These maroons were greatly feared by the colonial authorities and eventually entrenched themselves in fortified settlements deep in the forests. Their consistent and repeated attacks on isolated farms forced the Portuguese to abandon their plans to bring more European settlers to São Tomé.[22]

For the colonizers, worse still was to come. In 1595 a revolt on São Tomé erupted among the black captives under the leadership of a charismatic figure named Amador. More than half of the enslaved population (estimated at around 10,000 to 12,000) joined the movement, which was one of the first and largest revolts of this type in Atlantic history. The uprising lasted three weeks and led to the massacre of dozens of white and mixed-race settlers and widespread damage to sugar plantations. All the black captives in liberated territories were emancipated, and Amador was proclaimed king.[23] His rebels tried to storm the capital with 5,000 men but were eventually defeated. Yet the insurgents won a moral victory: slave-based sugar production was abandoned on the island in the aftermath of the rebellion, and Amador is now one of São Tomé's cherished national heroes.[24]

This was not an isolated example in these early stages. Europeans who attempted to travel into the African interior to capture men and women encountered stiff resistance. The sixteenth-century slaver Sir John Hawkins, one of England's first traders in human captives, recounted how 160 of his crew were cut down at Cape Verde, some 800 kilometres off the west African coast, in the late 1560s by local Africans who fired 'invenomed arrows' at them.[25] It was clear to African populations that self-reliance was the only way to survive encroachments from predatory imperial states, armies with superior firepower and equipment, and powerful slave traders and raiders. Those populations thus developed a range of defensive mechanisms to keep themselves out of harm's way. In many respects the most effective (and rational) response was to adopt a visceral suspicion of foreigners, and some communities took this xenophobia to its ultimate conclusion. For example, the Nones, who lived in the forested areas around Thiès in Senegambia, fiercely resisted attempts to subdue them and developed the habit of shooting at strangers, especially if they happened to be white. Another community of Sereer people in the region were described by a local missionary as passionate defenders of their liberty and independence, who believed that slavery was a 'crime' and did everything to protect their people from being kidnapped in their 'little republic of Ndieghem'.[26] The Lobi and Dagara of Burkina Faso and northern Ghana developed similar reputations. Further south, shipwrecked sailors were well advised to steer clear of the Diola of the Casamance, who would kill them on sight – until the Diola found out that the sailors could be ransomed.[27]

One of the most common forms of self-defence was through the organization of local militias. Writing in the eighteenth century about his native Igboland (in today's southeastern Nigeria), where African slave raiders were a constant menace, the anti-slavery campaigner Olaudah Equiano recalled: 'Our whole district is a kind of militia: on a certain signal given, such as the firing of a gun at night, they all rise in arms and rush upon their enemy.'[28] The main local slave traders in the region were the Aro people, in southeastern Igboland, assisted by Abam mercenaries who travelled inland to kidnap villagers and sell them into transatlantic slavery. Against them, all young men went through extensive training in militias during their adolescent years, learning to use 'fire-arms, bows and arrows, broad two-edged swords and javelins' – a training that many put to use in acts of resistance in the New World, and which their descendants still actively maintained a century later.[29] Roadblocks were mounted and expected hide-outs of assailants in forested areas were monitored. Some communities met the raiders with stones, to the consternation of the slavers, who seemed unprepared to face such opposition. One place still bears the Aro nickname (one can sense the indignation) 'those who throw stones at us'. The populations in Akwa (also in southeastern Igboland) formed vigilante groups armed with rifles, built towers where sentinels were posted, and their shots would alert villagers if raiders came within sight.[30]

Faced with increasing attacks from slavers, other communities came together in defensive alliances. One of the most enduring was the kingdom of So, initially formed by the regrouping of seven kingdoms seeking to escape raiding expeditions from Cotonou and Porto-Novo in the Bight of Benin ('So' meant rifle or weapon). Established in the sixteenth century, So developed several resistance camps in the hinterland, where militias were trained to repel attacks from Portuguese slavers and their local African allies. In the early eighteenth century, the kingdom was led by Linzé I, a powerful martial figure who directed a sophisticated network of anti-slavery military patrols on the Wewe river, the main waterway used by regional slave-raiding parties to travel up and down from the Atlantic coast. Linzé's patrols were called 'Achti' ('you are without life'), and they were manned by entranced warriors armed with poisonous javelins. These fighters carried out their patrolling duties chanting religious hymns to the beat of drums and gongs. They intercepted boats carrying captives, seized their crew and weapons, and ended the lives of many slavers. One of their war songs, still remembered today, was inspired by their killing of a Portuguese trader named Saba-do-Santos.[31]

Likewise the Umuchu, and the Isuochi and Nneato of Okigwe in present-day Nigeria, formed defensive confederations to pool their resources. A variant of the same principle among decentralized communities was the choice of a war leader in times of defensive conflict, as with the Wasulu, a people inhabiting a west African region that today spreads across Mali, Ivory Coast, and Guinea, who effectively confronted slave raids in this way.[32] These militias did not rely only on military force. Two further examples from communities in present-day Nigeria can be given. The inhabitants of Enugwu-Ukwu dropped poisoned food, water, and wine on the routes they knew the Abam raiders would use; the assailants perished in large numbers and their planned invasion was aborted.[33] Forced to flee from their original habitations by Abam slave raids, the Ebiri people moved to a new place where they were compelled to confront their attackers again, as they prepared to launch a full-scale invasion. The Ebiri militia defeated their assailants decisively, and this victory thereafter remained an integral part of their collective identity, so much so that they named their settlement Igbo Erughi, 'the town the Aro could not capture'.[34]

Another example of collective resistance came from the Kasena people, who lived in dispersed agricultural communities on the northern Gold Coast. The Kasena had no native tradition of slavery: they lacked a word for it in their own language, using a Hausa term instead. In the eighteenth and nineteenth centuries they protected themselves against persistent slave raids from neighbouring kingdoms, particularly the Asante; one of their preferred techniques was to greet their assailants with 'showers of arrows' with poisoned tips.[35] Communities developed specialized defensive techniques, often exploiting local topography to their advantage. The hill-based Eggon of central Nigeria were constantly on the look-out for slave raiders when they ventured towards the lowlands to gather wood or look after their crops, and they carried drums and trumpets that sounded the alarm as soon as the enemy was spotted; other communities used flutes and gongs. The villagers would then retreat to the hilltop from where they would launch stones, spears, poisoned arrows, and beehives.[36]

Water was an effective natural defence. Tofinu populations came together to escape the attacks of Dahomean armies and slave raiders in the eighteenth century, and they established themselves in lacustrine communities in southern Benin. The most famous of these havens is the town of Ganvié, whose name is widely accepted to mean 'safe at last'. The Tofinu used canoes to move around and over time developed extensive skills in naval warfare, repelling aggressors by relying on their dexterity with javelins, sledgehammers, swords, and harpoons; they also devised a 'particularly ingenious kind of Molotov cocktail'.[37] As we will see in the next chapter, many African communities possessed similar aquatic skills and they were widely deployed by fugitives escaping captivity in the New World.

Fighting back against attempted enslavement was effectively an act of war. In all these places, the warriors who carried out successful attacks against slave raiders were honoured – proof not only that resistance took place, but that these acts of self-defence were accorded a high status within their communities. Raided all year round both from the Sahel and southern Ghana, the Builsa peoples of upper eastern Ghana developed robust techniques of resistance, which they continue to celebrate in their annual Feok festival. These gatherings have helped to forge and pass on a heroic narrative of local struggles against enslavement, by dwelling on the strategies and tactics used by Builsa warriors to overcome their better-equipped adversaries. These idealized reconstructions are reinforced by full displays of the traditional armoury and regalia of the Builsa combatants as they went into battle: bows and arrows, spears, cudgels with specially designed serrated edges, horned helmets, smocks with amulets, and memorabilia such as heads, skins, jaws, and tails of wild animals; these objects were morale boosters as well as sources of spiritual support.[38]

Local communities further frustrated slave raiders by denying them easy access to their dwellings. The traditional style of housebuilding in the African outlands, in scattered hamlets typically close to agricultural lands belonging to family or clan members, gave way to the concentration of houses into ever-tighter units. This defensive pattern was already apparent in a sixteenth-century Portuguese account of a battle in Guinea between the slaver state of Cassanga (allied to the Portuguese) and the followers of a local chieftain, King Bambara. Those followers gained a decisive advantage over the Cassangans by regrouping their dwellings into 'fortified positions', which eventually allowed them to ambush and rout their enemies.[39]

Such defensive settlements became the norm in areas vulnerable to slave-raiding, with individual houses and collective habitations undergoing significant transformations. In coastal Guinea-Bissau, dwellings were 'large and well-built', with 'so many doors and rooms that they are more like labyrinths than houses'.[40] In villages in the region, houses were arranged in circles, and the cluster of homes was walled with tall timbers with pointed stakes, often with external ditches; there were sentinel towers and gates (called *tabancas*), which would be closed at night for added security.[41] In Wasulu territory the remains of some of these walls are still standing; they were made with mud, pebbles, and karité oil, and had holes that could be used by riflemen.[42]

Generally, the wall perimeter protected the village granary, which was often the first point of attack for slave raiders. The assailants would be deterred by these fortifications, as they lacked the means to sustain sieges for any significant length of time. Houses were frequently surrounded by high walls, although these barriers were not always effective against determined predators – Olaudah Equiano and his sister were captured in his native Igboland by a small party of three raiders who jumped over the external wall of his home.[43] The Builsa communities, like many others, developed the practice of sealing the top of their roofs with sand rather than grass, so that slave raiders would not be able to set them alight.[44] The houses of Senegambian communities were interconnected, to enable easy escape for their inhabitants, and so that neighbours could be warned of imminent danger. These houses typically had only one entrance and no windows, and openings of homes and town gates were very low so that several people could not enter at the same time;[45] the entrances to the dwellings of the Gurunsi were only 70 centimetres high.[46]

Such defensive provisions were not always sufficient, and, when the human and practical costs of resistance in long-established positions became too high, populations moved. Flight was a major form of resistance to enslavement in Africa. Natural conditions that offered greater safety from large armies were often chosen, such as forests, mountains, and hills, and swamps, mangroves, and lakes. Ganvié, for example, is generally believed to have been founded in the aftermath of the kingdom of Dahomey's brutal conquest of Allada (1724) and Ouidah (1727), with populations in the surrounding areas fleeing to avoid enslavement. Among the thousands of men and women who were sold into Atlantic slavery at this time were the Allada-native parents of Toussaint Louverture, the future revolutionary leader of Saint-Domingue. Dahomean soldiers were unfamiliar with canoes and were known to be poor swimmers, so water was seen as a particularly valuable protection.[47] Likewise, victims of slave raids in Gambia in the nineteenth century often fled to MacCarthy Island for protection.[48] The Balanta people in the Guinea-Bissau region were one among many groups known as *refoulés*: hinterland populations forced to flee towards the coast as a result of aggressions from Mandinka communities. The Balanta developed defensive military techniques that relied on the natural protections of mangrove-covered areas, allowing them to ambush and unsettle slave-raiding forces even when the latter enjoyed numerical superiority: the Mandinka word *balanto* means 'those who resist'.[49]

Higher ground was the other obvious place of refuge. From the sixteenth century onwards, communities in the Lake Chad area of western-central Africa became vulnerable to slave raiders from powerful regional empires, and they responded by moving their dwellings to more remote upland regions. The Mofou relocated to the hills of Mikiri, and then Durumi. The Toupouri fled to the Tekem mountains in Chad, where each of its twelve summits was settled by one of the Toupouri clans – a perfect match as the refugees happened to have exactly twelve clans.[50] These heights provided caverns that were used to hide, store food, and shelter cattle, especially for the Nyem-Nyem, who settled in the caves of Mount Jim, in the mountains of Galim. They even found two springs there, and their descendants in Cameroon still celebrate their effective resistance against slavers and later German colonizers.[51] Recent archaeological research at places of enslaved memory in Sankana, Gwollu, and Nzulezu in Ghana found surviving evidence of local communities using caves for shelter and religious purposes, and to forge weaponry and ammunition, including gunpowder.[52] Among the Builsa people, songs are still sung about retreating from slave raiders into rocky and cavernous areas, and then ambushing them. One refrain goes as follows: 'let someone be deceived to follow and die in the bush'.[53]

The practical challenges faced by these communities were extraordinary. But so were their responses. They put all the materials they could find to the fullest possible use: rocks served to fortify their dwellings, as weapons against their predators, and as we shall later see as sources of spiritual comfort and strength. They created defence systems based on plants: in Senegambia, many venomous shrubs were cultivated to provide an initial barrier against attack; thorny hedges were used as well, and sometimes village walls were reinforced with bristly plants.[54] The Nyem-Nyem built an underground tunnel that could lead them to a friendly neighbouring community in times of need. In the seventeenth and eighteenth centuries, when Mount Mandara became another major refuge, local communities built additional stone walls on the flanks to slow down the approach of the enemy. These walls ran along the borders of foothills and in concentric circles around the summits.[55] For many of these settlements, survival depended on producing food without individuals needing to travel to lower ground, where they might be more exposed. The Kabre of northern Togo had to face slave raiders from three different directions, so they retreated to mountain tops for protection. They evolved specialized farming techniques, building terraces and anti-erosion barriers, and developing intensive agricultural systems.[56]

Flight led to the creation of communities of runaways, which established themselves across west Africa from the seventeenth century onwards. The concept of marronage is much discussed in New World settings, but the scale and significance of this phenomenon in Africa have been under-estimated until recently. However, individuals, groups, and entire communities came together to form free settlements, whether to escape from an existing condition of enslavement, or from its impending threat by African states and slave-raiding forces. Mostly, people ran away 'because they did not consider themselves enslaved'.[57] These fugitive communities sometimes found refuge on islands, such as the numerous clusters located off the Upper Guinea coast. But many more proliferated on the mainland. Their populations were fluid, and sometimes their settlements proved short-lived, ending with further flight, destruction, or recapture. In many cases, however, these free communities endured over significant periods of time – years and even decades. In one instance, as will be seen later in this chapter, an entire region retained its reputation as a bastion for runaways for well over two centuries.

These settlements often survived long enough to feature on maps of the period, and their whereabouts were widely known among enslaved populations and free black people. Information circulated through word of mouth about how the more remote (or concealed) places could be reached, and networks of support developed to facilitate the runaways' transit to safety; these could be based on family ties, kinship, or religious and spiritual affinities.[58] Flight could be provoked by a wide range of circumstances, involving those individuals destined for the Atlantic trade as well as internal captives. The latter were liable to escape in the earlier phases of their bondage, when they typically had to endure the brutal process of 'breaking', which could involve branding and flogging.[59] Mistreatment could be systematic, a fate that was particularly common for agricultural or field workers, or when captives were forcibly incorporated into an African imperial militia, as frequently happened. At the same time, the physical constraints on internal African captives were generally looser, so some took the opportunity to flee when sent away on business (many were deployed as itinerant traders), or when their owners died. Most importantly, flight could be provoked by the threat or even the fear of being sold into chattel slavery. In the Angolan area, there were numerous reported instances of collective flight following the sale of one or more domestics, as well as stories about captives working in coastal farms and factories escaping en masse when they heard rumours that they were to be shipped to Brazil.[60]

Those who were captured and destined for coastal slave ports would attempt to flee whenever they could, whether immediately after being taken, during their transport by slave raiders in caravans or on canoes, or when they were being held in barracoons and camps at various staging posts on their journey coastwards. The physical circumstances that the captives faced here were extremely testing, and in themselves were inducements to flight: gruelling marches, severe weather, inhospitable regions, limited rations, and cramped holding areas. Captors tried to prevent flight by using restraints such as ropes, manacles, and neck harnesses.[61] But prisoners managed to escape in significant numbers anyway, either by breaking free through their own devices or with the help of local runaway communities. Even when they reached the coast and were penned in fortified holding stations, there were frequent attempts to flee. One of the many recorded episodes of this kind occurred at Cape Coast Castle in November 1730, when an incarcerated captive tried to saw the bars of his windows; he was known to have made several previous attempts.[62]

Runaway settlements were often formed after a specific act of resistance, such as a movement or an uprising of a particular group of people. In 1756, for example, a group of captives in Futa Jallon revolted and, declaring themselves free, migrated north-west towards Futa Bundu, where they created a fortified town called Kondeah. Despite repeated attempts by slavers to attack them, they survived and were eventually allowed to live unmolested until the late eighteenth century.[63] In northwestern Sierra Leone, a revolt of enslaved people in 1825 against local Soso elites was led by a man called Tamba; after killing their rulers they moved away and settled in a place that came to be known as Tambakka.[64] Runaway settlements could arise in the aftermath of a successful mutiny on board a slave ship: after one such insurrection on a Danish carrier in the mid-eighteenth century, a group of captives escaped and founded a free settlement on the mountains off the Sierra Leone coast. They were led by a Fula called 'Old Mano', and they managed to guard their freedom against external encroachment.[65] A few decades later, an insurrection on another Danish vessel, this time lying in the Rokel estuary in Sierra Leone, led to the formation of a free settlement a few miles from Conakry, in the hills; it was given the name of Deserters' Town.[66]

Runaway insurgencies always started locally, but they could spread across territories and even entire regions. One of the most dramatic episodes of this kind unfolded across the Upper Guinea coast in the later eighteenth century. It began with an uprising of Temne, Baga, and Bullom captives against the Mandinka ruling elites of the kingdom of Moriah, an important commercial centre whose agricultural production was dependent on a brutal regime of plantation slavery. Captives represented more than two-thirds of the population; they were seized to work in the rice fields and many of them were then sold to Atlantic slave traders after the harvest cycle. In addition to this physical oppression, the prisoners were victims of religious persecution; many of their spiritual beliefs and rituals were violently suppressed, and those accused of occult practices were routinely prosecuted.

In 1785, in the aftermath of one of these trials, a revolt of around seven hundred captives erupted, leading to the killing of local Mandinka rulers, whose decapitated heads were paraded in triumph; rice fields were set alight.[67] Led by their commander Tambee, the victorious rebels escaped, forming settlements in several different areas, the most significant cluster emerging among a group of villages at the foot of the Yangiakuri Hills. These dwellings were fortified and attracted a steady stream of runaways and free men and women from surrounding areas; they united in a common search to live in dignity, free from enslavement and the despotism of the regional monarchs and aristocrats.[68] Although the sources are not precise, it appears that several leaders emerged within the runaway ranks, one of whom was a warrior and spiritual leader named Dangasago.

The consolidation of the Yangiakuri rebellion posed a serious threat to slaving states in the region, which made several unsuccessful attempts to put down the insurgency during the next decade. The rebels not only defended themselves resolutely but fought back, visiting severe military and economic losses upon their foes. They exploited the divisions among surrounding political communities, playing off rival groups against each other, and for a while relying on the protection of a powerful Islamic holy man named Fatta.[69] Finally, after killing off Fatta, the Mandinka and their aristocratic allies formed a broad alliance in 1795, with the support of European mercenaries; in March 1796 they destroyed the rebel settlements following a lengthy siege. The rebels managed to inflict heavy casualties on their attackers (who lost more than half of their men), but in the end they were recaptured and sold into slavery. Dangasago was killed after being betrayed – although a small number of runaways commanded by another leader, Mamby, managed to survive in their settlement in Bena territory.[70]

Further south, perhaps the most remarkable example of fugitive resettlement was the province of Kisama, a largely arid geographical area situated in Angolan territory between Luanda and Benguela, ports that respectively transported the greatest and third-greatest numbers of captives in the transatlantic slave trade. From the late sixteenth century until well into the seventeenth, Kisama became a refuge for populations fleeing the slave trade and the wars that fed it in the Angolan interior. Kisama was exceptional in several respects: its salt mines were of the highest quality, and it was a haven that welcomed people escaping enslavement from a broad swathe of west-central Africa, as well as soldiers from regional armies and large numbers of women. And even though it produced highly skilled warriors, Kisama prioritized communal harmony and social and economic integration over the culture of war. Above all it rejected slavery and refused to engage in any aspect of the slave trade, unlike neighbouring states such as Ndongo and Kongo.

Although Kisama was politically decentralized, a strong *soba* (military and spiritual leader), Kafuxi Ambari, emerged from within the communities. Ambari was a charismatic local ruler and warrior who came to prominence in 1594 when he defeated much larger advancing Portuguese forces and made them abandon the fort they had built in the area. He enjoyed considerable authority over other *sobas*, without apparently establishing a formal hierarchy of rule. Ambari was able to maintain his region's distinct profile as a haven for skilled warriors and opponents of slavery. A report from the Portuguese governor of Benguela in 1631 noted sourly that the people living in Kisama 'do not participate in the [slave] trade, nor do they wish to become vassals'. In 1655 another report mentioned that Kisama was harbouring 'more than ten thousand slaves', and it was disrupting Portuguese commerce in the region as well as rejecting any contact with their missionaries.[71]

Kisama's autonomous regime was eventually compromised as wars and slave-raiding intensified in the later seventeenth century. But the example of freedom and resistance to enslavement it had set continued to reverberate throughout the Angolan region and beyond. Two centuries later, a report from the governor of Angola in 1850 recognized, not without a touch of admiration, that black people in the area had a 'natural' inclination to escape slavery.[72] By this point runaway communities had become so widespread that these settlements were designated by specific terms, such as *mutulos* or *quilombos*. They proliferated as the Atlantic slave trade in the region intensified from the late seventeenth century onwards, and administrative reports frequently referred to the presence of runaway communities both in coastal areas and in the hinterlands. These texts further observed that their populations came from different backgrounds and territories, and attracted enslaved field workers and former soldiers as well as free Africans. Kisama was still being described as a 'safe haven for runaways' from Luanda in the mid-nineteenth century.[73]

The emergence of charismatic leaders from within their ranks, such as Ambari, was key to the survival of these runaway communities. Another such figure was a *quilombo* leader named Calumba, a warrior and spiritual guide who established a free settlement around Benguela. Not much is known about him except that he was feared by the Portuguese and became such a powerful chieftain that he had the authority to appoint local

African rulers.[74] Strong leaders helped protect their communities by forging judicious political alliances with local African chiefs, despite the best efforts of government officials to prevent them. They inspired, by their own example, a wider culture of resistance against slavery, and helped nurture the particular qualities of these runaway communities: their resilience, their mobility and adaptability to local surroundings, and their expertise at raiding traders on their established routes.

Indeed, these communities disrupted the order that the colonial authorities were seeking to create. Traders often complained that inhabitants of *quilombos* would attack their caravans, while slavers would report that the runaways would intercept convoys of captives heading for the coast and free them. Even with the military support of local African forces, Portuguese authorities were unable to eradicate these *quilombos*, and after a succession of failed campaigns in the 1850s they estimated that more than 20,000 runaways were still living in settlements in the Angolan area. A significant proportion of these fugitives had acquired military skills, and at this point the Portuguese feared the runaways had become so powerful that they could attack and overrun Luanda itself. The colonial authorities were thus forced to accept co-existence and signed a treaty with the former captives, which guaranteed the existence of their *quilombos*.[75]

These patterns of runaway leadership, strength, and endurance were all in evidence in what was perhaps the greatest nineteenth-century revolt by African captives, the Bilali rebellion in the west African kingdom of Soso. By this point, the transatlantic slave trade was in sharp decline, partly due to its formal abolition by the British in 1807; this struggle was about the persistence of African slavery and the emergence of an indigenous abolitionist movement. The uprising began when Bilali, the son of King Alimamy Dumbuya and one of his captive concubines, was denied recognition by his family when the king died in 1838, contrary to convention and the king's express wishes. Bilali, a devout Muslim who had been given extensive Qur'anic and military training by his father, then fled with his family and supporters to the Tonko Limba region, where he was welcomed by the chieftains and given land to build a settlement. He named it Laminyah, and very soon its population swelled as it became a magnet for runaways from the surrounding Soso and Temne regions.

Bilali professed opposition to slavery and his followers pledged to support him and protect their community from attack. Over the next four decades, Laminyah and other runaway settlements that grew up around it effectively resisted incursions from African slaver forces, and Bilali established himself as a beacon of abolitionism in the area. In the early 1870s he was able to negotiate a settlement with neighbouring states that preserved his autonomy. The pan-Africanist Edward Wilmot Blyden, who travelled to the areas controlled by Bilali, wrote that the charismatic runaway leader had succeeded in 'forming a large powerful party, and in rousing among a large portion of the enslaved population not only a devotion to the idea of liberty at any price, but a strong attachment to himself and a hatred for all those who hold slaves'. Blyden referred to Bilali as the 'new Spartacus'.[76]

What sense can we make of the intellectual and spiritual sources of these resistance practices, and the ideas and values they expressed? Such a reconstruction is not easy, as the voices of these fugitive resisters have come through to us faintly – only indirectly, and typically mediated by the very people they were fighting against, or by European observers who, even with the best of intentions, lacked the necessary tools to appreciate the world views of the peoples they were writing about. For example, the British anthropologist Frederick Butt-Thompson described the late eighteenth-century Yangiakuri rebels as 'republicans'.[77] This label might seem obvious for a time when revolutionaries in Europe and the Americas were fighting for emancipation from monarchical rule in the name of equality and fraternity. More recent scholars such as Bruce Mouser have been more sceptical, specifically arguing that the Yangiakuri conflict was caught up in regional power struggles, and was much more complex than a binary struggle between slavers and resisters; Mouser deduces on those grounds that the rebellion was unlikely to have been 'democratic or republican'.[78] Both positions are problematic: the first because it mechanically transposes a European scheme of values onto the Yangiakuri conflict, the second because it seems to deny the possibility that African anti-slavery struggles could be expressing universal beliefs about freedom.

Equally unsatisfactory are attributions of general psychological dispositions to these African rebels on the basis of either their emotions or their alleged ethnic characteristics. For example, there are frequent references in administrative reports and slaver narratives to acts of resistance being provoked by fears of white cannibalism; these were often seen as the primary cause of slave-ship revolts, even though such claims are simplistic and typically fail to engage with the wider spiritual beliefs of the enslaved.[79] The attribution of martial or pacific characteristics to African ethnic groups became fashionable at the height of colonial slavery, although these classifications were largely arbitrary and grounded in racial and cultural stereotypes that are now discredited. Thus the Fon were seen as more inclined to active resistance than the Igbo, who were widely thought to be prone to depression and suicide.[80]

Yet more recent ethnographic evidence from west Africa, as high-lighted earlier, has shown that Igbo populations were no less pugnacious in challenging their attempted enslavement than other groups. As we will observe in later chapters, revolts and rebellions in the New World were carried out by captives across a wide range of ethnic communities. In any event, the real evidence that there was little discernible difference among African ethnic groups in terms of their rebellious propensities came from the practices of the slavers themselves: they warned each other constantly about the revolutionary dispositions of their captives, and often tried to stop prisoners from the same geographical area or ethnicity from carry-ing out breakaways or uprisings by separating them from one another, so as to prevent seditious communications.[81] Moreover, as we will later observe, these 'ethnic' markers were not fixed, and indeed could rapidly be transcended when individuals from different communities found them-selves facing a common predicament, such as the threat of enslavement, or the experience of captivity in a coastal barracoon or on a slave ship.

What of the great monotheistic religions such as Christianity and Islam? The only region with a significant Christian tradition was Kongo, whose rulers embraced the faith as from the late fifteenth century, and where there was no indigenous tradition of slavery before the arrival of the Por-tuguese. As we saw earlier, a robust international anti-slavery movement emerged in the seventeenth century, culminating in Mendonça's denunci-ation of chattel slavery to the Vatican as a violation of natural, divine, and civil law.[82] However, eventually the power of European enslavers and their political and religious allies prevailed in Kongo, and the forcible capture and sale of Africans became so widespread that the communities could no longer even protect their own. Catholic ecclesiastical hierarchies became actively complicit in Atlantic slavery, from its theological justifications as a form of divine redemption and persecutions of African religions to the forced baptisms of captives, the presence of churches in coastal slave forts (in some instances, as at Elmina, directly above the dungeons where prisoners were held), and the naming of slave ships after Christian saints. For example, there were British slave vessels called *Saint George*, *Saint Michael*, *Saint Paul*, *Saint Thomas*, and *Saint David*. In the eighteenth-century Mascarene Islands east of Madagascar, Lazarist missionaries not only defended the institution of slavery but owned slaves, and they sub-jected them to the same regime of physical punishments as were generally practised at the time.[83]

We have seen that Islam did not offer a blanket opposition to slavery, and many of the major Islamic caliphates were heavily engaged in the Atlantic slave trade, even though they did not sell members of their own

faith. But Islamic teachings could inspire and justify individual oppositions to slavery by dissenting figures: this was no doubt the case with
Bilali, for example. There were interesting instances of anti-slavery attitudes and practices among the lower Islamic clergy; so much so that in
coastal areas, many *marabouts* (Muslim clerics) were kidnapped and sold
into slavery by European colonial authorities, with the support of slave
traders. In eighteenth-century Senegambia, monarchs and aristocrats were
invariably allied with slaver interests, and they adopted harsh policies
that were resented by large sections of the population; in response, there
was an Islamic revolt against the slave trade in 1765. One religious leader
ordered all boats passing through his area to be inspected for captives,
and anyone capable of reciting verses of the Qur'an to be freed.[84] Other
marabouts set up villages along wooded areas that served as refuges, and
many runaways travelled long distances to reach these safe havens, where
they were treated on an equal footing. The names of these places bore
witness to the inclusive spirit that governed the life of these communities,
as well as the spiritual principles they cherished: 'here where no one can
reach them anymore', 'the place of abundance', 'here where we speak of
peace', and 'the village of free people'.[85]

Another way of thinking about the resistance of African captives is
to view it as an expression of black fugitive thought: confronting the
oppression of enslavement by devising strategies of survival, and creating
spaces (often concealed) where they could live autonomous lives; hence
the notion of freedom as marronage, which will be discussed later in the
book. Key sources of inspiration for these emancipatory endeavours were
the traditional religions that dominated collective life. These belief systems
were complex and highly differentiated across regions, but at their core
they shared several characteristics, especially the fluidity of the boundary
between the living and the dead, and the interconnectedness between the
secular and spiritual spheres. Also common was the reliance on access to
the divine through continuous revelation (visions, miracles, prophecies,
and cures) and prophetic intermediaries (ordinary people, such as ancestors, healers with specialized medical skills, spiritual figures who could
communicate with the higher world through possession, as well as community leaders endowed with special powers, such as *gangas* in Angola).[86]
This revelatory dimension was so powerful that it was embraced even
by followers of Christianity and Islam in Africa. Continuous revelation
meant that religious systems did not have fixed theologies but were constantly adapted and adjusted according to circumstance – and of course
the emergence of slavery had a major impact here.

Deities came in an elaborate range of forms: most religions subscribed to one general overlord, flanked by a large cast of lesser deities, who were worshipped in shrines or believed to be present in natural areas, such as rocks, pools, forests, and caves. Curiously shaped stones, for example, were widely seen as having particular powers, which could be harnessed by specialists. Natural objects could take on a spiritual form after a particularly decisive event: trees that had effectively served as a refuge from a slave-raiding attack would become sacred spaces, and thenceforth be integrated into the panoply of local divinities. Caves that provided a safe haven for local villagers would come to be seen as the homes of gods, and transformed into places of worship;[87] one of the gods still celebrated in contemporary Ganvié, namely Finondè, was a local guide who was believed to have sacrificed himself to prevent the attack of a group of slave raiders; the spot where he caused their boat to capsize became sacred.[88] Rock art from southern Africa shows that eighteenth- and early nineteenth-century fugitive groups depicted animals such as baboons and ostriches in their mountainous refuges. These creatures were seen in spiritual terms and believed to have special powers associated with protection and escape; the paintings were created by ritual specialists who served as war-doctors.[89]

African traditional religions accorded a central role to spirits, who were appealed to for a variety of public and private purposes and were believed to inhabit talismans or fetishes. These objects were very widely used in daily life; the Islamic variants were known as *gris-gris* (typically verses of the Qur'an encased in pouches), while the Yoruba-Fon peoples appealed to their *vodun* spirits in fetishes in the form of ceramic vessels; their higher god was sometimes called Vodu or Mawu. Water spirits were widely popular across west Africa, and they were reached through fetishes shaped as seahorses. All traditional African religions were highly syncretic. Yoruba-Fon peoples had a panoply of gods – such as Dangbe, the snake deity; Ogun, the god of iron, warfare, and hunting; and Legba, the director of life and death – but they were open to including European gods and saints in their worship.[90] In Luanda and across the Portuguese Atlantic world, fetishes were known as *bolsas de mandinga* (mandingo bags); these amulets were carried by captives to protect themselves from abuse by their masters, and were believed to have the power to stop weapons from penetrating the body.[91] This supernatural protective power was associated with west African *vodun* religions, as well as many local African deities and spirits; in Igbo territory the Ngwa community worshipped a war-god named Ike-Oha, who was believed to shield its devotees from bullet wounds.[92] As we saw earlier, warriors carried these amulets with them when they went into battle to defend themselves and their communities.

In many regions where local populations were vulnerable to slave raiders, *vodun* itself evolved into a philosophical system in which disciples were trained in martial skills, such as hunting, endurance running, swimming, and the mystical art of invisibility.[93]

This flexible and localized spiritual landscape offered obvious advantages to individuals and communities fighting enslavement. The openness of African traditional religions to all devotees prevented the imposition of any dogmatic or fatalistic narrative about slavery being in some sense 'natural'. The mobility and fluidity of these religions mirrored the very conditions of the rebels and runaways, and it enabled them (literally) to carry their spirits with them, and to find natural objects of religious worship wherever they happened to move. The emphasis on revelation and prophecy created opportunities, too, for charismatic war leaders, who could enhance their authority by surrounding themselves with supernatural auras. For example, Kafuxi Ambari's reputation in Kisama rested not only on his political, military, and diplomatic skills, but on the widespread belief that he could command the elements; farming communities would call upon him whenever droughts became a menace. His magical repertoire extended to casting malignant and even fatal spells on his adversaries. Thus, when the newly appointed Portuguese governor João Rodriguez Coutinho ventured to attack his territory in 1602, Coutinho died within six days, struck down by 'the illness of the country'. Both Ambari's supporters and Portuguese chroniclers credited this achievement to the rebel leader's supernatural powers, and indeed this moral victory had immediate practical consequences: for the moment, the colonizers abandoned their sweeping plans to conquer the territory.[94]

The connections between spiritual belief, ritual practice, and resistance were further in evidence in the realm of occultism. Divination was widespread across west Africa, and magical and healing practices were not the sole preserves of the enslaved, for they were used by people in all walks of life to protect themselves against evil spirits; divination included European participants and spiritual motifs drawn from Christianity and Islam. But the anti-slavery dimensions of the phenomenon were unmistakable. The enslaved turned readily towards African occultism because it was a form of spirituality despised and feared by the European slavers and Catholic ecclesiastical hierarchies. It was true that the slavers' fear of harm (to themselves and their captives through poisoning or evil possession) led to supernatural arts being represented as a form of 'devil-worship', and it resulted in the prosecution of priests and healers, a significant number of whom were sold into Atlantic slavery. However, this very repression reinforced the connection between occultism and slavery; the two grew enmeshed. Priests were treated as rebels, and, just as importantly, rebels were invariably accused of 'sorcery': the Yangiakuri revolt was denounced for its occult practices by the regional forces that eventually defeated it.[95]

This symbiosis had important consequences for the practice of occultism in Africa, which evolved over time to become the central spiritual underpinning of resistance to Atlantic slavery. It incorporated within its cosmology the imperative that all should be bound to deliver justice from enslavement, and from the massive social disruptions brought about by the European slave trade, such as mistreatment, malnutrition, disease, wars, and population displacement. It is notable that the elements which made up African conjuring rituals generally combined local components (animals, shells, powder) with objects referring explicitly to the slave trade, such as ropes, iron chains, whips, and trade cloth. It is against this backdrop that African beliefs about white cannibalism need to be understood. In the apt summary of one scholar, African occultism was the response of local spiritual systems to 'the most virulent form of witchcraft', which was the slave trade itself.[96] Among ordinary people in Africa, the association of slavers with evil was widespread. In his memoirs the nineteenth-century French-Italian slave dealer Théophilus Conneau observed that Africans viewed him as a 'Satan' and reported instances of women throwing handfuls of earth towards him, while uttering a short sentence. He believed this gesture was a form of exorcism aimed at 'driving the evil spirit from them'.[97]

Knowledge of the supernatural could be deployed for a range of purposes. Some were personal, such as providing comfort for sorrow, and healing mental and physical ailments. Others were more oriented towards protection of the community, such as the practice of turning to healers and priests to interpret predicaments and confront moments of danger. Communities threatened by imperial or slave-raiding forces often used diviners to find out about the timings of attacks: on the outskirts of nineteenth-century Luanda, for example, runaways paid a woman named Maria Sebastião to inform them about colonial troop movements; she was apparently so effective that the runaways lived 'without concerns'.[98] Likewise the Sandema people successfully turned to their earth priest Atankab to predict the impending attack of slave raiders. He carried out the divination at the community's holy shrine, and he announced his conclusions after seeing a vision that included 'guinea fowls without feathers'.[99]

Diviners could be recruited to help communities facing slaver attacks to ward off potential enemies. Intimidation of adversaries was a common device, as highlighted by another legendary episode in the Igbo resistance to slave-raiding. Enwelana, the priestly king of the Nri, was so appalled by the incursions of Aro and Abam slave raiders into his territory that he pronounced a ritual curse on them and declared their presence unwelcome. This excommunication did not completely stop the raids, but it increased the vulnerability of the raiders, as the curse was tantamount to a declaration of war, and one of its practical effects was to allow any member of the Nri to kill an Aro or Abam person without being accused of murder. According to oral tradition, the leading Aro slave raider was sufficiently moved to apologize to Enwelana for his predatory actions.[100]

Despite their concerted efforts to resist enslavement, in the end millions of Africans ended up being seized and transported across the Atlantic in slave ships. The conditions they faced were unimaginable to our modern sensibility. Men and women were separated, kept naked, packed close together, with the men enchained for long periods. Around a quarter of those on board were children. Many of the enslaved refused to submit and committed suicide, by rejecting food or throwing themselves overboard; mistreatment and disease led to the further deaths of an estimated two million captives.[101]

But notwithstanding the brutal treatment they experienced on these vessels, the enslaved did not give up their struggle for freedom, continuing their resistance in insurgencies that erupted aboard the ships ferrying them across the Atlantic. Often seen as isolated and desperate acts, these Middle Passage revolts spanned more than three centuries. One of the first known insurrections took place in 1532, aboard the Portuguese ship *Misericordia*, when the eighty captives seized control of the vessel, killed most of the crew, and steered themselves back to the Benin coast, where they disembarked; and one of the last documented insurrections occurred in 1865, aboard the Spanish vessel *Gato*.[102] Indeed, these systematic attempts at self-emancipation should be seen as the culmination of the different facets of African resistance we have documented across this chapter. In many instances, on-board revolts were led by men and women who had already taken an active stand against slavery in Africa, whether in the self-defence militias of their own communities, in runaway settlements, during the forced marches to the coast, or in the encampments and forts where they were held before embarkation.

One of the best examples of these continuities and overlaps was the Baga chief Tomba, who as we saw earlier led the opposition to slave raiders in the Rio Nuñez area, before being seized by them in 1721. He exacted a high price for his capture, killing two members of the raiding party that came to seize him. Following his abduction, he was brought to the coast, where a contemporary English eyewitness, a surgeon in the

Royal Navy, described his 'bold, stern aspect'. He observed that Tomba remained unbowed, despite enduring severe whippings by the slave raider who had detained him, an Englishman nicknamed (appropriately enough) Cracker. After being forcibly embarked on the British slave ship *Robert*, Tomba went on to instigate a revolt while the vessel was still near the African shores, with the help of several of his companions and a female captive who was able to smuggle a hammer down to the lower deck where he was held. Their plan was to break free from their bonds, neutralize the crew, release the 220 prisoners on board, and escape inland. The insurgents managed to reach the upper deck and kill three crew members, before the remaining crew emerged and contained the rebellion; Tomba's life was spared, but three of his fellow rebels were executed.[103]

Thanks to the SlaveVoyages database, which has drawn on archival sources to tabulate more than 36,000 journeys across the Atlantic between 1514 and 1866, with a specific column devoted to 'resistance', it is now clear that hundreds of such vessels experienced some form of insurgency on board.[104] The exact number will never be known, as captains often avoided reporting the revolts, since these reflected poorly on their command. Tomba's actions were in many respects characteristic of the overall pattern of rebellions. Most of these insurrections (75 per cent) took place when ships were close to the African shores; as with the *Robert*, they were far more likely to occur when the ship was carrying a large number of captives, and a relatively limited crew; and at nighttime, when only a small proportion of the crew were keeping watch. Tomba was a figure with extensive military training, as was no doubt true of his close associates, and this too was a standard feature of slaveship rebellions, which were generally instigated by captives with some military or combat experience.

Tomba and his fellow rebels were given critical assistance by the female captives, and this was a necessary condition for enabling an insurrection to be launched. Women (and children) used their greater freedom of movement on board to gather strategic information about crew movements and, when possible, locate and access weapons; in some instances they managed to poison the crew.[105] Women used their fetishes to try and protect their fellow captives and cast spells on the captain and crew members.[106] In some instances women were the primary instigators of rebellions, as revealed by the captain's log on the slave ship *Unity*, which made its way across the Atlantic in June 1770 after picking up 425 captives from Dahomey and São Tomé. There were three revolts, the first of which was led by women, two of whom died; the second uprising followed the death of a young woman captive; the surviving women were each given twenty-four lashes.[107] Evoking his experience of the Middle Passage in his memoir, Ottobah Cugoano mentioned an attempted insurrection that was to be carried out by women and children, with the full support of the men chained below deck. The plan was to burn the ship, so that all those on board would perish; death was deemed preferable to enslavement. However, in this instance the plot was thwarted.[108]

These slave-ship rebellions were complex affairs, nowhere more so than in the instances when captives were released following some kind of armed attack from African shores. A total of 101 such cases are listed in the SlaveVoyages database, from the seventeenth to the late eighteenth century, with around two-thirds resulting in the complete release of the captives. These listings are separate from the category of 'slave insurrections', where the rebellions originated exclusively from on board. The first documented instance of such an armed attack from the shore occurred in 1688, when a British ship that had picked up 251 captives from Calabar (present-day Nigeria) was successfully targeted by an African commando, and the prisoners were released. The final case on record was the attack on the Liverpool ship *Young Tom* in 1796, with the emancipation of all 359 captives. In between, we have listings of mostly British ships, except for a few French vessels, such as the *Grue* from Nantes, which was forced to release its 150 captives in 1776 after coming under attack. Some ships were struck on more than one occasion: such was the fate of the London schooner *Fly*, which was successfully targeted in 1774 and then again in 1792, with a total of 361 captives set free; it withstood a third attack in 1805. In 1753 the *Race Horse* was not only relieved of its 230 human captives but stripped of its contents; the vessel had to be 'recovered from the natives'. We do not know what happened to the crew, but there were only eight of them, which almost certainly facilitated the success of the rebellion.[109] It is very likely that similar incidents took place on Spanish, Portuguese, and Dutch ships, even though far fewer records have survived.[110]

The archives on which these tabulations are based (official notices, newspaper reports, diaries, insurance claims)[111] were not always precise about the circumstances in which these acts of emancipation took place. For example, we have little information about the external authors (typically referred to as 'natives') or the exact places where the incidents occurred. But the contemporary descriptions were clear enough: these voyages were 'cut off by Africans', the vessels were 'attacked from the shore', after which the captives 'disembarked in the old world'. Some spots were privileged: rivers and river estuaries appear in several instances, as in 1732 when news reached New England that a schooner had been intercepted off the Guinean coast by the people of Cassan. The captain John Major and most of his crew were killed, and the prisoners set free.[112] In 1742 the *Jolly Batchelor* (part-owned by the American colonial merchant Peter Faneuil) was anchored in the Sierra Leone river when it was attacked by a contingent of local Africans, who killed the captain named Cutler and threw him overboard, freed the seventy-five prisoners, and stripped the ship of its rigging and sails. The crew went in search of the emancipated captives, but found fewer than half of them; the rest had disappeared into the woods.[113] Captives from Madagascar frequently revolted; in 1775, out of 120 on board the French slave ship *Flore*, 104 of them carried out an insurrection, a few days after the vessel embarked from the north-east coast of the island. They overpowered the crew and steered the vessel back to their homeland, where they disembarked and made off with the cargo, as well as all the planks and pieces of wood they could carry away.[114]

On-board slave rebellions were far greater in number, and unlike the attacks that came from the shores, these insurgencies saw the comprehensive involvement of captives at all stages. Indeed, the fear of these uprisings was a leitmotif in the correspondence and memoirs of slavers. As one of them reflected: 'These [insurrections] are always meditated; for the men slaves are not easily reconciled to their confinement and treatment; and, if attempted, they are seldom suppressed without considerable loss; and sometimes they succeed, to the destruction of a whole ship's company at once . . . One unguarded hour, or minute, is sufficient to give the slaves the opportunity they are always waiting for.'[115] Although some uprisings took place spontaneously, when the captives suddenly found themselves in a favourable situation on deck (during mealtimes, for example), most were carefully planned and co-ordinated, despite the severe difficulties faced by the insurgents.

These schemes involved lengthy discussions below deck, the gathering of information, and on some occasions the recruitment of accomplices from among the crew, in particular African-born ship's hands and interpreters. Among the most elaborate plans of this kind was one hatched by an African sailor in 1728: he duped the British captain of the *Queen Caroline* into trusting him, went ashore, and returned with a group of local Africans, who promptly organized an attack on the ship. The rebellion led not only to the killing of most of the crew and the liberation of the prisoners, but also to the plundering of all the goods on board by locals.[116] In 1812 captives on board the Portuguese galley *Felix Eugênia* revolted just outside Benguela. They were assisted by the free and enslaved black sailors, who joined forces with their brethren against the white sailors.

The prisoners escaped, and although most of them were recaptured, the black sailors who helped them were never found.[117]

Aside from the obvious physical constraints, insurrections could be inhibited by the fact that the captives often came from different west African regions and territories, did not speak the same languages, and at times had histories of rivalry and conflict. Building trust under such circumstances was far from straightforward. Generally, the common predicament focused collective minds, and individuals who spoke several languages often acted as intermediaries; sometimes the ship's crew unwittingly helped, as with the English slaver *Postillion* in 1704. As it sailed down the Gambia river collecting prisoners for the Royal African Company, it handed the captives some musical instruments, with the intention of keeping them occupied. Soon the sounds of drums and string instruments were heard from below deck, and the crew thought that their captives had been pacified. Under cover of the music, however, the prisoners were planning an uprising, and although they did not fully succeed, many managed to jump overboard and reach the shore.[118]

This incident showed the importance of tactical deception, as well as turning all available resources to good advantage. A significant feature in this respect was the sheer range of weapons used. They included arms seized on board, such as guns, swords, knives, lances, and pikes, as well as utensils: axes, hammers, carpentry tools, cooking implements, buckets, shovels, scissors, razors, and files. In fact, any object that could be converted into an attack instrument was redeployed, and in certain insurrections some captives used pieces of wood such as planks and firewood logs, scraps of metal prised off the ship, food bowls, oars, as well as their own chains – and in at least one instance boiling water.[119]

The length of these engagements could vary. A well-timed and executed attack could achieve success rapidly, especially if it began with the neutralization of the captain, or by gaining effective control of the main deck. Other struggles could last several hours: in 1733 a letter from a slave-ship captain reported being ambushed by 'native forces' on the river Gambia at midnight, and the ensuing battle continuing until dawn. In this instance, although the insurgents were able to board the ship, they were pushed back.[120] One of the longest battles for control of a ship took place aboard the *Little George*, a Rhode Island sloop returning from Guinea in 1730 with ninety-six captives, thirty-five of whom were men. Three hundred miles into their journey across the Atlantic, at 4.30 in the morning, the men broke free from their chains and overpowered the guards, throwing them overboard. The captain and the rest of the crew managed to find refuge in a cabin below, where they endured a siege lasting nine days, during which they were subjected to a barrage of explosions and attempted incursions, surviving only on 'raw rice'. The prisoners were able to guide the ship back to African shores, where they ran it aground on the Sierra Leone river and disembarked along with the women and children.[121]

The most famous slave-ship rebellion occurred in the summer of 1839 off the Cuban coast on board the *Amistad*, a Spanish vessel carrying forty-nine men and four children (three girls and a boy). Beaten and tortured by the crew, the enslaved rebelled, killed the captain and cook, and seized control of the ship. Although this insurgency took place within the domestic Cuban slave-trade system, as the captives were being transported from one part of the island to another, the rebels involved were all African-born and part of a larger group of prisoners who had just been transported across the Atlantic from Sierra Leone on a Portuguese vessel, the *Teçora*. The incident acquired an international dimension when the rebels steered the ship on a 1,400-mile journey to the United States, where they were arrested and detained in a jail in New Haven, Connecticut, and charged with murder (see Plate 3). The Spanish owners of the ship sued for the return of their human 'property' and the case ended up in the American Supreme Court, which ruled in favour of the former captives; the survivors of the *Amistad* – by now reduced to thirty-five – were able to return to Sierra Leone in 1841.

Because of the sheer length of the legal proceedings, and the enormous public interest generated by the case across the Atlantic world, we know more about the *Amistad* rebellion than about any other slave-ship insurgency – and especially about the rebels themselves. During their long stay in the United States, they gave numerous interviews, met with many sympathizers, had their portraits drawn, and became heroes of the American abolitionist movement. Theirs are the only voices of African captive resisters that have reached us (more or less) directly. Until recently, however, their remarkable story has been told mostly from a North American perspective, as a celebration of its judicial system and the strength of domestic opposition to slavery, and a turning point in the history of American abolitionism. In Steven Spielberg's classic 1997 movie, the courtroom drama and the eloquence of John Quincy Adams eclipse by far the actions and motivations of the African rebels. Marcus Rediker's recent study has brought the resistance of the insurgents into proper perspective, and we can now see the insurrection in its full complexity, both as a carefully planned act of self-emancipation by the *Amistad* captives, and as a wider expression of the richness of their material, cultural, and spiritual lives in west Africa.

These qualities are already apparent in the intricate preparations that preceded the insurrection, which confirm this chapter's findings about the robustness of indigenous resistance to African slavery. The principal *Amistad* rebel leader Joseph Cinqué (Sengbe Pieh) hailed from Mani in southern Sierra Leone, where he was a military leader of some significance. His family clan included his wife and three young children, and his father was a local figure of authority. Cinqué was kidnapped by African slave raiders and taken to the coast, where he was sold to Spanish traders. His first encounter with one of the other main leaders of the rebellion, Grabeau, took place in Africa, in the Lomboko slave barracoon on the Gallinas coast, where they were both held for several weeks before being transported across the Atlantic on the *Teçora*. It was at this point – before they had even embarked let alone reached the Americas – that the two men began to discuss and organize their resistance. Cinqué's belief in freedom was absolute: in his exhortations to his comrades he would typically assert that death was preferable to enslavement.[122] Indeed, it transpired that Cinqué and Grabeau had first plotted a rebellion on board the Portuguese vessel, which had failed. The Sierra Leone region was the theatre of intense conflicts in the 1830s, and all the main *Amistad* rebel leaders were experienced warriors, familiar with the use of sabres and muskets. Some of these men had fought in mercenary armies, others in defensive engagements within their own communities.

But this shared military experience was not, in and of itself, sufficient to generate a common sense of purpose. The *Amistad* rebels were mostly from the Mende territory, but they consisted of at least fifteen other ethnic groups and so did not initially form a natural community. This sense of group solidarity emerged only through the discussions they held with each other on board the *Amistad*, where they deliberated about how to face up to their common predicament, and overcame their internal political and ethnic differences. These conversations were helped by the fact that the Mende language was spoken by most of the other groups. Another critical factor was the affiliation of the leading rebels with the Poro, an all-male secret society that played a central role in the social governance of west African communities.[123] One of the key functions of the Poro was to declare war, and this was the question the captives attended to in their final discussions below deck on the *Amistad*, as they tried to decide whether to carry out the insurgency. Not all the prisoners initially agreed that they should fight, and the final decision was only taken when everyone had reached 'unity', the key Poro principle of *ngo yela*.[124] In other words, the decision to launch the insurrection was reached by democratic consensus.

Thinking about the *Amistad* rebellion as an act of war offers important insights into the insurgents' beliefs and values. This fight was not only
about their predicament on the ship, but about slavery, and their desire
to live in freedom and dignity. Moreover, the specific way they fought for
their liberation was characteristic of the African traditions of war in which
they had been formed. They carried out their attack on a moonless night,
as was typical of Mende military practice. Once they found the weapons
on board (with the assistance, it should be noted, of the three little girls),
they chose to fight with cane knives, very similar to the cutlasses they used
at home. They launched a surprise guerrilla attack, using war shouts and
swinging their blades emphatically in an effort to intimidate their adversaries; this too was a standard tactic from home. Once they had killed the
captain, they beheaded him, as required by their traditional *kootoo* war
ritual. But, in keeping with their customs of war, they treated their surviving adversaries with humanity, including the two cruel Spanish men who
had bought them, Ruiz and Montes, to whom they even gave the same
food and water rations as the liberated captives were given.[125]

Indeed, what was striking about the behaviour of the *Amistad* rebels
throughout their ordeal was their effort to remain dedicated to their spiritual values. During the long journey to the United States, for example,
they repeatedly made offerings to Mama Wata, the female water spirit
worshipped by communities across west Africa. At one point when their
ship ran aground, they threw several manacles and chains overboard, as
well as the clothes they were wearing. They explained that the purpose of
the ritual was to 'break the charm' – which it clearly did.[126] They carried
protective amulets as well. Joseph Cinqué always wore a cord around his
neck, from which a small box was suspended. This was almost certainly
a *gris-gris* pouch, commonly used in Mende country, containing some
combination of cloth, earth, iron, animal skin, and an Islamic religious
inscription on a parchment.[127]

Opposition to slavery was both widespread and constant across west
African territories, from the earliest days of Atlantic slavery, as with the
São Tomé rebellion and Lourenço da Silva Mendonça's vigorous appeal
against human bondage to the Vatican, all the way through to the nineteenth century. This resistance was an indigenous phenomenon, expressing
the initiatives of individuals, groups, and communities operating on the
ground, drawing largely on their own material and intellectual resources,
and their instinctive opposition to enslavement. And as the *Amistad* insurgency brings out emphatically, this was a tale of conscious and purposeful
action, driven by group solidarities, and the search for individual freedom

and collective self-determination. In this sense, the rebellion led by Joseph Cinqué and his comrades sheds light not only on slave-ship insurgencies, but also on the richness of African challenges to enslavement.

This is, above all, a remarkable tale of African fugitive politics. All the facets of resistance evoked here involved working to defy and subvert the existing oppressive slave order – whether by raising and training a militia, waging war against European slavers and slave raiders, spurning the inducements and threats of powerful African states, fortifying village defences, seeking refuge in other areas, choosing or allying with a military and spiritual leader, appealing to spirits and deities for protection, targeting sailors, settlers, and trading caravans, and planning an escape from a slave barracoon or a breakout from a fort; and, as we have just seen, conceiving and executing uprisings on slave ships. Even the decision by individuals in west African communities to flee from their servitude and become runaways would typically be reached after a process that would have included taking soundings, learning about escape routes, weighing the risks of success, and considering the fate of family members who might be left behind. It is highly likely that many of those involved in rebellions, as in the *Amistad* case, were members of militarized secret societies that proliferated across west Africa from the seventeenth century onwards.[128]

Describing African resistance to slavery as a form of fugitive politics enables us, moreover, to confront accounts that, while acknowledging the reality of the resistance of the enslaved, end up depoliticizing it by ascribing it primarily to private emotions such as fear. Most of the populations targeted by slave raiders lived in dispersed communities with long traditions of self-governance and egalitarianism (in terms of a rejection both of centralized rule and of the institution of slavery itself), and they stood up to protect these established ways of life. Freedom and autonomy were thus tied to sentiments of collective dignity. During the final discussions among the *Amistad* captives, before they reached an agreement to proceed with the insurrection, one of the decisive interventions came from an old man named Lubos, who observed that 'no one ever conquered our nation, & even now we are not taken by fair means'.[129] Freedom was in this sense inseparable from honour. It was intimately connected to spirituality, too. Those who were taken fought for emancipation, for themselves and their fellow captives, refusing enslavement in the name of moral values that were integral to their understanding of themselves and the world. As one scholar of African religions put it succinctly: 'In classical African cultures, religiousness and a sense of the sacred permeated all dimensions of culture and human behaviour. It was from this sensibility, that of religiousness, that Africans derived the mandate and resources to revolt against enslavement.'[130]

This point can be made more broadly. In order to make sense of the underlying ideals of liberty and autonomy that drove the various acts of resistance, we need to appreciate the weight of slavery in African collective life, the profound violation it represented, and the political, social, military, religious, and cultural responses it called forth. These were not distinct but interconnected realms, and the links among them allowed resisters to draw on a wide range of moral and material resources. Military training was an integral part of social life; an insurgent leader was a person with prowess as a warrior and privileged access to the spiritual realm; scientific and religious knowledge could be put to social and military ends; and the universe of spirits and gods was inseparable from material struggles for existence and survival. Above all, war and spirituality were closely intertwined. In 1780 a revolt on a Portuguese slave ship headed from Mozambique to Mauritius was led by a man named Bororo, whose authority over the other enslaved captives rested on their recognition of his religious powers;[131] one of the main Yoruba words for 'war' or 'battle' was *ogun*, which was the name of the god of iron as well.[132]

How effective was this resistance? Those who stood up to the slavers on land and at sea often paid a heavy price for their bravery. Many lives were lost repelling attacks by African imperial armies and slave-raiding parties, and many more in the often gruelling marches that enabled vulnerable communities to relocate to safe havens in hills, mountains, and forests. Survival in runaway settlements was no doubt hazardous and many men, women, and children perished, or were recaptured. If we stay with the slave-ship cases, violent rebellions often resulted in high casualty rates among the captives, and when unsuccessful they provoked severe reprisals by the crew – and there were undoubtedly more failures than successes. Probably only around a quarter of the documented rebellions succeeded completely, in the sense that the enslaved were able to break free, take complete control of the ship, and disembark in Africa. In some instances, only some of the captives were able to escape; in others, the captives were unable to return to land because of their lack of navigational skills, and their ships were found drifting off the African coasts.[133]

But despite these unfavourable odds, African communities did not give up their struggle for freedom. Many of the groups that opposed slavery not only endured over time, but thrived: for example, the Balanta had a high population density during the nineteenth century and developed successful agricultural techniques.[134] And these acts of defiance were far more than symbolic. The determination to resist enslavement at all costs forced the slavers to remain on their guard, and to redesign the ships so as to make rebellions and suicides less likely, by creating a forti-fied 'barricado' within the deck area and increasing the number of crew members; these measures, in turn, led to an increase in the costs of slave-shipping (see Plate 3).[135] Marine insurance lawyers were forced to debate and take into account the humanity of the enslaved, and recognize their desire for freedom.[136] Most importantly, this resistance is thought to have significantly reduced the number of captives transported across the Atlantic. According to one scholar, as many as one million African men, women, and children were spared enslavement as a direct result of slave-ship resistance.[137] But this is a conservative estimate, as it does not include all those who avoided capture thanks to the defensive actions undertaken by fugitive communities across African coasts and hinter-lands. So the real figure of those who escaped enslavement because of the totality of these actions is much higher.

2

'The Most Natural Desire
of the Human Heart'

The maroon community of Palmares in northeastern Brazil was one of the most emphatic early manifestations of enslaved resistance in the New World. According to a contemporary Brazilian account, it was established by forty African-born people (mostly from the interior of the Angolan region) fleeing from Portuguese coastal settlements in the early seventeenth century. This founding group escaped captivity to form a republic of their own and to live 'free of any domination'.[1] Palmares grew into an independent military, social, and political force, which withstood repeated attempts to destroy it, first by Dutch forces and then after 1654 by the Portuguese. Its continued existence for well over eight decades posed a challenge to the system of colonial slavery in the Americas, and to the notion that European settlers had fully conquered these New World territories. This endurance attested to the captives' instinctive abhorrence of their condition, to their yearning to lead lives of liberty and autonomy, and to their commitment to struggle for these goals by all means available. As one Portuguese regional governor ruefully admitted, the self-emancipation of these men and women expressed the simple truth that 'freedom [was] the most natural desire of the human heart'.[2]

Palmares initially took its name from the wild palm trees proliferating in the area, which provided the refugees with most of their basic needs in terms of nourishment and shelter, while allowing them to trade with coastal settler communities. However, they also raided these places for weapons and tools, and sometimes destroyed sugar mills and plantations as reprisals for attacks against Palmares. Over time, the fugitive settlements developed into a network of nine main communities spread over a large area running parallel to the coast and linked by a common system of governance. At its height Palmares was thought to have a population of at least 10,000 – and possibly as many as 20,000. From the 1640s the territory had a single overarching ruler, Gana Zumba, who lived in a sizeable palace in the capital, Macaco. This leader was chosen on merit by the local chiefs and entrusted with the absolute power to wage war. Palmares was attacked regularly from the mid-seventeenth century and its inhabitants were constantly on a battle footing. After facing a series of such military campaigns, Gana Zumba signed a peace treaty with the Portuguese governor of the Pernambuco province in 1678. All the inhabitants who were born in Palmares would be granted freedom, provided they returned those who were fugitives to the authorities; the emancipated community would be resettled in a village in the Cucaú region.[3]

This compromise arrangement only lasted two years. It was rejected by many members of the Palmares community, who refused to follow Gana Zumba to the new settlement, and he was assassinated shortly afterwards; in 1680 Cucaú was invaded by colonial troops and its inhabitants were enslaved again. The dissidents were led by Zumbi, a charismatic warrior who had been a senior military figure in Palmares, and now assumed the role of commander. He formed another community, in Serra da Barriga, and this eventually became the new armed base for Palmares. Zumbi was described by a Portuguese official as a 'black man of singular valour, great spirit, and rare constancy. He is the overseer of the rest, because his industry, judgement, and strength serve ... as an example [to his people].'[4] Such was the dread Zumbi inspired among the Portuguese that the king wrote to him from Lisbon in 1685 offering him an amnesty in exchange for his allegiance. He turned down the offer and held out for a further decade until Palmares was finally overrun by colonial mercenaries in 1694. Zumbi was captured and killed a year later.

Information about African resistance travelled far, wide, and fast on both sides of the Atlantic, and proved hugely unsettling to Portuguese colonial powers. A letter from a Jesuit priest in 1597 warned prophetically that 'rebel negroes' might pose a threat to commercial activities in the Brazilian territories, as 'their relatives [had] done in São Tomé Island'.[5] Even at this early stage, captive resistance was a general and interconnected phenomenon, and it was understood as such by the enslavers. And so it was: among the enslaved population in San Salvador de Bahia, the main city in Bahia (and colonial Brazil's first capital), there was a sizeable contingent from São Tomé, and the patterns of behaviour of the rebels in northeastern Brazil were very similar to those we witnessed across African territories in chapter 1. Recently uncovered archival evidence has shown that Palmares was known and discussed in Africa, and Africa in Palmares. For example, many captives who rebelled against Portuguese rule in seventeenth-century Brazil had connections with Palmares, and they were subsequently exiled to Angola.[6] In this respect the parallels between Palmares and the Angolan-based fugitive resettlement of Kisama were

especially noteworthy. The two communities were broadly contempor-
aneous, and they were animated by the same visceral rejection of chattel
slavery. They attracted a wide range of refugees, and eventually came to
be led by charismatic leaders who confronted European colonial rule in
similar ways. It is likely that stories and myths about Kisama helped to
shape the cultures of resistance in early colonial Brazil.[7]

Indeed, given the predominantly Angolan origins of the captives forcibly taken to Brazil, and the sharp increase in Atlantic slave-trading
activities in the Kongo region in the seventeenth century, it is no surprise that African experiences and practices featured prominently in the
collective life and imagination of the inhabitants of Palmares. The term
quilombo, used to describe Palmares, was of central African origin. It
was derived from the Bantu term for a camp (*kilombo*) and referred to
warrior societies (primarily male) of different ethnic groups, brought
together by the disruptions caused by slave wars and forced migrations in
Africa. Many of the inhabitants of Palmares referred to their settlement
as 'little Angola' (Angola Janga or Angola Pequeña in Portuguese), and
we know that six of the nine villages, including the capital Macaco, had
Bantu names.[8] The practice of local chiefs in electing a principal leader
was common in seventeenth-century Angola, and the titles of the two
Palmares chieftains had multiple semantic connections with Africa. Gana
meant 'Lord' in Kimbundu, the language spoken by the majority of Africans brought to Brazil; and the term 'Zumba' was widely understood to
refer to an ancestral spirit or a Supreme Being.

The ways in which the inhabitants of Palmares confronted regular
attacks from the colonizers revealed defensive military skills that had
been tried and tested by African fugitive populations. Thanks to their
wide contacts with coastal enslaved communities, as well as Amerindian
groups, the Palmares political and military leadership knew when the Portuguese were preparing to attack them and were able to anticipate their
responses accordingly. The rebels mostly preferred to rely on guerrilla
tactics. They typically retreated into the jungle to avoid direct confrontation with the enemy, exploiting the terrain to their advantage by fighting
with light weapons and laying ambushes in swamps and thickly forested
areas. A lengthy report on the war waged by the Portuguese against Palmares, written in the late 1670s, concluded that military attacks had been
largely ineffective, and that the emancipated fugitives remained 'lords of
the forest'.[9] This dominion extended to cultivating enduring links with
some Brazilian colonists with settlements in or near Palmares, many of
whom paid regular taxes to the maroons in exchange for protection. One
of them, Cristóvão de Burgos, was a high-court judge in Bahia and one

of the province's wealthiest landowners. He maintained a long-term economic relationship with Palmares for over two decades and disagreed with the Portuguese policy of violent confrontation with the fugitives. In other words, there were long periods when Palmares had significant allies even within the local Brazilian creole colonial elite.[10]

The most remarkable feature of Palmares was that, as well as its indisputably African character, it evolved broader traits that eventually transformed it into a more dynamic and composite community. Its settlements were in Amerindian territories, and the Palmares fugitives forged an alliance with these indigenous Brazilians, developing close links with them.[11] This hybridity was true even of its military practices, which mobilized the human and technical skills of all inhabitants. Women fought alongside men, and the fortified military camp used for training soldiers and officers was called Subupira, an Amerindian name. There is little doubt that Native American defensive fighting techniques were incorporated into the war culture of Palmares: lances and bows and arrows were deployed alongside firearms. Although it was repeatedly designated as a 'black' settlement in Dutch and Portuguese documents, Palmares was in fact a cultural mélange. It became a magnet not only for African-born men and women seeking to escape from servitude, but also for Amerindians and poor whites fleeing from the violence of colonial society, destitutes, family outcasts, and those – such as Jews and African priestesses – persecuted for their spiritual beliefs. All these groups contributed to defining the character of the settlement. Its inhabitants dressed in animal skins and cloth, and exhibited a wide variety of hairstyles, including braids.[12]

No written records produced by the Palmares rulers have survived, but it is implicit from the available evidence that the principal language was Kimbundu, although others were spoken in the settlements.[13] This syncretic quality was likely, too, in the religious and spiritual cults followed by the locals, which probably combined Catholic principles with west African and Native American traditions. According to a contemporary account, Palmares had a church with a trained Catholic priest who performed baptisms, and the building's interior was adorned with statues of Jesus and the Virgin Mary. The church also contained a statue of Saint Blaise, an Armenian martyr who was warned to hide in the mountains to avoid capture – a suggestive example of how local fugitives adapted the Catholic cult to their specific situation. In 1689, in the wake of the anti-slavery case brought to the Vatican by Lourenço da Silva Mendonça, Pope Innocent XI authorized the 'blessings of Christ' to be taken to Palmares, even though the cleric he appointed refused to carry out the mission.[14]

At the same time, contrary to Catholic custom, polygamy was the norm in Palmares (the ruler had three wives), although this arrangement seems to have been based on the smaller number of women in the settlements rather than cultural preference. This 'Afro-Brazilian' melange was embodied by Zumbi himself. He was thought to have been born of black parents in Palmares in 1655 and captured as a young boy during a raid on the settlement by colonial forces. He was then handed over to a Jesuit priest in Porto Calvo, who baptized him and named him Francisco, and taught him Latin and Portuguese. Zumbi escaped back to Palmares in 1670 and was educated in the art of combat by an African warrior. At least one of his concubines was a white woman, captured during a coastal raid.[15]

The example of Palmares is evidence of the continuity of African inspirations for captive resistance after the Middle Passage. It typifies several wider features of this opposition: its manifestation from the earliest moments of New World slavery, its rejection of white settlers' belief in their natural entitlement to rule, its entrenched and warlike character, its social and cultural richness, and above all its expression through flight (marronage). Indeed, until the mid-late eighteenth century, maroons were the main embodiment of captive resistance across the Americas and the Caribbean. From the moment they landed in coastal ports on the Atlantic, and were put to work in towns, plantations, and mines, the enslaved tried to escape to areas that could not easily be reached by white colonists, such as secluded regions, mountains, forests, and marshes. Those who succeeded formed settlements that stood up to slavery by their very existence, as they essentially operated outside the framework of colonial institutions. They created a major security problem for the slavers, forming armed bands that raided their plantations and supply lines, carrying out attacks, thefts, and abductions. Maroon activity took several different forms. It could involve more individualistic behaviour and the retention of closer physical proximity to slave societies (including hiding in urban areas), as well as the organization of roaming armed bands. However, its most substantial version was the geographical separation exemplified by Palmares.[16]

Collective flight was so widespread across the early slavery period that a range of terms became common by the seventeenth century to designate these fugitive communities and their activities. The most widespread was 'maroon', derived from the Spanish *cimarrón*. This term originated in the Spanish colony of Hispaniola and referred to livestock that had wandered away from plantations. The expression was applied first to Amerindian runaways, and after that to African fugitives.[17] The Spanish referred to these runaway communities as *cimarrones*, and also *palenques*, cumbes, or mambises. The Portuguese, as we saw earlier, described them as quilombos, and mocambos, ladeiras, magotes, coitos, and (unsurprisingly) palmares. The Dutch talked of their runaways as boschneegers (bush negroes) or schuilneegers (hide negroes), while the French referred to theirs as nègres marrons. 'Maroon' became a standard English term, and there were also references to 'mountain', 'outlaw', and 'fugitive' captives.[18] These disparaging terms were not employed among the runaways, who, as we shall see, generally presented themselves as combatants, officers, and soldiers, and as warriors seeking to recover their natural freedom, refusing to accept the legitimacy of their capture and enslavement.

Challenges to the initial Spanish colonial settlements in the Americas highlight the pervasive nature of this type of resistance. One region with a robust early tradition of enslaved flight was Venezuela. In 1552, in the gold-rich region of San Felipe, a group of African and Amerindian mineworkers led by a black ladino (Christianized person from the Iberian peninsula) captive named Miguel escaped into the nearby mountains, where they established a fortified camp, which they used as a base to attack the Spanish mines and recruit more followers by invoking emancipationist ideals. Miguel declared to black captives that 'God had created them free as the rest of the peoples of the world'.[19] He was crowned king of the settlement, and his wife Guiomar became its queen. The community had around 180 people at its peak, and among its institutions was a religious centre where services were performed by a cleric appointed by Miguel. The rituals were probably a combination of Christianity and African spirituality. The community was culturally composite, and it was defended by a well-organized militia that included ladinos and African-born captives (bozales) wielding swords and spears as well as Amerindians armed with bows and arrows. Fighters painted their faces in black to intimidate the enemy.[20] Although Miguel was eventually killed in battle in 1555, when the Spanish mounted a successful attack against his community, his message of freedom continued to reverberate across the region.

The war analogy was particularly apposite for Panama, where African captives first arrived in 1513. Subjected to forced labour in gruelling conditions in gold mines, pearl fisheries, and construction work, they escaped in increasingly large numbers. The Spaniards' two principal settlements were Nombre de Dios on the Caribbean side and Panama City on the Pacific coast; between these two inhabited areas lay the remote mountainous territories where the runaways took refuge. The first significant maroon settlement was established in the early 1530s, a few years after revolts had broken out in Panama and the coastal town of Acla. The latter uprising provoked a further rebellion in Panama, where a group of black captives led by Damián conspired to escape and join forces with other maroons. The plot was foiled by the authorities, but it highlighted the close connections between runaway and rebellious activity. For urban captives, an established fugitive settlement could provide both a destination to aim for as well as a spur for insurgent action.[21]

By the mid-sixteenth century the maroons of Panama became entrenched in the hinterlands. Their bands posed a persistent threat to communications between coastal Spanish settlements, by both road and water; military campaigns against their *palenques* failed to eradicate them. These Atlantic fugitives united under the leadership of Bayano, a charismatic black ruler. He developed a following of over 1,000 men and women, who referred to their chief as their 'king'. The community was well organized, and observed Catholic rituals, again probably of African origin. After four failed military campaigns against him, Bayano was finally captured by deceit in 1558, having been promised recognition of his territory by the Spanish in exchange for ending his attacks.[22] Bayano's final fate is unclear, but it is believed he was pardoned and sent into exile in Spain, where he lived until his death. Yet the destruction of King Bayano's *palenque* only provided a brief respite for the beleaguered Spaniards. Fugitive activity resumed in the 1560s with even greater intensity, and the eastern maroon region of Panama was named 'the Bayano' by the Spanish.

A decade later, several other settlements had appeared, with an estimated population of over 3,000 freed captives. A raft of new leaders emerged, such as Antón Mandinga, who formed a mutually beneficial alliance with the English pirate Francis Drake. In the second Bayano war (1579–82), attacks against Spanish interests escalated, with plantations being targeted as well as towns. On one occasion, the rebels even entered Panama City and carried away many black captives, whom they promptly emancipated. The Spaniards rapidly concluded that they could not defeat the maroons militarily, so they began a series of negotiations with at least three distinct runaway communities. They offered them pardons and lands in which they could resettle, and the freedom to govern themselves and continue to choose their own leaders. By 1583 the pacification process had been completed, with over 5,000 fugitives pardoned and relocated. The details of these negotiations will be examined shortly, but the most important point is that these agreements recognized the maroons were no longer enslaved.

Three of those who received their freedom in this way in May 1579 were Francisco Berbesi, Antón Congo, and María Biafara, after living in the Cerro de Cabra bush in Panama for eight years. Such a long absence would have made them liable for the death penalty, but according to the court ruling that pardoned them they were now 'free of all captivity and servitude' and were granted 'the right, as free persons, to travel to all parts and places that they would wish, to engage in trade and commerce, to make their wills and testaments, and to do all other judicial and extra-judicial acts that free persons may'.[23] The three former fugitives were resettled a few years later in the free community of Santa Cruz la Real in Panama.[24] Long before Palmares, the maroons of Panama thus carried out the first successful African captive revolt in the New World: they forced the Spanish imperial authorities to treat them on an equal footing with rebels they typically denounced as men without honour and faith, and formally to recognize their freedom and autonomy. Their success was even more comprehensive, as the systematic and enduring rebelliousness of these fugitives compelled the Spaniards to halt the introduction of African captives to Panama.[25]

The first fugitive resettlement showed what the maroons could achieve. The community of Santiago del Príncipe came into being after a treaty approved in September 1579, which granted freedom to maroon leader Luis Maçanbique and his group of close followers in Portobelo. Maçanbique had travelled to Panama City a few months earlier with a document pledging loyalty to the Spanish, and proudly describing himself as 'Luis, king of the soldiers of Portobelo'.[26] The documents detailing the agreement showed that there were concessions on both sides. The Spanish devoted 20,000 pesos to the creation of the settlement, a significant financial outlay deemed 'excessive' by the Panama Treasurer.[27] Maçanbique was addressed as 'don Luis Maçanbique, principal *caudillo*' in the treaty. He was appointed as governor of the new settlement, and although he had to pledge loyalty to the Spanish Crown and assistance to the authorities in their fight against any runaways who might appear in his region, he was given extensive responsibility for maintaining social order. Maçanbique theatrically declared in the presence of a Spanish envoy that, 'There is no more "King don Luis Maçanbique ..." We have no other king than the [Spanish] King.'[28] The fact that he repeated this statement 'over six times' in front of his assembled community suggests that this proclamation was really intended for his visitor's ears.

The emancipated community was relocated to Santiago del Príncipe in 1580 and in October of that year the authorities took a census of its ninety-seven residents. The document is an extraordinary record of early maroon life in the New World, containing the names and origins of the inhabitants as well as brief but evocative physical descriptions. It lists the men, women, and children of the community, and the first female to be mentioned is 'Doña María, from the land of Bran, wife of don Luis Maçanbique, a woman tall, handsome face, who is thirty years old'. It was a young community: most of the men were in their thirties or forties, and the women in their twenties and thirties; there were seven boys and five girls, who were probably born in the Portobelo fugitive settlement. All seemed to be in relatively good health (as we will later observe, well-organized runaway communities had excellent supplies of home-grown agricultural produce). Yet some of the specific indications underlined the harsh lives these men and women had led. A number of men had battle scars on their arms and faces, and many had an ear cut off – one of the standard punishments meted out to captives by their owners.[29] As might be expected given the demographic profile of the men and women brought to Cartagena, the former fugitives hailed from a range of African regions, including Senegambia, Upper and Lower Guinea, and Angola. Indeed, the respondents all gave their origins using specific African designations: the majority were from the Zape ethnic group in Upper Guinea, while others described themselves as Casanga, Mocombo, Angola, Kongo, Enxico, Bran, Gilonga, Maçanbique, Bañon, Biafara, Mandinga, Jolofo, Biocho, and Caravali.

It was a very diverse group in cultural, linguistic, and religious terms, and it was a measure of their collective resolve that they had held together successfully for so long. This sense of unity was undoubtedly shaped by their commander, the *caudillo*-warrior-king Luis Maçanbique. His stature among his peers was highlighted by the Spanish official, who described him as the 'leader of the people'. The census listed the name of his servant, a woman named Agustina, who was 'tall, strong' and in her twenties. Her robustness was shared by her chief: twenty-seven years later, in the year 1607, Maçanbique was still in charge of the free black community of Santiago del Príncipe, at the reported age of 110.[30]

This pattern of spirited African resistance was also seen in sixteenth-century Mexico, where conspiracies sent waves of panic among the authorities. A plot in 1537 aiming to 'kill all the Spaniards and seize the land' prompted the interruption of black captive imports for eight years.[31] There were an estimated 2,000 runaways by the late 1570s – around a tenth of the African population. By this time the authorities here too were effectively in a state of war against insurgent captives and fugitives, mounting military campaigns against their settlements and passing a series of draconian decrees aimed at containing the threat they posed to Spanish authority. However, the measures proved costly and largely ineffective.[32]

One of the most remarkable fugitives was Nyanga, an African chief who was enslaved by the Portuguese and brought to Mexico sometime in the 1570s. He soon escaped and organized a well-protected runaway settlement in the mountains near the city of Orizaba, from where he launched regular attacks on travellers and plantations in the surrounding areas. For four decades 'the king of the cimarrones', as he was nicknamed, remained irreducible. He used guerrilla tactics to counter the numerical superiority of the Spaniards, exploiting his knowledge of the terrain to deceive them. By the early 1600s his *palenque* consisted of around eighty men (all runaways), twenty-four black or Amerindian women, and several children; they lived in sixty huts. Military expeditions against Nyanga failed until 1609, when the Spaniards finally managed to destroy his fortified settlement. But even then they could not fully subdue the mobile and hardy fugitives, who were able to retreat and regroup. Further incursions by the Spaniards failed to capture Nyanga and his military commanders, who continued to disrupt the slavers' economic activities in the region.

Finally, the weary Spaniards came to a settlement in 1618, conceding the key terms stipulated by Nyanga, which they had rejected in earlier negotiations. The maroons were no longer treated as outlaws and were given the right to establish a town of their own, which would be governed by a ruling council and a judge appointed by the 'warriors', as the fugitives called themselves. 'Captain Nyanga' was recognized as their leader, and his descendants would rule the community; only Franciscan monks would be allowed in the town, and no Spaniard would be permitted to live there permanently. In exchange, Nyanga and his warriors agreed to recognize the Spanish king as their sovereign, to return any captive who sought refuge in their midst, and to bear arms to defend Spanish rule if it was threatened. The establishment of the free community of San Lorenzo was thus a triumph for the black fugitives. One of Nyanga's conditions was the threat to return to hostilities if the community was not granted its royal charter within eighteen months; he even insisted that the costs of the church ornaments should be borne by the Spanish Crown. San Lorenzo still stands today and it bears the name Yanga after its founder, who is regularly honoured in local festivals and commemorations.[33]

While Spanish rule was being fiercely contested in Panama and Mexico, a similar pattern of fugitive resistance was developing in South America. This was the case especially in and around Cartagena de Indias, the principal Atlantic port of entry for captive Africans in the Spanish colonial provinces of New Granada. By 1610 around 80,000 African captives had been brought to Cartagena, mostly from the Senegambia and Gulf of Guinea regions, and increasingly from the Angolan area; the Portuguese, who became the principal suppliers of African forced labour to Spanish colonies, had established strong links with slave traders in this region. African captives were brought to work on plantations and as domestic servants, but mostly in the gold mines of the region. The Spanish settler population in Cartagena was outnumbered by the enslaved by a ratio of one to ten, and the colonists adopted a series of measures to protect themselves against rebellion and flight. These included bans on Africans walking unaccompanied in the streets, carrying knives, machetes or clubs, or having any dwellings outside their owners' residences. Any armed rebellion was punishable by death, and flight was not only banned but severely punished. A captive who ran away for under a month would be sentenced to a public flogging of 100 lashes. If the absence lasted over a month, his genitals would be cut off in public; and if over a year, the penalty was death. Maroons could be killed if they resisted capture by Spanish militias, and it was clearly implied that their physical elimination was the preferred outcome. These types of punishment against fugitives became the norm across the enslaved Americas.[34]

There were many plots and rebellions by the enslaved in Cartagena, but the most consequential uprising took place at the end of 1599. Initially a modest affair, it was led by Benkos Biohó, an African warrior who had been transported three years earlier from Guinea-Bissau, with his wife Wiwa, his daughter Orika, and his son Sando-Bohio. They were all captured in Upper Guinea and sold into slavery in Cartagena to a brutal master named Juan Gómez. Biohó and his family ran away with three black women who were close to his wife, along with nineteen other black captives. Using his navigation skills, Biohó canoed the group through the marshlands and into the safety of the tropical hinterlands. Before reaching their hideout, they ambushed the Spanish military and mercenary forces sent after them, killing the head of the search party – none other than his master Gómez – and several of their members. As Biohó's local fame grew rapidly, he soon attracted a large following of runaways from all the different African communities in the Cartagena area, and they referred to him as their 'king'. A contemporary Franciscan monk described him as 'audacious, brave and daring', and he was certainly an effective leader. Established in 1603, his main *palenque* at the foot of the Montes de María was called San Basilio.[35]

Apart from shielding the Montes de María fugitives from attack, Biohó and his militia launched raids on coastal towns and plantations, securing weapons and supplies, and liberating captives sent out into wooded areas to fell lumber.[36] Biohó and his maroons inflicted significant economic and political damage on the colony and held out for fourteen years, until the Spaniards negotiated a truce with them in 1613. It guaranteed the freedom of his San Basilio *palenque* from Spanish armed attack, and further allowed the former fugitives the right to enter Cartagena. This truce was broken by the next Spanish governor, who ordered the arrest and execution of Biohó in 1619 on the charge of conspiracy. It is not known whether the rebel-king had planned an uprising or whether the Spaniards invented the plot in order to rid themselves of a man who regularly came to taunt them in Cartagena, dressed as a Spanish gentleman, with a sword and gold dagger at his side. The sight of a black man in European garments would have been seen as provocation by the local white settlers – and it is likely that this was precisely what Biohó intended. He paid a heavy price for his 'arrogance', but the revolutionary tradition that the rebel commander had initiated endured in New Granada throughout the seventeenth century, and well beyond. The number of *palenques* grew, and the name of Biohó was adopted by several generations of maroon leaders, becoming associated with African resistance to slavery across the region.[37]

It should now be clear that the story of the runaway community of Palmares, with which this chapter opened, was singular in terms of its longevity but in no way exceptional. Indeed, when viewed comparatively, Palmares was not a starting point, but a continuation of established patterns of runaway resistance that originated in Africa and developed across the New World from the earliest moments of the European settler presence. These communities of self-emancipated men and women appeared in the 1500s, and were hardy, mobile, creative, and self-reliant, and organized themselves according to military and political principles. They combined African and Amerindian war techniques and often produced charismatic and talented commanders. Although the enslavers succeeded in destroying many of their settlements, others often quickly sprang up in nearby areas. These communities endured over significant periods of time in the seventeenth and eighteenth centuries, challenging the stability and legitimacy of the colonial system of production. These ongoing crises forced both the authorities and local settlers to devote considerable resources to tracking and finding fugitives, and in many instances to seek compromises with them. These accommodations ranged from de facto recognition of their settlements, establishing trading relations, reaching tacit non-aggression and explicit protection agreements, and in some instances concluding formal treaties.

In colonial Brazil, runaway communities proliferated in several regions, particularly the captaincy of Bahia, where the disruptive presence of *mocambos* and *quilombos* is consistently mentioned in administrative reports from the Palmares period all the way through to the late eighteenth century and beyond. The southern district of Cairú was a particular source of concern, with military expeditions launched against fugitive settlements in 1663, 1692, 1697, and 1723. None of these operations produced a decisive outcome. In 1692 bands of runaways sacked plantations around Camamú and threatened to seize the town. They launched a full-scale threat to the slave order in the entire Bahia region and provoked insurgent movements in other areas. In the end, the captives were defeated but their rallying cry was doubly haunting to the settlers: 'death to the whites and long live liberty'.[38]

In the Minas Gerais captaincy, the discovery of gold brought a massive influx of African bonded labour as from the early eighteenth century. Many fugitives escaped and established settlements across the region's interior. One of these settlements, Jacuí, grew into a community of 4,000 inhabitants. Although these maroons were invariably denounced as criminals by the authorities, many engaged in commercial activities such as farming, gold mining, and smuggling; they were in this sense informally integrated into local economies.[39] But the menace of revolution was never far removed. In 1719 Count Pedro de Almeida, the governor of Minas Gerais, uncovered a plot by Mina and Angola runaways from the Rio das Mortes mining district. These captives planned to take advantage of Easter celebrations to launch an insurrection to exterminate the region's white slavers. The maroons had created an underground organization that communicated through secret agents, appointed political and military leaders, and prepared for the insurrection by amassing and concealing weapons in the hills. The conspiracy was betrayed and the leaders were arrested. But the governor admitted, in his subsequent report to the king, that the Portuguese could not deprive the captives of their 'natural desire for freedom'. He added that stories and myths about Palmares continued to inspire rebels in his region, and to nurture in them sentiments of 'pride, boldness and courage'.[40]

In Guatemala, plantation and prison records likewise show a consistent pattern of flight by the enslaved. Planters in the early to mid-seventeenth century were compelled to devote significant resources to recapturing fugitives, and sometimes their frustration was apparent in their listings of their own captives. An Arará woman named Isabel, who was put on sale and purchased by a priest in 1621, was described by her enslaver as a 'crazy runaway'. In the early 1640s the authorities in the province admitted that maroons had been operating for seventy years in the mountainous terrain near the Golfo Dulce. These communities prospered by holding up mule trains travelling on the main commercial trade routes, and seizing wine, iron, clothing, and weapons. They often succeeded in enticing the African captives working on these convoys to join them. Local settlers became so frustrated with this wave of self-emancipation that they asked the Spanish authorities to halt the import of new captives into Guatemala on at least three occasions during the first half of the seventeenth century. Moreover, concerted efforts were made in the 1640s to reach agreements with maroon communities, using Franciscan monks as intermediaries, and apparently some of these overtures met with success.[41]

In Guadeloupe, likewise, where enslaved men and women were forcibly transported from Africa by the French in the seventeenth century, the authorities sent at least ten military expeditions against fugitive hideouts in mountainous regions between 1702 and 1777; all of them failed to eradicate the fugitives. One of these campaigns, in 1737, came in the wake of the discovery of a plot by maroons in the north-west to launch an insurrection, kill the white settlers, and take control of the colony.[42] Fugitive settlements were places of political and cultural improvisation, as with the Guadeloupean maroon settlement known as Camp des Kellers. Established sometime in the early nineteenth century, after a shipwreck, this community developed into what a French official called 'an independent republic'. It included African captives, creole-born black people and some whites, and its chief was a military and spiritual leader who was called 'king' but was chosen democratically. Among the significant figures who occupied this position were maroons named Mocachy, Bonga, and Martial, and one of these leaders in the early 1820s, Grand Papa, had been a fugitive since the mid-1770s.[43] The Camp des Kellers maroons remained undefeated until the second French abolition of slavery in 1848. They formed alliances with other fugitive settlements in Guadeloupe, and established a modus vivendi with neighbouring white plantations, trading goods and services with them and sparing them from attack. In return, the French settlers did not denounce them to the authorities.[44]

The isolation of fugitive communities was thus only relative – or, to make the same point differently, the separation was geographical but not human. Contact with colonial society took a variety of forms. Maroons often retained links with the plantations from which they escaped, especially if (as was often the case) they still had enslaved family members there. These links allowed fugitives to gather vital strategic information, particularly from women captives, about planned militia attacks against their settlements. Many of these incursions failed because maroons had been forewarned and simply moved away. We can observe the complexity of these connections in the case of the Mexican maroon community of Mandinga, founded in 1735 in the Oaxacan mountains by runaways fleeing from the region's sugar and tobacco plantations. They maintained close relations with livestock-feed gatherers from the coastal area where the port city of Veracruz was located. These gatherers sold products on behalf of the maroons, in exchange for a commission, and purchased supplies for them in Veracruz. The fugitives established good relations with several important members of the nearby town of Teutila, including the district magistrate and local white settlers, who employed the maroons to protect their lands and warehouses; in 1769 Mandinga was recognized as a free community.[45]

Among the most significant accommodations reached by colonial powers with fugitives were the 1739 and 1740 treaties signed between the British authorities in Jamaica and the colony's maroon groups. Organized around two communities based in different parts of the island – the Eastern or Windward maroons, based in the Blue Mountains, and the Leeward maroons of the Cockpit Country in the west – the Jamaican rebels had been fighting the occupiers intermittently for eight decades, inflicting serious and sustained damage to the plantation system. Although relatively few in number, they proved impossible to reduce because of their outstanding tactical skills. They swam up rivers to mask the scent of the hounds sent to find them, and disguised themselves in elaborate natural costumes to conceal themselves and ambush their enemies.[46]

The British were all the more worried by the early decades of the eighteenth century that there were around 80,000 captives in Jamaica, and they outnumbered white settlers by a ratio of ten to one. From 1730 onwards the enslavers launched a determined effort to wipe out the maroons, and they did manage to capture the village stronghold of Nanny Town in 1734. However, their own militias sustained serious losses and desertions, and by the mid-1730s they began increasingly to favour a negotiated settlement. One of the main maroon leaders, Cudjoe, later admitted that his forces were seriously weakened and had no option but to settle. However, the British were unaware of this.[47] The treaties required significant compromises on both sides. The British recognized the maroons as free people and granted them significant economic and legal autonomy; in exchange the former fugitives pledged to provide military assistance to the British forces, help them suppress any future rebellions, return escapees from slavery, and accept a British 'resident' in their settlements.

Two decades later, the Jamaican model served as a template for the settlements reached between Dutch authorities and maroon communities in Surinam, in northeastern South America. The Dutch took over the colony from the British in 1667 and brought in African captives to work the plantations. As elsewhere across the New World, they deserted in droves and sought refuge in the inhospitable tropical rainforests of the interior. They survived by growing their own crops and raiding settler farms; they were also successful in increasing the size of their communities by recruiting fugitives from the plantations. The guerrilla war of the Surinam maroons lasted over six decades, and by the late 1750s there were several thousand fugitives. Like the British in Jamaica, the Dutch realized that their interests would be better served by reaching an agreement. Three major treaties were concluded in 1760, 1762, and 1767: with the Djuka living along the Marowyne river, the Saramaka along the Suriname river, and the Matuari along the Saramacca river. The terms of the agreements broadly mirrored the Jamaican treaties, with the expectation that the maroons would return any runaways and help the Dutch pursue any new group of rebels. The three Djuka groups undertook not to combine their forces against the Dutch, and a white official was placed in their midst to ensure that this pledge was honoured. The bulk of Surinam maroons indeed upheld the treaties and came to be known by the Dutch as 'pacified bush-Negroes'. Only a newly formed fourth group, the Aluku (led by a fugitive named Boni), refused these terms and crossed into neighbouring French territory, continuing the fight against the colonial authorities until the mid-nineteenth century.

These agreements between European colonial powers and maroon groups in Jamaica and Surinam are often discussed in material terms, and from the perspective of strategic gains and losses on both sides. This is fitting given that these were wars with strong military and territorial dimensions. However, from the perspective of the maroons these arrangements were not only seen as pragmatic or circumstantial: they expressed spiritual commitments to live in peace with their former enemies. This was reflected in the sacred oaths that consecrated the conclusion of both sets of treaties in Jamaica and Surinam. After the written documents were signed in 1739–40 and in the 1760s, blood was drawn from the maroon leaders and the British and Dutch delegates present, and it was mixed with water or alcohol. In the presence of a religious leader, each party then drank the potion and swore that they would not fight each other again.[48] This 'blood covenant' was an established feature of the rituals surrounding political arrangements and alliance-making in the west African regions from which the maroons in Jamaica and Surinam originated. Their replication in the New World expressed the depth of their commitment to the agreements, and their sense of honour and pride in what they had achieved through their decades of struggle; the rituals can also be construed as a maroon way of drawing the Europeans into their spiritual world.[49]

*

How did runaway communities survive, and what kind of lives did their inhabitants lead? The answers varied according to time, size, territory, and the type of settlement. Dwellings, for example, could range from improvised huts to cottages neatly arranged in rows; in the El Cedro *palenque* in Cuba the houses had bedrooms and an individual plot of land.[50] Sylviane Diouf has made a valuable distinction between borderland and hinterland maroons, suggesting that the former operated in close proximity to plantations and existed in an effectively symbiotic relationship with them, whereas the latter were more autonomous and geographically secluded. The more developed types of dwellings were generally to be found in hinterland areas.[51]

Indeed, one of the overarching conditions for the endurance of a maroon community was its relative remoteness from plantation societies. As in the example of Palmares, the most secure settlements were in hinterland areas such as swamps, forests, hills, and mountains, which were difficult for colonial militias to reach. The Windward maroons formed their encampments in the Blue Mountains, the highest in Jamaica, with peaks reaching over 6,000 feet. Cuban runaways built their dwellings on piles over mangrove swamps, in areas which were so impassable that they were out of bounds even for specially trained maroon-hunting dogs.[52] In Panama, King Bayano's settlements were established on top of a steep hill in an area of thick jungle surrounded by mountains and were accessible only by two narrow roads. The dwellings of the runaways were at the top of the hill, and they dug deep trenches between the huts where they stored their provisions.[53] Booby traps of various kinds (buried spikes, quicksand pits, and dog snares) were often placed on roads and paths leading to these *palenques*.[54]

At the same time, mobility and adaptability were cardinal maroon virtues, and long-term survival depended on the fugitives' capacity to withdraw and scatter rapidly into the forests if confronted by a large-scale military attack. This could mean abandoning a settlement and returning to it later when the danger had passed. And if their dwellings were destroyed, they would simply build another settlement in a nearby area. The ideal area, from this point of view, was one combining remoteness from plantation societies with proximity to borders with neighbouring territories. When threatened, maroons would cross over into these areas and only return to their settlements once their assailants had left. For decades, Surinam maroons eluded Dutch forces in this way by slipping into French and British Guyana, and Saint-Domingue runaways did the same by moving across the border into the Spanish territory known as Santo Domingo. But, as we have already seen, remoteness was not the same as isolation: effective runaway groups developed close links with captive communities on plantations and in urban areas. In early nineteenth-century Bahia the *quilombo* leader Malomi João had a chief agent in the main town of Salvador who not only supplied him with information but also collected funds and food for his community.[55]

Effective fortification was another key condition of survival. The entrance to Bayano's settlements was garrisoned with palisades, following a defensive model that was widespread in Angolan *quilombos*. Depending on the size and complexity of the group, further internal fortifications were sometimes built, particularly at the heart of settlements where rulers and priests generally lived. Additional techniques were introduced to enhance protection. The capital of Palmares and many of its larger settlements were surrounded by stockades and pits studded with sharpened stakes – another example of the combination of Angolan and Amerindian defence techniques. This blend of methods was widely adopted by fugitives, even when their settlements were on a much smaller scale than Palmares. For example, the Buraco de Tatú ('Armadillo's Hole') *mocambo* in the Bahia region had around sixty-five inhabitants between 1743 and 1763. It was not very far from the regional capital Salvador, but the defensive network that protected access to the village was remarkable. The rear was blocked by a swampy dike, the height of an adult; the other three sides were shielded by sharpened spikes driven into the ground, as well as twenty-one pits with stakes covered with bush and grass. There was only one road into the *mocambo* and it was lined with hidden spikes and camouflaged traps. Entry and exit were possible only when the guard stationed inside the settlement lowered a set of planks to enable people to walk across the defences.[56]

Fugitive settlements needed to be self-sustaining, and their rural and forested areas provided ample supplies of fresh water and hunting game. Maroons commonly reared domesticated animals, mostly chickens and pigs and sometimes cattle. They fished in rivers and even in the ocean; their maritime skills were extensive, as we will see later. They raided nearby plantations for food, clothing, and weaponry, and made the most of the trades of the more skilled runaways, especially carpenters and blacksmiths; maroons in Berbice (Dutch Guyana) erected a forge where they produced their own spears.[57] Most importantly, fugitive communities developed extensive agricultural skills. In his Mexican *palenque* Nyanga cultivated a range of crops. As reported by a contemporary observer, these included cotton, sweet potato, chilli, tobacco, squash, corn, beans, and sugar cane.[58] Palmares in Brazil had a well-honed system of agricultural production and this eventually became the norm with many runaway communities. In nineteenth-century Cuba, for example, the Todos Tenemos settlement had a population of around two hundred fugitives, and its inhabitants communally farmed an area of 67 hectares of land, on which they grew 'bananas, taro, sweet potatoes, yucca, yam, sugar cane, tobacco, corn, ginger, greens and fruit trees'; in addition they had stores of rice and smoked meat.[59] These kinds of surpluses allowed many settlements to move beyond subsistence production and engage in trade or barter with local settler communities. This too was a trend initiated in Palmares, where the inhabitants manufactured baskets, hats, and a variety of utensils, and enjoyed such an abundance of food that they were able to trade their surpluses of corn, tobacco, and oil with frontier colonists in return for 'copious amounts' of arms, tools, and gunpowder.[60] Such plentiful supplies of food were in themselves a source of the appeal of established runaway settlements; colonial and settler militias often targeted them specifically in their attacks against maroon communities.[61]

The most fundamental quality of a lasting settlement was its capacity to maintain an effective and cohesive social organization. As we have seen repeatedly, many fugitive communities were led by charismatic figures, whose identification as 'kings' reflected the strong influence of west African political traditions on maroon cultures in the New World. Cudjoe's power over the Leeward maroons in Jamaica was based on the sheer force of his personality, as well as kinship bonds: he inherited his leadership position from his father and surrounded himself with several members of his close family.[62] Strong leaders governed with a firm hand, and used violence whenever necessary to protect their own positions and the integrity of their community. But while the stereotypical image of the maroon chief as a ruthless despot became widespread in colonial plantation societies, the reality was generally far different. Leaders were often chosen through democratic consultation (this too was part of west and central African traditions), and even those who were not picked in this way typically earned their position through merit and a record of proven achievements, as in the cases of Nyanga, Bayano, Biohó, and so many others.

Moreover, in larger settlements leadership was rarely exercised by one single individual. Enslaved communities across the Atlantic had active traditions of electing groups of leaders, and bestowing civilian, military, or monarchical titles upon them, and these practices were carried over into runaway settlements. There was often a separation between the war leader and the administrator. This was the case in Nyanga's community, where military command was entrusted to an Angolan fugitive, Francisco de la Matosa; such men were powerful figures in their own right and were responsible for the training of warriors. Likewise there were two different offices in the Buraco de Tatú settlement. The military commander was Antonio de Sousa, and the administrator was named Theodoro; it seemed they had equal status (both had consorts who were called 'queens').[63]

Many communities were administered by a senate or council: Nyanga's home had a large room that was clearly used for such meetings.[64] Biohó's *palenque* in Cartagena had an elaborate system of governance in which he was seconded by a war captain, a treasurer, a mayor, and a religious leader. His captain was a brilliant military commander named Lorencillo, who had escaped with him in 1599.[65] Again, Palmares was the most advanced example of this institutional complexity. By the mid-seventeenth century it was a confederation of at least nine villages, linked by a common system of taxation, and each with its own ruler and justice council, which oversaw the settlement of disputes and the communal distribution of land; the agricultural fields were irrigated with canals.[66]

Fugitives took care of each other and went to great lengths to protect members of their community. Bayano created a separate hideout in the jungle for women, children, and old people, which was discovered only when the Spaniards captured its leader.[67] A Cuban *palenque* was specially named Guardamujeres (Protect Women).[68] Bayano established his agricultural settlements in several different areas, all at some distance from his *palenque*, so that these communities could serve as a refuge if his central base came under fire.[69] At the same time, well-maintained security precautions were taken to protect settlements from external attack. Sentinels were posted to warn of the approach of enemies, and they communicated by sending runners, and by sounding the alarm with horns, drums, and conch shells, or imitating animal noises.[70]

Because maroons considered themselves to be in a state of war against the colonial order, generally any fugitive who was suspected of spying for settlers was executed, and vetting mechanisms were put in place to ensure the effective screening and integration of new arrivals. In Araguari in Amazonian Brazil, this task was entrusted to an overseer charged with monitoring the newcomers, who were only allowed to travel out of the settlement after at least a year. The Jamaican maroons too had a probation system.[71] In Palmares, fresh immigrants were interrogated by the justice council and allowed in if their bona fides were established. However, anyone who left the settlement without permission, or tried to abandon it and return to colonial life in the coastal areas, was hunted down and killed. Captives who were taken in raids on settler plantations were only treated as full members of the community once they had proven themselves by snatching another enslaved person.[72]

Spiritual practices and beliefs were an important source of cohesion in fugitive communities. Leeward and Windward maroons in Jamaica asked newcomers to swear a sacred oath not to betray the community they were joining. They had religious leaders, known as Obeah-men and -women, who served as public oracles and counsellors. They were consulted on all important decisions; we will learn more about these spiritual figures in the next chapter.[73] As we saw earlier, Christianity was the dominant religion in Palmares, as in many fugitive settlements across the Americas, especially when their inhabitants originated from the Kongo region. But there was a widespread adherence to traditional African beliefs and rituals. When the new settlement of Santa Cruz la Real in Panama was officially founded in 1582, it had a site dedicated for a church, but the two hundred former fugitives celebrated the event by 'a great party which lasted all night long, with dancing and drums according to their customs'; there is little doubt that these would have included invocations of African spirits and deities.[74] Africa remained present in life and in death: a maroon burial site in Cuba contained evidence of African magical-spiritual practices, highlighting the importance attached to traditional ways of honouring the dead in runaway communities.[75]

Given the broad range of African ethnic groups who ended up enslaved in the New World, and the development of creole communities over time, these spiritual rituals had a generic quality, so that they could resonate with everyone – including Christians – and it is likely that this fusion was found in maroon settlements.[76] For example, the late seventeenth-century Matudere *palenque* in the jungle around Cartagena, which had about 250 inhabitants, had a Catholic church decorated with paper images of saints. A Spanish cleric who visited the settlement after its capture by the authorities found that regular services were held in the church and at least some of the maroons were very well acquainted with Catholic rituals and beliefs. However, he added that African religious and spiritual traditions, such as the cult of ancestors and the celebration of natural spirits and deities, were also widely observed among the maroons.[77]

The role of women in fugitive communities merits closer scrutiny. The maroon phenomenon was long portrayed as an expression of conquering masculinity, typified by charismatic leaders and war captains, thus apparently relegating women to marginal and submissive positions in runaway societies. There was an undeniable sexual imbalance in most settlements: escape was easier for men, often because women had to stay behind to look after children and other family members. There was, moreover, some substance to the settler complaint that maroons captured black and Amerindian women against their will.

This was illustrated by the case of Antoinette, an enslaved woman taken in 1814 by a maroon raid in Berbice and held for eleven years in a fugitive camp in Demerara, then in Dutch Guyana. After being severely beaten for trying to escape, she eventually made her way back to her master in 1826, choosing a return to slavery over maroon life.[78] However, these abductions from places of enslavement were often carried out in connivance with black women captives – and there is some doubt in this respect about Antoinette's precise dispositions in 1814. In any event, maroons could carry out these raids precisely in order to bring back wives and children they had left behind. Pregnancy could cause women to stay behind, and sometimes to flee, as those who were expecting were not spared beatings and whippings. Many enslaved women did not want their children to live under the same conditions as they had – or even worse, be sold off and never be seen again.

There are, moreover, plenty of examples of women escaping from towns and plantation societies, and making their own way to fugitive settlements. At times they moved freely from one area to another, as with the enterprising woman captive in late seventeenth-century Barbados who managed, with the help of another house servant, to forge the signature of her master on a travel document. This allowed her to 'pass from place to place without being molested'.[79] In Antigua, women were notable among the early maroon resistance groups. Among them was one valiant and resourceful female rebel – her name was not recorded – who opposed the British 'by force and arms' and participated in the 1687 maroon insurrection that aimed to seize control of the island, with the assistance of plantation captives. Captured by the militia, she offered to act as a guide – and promptly absconded again.[80] Several maroon settlements were named after women, and in some instances they helped found them: the Matudere *palenque* was led by a fugitive named Domingo Padilla, who together with his wife Juana escaped from slavery in Cartagena in 1681 and created the settlement. In honour of her foundational role, and perhaps because of her fondness for fancy dress, Juana was known among the inhabitants as the *virreina* ('vice-queen').[81]

Court testimonies survive from five women recaptured from the El Portillo *palenque* in eastern Cuba in the mid-eighteenth century. They were all enslaved in the nearby town of Bayamo, and their time in the settlement varied from a few years to seventeen years, with equally contrasting ages and backgrounds. Mariana, aged thirty-five, was Carabalí; fifty-year-old María de la Caridad was Mina; Juana and Rosa, thirty-five and thirty respectively, were both Kongo; and thirty-year-old María Antonia was born in Jamaica, and had escaped with her two small children.

Pregnant at the time of her recapture, María Antonia gave birth in jail, but her baby died two days later. They all provided specific information about the contexts of their flight. Mariana was part of a group of eight captives (five men, two women, and a child) who all ran away at the same time, and clearly planned their escape together. Among the reasons María Antonia gave were 'bad conditions of captivity and bad food'. María de la Caridad's owner, an old woman of limited means and poor health, had promised to free her when she died, but her son had refused to honour the arrangement.

The common, recurring theme, however, was the cruelty they had faced. Mariana's mistress was 'never pleased' and punished her for 'trivial mistakes'. María de la Caridad was sanctioned by the son of her mistress without any justification. Juana felt 'plagued' by the brutality of her treatment. Rosa's mistress was her master's elderly mother-in-law, who was 'very hard to please' and found fault with her repeatedly, and María Antonia received 'much punishment' at the hands of her master. Interestingly, two of the women offered qualified views of their enslavement: Rosa observed that, in stark contrast with her mistress, her enslaver was a 'good man'. María de la Caridad had considerable affection for her old mistress, and even spent some of her own meagre resources on her. But there was little doubt that, for these five women, the freedom of fugitive life, even with its insecurity and pain, had remained preferable to the certain oppression of enslavement. María Antonia conveyed this sentiment when she testified that 'a good master makes for a good slave'.[82]

These five women did not discuss their life in the El Portillo *palenque* during their trial; this was of little interest to their interrogators. Women performed essential roles in maroon societies: they were central to their demographic growth and were the ultimate guarantors of their continuity over time. It was not uncommon in established settlements for several generations to live together. Maroon women like María Antonia acted as midwives and cared for children. They were generally responsible for small-animal husbandry, and for maintaining and harvesting the crops on which the settlements depended; all five women would have been involved in these activities. In general, half of the population of a maroon community was dedicated to agricultural labour, and most of these workers were women. Men were assigned to defence and construction, as well as hunting and fishing tasks. Agricultural work was arduous, and many settlements maintained alternative clearings that maroons could retreat to if their primary dwellings came under attack. These fields were often a considerable distance away from the main village. Maroon women actively supported military operations, carrying food, powder, and weapons, and nursing the wounded.[83]

Women played a major role in spiritual life, which often revolved around the African priestess, a key member of the community. Involved in all major decisions, the priestess provided a range of services, including healing and divination through possession, as well as the worship of ancestors, the honouring of spirits and deities through sacrifices, and the design of protective amulets. In the Buraco de Tatú settlement in Bahia, there were two priests, one of them an old woman who was clearly a repository of collective knowledge and wisdom for the community.[84] Examples of such figures would include Queen Nanny, the spiritual leader of the Windward maroons in Jamaica, who inspired the fight against the British, and will be further discussed in the next chapter. Less well known, but just as crucial, was the role played by the priestess Jaja Dandé in the conclusion of the 1762 peace treaty between the Saramaka and the Dutch. Dandé was the daughter of Ayako, one of the supreme chiefs of the community, and her father was bitterly opposed to any agreement with the whites, who frequently sent military expeditions against their settlements.

Indeed, Jaja Dandé's prophetic visions were crucial in helping her community manage these military threats during the first half of the eighteenth century, warning of approaching patrols and preparing the fighters for battle (the role was not purely defensive: priests and priestesses could propose attacks against enemy targets). Opposition to peace remained the dominant view among the Saramaka until another significant intervention from Jaja Dandé. After being possessed by her forest god Wamba, she announced that the time for fighting would soon end, and that it was to be followed by a lasting peace with the Dutch. This vision helped turn the tide of Saramaka opinion in favour of peace. Among the Saramaka who were moved by Jaja Dandé's prophecy was her son Abini, who later became one of the signatories of the 1762 treaty.[85]

Maroon women took part in military combat, as soldiers, officers, and commanders. In late sixteenth-century Cartagena, a Spanish maroon-hunting militia found itself engaged in a fierce battle with a battalion of black fugitives. The fighters included 150 women, armed with clubs and daggers; these African-born 'Amazons' were described as 'fighting more hardily than men', and were commanded by a woman warrior named Polonia.[86] There were cases of women ascending to leadership positions in the *quilombos* of Brazil. These included Filippa Maria Aranha in the Trombetas region, who forced the Portuguese authorities into submission.[87] A Berbice maroon community in the early nineteenth century consisted of fifty men and one single woman, who became their leader after her husband was captured.[88] Women fought in maroon insurrections. One of the many early nineteenth-century uprisings in Bahia was launched from the *quilombo* of Urubu in 1826, with the aim of converging on Salvador and killing its white inhabitants. Soldiers despatched to quell the rebellion were pushed back by insurgents armed with bows and arrows, knives, pitchforks, hatchets, and spears. Among the most valiant combatants was a Nagô woman named Zeferina, who rallied the fighters by constantly shouting 'Death to the whites! Long live blacks!' and deploying her archery skills against the colonial forces. Zeferina was one of the last to surrender, and she impressed her adversaries by her martial valour and imperious demeanour. The president of the province called her a 'queen'.[89]

Fugitives escaped by land and by water, exploiting the resources offered to them. In the history of slavery rivers and oceans have widely been perceived as spaces of captivity and death, particularly during the journeys to the African coast and the Middle Passage. But seas, rivers, and lakes were also gateways to self-emancipation and freedom, as we already saw in the previous chapter with the example of Ganvié, and earlier here with Biohó, whose canoeing skills were an essential instrument of his successful flight.

In the Caribbean island of Barbados, where plantation slavery had spread by the 1660s, African fugitives sought refuge in caves, gullies, and wooded zones. They increasingly absconded to the neighbouring Windward Islands of Saint Lucia, Saint Vincent, Tobago, and Dominica. These 'maritime maroons' were particularly attracted to Saint Vincent, as the island lay directly west of Barbados, lacked a European settler population, and could be reached with relative ease. A French priest who travelled there in 1700 reported that alongside the native Carib population, the territory was inhabited by 'negroes, most of whom have escaped from Barbados . . . in canoes or rafts'.[90] These black maroons grew in numbers and rapidly took control of the windward part of Saint Vincent, somewhat to the frustration of the Caribs, who invited the help of the British and the French to dislodge the new migrants. A small British invasion was attempted, but it was easily repulsed by the maroons. The Caribs then persuaded the French to mount a larger assault and promised them their full support. The attack took place in 1719 under the command of Major Poulain de Guerville, a senior officer from Martinique. Well prepared for this offensive, the Saint Vincent maroons confused the invaders by painting themselves red, like the Amerindian allies of the French, and retreating to the mountains, coming down during the night to ambush their troops. The promised Carib support failed to materialize, and French forces, weakened by dysentery, suffered significant losses and were forced into a humiliating retreat. Among the fatalities was their commander, Poulain de Guerville. During the first half of the eighteenth century, Saint Vincent consolidated its position as a bastion of maritime marronage.[91]

There were many other patterns of maritime escape from New World slavery. Spanish territories such as Florida, Cuba, and Puerto Rico were especially sought after because of the widespread belief that escaped fugitives would be granted asylum and treated as free people if they converted to Catholicism and pledged allegiance to the Spanish Crown. The welcome in Florida was uneven and at times ambiguous but many were able to enjoy protected status. In 1738 the Spaniards even founded a town for the fugitives, Gracia Real de Santa Teresa de Mose; the sanctuary policy was formally ended in 1790.[92] Between 1680 and the late eighteenth century, many hundreds of men, women, and children reached Cuba on a variety of vessels, fleeing from slavery in Jamaica, the Bahamas, Saint-Domingue, and British North America. They often travelled in sizeable groups.[93] In 1766 and 1767 alone, ninety-five people escaped from northern Jamaica into Cuba.[94] Puerto Rico was a source of flight during the first half of the eighteenth century, and the British Virgin Islands governor declared in 1754 that if this exodus were not checked it would ruin British sugar colonies; the sanctuary policy was ended in 1767 after the signing of a treaty with the British.[95]

In the Indian Ocean, captives from Madagascar who were forcibly transported to Ile de France (Mauritius) in the eighteenth century would take flight and attempt to return to their homeland in dugouts and *pirogues*, and many were successful. A source from 1749 – one of the earliest references to the *kreyol* language – indicates that the enslaved would often point in a westerly direction and exclaim 'Madagascar li là!' ('Madagascar is over there!'). The urge to escape enslavement was based on a yearning for freedom, as well as a spiritual belief among Malagasies that their soul could only rest if their body was buried in the land of their birth.[96] Flight from Mauritius became so common that in the late 1720s sentinels were deployed to guard sailing vessels on the island, and in 1785 local authorities were still warning boat and canoe owners to keep their vessels under close watch.[97] Such was the courage, determination, and sense of solidarity of these Malagasy maritime fugitives that if there were too many of them to fit into their escape canoe, they would take turns to occupy it, and swim alongside it for half of the four-day journey back to their homeland.[98]

Alarmed by these waves of maritime flight, colonial authorities went to considerable lengths to frustrate them. Several laws against the theft of 'shallops, boats and other vessels' were enacted in Barbados, and captives who were found guilty of such acts could face the death penalty.[99] Commercial or privateering vessels were warned that their owners would be prosecuted if they allowed fugitives to come on board, or employed them as sailors (some maroons made temporary bondage agreements with captains in return for being granted passage out of the territory they were fleeing). Across the British, French, Dutch, and Danish West Indian colonies, paddles, masts, and sails were required to be locked away. Even when they were not put to death, recaptured fugitives were subjected to brutal punishments, including whipping, branding, and the severing of ears and limbs. Vessels passing Guadeloupe were mandated to keep at least a league's distance from land, in order to discourage captives from escaping and swimming or sailing to them. Officials placed small coastguard vessels offshore to intercept those in canoes heading for Dominica (25 miles), Montserrat (35 miles), or Antigua (40 miles).[100] In 1706, Danish officials on Saint Thomas took the extreme measure of ordering the destruction of all trees in the island's primordial forest that could be cut down to make a dugout.[101]

The responses of the colonial authorities were entirely understandable. These maritime fugitive escapes were based not just on individual and collective determination but elaborate planning and sophisticated skills. The predicament the enslaved faced in the New World required men and women from different ethnic and regional backgrounds to co-operate in new ways: as we have seen, this sense of community often began on slave ships, when the captives called each other 'shipmates',[102] and continued as they sought to find or construct their escape vessels. Advertisements for the capture of runaways frequently mentioned the composite quality of maritime fugitives, as in 1738 when a slaver from South Carolina declared that his vessel had been stolen by two of his boatmen, 'an Angola Negro named Levi and an Ibo Negro named Kent'.[103] Many escapees fled in vessels that they themselves had built. This complex process involved selecting the right trees (silk cottonwoods were preferred), shaping the hull and paddles, and working out the optimal canoe length. These technical abilities played an essential role in making maritime marronage possible, and were generally carried across to the New World from Africa, where many communities developed extensive aquatic traditions in their struggles against slave raiders. Dugouts, for example, drew on African sailing techniques designed to maximize speed, agility, and sturdiness. They could be launched quickly and did not sink even if filled with water; they sailed well with and close to the wind, and typically carried human loads several times their own weight.[104]

As with so many other aspects of marron life, African maritime fugitive traditions were based on science as well as spirituality. A runaway dugout was much more than a precise assemblage of timber. It was invested in metaphysical qualities and was thought to possess a soul – as indeed were rivers and oceans. In many African cultural traditions, these aquatic expanses were the final resting places of ancestral spirits. Maritime escapes were thus seen as ways of re-engaging with the lives, customs, and ways of being of which the enslaved had been dispossessed. Religious and spiritual motifs were inscribed on canoes and boats, referencing aquatic deities such as Mama Wata, the African spirit who protected people from harm as they travelled across expanses of water, and guided them to safety and freedom (as we saw in the previous chapter, she was invoked by the *Amistad* rebels). Africa was thus present in multiple ways in the minds and imaginations of maritime fugitives. And for some escapees, it was an expressly stated final destination. In 1727 a Virginian planter reported that seven of his captives had stolen his canoe 'to regain home waters'. In 1734 a slaver from South Carolina likewise stated that three of his Angolan captives named Hector, Peter, and Dublin had robbed his boat in order to head for their homeland (and five other Angolans in the same state escaped with the same intention in 1761).[105] In 1775 four enslaved men and one woman made off with a 'small paddling canoe' belonging to the governor of Georgia; they were going to 'look for their own country'.[106]

These North American examples open up the broader question of marronage in the United States, which is far less exceptional than was once thought to be the case. As elsewhere in the Atlantic world, the territorial bases of American fugitives were geographically distinct: they spanned the American South, and particularly Virginia, the Carolinas, Georgia, and Louisiana. Thousands of statutes targeting maroons were enacted in these states between the late 1600s and the mid-nineteenth century. One of the first came into effect in June 1680, and it sought to proscribe captives from 'lurking in obscure places'.[107] Another important commonality was the predominance of Africans (as opposed to American-born captives) among the fugitives. In the eighteenth century, even as their proportion fell as a percentage of the enslaved population, African captives were significantly over-represented among fugitives in North America.[108] The other important, and related, characteristic was that African fugitives tended to take flight in groups: between 1790 and 1860 two-thirds of Africans ran away in cohorts of two or more, and one-third in groups of five or more. People left with members of the same ethnic community, but mixed groups were by no means unusual.[109]

Sylviane Diouf has recovered the distinct features of the 'maroon land-scape' of the American South. Runaways who remained in proximity to plantation areas hid in trees and cabins but most commonly in caves, living there for years and sometimes even decades; some of these underground dwellings had several rooms, furniture, and cooking stoves.[110] Most of these fugitives tried to remain hidden so as not to provoke attention, but a minority formed gangs which engaged in acts of theft and highway robbery that made them famous. As elsewhere across the New World these attacks against slaver interests reinforced the white-settler association between marronage and criminality. In the early 1820s one such gang was active in a large area around Georgetown in South Carolina, and it was led by a charismatic leader who eventually called himself Forest. Tall, slim, and light-skinned, he was an intrepid and ingenious figure, who protected himself from gunshot with a home-made bullet-proof vest. His audacious actions turned him into a legend among plantation captives in the districts where he operated. His band of maroons drew on a wide intelligence network that allowed them to elude capture until Forest was ambushed and killed in 1823.[111]

There were relatively few fortified camps on the *palenque* or *quilombo* models in the American South. Those that were established in the late eighteenth century, such as the Bas du Fleuve community south-east of New Orleans, and Bear Creek in Georgia, were rapidly destroyed by the authorities. The most enduring settlements survived in more remote hinterland areas, such as the Great Dismal Swamp, a large marshy area stretching from southern Virginia to north-east North Carolina. Although they were increasingly hunted down in the decades before Emancipation, hundreds of men and women – possibly up to a thousand – were able to survive there, building cabins and dwellings on stilts, and relying on the abundant wildlife for nourishment and clothing.[112] In 1770 an advertise-ment was posted for three runaway captives 'imported this last summer from Africa' who had escaped and were thought to be 'lurking' in the Swamp.[113] The area was the home of several generations of runaways, as well as a refuge for those escaping prosecution. A young black captive who killed a white man in the early nineteenth century disappeared into the Swamp and stayed there for at least forty-nine years.[114] We have no direct testimony of this kind of rugged lifestyle in North America, but a flavour of it is captured in the autobiography of the Cuban runaway Este-ban Montejo, who led a solitary existence in the woods until the abolition of slavery in Cuba in the late nineteenth century.[115]

Also singular to the North American fugitive experience was the absence of a major tradition of offensive maroon warfare against the slave order, of the kind widely seen across the Atlantic world. There were many rumours about the involvement of runaways in plots against whites, such as the 1765 South Carolina Christmas conspiracy and those of 1802 and 1821 in North Carolina. However, there was little evidence of any substantial maroon involvement in these plots, except perhaps providing hideouts for stockpiling arms and ammunition.[116] One of the key factors that might explain this absence of runaway revolutionism was the relatively small size of maroon groups, which were perhaps more conducive to separation and autonomy than confrontation. Moreover, the borderlands and hinterlands of the South were not the only available destinations for American fugitives. Many sought refuge in Northern states (until the 1850 Fugitive Law forced them underground), as well as in further territories such as Canada, Mexico, and the Caribbean – and, after 1804, Haiti. Seaborne escapes along the East coast were an integral part of this phenomenon, as runaways made their way to Northern cities through ports in the Carolinas, Virginia, and Maryland. Maritime marronage was thus part of the American tradition of opposition to enslavement.[117]

From the onset of Atlantic slavery, runaway communities were a major form of resistance across the New World. As with African opposition, it was by no means always successful, and for every individual taking flight the fear of capture and death was always present. These emotions have been powerfully evoked in literary works. In Patrick Chamoiseau's *The Old Slave and the Mastiff*, the maroon's experiences of physical and mental distress are likened to 'ruins which had once been sumptuous cathedrals'.[118] Yet many male and female runaways survived, and the settlements they created enduringly confronted the material and ideological power of their enslavers, and in some instances forced colonial authorities to recognize their legitimacy through formal peace treaties and tacit non-aggression agreements. Even when these compromises were not found, or not honoured (generally under settler pressure), and maroon communities remained essentially at war with the slavers, their sturdiness, inventiveness, and adaptability proved a constant source of anxiety for their oppressors. This ranged from the individual planter who feared losing his livestock and crops to runaway raiders and to regional authorities' worries about maroon-led rebellions and insurrections. In places such as north-east Brazil, Hispaniola, Jamaica, and Surinam there were constant and generalized fears that maroon activity was threatening the viability of colonial activity.[119]

These traditions of fugitive resistance could extend across significant periods of time, colonial regimes, and indeed oceans. Mauritius was colonized first by the Dutch in the seventeenth century, then the French in the eighteenth, and finally the British in the nineteenth. In addition to the maritime escapes mentioned earlier, inland maroon activity was constant throughout the three eras. More than half of the 105 captives initially brought to Mauritius by the Dutch in 1642 escaped into the woods. Indeed, one of the principal reasons for the Dutch abandonment of the island's colonization in 1710 was the systematic incidence of marronage among enslaved populations, accompanied by frequent and often devastating arson attacks. In June 1695 a group of maroons (including at least one woman, Espérance) carefully planned an assault that destroyed Fort Frederick Hendryk in Grand Port. In 1706 a major conspiracy involving captives and fugitives was uncovered, in which they planned to assassinate the Dutch settlers and burn down their houses.[120]

The French, who took over the island and established permanent settlements as from 1721, faced significant initial opposition from well-armed maroon bands, whose military skills enabled them to launch attacks against local garrisons in 1724 and 1732. The colonizers only got the situation under relative control through brutal repression, notably under the governorship of Mahé de Labourdonnais, who set up slave-hunting militias. These forces captured and killed the maroon leader Sans-Souci in 1739; this runaway from Mozambique had been a fugitive for over fifteen years. But even without such leaders, marronage persisted in Mauritius over the next hundred years.[121] Under the British, it is estimated that around 12 per cent of the island's nearly 80,000 captives were maroons during the 1820s.[122] In the final decades before emancipation, many of them found their way to the capital Port Louis, where they posed as free people, forging passes and manumission documents, and working as skilled artisans.[123]

While Atlantic and Indian Ocean runaways lacked the firepower to bring down slavery itself, and a considerable number of settlements were successfully dismantled by colonial authorities, they nonetheless managed significant accomplishments, against their enemies and for themselves. In addition to the treaties they forced upon their enemies, they survived countless military campaigns aimed at physically eliminating them, disrupted commercial and trade routes, killed scores of settlers and militia troops, sabotaged plantations and industries relying on forced labour, compelled their enslavers to halt the import of 'troublesome' ethnic groups (and in some instances, the import of African captives altogether), contested the territorial supremacy of colonial powers and settlers in the New World, and subverted the association of blackness with inferiority, turning it instead into a symbol of power. Military expeditions against runaway settlements were costly to the enslavers, and often required the levying of expensive taxes on local settlers. Given the acute material power imbalance between the fugitives and their enemies, these were prodigious achievements. There will be more to come later in the book.

Even more important is what runaway communities managed to effect for their own collective material and moral benefit. Drawing on the composite ethnic and cultural groups that typically formed their settlements, they nurtured their own military, intellectual, and technical aptitudes – particularly in the development of defensive martial practices and in guerrilla warfare. They were highly skilled in agriculture; these capacities often allowed them to create comfortable reserves, and trade with plantation societies, thereby achieving a de facto recognition. As with the complex *kreyol* languages that emerged in places such as Mauritius and Haiti, they invented new ways of communication, combining and building on the cultural resources they already possessed. Moreover, they managed their own affairs, and in many instances created systems of self-governance that matched and even surpassed those of colonial societies in terms of their complexity, their efficiency, their deliberative and representative qualities, and (most significantly) their humanity. In all of these arenas they recovered what slavery had taken away from them: a sense of dignity and self-worth, and a belief that life could have a meaningful purpose that they could at least help to define. This was true for fugitives in general, but perhaps especially so for the women.

Above all, the maroon quest for autonomy and emancipation expressed a powerful rejection of the institution of chattel slavery, one that was channelled through a distinct war culture and grounded in African spiritual understandings of the fugitives' place in the universe. It is sometimes claimed that before the Age of Revolutions in the late eighteenth century the enslaved had no real understanding of the concept of freedom, except in personal, self-interested, or 'ethnic' terms, and that their opposition to enslavement was thus at best conditional. The cumulative evidence from this chapter demonstrates that this view is incorrect. From the sixteenth century onwards, African fugitives appealed to universal ideals of freedom. They did so in their explicit calls for equality when they rejected the slavers' association of whiteness with superior values. Hence the frequent association of liberty, during maroon insurrections, with calls for white slavers to be put to death. They gave voice to both natural and divine conceptions of liberty, and their embodiment in legendary fellow rebels such as Miguel, Nyanga, Biohó, and Zumbi, who were idolized by generations of maroons. As we have seen, this natural desire of runaways for freedom was repeatedly acknowledged by the colonial authorities.

By their words and deeds, maroons inspired insubordination among communities of enslaved people, and other kinds of fugitive action – such as the large numbers of captive men and women who took flight to colonial towns where they successfully blended with free black populations. Their stories have not been evoked in this chapter, but these were equally remarkable tales of determination and courage. Ona Judge, one of the captives owned by George Washington, is a good example. She was born on his Mount Vernon estate in Virginia, and in 1789 he took her with him to New York City and then Philadelphia when he became President; she served as one of the maids attending his wife Martha. In May 1796, aged twenty, probably after hearing that she was to be given away as a wedding gift to Martha's ill-tempered granddaughter Eliza, she escaped on a sloop to Portsmouth, New Hampshire. Washington's associates put out an advertisement for the runaway, which described her as having 'absconded from the household of the President of the United States', and it expressed surprise at her flight. The President made concerted efforts to get her back, asking that she be returned 'by force if necessary'. Ona was able to escape from the clutches of the Founding Father. Interviewed by a journalist for a New Hampshire abolitionist newspaper in 1845, her simple words effectively summarized the defiance of Atlantic runaways across the ages: 'I am free now and choose to remain so.'[124]

3

Not to be Hurt by the White Men

The enslavement of millions of people in Africa and their forced transfer across the Atlantic was a violent and degrading process, in which slavers made every effort to dehumanize their captives and sever all links with their lives back home. Enslavement was about depriving its victims of their sense of self and personal dignity, and of anything that might afford them status, value, and honour. Moreover, once they reached the New World, captives were treated as barbarians lacking any of the trappings of civilization. Dispossessed of their African identities, they were given Christian names and often baptized by their new owners. Even the 'African' ethnic designations used by the slavers were broad abstractions, frequently bearing little resemblance to the ways in which men and women from Africa saw themselves. The same people were given different names: Yoruba-speaking captives from the Bight of Benin were called Lucumi in Cuba, and Nagô in Portuguese Brazil and French Saint-Domingue. Different people were called by the same generic name: frequently used to describe the origins of enslaved people, the term 'Guinea' covered an area corresponding to the entire west coast of Africa. In its brutal uprooting of its victims from their homelands, in the domination it exercised over them, and its intended ambition to annihilate their spirit, Atlantic slavery was thus rightly described as a 'social death'.[1]

However, the complete rupture that the slavers sought to provoke was never realized in practice. As we glimpsed in the previous chapter, African captives were able to preserve elements of their traditions and recreate, build, and act on them in the New World. Among these were their languages, their scientific and technical knowledge, their political conceptions and laws, their agricultural and military skills, their artistic and cultural practices, and their religious cults and imaginings. They spoke in native tongues when among themselves and members of their ethnic groups. Facial marks that were signs of noble, royal, or associational distinction in Africa continued to provide their bearers with some recognition, at least among their fellow captives. Military captains who had fought in African wars still commanded the loyalty of their former soldiers in the Americas. Herbalists deployed their skills for medicinal purposes, using their existing knowledge of plants and adding New World flora to their repertoire. Men and women with religious training and divination skills were treated with respect and were sought out and consulted in towns and plantations.

Indeed, this process of cultural retention and development, which amounted to a 'social resurrection',[2] was notable in the spiritual realm. As we saw in chapter 1, west and central Africans embraced a rich and diverse spiritual life, which included monotheistic religions such as Christianity and Islam as well as traditional forms of belief. These systems were not closed and often interacted with each other. When they came to the New World the enslaved did whatever they could to hold on to these religious practices and spiritual values, often combining them in innovative ways. One widely reported fact summarizes their determination. During the Middle Passage, prisoners were stripped of their clothing but kept their bracelets, necklaces, and amulets, many of which had Arabic inscriptions and were believed to have protective and supernatural qualities. Two of the major African traditions preserved by captives in the New World were the Islamic faith and the traditional belief system known as Obeah. These belief systems were markedly different from each other in their make-up (Islam, unlike Obeah, was monotheistic) as well as in their rituals. Moreover, Islam was based on written holy texts, whereas the knowledge of Obeah practitioners seems to have been maintained and transmitted orally. Women were often important figures in Obeah, whereas the key agents of Islamic rituals and beliefs in captive communities were typically male.

Yet these two faith systems overlapped. Their African origins were rooted in the cultural practices of ordinary people, and the flexibility of these faiths allowed them some degree of improvisation, and the ability to draw people from different backgrounds and groups together. They both provided mental refuges for the enslaved, furnishing them with autonomous spaces where they could escape – however briefly – from the violence dominating their lives, and seek some measure of bodily and spiritual healing. These protective qualities were associated with Brazilian Candomblé as well – a religion originating among African slaves in Brazil, combining African, indigenous, and Catholic elements – although it has much less of a direct association with enslaved resistance.[3] Obeah and Islam were also sources of dissent and rebellion. They empowered rebels to devise plots and foment insurrections, equipping them with practical and moral instruments to bind their fellow conspirators together and confront their enemies, while seeking to neutralize their superiority in material force and firepower. In many instances, these faiths armed the insurgents with the belief that they were invulnerable and could be protected even from the lethal weapons they faced. It was said of Tacky, the principal leader of the 1760 revolt in Jamaica, that he could 'not possibly be hurt by the white men, for that he caught all the bullets fired at him in his hand, and hurled them back with destruction to his foes'.[4]

The African knowledge and belief system known as Obeah originated among the social practices of west African peoples. Although there is no agreement about its linguistic origins, it was particularly associated with the culture of the Akan people in the Gold Coast,[5] and referred to the activities of persons with specialized knowledge of chemical and supernatural forces that could be used for bodily healing and divination.[6] Obeah first appeared as a specific term in European colonial writings in the early eighteenth-century Caribbean, but it was almost certainly present among the practices of the enslaved from an earlier date. Obeah was in effect a catch-all term referring to medical practices as well as the invocation of various supernatural forces from west Africa; there was considerable overlap and interplay among them. Spirits were summoned to help bring about desired outcomes, such as healing, protection, recovery, threat, and harm. These results were achieved through magical objects and substances, which included mirrors, wooden effigies, amulets, herbs and plants, stones, powders, and potions. Among the most common spirits was the river goddess known as 'Mama Wata', whom we encountered in previous chapters. This deity was particularly prominent in the Caribbean, where she was invoked through a dance ritual.[7]

The practice of Obeah (which had several proximate spellings, such as 'Obia') came to be widely disseminated among captive communities in the British, Danish, and Dutch Caribbean, and in the Americas. It was present in the French Caribbean as well, although this has received much less attention, and was generally referred to as 'conjuring' in North America. In Jamaica a distinction was sometimes made between Obeah as a form of 'bad magic' and Myal as 'good magic'. But it is most likely that this was simply a different way of describing the same phenomena, based on misconceptions rooted in Western Christianity.[8] Obeah was practised by priestly figures, commonly referred to as Obeah-men and Obeah-women. These charismatic individuals enjoyed a special status in New World captive communities. Their cultural and linguistic skills often enabled them to navigate across the major ethnic divides. They operated as intermediaries among different groups, and in particular between plantations and maroon areas. They were respected and often feared for their extensive knowledge and their divination powers.[9] Obeah beliefs and rituals helped to sustain enslaved communities by offering a practical avenue for healing various physical and moral ailments, and an African sacred system flexible yet robust enough to deflect missionary attempts to dismiss the captives' traditional 'superstitions' and assert the superiority of Christianity.[10]

The social value of Obeah to enslaved communities in the Caribbean and the Americas was widely recognized in the writings of eighteenth-century naturalists. They observed that captives relied on Obeah to alleviate their sense of loss, solve their practical problems, and cure their diseases with natural ingredients such as leaves, barks, and roots – a particularly important function in a context where access to medical facilities was very limited for the enslaved. One of the first European chroniclers, Griffith Hughes, described Obeah figures as 'Physicians and Conjurors ... of a sort' who could control the supernatural forces believed to cause harm and misfortune to individuals. He witnessed a woman captive healed of her rheumatism by a 'magical apparatus' consisting of water, leaves, and soap. A belief in these types of cure was widespread across New World plantations and not only among the enslaved communities; many slavers were known to rely on them, including for their personal medical needs.[11] Even as he condemned it as a form of occultism, a French planter in Martinique offered this striking description of Obeah's medicinal qualities: 'I do not believe in sorcery. But I do believe in certain sciences, certain recipes [the Obeah healers] preserve mysteriously, and that surprise and disturb us, just as in the Middle Ages our ancestors were left surprised and disturbed before the most basic experiments in physics or chemistry.'[12]

As captives turned to Obeah for protection from moral and material harm, the guidance of Obeah priests was essential. The American abolitionist William Wells Brown described one such figure, Dinkie, a powerful force on the plantation, who typically wore a snake's skin around his neck, and had a petrified frog in one pocket, and a dried lizard in another.[13] Frederick Douglass likewise related how he was advised by one of his fellow captives, Sandy Jenkins, a 'clever soul'. Jenkins was a conjuror, and he recommended that Douglass should carry a particular root on his right side to prevent the abuse he was suffering from his cruel master, Edward Covey. The charm apparently worked, although Douglass played down this success in his later recounting of the story.[14] Captives widely used such roots, as well as magical powders and amulets, as defensive implements against the violence they encountered on plantations, or to deflect anticipated punishment – for example, the whippings they might receive for leaving their masters' premises without permission.

Approached by a group of mistreated captives in Kentucky, the conjuror William Webb told them to gather a particular type of root and collect it in bags. He then asked them to walk around their own quarters a few times, before carefully laying the bags outside their master's lodgings. These Obeah bundles were often planted in sensitive places, either for defensive aims (to effect a change in the behaviour of white settlers) or offensive purposes (to cause harm to individuals or plantation livestock). The object of the exercise in this instance was a combination of the two: to induce the white settler to dream that those he had enslaved were gaining revenge and punishing him for his past wrongs. We do not know for certain whether this moral fear was actually generated. But this slaver's treatment of his workforce improved considerably after the Obeah intervention – as indeed did conjuror Webb's prestige among them.[15]

Obeah's implicit challenge to the institution of slavery could easily become an explicit one. Obeah priests were frequently suspected of encouraging those attempting to escape and join maroon communities. In Westmoreland parish in Jamaica, planters identified one such figure, Plato, as the source of the desertion of their captives. They launched a campaign to capture him, even as they could not help but notice his charismatic qualities. In the words of one settler, Plato was seen by women runaways as a source of 'freedom, protection and unbounded generosity'.[16] Observing the practice of Obeah in Pennsylvania, the Swedish botanist Peter Kalm noted instances of its violent use by some of the enslaved against their own brethren – particularly those who had become too close to their masters, or had adopted manners and habits that were too 'European'.[17] Some Obeah rituals involved whippings, beatings, and other forms of violence against captives, particularly to cure them of their 'evil spirits'. These rituals could often lead to serious injuries and even death.[18]

Spells could be cast on entire groups of enslaved people, causing them to lose their lives or become melancholic and despondent. Such symptoms were frequently blamed by slavers on Obeah. In 1775 a Jamaican planter suffered several deaths on his estate, with many other captives battling with a 'mysterious illness' that sapped their energy. All attempts at treating these ailments by conventional medical means failed. Eventually the source of the problem was identified as an eighty-year-old woman captive from Benin, who turned out to be a seasoned Obeah practitioner and had cast a spell on the plantation. She was identified by her stepdaughter, who was also struck down by the mystery disease. A search of the old woman's house found 'hundreds' of ritual materials carefully concealed in her roof and the crevices of her walls, including rags, feathers, cat and dog teeth and bones, glass beads, and eggshells filled with viscous substances.[19]

Women were often practitioners of Obeah in west Africa and this pattern seems to have continued in the New World, where they could charge considerable sums for their services. They were also involved in revolutionary activity. Among the key advisors of Atta, one of the principal Berbice captive leaders (along with Cuffy) in 1763 was a female practitioner of Obeah named Pallas, whom the Dutch authorities described as 'an instigator of the rebels through pretend magic'.[20]

In an effort to discredit the practice of Obeah, slavers repeatedly associated it with black magic, and later with poisoning.[21] In Bermuda a mixed-race woman named Sarah (Sally) Bassett was sentenced to death in 1730 for attempting to murder the two white owners of her enslaved granddaughter Beck. The poisonous substances she was alleged to have introduced in their house included roots and toad toxins, which were intended to bring about a slow wasting away of the body – a technique familiar to Obeah practitioners in Africa.[22] Writing about British-controlled Jamaica, the Methodist missionary John Shipman claimed in 1820 that 'Obeah people know best how to make up a poison properly'.[23] Livestock were often targeted on plantations, as were humans, both old and young. This happened in the French Caribbean, as we shall see, and in Jamaica as well. Enslaved nurses on the island were believed to have fallen under the spell of men and women practising Obeah, and the nurses were blamed for the death of white children, as well as the distribution of drugs and medicines intended to cause abortions; many were prosecuted.[24] The line between poison and medication was sometimes hazy, and in many west African languages (such as Fon and Igbo) the same word was used for both.[25] Sometimes these acts were driven by personal revenge rather than opposition to the institution of slavery. In another Jamaican case, a butler poisoned the well used by his white owners because they had demoted his sister, whom they no longer trusted to look after their children. The butler had responded by throwing a chicken into the family well, with its beak and claws cut off. He was seen with a phial containing a green liquid, no doubt obtained from an Obeah priest.[26]

References to such conspiratorial Obeah networks can be found in slaver writings and colonial records from the early eighteenth century. They typically came to light in the aftermath of enslaved revolts and insurrections in the Americas, when captured rebels and their alleged accomplices were put on trial. No fewer than twenty significant rebellions can thus be connected to some form of Obeah revolutionary activity in the British, Dutch, French, and Danish Americas, in the United States, Dutch Guyana (Berbice), the Virgin Islands, Jamaica, Barbados, Antigua, and Martinique. In the United States, African spiritualist presences can be detected in the New York revolts of 1712 and 1741, as well as the Richmond and Charleston uprisings of 1800 and 1822.[27] All of these rebellions had significant mystical dimensions – especially in terms of the west African origins and spiritual inclinations of some of their leading figures, as well as the specific beliefs and revolutionary practices of the rebels. One of their most characteristic features was their Obeah-induced conviction in their physical invulnerability, which they sought to instil in all those around them.

The April 1712 New York rebellion was carried out by around twenty-five to thirty men, mostly African but including a small number of Amerindians. They armed themselves with swords, clubs, knives, and guns, and set fire to a building in New York, then proceeded to ambush those who came to put out the blaze. Nearly one-fifth of the city's population at the time was African, and the rebels hoped to provoke a general uprising. Its ultimate aim was, in the words of a contemporary clergyman, to 'destroy all the whites in order to obtain their freedom'. The rebellion was contained, but ten whites were killed and another twelve wounded. The uprising – the first on such a scale in North America – caused a movement of panic across the colony. One of the rebel leaders was Peter the Doctor, a free African labourer who drew on his spiritual knowledge to galvanize the insurgents, conducting a blood oath to seal their collective resolve and rubbing a magical powder on their clothing to make them 'invulnerable'. Peter's key role can be deduced from the fact that he was the only conspirator who was a free person; all the others were captives. Moreover, his 'Doctor' nickname was a common reference to Obeah priests in the Caribbean.[28] He was likely of Akan culture (at the time described as 'Coromantee'), from the Gold Coast region, as were a preponderance of the twenty-eight rebels who were put on trial.[29] The effectiveness of Peter's conjuring art may remain mysterious. But there can be no denying his diplomatic skills: whereas three-quarters of those tried for their involvement in the conspiracy were executed, Peter the Obeah-man managed to secure his acquittal and discharge.[30]

Akan rebels were prominently involved in several ensuing New World revolts, such as the 1733 rebellion on St John in the Danish Virgin Islands. During this insurrection, a group of Akan captives (identified locally as 'Aminas') plotted to emancipate themselves and create a polity dominated by their community on the island. They killed forty whites, burnt around eighty-five plantations as well as many sugar-producing facilities, and managed to take control of the territory. They ruled for six months before being overcome by a combined military force of French, Swiss, and Danish troops. Most of the leaders of the revolt committed suicide, in accordance with their belief in spiritual transmigration.[31] Three years later another Akan-led conspiracy was uncovered in British Antigua, under the leadership of a charismatic Ashanti captive called Court, also known among the enslaved as Prince Klass. Hatched over a long period, the plan was to blow up a building where many of the island's planters were gathering for a ball in honour of King George II, and then launch a general insurrection that would overthrow the white settlers and proclaim Klass as the new king. The conspirators swore an oath of loyalty involving an African war dance with shields and the ingestion of a potion made of blood, graveyard dirt, and rum. The ceremony was overseen by two Obeah-men named Caesar Mathew and Quawcoo Hunt.[32]

Soon afterwards, another attempted conspiracy in New York revolved around a series of fires that broke out in the city between March and April 1741. Although details of the plot remain sketchy, the authorities claimed the conspirators were – again – planning to burn down the city and kill its white inhabitants. Here, too, the link among the thirteen men arrested, in addition to their professed hatred of slavery, was their common Akan origin. At the ceremony where they had sworn an allegiance to the conspiracy, they pledged that it would include only 'their countrymen'.[33] One of the most fascinating figures to emerge in the records of these plots was a captive named Will Ward. He was implicated in all three of these conspiracies, first in St John (where he participated in the insurrection), then in Antigua (where he was part of its leadership), and then finally in New York, where he was among the men who took the loyalty oath, administered by 'a little man with a long gown'.[34] Ward exemplified the way in which enslaved rebellious activity was already operating transnationally across New World borders in the early eighteenth century.

One of the most dramatic and mysterious Obeah conspiracies unfolded in French-controlled Martinique in the early nineteenth century. By 1819, as a wave of deaths and illnesses mounted across the island, Martinique was in crisis, and the authorities blamed it on the wide-ranging powers of 'Obis', priest-like figures whom they likened to sorcerers. The colonists claimed that Martinique was the target of a conspiracy seeking to destroy the plantation system through the widespread use of poison to kill or harm livestock, fellow captives, and white settlers. The driving force behind the plot, they believed, was an underground Obeah leadership with a network operating across Martinique, complete with sacred oaths, initiation rites, and secret signs. These Obeah leaders exerted their influence through mystical and coercive powers. They drew the enslaved elite into their orbit, in particular overseers, slave drivers, chambermaids, and children's nurses, who carried out the poisonings at their behest. Some colonists claimed the leaders used arsenic-bearing peddlers who travelled across the colony as couriers, while others thought they relied on ethnically based cultural associations.[35]

According to an official report drafted in early 1827, the casualties were high. Over the previous five-year period, around 5,000 black captives and seventy-three white settlers had been killed, and more than 8,000 animals. The deaths continued even after the authorities launched a fierce wave of repression from mid-1822, trying large numbers of captives in special courts and executing more than six hundred of them, and condemning over a thousand to the galleys, forced labour, or deportation. It remains unclear whether this 'special masonry dedicated to poison',[36] as one planter called it, really existed. None of the Obeah ringleaders were ever identified, although it is conceivable that they were among those who were executed or banished. But there is no doubting Obeah's ideological power. It poisoned the minds of the white population and the French authorities with paranoia and confusion, undermining the economic capacities of the plantation system and the slavers' trust in their own captives.

Jamaica was the theatre of Obeah's most direct and enduring association with rebellious activity. Its spiritual and practical presence was felt in all the colony's major captive revolts of the eighteenth and nineteenth centuries, from the First Maroon War of the 1730s to Tacky's Revolt in 1760, all the way through to the Boxing Day rebellion of 1823 and beyond. Such was the scale of the perceived Obeah threat to the slaver order that Jamaica led the way in its criminalization, passing a series of legislative acts against its practice – first in 1761, three more times in the late eighteenth century, and then again in 1816. Carrying out any Obeah ritual became a capital crime, and from 1792 it was explicitly linked to poisoning. The mere possession of Obeah paraphernalia such as feathers, broken bottles, parrots' beaks, and alligators' teeth was punishable by death.[37] The Jamaican enslavers' fear is not hard to fathom, as their understanding of Obeah was based from the outset in their experience of rebellions by the enslaved. The first recorded use of the term in Jamaica appears in early eighteenth-century letters and documents relating to the runaway maroon leader known as Nanny, where she is referred to as an 'old Obeah woman'.[38]

Nanny – variously known as Granny Nanny, Grandy Nanny, and Queen Nanny – was a Jamaican runaway of Akan-speaking Ashanti origin. She is thought to have been of royal descent and was trained in the art of guerrilla combat. After coming to Jamaica as a teenager (probably enslaved) she escaped to the eastern mountainous interior, where she set up a group of runaway settlements, known by the early 1720s as Nanny Town. Queen Nanny became one of the main leaders of the Blue Mountain maroons, a hardy group of African-born and Taino rebels who raided plantations, killing white settlers and liberating their captives: around a thousand were set free. They were able to withstand repeated British military expeditions thanks to their effective defensive war techniques, relying on surprise attacks and ambushes and exploiting the natural habitat to their advantage. In the end, as we saw in the previous chapter, the British were forced to sign peace treaties with the rebels in 1739–40, recognizing their claims to live in freedom and providing them with sizeable land grants. In exchange, these maroons laid down their arms and pledged to return runaways to their owners and assist the British in putting down any future captive rebellions.

Despite these provisions for collaboration, which would complicate relationships between free and enslaved Jamaican communities, Queen Nanny became a legendary figure of the First Maroon War. Her authority rested both on her military talents and on her Obeah powers, which her fighters and followers saw as God-given; for them, these two elements were intimately connected. She was thought to rely on her spiritual and divination powers to anticipate the moves of her adversaries and render her invulnerable in battle. According to her legend, this allowed her to take them out in combat with a machete, and also to catch bullets and cannonballs and throw them back at the British soldiers (in one version, she caught them between her buttocks and farted them back). Stories circulated about a magical vessel described as 'Nanny's Pot', a boiling utensil without a flame under it, which unsuspecting British soldiers would be lured towards. When they leaned over, they would fall into it; this was probably a myth created after a successful ambush involving a waterfall.[39] Queen Nanny's protective and healing powers were widely celebrated among maroons. They credited her with the ability to treat the sick with plants and herbs, accelerate the growth of crops to feed her troops, and ward off evil from her people – as in the belief that if a white person went to Nanny Town they would be struck dead.[40]

The series of conflicts in 1760 known as Tacky's Revolt were in direct continuity with the First Maroon War. Its principal leader, Tacky, was, like Nanny, of Akan culture. He was from the Fante community, and a senior political and military figure in Africa before his capture and enslavement. After escaping from servitude in Jamaica, he planned his insurrection for a year, and launched his uprising on Easter Monday in April 1760, with the aim of taking over Jamaica from the British and creating an African state.[41] How far the conspiracy was unified or driven by Obeah in a broader sense remains unclear, but Tacky was (like Queen Nanny) also believed to possess the Obeah power of catching bullets and firing them back at the enemy. It is known that his entourage included several Obeah priests, who grafted elements of divination onto the planning and execution of the insurgency, and administered the 'solemn oath' to the conspirators.[42] Familiar Obeah rituals of self-protection were in evidence as well – one of the insurgents testified after his capture that he 'administered a powder which, being rubbed on their bodies, made [the rebels] invulnerable'.[43] This prisoner faced his executioners with defiance, declaring that it was 'not in the power of White people to kill him'.[44] Further signs of Obeah influence in the 1760 rebellion included the capture of an Obeah-woman named Cubah in Kingston, who was reportedly crowned queen by local insurgents.[45] The uprising was eventually contained, and Tacky killed – ironically with the decisive help of maroon troops. A smaller group of insurgents continued to fight until the end of the 1760s.[46] One of the turning points in the rebellion's defeat was the capture, execution, and public display of an Obeah-man by the British, which is widely thought to have demoralized the rebels. This confirmed the physical and spiritual centrality of Obeah for the insurgents, not to mention its indisputable fascination for the imagination of their adversaries.

One of the most detailed accounts of the performance of Obeah rituals in revolutionary Atlantic settings comes from the Boxing Day conspiracy in Jamaica, an enslaved revolt that was planned to begin in late December 1823. A group of African captives in the parish of St George had been meeting regularly under the pretence of praying and dancing. In fact, they were organizing a mass uprising aimed at eliminating the island's white slavers and destroying the plantation system in the colony. The authorities pre-empted the rebellion, and twenty-four revolutionaries were captured by the Jamaican militia and put on trial between January and April 1824. One of the principal leaders was identified as 'Obeah Jack', an African-born runaway who had been detained in February 1823. He was from the Guinea region, and his skills as a healer were widely recognized at the time – one of his co-conspirators called him 'Doctor'. Jack was one of the three main organizers of the conspiracy, and officiated at the main Obeah rituals that bound the insurgents together. These included a ceremony in which he killed a fowl and boiled it in water, and then rubbed the faces of the conspirators with the liquid. He claimed that this substance would act as a shield preventing white people from uncovering their plans. One of Obeah's key functions was to insulate the minds of the enslaved.

A few days later Jack prepared another potion, which was drunk by the rebels during their oath, which he administered. The drink contained a mixture of rum, gunpowder, human blood, and dirt that had been stepped on by a white man. He rubbed everyone's face with a wild-sage bush, noting that according to his native African tradition this plant would give them the 'spirit to overcome the white people'. It would further endow them with magical powers, including the ability to catch bullets in their hands – a power that he claimed he personally possessed. Among the other objects Jack produced was a mirror, a familiar implement for Obeah priests, which allowed him to exercise his divination skills. He brought a small wooden coffin containing hair taken from white men; a charm was meant to be more effective if it included something from the body of its intended victims. The coffin was to be buried in the ground on the day of the insurrection and was intended to cause fatal harm to any white person who passed by it. Several Obeah items were found in Jack's house, including a series of effigies, four knives, two bits of bone, a small stone, a nail, and some guinea pepper. We should mention – and this too was a general characteristic of Obeah priests – that Jack's role was not purely confined to the esoteric realm. He was involved in the military planning and drilling of the insurgents, and personally supplied many of the guns that were to be used. He was sentenced to death and executed, but his activities demonstrated that the African traditions of rebellion which emerged in Jamaica in the early 1700s were still very much alive more than a century later across the Atlantic world.[47]

Islam was an equally enduring source of strength for captives in the Caribbean and the Americas. Like Obeah, this religious, legal, and cultural system was brought to the New World from west Africa, and it is estimated that between 15 and 20 per cent of all African captives in the transatlantic slave trade were Muslims. The first captives taken to the Americas by the Spaniards in the early sixteenth century were mainly from the Senegambian and Upper Guinean regions. Most of them (Wolofs, Mandinkas, Fulanis) practised the Islamic faith, which was already well established in these areas. One of the common terms for Muslims in the Spanish Americas, and later in the American South, was 'Mandingo'; they were sometimes referred to as Moors. Later, the principal agents of this Islamic transmission were Hausa- and Yoruba-speaking communities sold into Atlantic slavery after being caught up in the military and religious conflicts that engulfed the Lower Guinean region from the eighteenth century onwards. The principal destinations of Muslim captives varied over time but significant groups were taken to the French Caribbean, Brazil, the American South, and Cuba. There were Muslims among the *Amistad* rebels, discussed in chapter 1; the Irish abolitionist Richard Robert Madden reported that one of them knew how to recite prayers in Arabic,[48] and another captive testified that his father was a *marabout*.[49]

The dominant strand of African Islam was Sufism. This mystical approach stressed the value of social cohesion, ritual observance, and the intimate nature of the connection between believers and Allah; these characteristics helped the enslaved retain their religion after they crossed the Atlantic. In this sense, Islam shared several other similarities with Obeah. It was both a source of refuge as well as potential rebellion and remained true to its African origins – especially as African Islam at times retained powerful attachments to traditional religions and spiritual practices, including divination and the use of magic potions and amulets. And like Obeah, Islam was strengthened by the cultural and religious hostility it encountered in the New World, particularly from Christianity.[50] Above all, Islam was a common denominator across and among African ethnic groups, which often had little else by way of shared traits – except on occasion a history of rivalry and conflict. Noting the presence of 'Mohamedan' captives in the Caribbean port of Cartagena de Indias in the early seventeenth century, a Spanish missionary observed that they came from different regions, but were drawn to each other through their affiliation to the Islamic faith.[51]

Several factors facilitated the survival and growth of Islam in the Americas. One of the attributes of Islamic communities in west Africa was their high rate of basic literacy, produced by the extensive network of Qur'anic schools (*madrasas*). Many Muslim captives could read and write, both in Arabic and in *ajami*, the generic name given to their own language transcribed in the Arabic alphabet. Some left memoirs.[52] This literacy played a significant role in enabling them to preserve and celebrate their cult, to communicate with each other and create faith-based networks, and to convert non-Muslim captive and free populations. These connections were helped by the presence of a dynamic contingent of noblemen, warriors, traders, and artisans among Muslim-bonded people.[53]

Many of these captives had practical skills that they were able to use to their personal advantage in the New World. This was the case with Salih Bilali, who was taken from his homeland in the kingdom of Massina (in Upper Niger) and brought to the American South in 1800. By 1816 he had become the head driver on a plantation at Cannon's Point, on St Simons Island in Georgia. Bilali's enslaver trusted him and left him in charge of the plantation, sometimes for months at a time. Although he was called 'Tom', and even helped defend the plantation against British attack in 1813, Bilali's contempt for 'Christian dogs' was undiminished. He remained a devout Muslim, wearing a fez and kaftan, praying daily, and observing the Muslim holy calendar.[54]

Intellectual classes were particularly well represented among New World Muslims. This was because African Islam was an especially mobile religion, making its practitioners vulnerable to slave raiders and criminal gangs. Among the groups preyed upon were pilgrims travelling to Mecca, and teachers moving from one area to another. Also targeted were students and clerics journeying (often across considerable distances) to reach their schools or to find writing paper. Some of these religious figures, such as the *marabouts*, led nomadic existences, devoting themselves entirely to study, teaching, and travel, and carrying their books and manuscripts with them. Their hostility to slavery in Africa made them vulnerable to European slavers, as we saw in chapter 1. But these Islamic holy men could just as easily be caught in the crossfire between rival imperial states. A *marabout* named Tamerlan thus recounted to a French officer in Saint-Domingue how he was recruited by an African king to teach his son. As he accompanied the prince one day, their convoy was ambushed and the young boy was killed. Taken into captivity, Tamerlan was marched to the coast on a three-month-long journey and sold to European slavers.[55]

The most immediate challenge that Muslim Africans faced in the New World was the denial of Islam's legitimacy as a religion, accompanied by systematic attempts to convert them to Christianity. Their resistance to being treated as 'infidels' was immediate, with missionaries frequently venting their frustration at the captives' refusal to abjure their faith. A French Jesuit, posted in the Caribbean from 1693 to 1705, recommended not bringing Muslims to the islands, 'for they never embrace the Christian religion'.[56] It is easy to appreciate why Muslims held on to their faith with such tenacity. Their religion was often their only substantive connection with the families they had left behind and their former life in Africa. Moreover, the Christianity imposed upon them in the New World was directly tied to their enslavement, and so was as alien in spirit as it was brutal and humiliating in form. In his memoirs, Mohammah Gardo Baquaqua described how the owner of the Brazilian plantation where he was taken would gather his five bonded workers and subject them to Catholic worship twice a day, forcing them to perform its holy rituals in front of his house, next to some holy icons made of clay: 'We all had to kneel before [the icons]; the family in front, and the slaves behind. We were taught to chant some words which we did not know the meaning of.

We also had to make the sign of the cross several times. Whilst worshipping, my master held a whip in his hand, and those who showed signs of inattention or drowsiness, were immediately brought to consciousness by a smart application of the whip.'[57]

Muslims frequently managed these situations by giving the outward appearance of conformity, seeming to embrace Christianity to make their daily lives easier, while at the same time holding on to their Islamic faith and practices. These 'pseudo-conversions' were widespread in North America as well as in Brazil, where Catholicism became the official faith after independence in 1822 and the religions of the enslaved people were declared illegal.[58] The captive Senegalese Muslim scholar Omar ibn Sayyid, who arrived in Charleston, South Carolina, in the early nineteenth century, was baptized in a Presbyterian church in 1820. However, he continued to celebrate the Prophet in his prayers and his writings, and his 1831 memoir began with an invocation to 'Lord Mohammad'. Islam survived in the New World because believers learnt to operate furtively and even secretly so as to adapt themselves to these constraints. Despite the overwhelming odds they were able to uphold their faith and preserve the wider culture in which it was rooted, with intellectual connections to Islamic traditions in North Africa and Iraq.[59]

Thus even though they were frequently given Christian names by their owners, many kept their original Islamic names when among themselves, and, as a Christian writer from South Carolina reflected sourly in the early nineteenth century, they 'taught the [Qur'an] to their children'.[60] When possible, as with the case of Bilali, they wore Islamic dress (caps, veils, trousers), and silver rings, bracelets, and talismans. Literate Muslims learnt how to make their own writing implements, copied verses of the Qur'an, and helped disseminate the holy texts among the faithful (sometimes disguised as Christian prayers). Even after three decades of servitude in Jamaica, Muhammad Kaba was able to produce a fifty-page manuscript in Arabic.[61]

Above all, Muslims practised the key tenets of Islam. They did their best to pray daily, even if they could not always be as punctilious as the unnamed Muslim captive from Charleston mentioned in the memoirs of Charles Ball (a fellow enslaved person who was Christian). Ball saw this man praying five times a day, 'always turning his face to the east, when in the performance of his devotion'.[62] In many instances, these prayers were recited individually and in secret – or at the end of the day's forced labour, when the captives returned to their dwellings. But some Muslims in the New World organized themselves to hold group prayers in 'makeshift mosques' – a hut, a room, the house of a free Muslim. In Jamaica many met in secret to recite and pass on verses of the Qu'ran by word of mouth.[63] They engaged in the practice of almsgiving (*zakat*), and most remarkably fasted during Ramadan, even though the Qur'an allowed exemptions for those in their circumstances (being away from home or engaging in strenuous physical labour). In nineteenth-century Bahia in Brazil, where there was a large Muslim population, there were two established periods of fasting, each lasting twenty-nine or thirty days: one for the mass of believers and the second for the *marabouts*.[64]

The fifth pillar of Islam, the pilgrimage to Mecca, was obviously unattainable for Muslim captives in the New World. But they kept the holy shrine in their minds and prayers, and adapted a reference to it in one of their religious rituals, the ring shout. This dance became widespread in the American South, as well as in Trinidad and Jamaica. It involved men and women turning counterclockwise in a circle around a sacred object while clapping their hands and shuffling their feet. This may have been a local adaptation of the Arabic 'sha'wt', the term designating one tour of the Kaaba, the stone building at the centre of Mecca.[65] Alternatively, the practice could be derived from the Sufi 'shawq', a sense of longing for the divine that here found its full expression in this ecstatic ritual.[66]

From the outset, therefore, Islam was a spiritual and cultural refuge for New World Muslims – although it was not confined to these defensive roles. Like Obeah, it could inspire dissent and rebellion. This was demonstrated in one of the first major New World revolts, which occurred in the Spanish empire on the Caribbean island of Hispaniola, where Christopher Columbus landed in 1492. From the early sixteenth century, as they moved from gold mining to the production of sugar, the Spaniards imported Africans from Senegambia and Upper Guinea in increasingly large numbers to work on their plantations. They referred to these Muslims as 'Mandingos' and sometimes 'Wolofs'.[67] These captives worked under gruelling conditions – squalid lodgings, inadequate nourishment, severe physical punishments – and loathed their harsh treatment by the Spanish settlers. Many of Hispaniola's enslaved people were literate, and moreover were skilled warriors and horsemen. The arrival of a large contingent of Wolof captives on the island in 1520 and 1521 further heightened the tension, thereby creating the effective conditions for an insurrection.

On Christmas Day 1521 a group of twenty Wolofs – their names have not survived in the records – rebelled on the plantation of Governor Diego Colón, the son of Christopher Columbus. As they moved across the territory the insurgent numbers grew to over a hundred. They killed a dozen settlers and devastated their plantations, and advanced towards the capital Santo Domingo, where they were eventually confronted by Spanish colonial forces. Although unable to take the capital, the rebels regrouped and escaped to the nearby Baoruco Mountains. Here they joined forces with Amerindian fugitives, who had themselves risen against the Spanish in 1519 under a leader named Enriquillo. For the next fifteen years this alliance of African Muslims and Taino Native Americans formed a powerful maroon community in the mountains. Its numbers grew from a few hundred to over 4,000, and within a few years they dominated most of the territory, confining the settlers and colonial authorities to the capital and its immediate surroundings, and launching raids against plantations.[68] The Spaniards only defeated this coalition by signing a separate peace treaty with Enriquillo. The Africans remained irreducible, and by the 1540s the Wolof maroons had developed their own cavalry with horses stolen from settler ranches. The 1521 Wolof rebellion led the Spanish Crown to impose a ban on migration to the New World of 'slaves suspected of Islamic leanings'. One of its edicts described Wolof Muslims as 'proud and disobedient, agitators and incorrigible'.[69]

This rebellious spirit was subsequently confirmed in several ways – starting from the moment African Muslims boarded the vessels that took them to the New World. They were among the groups who sought most actively to escape from servitude during the Middle Passage. Captives from Sierra Leone and Senegambia – territories with significant concentrations of Islamic 'Mandingo' populations – were three to five times more likely to carry out a shipboard insurrection than captives from other west and central African regions. These revolts experienced higher than average casualty rates, suggesting a greater willingness among the resisters to die rather than be enslaved.[70] Muslim Africans continued to spearhead resistance to Spanish rule in the Americas. In Panama from the late 1570s, an African known as Anton Mandinga became the leader of a group of runaways who challenged the Spanish authorities in the locality of Bayano for at least four years, until they surrendered in 1581.[71]

Runaway notices show similar patterns. In eighteenth-century French Saint-Domingue there were regular advertisements in the colonial press detailing the names and characteristics of maroons; many Muslim names appeared here, sometimes with specific evidence of their rebellious disposition. One such figure was a man recaptured in the town of Saint-Marc in 1766. He could only be described by his ethnicity as a 'nègre Madingue', as he refused to identify himself or to give the name of his enslaver, and seemed to have erased the branding marks on his skin.[72] Federal and state court records from the United States reveal the names of many Muslim defendants.[73] In French Louisiana, where a considerable number of captives (up to two-thirds, according to some estimates) were brought from Senegambia, legal records and runaway notices likewise list several Muslim names of Arabic origin, including Mohammad, Fatima, Yacine, Moussa, Baraca, and Bakary.[74] In other instances the names mentioned are Christian, but the likely Muslim identity of the maroons can be deduced from their territory of origin, as in the 1802 notice calling for the return of a runaway named 'Pierre-Marc', who was from Senegal. As with many such fugitives he was a man of many talents, for the text mentioned that he spoke Spanish, French, and English.[75]

Along with Louisiana, the states of the American South with high concentrations of Muslim captives were South Carolina and Georgia, and their records provide sustained evidence of dissent. Eighteenth-century advertisements for the capture of runaways list clearly identifiable Muslim names such as 'Mahomet' (Muhammad), 'Bullaly' (Bilali), 'Bocarrey' (Bakary), 'Walley' (Wali), and 'Mamado' (Mamadu).[76] Some runaways in South Carolina who were described as 'Mandingo' were acting as interpreters, suggesting the presence of a sizeable cohort of their fellow countrymen.[77] Notices made specific references to the fierce dispositions of the escapees, like the 1772 description of 'Homady' (Amadi) as 'having a sulky look'. Appearances could be deceptive, though, as the docility of some captives was often a ploy to get their owners to lower their guard.

This tactic was most probably achieved by the runaway named Mustapha, commonly known as 'Muss', who absconded from North Carolina in 1808 while still being described by his unsuspecting owner as 'polite and submissive'.[78] Interestingly, considering the alliances made during and after the Wolof rebellion of 1521, some of these Muslim runaways sought and found refuge among Amerindian communities. One such Georgian fugitive was named Homady (Hamadi), and after an absence of three weeks he was believed to be 'harboured among the Indians'. Another runaway, named Mahomet, managed to escape for three years until he was sighted in 1774 near a Native American reservation. Many of these fugitives aspired to go much further, and travel back to their African homelands. The notice for the runaway Jeffray (whose Muslim name was Ibrahim) specifically mentioned that he had pledged to take flight at the first opportunity in order to 'get on board some vessel'.[79]

Amulets were regularly used as an expression of Islamic belief as well as social and cultural influence in the New World. Originally associated with the Mandinka peoples around the Niger and Senegal rivers, who formed a large percentage of the Africans enslaved in the early years of the slave trade, these objects, their creators, and their effects were often generically referred to as 'Mandingo'. They were a key feature of popular culture in west Africa, as we found in chapter 1. Among its most widespread talismans were the *gris-gris* amulets that drew from Islam's occult dimensions through the practices of astrology, astronomy, and divination. There were believed to be connections between Islamic texts and letters, stars, and numbers, and this specialized knowledge was held and disseminated by clerics and *marabouts*, who were said to be able to interpret the skies. Islamic amulets were noticed by early European travellers in west Africa: in 1625 the trader André Donelha observed that one of his Senegambian acquaintances wore 'amulets of his charms'.[80]

These objects were used for a variety of healing and protective purposes, and typically consisted of a folded, written piece of paper sewn in leather. The parchment bore kabbalistic signs, numbers arranged in a grid, or excerpts from holy texts; the pouch could contain other material. Amulets were worn on various parts of the body (around the neck, arm, waist, ankle, or knee), or placed in specific spots (above doors or under beds). Pieces of paper with Qur'anic text could be dropped in water and after the ink was dissolved the liquid could be drunk as a potion or used on the body to protect against evil spells.[81] These talismans and charms were widely used in west Africa, and not only by Muslim populations. They were eagerly sought by non-Muslims, and in many African monarchies Islamic amulets and fetishes were associated with the symbols of power. This cultural syncretism was in evidence in the religious realm as well. In Muslim societies Islam was frequently combined with traditional African forms of spirituality. Among Muslim Yorubas, for example, religious authorities tolerated membership of secret societies such as the Gelede, who worshipped female ancestors, and the Egungun, who practised a cult of the dead.[82]

As we saw earlier, African enslaved populations were so attached to these amulets that they frequently managed to retain them during their enslavement and captivity, and carried them on the journey across the Atlantic. In the New World the link between the objects and their place of origin was preserved, although (as in Africa) the practice of amulet-wearing was widespread across slave societies more generally. In Brazil the amulets were called *bolsas de mandinga* (Mandingo bags), and the *marabouts* who made and sold them were reputed for their ability to harness supernatural powers.[83] 'Mandinga' was one of the many terms associated with occultism and rebellion in the Americas; there were numerous instances of captives deploying these objects for self-protection, and against slavers, drivers, and overseers.[84] Indeed, this very association of amulets with rebelliousness was brought across from Africa, where the subversive connections between fetishes and Islamic holy men were widely known and feared by European slavers. As an employee of the French slave-trading Compagnie du Sénégal wrote in the eighteenth century: '*marabouts* who give and bless *gris-gris* are very dangerous for the slave traders, and if some are among the slaves, it is almost certain there will be some seditions or revolts. They always promise them that they will overcome the Whites.'[85]

The revolts of enslaved people in the Americas were driven by local and regional factors, and as we shall see in the following chapter the Haitian revolution would prove to be one of the major drivers of insurrection in the nineteenth century. But these rebellions could be spurred by political and religious upheavals in west Africa. One of the most significant of these was the Islamic *jihad* (holy war) launched in 1804 by Usman dan Fodio against the oppressive rule of the Sultan of Gobir over the Fulani people. This Islamic reform movement soon swept across the entire Sahel region and led to the creation of the Sokoto Caliphate in 1809. This Islamic expansion then continued southwards in the ensuing decade. It led to further conflicts across a large swathe of west African territory from the Sahara to the Gold Coast, and the capture and enslavement of thousands of men and women, many of whom were Muslim – especially Fulani, Yoruba (Nagô), Bornu, and Hausa. These captives had often fought in these local wars, and in some cases had substantial combat experience and military skills. They ended up being sent in droves across the Atlantic to Cuba and Brazil (mainly to Bahia), where they became enmeshed in a series of insurgent movements during the first half of the nineteenth century. This African-Islamic nexus therefore shaped both the form and the substance of these rebellions in the New World. Indeed, they were acts of war that followed in direct continuity with the captives' battles in west Africa.[86]

More transatlantic captives were sent to Cuba during the first half of the nineteenth century than to any other territory in the Americas,[87] joining the west African Muslims who had come to the Spanish colony in successive waves from the sixteenth century onwards. Because of the ways in which records were kept in Cuba, and the long tradition of denying any legitimacy to Islam, gauging the depth of their involvement in rebellious activity is not easy. But some of the rebels identified by the Spanish authorities were clearly Muslim: for example, a mid-eighteenth-century report on a runaway settlement included Mandinga names.[88] The captives who arrived in Cuba in the wake of the nineteenth-century west African conflicts were Islamicized, in the sense that they both came from regions with large Muslim populations and were in many instances directly involved as combatants in religious wars. It is therefore highly likely that many participated in the series of African-led Cuban revolts and uprisings against Spanish slavers. These began in the mid-1820s and continued until the mid-1840s, during which there were more than forty such insurgencies.[89] After the 1833 rebellion in Banes, west of Havana, which involved over three hundred captives, many of whom had just landed from Africa, the identities of the rebels were recorded and they included common Muslim names.[90]

These west African influences were further apparent in the types of weapons used by rebels in Cuba, which included shields, knives, sickles, machetes, spears, and bows and arrows.[91] The paraphernalia of war deployed by the insurgents was inspired by west African war rituals, with a profusion of drums, parasols, flags, and crowns, generally prepared by Hausa, Fulani, or Mandingo holy men.[92] Islamic amulets were conspicuous as well, and were carried by the insurgents to protect themselves from harm. Material found on insurgents throughout the first half of the nineteenth century included pieces of paper with passages of the Qu'ran in Arabic, as well as pouches containing an assortment of material such as earth, bones, pieces of glass, birds' feathers, animal remains, and shells. Many participants in the Cuban conspiracy of La Escalera, which unfolded in 1843–4, carried such amulets with them. One of them declared that 'with those charms they could go to war with the whites, and that the whites would not be able to defeat them, as the charms would protect them from bullets and machetes'. Among the leading figures in this conspiracy was a west African *marabout* named Campuzano Mandinga, widely known as the 'Great Sorcerer of Matanzas'; he was one of the main suppliers of amulets to the rebels.[93]

After Cuba, the major New World destination for Muslim captives in the first half of the nineteenth century was Brazil, especially the northeastern region of Bahia. Islam was not the dominant religion among Africans in the territory, but the Muslim community there was sizeable and highly literate.[94] The first attempted anti-slavery rebellion occurred there in 1807, just three years after the launching of the Fulani *jihad* in west Africa. In that year alone 8,000 mostly Muslim Hausa, Nagô, and Ewe captives were brought to Bahia. Brazilian authorities received advance warning of the 1807 rebellion and were able to arrest the organizers before it began. The material found by the police suggested that in this instance, as in all subsequent cases, the revolts were carefully planned and were driven by the quest for emancipation and a return to Africa. There was an elaborate clandestine organization, and the plan was to capture the ships in the harbour and orchestrate a massive flight back to their homelands. In this sense, it was an insurrection combined with a collective act of maritime marronage. The searches of suspects' houses led to the discovery of bows, arrows, knives, pistols, rifles, and talismans written in Arabic. Among the material the Muslim rebels had prepared for combat were Mandingo bags that they believed would protect them from injury.[95]

This pattern of Islamic-led insurgency in Bahia continued for the next three decades. A few of the rebellions took place in urban settings, as in 1814 in the fishing town of Itapoã. Here six hundred African captives, freedmen, and maroons led by a Hausa commander staged a revolt that left fourteen whites dead. In 1830 a group of Nagô Africans attacked three hardware stores in the principal town of San Salvador de Bahia, seizing swords and knives. The group – now numbering over a hundred – moved to the slave market, where they freed several captives and attacked the police station; the rebels were eventually defeated but some managed to escape.[96] Most of the uprisings, however, took place in sugar plantations around San Salvador de Bahia, starting in 1808 when a group of Nagô and Hausa captives escaped from their plantation. After being joined by another party of runaways, they proceeded to attack the town of Nazaré das Farinhas, and for months afterwards the rebels controlled the surrounding areas, launching raids on local plantations. Between 1816 and 1830 there were another sixteen such uprisings in Bahia: Muslim captives participated in all of them, and were identified as leaders in at least five.[97] The most elaborate involved the Urubu maroon settlement on the outskirts of San Salvador de Bahia. It was a well-organized community whose members carried out religious rituals. As noted previously, they were led by a Nagô woman named Zeferina, an African warrior who used her expertise in archery to rally her comrades. Their objective was to provoke an uprising among the enslaved in Salvador, kill the white slavers, and gain their freedom.[98]

In the early hours of the morning of 25 January 1835 several hundred Muslim conspirators launched an insurrection in San Salvador, which has been described as 'the best-planned and most daring slave uprising in American history after the Haitian revolution'.[99] The rebels were dressed in traditional white Islamic garments, the symbols of purity, and wore rings of silver and iron; they took to the streets armed with lances, knives, swords, and some firearms. To the sound of beating drums they attacked the National Guard and police buildings, and attempted to storm the jail where Pacífico Licutan, one of the respected Muslim elders, had been held since November 1834. Their plan, which had been prepared for several months, was to set fire to as many buildings as possible, then attack the forces that would come to extinguish the flames. The city insurgents co-ordinated their plans with rebels from the plantations, who were expected to join them later in the day, so that they could take control of the surrounding areas after seizing the city. The police got wind of the plot, so forcing the rebels to launch the movement prematurely, which led to its military defeat at the hands of the colonial infantry and cavalry.[100]

There is still much debate about the 1835 Bahia uprising, and whether it was an extension of west African *jihad*, an ethnically based revolt led by the Nagôs, or a New World conspiracy uniting different groups of captives and free people. There were elements of all three, but in a more basic sense it was about waging war against slavery. Most of the leaders of the insurrection were captives,[101] and there were many references among the insurgents to 'making war to [*sic*] the whites'.[102] There was little doubt that Islam was a unifying force. A majority of the insurgents were Nagô Muslims, and the rebellion was planned towards the end of the month of Ramadan. As with so many other rebellions by the enslaved, religious gatherings provided an ideal cover for the conspiracy. Some of the rebels taught in Qur'anic schools operating in Bahia at the time.[103] Prayer books were found on the insurgents, such as a 102-page booklet bound in leather that included verses from the Qu'ran. The text included a call to be rescued from 'this town, whose people are oppressors', and an illustration in the form of a ship with people on board, beneath which was the inscription 'Muhammad messenger of Allah, may Allah bless him and give him salvation'. Another document found among the conspirators invoked the name of the Prophet, noting that blood had to be shed and that 'we must all have a hand in it' (see Plate 2).[104]

It later emerged that the organizers included several imams, whose chief Abubakar managed to keep his identity concealed from the police even after the insurrection had occurred. These religious men had produced amulets that they supplied to the fighters. One of them had been written more than a year and a half earlier and was thought to 'protect the body from all weapons'. This charm's operation was to be reinforced by writing the prayer on a slate, washing it away with water and drinking the liquid.[105] The maps and messages found on the fighters contained occult Islamic annotations, including circles, signs, and numbers. At the same time, this was not a *jihad* in the strict sense, as its primary goal was not religious but political: the rebellion was directed against the enslavers. To this end, the Islamic conspirators of Bahia created a revolutionary network that was able to build bridges among different sections of the black population, while creating links with plantation captives and maroons.[106]

Obeah and Islam both challenged Atlantic slavery in ways that went to the heart of the power it sought to exercise. They confronted its material force, rejecting the cultural and racial superiority on which it claimed to rule the lives of the enslaved, and disrupting the relationships that white settlers thought they had securely built with their most trusted captives. Obeah and Islam elicited very similar responses from the slavers, a downward spiral that began with indifference, then turned to contempt, soon followed by fear which could at times border on panic.

The poison scares associated with Obeah became an obsession in many parts of the Caribbean, and the Brazilian authorities were so shaken by the 1835 revolt that they sought to expunge all forms of Islamic activity from their territories. They confiscated documents written in Arabic from various provinces and sent them to Rio de Janeiro for translation; one suspicious letter from Recife turned out to contain marriage vows.[107] In 1853 the Brazilian police arrested an African-born Yoruba former captive named Rufino in Recife on suspicion of conspiracy, and they found a collection of Arabic manuscripts at his home. He was a religiously educated diviner and an *alufa* (spiritual leader), providing services to a wide cross section of locals, including whites. His portfolio included casting spells to make people fall in love, and he told his interrogators that he refused to abjure his religion, even if he were to be 'sent to the gallows'. Rufino was almost certainly not a revolutionary, but his pride in his African origins and the steadfastness of his Islamic faith were in themselves challenges to the established order in mid-nineteenth-century Brazil.[108]

Obeah and Islam both provided a refuge for the enslaved, as well as direct inspirations for their conspiracies and rebellions. Even though a collective uprising amounted to more of a challenge to the slavers than supernatural rituals, we should not under-estimate the significance of these acts of spiritual devotion. Slavery was as much about crushing the minds of the enslaved as dominating their bodies, and the fact that so many men and women were able to retain their own spiritual moorings is significant. All the more so because Obeah and Islam highlight one of the consistent themes in the early part of this book: the African character of resistance in the New World. This was evident in the presence of predominantly African-born groups among the rebels, such as the Akan and Yoruba peoples; the emphasis they gave to African rituals and forms of spirituality (solemn oaths were a traditional form of homage to ancestors in many African societies); their use of west African techniques of war; and the revolutionary impacts of specific cohorts of combat-hardened Muslim captives in the wake of the Fulani *jihad* in the early nineteenth century, especially in Cuba and Brazil. Newly arrived Igbos were thought to be behind the wave of poisonings in Martinique in the 1820s. All of these influences contributed to give insurgents the strength to face up to their enemies with composure and defiance, and even a sense of physical invulnerability.

Moreover, the separation between mind and body was not greatly relevant in the world view of the enslaved. As we have seen, spiritual beliefs were integral to their revolutionary activities, both through their capacity to provide the rebellions with important leadership figures, and because Obeah and Islam were already in a significant sense operating underground in the New World. The concealed and secretive qualities of these spiritual systems, necessary to keep themselves insulated from the slavers' gaze, were invaluable assets for the organization of the conspiracies. We might say they facilitated their art of subterfuge, even though of course not all practitioners of Obeah and Islam became active dissidents. The appeal to religious and spiritual forces was an essential part of the conspiracies, shaping the imperative of resistance as well as their most practical aspects, right down to the precise timing of an insurgency, the buildings and people targeted, the specific route to be taken by rebels, and of course the protective amulets they wore. To make the same point differently, spirituality was at the very heart of the resistance of the enslaved, and intimately connected to the organization of rebellions, a theme that will re-emerge throughout the rest of the book.

Of the two sets of beliefs, it might be tempting to view Islam as a superior source of resistance to the extent that it was more organized, rested on a more coherent doctrine, and relied on a clearly identifiable group of devoted missionaries, the *marabouts*. Obeah, in contrast, was hazier, and its supernaturalism seems quaint to our modern sensibility. If evaluated in terms of its revolutionary outcomes, it appears to fall equally short: its twigs, feathers, and bones appear flimsy when set against the slavers' brute material power, and with the possible exception of Tacky's Revolt none of the rebellions with significant Obeah involvement seem to have made much headway, and the Jamaican Boxing Day conspiracy ended before it even began. Indeed, there is a tendency to dismiss the conspiracies of the early to mid-eighteenth century as principally the product of settler fantasy rather than real revolutionary ambition. But this misses the point that these fantasies were themselves the results of Obeah's remarkable power to take hold of minds and imaginations not only of captives but also of their oppressors. The healing and even the supernatural powers of Obeah-men and Obeah-women were widely believed, including among Caribbean whites. The records of the ruling Council of Martinique affirmed in the 1820s that African sorcerers could kill by touching something with their hands, or by getting people or animals to walk over a poisonous package buried deep in the ground. These claims were couched not as conjectures but as statements of fact.[109]

Obeah was a significant force in the struggle against Atlantic slavery. It helped maintain the captives' material and spiritual connections to their African homeland, and offered them a space in which they could at least shield themselves from the oppression they faced, and seek remedies for their illnesses, injuries, and losses. As a specialist of the Jamaican enslaved religious experience put it, Obeah 'inspired Africans to refuse dehumanization and oppression and to pursue freedom, control of destiny, and well-being as signs of the life to be experienced on earth'.[110] In fact, its lighter footprint and lack of a unified doctrine effectively gave Obeah an advantage. It enabled Obeah to adapt to different local environments, arguably with greater ease than Islam, and to operate comfortably across enslaved communities. Indeed, it was able to do so not just in large urban settings, of the kind that made possible the Bahia uprising of 1835, but in small towns as well as in plantations and maroon settlements. Despite its criminalization from the 1760s onwards, Obeah proved remarkably resilient over time, reproducing itself in Caribbean and American societies; it gained strength and power even as the number of African-born people declined in many slave societies.[111]

The ways in which this transmission and reproduction took place have not been studied in depth, owing to the lack of sources. But there is little reason to doubt that processes of apprenticeship similar to those that enabled the training of healers and diviners in Africa were reconstructed in New World enslaved communities. This raises fascinating questions about the mobility of Obeah-men and Obeah-women, as well as Obeah's capacity to exist alongside Christianity, to feed off it, and to appeal to 'creole' captives, who had no direct experience of Africa. Obeah had this staying power because it gave the enslaved a sense, if not of agency, then at least of possibility: that they could find a way of reclaiming some control over their destiny. Obeah was, moreover, as we have seen, one of the rare spaces in which women could exercise considerable material and spiritual power. Obeah-men and Obeah-women helped raise the political consciousness of the enslaved, giving them a sense (however fleeting) of what it might mean to recover their liberty and live a life free from servitude.

Many of these qualities shine through in *Hamel, the Obeah Man*, a fictional work published in 1827 by an English writer who had travelled to the Caribbean a few years earlier. The novel is set in Jamaica in the early 1820s, at a time of rising enslaved rebelliousness locally and abolitionist advances in London. Although it is written from a white anti-abolitionist perspective, there is a looming sense that the slavers' days are numbered. One of the main characters is Roland, a Christian missionary who becomes entangled in a captive conspiracy and is eventually killed.

The main protagonist is the eponymous Hamel, the Obeah-man, a mercurial black captive who spends part of his time in a cave, from where he dispenses his charms, and holds sway over his brethren thanks to his 'magic talents'. He displays 'perfect confidence'[112] and controls other figures and events, largely manipulating them to his own ends, even though these are somewhat mysterious.

But this opaqueness is presented as integral to Hamel's personality and his spiritual craft, which remain completely outside the realm of colonial power, and beyond its reach. In all these respects the novel offers a favourable portrayal of Obeah, particularly in its capacity to shape individual and collective destinies, for both good and ill. Moreover, there are passages – spoken by Hamel himself – that criticize colonial slavery and Christianity, as when he ironically asks the missionary whether 'fasting or reading prayers will compensate for injuries done to man'.[113] Haiti is hailed as 'the land of freedom'.[114] Hamel supports and then betrays the enslaved rebellion in Jamaica, but his autonomy and sense of pride survive intact, and the novel ends with him leaving Jamaica to return to his African homeland.

4

Full of Resolve and Determination

The greatest Atlantic anti-slavery insurrection was launched in 1791 in the French colony of Saint-Domingue. The revolt led to abolition of human bondage there two years later and the founding of Haiti in 1804 – the world's first independent black postcolonial state. This mass uprising was a culmination in three overlapping senses. It was the most radical manifestation of the Age of Revolutions in the Atlantic world, which saw democratic mobilizations against tyranny and the creation of new political institutions based on the principles of popular sovereignty and collective self-determination. Furthermore, the events in Saint-Domingue expressed, with exceptional force, all the main anti-slavery currents (African, maroon, and spiritual) identified in the preceding chapters. Finally, the uprising came at the end of a series of sustained challenges directed at Spanish and then French colonial slavery on the island of Hispaniola, which had lasted for over three centuries.

The symbol of these rebellious traditions, and in many ways the principal architect of Haitian self-determination, was the mid-eighteenth-century maroon leader François Makandal. Like so many of the men and women we have already encountered, Makandal was a fugitive. He left no direct written records, and everything we know about him comes from the material gathered during his trial in the late 1750s, from oral traditions in Saint-Domingue, and from eighteenth- and nineteenth-century French and Haitian accounts. It is thought that he was born into a ruling family from the Upper Guinea region (he was likely from Senegambia or Sierra Leone), and that he was an Arabic and Mende speaker brought up in the Islamic faith.[1] He was probably a *marabout*, and highly cultured, with skills in music, painting, sculpting, and medicine. Enslaved while fighting in a regional war in west Africa, Makandal was brought as a captive to Saint-Domingue, where he acquired an island-wide reputation as a botanist and healer. After losing an arm in a sugar-mill accident he escaped into the Limbé highlands in the northern province sometime around 1740.[2]

Here the 'old man of the mountains', as Makandal became known, emerged as a charismatic maroon leader. He remained at large for well over a decade (eighteen years, according to some accounts), developing an immense following across the colony's northern plantations. Makandal cultivated this support by addressing secret nocturnal gatherings, where those in attendance danced the *kalinda* and listened to his blistering speeches. These mystical orations lamented the massacre of native Taino Amerindians in Hispaniola, and predicted the overthrow of slavery and white rule and the empowerment of the black population in the colony.[3] Makandal relied on coloured scarves to convey these thoughts: thus he used olive or yellow to evoke the experiences of the Taino people. He was a mesmerizing figure for his supporters and adversaries alike. His close followers called him 'the Prophet', and they went through an initiation rite in which they were struck with a machete to test their capacity to withstand pain. A report compiled by the French judge who prosecuted Makandal described him as a 'captain of his country, a confident man, with a lively gaze and firm gestures, full of resolve and determination, agile and with an uncommon force of body'.[4]

Makandal professed to be mandated by God, and his supporters often repeated that he was second only to the Almighty. Amulets or fetishes were an essential ingredient in his revolutionary repertoire, so much so that he was seen as a 'sorcerer of the first order'. He assembled talismans in pouches that included Qur'anic texts, and human bones, nails, and roots. His rituals included Catholic features such as holy water, communion bread, and small crucifixes, over which Makandal prayed with the incantation 'Alla Alla', repeated several times. He wore his own *gris-gris* under his hat, and many claimed to have witnessed the elements it contained being summoned to life: 'All agree that the fetishes of François Makandal wriggled on their heads when they speak to them; some even said that the fetishes cried like chicks.'[5] Makandal's name was associated with Islam, but the prayers of this Prophet's disciple included references to Jesus Christ and Bondyé, the supreme Lord of the Vodou religion. Indeed, a key part of his appeal to the enslaved was the unifying quality of his spiritual system. It sought to draw in as many captives as possible, irrespective of their ethnic, geographical, and religious affinities, or whether they were colonial-native creoles or African-born. Two of Makandal's closest associates, Teyselo and Mayombé, were Kongos, a community that was predominantly Christian.

Makandal's challenge to colonial enslavement culminated in a conspiracy to poison Saint-Domingue's white settlers as well as the black captives who were loyal to them. When he was arrested in December

1757 at the Dufresne estate, where he had come to attend a celebration organized by its enslaved workforce, Makandal was accused of using his botanical knowledge to create lethal poisons, and of relying on a network of agents recruited from among hawkers and house domestics to introduce these toxic substances in their masters' food, preferably when they hosted large dinners. According to a contemporary source, Makandal used three different types of poison. One of these was a plant-based powder so violent that its victim was instantly killed, while another provoked a debilitating illness that could last up to a year, followed by death.[6] His network was believed to have operated extensively in the districts of Limbé, Port-Margot, Souffrière, and Borgne over a three-year period. Makandal planned to eliminate the population of Cap-Français by poisoning its water wells, and then attacking the city with his lieutenants. His chief Cap agent was a woman named Marianne, who was in contact with Makandal's wife Brigitte. Well versed in the manufacture of amulets, Brigitte too was believed to possess supernatural powers, including the ability to make fetishes move on the head; she was one of her husband's main couriers. Female house captives were notable among the group of 140 people who were arrested and tried as Makandal's accomplices. Strategically positioned as domestics, they played a critical role by receiving the poisonous material from Makandal, Brigitte, or one of their associates, transporting it to different areas, and introducing it into the slavers' households.

The full contours of Makandal's conspiracy remain hazy, and continue to be debated to this day, with some historians disputing whether he was a revolutionary leader.[7] But there were strong echoes of the Atlantic maroon resistance tradition in his approach. He understood that political and ideological unity among the enslaved was indispensable to challenge French settler rule in Saint-Domingue. He developed methods for operating underground, for identifying the most vulnerable aspects of the settler order, and for finding ways of turning his material power deficit to his advantage – especially by stoking the slavers' fears and insecurities. In keeping with the dominant strand among Atlantic maroons, he was completely opposed to slavery, and he believed that only the physical elimination of white settlers could ultimately safeguard the rights of his black brothers and sisters. Like the Obeah priests elsewhere in the Atlantic, Makandal's conception of life and death was grounded in his animist beliefs, his African expertise as a healer, and his moral understanding of the universe.

Moreover, the collective psychosis that Makandal and his followers produced in Saint-Domingue (and beyond) was real. White settlers wondered whether the captives in whom they had placed the greatest faith – their slave drivers, coachmen, cooks, nursemaids, and other house captives – could be secretly planning their demise; future events would show that they were right to be apprehensive. Frantic accounts of the plot circulated in the colony, systematically inflating the number of victims, until the figure reached 6,000. This was an exaggeration, no doubt, but it confirmed the apocalyptic power that the rebellious prophet had come to exercise over the settlers' imagination. His fetishes would be dancing on the French slavers' heads for some time to come. At five in the afternoon on 20 January 1758 he was burnt at the stake. By this time Makandal had already become a legend, his name synonymous with maroon, healer, priest, poisoner, and agent of mass disorder. Even before his death, fetishes in Saint-Domingue were being called 'macandals'.[8] He proclaimed that if the French tried to kill him, he would turn himself into a bird or insect and fly away, in an ultimate act of *marronnage*.

And indeed, after the executioner lit the pyre, Makandal somehow managed to break free from the pole to which he was tied, and walked several yards until he was recaptured and thrown back into the flames. The incident – unprecedented in the annals of public executions in the colony – only lent further credence to his prophecy. His Islamic culture remained integral to his myth: a memoir published in 1779 described him as 'a Mohammed at the head of a hundred outlaws taking refuge in the deserts of Arabia, and preparing the conquest of the Universe'.[9]

Makandal's resistance movement captured the particular combination of popular forces that came together in the late eighteenth century to make the Haitian revolution possible. He operated in Saint-Domingue's northern plain, the colony's most populated region that later became the epicentre of the enslaved insurrection. The captive elite he appealed to and among whom he recruited his followers played a critical role in the 1791 uprising. He was, like so many Atlantic enslaved revolutionaries, a leader who emerged from the realm of healing and divination – a crucial underpinning of these types of revolts, as we saw in the previous chapter. Makandal combined *vodun* religious practices from different west and central African regions in a synthesis that was one of the distinctive characteristics of Saint-Domingue's emerging *vodou* tradition. This inclusiveness was essential to Makandal's revolutionary success, as it encouraged secret meetings, broke down barriers among different ethnic groups, and created powerful bonds among those who were initiated into his movement.[10]

Makandal served as the link between the Haitian revolution and the historical antecedents of resistance in Hispaniola itself, from the very onset of Spanish colonization. As we saw in chapter 2, the efforts by Spanish authorities to control the territory faced fierce opposition, particularly from the Wolofs, whose 1521 uprising was one of the first major African insurrections in the New World. But it was not only African-born captives who rebelled against the Spaniards. Archaeological evidence from cave systems suggests that there was a strong alliance between African and Taino Amerindian insurgents in Hispaniola during the first half of the sixteenth century. Both groups shared knowledge about the island's topography and their respective beliefs, developing joint tactics to resist Spanish slavers.[11] Caves were still being used as hideouts by African and Taino runaways in the early seventeenth century, and maroon resistance drew on these African and Amerindian traditions of opposition thereafter.[12] And so when Makandal was waving his collection of coloured scarves to his audiences in the northern plain in the mid-eighteenth century, he was directly appealing to this tradition of solidarity among captive communities in Hispaniola, first under Spanish rule and then later in French Saint-Domingue.

Makandal's maroon heritage too was part of a much longer local tradition; indeed, one Haitian scholar has argued that 'marooning is the dominant feature of all Haitian history'.[13] We saw that the term 'maroon' had its origins in Hispaniola, and it has been suggested that the Spanish word *cimarrón* was perhaps inspired by the Taino term *simaran*. In the Arawak language this refers to the ongoing action of an arrow in flight – an image suggesting both escape and combativeness.[14] One of the earliest recorded mentions of maroon activity in Hispaniola dates to 1503, when the governor, Nicolás de Ovando, complained that runaways had found refuge in the mountains and that troops sent in their pursuit could not find them. Although the Spaniards had some successes – a fugitive settlement was razed in 1522 – African maroons posed such a challenge that by the 1540s the authorities referred to their military expeditions against them as a 'war'. These escaped captives operated in the northern plain (already a hotbed of revolutionary activity), and in Môle Saint-Nicolas, Tortuga, the Artibonite valley, and the Baoruco Mountains. They organized militias that regularly raided Spanish plantations, raised livestock, and grew crops. The maroons established trading connections with each other and with other free and enslaved Africans still living in Spanish communities, who helped recycle the goods seized from the settlers.

Makandal had a string of sixteenth-century maroon predecessors. They included leaders such as Sebastian Lemba, Diego Guzman, Diego Ocampo, Miguel Biafra, and Juan Criollo, who established effective control over significant parts of Hispaniola, and forced Spanish settlers to travel only in large groups. Lemba was in many respects the most flamboyant of these rebels. He was a Kongolese blacksmith with extensive military skills, who set up his camp in the Baoruco Mountains. He organized his bands of African and Taino fighters to attack Spanish settlements, holding out for fifteen years. When the Spaniards eventually captured and killed him in 1547, they cut off his head and placed it outside Santo Domingo as a warning to potential rebels. However, the legend of 'Captain Lemba' remained powerful among local enslaved communities, and it is likely that Makandal would have spoken about him in his speeches.[15] Around the mid-1500s nearly two-thirds of Hispaniola's sugar plantations had been destroyed by the maroons, and there were an estimated 7,000 fugitives in different settlements across the island.[16] The northern territories – where Makandal would later operate – remained constantly beyond Spanish control, despite repeated and costly efforts to subdue the maroons militarily. Throughout the initial period of the Spanish presence on the island, the African population – amounting at its peak to around 20,000 to 30,000 – thus included a significant community of self-liberated men and women.[17]

Indeed, these fugitives posed such an enduring threat to the colonists that in the early seventeenth century the Spaniards decided to abandon their settlements in the northern and western parts of Hispaniola. This maroon victory set the stage for Makandal's subsequent call to expel the whites, itself later enacted by the Haitian revolutionaries after 1804. At the same time – and this is what made him such a potent figure – Makandal epitomized the African inspirations of resistance we have mapped out in previous chapters. A large number of the captives forcibly brought to Saint-Domingue in the eighteenth century were combatants caught up in the regional wars between rival African states. From the 1750s onwards, as the French increased their imports of bonded labour into the colony, West Central 'Kongo' Africans became the largest group. Captives from this region were traded as a result of the political conflicts in the kingdom of Kongo between the 1760s and 1780s, which led to the overthrow of King Pedro V and his allies. In the same period many captives brought to Saint-Domingue from the Bight of Benin were prisoners from the ongoing wars among African empires in the region, particularly between Dahomey and Oyo.[18] Around a third of these were Nagôs/Yorubas, whose military skills were extensive. Likewise, among the Senegambians who were forcibly transported to Saint-Domingue were Minas, who were reputed for their excellence in handling firearms.[19]

Makandal's rebellious activities were thus steeped in his African political and religious heritages. He was brought to the French colony during the first half of the eighteenth century, when the Upper Guinea region, from where he most likely originated, supplied one of the largest groups of captives brought to Saint-Domingue. As we saw in chapter 3, there was a long tradition of popular opposition to slavery in this African region, often inspired by Islamic rebels, and in the 1720s and again between the 1760s and the 1780s there were *jihads* seeking to end the slave trade in Senegambia. Makandal's invocation of Islam as part of his emancipatory message thus had deep roots in his native African soil.[20]

Makandal's conspiracy unsettled Saint-Domingue's European slavers, and in its wake the authorities issued a series of restrictions in an effort to suppress any further agitation. In 1758 the making, selling, and distributing of *macandal* fetishes were banned, and any planter who allowed nocturnal *kalinda* dances on his property was liable to a fine of 300 *livres*. In 1764 free and enslaved black people were prohibited from practising medicine, and in 1777 the police forbade captives from congregating during the day or night for the purposes of weddings and funerals. Drumming and singing were expressly banned (these provisions already existed in the 1685 *Code Noir*, the royal decree that regulated slavery in the French empire). None of these measures proved effective, and enslaved gatherings of various kinds continued between the 1760s and the 1780s, as did rumours of poisoning conspiracies fomented by Makandal's surviving agents and sympathizers. The revolutionary leader's spirit continued to inspire rebels. A Kongolese runaway named Eustache was reported missing in 1766 from the plantation where he was held in bondage in Dondon. It transpired that he had been calling himself 'Makandal' in previous years.[21] In 1781 a captive named Jean-Baptiste escaped from a plantation in Plaisance. The report described him as a 'thief and *macandal*', *macandal* being here synonymous with 'poisoner'.[22]

In the run-up to the revolution, Makandal's fugitive aura continued to inspire runaway activity across the colony. There were just under 13,000 advertisements for the capture of maroons published in Cap-Français and Port-au-Prince between 1766 and 1791. The length of the reported absences ran the full spectrum of *marronnage*, from three days to over ten years. A significant majority of the runaways were men aged over sixteen (80 per cent), and mostly African-born (62 per cent). Well over half were west-central African 'Kongos', the dominant ethnic group in late colonial Saint-Domingue. A majority (60 per cent) escaped alone, while 40 per cent fled with two or more companions. The single escapes were typically by Saint-Domingue native 'creole' captives, whereas most of the group flights were undertaken by Africans. There was a greater likelihood of people taking flight with members of their own community (25 per cent of the total), but 15 per cent of the groups were ethnically mixed. These composite cohorts were on the rise in the decade before the Haitian revolution, suggesting both an increase in collective anti-slavery consciousness and an enhanced belief that escape could be successful.[23] One of the largest breakaways took place in October 1789, on a plantation in Borgne, when twenty-two Africans from six different ethnic groups escaped: Kongos (the relative majority, again), Mandingos, Minas, Igbos, a Senegambian woman and a Bambara man, along with one creole woman.

The French colony did not, however, generate the type of fortified runaway communities seen elsewhere in the Atlantic world. Indeed Maniel – the one large-scale fugitive settlement located on the border between French Saint-Domingue and Spanish Santo Domingo – had a fixed population of only a few hundred, and eventually negotiated a peace agreement with the French and Spanish authorities in 1785.[24] One explanation is that the possibility of flight into Spanish territory made such fortifications unnecessary. Moreover, Saint-Domingue provided ideal habitats for external as well as internal escape: over thirty rivers flowed from its mountains to the coastlines, and the colony was made up of over 800 miles of coastline. Because of the ruggedness of the interior, shipping was the primary method of communication between different parts of the territory. Captives with swimming and seafaring skills were able to use these conditions to their advantage, for example by jumping off vessels as they approached their coastal destinations and swimming ashore, before disappearing into wooded areas.

Among the vast contingent of Saint-Domingue maroons were sailors, many of whom took flight after being brought to one of the colony's many ports from other Caribbean islands. Their expertise was highly prized by candidates for maritime escape. Advertisements for the capture of runaways frequently mentioned such attempted aquatic escapes by fugitives: two women thus left Les Cayes in a canoe in 1767, one of them with a two-month-old child. In 1788 a Jamaican captive named Quaco escaped, again from Les Cayes, along with two other fugitives, after having been sold to a French planter.[25] These expeditions were often collective enterprises: in 1791 six captives (four men and two women) of the Nagô and Arada nations made off with a fishing boat belonging to a French settler.[26]

The mobility patterns of Saint-Domingue's maroons corresponded to the general tendencies we described in chapter 2. Some headed to mountains and remote areas, whereas others left rural areas to find refuge in cities such as Cap-Français, where hundreds of runaways were hiding in plain sight by the late 1780s, particularly in the neighbourhood of Petite Guinée, where free people of colour lived. Others still lingered near the places from where they escaped, in order to remain close to family members who were unable to flee with them.[27] Saint-Domingue had its fair share of maroon bands, many of which raided local settler communities from the beginning of the 1700s all the way up to the decades prior to the revolution. Sometimes they went on the offensive: in 1741 the town of Mirebalais was attacked by maroons.[28] In the early 1770s a gang of around three hundred fugitives led by a maroon named Thélémaque Canga operated effectively in the area around Fort-Dauphin; they were only captured in 1777.[29] Mountainous areas in the north with strong runaway presences were given evocative maroon-inspired names, such as Piton des Nègres, Piton des Flambeaux, Piton des Ténèbres, and Tête des Nègres.[30]

Makandal's most flamboyant successor was a Kongolese former captive named Pierre. Calling himself Dom Pedro, he roamed across the southern Petit-Goâve parish with his followers in the late 1760s, raiding plantations, poisoning animals, white settlers, and 'loyal' captives, and punishing all those who stood in his way. He wore tails on his head and had a long lock of hair on each side of his face. Dom Pedro invented a vodou ritual that was named after him (petro), involving a pantheon of 'hot' spirits, a heightened drumbeat, and the addition of crushed gunpowder into rum to generate an intensified sense of exaltation (the potion killed some of those who drank it). The initiation rites for the petro brotherhood were extremely challenging, and they included the infliction of torture – a traditional form of African ritual purification and a way of testing the aptitude of potential sect members not to divulge compromising information. Dom Pedro called on captives to join his fraternity and revolt against the whites, and he carried a large stick or on occasion a whip that he used against plantation slave drivers.[31] Although he was eventually killed by the authorities, the name Dom Pedro became another synonym for resistance and poisoning in late colonial Saint-Domingue.[32]

The year 1791 marked a new phase in Saint-Domingue's enslaved resistance, with the unfolding of a massive insurrection across the northern territories' plantations. Two years earlier, the colony's captives had greeted the French Revolution with cautious enthusiasm, and the expectation that at least some of the civil and political rights granted to the French people would be extended to them. Many even believed rumours that the French king could support reforms to the Code Noir, which would reduce the severity of their punishments and lighten their workload. However, the National Assembly in Paris was dominated by the powerful colonial lobby, which saw the slightest concession to people of colour as a betrayal of their interests. In March 1790 the legislature adopted a decree criminalizing any criticism of human bondage and putting the 'properties' of the colonial settlers (including the people they enslaved) under the protection of the nation. A year later, in May 1791, French parliamentarians recognized the constitutional basis of slavery, and gave white settlers an effective veto over any reforms. Local assemblies in Saint-Domingue vehemently opposed any change to the status quo, and they asserted that the 1789 Declaration of the Rights of Man could not be applied to Saint-Domingue. Those suspected of sympathy for captives were denounced, publicly humiliated, and in some cases murdered. As one of the leading *colons* put it: 'in Saint-Domingue there can only be masters and slaves'.[33]

Faced with this uncompromising hostility from both French revolutionaries and local white settlers, and the equivocation of the colony's mixed-race leaders such as Vincent Ogé, who refused to support immediate emancipation, Saint-Domingue's black captives launched their own anti-slavery insurrection in August 1791. The revolt was initiated in the wake of two meetings. The first, held on 14 August at a plantation in Morne-Rouge, was a gathering of the enslaved elite (drivers, coachmen, house domestics) from around a hundred northern plantations, each represented by two delegates. They were part of a 'vast network' that had been meeting regularly on Sundays in order to plan the uprising.[34] The second, around a week later, was the famous 'Bois-Caïman' ceremony, in which the conspiracy was sealed in a religious ritual.[35] One of the principal insurgent leaders was Dutty 'Zamba' Boukman, a man of enormous physical stature who was a former slave driver and coachman, a fugitive, as well as an African priest. Boukman officiated at Bois-Caïman, along with the priestess Cécile Fatiman, a mixed-race woman with green eyes and wild hair, who was the daughter of a Corsican prince and an African-born woman. Boukman's peroration to the assembled captives contrasted the 'God of the white men', who called upon the *colons* to commit crimes, with the God of the enslaved, who was now demanding 'revenge'. He urged the captives to 'listen to the voice of liberty which speaks in the hearts of all of us'.[36]

The start of the Haitian revolution was the apotheosis of the Makandalist tradition. Although some historians have downplayed the connections between Saint-Domingue's runaway culture and the 1791 uprising,[37] the links are evident enough, politically and spiritually. The movement began in the northern plain, where the 'old man of the mountains' had held sway. It is tempting to see his spirit, from beyond the grave, guiding the delegates to the Morne-Rouge plantation where the insurrection was planned. This property belonged to Lenormand de Mézy, one of the wealthiest *colons* in Saint-Domingue, who also owned the Limbé plantation where Makandal himself had been enslaved. The insurgency was directed squarely at the white settlers, as Makandal had preached, and utterly rejected their beliefs and values, and their very presence on the territories they claimed to rule. In this sense the 1791 uprising returned to earlier patterns of African and Taino resistance against European colonizers in Hispaniola.[38]

There was more: Boukman was both a religious and a political leader, just like Makandal, and like him he went from being a trusted member of the captive elite to a runaway and then a revolutionary. Moreover, Boukman and his comrades followed Makandal's lead in assembling a powerful underground movement that united rebels from maroon camps and plantations in the common pursuit of freedom. The religious rituals of captives in Saint-Domingue during the second half of the eighteenth century were elaborated around African-inspired communal principles forged in maroon camps. Runaways were initiated into fugitive communities through dedicated ceremonies and swore not to betray their brothers; this oath was generally administered by the commander of the settlement, who typically combined the functions of priest and healer, and was involved in the creation of protective amulets. Saint-Domingue's maroon culture thus contributed significantly to the revolution by developing practices of secrecy as well as a common sense of moral identity and political purpose among enslaved people.[39]

This emerging *vodou* tradition, which combined west African, Caribbean, Catholic and Taino spiritual elements, would become a powerful force in the Haitian revolution, performing a subversive role similar to that of Islam and Obeah. Except that Saint-Domingue's spirituality was much more potent, as it was centrally defined around, and in opposition to, slavery, in a way that was true of neither *vodun* traditions in west Africa nor Islam and Obeah in their Atlantic settings.[40] Moreover, this intellectual subversion happened on a much grander scale in Saint-Domingue than in any other rebellion: in terms of the sheer number of enslaved people involved, and the scale of their emancipatory objectives. African practices and beliefs may have been an important element in enabling this collective action, but the ultimate objective here was to liberate the black people of Saint-Domingue by achieving a radical separation of the captive elite from the plantation system. This too was a process that Makandal had envisioned and initiated, and the 1791 revolt was its logical culmination.

The eclectic ritual that Boukman performed in 1791 appealed to the sensibilities of African and creole captives from different backgrounds and traditions, in the same way as Makandal had done earlier. Both men included Islamic elements in their rituals, and it has been claimed that Boukman's name may have been a corruption of 'bookman', a widely established designation for Muslim religious figures in Africa. And just as Makandal brought his African experiences to bear on his revolutionary thinking, Boukman was captured and taken to Saint-Domingue from Africa via Jamaica. It is likely that his belief in the imperative of unity among the enslaved would have been reinforced by the historical divisions between Jamaican maroons and plantation-based insurgents, which as we saw in the previous chapter had weakened anti-slavery opposition among captives and contributed to the defeat of Tacky's Revolt in 1760.[41]

The remarkable scale of the 1791 Saint-Domingue insurrection can be gauged by these simple figures: at its start in mid-August the rebels numbered around 1,500; by 24 August, as they were joined by captives from nearby plantations, they increased to 3,000; three days later they had reached 20,000, divided into three armed groups. By late September, the combatants had grown to 50,000, and by the end of November they were thought to number 80,000. The insurgents formed the largest army of captives in the history of the Atlantic world (the total number of enslaved people in the northern province was roughly 170,000 at the time). This was an unprecedented democratic uprising, expressing the collective will of the captives to be free. And given that almost all these men and women had come from plantations that they had deserted, the revolt had effectively become a mass maroon insurrection. The rebels armed themselves with rifles and ammunition taken from the slavers, as well as anything they could use for offensive purposes – sabres, knives, clubs, poles, farm implements, and even kettles. They set fire to the plantations, destroyed settler homes, factories, irrigation systems, and tools, and killed hundreds of white men, women, and children. These were gruesome massacres, but they often repeated the same forms of violence they had experienced at the hands of the French settlers. The insurrection swept like wildfire and the rebels soon controlled most of the northern province, except for Cap-Français, which they tried to capture three times without success.[42]

The fighters were organized in different bands under local military commanders, based in camps in remote areas. Boukman, the charismatic early leader of the insurrection, was killed in November 1791. His death was greatly mourned by his comrades. He was replaced by Jean-François, a highly intelligent commander who had spent most of his life in bondage, and Biassou, a popular leader with a fiery temperament. As elsewhere across the Atlantic world, many of Saint-Domingue's combatants were trained warriors from Africa, or had some combat experience. They relied mainly on guerrilla tactics, avoiding direct military confrontation whenever possible, and using camouflaged traps, obstructions, and ambushes. Their troops marched to African martial music, uttering piercing war cries and screeching sounds to intimidate and disorient the enemy.[43]

Some of these local rebel captains were striking figures, perhaps none more so than Halaou, a Yoruba commander who became one of the leaders of the Cul-de-Sac insurgents. He was a man of colossal physical stature and Herculean strength, who always carried a big white cock which he claimed directly transmitted the wishes of the heavens.[44] Another remarkable commander was Romaine Rivière, a free black planter who became the leader of the Trou Coffy insurgents. His forces briefly held the southern towns of Jacmel and Léogâne. Calling himself 'Romaine-la-prophétesse', Rivière dressed in women's clothes and developed a cult that combined royalism, African spiritualism, and Catholicism.[45] Many of these local fighters were Kongolese steeped in Catholic traditions: their commanders were called Sainte Jésus Maman Boudier, Sainte Catherine, and Saint Jean Père l'Eternité.[46] Cross-dressing was not all in one direction: there were numerous cases of runaway women who wore men's clothing, such as Magdelaine, a twenty-nine-year-old enslaved woman from Petit-Goâve who was lured away by the *vodou* priest Hyacinthe, and was 'in the habit of dressing up as a man'.[47]

Among the fighters were several women known for their daring, ruthlessness, and extreme hostility towards the slavers. Healers and priests were deployed as well, providing charms to protect fighters from harm and casting spells on their adversaries.[48] By 1792 this was still an all-out war, on both sides. Negotiations between the insurgents and the authorities in late 1791 broke down (Saint-Domingue's colonists wanted nothing short of unconditional surrender), and in any event the rank-and-file revolutionaries remained implacably committed to the destruction of the white order. As a French royalist observed in early 1792, his frustration mingled with grudging admiration: 'the bravery of these Africans is unbelievable . . . they are vigorous, stubborn, and full of rage in this war'.[49] For their part, the rebels expressed their sentiments more succinctly in the uncompromising Makandalist slogan inscribed on their battle flags: 'bout à blancs'.[50]

The insurrection dealt a crippling blow to Saint-Domingue's slavers. Hundreds of white settlers were killed, often by the very slave drivers, coachmen, cooks, and butlers they most trusted, and thousands of others fled to neighbouring Caribbean islands or to the United States, never to return. The production of the colony's precious commodities such as sugar, coffee, and indigo went into steep decline, and eventually collapsed. By the mid-1790s, exports had ceased altogether. Neither the French authorities in Paris nor the local settlers could imagine the restoration of the colony's former status as the 'Pearl of the Antilles'. As in post-revolutionary France, where feudalism was destroyed, the old order in Saint-Domingue was well and truly shattered.

But the revolution was far from secure. Slavery was still the law of the land, and its general abolition still seemed inconceivable, even to many insurgents. The proclamation of the Republic in France in September 1792 did little to alter the hostility of French authorities towards the black rebels, whom they continued to denounce as 'brigands'. Spain and Britain, ensconced across the border in Santo Domingo and in nearby Jamaica, kept a watchful eye on events, hoping to exploit the circumstances to the detriment of French interests. Having broken their chains, Saint-Domingue's revolutionaries now needed to maintain their momentum and avoid the mistakes that had derailed previous Atlantic insurrections. In particular, they had to stop themselves from being overrun or forced to accept compromises that would ultimately reinforce the slave order – as with the maroons in Jamaica. Equally imperative was the need to maintain unity within the insurgency and among the captive population more generally, and prevent personal conflicts, ethnic antagonisms, and territorial rivalries from spilling over. The threat of African or mixed-raced separatism continued to lurk in Saint-Domingue's revolutionary politics throughout the 1790s. Above all, the revolution had to show itself capable of producing what had often eluded Atlantic anti-slavery movements: a leadership that could hold the rebels together, keep their domestic and foreign enemies at bay, and offer a coherent vision for a new order.

Salvation often comes from unexpected quarters, and the man who emerged from the insurgent ranks to guide Saint-Domingue through the decisive phases of its struggle for emancipation was perhaps modern history's most unlikely revolutionary. In 1792 he was still known as Toussaint Bréda, following the name of the sugar estate in the northern province where he had been born into slavery, and laboured at first as a humble shepherd. Unlike Boukman and many Atlantic leaders, he was not physically imposing – as a young boy he was so frail that he was nicknamed 'Fatras-Bâton'.[51] At Bréda he was no firebrand, and had risen to become the coachman and principal assistant of the estate manager Bayon de Libertat, who had emancipated him sometime in the mid-1770s. One of the few documents mentioning his pre-revolutionary existence, a plantation register in 1785, described him as 'handy for treating animals, and gentle in his manners'.[52] Indeed, his profile seemed markedly different from the colony's African-born captive majority. Not only was he a freeman, but he was born in Saint-Domingue, and so, unlike many of the 1791 insurgents, he had no military training or experience of African warfare.

Yet what Toussaint may have lacked in these respects was more than amply compensated by his other qualities. He was intelligent and inventive, and blessed with a remarkable memory. In his youth he attended a local Catholic church that welcomed captives and recognized the moral equality of all people. His religious and cultural upbringing thus furnished him with a deep sense of humanity, and a belief that there was a capacity for goodness in all people – even former enslavers. Although he had lived his entire life on a plantation, he was nonetheless imbued with what we might call the maroon spirit. One of Toussaint's most famous sayings was: 'I was born a slave, but nature gave me the soul of a free man.'[53]

He learned the science of herbal medicine from his father, a senior official in Allada who had been enslaved and brought to Saint-Domingue after the defeat of his kingdom by Dahomey. Toussaint thus shared the predilection of African-born captives for healing, and their understanding that physical well-being and moral health were intimately connected. His natural sense of freedom was nourished by his equestrian skills: he was an accomplished horseman, and he spent much of his time as a young adult galloping across the plains and hills of the northern province; even when he became the colony's main political and military leader, he was always on the move. Very much in keeping with this maroon sensibility too was Toussaint's belief in the virtues of discipline and secrecy, and the importance of agricultural production for the common good. His knowledge of Saint-Domingue's ecology was encyclopaedic and acquired entirely from experience.

To make the same point differently, Toussaint was living proof that divisions between freemen and captives, Saint-Domingue creoles and African-born *bossales*, followers of Christianity, Islam and other African religions, and maroons and plantation or town captives, were exaggerated; there was no 'creole' sphere that was completely distinct from these other dimensions.[54] Take, for instance, Toussaint's imaginative engagement with Makandal's heritage. At first glance, the two figures seemed worlds apart. They lived completely different lives, Toussaint on the estate and Makandal in the mountains, and Toussaint's overall aims and methods could not have been more dissimilar to those of his revolutionary predecessor. He did not seek to eliminate whites from the colony, and poison was never part of his repertoire; moreover, spilling the blood of his black brothers was abhorrent to him, in contrast with Makandal. As a young man (he would have been in his late teens in 1758), Toussaint probably attended the execution of Makandal in Cap-Français, which was not far from Bréda, and the old prophet's capture would have shaped Toussaint's own belief that a less combative and more inclusive method was needed to bring down the slave order.

And yet the two revolutionary figures had a great deal in common. Both came from families that were part of the ruling elite in Africa. Both were deeply religious, and Toussaint resolutely embraced Makandal's ambition to work across religious, ethnic, and territorial divides to unite the captives of Saint-Domingue around the goal of emancipation. He shared Makandal's belief that the captive elite could be detached from the settlers – indeed Toussaint himself was the embodiment of this subversion. Also shared by both men was a dedication to creating brotherhoods and underground networks across the colony's plantations, and combining different political and cultural traditions from both sides of the Atlantic in order to maximize the appeal of their revolutionary message. Like Makandal, Toussaint was a powerful orator, capable of moving his audiences with his fiery rhetoric, his use of colourful symbols and metaphors, and his invocation of African spirits. In fact, many of his followers among the enslaved believed Toussaint was a holy man with magical powers, a reincarnation of the revolutionary prophet.[55]

All of these qualities were captured in mid-1793, when the Bréda coachman changed his name to Toussaint Louverture. His new *nom de guerre* was first and foremost a confirmation that his old plantation life was behind him, and that he was now taking charge of his own fate, as well as that of his own people. In one of his first proclamations, he pledged his commitment to emancipation, declaring: 'I want freedom and equality to reign in Saint-Domingue.'[56] 'Ouverture' means 'opening' in French, and he sought to signal to the colonial authorities that he could breach their defences, while being receptive to conciliation. Contemporary French accounts suggest that the message was received: a local commissioner, exasperated by Toussaint's repeated seizing of French positions (often by stealth), is believed to have exclaimed: 'comment cet homme fait donc ouverture partout!'[57] This was precisely the kind of calculated ambiguity that later became Toussaint's hallmark as a revolutionary leader. But his pitch to the black people of Saint-Domingue was unequivocal: if they followed his lead, a brighter path lay ahead for them. He underlined the point with an astute nod to an African tradition. Toussaint would have understood that most of the 1791 insurgents would connect his new name with one of their most revered *vodun* deities, Papa Legba, the spirit of the crossroads who acted as the conduit between mortal and divine worlds, and who opened the gates of destiny.[58]

The years 1793–4 were momentous both for Toussaint Louverture and the cause of emancipation. In August 1793, under pressure from the self-emancipated insurgents, and a deteriorating military position in the face of Spanish and British military offensives in Saint-Domingue, local French republican officials decreed the abolition of slavery in the colony, and a year later the Convention in Paris abolished human bondage altogether. France thus became the first major colonial power to end enslavement – a significant landmark in the history of abolition, although this emancipation would only last less than a decade. It would be reversed after Napoleon Bonaparte's full-scale military invasion of Saint-Domingue in 1802 and subsequent restoration of slavery in French colonies. This aggression would lead to another mass uprising, and the final revolutionary war of liberation, ending with the proclamation of Haitian independence in 1804. For Saint-Domingue, however, the period between 1794 and 1802 was crucial: it allowed the revolution a window to develop its collective democratic spirit through mass organizations, build new institutions and laws, and prepare its people for their final conquest of sovereignty in 1804. These years were decisively shaped by Toussaint Louverture.

After a brief spell as a Spanish ally, Louverture joined forces with the French republicans in 1794, and became the leader of the black revolution in Saint-Domingue. He charted an original course that sought to consolidate its political and military gains, while slowly encouraging the emergence of a new sense of Saint-Domingue's collective self. His vision consisted of several interconnected elements, the first of which was that Saint-Domingue's white, mixed-race, and black people formed a legitimate political community, which existed in its own right (Toussaint would often refer to the colony as 'mon pays'). As he put it in one of his early proclamations, addressed to his mixed-race 'brothers', many of whom had been slavers: 'equality cannot exist without liberty, and for liberty to exist we need unity'.[59] This union included the colony's white settlers, and was perhaps the boldest component of Louverture's dream. It envisioned a state of affairs no previous Atlantic enslaved insurgency had aspired to or even imagined: the forging of a constructive relationship between the emancipated and their former enslavers, on the basis of civil equality, forgiveness, and mutual respect. Or as Toussaint summed it up, he wanted to create a 'single family of friends and brothers' in Saint-Domingue.[60]

This fraternal objective was closely tied to his second goal: holding the now emancipated black community together, both in the negative sense of preventing any escalation of ethnic and cultural divisions, and in a positive perspective, enabling them to demonstrate their competences across a range of public and private activities. Black people were appointed as judges, administrators, schoolteachers, and municipal councillors. He believed his brothers had a duty to be exemplary: 'we the black people are the strongest and it is up to us to maintain order and tranquillity, and to set the right example'.[61] This was related to Louverture's other ambition: to manoeuvre Saint-Domingue into a position where it could manage its own political and economic affairs, and develop commercial ties with regional powers such as the United States and Jamaica on the basis of their reciprocal interests – even if these ran counter to French policies.

This delicate balancing act proved indispensable in the later 1790s, when Saint-Domingue needed British and American support to break its economic isolation. It led to fruitful trade agreements, and the siting of British and American consular officials in Saint-Domingue – a badge of international respectability that was another unprecedented achievement for a regime born out of a captive insurgency. But even though he encouraged his new partners to think that he wanted independence, Louverture believed that Saint-Domingue should retain close ties to the French Republic, at least in the short term. He sincerely identified with the republican principles of liberty, equality, and fraternity, although his own formulation of brotherhood was much broader and richer; he sent his two older sons Isaac and Placide to be educated in France. This did not mean, as his critics claimed, that he was subservient or beholden to his French allies, or that his political and intellectual horizons were limited only to France. Indeed, he was proud of Saint-Domingue, the creative and indomitable spirit of its people, and the revolution's 'crazy dream' to combine the best of European, African, and Caribbean traditions.[62] He frequently made positive references to the Jamaican maroons, and the way in which they had forced the British colonial authorities 'to make treaties with them'. In a sense this maroon recognition of autonomy was what Toussaint was trying to achieve, on a grander and more self-sufficient scale, in his own dealings with the French.[63]

But Louverture was not prepared to follow the Jamaican maroons in helping the authorities preserve the wider system of slavery. Indeed, a leitmotif in his speeches throughout this period was the irreversibility of emancipation, and the certainty that the black population of Saint-Domingue would fight to the death if any European colonial power attempted to bring back human bondage. In the words of Toussaint, his people would prefer to 'bury themselves in the ruins of their country rather than face the prospect of a restoration of slavery'.[64] To strengthen

Saint-Domingue's social cohesion, Toussaint relied on institutions that
would govern the colony in the best interests of all sections of the community. After pushing successive French administrators out, Louverture
himself assumed control of Saint-Domingue's colonial administration. He
oversaw the development of municipal councils that worked effectively
to improve the lives of local communities; this too was a major achievement of the Louverture era. These governance reforms culminated in
the promulgation of a new constitution in 1801, which appointed Toussaint governor for life, while still retaining the colony's links to France.
The third article specified that 'there can exist no slaves in this territory,
where servitude is forever abolished and all men are born, live and die
free and French'.[65]

This collective popular attachment to freedom was one of the most
remarkable features of the Haitian revolution, and was reflected in the
development of an extensive democratic culture in Saint-Domingue
during the 1790s. Emancipated by the French Republic, its black citizens
were thoroughly imbued with revolutionary principles, and considered
themselves to be free and self-governing agents, who had begun to shape
their collective destiny as from the 1791 insurrection. Women in southern
plantations, for example, vigorously contested their treatment by French
authorities in 1793–4.[66] It was this popular spirit of republican autonomy
that underpinned and empowered Toussaint Louverture's leadership, and
it further thrived in plantation brotherhoods, National Guard meetings,
and local assemblies where black citizens came together to resolve conflicts and discuss matters of interest. As a French official who observed
these gatherings reported, their meetings were conducted in an African
style of democratic deliberation, in which participation, experience, and
consensus were valued; these discussions were carried out in a manner
that combined 'order, sagacity, and secrecy'.[67]

This democratic citizenship could become confrontational, especially against French officials if they were thought to be acting against
the public good. Black communities were particularly sensitive to any
issue that reminded them of their enslavement, which was the touchstone
issue in French colonial politics throughout the 1790s. Toussaint Louverture was supported by the newly emancipated because he was seen as
the defender of their interests in this respect. When he came into conflict
with the French colonial administrator Gabriel de Hédouville in 1798
over his proposed treatment of agricultural labourers, a large body of
revolutionary citizens mobilized against the French administrator and
helped Louverture force him off the island. In their speeches and slogans,
these men and women reclaimed the language of the 1789 Declaration

of the Rights of Man, proudly claiming to exercise the democratic rights afforded to them by the French constitution. They saw themselves as active citizens, fully entitled publicly to intervene in matters of state. Just to prove the point, one petition from the commune of Marmelade listed the names of more than a hundred signatories, while another document signed by the black citizens of Petite-Rivière affirmed that 'the rights of man are inalienable and unalterable'.[68]

This popular democratic spirit was an independent social force, which could even turn against Saint-Domingue's revolutionary leadership. Louverture's closeness to the white planters was resented by many of the former captives, particularly in light of his most controversial policy: the retention of the colonial plantation system. Toussaint expected those formerly enslaved to operate as wage labourers, working hard for the common good in order to regenerate Saint-Domingue's economy. In order to achieve this objective, the revolutionary leader eventually imposed a draconian system of discipline on the plantations. His agrarian policies became increasingly unpopular with the now emancipated black majority, and many fled their plantations into a new form of marronage, and became rebellious in the late 1790s, despite sharing Louverture's Afro-Catholic faith.[69] But Louverture remained inflexible, and maintained that black labourers could not expect special rights or privileges: 'blacks, people of colour, and whites, when they submit themselves to the laws, should be protected by them, and they should equally be punished when they violate them'.[70]

Toussaint's justification of black freedom was grounded in their self-emancipation in 1791, as well as his military leadership of Saint-Domingue's predominantly black troops. The creation of a mighty army of brave republican warriors, as his commander called them, was arguably the greatest single Louverturean contribution to the Haitian revolution. He transformed his hardy but bedraggled combatants of the early 1790s, most of whom came from local maroon bands and plantation insurgents, into a united and effective force that defeated local slavers and their Spanish and British allies. He led by example, and was the epitome of the charismatic military leader, driving his men into battle, sleeping only a few hours every night, and travelling vast distances at breakneck speed. He instilled in his soldiers the virtues of 'honour, subordination and discipline', and trained them to fight using a combination of European and maroon guerrilla tactics, such as deceptions, psychological intimidation, and ambushes. They often drew on Toussaint's remarkable knowledge of Saint-Domingue's terrain to overpower their adversaries. Always attuned to the appeals of Makandalist symbols, Toussaint wore a red handkerchief around his head, a symbol of Ogun Fer, the west African spirit of iron, war-fare, and hunting who led his followers into combat and kept them safe.[71]

Louverture was appointed commander-in-chief of the republican army in 1796, and recruited the most talented warriors he could find from all sections of Saint-Domingue. His troops were made up of whites, mixed-race and black people, and among the black officers were creoles as well as African-born *bossales*; in this sense, his army was a microcosm of the integrated political community he sought to build. Although his republican troops became the principal military force in the colony, Toussaint had to contend with sectarian divisions, especially in efforts by the southern mixed-race leader André Rigaud to challenge his leadership. The ensuing conflict left a bitter legacy in the relationship between black and mixed-race communities. A range of maroon combat forces emerged in the aftermath of the 1791 insurrection; many of these bands were organized along African ethnic lines, so were often reluctant to work with Louverture because of his co-operation with whites. For example, Toussaint's relationship with Macaya, the Kongolese leader of the Acul fighters, was particularly difficult. In 1793 Macaya rejected any collaboration with the French republicans, and he described himself as a subject of three kings: Kongo, France, and Spain. By the mid-1790s he was calling for the death of all white settlers, and he was briefly detained by Toussaint; he later vigorously opposed his labour policies. Even though they had the Catholic faith in common, Macaya's Christianity was much more mystical than Louverture's, and he believed in a far more limited form of government, and in taking decisions through collective group deliberation.[72]

Although Macaya was one of the African-born maroon leaders who remained outside the Louverturean tent during the 1790s, many other 'Kongos' were successfully brought inside it. They included able commanders such as Petit-Noël Prieur, Mademoiselle, Sylla, and Jean-Baptiste Sans-Souci, who were all incorporated into Toussaint's army and became senior commanders. The most compelling of these maroon figures was Sans-Souci, an old acquaintance from Toussaint's Bréda days. He rose to the rank of colonel, becoming one of the most powerful military leaders in the northern province by the late 1790s. Sans-Souci assisted Toussaint in several important political operations (notably the expulsion of the French agent Hédouville in 1798), and remained loyal to him until the very end.[73]

Indeed, Toussaint's senior officers included men who would play a vital part in the Haitian revolution, especially Jean-Jacques Dessalines, a formidable commander whom Toussaint entrusted with his most important military operations. The most critical of these battles was the ongoing fight against the Spanish and British, and their royalist allies. By the end of 1794 they occupied strategic portions of the northern, western, and southern territories (including Port-au-Prince). Toussaint's fighters took them on and drove them out of the colony by 1798, despite being under-equipped and often lacking the barest of necessities, such as food supplies and clothing (in one of his campaigns in 1797, Toussaint's soldiers were given a daily ration of three biscuits).[74] In 1801, Toussaint led a military expedition into neighbouring Santo Domingo, and expelled the Spaniards from the territory, placing the entire island of Hispaniola under French republican rule.

The military rout of the British was a particularly notable victory for Saint-Domingue's black army. Toussaint and his men overcame an enemy with vastly superior resources: the British spent £10 million to retain their position in the colony. Assisted by the ravages of yellow fever Toussaint's men inflicted severe losses upon his adversaries: around 20,000 British soldiers died during their five-year campaign. Toussaint presented these efforts to his men as wars against foreign occupiers seeking to re-enslave them, and as necessary struggles to create a better Saint-Domingue for all its citizens. As he once told his soldiers: 'we fight for our freedom, which is the greatest of riches we can aspire to, and we have to preserve it for ourselves and for our children'.[75] One of the many effects of Toussaint's military accomplishments was to bolster the martial image of black people in the colony and across the Atlantic world; this was reflected in a popular saying in late eighteenth-century Saint-Domingue, directed at whites: 'zautres pas capable battre la guerre contre nègres'.[76]

In the end, despite all these achievements, and his hope that he had done enough to deter his adversaries, Toussaint Louverture failed to prevent the French military invasion of Saint-Domingue. In late 1801 Napoleon sent a large army to reconquer the colony and purge its black military and political leaders. Toussaint rapidly assembled his forces when he saw the French fleet on the horizon, and he led a spirited resistance in the early months of 1802. He was treacherously captured after signing an armistice with the French in May, and was deported to the Fort de Joux in eastern France, where he died a year later. He had counted on a war of attrition, and the expectation that the French would eventually succumb to disease (as had the British). Like many charismatic leaders, and indeed like his nemesis Napoleon, he was undone by his faith in his own powers and good fortune – and perhaps even more by his trust in the honourable behaviour of the French military, of which he was after all a distinguished commander. Louverture was not the first black Atlantic leader to have been betrayed after signing an agreement with European slavers.

The Haitian war of independence, the climax of the revolution in French Saint-Domingue, was therefore fought without Toussaint Louverture. In a sense this was fitting: complete sovereignty was not part of his vision for his country, at least immediately. But he could take credit for preparing his army and his people to cherish their emancipation and resist any foreign attempt to restore slavery in Saint-Domingue. The mass uprising that erupted in the northern province in mid-1802, following news of his capture and the restoration of slavery in neighbouring Guadeloupe, prepared the ground for the eventual defeat of the French. Louverture's shadow remained present throughout the course of the war in 1802–3. His successors' military tactics against the French mirrored those he had enunciated in the early months of 1802, and which in effect harked back to the maroon warfare of the early 1790s: a scorched-earth policy, accompanied by the systematic destruction of the economic apparatus of the colony (by the end of 1802, sugar production had completely halted), the retrenchment of rebel forces on higher and remote ground, and the use of guerrilla tactics and popular insurgencies against the occupying forces. Most importantly, Toussaint had always advocated a united front of black and mixed-race people. This principle was eventually adopted in October 1802, when leading local military figures such as Dessalines and the mixed-race commander Alexandre Pétion (who were still serving in the French army) defected to the resistance. Dessalines became the commander of the Armée Indigène, and as Saint-Domingue's most experienced warrior he was perfectly suited for the position – especially as he had declared in 1800 that a French invasion, were it to come, would be greeted with an insurrection of the whole people of Saint-Domingue, 'the men and women all united together'.[77]

This collective democratic spirit was one of the most remarkable features of the Haitian revolution. It was further manifested in the ways in which it produced its leaders from the ranks of the emancipated population, drew the mass of ordinary people into the public arena, gave them a sense of belonging and shared destiny, and prepared them successfully to defend their freedom against the French slavers. From the outset, revolutionary citizenship was in this sense intimately bound up with resistance against enslavement. These qualities were reflected, too, in the prominence of women, from the early 1790s all the way through to the war of independence. As we saw earlier, women were already an integral component of Makandal's conspiracy, with his wife Brigitte and the network of female poisoners. Among the remarkable figures who emerged in the late eighteenth century was Toya Montou, a Dahomean warrior who was captured and enslaved in Saint-Domingue, where she ended up on the

1. (Left) Statue of the anti-slavery combatant Solitude in Paris; she holds up a copy of the 1802 revolutionary proclamation of the anti-slavery rebels in Guadeloupe.

2. (Below) Two pages from a booklet found on an insurgent during the 1835 Bahia uprising in Brazil. It contains citations from the Qur'an, prayers and Islamic religious inscriptions. The page on the right begins with a reference to the Prophet Muhammad. Such booklets were carried by educated people in West Africa and the Americas to express and reaffirm their faith.

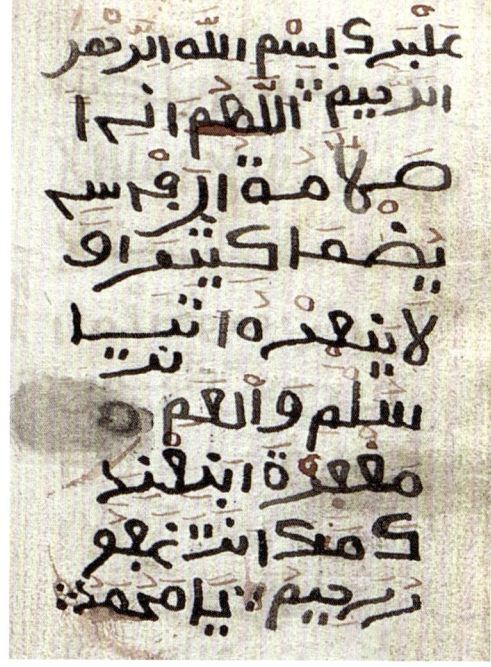

REPRESENTATION of an INSURRECTION on board A SLAVE-SHIP.

Shewing how the crew fire upon the unhappy Slaves from behind the BARRICADO, erected on board all Slave ships, as a security whenever such commotions may happen.

3. Resistance on the seas: (left) an eighteenth-century drawing of a slave ship insurrection and (below) a nineteenth-century lithograph about the Amistad revolt, showing Joseph Cinqué speaking to his fellow-rebels on the day the vessel was seized by the American Navy and escorted to New London in Connecticut. The three young enslaved girls who assisted the insurgents are in the centre; the Spanish slavers José Ruiz and Pedro Montes are third from right and far right respectively.

A Rebel Negro armed & on his guard.

4. A late eighteenth-century maroon rebel from Surinam, armed with a firelock and a hatchet, with two of his fugitive companions in the background. The skull and bones at his feet represent his enemies. The image conveys the maroons' adaptability, as well as their vigilance and resilience.

5. The struggles of the enslaved in the parish of Trelawney in colonial Jamaica during the Second Maroon War (1795): (above) British forces attack Trelawny town, one of the maroon strongholds, and (below) a group of maroons ambush British troops on an estate.

6. Two folios from a Mandingo bag made for protection and healing by the African-born captive José Francisco Pereira in the early eighteenth century. Pereira was enslaved in Brazil and then Portugal, where he was arrested by the Inquisition in 1730 for 'sorcery'; the images relate to Christ's crucifixion and illustrate the syncretic nature of slave religions and the complex links between spirituality and anti-slavery resistance.

7. A Brazilian Obeah man, by the French painter Jean-Baptiste Debret (early nineteenth century). Obeah was an African-originating spiritual system appealing to natural and supernatural forces for healing, poisoning, protection and divination; the image again highlights the range of cultural combinations which were at play as African spiritual practices crossed over to the Americas.

8. A divination ceremony in Brazil painted by Zacharias Wagener, a German mercenary who worked for the Dutch East India Company in the seventeenth century. The scene depicted here is a ceremony involving ancestral spirit possession.

9. A Kalinda dance in the United States, late eighteenth century. The image is meant to convey the harmony of plantation life, with the enslaved dancing merrily under the benevolent gaze of the white owners. In reality, gatherings of this kind were often a cover for rebellious and revolutionary activities.

10. A contemporary depiction of enslaved rebels in action during the 1831–2 Baptist uprising in Jamaica, here seen attacking and setting fire to the Roehampton estate in the parish of St James.

11. A sketch from a flag taken from the insurgents during the 1816 Bussa revolt in Barbados, expressing the rebels' aspiration for freedom, dignity and happiness, and at the same time a desire to retain friendly ties with the British crown.

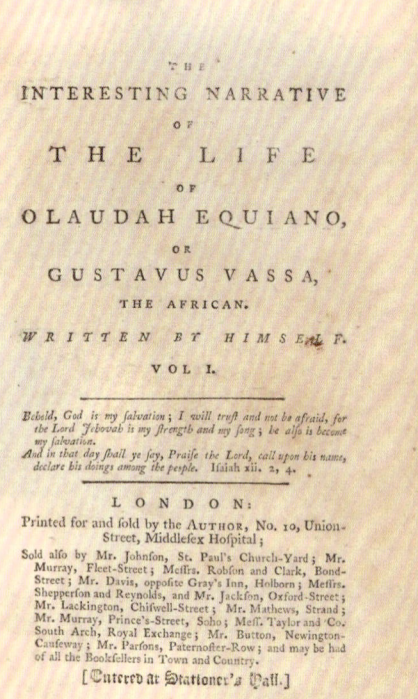

THE
INTERESTING NARRATIVE
OF
THE LIFE
OF
OLAUDAH EQUIANO,
OR
GUSTAVUS VASSA,
THE AFRICAN.
WRITTEN BY HIMSELF.
VOL I.

Behold, God is my salvation; I will trust and not be afraid, for the Lord Jehovah is my strength and my song; he also is become my salvation.
And in that day shall ye say, Praise the Lord, call upon his name, declare his doings among the people. Isaiah xii. 2, 4.

LONDON:
Printed for and sold by the AUTHOR, No. 10, Union-Street, Middlesex Hospital;
Sold also by Mr. Johnson, St. Paul's Church-Yard; Mr. Murray, Fleet-Street; Messrs. Robson and Clark, Bond-Street; Mr. Davis, opposite Gray's Inn, Holborn; Messrs. Shepperson and Reynolds, and Mr. Jackson, Oxford-Street; Mr. Lackington, Chiswell-Street; Mr. Mathews, Strand; Mr. Murray, Prince's-Street, Soho; Messr. Taylor and Co. South Arch, Royal Exchange; Mr. Button, Newington-Causeway; Mr. Parsons, Paternoster-Row; and may be had of all the Booksellers in Town and Country.

[Entered at Stationer's Hall.]

12. (Above) Olaudah Equiano's *Interesting Narrative* (1789 edition), one of the most famous slave memoirs of the eighteenth century, with multiple editions in Britain and several translations in Europe.

13. (Left) A statue of Denmark Vesey in Charleston, South Carolina, dedicated in 2014 after nearly two decades of community campaigning. A freedman, skilled carpenter and church leader, Vesey was one of principal architects of a major anti-slavery conspiracy uncovered in Charleston; he was tried and executed in July 1822, along with thirty-four of his compatriots.

Duclos plantation, taking under her wing a young captive named Jean-Jacques, the future Dessalines. They both shared a fierce hatred of slavery and a determination not to be broken by it. Toya commanded a group of rebels after the 1791 insurgency and fought bravely before being captured. Dessalines considered Toya as his aunt – in effect, a second mother – and she is thought to have educated him about his African heritage; she also passed on some of the combat skills she had acquired in Africa.[78]

A large number of women played an active part during the war of independence, carrying out arson attacks, growing food, helping to transport weapons and ammunition, and spying against the French; in a further echo of Makandal, two female black nurses were convicted of poisoning soldiers in their care.[79] There were women fighters: rank-and-file combatants, largely drawn from among the agricultural workers, as well as officers such as Sanité Belair, who became a sergeant and then a lieutenant in Louverture's army. She was one of the leaders of a popular uprising against the invading French forces in the Verrettes mountains in August 1802, alongside her husband Charles. Feared by the occupying troops for her bravery and her determination, she rallied the populations of the Artibonite department to the resistance cause (including many women) before being captured and executed. During a campaign against another insurgent leader, a French officer reported the presence of women rebel fighters.[80] A similar fighting spirit was displayed by Marie-Jeanne Lamartinière, a mixed-race woman who became one of the heroines of the siege of the Crête-à-Pierrot fort, in which the heavily outnumbered rebel forces (including many women fighters) inflicted heavy casualties on the French troops. Dressed in a mamluk outfit, Lamartinière continually resupplied the defenders with gunpowder and ammunition; she frequently shot at the French herself.[81]

The war was an unmitigated disaster for Napoleon's forces. Their troops were decimated by yellow fever, just as Toussaint had predicted, with the commander of the invading forces Charles Victoire Leclerc (Bonaparte's brother-in-law) dying of the disease in November 1802; an estimated 50,000 French soldiers lost their lives during the conflict. Leclerc fought with increasing desperation, and as his black troops defected in ever larger numbers he carried out mass killings of his own forces in an attempt to prevent them from going over to the rebel side. The entire 6th Colonial Regiment was drowned in the Cap harbour, and Leclerc added a further cohort of black men, women, and even children to the list. The recipe he advocated for defeating the insurrection was genocidal: 'we must destroy all the blacks in the mountains, men and women, keeping only the infants less than twelve years old; we must also destroy half those on the [northern] plain ... without this the colony will never be quiet'.[82]

Leclerc's successor the vicomte de Rochambeau requested permission to restore slavery in Saint-Domingue in January 1803. He continued and amplified the barbaric methods used by his predecessor, carrying out mass drownings of prisoners and people suspected of sympathy for the resistance cause, and importing a special breed of bulldog from Cuba specially trained to attack and devour humans. But even such extreme measures could not impede the momentum of the insurgency. By now the resistance consisted of an integrated army under a unified command, and independent insurrectionary movements across the colony, under the leadership of African maroon rebels such as Sylla, Sans-Souci, Petit-Noël Prieur, Macaya, and Lamour-Dérance (the first three of these insurgents, as we saw earlier, had long been close allies of Louverture). After suffering their final defeat at the battle of Vertières in November 1803, the French capitulated, and in January 1804, Haiti's first ruler, Dessalines, proclaimed the independence of the new state, celebrating the achievement of his people who had dared to be free.

Democratic revolutions always generate a range of contending visions of the future among their leaders, and among the politicized masses, and Saint-Domingue was no exception. There were different views across the colony about its future relationship with France, the place of the *colon* and mixed-race minorities, and the social and economic role of plantation labourers. One of the most charismatic black military leaders, Toussaint's nephew Moïse, believed his uncle was too generous with the white elite, and too harsh in his dealings with labourers, among whom he had a strong following in the northern province. After being implicated in a peasant rebellion in October 1801, in which several hundred whites were killed, Moïse was arrested, tried, and executed.[83]

Many senior black commanders and officials, such as Henri Christophe, had been sceptical of Toussaint's attempts to distance the colony from France. Dessalines too was wary of this policy of autonomy, but for the opposite reason: he wanted full independence, and believed (like Moïse) that there was no place in the new state for whites. Between February and May 1804 several thousand of the remaining French *colons* were massacred, and Dessalines issued a fiery proclamation justifying the killings in the name of retribution: not only for the crimes perpetrated by the French in Saint-Domingue, but for those committed by slavers since the beginnings of colonialism in the New World. The new Haitian people were defined as a black nation, made up of black and mixed-race people, and the 1805 constitution banned any white person from owning property. As Dessalines put it: 'I have avenged America.'[84]

This was an emphatic and, in the circumstances, a necessary break from the Louverturean vision, and it is instructive briefly to compare the differences between modern Haiti's two founding fathers. The rupture between them should not be overplayed. Both were former captives, and rose to their positions of supreme leadership through the 1791 revolution. Both drew their energy and inspiration from the emancipated masses and understood that their own power ultimately rested on the collective will of the people. In this sense, both leaders expressed and channelled the formidable democratic energy of the Haitian revolution. Moreover, Dessalines was Louverture's most gifted military disciple, and despite his publicly expressed criticism of Toussaint after independence, he essentially continued his predecessor's agrarian and foreign policies. He was particularly careful to stress, as Toussaint had done, that Haiti had no wish to export her revolution. The basic difference between them was their contrasting sensibilities on the issue of slavery. This was not a matter of principle: both men absolutely opposed human bondage, and both devoted themselves to preventing their people from being re-enslaved. This was the cornerstone of Toussaint's policies as a military and political leader throughout the 1790s, culminating in his 1801 Constitution that proclaimed the abolition of slavery for ever, as we saw earlier.

But in this sense Toussaint's approach to slavery was more abstract: this arguably gave him an edge over Dessalines in the sense that he better understood its systemic nature, and therefore the strategic difficulties which would arise if Saint-Domingue were to try to go it alone, and so become a beacon of emancipation in the Atlantic world without the support of at least one major imperial power. Haiti's post-independence isolation was arguably a vindication of Toussaint's caution. But this approach blunted Toussaint's sensitivity to the immediate and human effects of his harsh labour regime, and the way it reminded many labourers of the servitude they had experienced before 1791. Dessalines, on the other hand, had a better understanding of how little the racial attitudes of Saint-Domingue's *colons* had really changed. He also had a more profound appreciation of the brutal realities of slavery, which he had personally experienced, as reflected by the scars still visible on his back at the time of the revolution. He therefore saw with greater lucidity than Toussaint that the complete eradication of enslavement in Saint-Domingue – in practice as well as in spirit – would be much harder to bring about in the presence of a sizeable white settler community. In this sense he followed the logic of daring to be free to its conclusion.

This triumph of the soon-to-be Emperor Dessalines (he was crowned in October 1804) marked something much deeper. It saw the resurgence of the radical popular spirit of the 1791 insurrection ('bout à blancs' could well have been a Dessalines slogan), and even more ardently the revival of Makandal's revolutionary tradition. It was a measure of its potency that it was able to shape the outlook and style of leaders as different as Toussaint and Dessalines, but its greater influence was undoubtedly on the latter. Both Dessalines and Makandal were strong, determined, and ruthless – Dessalines co-operated with the French to allow Louverture's capture. Like Makandal, Dessalines explicitly appealed to an indigenous pattern of maroon anti-slavery resistance that harked back to the Taino Amerindians. The name he chose for the new state, 'Haiti', was the Arawak designation of their territory as the 'land of the mountains'. And in contrast with Louverture's dalliances with French ideas and values, Dessalines was openly contemptuous of the 'murderous nation' that had ravaged his country, and was robustly African in his cultural preferences (he loved African music and drums, like Makandal).[85] Dessalines had no scruples, either, about spilling black blood; he used poison against his enemies, like Makandal, and purged many black leaders who had played a vital role during the war of independence, even though he was culturally and spiritually closer to them than any of the other revolutionary leaders. His vision of Haiti as a black nation free of any European contamination exactly matched the prophecy of the old man of the mountains. And just as Makandal had used different-coloured scarves to represent his vision of Saint-Domingue's past and future, Dessalines is believed to have designed the new Haitian flag by ripping out the white strip from the tricolour, leaving only red and blue.

Like Makandal, Dessalines symbolized the spiritual syncretism of Haiti's democratic revolution: he married his wife Claire-Heureuse in a Catholic church in Léogane in 1800, and practised divination (a contemporary French source described him as taking regular advice from a 'council of macandals'[86]). Dessalines was a *houngan* (*vodou* priest), and he galvanized his troops by affirming that they should not fear death, as it would allow their spirit to be reunited with their African homeland, where they would find 'Papa Toussaint' (the former commander remained popular with his soldiers).[87] Dessalines' rule was short-lived: he was assassinated by disaffected members of his administration in October 1806. But his place in Haitian popular memory was already assured by this point; he went on to join the pantheon of Haitian *lwas*, and was celebrated in an early twentieth-century song as the ultimate warrior and providential saviour of his people: 'He is bringing new magic. He is bringing muskets, he is bringing bullets . . . He is bringing cannons to chase away the whites.'[88]

*

The Haitian revolution captured the collective imagination of the Atlantic world. Its embrace by enslaved, mixed-race, and free black people began before the revolution and independence, in the immediate aftermath of the 1791 insurrection. News of the rebellion spread across the Caribbean, carried through ports by sailors, soldiers, dock workers, captives, as well as settlers fleeing Saint-Domingue.[89] Information travelled fast: by September 1791, a few weeks after the rebellion had begun, there were reports of Jamaican captives having composed songs in its honour.[90]

The uprising was a topic of animated conversation: in the summer of 1793, American planter John Randolph overheard two captives talking outside his home in Richmond, Virginia, with one marvelling at the fact that 'blacks had killed whites on the French island a little while ago'; similar conversations were occurring across the Atlantic world.[91] The pillars of the slave order talked about the insurrection too, but in a very different way. A white planter in the British colony of Tobago complained in 1794 that captives had become imbued with ideas about 'fraternity' and now believed themselves 'equal to their masters'. He feared that they would soon band together to 'exterminate the proprietors', as had happened in Saint-Domingue.[92] For these folks, Saint-Domingue became the stuff of nightmares: Simon Taylor, the wealthiest sugar baron in Jamaica, 'tossed and turned in his luxurious bed linen, suffering repeated bouts of fever' as he imagined Toussaint and his revolutionary comrades arriving on his plantation to slit his throat.[93]

As the revolution began to take shape from the mid-1790s around the military exploits and administrative reforms of Toussaint Louverture, captives in the Atlantic world celebrated Saint-Domingue as an example of black popular power in all its forms. In the Dutch colony of Curaçao in the southern Caribbean, an enslaved uprising in 1795 was directly inspired by events in Saint-Domingue; Louverture and his black republican commanders were idolized by local insurgents, many of whom named themselves (and their children) 'Toussaint'.[94] A song in honour of the principal leader of the rebellion, Captain Tula, stressed that women were fully engaged 'in the fight'.[95] Jamaican captives too continued to be creative, composing songs in honour of Saint-Domingue's policies of racial equality; one refrain underlined that 'black, white and brown' were 'all de same'.[96] When Louverture removed French colonial administrator Léger-Félicité Sonthonax in 1797, the news triggered an insurrection in neighbouring Guadeloupe, even though it was under French rule and slavery had been officially abolished. However, rebels in Guadeloupe's Marie-Galante and Lamentin resented the economic power of the békés (white settlers), and they called on plantation workers to challenge it.

The insurgents explicitly cited Saint-Domingue as a justification of their actions, further noting that 'everyone there does what they please, and all those in command are blacks' and 'white women go with the blacks' (stories about Louverture's numerous white mistresses had obviously spread far and wide).[97]

The 1791 revolution was much talked about in the United States, especially in eastern cities like Philadelphia where there were many refugees from Saint-Domingue. The presence of these 'French negroes' on American soil became a source of concern to white slavers, with growing fears of revolutionary 'contagion'. Several states and cities banned the entry of Caribbean captives, or passed laws to expel those who were already there: in Baltimore in 1797 a law called for the forcible removal of any 'French' black or mixed-race captive, at the city's expense, citing their 'disorderly conduct ... dangerous to the peace and welfare of the city of Baltimore'.[98] In 1799 Thomas Jefferson, himself a slaver, denounced Toussaint Louverture and his republican associates as 'cannibals of the terrible Republic', warning that their 'missionaries' could provoke a 'combustion' in the United States; when he became President, Jefferson refused to recognize Haiti.[99]

African Americans, for their part, welcomed the emancipation decrees passed by the French. In the mid-1790s a group of 'coloured citizens of Philadelphia' drafted a letter thanking the National Assembly in France for ending slavery in the French Caribbean; the 1791 rebellion was not mentioned specifically, so as not to antagonize local whites, but the text referred to Saint-Domingue's former captives as their 'brothers'. Some African Americans began to address each other as 'citizen', following the French revolutionary convention.[100] When a white mob attacked a group of black people in Philadelphia, they defended themselves and called out 'Show them San Domingo.'[101] The number of Saint-Domingue-born runaways in the United States rose: during the period between 1791 and 1805, New York City newspapers issued at least forty-seven advertisements for the capture of French-speaking fugitives – a considerable increase from previous decades; similar patterns were in evidence in other American cities.[102] In 1794 Crispin, a sixteen-year-old captive belonging to the prominent Philadelphia merchant Stephen Girard, escaped and found his way to Saint-Domingue by boarding a ship and disguising himself as the bonded servant of a Spanish traveller. Girard asked for his return but was told in no uncertain terms by the Saint-Domingue governor Étienne Laveaux that Crispin was now in a 'land of liberty'.[103]

As the decade advanced, African-American expressions of enthusiasm for the Louverturean revolution in Saint-Domingue became bolder, both in words and deeds. In 1797, in an address to the Boston African Masonic Lodge, the black abolitionist leader Prince Hall invited his audience to take inspiration from the new republican order in the French colony, and expressed the hope that the racist insults they were experiencing daily on their city streets would soon end. Pointedly referring to the 1791 revolution in Saint-Domingue, he remarked that 'the darkest is before the break of day' – in other words, America could well follow the path of her black French brothers.[104] In the American South, this message had already been clearly received. In Charleston, South Carolina, there was a wave of arsonist conspiracies between 1795 and 1798, all principally involving captives originating from Saint-Domingue. The 'French Negroes' involved in the 1798 plot, as described by the authorities, were led by two enslaved people named Figaro and Jean-Louis; they planned to set fire to the city and 'act here as they had formerly done in St Domingo'.[105] This was a reference to both emancipation and the destruction of white properties after the 1791 revolution. In New York, when a former white woman settler from Saint-Domingue tried in 1810 to remove to Virginia a group of captives she had brought with her from the French colony a few years earlier, she was taken to court by the local abolitionists, and several hundred demonstrators – Americans as well as émigrés from Saint-Domingue – protested outside her house, some armed with clubs. They were dispersed by the local guard, after threatening to 'burn the house, murder all the white people in it and take away a number of black slaves'.[106]

An even more elaborate plot came to light in 1800, when captives in and around Richmond, Virginia, planned an insurrection inspired by events in Saint-Domingue. Under the leadership of a literate twenty-four-year-old enslaved blacksmith named Gabriel, an admirer of Toussaint Louverture, they met in cabins, blacksmith shops, and around local waterways, and gathered muskets, gunpowder, and knives. 'Uncle Gabriel, war de chief of da Insurgents', as the popular song later characterized him,[107] had technical skills that enabled him to manufacture weapons, and to appeal to the African god Ogun, the deity of iron, warfare, and hunting (who as we saw earlier was one of Louverture's favourite African deities). It is very likely that among those involved in the conspiracy were African-born as well as Saint-Domingue captives who had arrived in large numbers in Virginia after 1791, and whose values and beliefs were shaped by similar religious and spiritual sensibilities.[108]

Gabriel's plan was to put together an army of rebels on 30 August 1800 and march on Richmond to instigate a general insurrection. The aim was to kidnap the state governor (the future president James Monroe) and hold him hostage until he agreed to declare the abolition of slavery in

Virginia. The plot was betrayed and many of the conspirators, including Gabriel, were executed. But its organization, as well as the subsequent Easter plot of 1802 by one of Gabriel's followers, was evidence of the potency of 'revolutionary San Domingo' in the imagination of African Americans and black Atlantic communities more generally, as we shall discover in the next chapter.[109]

5

Land of Liberty

The Haitian revolution had momentous and wide-ranging impacts on the Atlantic world, both for its captives and for those attempting to preserve the system of chattel slavery. One of its immediate consequences was the enacting of legislation in 1807 in the British Parliament to ban the trade in enslaved people. This measure is typically discussed as the first major vindication of liberal white abolitionism, and it was without doubt a landmark moment for the anti-slavery campaigns that had developed in Britain from the late eighteenth century. Moreover, the timing of this ban – three years after Haitian independence – suggests an intimate connection with the collapse of French slavery in Saint-Domingue, as well as with the earlier defeats of the British at the hands of Louverture's black army. During the second reading of the Bill in February 1807, Prime Minister Lord Grenville was candid about the best way to avoid a recurrence of such convulsions in British colonies: 'so far from the abolition of the Slave trade having a tendency to produce those horrors in our islands, I contend that it is the only measure that can prevent them . . . the abolition of the trade is the only way of avoiding, in our own islands, the horrors which have afflicted St. Domingo'.[1]

As we saw in the previous chapter, the fear of a repetition of Saint-Domingue's 'horrors' provoked a generalized panic among European and North American slavers. The insurrections that destroyed the 'Pearl of the Antilles', and the further plots and uprisings they triggered across the Atlantic, led many of them to conclude that slavery in the American South and in British colonies would best be preserved by cutting off the supply of African captives, widely seen as the most disruptive section of the captive population. Indeed, to underline the connection further, a similar ban on trading in enslaved Africans came into effect in the United States at the end of 1807. President Jefferson imposed a trade embargo on Haiti in the same year. He broke with the support given by his predecessor John Adams to Toussaint Louverture, refusing to recognize the new state.

American states had an established tradition of imposing curbs on the slave trade in the eighteenth century in the wake of African-led domestic captive revolts, or the fear of their occurrence.

In this sense, enslaved people in the Atlantic could take little comfort from the British and American bans of the African trade, as they were not presented as the prelude to an immediate ending of slavery itself – quite the opposite. To quote Lord Grenville again: granting liberty to slaves in the colonies would be a 'poison of the most baleful nature' in light of their 'ignorance and barbarism'.[2] In effect these bans consolidated New World slavery in the colonies rather than eliminated it. This point was reinforced by the exponential growth of the African slave trade in Cuba and Brazil during the first half of the nineteenth century. British individuals and institutions continued to be involved in this trafficking, as slave merchants, suppliers of credit, and providers of vessels and insurance.[3]

Given this reactionary Atlantic context, it is no surprise that enslaved and free black communities looked to Haitian-inspired revolutionary ideals after 1804. With the restoration of slavery in French colonies, people of African origin could turn only to Haiti for a coherent and effective source of ideas about freedom, military valour, dignity, and sovereignty. After the assassination of its founder Dessalines in 1806, the new state was divided until 1820 into two rival political entities: a northern government under Christophe (crowned King Henry in June 1811) and a southern Republic under Pétion. Both men had played major roles in the struggle for national independence, and despite their personal and ideological differences they were strongly committed to its revolutionary values. On the surface, the Haitian authorities publicly adopted a policy of non-intervention in the internal affairs of their neighbours; this principle was reaffirmed in successive constitutions. However, as in the Louverture era, when a similar principle did not prejudice Saint-Domingue's revolutionary aura among Atlantic rebels, post-independence Haiti became a beacon for black emancipation. In 1806 the French colonial authorities in Martinique reported the discovery of a conspiracy across the region to overthrow white rule in British and French colonies and introduce a Haitian-type political system.[4] Even though its leaders did not seek direct confrontation with foreign slaver states, Haiti's mere existence stood as a direct challenge to everything they stood for. Moreover, it developed a distinct language and policies about citizenship as well as universal rights such as freedom, equality, and justice. These became the cornerstone of a new black internationalism that emerged around Haiti. How its notions of individual and collective empowerment were recognized, imagined, and acted upon by free black people as well as enslaved communities in the Atlantic world will be the central theme of this chapter.

This internationalism began in Haiti itself. One of the early objectives of post-independence authorities was to secure the return of Saint-Domingue's native black people who were taken out of the country by fleeing white settlers when they went into exile after the 1791 uprising. This issue had already been raised by Toussaint Louverture in the 1790s, after captives started taking cases to the American courts, with some limited success. Soon after independence Dessalines brought up the matter again, offering to pay American captains to bring back to Haiti any black Saint-Domingue citizens based in the United States.[5] His successor Pétion made a similar request from the Spanish authorities in Cuba, asking for the return of formerly enslaved black men and women who had been forcibly taken to the island during the revolutionary era and who now wished to return to their native land as free citizens. Pétion called them 'Haitians', and at least ten Cuban ships carrying black returnees arrived in Port-au-Prince and Jérémie in mid-1809.[6]

Even more daringly, this policy of inclusiveness was extended to people of African origin with no native or historical connections to Haiti. Black sailors who expressed the desire to remain in Haiti – and there were many – were welcomed with open arms and given Haitian citizenship. In 1814 American officials accused Pétion of 'seducing' sailors of all nationalities with these offers. This condemnation came after a black sailor born in Martinique and living in New Orleans decided to stay in Haiti: he declared himself to be a Haitian, even though he had never lived there. Visitors to Haitian towns observed the presence of sizeable numbers of maritime maroons who had fled enslavement from neighbouring islands in boats and canoes. The British consul in Port-au-Prince observed that 'a very large proportion of the population . . . [consisted] of refugee slaves from the British colonies'.[7]

Black internationalism further extended to challenging the Atlantic slave trade, which continued despite the British and American bans. Through the 1810s, Haitian warships intercepted slave-trading vessels from Africa bound for neighbouring islands and freed their captives. The liberated men and women were publicly welcomed and informed that they were 'free and among brothers and compatriots'.[8] This general asylum policy was formalized in article 44 of Pétion's 1816 Haitian constitution: 'All Africans and Indians, and the descendants of their blood, born in the colonies or in foreign countries, who come to reside in the Republic will be recognized as Haitians.'[9] Shortly afterwards, this internationalist principle was tested when seven Jamaican sailors absconded to southern

Haiti with their English slaver's vessel. Despite the latter's arrival in Haiti to recover his properties, he was able to leave only with his boat. The sailors were granted asylum, because they had come to a land where slavery had been abolished. It emerged that the seven sailors were well informed through Haitian contacts and local networks in Jamaica about the emancipation they would secure if they fled to Haiti. They were attracted, too, by the possibilities of gaining access to farmland and a military career.[10]

Contrary to the general view of its early post-independence years as a time of division and retrenchment, and notwithstanding the racial discrimination it systematically encountered in its dealings with the nineteenth-century international order,[11] Haiti established a strong intellectual and political presence in the Atlantic world in the arena that defined its *raison d'être*: freedom from servitude. This presence was not only theoretical. Through the specific policies and laws that they adopted, Haitian governments enabled the self-liberation and emancipation of thousands of captives who found refuge and sanctuary on their territory after 1804. And as the case of the seven Jamaican sailors illustrated, the existence of the Haitian state stimulated ideas, plans, and schemes among bonded and free black people in the Atlantic world about freedom, and how it could be most effectively realized for themselves, their families, and their communities. This prospect now included a new, revolutionary form of maritime marronage for Atlantic people of African descent: one that could end with finding asylum in the land of liberty.

It was not easy for the enslaved to make their way to Haiti, but free black people did come from across the Atlantic, some in significant numbers. It is estimated that between 6,000 and 13,000 African Americans emigrated to Haiti from the United States in the 1820s. Many eventually returned to America but their journey was evidence of the appeal of the new state to black Atlantic communities.[12] And for those who could not make the journey, Haiti was an enormous source of self-affirmation and pride. Indeed, if republican Saint-Domingue had provided martial inspiration and mobilization for Atlantic slaves, the birth of the Haitian state in 1804 took this enthusiasm to an even higher plane. The defeat of the Napoleonic army, the mightiest military force in Europe, as well as the creation of an independent political community in which slavery was constitutionally banished, and every citizen was black, gave Haiti a special place not only among the enslaved but across a wide spectrum of progressive and enlightened opinion in Europe and the Americas.

Of course, free and enslaved black men and women were particularly triumphant. Some wrote articles celebrating the birth of the new state. In

May 1804 an anonymous African-American writer saluted the Haitians as a 'united and valiant people' and drew parallels between their struggles and the fight for emancipation and justice for black people in the United States.[13] In Philadelphia the anniversary of Haitian independence (1 January) was quietly celebrated in black churches. Stories about the war of independence were disseminated in newspapers and pamphlets. In addition, news about Haiti was carried across the seas by black sailors and former combatants, who contributed to the emergence of a veritable industry of revolutionary paraphernalia across the Atlantic – cheap prints, buttons, military jackets, necklaces, and portraits of leaders. The docks of Havana were one of the many places where such Haitian images and artefacts circulated.[14] This material could become a matter of concern to white authorities, as when black and mixed-race militia officers in Rio de Janeiro were found wearing miniature portraits of Dessalines around their necks in 1805.[15]

Haiti was a symbol of black power, and an inspiration for revolutionary action. After an attempted insurrection in February 1814 in the province of Bahia in Brazil, captives were overheard discussing plans for the next rebellion. In the words of terrified local merchants, 'they speak and know of the fatal success on the island of São Domingos [Haiti], and other rebellious speeches are heard, saying that by St John's day [23–24 June], there will be no whites or mulattos left alive'.[16] This kind of 'Makandalist' talk, aiming at the complete elimination of white settlers and their collaborators, highlighted the impact of Haiti on the political consciousness of the enslaved. This influence was confirmed two years later, when planters and merchants in São Francisco reported that the 'spirit of insurrection is seen among all types of slaves, and is fomented principally by the slaves of the city [Salvador], where the ideas of liberty have been communicated by black sailors coming from Saint-Domingue'.[17] This fear of Haitian revolutionary contagion was so pronounced in Brazil that it was given its own term, denoting (imaginary or real) expressions of social revolt involving free or enslaved black and mixed-race people: *haitianismo*.[18]

The martial reputation of the new Haitian rulers was heartily welcomed in Trinidad, where French-speaking captives were heard singing songs in honour of the revolution after the declaration of independence, including one with this engaging refrain: 'Pain nous ka mangé / C'est viande béké / Di in nous ka boué / C'est sang béké.'[19] This was mostly playful bluster, lampooning slaver stereotypes about African barbarity, but there was more. Here, as in Brazil and elsewhere in the Atlantic world, the victory of Dessalines gave challenges to slavery a more resolute character, and a comprehensively radical tone. The complete elimination of white settlers, as in Haiti, was now frequently acknowledged as the stated aim of rebels. In Jamaica, when a group of Africans revolted in St Mary's parish in 1809, it emerged during their trial that their objective was to 'rise and put all the Bukras [whites] in the sea, in the same fashion as the French negroes had done in their country'.[20] Haitians visited Jamaica in the early years after independence; they were frostily received by the authorities, who suspected them of being 'dangerous in character and disposition'.[21] Many of these visitors had participated actively in Saint-Domingue's emancipation and war of liberation. They were more than eager to share their revolutionary knowledge with their Jamaican brethren, and to encourage them to stand up for their rights or to escape to Haiti – as others were doing across the Atlantic.

We can glimpse the tenor of these conversations from the trial of the 1823 Boxing Day conspirators in Jamaica, discussed in the previous chapter. Alongside 'Obeah Jack', one of the plot's main organizers was Haitian-born Jean Baptiste Corberand, also known as Dimanche (Sunday). According to one of the witnesses, Corberand had come from Haiti on purpose to 'stir up the negroes'. He was a 'fine-looking tall young man', who wore a crucifix around his neck. He celebrated Haiti as a land of absolute freedom for black people, where 'every man did as he liked'.[22] He lectured the conspirators about the revolutionary war against the French, which he had not fought in, but clearly knew about from his family and from acquaintances. One of the points he specifically discussed was the ways resistance groups communicated by using African sound instruments such as conch shells.

There was considerable overlap between Haitian *vodou* and the Obeah rituals practised by the 1823 conspirators. As we have seen, one of the strengths of the Haitian revolution's appeal was this capacity to tap into African religious traditions among Atlantic captives. Corberand's messages to his Jamaican friends combined metaphysical and political themes. He told them they should not fear death, as their existence was part of a greater natural order that was guided by spirits. Evidently, like many nineteenth-century Haitians, he combined the Christian faith, as reflected in the cross he wore around his neck, with traditional African beliefs. Corberand added that Jamaicans should feel no remorse about eradicating the whites from their land. Many Haitians had lost their lives during the revolution, but they eventually got rid of the 'Bukras' (white settlers), and that was how they destroyed slavery in the end. If they wanted freedom in Jamaica 'the English negroes must do the same'.[23]

*

These Haitian-inspired episodes from different parts of the Atlantic high-lighted the intellectual dynamism and adaptability of the revolution in the years after 1804. In the imagination of both enslaved and free black people, Haiti stood for several general principles such as emancipation, territorial sovereignty, black empowerment, racial equality, and justice. But there was no single interpretation of what the Haitian revolution meant. Moreover, its appeal could coexist with contrasting ideals, rang-ing from African imperial power, European republican principles, South American emancipation from Spanish rule, and American-style constitu-tional government to the retention of links with the colonial metropole. These 'Haitian' motifs were amalgamated with a wide range of local beliefs, ideas, and cultural attitudes. Insurrections tended to occur when the Haitian revolution's general anti-slavery principles happened to com-bine, at the right moment, with favourable regional conditions as well as propitious factors. Rumours of external interventions, too, could play an important role in encouraging these confrontations.

One of the most fascinating examples of this mélange was the cap-tive revolt in Louisiana of 1811. This uprising took place in America's newest territory, acquired in 1803 from France. It began just outside New Orleans on the banks of the Mississippi river, in the parishes of St John the Baptist, St Charles, and Jefferson. The rebellion lasted only two days – between 8 and 10 January – and was brutally suppressed by local militias and federal forces. But with around five hundred participants (both men and women), a complex organization, and a dedicated leadership, it can be described as the largest insurrection of its kind in the United States to that date. The previous revolt on this scale in the United States was Gab-riel's attempt in Virginia in 1800, and it would be another decade before Denmark Vesey's planned insurrection in South Carolina. What unfolded in Louisiana was therefore not part of a connected pattern, but very much tied to specific events in the region. Key among these developments in the first decade of the nineteenth century was the sudden influx of Kongo cap-tives into Louisiana from South Carolina (which had resumed the import of enslaved Africans in 1803, after the ban imposed by Congress during the Revolutionary War). It is estimated that by 1811 more than half of the enslaved people in Louisiana had been born outside the territory.[24]

These captives originated from Africa as well as the Caribbean, and many came specifically from Saint-Domingue. They joined an underclass of Amerindians, maroons, outlaws, and political dissidents operating in the New Orleans area. In the years before 1811, planters reported inci-dents in which these recently imported enslaved people threatened white settlers; one group boasted that Louisiana settlers would suffer the same fate as those of the former French colony.[25] The governor of New Orleans, William Claiborne, repeatedly expressed fears that the territory would become 'another San Domingo'.[26] To this already explosive atmosphere were added a large cohort of some 9,000 French refugees who arrived in Louisiana in 1809, after being expelled from Cuba. This was their second exile, as they had initially come to Cuba as refugees from Saint-Domingue, and more than two-thirds of them were black or people of colour. These were mostly captives, with strong ties and affinities with their country's revolutionary past; as we shall later see in chapter 8, many were directly implicated in the wave of Cuban uprisings of the 1790s and early 1800s. A significant number of these Saint-Domingue-Cuban people ended up in the parishes where the 1811 insurrection was to be launched.[27]

There were thus multiple Saint-Domingue backdrops to the 1811 Louisiana revolt, and these connections can further be surmised from what we know about the insurgents. We have to make sense of their actions mostly by inference, as very few testimonies from the leading rebels have survived. Their leader was Charles Deslondes, a mixed-race slave driver from the Manuel André plantation, who was thought to have been born in Saint-Domingue. There were suggestions (but no solid evidence) that there were veterans of the Haitian war of independence among the rebels. Contemporary accounts of the insurgency suggest that Charles and a small group of plotters carefully organized the rebellion, and that they probably had connections both with maroon groups in the area and with fellow plotters in New Orleans. They began as a relatively compact group, increasing their numbers by rallying captives to their cause as they attacked a series of plantations. Their progression towards New Orleans was halted on 10 January when they were cut off by white forces. Among the reasons for their rapid military defeat was their failure to find the large cache of weapons they had hoped to seize from the Manuel André plantation.[28]

The composition and combat style of the insurgents combined the African and indigenous elements of warfare that were seen in the early moments of the 1791 revolt in Saint-Domingue. The insurgents were a coalition in the broadest possible sense: drivers and field slaves, African-born and creole, black and mixed-race, men and women. But just as in Saint-Domingue, it seems that the elite among the enslaved – like Charles – played a key role. The combatants were well-drilled and disciplined, with officers riding on horseback, instructing fighters who had clearly been given some kind of guerrilla training, which enabled them to advance swiftly and silently when necessary. However, at certain moments they also chanted war cries, and deployed flags and drums. All these elements, which probably included religious practices and rituals, are likely to have been drawn from Kongo war traditions.[29] The objectives of the insurgents in 1811 are difficult to reconstruct fully, and will never be known for certain. But as in Saint-Domingue, it was clear that this was a revolt against the institution of slavery itself: Jupiter, a Kongolese insurgent slave who was captured, testified at his trial that the rebellion's goal was to 'kill the whites'.[30]

What the rebels hoped to achieve once they reached New Orleans is unclear. Some claim that Charles had planned to link the plantation movement with anti-slavery dissidents in the city, overthrow the local white authorities, and proclaim general emancipation across the territory. Others believe that he wanted to create a sovereign state in Louisiana on the Haitian model.[31] There is the tantalizing suggestion that had this effort to capture New Orleans failed, the rebels' fall-back plan was to commandeer several vessels and set sail for Haiti.[32] We can further conjecture that if their plan had succeeded, this option of emigration to Haiti would have been made available to those who wished to take it up. In any event, we can be sure that as they surged through the Louisiana plantations dreaming of emancipation and racial equality, Charles and his comrades-in-arms had the land of liberty in their thoughts.

Meanwhile Haiti's internationalism was given a new impetus by Simón Bolívar's war of liberation against Spanish rule. After the collapse of the First Republic in Venezuela in 1812, Spanish republican patriots began to escape to Haiti, where they were given asylum, establishing small expatriate communities in the southern towns of Jacmel, Jérémie, and Les Cayes. The fall of Cartagena in 1815 brought a fresh wave of refugees, bringing the total number of republican exiles in Haiti to around 2,000; some were based in Port-au-Prince.

In December 1815 Bolívar arrived in Haiti, where he was warmly welcomed by President Pétion. The two men met in Port-au-Prince in early January 1816, shortly after the celebrations for Independence Day, and following further meetings and exchanges of letters the Haitian president agreed to provide Bolívar with material support to relaunch his campaign against the Spaniards. When Bolívar left Les Cayes in March 1816, he was equipped with 6,000 rifles with bayonets and ammunition, vessels, and a portable printing press. He was accompanied by a contingent of Haitian soldiers, sailors, and volunteers.[33] This first effort failed, and Bolívar was forced to head back to Haiti, this time to Jacmel, from where he initiated a further bid to reconquer Venezuela in December 1816. This second operation, which followed a different strategy of capturing hinterlands rather than coastal areas, was successful; it was materially supported by the Haitians as well. Bolívar went on fully to liberate Venezuela, as well as New Granada (Colombia and Panama) and Quito (Ecuador). The assistance of Pétion and Haitian volunteers was thus critical to securing the independence of Spanish-controlled territories in South America from colonial rule.[34]

Bolívar's brief stay in Haiti was materially as well as intellectually significant. His later project for the Bolivian constitution drew at least some of its rhetorical inspiration from Pétion's 1816 text, which Bolívar celebrated as laying the foundations for a 'sublime republican order' in which liberal principles were reconciled with strong leadership.[35] This was a somewhat optimistic reading, especially as Bolívar was obsessed that Haiti would inspire racial divisions within his own liberation movement, and in particular tensions between *criollo* whites and mixed-race and black people. He later spoke of the 'Africans of Haiti, whose power is stronger than primeval fire'.[36] In 1817 he executed one of his senior mixed-race commanders, General Manuel Piar, who had been in exile with him in Haiti, on trumped-up charges of wishing to eliminate whites and create a black and mixed-race republic in South America. The news was greeted with sadness in southern Haiti, where Piar was known for his 'Haitian heart' – which no doubt contributed to his fall from grace in the eyes of the Liberator.[37]

More significant for our purposes is what Bolívar's exchanges with Pétion in 1816 reveal about Haitian black internationalism at this juncture. When Pétion agreed to provide Haitian military assistance to Bolívar, the Haitian president was in a position of relative strength, and asked the Liberator for two commitments in return. The first, which is widely known and commented on, was the abolition of slavery, which Bolívar agreed to (but he backtracked quickly, and the 1819 Angostura Congress that appointed him president made no mention of abolition). The second pledge was that any Africans taken from slave-trading vessels by insurgent republican privateers would be turned over to the Haitian government; Bolívar made a commitment to do so.[38]

It is not known whether Bolívar honoured this second part of the agreement, but in any event Pétion's insistence on its inclusion demonstrates the Haitian state's ongoing dedication to supporting emancipation and liberating Africans from the slave trade. This black internationalism reverberated across the Atlantic and beyond, and further boosted the virtuous reputation of the Haitian revolution. This was shown by the appeal addressed to the 'illustrious and generous' Haitian people by a committee of Greek republican patriots based in Paris in 1821, a few months after the start of the Greek war of independence. Written at the suggestion of Henri Grégoire, the revolutionary cleric and abolitionist who was France's most dedicated promoter of the Haitian cause (see Plate 14), the letter pleaded for Haitian military support against the Ottomans: the request was for 30,000 guns as well as a battalion of 'brave Haitian soldiers', whose arrival on Greek soil would 'terrify' the enemy.[39] In the same year a former Jacobin pamphleteer publicly urged the French king to embrace the Haitian nation, not least because of its 'formidable citizen army'.[40]

A conspiracy uncovered in Charleston, South Carolina, in the summer of 1822 shared some similarities with the Louisiana revolt. It was a sophisticated scheme, conceived by a group of free black people and captives from different African backgrounds, and combining Christian and traditional African beliefs. It occurred in a state that was heavily dependent on slave labour, and as we saw had reopened the African slave trade in 1803, provoking significant strains on its social fabric. One major difference, however, was the primary site of the conspiracy. Whereas the Louisiana revolt was plantation-based, the South Carolina plot was conceived and planned to be executed in a city (although with the hope of additional rural reinforcements) – and indeed in an area with a sizeable black majority. In 1820 the Charleston district had around 19,000 whites, 3,500 free black persons, and 57,000 enslaved people, most of them recently brought over from Africa by force.[41]

While urban black captives still faced harsh conditions, they were comparatively freer, and had more opportunities to move, think, and congregate than those on the plantations. Moreover, there was an established black revolutionary tradition in Charleston from the 1790s, inspired by the events in Saint-Domingue: it was therefore an ideal cocoon for the propagation of Haitian revolutionary internationalism. Charleston had multiple historical connections with the French colony, from 1791 all the way through to Haitian independence and beyond. In 1793 several thousand French settlers found refuge there, after the destruction of Cap-Français, and whites lived in general fear of a repeat of such 'horrors', while black populations kept a keen eye on developments across the Caribbean sea, hoping that they could repeat the emancipation achieved by their brothers.[42] As we shall see, Haiti was a powerful, active, and recurring presence in the minds of the plot's principal leaders.

As with Louisiana in 1811, there are many elements of the Charleston conspiracy that remain unknown. Still, its general outline is clear: the plan was to launch an insurrection in the city, in which the rebels, divided into six attack groups and armed with pike heads and bayonets specifically designed by local blacksmiths, would set fire to various strategic positions across the city. They were to break into local arsenals, rob some banks, and, after the arrival of rural support from the plantations (one of the organizers hoped the rebels would number several thousand), move to the waterfront and execute a mass escape to Haiti. Unfortunately, in mid-June two captives betrayed the scheme to the authorities, who immediately carried out a wave of arrests: 131 men were taken into custody. The ensuing trials, which lasted five weeks, provide much of the source material for understanding the Charleston conspiracy. In their aftermath thirty-five men were sentenced to death, among them the main leaders of the conspiracy: Monday Gell, an Igbo harness-maker; Gullah Jack Pritchard, a diviner and priest of Angolan origin; Peter Poyas, a skilled ship's carpenter; Rolla Bennett, the manservant of the governor Thomas Bennett; along with the man described in the official judicial report as 'the author and original instigator of this diabolical plot': Denmark Vesey.[43]

Along with Nat Turner, who will appear in a later chapter, Vesey is one of the most striking anti-slavery figures in American history. Little is known about his early years. He is thought to have been born on the island of Saint Thomas around 1767, although there are suggestions he may have been a native of the Gold Coast. He was bought as a young child by Joseph Vesey, a sea captain and slave merchant, who named him Telemaque. He worked as his assistant and eventually accompanied Vesey when he settled in Charleston in the early 1780s. The young man became literate and in the course of his work for Vesey learnt Danish *kreyol* and French. In 1799 Telemaque won a $1,500 lottery, which enabled him to buy his freedom; he paid Vesey $600 and used the rest of the funds to open a carpentry shop, taking the name Denmark Vesey. He established himself as an authoritative figure in the Charleston black community, with connections to all the principal African ethnic groups (Akan, Igbo, Gullah, Gambian, 'French' from Saint-Domingue, as well as American-born).[44]

In 1818, frustrated with the resentful attitude of Presbyterians towards their black members, Denmark Vesey helped found an independent African Methodist congregation. This 'African church', in which Vesey was a lay preacher, was systematically attacked both verbally and in action by the white authorities from its inception. In one incident, the city guard detained 469 black congregants of the new church. Although his business was successful, Vesey's personal life as a free black person was intensely frustrating, as his first wife Beck and second spouse Dolly remained enslaved,[45] and therefore so were his children. He began planning the Charleston uprising several years before 1822, using his contacts with the enslaved as well as his commercial and religious networks to build support for a collective uprising against slavery. He held meetings at his house, some under cover of night classes, and at various other places in and outside the city. In the final months he gave up his job to devote himself fully to enlisting recruits.[46]

Vesey's revolutionary views were profoundly shaped by his Christian faith, and in his sermons he often quoted passages from Scripture. His religious thought was long believed to have been based on the Old Testament, but in fact he did not exalt any one part of the Bible over another, and indeed the African church had forged a flexible religious doctrine based on both Christian and west African values.[47] This inclusiveness was further enhanced by Gullah Jack, a close friend of Vesey and one of the principal co-conspirators. Jack was an African-born healer who was widely known in Charleston's black communities, and he played an invaluable role in appealing to fellow Africans. Like the Obeah priests we encountered earlier, he used magical rituals for divination and protection purposes. Among the objects he supplied recruits to the rebellion were crab claws, which he assured them would heighten their courage, and prepare them for their flight across water.[48] Gullah Jack's magical talismans would make the insurgents invincible, like him: hence his reputation as 'the little man who can't be killed, shot, or taken'.[49]

Denmark Vesey's revolutionary vision was not nourished only by his Christian faith. The Haitian revolution played an equally important role in shaping his political thought, as well as his specific plans for the 1822 insurrection. His own connections with Saint-Domingue were multiple. He was enslaved there for a year, in the early 1780s, and Joseph Vesey had conducted extensive business with the French colony, and he received French settlers (and, after 1791, émigrés) at his house in Charleston. They would have discussed the 'horrors of St Domingo', and Denmark (or Telemaque as he was at the time) would have listened in, no doubt drawing his own conclusions. The black revolution was extensively covered in the Charleston press, and in 1797 the *City Gazette* published one of Toussaint Louverture's speeches to his troops, as the war against British occupation reached its climax. The commander-in-chief's address was replete with religious references and framed the conflict with the British as a war against human bondage: 'O Lord who are infinitely amiable, and who lovest us infinitely, suffer not that we should live in ignorance and slavery.'[50] We do not know that Telemaque read this speech, but information about Saint-Domingue's revolution was widely available in Charleston in the late eighteenth century. It is very likely that his fascination with the Haitian revolution, and his belief that anti-slavery and Christianity should be combined, were shaped by Louverture's distinct blend of republicanism and Catholicism.

Denmark Vesey discussed Saint-Domingue and Haiti with his comrades throughout the preparatory phase of the insurgency. Among the captives he recruited were a group of several hundred 'French' black people who were brought to Charleston from Saint-Domingue in the 1790s.[51] They were mostly to be found on plantations north of the city, along the Santee river, in an area known as the 'French Santee'.[52] He read out passages from newspapers and pamphlets about the Haitian revolutionary fight against slavery, as well as contemporary articles about Haiti (for example, President Boyer's successful expulsion of the Spaniards from Santo Domingo in February 1822).[53] For many of the African-born captives, this must have been their first encounter with the Haitian revolution, although many Africans already had extensive experience of warfare. Vesey made sure he gave his recruits a thorough revolutionary induction. When he needed to provide them with an example of steadfastness, he invariably picked Haiti: 'we must unite together as the people of St Domingo'.[54] He helped them imagine something that would have seemed inconceivable to most: black people coming together to confront American slavers and overpowering them. He often stressed the 'exceptional' Haitian example in this respect, as they had decided to 'turn and fight the white people'.[55] This struggle had to be comprehensive: he insisted that it was important 'not to spare one white skin alive', emulating what the Haitians had done at the end of their war of independence. Vesey clearly approved of Dessalines' extermination of the French settlers in 1804.[56]

In order further to bolster the spirits of the rebels, Vesey followed many other Atlantic slave insurgents in holding up the promise that military support would be forthcoming from Haiti. At one gathering he told his listeners that 'a large army from St Domingo and Africa were coming to help us, and we must not stand with our hands in our pockets'.[57] It is important that he mentioned an African army, as this image would have made sense to many of the African-born rebels he was appealing to. Indeed, his planned insurgency effected a remarkable fusion of different African groups.[58] There was no such promise of military support from Haiti, as far as is known, but Vesey did write at least two letters to President Boyer detailing the sufferings of black people in the United States, and requesting assistance from his government.[59] This may seem naive, except that Boyer's predecessor and protector Pétion had helped Bolívar a few years earlier, as we saw. It was not unreasonable for Vesey to think that Haiti might consider supporting an insurrection against slavery – especially one led by black people against a white community that had enslaved so many men and women from Saint-Domingue in the past.

Haiti was thus an integral element of the 1822 Charleston conspiracy, while serving as the final projected destination of the rebels – a plan that should be seen in the wider context of Haitian efforts to appeal to African Americans to emigrate there. Haitian authorities promised not only a warm welcome but access to farmland and citizenship; the latter had been formalized in Pétion's 1816 Constitution. There was considerable discussion of the merits of Haiti in the American progressive press in the early 1820s. An article in the *Columbian Sentinel* described it as the best place for 'emancipated people of colour ... active and brave men, determined to live free, or die gloriously in the defense of freedom'.[60] Denmark Vesey was already notionally 'free', as he had gained his emancipation two decades earlier – but this liberty was heavily circumscribed by the racial and religious discrimination that black communities faced, and by his own inability to protect his children from slavery. Unlike many African-American abolitionists, and no doubt because he was a black internationalist, Vesey seemed to have no interest in transforming the United States from within. Rather, he sought to find a home in a country where slavery had been irrevocably abolished, and where all citizens were defined as black people, wherever they came from. For him, that was the ultimate land of liberty.

One of the longest maroon rebellions took place on the island of Dominica. Sandwiched between the French islands of Martinique and Guadeloupe, Dominica was a contested terrain for Anglo-French rivalry during the second half of the eighteenth century, until the British eventually consolidated their position in the early 1780s. They considerably increased the import of African enslaved people in order to expand sugar production, with nearly two-thirds originating from the Bight of Biafra. Marronage immediately became widespread, with runaway settlements established in the island's mountainous and wooded interior (two-thirds of Dominica was covered in rainforests). These areas of self-emancipation followed the classic pattern, with small villages typically perched on high ground, surrounded by pits, pickets, and pikes, their inhabitants living in well-organized communities, and carrying out regular raids on coastal settler plantations.[61]

In 1784–5 an already tense situation was exacerbated by the introduction of an additional 5,000 African captives to the island, leading to the First Maroon War, in which several hundred runaways fought the British. The maroons were divided into separate combat groups, each with their own commanders. One of the most charismatic figures was Balla, a Mandinka prince forcibly brought to Dominica in the 1760s. Balla became a military and spiritual leader of his community. Much like Makandal, he was brought up in the Islamic faith but developed rituals that appealed to a range of west African religious traditions, and he himself practised Obeah. Among the tokens he carried with him was a lock of hair taken from a settler he had killed, after torching his plantation, and he declared that his stated goal was to expel the 'British dogs' from the island. His campaign for emancipation ended only when he was captured and executed in 1786.[62]

Prince Balla left his mark: the maroons intensified their struggles in the following decades, challenging the British with a further insurrection in January 1791, a few months before the massive uprising in Saint-Domingue. Under the leadership of a captive named Pharcelle they planned to overthrow the plantation system and 'kill all the white people'. They spurned efforts by the French revolutionary envoy Victor Hugues to enlist them on their side in the mid-1790s, as they understood that the French were merely looking for local allies in their fight against the British, and were not fully committed to racial equality (as we will see, they were right to be suspicious).[63] The first of many Dominican bans against the practice of Obeah was enacted in 1788. It was singled out for promoting 'mutiny and rebellion', as well as for administering poison to both slaves and free black people.[64]

The intensification of the conflict between the British and the maroons of Dominica was partly driven by the presence of a large contingent of Igbo captives, who were strongly predisposed towards marronage. The Igbos had no internal tradition of slavery in their African homelands, and preferred organizing themselves in small-scale societies without strong individual rulers. They were particularly close to nature and many of their spiritual beliefs were associated with water: Dominica's 365 rivers and streams provided them with an ideal habitat.[65] The Igbos were known as the 'flying Africans', as they believed in the transmigration of the soul after death. This made them more likely not only to engage in resistance but also to risk extreme physical danger, as they did not believe that death ended their lives.[66]

These Igbo values shaped the collective outlook of Dominican fugitives, particularly their independent spirit and refusal to compromise. The Igbo maroons began to forge an alliance with plantation captives, some of whom deserted their farms while others brought a regular supply of provisions and weaponry to the fugitives. By the end of the first decade of the nineteenth century, the number of maroons had doubled, and their systematic degradation of the plantation system had severely damaged the economy, with many whites fleeing the island.[67] The British authorities were forced to commit thousands of pounds to raising a militia, and to launch a second war against the fugitives. They eventually won this 'war of extermination' in 1814, after hunting down the maroons in their remote encampments. The main leaders of the movement, such as Elephant, Moco, Gabriel, Quashie, and the veteran Jacko, who had been in the bush for forty years, were all captured by this militia and either killed or deported.[68] Among those executed were two women, Vieille Ebo and Zabet, who were accused of being fugitives for over ten years, and of practising Obeah.[69]

The revolts in Dominica shared many of the characteristics of the early Haitian revolution: a significant presence of African-born captives, an emphatic rejection of white settlers who kept them in bondage, a complex military and political organization, a vocation for freedom based on composite spiritual beliefs, and a courageous disposition expressed either in maroon-style guerrilla tactics or in plantation-based revolts – and eventually a combination of both. There is no direct evidence that the events in Saint-Domingue and Haiti shaped the Dominican revolts, but these connections are easy to see. The final wave of maroon revolts in Dominica in the first decade of the nineteenth century coincided with the immediate aftermath of the Haitian war of independence, which had provoked a general rise in expressions of enslaved rebelliousness across the Atlantic. In fact, there were violent clashes between Dominican maroons and the British in 1808, and again in 1810. The ideology of the maroons became further entrenched as one of implacable opposition to any accommodation with the British and to the very notion of white rule; attempts to broker a Jamaican-style agreement were rejected by the maroons.[70]

To make the same point in 'Haitian' terms, the Dominican maroons were Makandalist, but not Dessalinist. They cherished their autonomy but wanted to be free and self-sufficient, and they had no interest in holding power in a centralized state. (This African-originating tradition of self-governance echoed an important minority strand within the Haitian revolutionary movement, embodied by Macaya; it was contained by Louverture and eventually defeated by Dessalines.) At the same time, the ideas of Dominican maroons about slavery and emancipation, their spiritual beliefs, and their absolute distrust of white settlers were very much in harmony with what became the dominant Haitian revolutionary tradition. The connection was made by the British governor of Dominica in December 1791, shortly after the launch of the insurrection in Saint-Domingue, as he expressed his concern about the revolt's potential impact on the island. He warned against the arrival of 'vagrant and disorderly persons and slaves' or any 'improper communication' between Antillean revolutionaries and the local captive populations.[71]

As elsewhere in the Caribbean, the ideas, stories, and myths about

Haitian revolutionary achievements undoubtedly found their way to Dominica. There were extensive maritime connections operating both ways between the island and the upper Antilles. A succession of enslaved people found refuge on Dominica by canoe from nearby islands, or took flight from Dominica to these destinations when circumstances were more propitious. The maroon leader Pharcelle was known to be a regular visitor.[72] More significantly, the Dominican harbours of Roseau and Portsmouth operated as free ports, welcoming ships of all nations. As from the late eighteenth century, these coastal towns received contingents of black sailors from the Antilles and from North America, bringing news of the Saint-Domingue revolution and the Haitian war of independence.[73] After 1804 many of these sailors would have been Haitian, and they would have shared information and updates about the latest developments in the land of liberty. We can imagine that the rebel captives of Dominica had heard about Dessalines' motto, which effectively became their own: better death than enslavement.

As the maroon war in Dominica was reaching its end, an intense – if short-lived – captive revolt was brewing in another nearby sugar-producing British colony: Barbados. On 14 April 1816 – Easter Sunday – an enslaved uprising began in the southeastern parish of St Philip, spreading to the southern and central regions. More than half of the island was rapidly engulfed in the rebellion. The plan of rebel combatants, who numbered around 4,000, was to launch an initial wave of arson attacks, setting the stage for a confrontation with the authorities and the creation of a revolutionary government that was committed to general emancipation. The insurgents managed to cause extensive damage to plantations and properties, estimated at £175,000; a quarter of the sugar crop was destroyed. A rapid intervention of the local militia and imperial forces stationed on the island prevented the uprising from spreading further, and the rebellion was suppressed within four days, with around a thousand insurgents either killed in battle or executed after trial. This was the only major insurgency of its kind in Barbados – but it expressed a radical rejection of enslavement. According to the local British military commander, the rebels believed that 'the island belonged to them and not to the white men whom they proposed to destroy'.[74]

Again, there were parallels as well as contrasts with the early phases of the Haitian revolution. As in Saint-Domingue in early 1791, the organizers of the Barbados uprising were mostly from the enslaved elite (drivers, artisans, and domestics) and a number were literate. There was a considerable rise in marronage in the years preceding the 1816 uprising, and the bulk of these fugitives were part of the captive elite.[75] The organizers of the revolt worked collectively, and across the southern and central parishes they formed a co-ordinating network that met regularly and established detailed action plans to collect weapons, recruit support from among plantation slaves, identify potential targets, and form a government. In a striking echo of the beginning of the Saint-Domingue 1791 uprising, the final meeting convened two days before the insurgency, on 12 April, was held under cover of a social gathering. Both the planters and authorities had no suspicions and were taken by complete surprise by the revolt.[76] As in Saint-Domingue, women were active in the movement, and many were executed. A prominent Barbadian planter believed they were at the forefront of the insurrection; a few days before the uprising an enslaved woman abused him verbally and told him that he and his kind 'would have it'.[77]

Differences were notable as well. Whereas the majority of the Saint-Domingue captives were African-born, in Barbados (which had been under British control for 189 years) over 90 per cent of the enslaved population was creole.[78] Given this preponderance, the rebel commanders were almost entirely drawn from the black creole population, but with some important exceptions. The spreading of insurrectionist propaganda was entrusted to three free literate men of colour: Cain Davis, Roach, and Richard Sarjeant. Davis reportedly told enslaved audiences, whom he addressed on Saturdays, that if they wanted freedom they 'must fight for it'.[79] The post of governor in the future revolutionary government was to be entrusted to Joseph Pitt Washington Francklyn, a free person of colour who was the illegitimate son of a small planter and Justice of the Peace in the Saint Philip parish.[80]

The only African-born figure among the rebel leaders was Bussa, the head ranger (slave driver) at the Bayleys plantation in Saint Philip, one of the epicentres of the uprising. Little is known for certain about his precise origins, but he probably hailed from the Bussa nation, a faction of the Mande people who were known for their trading and administrative skills.[81] Although his age is unclear, it seems he was in his late fifties at the time of rebellion, and had been on the Bayleys plantation since childhood.[82] There has been much debate in Barbados about the respective roles of Francklyn and Bussa. The latter has emerged in national memory as the revolt's principal leader, although this view does not follow clearly from the judicial testimonies of other captives (Bussa was killed during the fighting, so none of his own utterances have survived). It is reasonable to conclude that both men were significant figures – Francklyn on the political side and Bussa on the military.[83]

The role of religion in the Barbados uprising was long dismissed, and indeed its leading historian has claimed that 1816 was 'essentially a secular rebellion'.[84] If correct, this would be another contrast with Saint-Domingue, where there were powerful religious underpinnings to the 1791 insurrection. But there are grounds for revisiting this interpretation. Obeah was widespread in early nineteenth-century Barbados, so much so that there was an Obeah-man on almost every estate.[85] Bussa was African-born, and one of the principal leaders of the 1816 uprising; in all similar revolts of this kind, traditional African beliefs and religious rituals featured prominently. It would be hard to understand why Barbados would be an exception. Indeed, there are references in the Barbados Assembly report on the uprising to regular social gatherings held by captives in preparation for the insurrection, and Bussa was specifically seen dancing with several other rebel leaders on Good Friday, just a few days before the insurrection. These sorts of events (as in Saint-Domingue in August 1791) provided an ideal cover for spiritual ceremonies.[86] Even though Barbadian captive society was creolized by the early nineteenth century, Obeah beliefs and rituals survived and prospered on the island. As we saw in chapter 3, one of Obeah's essential characteristics was its capacity to reproduce itself across generations. Evidence of the significant role of Obeah in 1816 can be further deduced from the fact that two years later, in 1818, the Barbadian authorities amended existing anti-Obeah laws to deal with its potential as a 'force for insurrection'.[87]

Settlers in Barbados were not interested in publicly exploring the domestic sources of the revolt. It was more politically expedient for them to pin the blame on British abolitionists in London, who in 1815 introduced a Bill in the Commons requiring the registration of all captives in British colonies; this legislation was intended to prevent the illegal import of Africans. The local Barbados Assembly had discussed and rejected the Bill in November 1815. However, there was a widespread belief among local whites that the proposed legislation had both raised expectations among the enslaved and been deliberately misrepresented by rebel leaders in Barbados as a law to abolish human bondage. Cain Davis allegedly stated that 'the Queen and Mr Wilberforce had sent out to have [all the captives] freed, but that the Inhabitants of the island were against it'.[88] Another version of this rumour was that the Queen was a black woman.[89] A flag from the 1816 rebellion depicts the monarch approving the insurrection, and the British withdrawing from the island; emancipated black people are shown wielding social authority and political power. (See Plate 11.) These sorts of stories may indeed have been a factor in prompting the revolt, although they would not explain why Barbadian captives alone rebelled, despite not being the only ones affected by the 1815 legislation.[90] The strongest underlying reason for the rebellion was their widespread desire to overthrow the plantation system, and gain their freedom. In September 1816 a second revolt was planned by another group of elite captives; it too sought to secure general emancipation and, according to a local British officer, make the liberated black people the 'masters of the island'.[91]

The spirit of the Haitian revolution loomed above the Barbados slave revolt, as a menace as well as an inspiration. For white settlers and British troops on the island, Haiti was a constant negative reference, characteristically described as the 'horrors of St Domingo', and invariably invoked to illustrate the perils of abolitionism. More concretely, it was a grim reminder of what would happen to them if the revolution were to succeed. For the captives, in contrast, Haiti was associated with power, military might, and freedom. As with many other Atlantic rebellions, there were rumours that the Haitian army would come to the assistance of the rebels. In one military encounter at the Bayleys plantation, the insurgents were faced with a black British regiment, and seemed to have thought for a moment that these Haitian reinforcements had arrived.[92] Probably planted by the rebel organizers, the rumour reached the white settlers too: articles appeared in the local Barbadian press at the time of the uprising mentioning the sighting of Haitian ships 'steering towards Barbados'.[93]

But Haiti's overriding image was as a symbol of black empowerment. One of the woman organizers, Nanny Grigg, spoke to her fellow conspirators about the necessity of standing up for their freedom, 'otherwise they would not get it'; the only way to do so was 'to set fire, as that was the way they did it in Saint Domingo'.[94] The justification for the elimination of white settlers, too, came through the Haitian example. When another slave, James Bowland, was informed by the organizers of the rebellion that they were being denied their liberty by the Barbadian whites, he was told they had to fight for it 'in the same way that they had done at Saint Domingo'.[95] Haiti's magical aura appealed to the imagination. Cuffee Ned, another 1816 rebel, knew that there was a place in the West Indies where those held in bondage had broken their chains. He could not remember the exact name of this land of liberty but gave it his own, evocative shorthand: *Mingo*.[96]

Seven years after the Barbados uprising, a revolt erupted in Demerara, another British sugar-producing colony. The Dutch, French, and British vied for possession of this territory on the northern coast of South America, which changed hands six times between 1760 and 1803, at which

point the British finally secured control. Approximately 20,000 additional
African captives were brought into the colony in the years before the abolition of the slave trade in 1807; just over half of the enslaved population
were African-born at the time of the rebellion.[97] Demerara's uprising is
often mentioned as the second in the trilogy of insurrections that preceded
the abolition of slavery in Britain, starting with Barbados in 1816 and
ending with the Great Revolt of 1831–2 in Jamaica.[98]

The Demerara revolt of August 1823 shared certain similarities with
events in Barbados: the rebels were plantation-based on the colony's eastern coast. There had been plans to involve the western plantations, as
well as captives in urban areas, but they did not materialize; the maroon
communities in Demerara were not associated with the movement. The
uprising lasted only two days before being brutally suppressed. As in Barbados, the ensuing repression was fierce and went on for several months,
and fifty-one death sentences were handed out. The revolt took place
against a backdrop of enhanced abolitionist activity in London, which
exacerbated local settler opposition to any change to the slave regime.
There were similar rumours of emancipation having been granted by the
monarch but being withheld by the planters and governor. This time,
these rumours were based on discrete ameliorations to the conditions of
the enslaved, which had been agreed by the British government in May
1823: for example, women could no longer be flogged, nor the whip used
in the fields. Instructions to this effect reached Demerara in July, but the
local governor, John Murray, did not make them public, triggering an
escalation of rumours among the captives, some of whom decided to
challenge the authorities by force. The plans for the insurrection were
finalized on Sunday 17 August – one day before the start of the uprising.[99]
As with Bussa, the principal leader of the Demerara revolt, Quamina, was
a Coromantee; he was an African-born skilled artisan, highly respected
among enslaved communities.

But differences with Barbados were significant too. One of the main
figures associated with the rebels was a white British missionary, John
Smith, who had arrived in Demerara a few years earlier to head the Bethel
Chapel at 'Le Resouvenir' plantation. Sent to promote literacy and Christian beliefs among captives, Smith became an ardent defender of their
interests in Demerara, and these men and women flocked to his services
whenever they could and even though they were physically punished for
doing so. At times his chapel had five to six hundred attendees. Smith had
appointed Quamina as one of his deacons in 1817. Both men were accused
of instigating the 1823 rebellion, and it was claimed that the insurgency
was planned in the Bethel Chapel. They were sentenced to death; Smith

died in prison while Quamina was shot and killed in September after refusing to surrender. The Christian dimension of the insurrection was not the only difference with Barbados. The arson and damage to property was much more limited in Demerara, and the violence against settlers was largely confined to using whips and putting them in stocks. Only a handful of whites were killed and most captives opposed violence against the white planters and managers.[100] There was no alternative government-in-waiting, either, although one rebel later testified that if the rebellion had succeeded, Quamina would have been crowned 'king', and his son Jack (another leading figure in the revolt) governor. Hostile testimony used at the trials, and clearly intended to incriminate the pastor, claimed that Smith was to become the 'emperor'.[101]

A further contrast with Barbados was the degree of unity among rebels about objectives and methods. Quamina was widely respected as a calm and measured person, a 'man of reason', whereas his son Jack was described as clever, charismatic, and strong-willed – a 'man of passion'.[102] Jack clashed with his father before the insurrection, calling him 'an old fool', and urging the captives to 'hold a council about taking hold of the white people'. Quamina, for his part, seems to have tried his best to stop or at least delay the uprising, until the announcements from Britain could be made public. These temperamental differences, and other evidence from the behaviour of the rebels before and during the insurrection, indicate that there were varying opinions among the plotters, first about the desirability of the insurrection itself (at least one mentioned what had happened in Barbados), and then about what they should be trying to achieve if they acted to claim their rights. Some pushed for modest goals, such as an increase in the number of rest days, whereas others wanted immediate and general emancipation.[103] This was not necessarily an absolute fracture, and could simply have been a difference between tactics and strategy. Very similar divisions existed in the early moments of the 1791 revolt in Saint-Domingue between the leadership and the rank and file, but they did not prevent the insurgents from eventually securing emancipation in the end. But these conversations highlight a point often overlooked in the rush to categorize the political beliefs and values of the enslaved: these were not homogeneous, and they accommodated a range of diverse and sophisticated views.

There were further layers to this complexity. The story of the Demerara revolt is generally viewed through the prism of Pastor Smith and his valiant attempts to spread Christianity among the enslaved (he became a martyr for the abolitionist cause in Britain). However, the majority of the bonded people – including the men and women who came to his chapel – were immersed in a material and religious culture that remained profoundly African. How this world view shaped the rebellion is hard to pin down precisely, but all the evidence we have accumulated so far about Atlantic slave revolts with significant African-born captive participation indicates that it was likely to have been a major contributory factor. Many of those accused of conspiracy in Demerara were Coromantee or had Coromantee names, like Quamina himself. But the list of men arrested and executed for participation in the rebellion included Quashie, Quamine, Cudjoe, Quabino, Quacow, Quaw, and Cuffee – all common names in the Gold Coast.[104]

This Akan dimension has not been much explored in connection with the Demerara revolt, except as a source of the social bonds that may have brought these men and women together in the first instance. In addition to kinship, there would have been political elements as well: as we saw in chapter 3, Akan-speaking captives had a long tradition of fighting enslavement in the New World. It is likely that Akan beliefs and rituals featured in the planning of the Demerara insurrection, and perhaps shaped the outlook of the more radical elements among the conspirators – for instance by encouraging them not to depend for their salvation on the actions of white men; pride and self-reliance were key Akan values.[105]

We can further speculate that many of the active plotters subverted the framework provided by John Smith's Bethel Chapel to organize the rebellion. The Christian Church effectively became a conduit for secret-society revolutionary activity, in the same way as social gatherings such as dances or funerals. This hypothesis gathers even more force if we remember that Obeah was widely practised in Demerara in the early nineteenth century, and was a lived spiritual and cultural practice among enslaved people in the British and Dutch Caribbean, and in Martinique, in the 1820s. None of these Obeah activities – whether for healing, divination or conspiracy – would have been picked up or understood by Pastor Smith, as the enslaved would have known that Christian missionaries were contemptuous of such practices. In fact, hostility to the 'superstitions' of Obeah was fully shared by both slavers and Christian missionaries.[106]

The black internationalism that emerged through and in the aftermath of the Haitian revolution was remarkable. It took shape around the events in Saint-Domingue in the 1790s, and then in the constitution of the Haitian state, the world's first black postcolonial political community. Its key characteristics were its dedication to emancipation and racial equality, open and inclusive citizenship, cosmopolitanism and willingness to grant asylum to refugees of all descriptions, and a brief but decisive intervention in Simón Bolívar's war of liberation against Spanish colonialism. Even the divisions within the Haitian body politic in the years after independence, with the separation of the country into Henri Christophe's northern kingdom and Alexandre Pétion's southern republic, arguably enhanced Haiti's aura. These fractures enabled its appeal to cut across royalist and republican sensibilities among black and mixed-race communities, and even play to both.

But what made this black internationalism so potent was that it was sustained by ordinary men and women across the Atlantic. It came alive in the words, deeds, thoughts, and imaginings of enslaved and free black and mixed-race people, who helped disseminate a collective body of knowledge – we could call it a popular encyclopaedia – about the Haitian revolution as well as insurrections by captives in other areas. Its material culture was not extensive[107] and so information circulated mostly by word of mouth, within families, networks, and communities, and through travellers, sailors, dock workers, soldiers, and artisans. It was an oral and visual rather than a written tradition, embedded in songs, music, images, and artefacts, and stories, tales, and myths about the revolution's heroic leaders and the achievements of the Haitian people. It was in this spirit, for example, that the African-American composer Francis Johnson wrote a 'Recognition March of the Independence of Hayti' in 1820, dedicated to President Boyer.[108]

When captives chose to rebel against their oppressors, a similar repertoire was activated and often played a defining role in the thinking of insurgent leaders – and, for some, the choice of their final destination. All the rebellions had Haitian-style general emancipation as their primary goal, although how this liberty was to be achieved could vary considerably, depending on circumstances as well as local preferences: the options included self-emancipation (Dominica), coercing colonial authorities into granting freedom (Demerara), capturing sovereign power (Louisiana), breaking free from colonial rule and creating a state on the Haitian model (Barbados), and taking flight to the Haitian land of liberty (Virginia). We saw that many individual and collective migrations to Haiti took place in the post-independence decades.

These struggles for emancipation had the Haitian revolution at their core: in some cases as a direct inspiration for action, and in others by providing a loose framework (as with 'Mingo') for imagining a different possible world, in which black people were autonomous and ruled themselves without the interference of overlords. The example of Nanny Grigg suggests that women felt empowered by what they heard about the Haitian achievements. Also significant were the revolutionary contributions of the Saint-Domingue/Haitian diaspora, as shown in the examples of Charles Deslondes in Louisiana, Corberand in Jamaica, and the cohort of black 'French from Saint-Domingue' revolutionaries recruited by Denmark Vesey in Virginia.

This spontaneous, popular black internationalism helps explain why the Saint-Domingue revolution was so terrifying to the slavers, and accounts for the uniformly heavy-handed and brutal way in which the plots and rebellions we have described were handled by the authorities. Military violence was disproportionately used in the conflicts, especially in the early moments of the Demerara uprising, when the movement was still largely peaceful and the leaders seemed to be opting for non-violent strike action, and many of the rebels were actively protecting white settlers from violence.[109] After the rebellion was suppressed, British officers carried out summary executions of 'ringleaders' in several plantations, often killing slaves who had barely participated in the events, and epitomizing the dismal tradition of British colonial overreaction, which stretched well into the twentieth century. The purpose here was 'terror not justice'.[110]

This was not an isolated case: goaded by fearful white settlers, authorities everywhere responded in extreme ways, as shown by the executions of captives who did not participate in the rebellions, as well as large numbers of fugitive men, women, and even children. Coercion and torture were systematically used during the interrogation of rebels in Virginia, Barbados, and Demerara, in the last case to fabricate incriminating evidence against Pastor Smith and the Bethel Chapel. Martial law was imposed for several months in Barbados and Demerara, while in South Carolina a law was passed requiring black sailors to be incarcerated while their ships docked in Charleston harbour. Symbolic of this slaver brutality was the fate of most rebel leaders. In Louisiana, in addition to the dozens of rebels killed in combat, the captured leaders were executed and decapitated, and their heads placed on poles above and below New Orleans, and all the way up the Mississippi to the plantation where the insurrection began.[111] Similar gruesome displays of heads occurred in Barbados and Demerara. Many of the Dominica maroons were killed, and those who were executed after trial suffered the same fate as the other rebels: their heads were cut off and exposed on poles at various places on the island.[112]

Extreme settler violence did not deter the enslaved in previous centuries, and failed to break their resolve at this point. In fact, from a broader perspective, we can now better appreciate the enduring nature of resistance in the history of Atlantic slavery, and Haiti's place in the pattern of Atlantic revolutions. Historians have conventionally distinguished two types of captive revolt: 'reconstructionist' rebellions, in which slaves were thought to be essentially seeking to recreate their African traditions, and modern insurrections, driven by general ideas about freedom, introduced by the Enlightenment and the revolutions of the late eighteenth century.[113] By presenting the events in Saint-Domingue as derivative of European and American ideas, this distinction was long used to minimize the impact of the Haitian revolution. However, even with the greater recognition that Haiti now enjoys as one of the main pillars of the Age of Revolutions, this opposition remains problematic. As we have seen in earlier chapters, ideas of universal freedom were woven into the fabric of captive revolts from the very outset. Moreover, these conceptions of liberty did not just travel from Europe to the Americas, but from Africa to the Americas, from early traditions of resistance in one area to later ones, and from one place of revolt in the New World to others. The Haitian revolution was a powerful example of these cross-currents, but there were many others; in this respect, we are only beginning to grapple with the intellectual richness of the rebellions of the enslaved, and the complex interconnections among them.

Moreover, as we have seen here, and as will be further underlined in the second half of the book, enslaved rebelliousness was not grounded in a single geographical source in terms of its ideas, but was typically an amalgamation of different external, regional, and local influences. Its potency ultimately rested on the degree of organization, mobilization, and leadership of local networks of resistance, and how they came together to advance their collective objectives. If we return to the Demerara rebellion, this becomes very clear: the Bethel Chapel was a conduit for the captives, and their sense of purpose rested on their capacity to forge intellectual and affective links among different local groups. Social solidarity among the enslaved, to make the same point differently, was the key underpinning of resistance.

This ties in with the other major problem with the conventional dichotomy between traditional and modern rebellions: its under-estimation of the African and pan-African contributions to emancipation. Africa was not an antithesis to 'modernity', but an important source of ideas of equality and individual and collective autonomy. These ideas emerged through the extensive forms of resistance that developed on the continent itself, the African-inspired material cultures and spiritual beliefs which were recreated in the New World, as well as the military experiences and practices that African captives brought with them, and deployed in their rebellions. These emancipatory African ideals were present well before the late eighteenth century, and long afterwards, as seen repeatedly in this chapter, or again in the insurrections in Brazil in the early decades of the nineteenth century that culminated in the 1835 Bahia uprising. The weight of African-inspired military and cultural traditions remained powerful across Cuban slave revolts, as we will see in chapter 8.

In other words, the black internationalism that emerged after the Haitian revolution had a large African component. This is one of the ways in which the revolution shaped an alternative universalism, which was different from the rights-based traditions that emerged out of the French and American Revolutions.[114] Taken cumulatively, these African emancipatory influences were present throughout the long history of Atlantic slavery, and were thus more decisive in shaping enslaved resistance ideals of freedom and autonomy than European ideas and values, whose impact was confined to the Age of Revolutions. Indeed, all these pan-African dimensions were pivotal to the success of the Haitian revolution itself, from Makandal through the 1791 revolt to Dessalines, without forgetting the international black identity of the postcolonial Haitian state. And so it was entirely fitting that as he went around Charleston rallying his recruits in the early 1820s, the pan-African Denmark Vesey held up the prospect of forthcoming military support from Haiti, the land of liberty, as well as from Africa, where the resistance all began.[115] This transatlantic horizon is conjured up in the bold and melancholic composition that was sung at meetings convened in Charleston by Vesey:

> Hail! All hail! Ye Afric clan,
> Hail! Ye oppressed, ye Afric band,
> Who toil and sweat in slavery bound
> And when your health and strength are gone
> Are left to hunger and to mourn
> Let independence be your aim,
> Ever mindful what 'tis worth.
> Pledge your bodies for the prize,
> Pile them even to the skies![116]

6

Man and Brother

Within just over a year of each other, two men who made the great individual contributions to ending British slavery died: the enslaved Jamaican preacher Samuel Sharpe, who was executed by the colonial government in May 1832, and the English parliamentarian William Wilberforce, whose life ended peacefully in London in July 1833. The two men never met, but in very different ways both dedicated their lives to the fight against human bondage and helped mobilize large groups of men and women at critical junctures. Their impacts were significant: Wilberforce was the prime mover behind the 1807 ban on the slave trade, and Sharpe led the Baptist insurrection that erupted in the final days of 1831 in Jamaica – a revolt which eventually forced the British authorities to pass the Abolition Act in 1833. Both men were profoundly Christian, and they drew the primary inspiration for their anti-slavery beliefs from their faith. On the subject of human bondage both Wilberforce and Sharpe were talented orators, who could move their audiences by the power of their eloquence. Last but not least, both men became national heroes in their homelands. British abolitionism has remained closely associated with the name of Wilberforce, while 'Daddy' Sharpe went on to become one of the most celebrated icons of postcolonial Jamaica.

Yet both men also symbolize the contradictions and paradoxes of the fight against slavery in Britain in the early decades of the nineteenth century. They were somewhat blinded by their trust in the honourable behaviour of those they were dealing with, or just in their rationality. Wilberforce over-estimated the capacity of his fellow parliamentarians and colonial settlers to appreciate that slavery was not in Britain's interest, while Sharpe seems to have believed that passive resistance by Jamaican captives could be sufficient to effect changes in British colonial policies. Neither of them was able to retain full control of the mobilizations they initiated, which ended up taking different forms from what they had originally intended. Wilberforce's commitment to gradual abolition was superseded in the later 1820s by demands for immediate emancipation. Sharpe's ardent desire to eschew violence – he made his recruits swear an oath to remain 'peaceable'[1] – was swept away by the revolutionary turn rapidly taken by events in Jamaica. The final version of abolition adopted by Parliament in 1833 was a compromise, which was welcomed by none of the principal parties involved. It was bolder than Wilberforce's evolutionary approach, in that it held up the promise of general emancipation for all captives in the short term. Although he was no longer alive by that point, Sharpe would have seen the 1833 settlement as a betrayal, for it failed to engage meaningfully with the rights and expectations of the enslaved, and it provided financial compensation only for enslavers.

This contrast between these two eminent anti-slavery campaigners sets the stage for this chapter, which marks a departure from the approach adopted in the book up to this point. So far, we have concentrated almost exclusively on the thoughts and practices of the enslaved, and seen the world from their perspectives, and their struggles to free themselves from slavery. Here, in order to make sense of the end of slavery in Britain, we must closely examine its metropolitan abolitionist movement, as well as the institutional and cultural power of the pro-slavery forces. The battle between advocates and opponents of slavery was not a simple binary opposition. There were a range of views among abolitionists, as well as in the pro-slavery camp, and at times the views and assumptions of these two white groups overlapped significantly. Moreover, the way slavery ended in Britain reflected one of the greatest limitations of British abolitionism. After four decades of campaigning, white reformers and black captives still lived in completely different worlds, both practically and intellectually.

In fact, the relationship was entirely one-sided. As they confronted the slavers in the colonies, black revolutionaries like Sharpe kept a close eye on British political and intellectual life, reading the national press and monitoring debates within the abolitionist movement. In contrast, Wilberforce and his fellow white abolitionists – the 'Saints', as they were called – had a very limited understanding of the demands, expectations, and world views of the enslaved. Their abhorrence of human bondage was sincere. But despite their rhetoric of humanity and brotherhood they did not view the enslaved as their equals, and long resisted calls from anti-slavery campaigners for an immediate end of slavery. These dissonances expressed themselves across the struggles for emancipation in Britain and in the colonies, limiting the movement's effectiveness, and paving the way for a settlement that was heavily skewed against the interests of the enslaved.

*

The British Parliament passed the Abolition Act in August 1833. Scheduled to take effect on 1 August 1834, the legislation would eventually emancipate around 800,000 enslaved people in the British Empire, most of whom were from the Caribbean colonies. The Bill was the product of a lengthy process of parliamentary deliberation and committee consultation, during which a range of views were aired about the best way to end slavery without injuring British economic interests, at home and in the colonies as well. Thirty-two witnesses were approached to give testimony: they included sea captains, attorneys, plantation owners and missionaries – but not a single person who had been, or was still, enslaved.[2] Much of the discussion centred around assuaging settler anxieties about their loss of power, and their fears of meeting the same grisly fate as the French *colons* in post-independence Haiti. This precedent 'lingered menacingly in the minds of men who formulated plans for British emancipation'.[3]

It was thus no surprise that the final version of the Bill was largely favourable to slaveholder interests. The sum of £20 million (increased from the original proposal of £15 million) was allocated to slavers across the Empire as compensation, while the former slaves received nothing. In fact, the newly emancipated remained enmeshed in a coercive system of 'apprenticeship' with their former owners in the colonies, which was initially meant to last up to six years. Its stipulations were exploitative, as in the expectation that they would continue to provide unpaid labour, and they were widely understood as a continuation of the previous system of bondage. These measures provoked widespread resistance and were abolished in 1838 – the actual moment slavery formally ended in the British Empire. Compensation was handed out to some 46,000 British slavers, highlighting the pivotal nature of slavery in the national economy.[4] In order to raise the colossal sum needed (which represented 40 per cent of its budget) the British government had to borrow and only finished repaying the interest on this loan in 2015. In other words, slavers were compensated through general taxation by generations of ordinary British men and women, including many people of Afro-Caribbean descent.[5]

The 1833 Abolition Act came about through the convergence of several social and political forces in Britain, particularly the emergence of an effective public campaign for an immediate end to slavery, as we shall see later in the chapter. But its most immediate and direct cause was the massive insurrection of captives that erupted in Jamaica in December 1831. Throughout that year the British government was still firmly committed to a policy of gradual reform ('amelioration') of slavery, and it remained locked in a stand-off with Caribbean colonial assemblies. These bodies were dominated by planter interests, which were obstinately refusing to implement even modest adjustments proposed from London, such as a ban on the flogging of female captives and the recognition of enslaved marriages. In effect, slaveholders held a veto on any changes to the system of colonial slavery. The December 1831 uprising smashed through this lock, as it destroyed the slavers' argument that the status quo was the only way to preserve order in the colonies, and that their local judgement was superior to the meddling of metropolitan administrators and missionaries. The uprising inflicted significant damage to sugar estates in Jamaica's western parishes, with whites fleeing en masse to coastal areas. Fourteen settlers were killed and hundreds of captives died in skirmishes with troops and later by public execution, with the property losses estimated at £1,500,000.[6] As with the previous major Jamaican revolt of 1760, colonial militia forces and soldiers proved inadequate and the authorities were forced to call upon the assistance of the maroons, invoking the stipulations of the eighteenth-century treaties (outlined in chapter 2). The intervention of the former maroon captives finally ended the uprising – a further humiliation to British power and prestige.

The Jamaican insurgency was the culmination of the series of Atlantic uprisings that followed the Haitian revolution. It bore several similarities to its immediate predecessors in Barbados in 1816 and Demerara in 1823. The rebellion involved around 60,000 enslaved people, one-fifth of their total number in Jamaica. As in the two earlier instances, rumours circulated across the colony beforehand that the king had granted emancipation but freedom was being withheld by the local authorities. As in Barbados, the enslaved population in Jamaica was largely creolized. There was, furthermore, a great deal of missionary activity, involving several Protestant denominations, as in Demerara. All of them were committed to increasing the education and religious instruction of the enslaved in the face of strong opposition from settlers and colonial administrators. Although Jamaican authorities and anti-slavery campaigners blamed Baptist missionaries and metropolitan abolitionists for inciting the conflict,[7] the impetus for the uprising, as in Barbados and Demerara, came from within the local captive community itself, several thousands of whom could read and write.[8]

Samuel Sharpe, the charismatic leader of the rebellion, was an original thinker who had come to his own conclusions that the revolt against slavery was justified by the Bible.[9] Literate and well-versed in the history of earlier insurgencies in Jamaica as well as the wider region, he followed his predecessors Bussa and Quamina in recruiting organizers from among the captive elite (craftsmen, drivers, boilers). Sharpe established an underground network whose members combined radical Baptism with traditional west African social and spiritual practices.[10] Many of the local rebel leaders were practitioners of African religions, and it has been persuasively argued that the 1831 rebellion was driven by Obeah 'under the mask of Christianity', as demonstrated by the importance of dreams and visions among the native Baptists, and the prevalence of oath-taking among the leading conspirators.[11] The connections with the wider Atlantic revolutionary tradition were present in the minds of local whites. Describing the early moments of the uprising, a local clergyman observed that many were convinced Jamaica was about to witness 'a renewal of those terrible scenes of cruelty and massacre which had taken place in St. Domingo a few years before'.[12]

Sharpe's political and spiritual utterances did not directly refer to the Haitian revolution, but there is no doubt that he knew of it and fully embraced its emancipatory ideals. At the same time, he closely followed events in Britain, and he was aware that the abolitionist cause was gaining momentum in the late 1820s and early 1830s. As an enslaved deacon who worked for his pastor Thomas Burchell at the Baptist Church in Montego Bay, Sharpe was passionate about ending slavery, and he preached that no group had the right to hold another in bondage.[13] He believed that the natural equality of men was grounded in holy Scripture, and that God was on the side of the enslaved. He told those he recruited that protest-ing against human bondage was a matter of 'assisting their brethren in the work of the Lord . . . this was not the work of man alone, but they had assistance from God'.[14] He urged them to fight for their freedom, telling a group of conspirators that 'if the black men did not stand up for themselves, and take their freedom, the whites would put them out at the muzzles of their guns, and shoot them like pigeons'.[15]

Sharpe sought to achieve his ends by non-violent strike action, at least in the first instance. His plan was for the enslaved to refuse their labour at the height of the cane harvest in December in order to force the planters to pay them. The strike nonetheless rapidly escalated into a full-blown confrontation, partly because many on his own side did not believe peace-ful resistance would suffice.[16] (These contrasting views among insurgents were another strong parallel with events in Demerara.) Before his exe-cution, Sharpe spoke to a British missionary, expressing regret for the violence, but not for standing up for his freedom and that of his brothers. Sharpe asserted his belief in God, justice, and liberty, and was adamant that he would prefer to 'die upon yonder gallows than live in slavery'.[17] It was clear that had he lived he would have continued the struggle to free his people from servitude, and that this journey would have drawn him fully into confronting British colonial rule. Many insurgents declared that their aim was to live in a society in which they made their own laws, and a captured rebel testified that Sharpe's ultimate goal was to drive the whites out of Jamaica.[18] Even if these may not have been his actual words, they bore witness to the sentiments of autonomy, solidarity, and brotherhood that animated the black Baptist revolutionaries in Jamaica.

Britain and the British colonies had a historical and deep-rooted association with slavery. By the time of Samuel Sharpe's birth in Saint James's parish in 1780, the British had already been in control of Jamaica for about 125 years. English forces initially arrived on the island in 1655, when they expelled the Spaniards and created a plantation economy there, importing large numbers of African captives. Britain was already by then heavily involved in the traffic of kidnapped Africans, with the presence of traders in west Africa as well the emergence of an enslaved workforce in Restoration London. Resistance was already an established and visible phenomenon: there were over two hundred newspaper advertisements for the capture of African and South Asian runaways between 1655 and 1704.[19]

This engagement with the slave trade increased exponentially with the creation of the Royal African Company in 1672, actively sponsored by King Charles II. From its foundation to the early 1720s, the Company shipped around 150,000 African captives, mostly to the Caribbean. It controlled around a third of the slave market, and forcibly carried more men, women, and children across the Atlantic than any other single institution during the entire history of the slave trade. As its name indicates, the Company was fully supported by the British monarchy. Its first governor was the Duke of York, who acceded to the throne in 1685 as King James II. Many of the African captives were branded with the initials 'DoY' on their chests.[20] This dominant British position in the Atlantic system was maintained throughout the eighteenth century, all the way through to the abolition of the slave trade in 1807. By this point, the British had trafficked over three million captives into slavery, encountering intense enslaved resistance at all stages.

Just as profound was the impact of slavery on British public institutions, as well as on the fabric of the nation's economic and social life. This too began from the outset, starting with the monarchy. Before the creation of the Royal African Company, in the early part of Elizabeth I's reign, the English government had encouraged and promoted the slave trade, while the queen herself partook in the profits. In 1564 she sent a squadron to purchase slaves in west Africa. Such historical examples forged a strong connection between the monarchy and the institution of slavery, and they were often cited by pro-slavery advocates in Parliament.[21] From the late seventeenth century, the British state issued licences for slave ships, and used its political, economic, and legal powers to promote Atlantic colonial trade and keep its proceeds in the hands of British shippers, merchants, and financiers. For example, the Royal African Company's forts in Africa were maintained by a 10 per cent tax levied on goods exported to Africa, paid by merchants involved in the trade. The slave-ship market was dominated by British vessels, and from 1640 to the early nineteenth century Lloyd's of London was the global centre for insuring this industry. One insurance claim related to the slave ship *Zong*, whose crew, fearing that their supplies of drinking water had fallen too low, had deliberately thrown overboard more than 130 captives taken from the Gold Coast in 1781. This incident caused such an uproar in Britain that it provided initial momentum to the abolitionist movement.[22]

The Church of England too endorsed British slavery, producing slave bibles which were heavily edited to remove all references that could be interpreted as opposing human bondage or encouraging emancipation.[23] The Church invested in companies that profited from the slave trade, such as the South Sea Company, which transported over 40,000 African captives on its ships from 1714 to 1740. Among the properties the Church inherited was the Codrington estate in Barbados, one of the most brutal on the island, maintained through the labour of hundreds of captives, many of whom resisted by escaping into marronage.[24] The Codrington plantation was taken over by the Church in 1710 and managed by the Anglican Church's missionary organization. In overall terms, investments in slavery and in the slave trade earned the Church an estimated £1.3 billion in today's value. Similar stories could be told across British society, with millions of Britons benefiting from the economic activities that evolved around slavery, from running plantations, commercial and mortgage financing, and building ships, to importing and processing slave-grown crops. Sugar became by far Britain's largest import in the eighteenth century, revolutionizing tastes, developing consumer culture, and promoting technical innovations. Slavery was foundational to the modern British economy.[25]

However, from the later decades of the eighteenth century, Britain's role as a leading slaving power was increasingly contested domestically. Public opposition to human bondage and the slave trade in Britain led to effective campaigns for the boycott of sugar and rum in the early 1790s; it was estimated that half a million people took part in the boycott.[26] In response to this challenge, powerful and well-organized pro-slavery advocates emerged, both in the colonies and in the metropole. Settlers paid

lobbyists to represent their interests in Parliament, and eventually colonial planters and sugar merchants in Britain coalesced to form the 'West
India interest', which became the dominant public voice in defending
slavery. From the late 1780s, this lobby formed a committee to counter
anti-slavery arguments, establishing a combination of pro-slavery and
anti-abolitionist narratives that typically celebrated the economic benefits of slavery for the British people, the strategic importance of colonies
for British imperial power, and the historical association of slavery with
British political and economic institutions. These arguments included a
specific set of justifications for slavery, including references to the Bible,
long-standing British practices, and paternalistic arguments about the
moral and material protections afforded to captives by their masters. As
the Member of Parliament Thomas Hughan put it: 'there did not exist a
more happy race than the slaves in our colonies'.[27]

Indeed, slavery was often presented as a form of Christian salvation,
rescuing unfortunate Africans from the double tyranny of brutal kings
and 'revolting superstition'.[28] Another argument frequently deployed
was that captives would refuse to work if they were emancipated. The
Duke of Wellington asserted that 'men . . . in tropical climates' were
only willing to engage in labour to acquire the 'common necessaries of
life', after which they sought only to 'repose in the shade'.[29] This slavery narrative was forged around specific moments and episodes that
symbolized captive resistance, such as the French Revolution, the 1791
insurrection in Saint-Domingue, and Haitian independence. Supporters
of abolition in Britain were compared to Jacobins in France.[30] Slavery
was closely tied with the protection of British interests in the Caribbean, and the large contingent of British sailors – estimated to number
around 25,000 – were often presented as a major source of employment
in coastal ports such as Liverpool, as well as a key supplier of manpower
to the Royal Navy.[31]

These claims were echoed by well-disposed members of the political
class in the Commons and the Lords, particularly landowners, bankers,
businessmen, judges, journalists, and lawyers. These men campaigned
vigorously against the abolition of the slave trade, and after 1807 against
emancipation. One of the essential justifications they invoked was that
captives had been legally acquired and were recognized as the private
property of their owners, and these rights could not be taken away without damaging the institution of private property itself. This view of the
enslaved as chattel was widely shared – including by many abolitionists.[32]

In these battles against abolition the West India lobby could count on
allies at the highest level of British politics. In the early decades of the

nineteenth century these included figures such as Robert Peel, the Duke of Wellington, and George Canning, who gave a speech in 1824 likening African captives to Frankenstein's monster, a being 'in the maturity of his physical passions, but in the infancy of uninstructed reason'.[33] Major British policies relating to slavery, such as 'amelioration', which sought to make modest improvements in the conditions of captives, were initiated by planters in the late eighteenth century, and adopted by British governments largely as a ploy to appease abolitionists.[34] Moreover, every British monarch from Queen Anne in the early eighteenth century through the four Kings George to William IV, who was the sovereign at the time of abolition, were firmly committed to slavery. Many had close links with Caribbean planters, and actively opposed abolitionism.

Many clerics and several writers, such as James Boswell, justified slavery by claiming it was divinely ordained – but the real 'bible' of the slavers was written by the Jamaican slaveholder Bryan Edwards. Published in 1797, his *Historical Survey of the French Colony in the Island of St. Domingo* painted an apocalyptic portrait of the destruction of white settlers by the insurgents after 1791. This work shaped the abolitionist debate not just by raising the spectre of the 'horrors of St Domingo', but by associating captive rebellions with white abolitionism. Edwards speciously argued that the 1791 revolt in the French colony was inspired by Parisian abolitionists.[35] Pro-slavery advocates blamed revolutionary uprisings in the colonies, as in Barbados in 1816 and Demerara in 1823, on abolitionists and even suggested that the mere fact of discussing emancipation in London could provoke unrest.[36]

During parliamentary debates, pro-slavery advocates routinely associated opposition to enslavement with anti-British sentiment. In 1804 the anti-abolitionist parliamentarian John Fuller thus accused Wilberforce of despising the 'opulence' that slavery had brought to Britain, and seeking to undermine the monarchy, the constitution, and the empire.[37] Indeed, and perhaps most importantly, the defence of slavery was intimately connected to Britain's standing as a global power. During the Revolutionary and Napoleonic Wars Britain captured Trinidad, Demerara, Essequibo, and Berbice, and then Mauritius in 1810. All these territories had captives and provided new markets for British slaveholders. Arguments about how best to stabilize and protect Britain's colonial empire could thus have major implications for the slavery issue. This nexus was illustrated by Britain's military intervention in Saint-Domingue between 1793 and 1798, which effectively turned into a war to restore slavery, and led to the loss of at least 20,000 British soldiers. Ironically, the Prime Minister who presided over this debacle was William Pitt (the Younger), who in 1792 had made an eloquent speech in Parliament calling for the abolition of the slave trade, 'the greatest practical evil that ever has afflicted the human race'.[38]

The first anti-slavery petition was submitted to Parliament in 1783, by a group of English Quakers. The debate for and against slavery gathered momentum during that decade, especially through the publication of pamphlets that challenged the economic and moral foundations of pro-slavery arguments. Writing from a Christian perspective, Charles Crawford observed that slavery was incompatible with the Gospel's injunction: 'Thou shalt love thy Neighbour as thyself.'[39] William Roscoe added that the African slave trade was a violation of the 'natural and inalienable rights' of all humans.[40] Anti-slavery views were also actively promoted in children's literature.[41] There were collective mobilizations across Britain, which included the campaigns for boycotting sugar and rum, as we saw earlier, and by the early 1790s over 1.5 million people had signed abolitionist petitions. Opposition to slavery became one of the important ways through which Britons reflected on their sense of collective self in the decades that followed.[42]

While this hostility to slavery enjoyed popular support and provided the foundation for the later resurgence of mass anti-slavery sentiment in the 1820s and early 1830s, the leaders of the British abolitionist movement essentially focused their energies on ending the slave trade. Two figures emerged to play leading roles in this campaign in Britain: the evangelical Christian Member of Parliament William Wilberforce and Thomas Clarkson, an Anglican deacon who in 1787 was one of the founders of the Society for Effecting the Abolition of the Slave Trade. Clarkson travelled across Britain displaying thumbscrews, shackles, and other instruments of torture he had collected. His language sought to elicit sympathy for the victims of enslavement, and to generate a sense of indignation against the 'wickedness' of the slavers.[43] Wilberforce first introduced a Bill to abolish the slave trade in 1791, when it was overwhelmingly defeated, and he tried again in 1792, and once more in 1793, also without success. Parliament finally passed the Slave Trade Act in March 1807.

Even in its own terms the 1807 Act's abolitionism was qualified: it banned the import of Africans but still permitted an internal trade of captives within British colonies. In fact, by 1833 the overall number of men and women in bondage in the British Empire had increased, compared to 1807. Further, neither Wilberforce nor Clarkson was in favour of full emancipation at this stage, and were in fact at pains to distinguish it from abolition. Clarkson testified to the House of Commons that he had

no plans for 'freeing the negroes', while Wilberforce argued that emancipation would be 'premature' – a position he would continue to hold
until the final years of his life. In his 1807 pamphlet on the abolition of
the slave trade he argued that granting immediate freedom to the 'poor
degraded Negro slaves' would ensure 'not only their masters' ruin but
their own'. He characterized independent Haiti as being in a state of 'wild
licentiousness'.[44] One of Wilberforce's central preoccupations was not to
antagonize British enslavers but to protect their interests: hence his gradualist approach to ending human bondage. Indeed, his ultimate solution
to the issue was to appeal to the British commercial spirit, and to rely on
the slavers' sense of financial self-interest. If the supply of captives from
Africa was cut off, he believed, planters would be compelled to treat their
enslaved labourers in a more humane way, as they would not be able to
replace them so easily. This would foster closer bonds between masters
and captives, allow the latter to build families and embrace the Christian
faith, and thus to attain the 'manly maturity' that was the essence of 'true
liberty'.[45]

Underpinning this enlightened paternalism was a desire to safeguard
British imperial interests, and a racialized view of African captives as biologically and culturally inferior beings. In Wilberforce's words, their minds
were 'uninformed' and their moral characters 'altogether debased'.[46] This
portrayal of Africans as uncivilized wretches who were unfit for freedom
had a long pedigree in British and European Enlightenment thinking. The
philosopher David Hume had observed that negroes were 'naturally inferior' to white people, and they were incapable of any kind of 'ingenuity'.
Immanuel Kant agreed, adding that even free black people had failed to
demonstrate 'any praiseworthy quality'.[47] This view was widely embraced
among the colonial plantocracy. Thus for the Jamaican settler Edward
Long, one of the most vociferous defenders of Atlantic slavery, Africans and Europeans were two different species, and Africans lacked any
'moral, intellectual, and artistic capacity'.[48] Abolitionists like Wilberforce
and pro-slavery white settlers had much else in common. They shared the
belief that Africans were prone to 'rebellions and suicides', and colonization was the only way to protect them from degeneration. They further
agreed that the best long-term guarantee of colonial amelioration was
the development of a creole culture among captives. In other words, the
further the enslaved were from Africa, physically and culturally, the more
quiescent they would become.[49] Wilberforce was proved wrong here too:
this false dichotomy between loyal creoles and rebellious Africans was
exactly what the creole-dominated colonies of Barbados and Jamaica
challenged in their uprisings.

Freedom, in short, was not an end that enslaved Africans could pursue by themselves, for themselves. Clarkson was very careful, in his 1788 pamphlet based on testimonies of sailors involved in the slave trade, to present slave-ship insurrections as evidence of the violence of the system, rather than attempts by the captives to liberate themselves.[50] This paternalism was not greatly different in principle from the views of the pro-slavery planters concerning the benefits of enslavement, and the necessity of emancipating them only once they had been 'civilized'.[51] The related notion that slaves needed to undergo an apprenticeship as a prelude to emancipation was widely shared by abolitionists; it was first floated in *The Just Limitation of Slavery in the Laws of God*, a pamphlet written by the abolitionist Granville Sharp in 1776.[52] This limited conception of their humanity was reflected in the clay medallion designed by Josiah Wedgwood for the slave-trade abolition campaign. It featured an African kneeling in chains, with the accompanying legend: 'Am I not a Man and a Brother?'[53] The image was striking and clearly helped the broader dissemination of the abolitionist message in late eighteenth-century Britain and in the United States. However, its depiction of Africans as helpless supplicants reflected the reality that white-abolitionist brotherhood was not based on any meaningful sense of equality.

In his 1788 *Essay on the Impolicy of the African Slave Trade* Clarkson argued that the suppression of the slave trade would create a dynamic economic relationship between Britain and Africa, a 'new commerce' that would lift the 'insuperable impediment[s] to the civilization of the Africans'.[54] This too was an uncomfortable parallel with the slavers' view that bondage was a blessing for Africans, as it provided them with work as well as religious salvation. In this context, in 1807–8 the abolitionists founded the African Institution, which was tasked with promoting the 'civilization' and 'happiness' of the African continent through education reforms, the establishment of industries based on virtuous free labour, and commerce not dependent on enslavement; mainly because of the lack of funds, it made little headway. The organization sought to promote ameliorations to the slave regime in the colonies but none of its efforts had any impact on the treatment of captives or their living conditions.[55]

The Haitian revolution was the most interesting barometer of Wilberforce and Clarkson's views about emancipation. Although he came to admire Toussaint Louverture for his religiosity and credited his lieutenants for defeating the French and executing their grand scheme for emancipation, Wilberforce initially saw the events in Saint-Domingue as vindicating his arguments that enslaved Africans were creatures of passion rather than reason. He viewed Haiti as a potential source of regional disorder, and therefore a likely cause of destabilization for Jamaica.[56] Likewise Clarkson's pamphlet on the revolt in Saint-Domingue, written shortly after the outbreak of the 1791 uprising, simply repeated his claim that the slave trade caused insurrections. He furthermore went to great lengths to deny that British abolitionists were in any way responsible for inciting the rebellion.[57]

In 1814 the Haitian king Henri Christophe, who had always been something of an Anglophile from the Saint-Domingue era (he was born in a British colony), initiated a correspondence with Wilberforce, and a year later with Clarkson. Both men responded and became involved in efforts to set up a handful of elite educational establishments in northern Haiti.[58] Wilberforce emphasized the importance of religious education and arranged for five boxes of English and French bibles (the unredacted versions, one assumes) to be sent to Haiti. He also mailed Christophe copies of *The British Encyclopedia*, histories of the Inquisition and the Jesuits, and a book entitled *Dialogues on Political Economy*.[59] He seemed entirely unaware of Saint-Domingue's rich and sophisticated history in agriculture, sending Christophe two iron ploughs to enhance crop production.[60] As in all other matters, Wilberforce's view of Haiti was underpinned by his evangelical hope that the new state would become a beacon across the Atlantic world for 'Christian moral improvement'; he apparently prayed for Christophe every day.[61]

Both Wilberforce and Clarkson supported diplomatic efforts to dissuade the French from attacking and re-enslaving Haiti. At the Vienna Congress in 1815, France demanded (and obtained) the right to reclaim Saint-Domingue by force. Three years later at Aix-la-Chapelle the French backed down, and formally abandoned the slave trade (although French ships remained involved in the trafficking of captives throughout the 1820s).[62] Clarkson was quick to claim credit, although he was primarily motivated by the damage such a conflict would have on the international campaign to garner support for the British slave-trade ban. In any event it is hard to imagine that even the French would have risked another foolhardy military venture across the Atlantic at this point, after the trouncing of their army by the Haitians, and the Waterloo debacle at the end of the Napoleonic Wars.[63] In the final years of Christophe's rule Clarkson became one of his unofficial advisors. By this point the king's deeply unpopular reign was descending into tyranny (he committed suicide in 1820 rather than risk assassination or a coup; his son and heir was assassinated ten days later). Nevertheless, the exchanges show that the British abolitionist seemed genuinely willing to help Christophe further Haitian national interests. After Alexandre Pétion's death in 1818 from yellow fever, for example, Clarkson urged Christophe to seek reconciliation with his successor Jean-Pierre Boyer.

But Clarkson's advice often showed scant understanding of the Haitians' sense of pride and sovereignty after their hard-won independence. For example, Christophe asked Clarkson to use his good offices in London to help Haiti gain British diplomatic recognition, which had not materialized despite a growth in trade between the two countries after 1804. Such a move would moreover have marked a return to the co-operation of the late Toussaint Louverture era, when the commander-in-chief had signed a trade agreement with the British and sanctioned the establishment of British consulates in Saint-Domingue. Clarkson replied in 1818 that diplomatic recognition would be premature, as it would offend the French government and weaken the recently restored king, Louis XVIII. These were hardly convincing arguments: offending the French had not bothered the British at all in the late 1790s, quite the opposite.[64] Responding to a similar request from Christophe to promote Haitian recognition, Wilberforce was even more evasive, stating that this was a matter for the House of Commons, and that too many of its members were still 'strongly prejudiced' against Haiti.[65] After Christophe's death, Wilberforce commented in a private letter that 'there was never a monarch more unfeignedly desirous of promoting the improvement and happiness of his people'. However, he had been unwilling to help Christophe and Haiti by saying so publicly.[66]

Even more revealing was the advice given by the two British abolitionists about how Haiti should deal with the French, who were continuing to make threatening noises about their former colony, and still refusing to recognize it officially. With the support of Wilberforce, Clarkson pressed Christophe to pay the French an indemnity to compensate planters for their property losses in Saint-Domingue, in exchange for their acknowledgement of Haitian independence – a move that the king firmly refused to countenance.[67] Even after this refusal, Clarkson duplicitously continued to suggest to the French that Christophe was open to compromise on this point.[68] Fourteen years before British emancipation, the idea of compensating slavers for their losses was already fully endorsed by Britain's chief abolitionists, even as they condemned the immorality of the slave trade, and were denouncing slavers for treating their captives as chattel. This in many ways summed up the thinking of early British abolitionist leaders: the recognition of black sovereignty was always untimely, and the welfare of white planters – whether British or French – took precedence over the collective good of black Atlantic communities.

*

For the most part, as we have already seen, the public conversation about slavery among British abolitionists was conducted without any significant input from the captives themselves, or from men and women who had been previously enslaved. But even if they were not in Parliament, black people were present and visible in Georgian Britain, with a population of around 15,000, generally based in London, and mostly working as servants, pages, housekeepers, and launderers.[69] A small number became well known, as with Ignatius Sancho, a self-educated former enslaved man who wrote poetry, plays, and music, and established himself as a successful grocer. He wryly described the trials of his attempted assimilation into British society in his *Letters*, a best-selling work published in 1782, two years after his death.[70] A black slave-narrative tradition also emerged in the second half of the eighteenth century, making a brief but powerful intervention in the public discussion about abolition and emancipation. One of the very first works of black autobiography to appear in the English language was James Albert Ukawsaw Gronniosaw's *Narrative*, first published in Bath in 1772.

Gronniosaw was an African prince who originated in the Borno region of west Africa, a Muslim enclave that had been ruled by his grandfather. Captured and sold into slavery in the Gold Coast, Gronniosaw was bought by a Dutch trader, who shipped him to Barbados. From there he was purchased in the late 1730s by a member of the Van Horne dynasty, a powerful Dutch family in the New York area. Then he was sold on again, this time to a Calvinist preacher, Theodorus Jacobus Frelinghuysen, who introduced Gronniosaw to his fierce millenarian theology. After Frelinghuysen's death, Gronniosaw made his way to England around 1763 to find George Whitefield, one of the major Calvinist preachers of the era who had been a close friend of his American master. Whitefield took Gronniosaw under his wing and introduced him into the upper reaches of British Calvinism, where he came under the patronage of Selina Hastings, the wealthiest and most influential figure from this milieu. Hastings, to whom the *Narrative* was dedicated, paid for the amanuensis who took down Gronniosaw's story and produced the text, and its vision of spiritual redemption conformed with her religious world view; in short, the book was written for and published by Calvinists.[71]

The *Narrative* is nonetheless a compelling black autobiographical work, especially in its vivid renderings of Gronniosaw's experiences of racial exclusion in Britain in the final stages of the book. This awareness of his difference first dawns on him on the slave ship carrying him across the Atlantic, when he attempts to converse with the copy of the Bible used by the captain to read out to the captives. Unable to elicit a response from the Holy Book, he concludes that 'every body and every thing despised me because I was black'.[72] This lament captured the exclusion of the black voice from the Western intellectual tradition, and the alienation of non-Christian Africans from divine grace.[73] From this moment on, the book becomes the story of Gronniosaw's quest for Christian spiritual redemption, already intimated in his glossing over the Islamic faith in which he was brought up, and his extraordinary interjection to the Dutch slave trader who buys him: 'Father, save me!'[74] Convinced that he should embrace Christ, Gronniosaw fears that Jesus will not wish to receive a 'sinner' like him; after his conversion he becomes reconciled to his own enslavement, admitting that he 'would not have changed situations for the whole world'.[75]

The *Narrative* thus does not call for the abolition of slavery, and its message about human bondage is agnostic at best – a paradox for a text that helped found the tradition of black emancipatory writing, but entirely in line with the views of slaveholding British Calvinists such as White-field and Hastings. Although they were opposed to any ill-treatment, they thought that the enslavement of Africans was ultimately a benevolent activity, freeing the captives from paganism.[76] This belief in the priority of religious liberation over physical emancipation underscored the difficulty for black subjects to acquire any kind of visibility in Britain. This position was not far removed from Wilberforce's own view that captives should not be freed until they reached 'maturity' – in effect, it was a religious version of the same proposition. This convergence was one of the many ways in which the line between pro-slavery and abolitionist positions was effectively blurred, and it further explains why leading abolitionists were so reluctant to acknowledge the demands for immediate emancipation expressed by the enslaved.

Gronniosaw's stylistic influence is apparent in the most famous piece of African writing published in the West in the late eighteenth century, Olau-dah Equiano's *Interesting Narrative* (1789). Appearing as the movement to abolish the slave trade in Britain was under way, the text significantly contributed to its momentum and visibility. Equiano's work went through nine British editions in five years, and appeared in Russia, Germany, Holland, and the United States. In 1791–2 the author embarked on speaking tours in Ireland, Scotland, and England.[77] His life story shared several similarities with Gronniosaw's: the forced travel from Africa to the Carib-bean and the United States and eventually Britain, where Equiano bought his freedom in 1766. Michael Henry Pascal, the British naval officer who was his last enslaver (and named him Gustavus Vassa), took Equiano with him on his travels in the Mediterranean, the Caribbean, and Britain.

He allowed his captive to pursue his education and acquire specific skills such as numeracy and ship navigation. The sea plays an essential role in Equiano's account: a place of horror (the account of the Middle Passage is one of the text's most powerful episodes) and at the same time adventure, discovery, redemption, and enchantment. Water reveals fundamental truths to him, and this is arguably one of the ways in which he remains intimately connected to his African heritage.[78]

Unlike Gronniosaw, Equiano is not reticent about the ills of slavery. He condemns the barbarity of the slave trade, and clearly calls for the abolition of slavery itself at the end of the book, stating that such an outcome would be a 'universal good'.[79] Echoing Clarkson, his solution to the loss of earnings from colonial slavery is to imagine a system of free trade with the populations of Africa, who would grow in number as a result of abolition and create a large market for British manufactures.[80] However, this is the point at which another logic asserts itself, significantly overlapping with Gronniosaw's text: Equiano too is primarily concerned with spiritual liberation. His trajectory essentially repeats the pattern laid out by his distinguished predecessor, starting with physical captivity, dejection, and sin, moving on to repentance, and ending with a new spiritual birth through the rediscovery of Christ, and a call to evangelize.[81] Indeed, the illustration that opens the *Interesting Narrative* is a direct homage to Gronniosaw's lament about the closure of the Holy Book to him. It depicts Equiano dressed as an English gentleman, his finger delicately (and somewhat boldly) laid on a Bible open on the passage that gave him the revelation to be 'born again' (see Plate 12).[82] This time, the Holy Book speaks – but only to confirm the message imparted to Gronniosaw: everything that had happened to Equiano (including his enslavement) was part of a providential plan, guided by 'the invisible hand of God'.[83] It is thus easy to understand why, with its priority given to a specific type of spiritual liberation, its evangelical sensibility, and its commitment to the spirit of commerce, Equiano's work could appeal equally to Selina Hastings and Clarkson, both of whom sponsored his book.

The *Interesting Narrative*'s opening chapter on Equiano's early years in Africa has been a source of controversy. One leading scholar has uncovered two contemporary documents (baptismal and naval records) in which his place of birth appears to be listed as South Carolina. He concluded that his Igbo origins were fictitious, and that Equiano was in fact an American-born slave of African ancestry, who invented his Igbo past in order to make his story more compelling, to provide the kind of Africa-centred account that British abolitionists were calling for at the time, and to secure his own personal financial gain (all the profits on the sales of his book came to him).[84] Even if he fictionalized his origins – and the case is not conclusive – there is little doubt that Equiano felt a strong connection with the African continent, and in 1779 he petitioned the Bishop of London to be sent as a Christian missionary to Africa (his request was rejected). In 1788 he wrote to Queen Charlotte on behalf of his 'African brethren' to lobby for support for a Bill to ameliorate the conditions of slaves.[85] He signed his letters 'Gustavus Vassa, the African'.[86]

Moreover, far from the common trope of Africa as a land devoid of culture and civilization, the *Interesting Narrative* paints a generally sympathetic picture of the history, laws, and customs of the Igbo people, stressing their orderly governance, the simplicity of their lifestyle, their agricultural skills, and their robust, warlike practices, as well as their relatively benign forms of slavery, in sharp contrast with the brutality of the Atlantic system of human bondage. He highlights their attachment to their cultural practices: 'we are almost a nation of dancers, musicians and poets'.[87] Here, and elsewhere in the book, Equiano draws in his white readership by adopting a rhetorical strategy that plays into dominant stereotypes about Africans, as does his dismissiveness of African pagan religions, and the 'credulity and superstition'[88] which allowed magicians and diviners to play important roles in Igbo social life. But Equiano concludes by comparing the 'primitive' state of his people to that of the early Israelites, claiming that African genealogy can be traced back to Abraham. Through this insertion of his people into the biblical tradition, Equiano affirms both Africa's essential humanity and its legitimate place in world civilization. This position enables him to refute 'the prejudice which some conceive against the natives of Africa on account of their colour'.[89]

The most remarkable anti-slavery treatise from this period was Ottobah Cugoano's *Thoughts and Sentiments*, first published in 1787.[90] Cugoano's life is not as well documented as that of Gronniosaw and Equiano, and there are few traces of his existence after 1791. He was from Ajumako in the Gold Coast, and his father and family were among the 'chief men' in the community. Captured and sold into slavery at the age of thirteen, he was first shipped to Grenada, where he was eventually purchased by a Scottish plantation owner who brought him to England in 1772. Here he was emancipated in the wake of the 1772 Mansfield ruling, which determined that slavery was not supported by British statute or by common law. Cugoano was baptized and took the name John Stuart. In the 1780s he became a campaigner against slavery, working closely with the abolitionist Granville Sharp, and collaborating with Equiano. Both men published their books within a few years of each other, and they shared the same Christian evangelism.

Cugoano's literary style draws heavily on biblical rhetoric and phrasing, and he frequently quotes from Scripture, asserting from the very outset of *Thoughts and Sentiments* that 'God who made the world hath made of one blood all the nations of men that dwell on all the face of the earth.' It therefore followed that 'it never could be lawful and just for any nation, or people, to oppress and enslave another'.[91] There is also, as with Equiano and Gronniosaw, the same acknowledgement of the providential dimension of enslavement: his capture was 'what the Lord intended' for his good.[92] But this is no prelude to any sort of equivocation about human bondage: this is a vehement text, in which Cugoano endorses the right of the enslaved to resist their captors, and be given 'adequate reparation' for the harm inflicted upon them. He not only calls for a 'total abolition of slavery', but demands that it should be preceded by 'days of mourning and fasting' so that the British nation may atone for its heinous sins against Africans.[93] These atrocities were all the more appalling to Cugoano in that they were carried out by 'those robbers, plunderers, destroyers and enslavers of men [who] call themselves Christians, and exercise their power under [a] Christian government and authority'.[94]

Thoughts and Sentiments both operates within the literary conventions of the slave narrative and radically unsettles them. Although Cugoano opens the book with some autobiographical material about his enslavement, and it describes the 'cruel beatings and lashings' he endured in Grenada, the book dwells little on his personal fate, and makes no appeal to sentiment. Instead, it rapidly moves to a higher level of generality, rebutting the pro-slavery arguments of the West Indian planter James Tobin, and grounding Cugoano's call for freedom in his humanity. He embraces his blackness fully, but refuses to be defined by it; as he puts it: 'there are no inferior species, but all of one blood and of one nature'.[95] This common humanity has a divine origin: 'God who made the world, hath made of one blood all the nations of men that dwell on all the face of the earth.'[96] (This view was one of the theological pillars of black Christianity among the enslaved, and was later echoed by figures such as Sam Sharpe.)[97] The emancipation that Cugoano seeks is not for his black brethren only, but for the working people of Britain as well, whose exploitation he condemns: 'it is evil with any people when the rich grind the face of the poor'. In his view, 'every civilized nation' has a duty to provide 'some general and useful employment . . . for every industrious man and woman'.[98]

Cugoano, like Equiano, makes every effort to correct slaver stereotypes about Africa, starting with the conventional trope that Africans find bondage 'natural' and socially acceptable, to the extent of selling their own wives and children. With respect to the first, he argues that Africans cherish their freedoms and rights just as emphatically as Europeans, and they are distressed when one of their family members or friends is captured; this happens not because ordinary Africans believe in slavery, but because of ongoing 'wars and feuds' among African rulers. Indeed, Cugoano stresses that the only Africans who believe in slavery are the 'wicked and profligate princes and chiefs' who have developed a stake in the system, along with slave procurers ('a species of African villains') – thanks in no small measure to the corrupt inducements of European slave merchants.[99] Moreover, Cugoano highlights the relatively benign treatment of captives in Africa compared to the Atlantic system, and pointedly puts African communal solidarity ahead of European mercantile individualism in respect of the support given to vulnerable sections of society: 'We want many rules of civilization in Africa; but, in many respects, we may boast of some more essential liberties than any of the civilized nations in Europe enjoy; for the poorest amongst us are never in distress for want.'[100]

Cugoano closes with a vivid warning of the revolutionary calamities that will befall the British if they hold on to their system of colonial slavery, conjuring an image of a natural cataclysm so powerful as to break mountains, rocks, and trees. This popular revolutionary 'vengeance' is a very real prospect, and there is no doubt that Cugoano believes it would be a just retribution. But he neither embraces violence nor believes it inevitable, especially as colonial slavery is an economic liability for Britain, leading only to corruption, massive state expenditure, and increases in the national debt to protect narrow slaver interests. Indeed, his apocalyptic vision of a 'universal calamity' is marshalled for reformist purposes: Cugoano holds out the possibility of the continuation of the 'grandeur and fame of the British empire', but one founded on principles of 'Christianity, equity, justice and humanity' as opposed to slavery and domination. This scenario of a reformed empire could produce the 'greatest happiness' across the globe and make Britain a beacon for all progressive nations. And in line with the thinking of political economists like Adam Smith, and Jeremy Bentham's utilitarianism, he argues that this cosmopolitan order would be entirely compatible with British self-interest; he endorses Clarkson and Equiano's visions of the abolition of the slave trade opening the door to 'a very considerable and profitable' commercial relationship between Britain and Africa.[101]

These three black narratives made powerful interventions in the British abolitionist debate in the later eighteenth century. Gronniosaw, Equiano, and Cugoano challenged widespread views – held by both slavers and abolitionists – about the barbarity of Africans, and robustly asserted their full and unqualified membership of the human race. With his sophisticated conception of his overlapping Black, British, and Christian identities, Cugoano anticipated modern ideals of multiculturalism and pan-Africanism. His universal humanism was one of the very few eighteenth-century philosophical texts that addressed racial and economic inequality as part of a general theory of human progress, while seeking to move beyond race as a defining human category. The full place of this piece of writing in the canon of the radical Enlightenment is yet to be fully acknowledged.

Through their specific and general accounts, these writers exposed the cruelty of the slave trade, and undeniably helped turn the tide of British opinion against it; they thus contributed to the wider intellectual and political push that culminated in the 1807 Abolition of the slave trade. By separating slavery from colonialism, they invited the British to think about a world in which their empire could thrive without human bondage. Their influence was practical as well: Equiano's campaigns brought the abolitionist message to Parliament, and to working-class associations.[102] Alongside other black advocates who called themselves 'Sons of Africa', he wrote letters against slavery that were published in the British press.[103] One of Cugoano's specific recommendations was to use British naval power to police the ban on the African slave trade through the interception of merchant ships carrying human cargo – a policy that was eventually adopted after 1807 with the creation of the West Africa Squadron.[104]

Despite these achievements, these biographies did not undermine British stereotypes about blackness. This was perhaps too much to expect, at a time when pro-slavery and racist views were still deeply entrenched in British Establishment circles, as well as in wider society; King George III once mockingly asked Wilberforce at a levée how his 'black clients' were doing.[105] These texts unwittingly played into the dominant vision of black subservience. Their emphasis on the providential nature of their enslavement, and on Christianity as the primary source of African redemption, bought into the racial stereotype of black inferiority. It buttressed the standard view of Africans as culturally and spiritually debased people, and kept the reins of their material and spiritual liberation firmly in the colonizers' hands. Even the existence of strong indigenous Christian traditions in Africa (as in Kongo) was not acknowledged. The hierarchical relationship between Europeans and Africans went unchallenged, and was arguably strengthened, with the erasure of the texts of both Equiano and Cugoano from British abolitionist discourse by the end of the eighteenth century.

Despite Equiano's efforts to engage British Members of Parliament, black abolitionists were not invited to testify about the slave trade in the early 1790s, and there is no evidence that Wilberforce met Equiano, or read his book – even though Wilberforce's views about Africa would have been directly challenged by the opening chapter of the *Interesting Narrative*. Cugoano was the strongest voice of the three slave-narrative writers on the question that truly underpinned the ideal of brotherhood: emancipation. Gronniosaw's silence on the issue, and Equiano's brief reference to it, allowed Wilberforce and Clarkson to keep the focus of the abolitionist movement exclusively on the slave trade in its early decades. After 1807 this narrow horizon further allowed them to rely on their doctrine of gradualism, and the pipe dream of colonial planters acting on their enlightened self-interest to improve the treatment of their captives. To make the same point differently, black narratives were not powerful enough to draw British abolitionist leaders closer to the humanity of the African captives, and to compel those abolitionists to pay closer attention to the thoughts and beliefs of enslaved black Christians in British colonies, as they pushed for general emancipation in the early nineteenth century.

After 1807, British abolitionism made little headway for at least a decade and a half. Emancipation was not on its agenda and in the early 1820s its mainstream advocates were still holding the general line of piecemeal reforms and a gradual end to slavery. Slavery was still denounced in vehement terms: in a pamphlet published in 1823, Wilberforce savaged the system for its injustice, immorality, and cruelty.[106] But there was an equally strong emphasis on protecting British interests and on the continuing need for a paternalistic oversight of captives. This was practically illustrated by the policies pursued in Sierra Leone. Founded in the late eighteenth century on an explicitly anti-slavery mandate, the British trading outpost of Freetown was populated by the surviving former North American loyalist slaves who had fought on the British side during the American War of Independence; they were joined in the late 1790s by exiled rebel Jamaican maroons. The 'Province of Freedom' embodied the idealistic hopes of anti-slavery campaigners who believed in the possibility of fostering new forms of British commerce in Africa based on free labour. Freetown's first governor John Clarkson (the brother of Thomas) was a British naval officer who accompanied the loyalists on their tumultuous journey from America back to Africa in 1792. He was a dedicated abolitionist who saw himself as the 'personal saviour' of the former slaves.[107]

In 1808 Sierra Leone became a British colony, and Freetown served as the base for the Royal Navy's West Africa Squadron, which patrolled the African coasts and attempted to enforce the ban on the slave trade.[108] Over 80,000 captives were thus freed over the course of the nineteenth century and saved from enslavement in the Americas. However, these 'liberated Africans' were not returned to their homelands. They were brought to Sierra Leone, forcibly resettled there, and put to work as soldiers and manual labourers; some of these soldiers were taken across the Atlantic and ended up in the British West Indies, where they enforced the slave regime until abolition. The freed slaves in Sierra Leone remained wards of the state and were subjected to exploitative working conditions.[109] The villages set up to accommodate them became areas of resistance and fugitivity during the first half of the nineteenth century.[110]

This insistence on controlling and 'civilizing' Africans freed from enslavement was consistent with British abolitionist thinking. This approach was summed up by the title of a pamphlet published by Clarkson in 1823: *Thoughts on the Necessity of Improving the Condition of the Slaves in the British Colonies, with a View to Their Ultimate Emancipation*. What exactly was meant by 'ultimate' was unclear, except that it was obviously not immediate, and was to be achieved 'by degrees', to allow captives to be educated for the 'right use of their freedom ... as through a preparatory school'.[111] Echoed in Wilberforce's 1823 pamphlet, this was still basically the same colonial view as expressed during the campaigns of the early 1790s. Captives were expected to meet a set of benchmarks before they were deemed fit for liberty, or even any kind of basic social interaction.[112] When Wilberforce received members of the African and Asiatic Society for a dinner at his home, there were separate tables for the host and his invitees, while the black and white guests were partitioned by a curtain.[113]

Gradualism was the dominant approach among abolitionist associations in Britain. Similar stances were taken by the Liverpool Society for the Amelioration and Gradual Abolition of Slavery, founded in October 1822 by the wealthy Quaker and East Indian sugar merchant James Cropper, and by the Society for the Mitigation and Gradual Abolition of Slavery, established in January 1823 by Wilberforce, Zachary Macaulay, and the parliamentarian Thomas Buxton. This organization, popularly known as the British Anti-Slavery Society, proposed a programme for a more 'humane' system of enslavement in May 1823, which included the emancipation of children. The key stipulation was that any changes to the overall system of human bondage were to take place with 'due regard to the well-being of the parties concerned' – in other words, captives as well as planters. By including the interests of the slavers in the equation, the proposal effectively gave colonial settlers a veto over any reforms.[114]

The West India interest paid little attention to these suggestions, and even denounced some very modest resolutions proposed by Foreign Secretary George Canning in Parliament in 1823 to improve the material conditions of the enslaved.[115]

The extent to which British abolitionist leaders were at this point still fixated by pro-slavery arguments was illustrated by Thomas Clarkson's convoluted appeal to emancipation in Saint-Domingue to help make his case for gradualism. This was a delicate exercise, not least because in this instance freedom had been decreed in 1793 immediately and for everyone – the opposite of what Clarkson and his colleagues were arguing for. Moreover, the image of 'the horrors of St Domingo' was still commonly invoked by planters and British political leaders. It was summoned as a warning both against immediate emancipation and of the possibility of revolutionary contagion spreading to Jamaica (the latter view, as we saw earlier, was held by Wilberforce himself). At the same time, Haitian emancipation was obviously irreversible by the early 1820s, and a reality that could no longer be ignored by those claiming to be opposed to slavery. Clarkson navigated his way through this conundrum by blaming the massacres of the early 1790s on French Revolutionary Jacobinism, and the conflict between white and mixed-race planters. He also ignored the killings of French settlers by Jean-Jacques Dessalines in 1805, carried out in the very spirit of retribution against the planters that terrified so many in Britain.[116]

One of the other great British fears about Saint-Domingue was its embodiment of the notion of black empowerment. As we saw earlier, the idea that men of African descent were capable of self-governance was unsettling to British elites, including many on the abolitionist side. This was because of the widespread fear that black people in British colonies would embrace complete self-determination if given their freedom, and promptly massacre the white settlers as Dessalines had done. Clarkson defused this mine by presenting a glowing picture of life in late colonial Saint-Domingue under Toussaint Louverture's rule. This was a period of general order and prosperity, thanks to the labour regulations introduced by Toussaint, which Clarkson claimed upheld discipline on the plantations 'without invading the liberty of individuals'.[117] This was a rather optimistic version of events. In truth, as we saw in chapter 4, agricultural workers could no longer sell their labour freely in the late Toussaint era, and his policy was widely resented among former captives.

Because he needed to steer clear of any thought of black self-determination, Clarkson insisted that Louverture was a loyal French colonial administrator. He glossed over Louverture's repeated conflicts with the French authorities, culminating in his 1801 Constitution, which effectively made Saint-Domingue an autonomous self-governing entity within the French Empire. Instead, Clarkson stressed the idyllic and hierarchical nature of colonial life in the Toussaint era, when white planters lived peacefully on their estates, and 'the Negroes, though they had been all set free, continued to be their labourers'.[118] In fact, Clarkson went on to add that Toussaint's labour regulations were essentially kept in place by all his successors, from Dessalines to Boyer, thus ensuring 'tranquillity and order' in the country's plantations.[119] Again, this was a way of skirting around the whole issue of Haitian independence, and giving credit to French colonial rulers for striking the perfect balance between planters and free labourers. By this sleight of hand, Clarkson was able to offer the essential argument that mattered for his purposes, namely that emancipation had not challenged white-settler and colonial interests, or, as he put it, in the thirty-year period following 1793 the free men and women of Saint-Domingue 'never abused their liberty'.[120]

This doctrine of gradualism was unsatisfactory to those both in Britain and in the colonies who believed that slavery should be immediately abolished. Thanks to the pressure from Wilberforce and Clarkson, the terms of the debate about slavery undoubtedly shifted. After 1807 the pro-slavery narrative dwelled less on justifying human bondage, often acknowledging its moral inadequacy, and even conceding that its most brutal aspects needed to be mitigated (hence 'amelioration'). However, on the ground any concrete proposals to curb the violence meted out to the enslaved – or even to uphold existing protective regulations – were actively resisted by local slavers, usually with the support of British colonial officials. A specific example can illustrate this phenomenon. In Mauritius, as we saw in chapter 2, enslaved resistance principally took the form of marronage, which caused ongoing problems for planters. When the British took over the control of the island from the French in 1810, the first governor, Robert Farquhar, asked the authorities in London to exempt the island from the ban on the slave trade, which was bitterly opposed by local slavers. This request was denied. However, the illegal traffic of captives continued apace, and the British authorities initially showed little interest in improving the conditions of captives, especially if these changes might antagonize the local French settlers.[121]

Finally, in the late 1820s, the British authorities appointed a 'Protector of Slaves', an official who was tasked with ensuring legal codes and ordinances were respected. Captives could complain to his office if they felt ill-treated. Settlers on the island objected to this new form of accountability, and 122 of the 182 complaints brought by the enslaved to the

Protector in the first year were dismissed. The entire process was skewed against the enslaved, and was designed to give greater credibility to the testimonies of slavers, managers, and overseers, whose mere word was generally sufficient to have a complaint rejected. Many of the complainants ended up being punished for allegedly making false accusations. Far from affording them any new protections, 'amelioration' left a bitter aftertaste for most of the enslaved population in Mauritius.[122]

The real shift in British anti-slavery thinking, however, came with the August 1823 rebellion in Demerara. Its fierce repression again brought home the brutality of colonial slavery and the inadequacy of British policies. The death of Pastor John Smith in prison turned him into a martyr for the abolitionist cause. The London Missionary Society published a full account of his trial as well as a range of personal documents defending the 'memory of a pious and persecuted man'.[123] The events in Demerara created space for the emergence of more militant voices within British abolitionism, with women campaigners often taking the lead. Women had been a specific focus of first-wave abolitionists in the early 1790s, particularly in the campaign against the consumption of 'blood sugar', which was deemed an affront to the 'virtue and honour' of English ladies. Equally, the rhetoric of the horrors of slavery was mobilized in Mary Wollstonecraft's more radical feminist perspective, with the subjugation of women being equated with a form of patriarchal enslavement.[124]

In 1824 the frustration with gradualism culminated in the pamphlet published (anonymously) by the radical English Quaker Elizabeth Heyrick: *Immediate, Not Gradual Abolition; or, An Inquiry into the shortest, safest and most effectual means of getting rid of West Indian Slavery*. Although careful to pay homage to the work of Wilberforce and Clarkson, the text was a vigorous polemic against the moral and practical failings of gradualism (see Plate 14). Heyrick lamented its time lost in endless petitions and fruitless parliamentary discussion.[125] She condemned its hypocritical demand that other nations desist from the slave trade, while British captives continued to be exposed to injustice and cruelty.[126] She censured the placing of enslaved and slavers on an equal footing, even though there was no possible comparison between their respective situations, and 'common equity' required that those whose suffering was greater be given absolute priority.[127] Heyrick further denounced the undue deference to slaver 'interests and prejudices', particularly about the violent consequences of immediate emancipation.[128] She pointed out, finally, the hollowness of the argument about captives' lack of maturity, which was simply an excuse to defer emancipation indefinitely.[129]

One of the strongest themes running through the pamphlet was the extent to which abolitionists had deliberately and unconsciously absorbed pro-slavery arguments. Heyrick believed that abolitionists should embrace immediate emancipation, which was the 'true Christian principle', and recognize the civil rights of the former captives. Rather than concentrating on planters' losses, in a dramatic reversal of perspective she argued for compensation to be given 'in the first instance ... to the *slave*, for his long years of uncompensated labour, degradation and suffering'.[130] She also called for a resumption of the campaign to boycott West Indian sugar, which would spread from house to house, city to city, and eventually become a mass movement across Britain. She believed such a collective popular force would land a 'death blow to West Indian slavery'.[131] Unlike moderate abolitionists who tended to avoid direct confrontation with slavers, Heyrick was forthright about the West Indian planters who benefited from the proceeds of slavery, calling them 'culprits ... [who] too long have ... fattened on the spoils of humanity'.[132] A key part of her argument was that abolitionism was about morality and not about material interests. She noted that the planters had been doing everything in their power to block the modest reforms proposed by Parliament. This delaying tactic had actually strengthened the system. Slavery therefore had to be 'crushed at once, or not at all'.[133] Immediate abolition was thus the better policy in all respects: wiser, safer, more rational, and more politic, as well as more just and humane.[134]

The illustration used for the cover of the first edition of *Immediate, Not Gradual Abolition* featured an African man with a discarded chain and a broken whip at his feet. Framed by the words 'I am a man, your brother', the image was a conscious subversion of the iconic Wedgwood medallion and caption, which had shown an enslaved man kneeling and in chains. In contrast, Heyrick's emancipated person is upright, and staring straight at the reader.[135] Her pamphlet inspired many abolitionists, in particular women's groups. Between 1825 and 1833 at least seventy-three women's associations became actively engaged in anti-slavery campaigning, distributing books and pamphlets, and creating artefacts such as work bags, pin holders, and samplers.[136]

In 1827 the Sheffield Female Anti-Slavery Society became the first British anti-slavery organization publicly to call for immediate abolition. Prompted by another Heyrick pamphlet, *An Appeal to the Hearts and Consciences of British Women* (1828), the consumer boycott of sugar was relaunched and is thought to have attracted higher public support than the campaign of the early 1790s.[137] With women's voices again leading the way, a heated meeting of the Anti-Slavery Society in May 1830 voted to drop the terms 'mitigation and gradual abolition', and instead call for the 'entire abolition' of slavery.[138] In 1831 younger members of the Society set up the Agency Committee, which sent out campaigners across Britain to make the case for immediate abolition. Heyrick died in 1831, so she did not live to see the formal end of British slavery. But the push she initiated finally made its way into the political mainstream with the 1832 Reform Act, which created many new constituencies in industrial cities such as Manchester, Sheffield, and Leeds. Some 204 of the newly elected MPs pledged to support immediate abolition, and a year later, after the Jamaican uprising, anti-slavery petitions to Parliament gathered 1.3 million signatures – a quarter from women's organizations.[139]

Throughout its long campaigns from the 1780s to the early 1830s, and in their aftermath, British abolitionism was seen in contrasting ways. For its opponents at the time, it was an irresponsible and ultimately dangerous idea, 'injurious' as one pamphleteer put it in 1826, 'to the character and prosperity of the British empire'.[140] For its defenders, it was a heroic moral crusade, embodied by titanic figures such as Wilberforce and Clarkson, to rid the British nation of an evil and barbaric practice. After the 1830s, abolition became a pillar of the British state's self-identity, and in the Victorian period it underpinned national prestige and the projection of imperial power.[141] This was one of the reasons why, for its later Marxist critics such as Eric Williams, abolition merely provided a humanitarian gloss to a change driven by the adjustments and global needs of British colonial capitalism rather than ethical or sentimental considerations.[142]

The British model of emancipation provided the template that was followed in subsequent decades by the French, Dutch (in Surinam), Brazilians, and the Spanish in Cuba. In all these instances compensation was paid only to slaveholders.[143] In the longer run, the other lasting legacies of slavery on British colonialism included the establishment of a system of coercive indentured labour enforced by state violence. In Mauritius, the last British colony to emancipate its captive population, the abolition of slavery in 1835 was followed by the massive introduction of indentured labourers from India, whose treatment during the second half of the nineteenth century used many techniques borrowed from the system of enslavement. Labourers who escaped were pursued by the British authorities and the white plantation elite under vagrancy laws modelled on maroon-hunting provisions.[144] Slavery generated the myth of the civilizing mission, effectively repackaged as a humanitarian exercise during Victorian colonial advances into Africa. Slavery was furthermore at the root of the doctrine of native immaturity, used by the British to deny sovereign rights and self-determination to colonial peoples well into the twentieth century.[145] In all these respects, and notwithstanding the valiant efforts of Sam Sharpe and the struggles of many generations of captives, the spirit of slavery lived on in the practices, policies, and imagination of British colonialism.

From the perspective of Britain's 800,000 captives, 1833 was both a victory and a defeat. A victory, because without their continued resistance, and in particular the insurrections in Barbados, Demerara, and Jamaica (with the Haitian revolution looming in the background), there would have been no emancipation at all. It was on the immediate agenda of neither the British government nor the abolitionist leadership – not to mention the slavers. It was in this sense a remarkable achievement. But 1833 was a defeat as well, because while strong enough to provoke this immediate change, the enslaved did not gain full recognition of their rights, and they lacked the power and sufficient metropolitan support effectively to shape the content of the settlement, which was largely injurious to their interests.

The continuities between slavery and the post-emancipation eras are hard to ignore. If we stay with the Jamaican example, freedom brought little change to the social and economic conditions of black colonial populations. In the post-1830 decades they still suffered from poverty, exploitation, and racial and cultural discrimination. Although Jamaicans were now British subjects nominally entitled to legal and political rights, they were in practice often denied them by repressive and exclusionary regulations, even though they demonstrated publicly for greater democratic inclusion.[146] In 1865 the Morant Bay rebellion erupted in southeastern Jamaica as a direct consequence of these injustices, and its leader the Baptist activist Paul Bogle drew a direct line between this revolt and the unsatisfactory ending of slavery in 1838.[147] History repeated itself: the 1865 uprising had strong support from the Baptist Church in Jamaica, now predominantly black, but was brutally put down by British military force, again with the complicity of Jamaican maroons. The continuities did not end there. Bogle was an admirer of the Haitian revolution, and many Morant Bay insurgents aimed to overthrow the British colonial system and create an independent black state on the Haitian model. Like Samuel Sharpe, Bogle was captured and executed, and he too has become a Jamaican national hero.[148]

If we turn back to Britain, abolitionism was in one sense a story of continuous and expanding public support, despite the stiff opposition it faced domestically. Although its power declined in the 1820s, the West India interest reflected the profound penetration of slavery into the social and economic fabric of British life. These pro-slavery attitudes and assumptions among elites and across society were intimately connected to wider conceptions of British imperial power. Slavers repeatedly claimed that the Caribbean colonies were essential to British national interests, and that abolitionists were undermining them. Further complicating matters, emancipation was achieved first in Saint-Domingue in 1793 and then confirmed by the French revolutionaries a year later. For many in Britain, this tainted the anti-slavery cause with Jacobinism. More importantly, it led to a prolonged, costly, and fruitless British military intervention to restore slavery in the French colony between 1793 and 1798, severely limiting the scope for abolitionist activity in Britain at this time. Haitian independence in 1804, with its assertion of black sovereignty and massacres of French settlers, was then mobilized by anti-abolitionists to justify their claim that any meaningful freedom granted to British slaves would have similar consequences.[149]

Yet opposition to slavery became increasingly widespread not only among the urban middle classes, but also among women, young people, and in working-class communities. Indeed, the movement was never as strong in Britain as in the early 1830s, when it commanded the support of a large cross section of society, and the endorsement of a sizeable body of parliamentarians.[150] Yet at the moment of its legislative triumph, the arrangements for emancipation fell short of the hopes of its active enthusiasts. The arrangements were seen as a betrayal by the captives themselves, especially with the Abolition Act's failure to treat them with dignity, and the massive compensation it handed out to the slavers. This happened because the 1833 Act, even though pushed through by mass opposition to slavery both in Britain and in the colonies, was still profoundly shaped by pro-slavery assumptions and interests. Compensation was handed out for service lost, thus vindicating the slavers' belief that human bondage had been legitimate, and indeed that the enslaved were simply chattel. Moreover, the apprenticeship scheme reaffirmed the view, shared by slavers as well as most white abolitionists, that Africans lacked the maturity necessary to be granted their full and immediate freedom.

Both the strengths and limits of mainstream abolitionism came down to the gradualist approach followed by Wilberforce, Clarkson, and Buxton. These men deserve credit for the dogged determination with which they pursued their crusade against the slave trade. But they were unable to adapt their strategy to the rise of enslaved resistance in the colonies, and to the captives' demands not just to be freed from slavery but to be empowered. Abolitionist leaders were hampered by their fear of slave revolution, while their desire to accommodate and eventually win over the majority of white settlers to the abolitionist cause proved unsuccessful. Even though they disagreed with the way captives should be treated, planters and mainstream abolitionists broadly converged in their belief that the enslaved were not yet ready for freedom because of their morally 'degraded' character.[151]

This position continued to be held by mainstream abolitionists for well over forty years, until they were forced by the Barbados and Demerara revolts and pressure within their own ranks to shift to a policy of immediate emancipation. It was facilitated by the erasure of the enslaved from the movement that claimed to champion their interests. The curtain behind which Wilberforce hid his black guests was a perfect metaphor: metropolitan abolitionist leaders struggled fully to embrace their professed ideals of humanity and brotherhood. Their moral opposition to slavery was sincere. But they also saw captives as weak creatures, with barely the capacity to reason, let alone formulate considered views about their rights and interests, and their future place in a post-slavery British Empire. Part of this erasure was driven by religious evangelism, and the conviction that Africans needed to be rescued from their pagan spiritual beliefs. The only way black narratives were able to break through – briefly – into the abolitionist conversation in the late eighteenth century was by buying into this doctrine of Christian salvation. Wilberforce had an equally dim view of Hinduism, which he compared rhetorically to a form of enslavement, likening it to 'one grand abomination ... the most foul, degrading and bloody superstition'.[152] In 1825 the Anti-Slavery Society damned Haiti with faint praise, noting that it was slowly 'advancing in intelligence, respectability, and wealth'.[153] No significant figure from the British abolitionist movement visited the country before 1833.

There was something deeper. British abolitionist leaders could not come to terms with the idea of black men and women as free people acting to defend their interests. It was understandable, and a quiet source of satisfaction, when the liberation of the enslaved happened to the detriment of the French. But in the minds of British abolitionist leaders self-emancipation, whether individual or collective, remained taboo before 1833. The enslaved narrative literature was enriched in 1831 with the publication of *The History of Mary Prince*, the first autobiography by a black woman. Her horrific experiences of enslavement in Bermuda, Turks Island, and Antigua were used by abolitionist campaigners to highlight the plight of enslavement. Yet here too the author was constrained by the literary and political conventions of her time. The published version of Mary Prince's tale was focused entirely on personal suffering, and all the passages highlighting her own agency and her subversion of the patriarchal system to her own ends were removed.[154] Ultimately, it was left to the indomitable Elizabeth Heyrick to give voice to the new abolitionist imperative: 'The slave has a *right* to his liberty, a right which it is a crime to withhold.'[155]

7

The Rights of Man are Inalienable

Compared to Britain, the formal end of slavery followed a longer and more convoluted course in France. Human bondage was abolished twice: first in 1794 and then, after the restoration of slavery by Napoleon Bonaparte in 1802, definitively in 1848. But there were echoes of the British case too, in particular the intellectual frailties of mainstream liberal metropolitan movements, and the reluctance of successive governments in France to confront the issue of general emancipation – except when faced with a crisis provoked by the resistance of the enslaved. Indeed, the fierce, varied, and creative oppositions of the captives in the colonies were a constant feature of the French experience throughout the period between the French Revolution and 1848.

It is sometimes written that the challenge to slavery stemmed directly from the 1789 Revolution. As one historian has claimed, 'between 1789 and 1792 those on the political left believed that the universal principles of the Declaration of the Rights of Man should be extended to the colonies'.[1] In reality, French Revolutionary leaders showed no initial inclination to promote the rights of black captives. Their only focus during these early years was on empowering the mixed-race minority in the colonies, many of whom were slavers. As we saw in chapter 4, it was the enslaved themselves who seized upon the emancipatory potential of the 1789 Declaration, effectively incorporating its universalist language into their own local mobilizations against the slave order. A radical emancipatory movement flourished in Saint-Domingue, blending European, African, and Caribbean ideals of liberation. It was symbolized by the black insurgent captured in late 1791 with a *vodou* fetish around his neck, while his pocket was filled with revolutionary pamphlets printed in France. Fortified by the transformation of Saint-Domingue under Toussaint Louverture and the revolts in other French colonies in the 1790s, this democratic grassroots anti-slavery tradition became a powerful and autonomous force.[2]

This resistance had to contend with republican lawmakers, administrators, and intellectuals in metropolitan France, whose views were often at variance with those of black and mixed-race revolutionaries in the colonies during the 1790s. As we have seen, this gap was often based on racial prejudice, although the republican transformation of the French colonies saw the emergence of European figures who were dedicated to black emancipation and worked constructively with black political leaders. In Saint-Domingue, such men included Governor Étienne Laveaux, Louverture's close ally, who subsequently played a major role in shaping colonial legislation in the French Assembly as a neo-Jacobin member during the later 1790s. Laveaux oversaw the 12 Nivôse an VI (1 January 1798) organic law that integrated the French colonies by instituting a departmental regime. He strongly believed in the equal civil and political rights of black and white inhabitants.[3] A similar egalitarian spirit was embodied by Charles Vincent, a civil engineer based in Saint-Domingue from 1786 to 1801. He spoke fluent *kreyol* and was widely admired by the colony's black revolutionaries; Louverture regarded Vincent as a 'republican brother' and entrusted him with important missions in the colony and in France.[4]

But the majority of officials sent to the colonies from Paris after those enslaved by France were legally freed in 1794 did not share this racial egalitarianism, and therefore had more antagonistic relationships with local black populations. For example, Victor Hugues, the Republic's envoy in Guadeloupe between 1794 and 1798, believed that the *nouveaux libres* (as the former captives were known) were still steeped in 'African barbarity and natural ferocity', and lacked the intelligence to enjoy the full rights of French citizens. He developed a framework for colonial governance that combined limited post-emancipation civil rights with policies of labour coercion and racial exclusion.[5] Former captives who had fought to defend the colony against British attack were disarmed and in many cases imprisoned, and even those who met the property qualifications to vote were denied their right.[6]

In Saint-Domingue, the most revealing of these conflicts was the battle between Toussaint Louverture and Léger-Félicité Sonthonax, who was sent from Paris in May 1796 to administer the territory. In principle, the two men were perfect allies. Louverture had by this point emerged as the most powerful local republican leader, while Sonthonax was a dedicated abolitionist who had written the August 1793 decree that had formally ended slavery in Saint-Domingue (he called himself 'the father of general liberty'). It was followed by the February 1794 general abolition voted for by the Convention in Paris. Yet the relationship between Louverture and Sonthonax rapidly broke down. Just over a year later the French administrator was forced to abandon his post and return to Paris.

The disagreements between the two men revealed the limits of metropolitan republicans' understanding of black empowerment. At an abstract level Sonthonax was sincerely committed to abolitionism and racial equality. But once in Saint-Domingue he behaved like a bullish colonial overlord, adopting a patronizing attitude towards Louverture, correcting his spelling mistakes, and lecturing him about European military history. He repeatedly cast doubt on the dedication and fighting capacity of Saint-Domingue's black soldiers, once telling a fellow white officer that 'blacks chase after military positions so that they can procure more liquor, money, and women for themselves'.[7] Sonthonax was contemptuous of Louverture's religious beliefs, claiming that he was 'beholden to priests'. After their rupture Sonthonax returned to France, where he became a bitter critic of Louverture, describing the black leader as 'a thick-headed man, as lowly as his first occupation as a slave herdsman; he normally speaks *kreyol* and barely understands the French language.'[8]

In other words, Sonthonax believed that his authority rested not only on his status as an envoy of the French Republic, but on his evident cultural and racial superiority as a disciple of the Revolution and as a white person. In his private correspondence with his superiors, Sonthonax was even more candid about the racial inferiority of the *nouveaux libres*: 'to organize general liberty with profit and to avoid making the inhabitants of [Saint-Domingue] a horde of savages without laws or manners, the European must command here'. Black political sovereignty, in the view of the French abolitionist envoy, was an utter abomination. Sonthonax predicted that if the colony were to be administered by its local leaders it would be 'for ever lost to the Arts, Civilization, and Agriculture'.[9] This was a common view among republican metropolitan envoys to the colonies in the late 1790s. Étienne Burnel, the agent of the Directory sent to Guyana in 1798, affirmed that it would be 'a long time' before the emancipated black populations could attain the 'degree of civilization necessary to become French citizens'. Until then, he concluded, they would continue to require 'the active surveillance of white Europeans'.[10]

In the aftermath of emancipation, French metropolitan and black colonial citizens thus drew upon an apparently common stock of universal political concepts such as liberty, justice, equality, and fraternity. But they invested them with very different meanings. This contrast was most tellingly expressed in the ways the abolition of slavery itself was represented. For the former captives, emancipation was at the heart of their political struggle for freedom. It had been initiated by their collective revolt in 1791, and it was reaffirmed during Saint-Domingue's victorious military operations against Spanish and British occupying forces. Emancipation was thus an immediate and concrete reality, which defined their citizenship and was inherently associated with black empowerment and dignity. For metropolitan French republicans, emancipation was one element in a broader constellation of principles that defined the hierarchical colonial order. It was further seen as part of an ideological process that had been driven by the Revolution, and as a projection of French power and prestige.

These differences were vividly expressed in the late 1790s, when the French officially marked the anniversary of the February 1794 abolition with commemorative ceremonies, held both in the metropole and in the colonies. Now back in Paris and elected to parliament, Laveaux marked the Fête du 16 Pluviôse in 1799 by proclaiming how the Republic had 'created a million new humans' by virtue of a 'single strong and precise idea'.[11] In Saint-Domingue, a similar approach was adopted in celebratory speeches delivered by local French republican officials. In the town of Môle Saint-Nicolas, the address was given by the municipal clerk, a man named Rochefort. The narrative he produced for the occasion is fascinating both for the way he reimagined French abolitionism, and for what remained unspoken. As might be expected, he portrayed the 1794 legislation as a triumphant expression of the French republican principles of equality and fraternity, and as a salutary destruction of racial prejudice.

At the same time, the event was completely detached from its historical context. Rochefort presented abolition not as part of a political process but as the victory of Enlightenment 'reason' and a return to a 'natural' state of human perfection. In this abstract and idealized account there was no mention of the institution of slavery itself, nor of the fact that the 1794 French legislation had been prompted by the abolition in Saint-Domingue the previous year. Indeed, the greatest silence surrounded the 1791 slave revolt, which had started the whole movement and was seen by black republicans in Saint-Domingue as the foundation of their revolution. Rochefort erased this uprising completely from his story. Even for the most progressive metropolitan republicans, the self-determination of black citizens remained a difficult issue.[12]

These tensions between French metropolitan abolitionism and black republican anti-slavery were exemplified in the actions of the Société des Amis des Noirs (Society of the Friends of the Blacks), formed in Paris in February 1788. Among its founders were two men who would become leading figures of the Girondist faction that dominated French national politics in the early years of the Revolution, the journalist Brissot de Warville and the lawyer, writer, orator, and statesman Mirabeau. They were soon joined by the *philosophe* the marquis de Condorcet, the banker Étienne Clavière, and the cleric Henri Grégoire, along with dignitaries such as the marquis de Lafayette, the hero of the American Revolution. The total membership was around two hundred, mostly drawn from the liberal nobility, the literary sphere, and the world of finance.[13]

Invoking the 'sacred rights of humankind', the purpose of the Société des Amis des Noirs was to help end France's involvement in the international slave trade, the 'monstrous assemblage of injustice and cruelty' that led to the capture and sale of thousands of Africans to French slave traders.[14] Pledging to make its case 'with moderation', the Société highlighted the positive examples set in the United States by Quaker campaigns against the slave trade, and by abolitionist movements in Britain.[15] It firmly rejected any immediate empowerment of the enslaved, especially by means of a 'revolution'.[16] In the 1780s, Condorcet wrote a pamphlet in which he described African captives as people who had lost their natural rights, and who could be a danger to themselves and others if they were to be empowered. He compared them to 'very young children, madmen or idiots'.[17]

From the outset this Parisian strand of French anti-slavery activity was profoundly shaped by its British counterpart. The Société des Amis des Noirs was modelled on the Society for the Abolition of the Slave Trade founded in London in May 1787, as we saw in the previous chapter. Brissot de Warville had been in the English capital in the autumn of that year and had become involved in the organization's activities. The British had encouraged the formation of a French association, as well as the strategic focus on the slave trade rather than immediate emancipation. In August 1789 – a month after the Revolution – Thomas Clarkson travelled to Paris to provide further advice and support. He held many meetings with French leaders but achieved frustratingly little during his six-month stay.

Despite Clarkson's long correspondence with Mirabeau (at one point he wrote to him every day), the French revolutionary orator did not deliver a speech about abolition in the legislature, even though he prepared one; the Assembly did not vote on the issue.[18] When Clarkson returned to London he arranged for British philanthropists to send funds to French abolitionists, and by 1790 over thirty British pamphlets against slavery and the slave trade had been translated into French and distributed in France.[19] Many members of the Société des Amis des Noirs produced their own texts, which made the case for severing the connection between colonialism and slavery. These writings imagined a new post-slavery relationship between France and the African continent, based on the promotion of industry, education, and trade. The proposals were framed in the characteristic colonial language of the need for Africans to be 'civilized'.[20]

The English connections of the Société des Amis des Noirs, as well as its elitist design, moderate purposes, and philosophical elevation, were ill suited to the fast-moving pace of the early years of the French Revolution, both in Paris and in the colonies. Many of the Amis des Noirs pamphlets reached the colonies, where they were appropriated by enslaved and free black groups demanding immediate emancipation. In October 1789 in Saint-Domingue, the colonial governor lamented the continuing circulation of 'books from Europe concerning liberty', despite his administration's attempts to stop them. He found that local captives had reinterpreted the French Revolution, saying to each other that in France 'the white slaves have killed their masters and that now they are free, they govern themselves and have recovered possession of the land'. They expected to carry out a similar programme in Saint-Domingue.[21]

Martinique-based captives received letters from Paris announcing the imminence of emancipation. There were reports of enslaved people gathering in sessions to hear readings of revolutionary pamphlets, and a free black named Casimir wrote to the governor in late August 1789 on behalf of the 'entire nation of black slaves' demanding 'freedom justly earned after a century of suffering and ignominious servitude'.[22] In May 1791, after a period of unrest, and just a few months before the great insurrection in Saint-Domingue, there was a revolt of enslaved people in Saint-Pierre on Martinique.[23] Rumours of immediate emancipation provoked plots in Guyana and Guadeloupe, where the governor reported the suppression of an insurrection in April 1790.[24] French abolitionist writings were seen as so seditious that they were banned in early 1790. A similar prohibition was introduced in Saint-Domingue in September 1791.[25]

Faced with accusations of undermining order in the colonies, the Société des Amis des Noirs blamed the unrest on the intransigence of planters. A pamphlet by Grégoire – the most radical member of the group, who was truly dedicated to emancipation and racial equality – prophetically warned that peoples who were deprived of their liberty would reclaim it for themselves.[26] But most members of the Amis des Noirs were not willing to endorse black self-emancipation, and their lofty universalism soon began to unravel. A proclamation written by Brissot in early 1790 in the name of the Société insisted that their only purpose was to end the slave trade, and not to bring about immediate emancipation or even consider granting political rights to the enslaved. Such ideas, they protested, had 'never entered' their minds. Using the exact formula of British abolitionists, Brissot added that the 'immediate emancipation of black people not only would fatally damage the colonies, but would be a poisoned gift for the slaves, given the state of barren abjection to which they have been reduced; it would be tantamount to abandoning to their own devices young children in their cradles, or beings who are mutilated and powerless'.[27] This demeaning characterization, repeatedly used by Brissot and other French abolitionists, was also a direct echo of the earlier pamphlet by Condorcet.

In early 1791 the Amis des Noirs went as far as supporting the granting of citizenship to free people of colour. This measure was approved by the National Assembly in Paris in May 1791, but was then overturned in September, with the uncompromising white colonists being given the right of veto over any such changes. But French abolitionists still rejected immediate emancipation, even though human bondage was seen as 'incompatible with the ideal of a free society'. They maintained that freedom had to be brought about gradually and in degrees, through 'a reconciliation of the interests of humanity with those of slavers'.[28] In a speech to the National Assembly, Condorcet called on the deputies to 'prepare' for the destruction of slavery. But he left the timing of the process open-ended, and effectively pushed it into the distant future. In his earlier pamphlet, he had envisaged a horizon of up to seventy years.[29]

These Parisian sophistries were interrupted by the mass uprising in Saint-Domingue, which began in August 1791. Denied the freedom and rights of citizenship proclaimed by the 1789 Declaration of the Rights of Man, and ignored by the Parisian elites who claimed to be advocating for their interests, the enslaved took their destinies into their own hands, launching the insurrection which started the Haitian revolution. One of its immediate casualties was the Société des Amis des Noirs, which went into hibernation sometime between late 1791 and early 1792[30] – but not without a final display of bad faith. In late October 1791, as the news of Saint-Domingue's enslaved insurrection reached Paris, Brissot blamed the movement on a 'great scheme' fomented by royalist conspirators. It was inconceivable to him that black captives could organize and execute a mass rebellion on this scale, 'given their character' and their lack of 'chiefs, military training, and discipline'.[31] The leader of the Amis des Noirs could still only picture black slaves as 'mutilated and powerless'. His practical response to the uprising was to call for the arming of the people of colour, so that they would join forces with white settlers to defeat the slave rebels. The Amis des Noirs thus ended the first phase of its existence by advocating a reactionary alliance of slavers – the only way to prevent the 'ruin of the colony'.[32]

The Société des Amis des Noirs played no further role in the process leading to French emancipation in 1794. By an ironic twist, when Brissot was put on trial and executed by the Jacobins in 1793, one of the charges was that he and the Girondins had promoted the anti-slavery rebellion in Saint-Domingue. Not only had he done nothing of the sort, but the proclamation of 'general liberty' was initiated by the Saint-Domingue slave insurrection itself. It was this rebellion that forced Sonthonax and the French authorities in the colony to proclaim the abolition of slavery in 1793. Six months later the French legislature unanimously passed the decree of 16 Pluviôse, which declared that 'slavery of Negroes is abolished in all colonies', and that 'all men, without distinction of colour, domiciled in the colonies, are French citizens and will enjoy all the rights guaranteed in the constitution'.[33] Among the legislators present was Saint-Domingue's Jean-Baptiste Belley, an African-born former captive who was the first black member of France's parliament. He delivered a passionate speech in favour of abolition.

From the start, this first abolition was met with intense hostility by European settlers across French colonies. The 1794 law was applied in Guadeloupe and Guyana, but not in the Indian Ocean territories of Réunion and Ile de France (Mauritius), where the colons, backed up by local officials, refused to implement it, dragging their feet for several years. The emancipation legislation was ignored in Martinique and Tobago as well, as they were both in British hands in 1794. In France opposition to abolition began to gather momentum in the second half of the 1790s, due to the rise of conservative forces associated with the metropolitan colonial lobby. These groups, which had remained implacably opposed to emancipation and the granting of political rights to black citizens, eventually helped Napoleon Bonaparte in his rise to power through his coup d'état of 18 Brumaire in 1799.

The opening salvo in this reactionary movement was fired in a 1796 pamphlet by François Barbé de Marbois, the last pre-revolutionary intendant (governor) of Saint-Domingue, who remained a vigorous champion of the old order, and later became a member of Bonaparte's Council of State. 'Let me have the courage to affirm it,' he asserted, 'better a return to a useful and well-organized slavery, as it existed for centuries, than the shapeless and anarchical turmoil with which it has been replaced!'[34] Men such as Barbé typically referred to the post-emancipation situation in the colonies, and in particular in Saint-Domingue, as chaotic. He stridently opposed the empowerment of black citizens and agitated for a return to 'order'. This was a euphemism that encompassed the reassertion of white rule, the removal of black military officers and restriction of black civil and political rights, and the restoration of slavery. All of these policies were eventually adopted by Bonaparte, underpinning his invasion of Saint-Domingue in 1801, and his reimposition of human bondage in Guadeloupe and Guyana a year later.

These counter-revolutionary views were fully aired in the French legislature, where the colonial lobby had a sizeable following. In 1797 one of its spokesmen, Vincent-Marie Viénot de Vaublanc, caused a stir with a blistering denunciation of post-revolutionary French colonial policy. Viénot was a royalist who hailed from a slaveholding family that had lost its fortune in Saint-Domingue. Three years after the universal abolition of slavery in France, he denounced the rise of black military and political power in the colony under Louverture's leadership, arguing that since abolition the territory had descended into violence and anarchy. He now claimed that Saint-Domingue was no longer being governed in the interests of its European settlers, whom he called 'the real Frenchmen'. The racial subtext here was clear: white rule needed to be restored, as well as slavery if necessary, and black people had to be removed forthwith from commanding positions in the military.

Étienne Laveaux, who was an elected member of the French legislature at this time, responded with a powerful speech in which he defended his own record as a colonial administrator, and rebutted the 'vile slanders' of Viénot de Vaublanc. He reaffirmed his commitment to the new political order created by the emancipation law of 1794, and proudly pointed out that he was held in high esteem by the colony's black citizens.[35] Back in Saint-Domingue, Toussaint Louverture too joined the fray with a pamphlet in which he methodically refuted Viénot de Vaublanc's arguments, denouncing the 'barbaric cupidity' of those Europeans who had established chattel slavery in Africa, and offering a robust defence of abolitionism. His *Réfutation* is a unique text in the history of black narratives, championing emancipation from the perspective of a former captive not only in principle but by demonstrating what emancipated people had accomplished practically as French citizens since 1794.[36]

Toussaint's 1797 text was prescient. Bonaparte went on to recruit Viénot de Vaublanc into his Senate, and he invoked an almost identical panoply of arguments as the French *colon* to justify his invasion of Saint-Domingue in 1801. In fact, the reactionary shift in French colonial policy was already apparent in Bonaparte's Constitution of 22 Frimaire, adopted in December 1799, which contained no declaration of rights and did not grant automatic citizenship to those born in the colonies. The text created a legal grey area that allowed for the effective enslavement of certain categories of people, such as household servants. Article 91 of the Constitution also moved away from Laveaux's republican universalism, stipulating that arrangements for colonial governance would be based on 'special laws' – an expression widely interpreted to open the door to the reintroduction of slavery. Laveaux himself was explicitly targeted by Bonaparte. Appointed as the French commissioner in Guadeloupe, he was arrested upon his arrival in 1800, on Bonaparte's orders, and sent back to France.[37]

France's new ruler surrounded himself with pro-slavery advisors, who reinforced his prejudices against newly emancipated citizens. Among his new recruits in the Council of State were the colonial lawyer and planter advocate Moreau de Saint-Méry, who had been an influential member of the pro-slavery Club Massiac in the early years of the Revolution, and Pierre Victor Malouet, a *colon* who had signed a convention with the British in 1793 inviting them to invade Saint-Domingue in order to restore human bondage. In October 1801 Bonaparte appointed Denis Decrès as his Minister of the Navy, and he too believed that the 1794 abolition had been a mistake. A year later, when justifying the restoration of slavery to his entourage, Bonaparte expressed his thinking in unambiguously racist terms: 'I am for the whites, because I am white; I have no other reason, and this one is good enough. How can we have given liberty to Africans, to men without civilization, who had not the slightest idea of what a colony, or for that matter what France, was?'[38]

The unravelling of the first abolition was thus largely driven by the reactionary political turn that accompanied Bonaparte's rise to power.[39] But the restoration of slavery was further facilitated by the weak and contradictory nature of French abolitionism, and its regressive views concerning black empowerment. The ineffectual character of the Société des Amis des Noirs in the early years of the French Revolution, its association with the defeated Girondist faction, and its absence of a popular base meant that the advocacy of metropolitan abolitionism was isolated from the emancipatory elements in the French revolutionary movement, and disconnected from the black men and women working to achieve and sustain freedom in the colonies. The growing divergences between metropolitan and colonial conceptions of black empowerment in the 1790s added to these existing divisions, preventing abolitionists from speaking with a unified voice. In the years preceding Bonaparte's *coup d'état*, these strains were further apparent in the brief re-emergence of the Société des Amis des Noirs between late 1797 and early 1799. The organization's ninety-two members now included Jacobin abolitionists such as Grégoire, as well as former Saint-Domingue colonial administrators Sonthonax and Laveaux, together with some black elected representatives such as Étienne Mentor. The Société's remit was to defend emancipation by promoting deeper civic integration in the colonies, and by helping to revive the international campaign against the slave trade.[40]

Largely devoted to philosophical and technical discussions, the Société's meetings had little concrete impact on French opinion and failed to counteract the rise of pro-slavery forces in national politics. The abolitionist principles of some of the organization's more conservative affiliates were soft, to say the least: for example, one of its important members was Daniel Lescallier, a senior official in the French colonial administration, who had been an enthusiastic abolitionist in the early 1790s and had unilaterally decreed the end of slavery in the French outposts in India. He supported Bonaparte's coup and joined the Council of State in 1799. Lescallier was appointed as colonial prefect in Guadeloupe in 1801, and a year later oversaw the reintroduction of slavery in the colony.[41]

Although not a member of the Société des Amis des Noirs, Victor Hugues, the champion of emancipation in Guadeloupe in the 1790s, went back to Guyana in 1800 and implemented the restoration of slavery in 1802.[42] The united front between metropolitan and colonial abolitionists was further splintered over the trajectory of the revolution in Saint-Domingue. Sonthonax, who played a prominent role in the Société, never forgave Toussaint Louverture for his humiliating expulsion from the colony. His hostility towards Toussaint's regime went as far as supporting Rigaud's attempt to overthrow the black revolutionary leader in the late 1790s. These actions caused Laveaux and Grégoire (who remained firmly loyal to Louverture) to distance themselves from the organization.[43]

Under the influence of Sonthonax, the Société des Amis des Noirs became principally focused on the interests and welfare of the *colons*. This new priority was apparent in a speech that he delivered in February 1799, at a special meeting of the society to mark the official anniversary of 16 Pluviôse. The 'father of emancipation' celebrated his own role in the abolition decree of 1793, and paid a glowing tribute to French colonial settlers, many of whom, he claimed, had taken pains to 'lighten the burden of slavery' before 1789 'by a soft and moderate regime'. Using language that was entirely drawn from pro-slavery rhetoric, Sonthonax went on to laud the 'paternal' role of *ancien régime* French planters in overseeing the welfare of their captives, a function which was now continuing as they became the 'educators' of France's black citizens in the colonies.[44]

In this revisionist account of abolitionist history, revolutionary black citizens were again infantilized, and the century-long violence of French Caribbean slavery was transformed into a benign form of paternalism. By downplaying the difference between *ancien régime* slavery and the Revolution, this kind of language by metropolitan defenders of abolition objectively facilitated Bonaparte's restoration of human bondage – a verdict later echoed in Grégoire's terse obituary of the Société des Amis des Noirs: 'death by lethargy'.[45]

The restoration of slavery in French colonies began with the law of 20 May 1802, which brought back human bondage in the Indian Ocean territories, and in Martinique, Saint-Martin, Saint Lucia, and Tobago, which had been returned to France by the British after the Treaty of Amiens in March of that year. In case there was any doubt about the racism behind his policy, in early July 1802 Bonaparte banned all persons of colour from entering French metropolitan territory. In mid-July he ordered the reintroduction of slavery in Guadeloupe; and another decree in December of that year made similar provisions for Guyana. These measures effectively brought French colonies back under the *ancien régime*'s Code Noir, with most of the emancipated men and women losing the rights they had gained after 1794.

Even from the narrow perspective of French power, this counter-revolution proved catastrophic. News from Guadeloupe rapidly reached Saint-Domingue, where it galvanized popular resistance to the occupying army of Charles Victoire Leclerc (Napoleon's brother-in-law whom we encountered in chapter 4), soon bringing about a general uprising that eventually defeated Bonaparte's troops and led to Haitian independence. Much less commented on, but equally disastrous, were the consequences of re-enslavement elsewhere in the French Empire. As we shall soon see, the removal of citizenship took away any incentive for local black populations to fight for the French Empire, as they had done so valiantly in the 1790s. This contributed to the collapse of French colonial rule across the Caribbean and the Indian Ocean. In 1809 the Portuguese and British captured Guyana, and a year later Guadeloupe, Martinique, Réunion, and Ile de France fell into British hands, followed in 1812 by the Seychelles. By this point, a decade after the restoration of slavery, Napoleonic France had no overseas colonies left. The French only recovered Martinique, Guadeloupe, Guyana, and Réunion as part of the allied settlement following Bonaparte's defeat in 1815.[46]

These losses were not merely the product of external factors. This reimposition of slavery in French colonies encountered considerable local resistance. The most emblematic case was Guadeloupe. Here, black citizens had been emancipated in 1794 and drew on their revolutionary traditions of mobilizing for their rights throughout the 1790s – against white slavers, against the British invaders in 1793–4, and then against the French Republic itself later in the decade. In the early 1800s, French agents initiated an aggressive policy of reducing the power of people of colour in the army. When these initiatives backfired, Bonaparte sent a military expedition to restore slavery. It arrived in Guadeloupe in early May 1802, and its commander Antoine Richepance immediately moved to disarm the colony's black troops. A group of several hundred soldiers revolted and headed to Basse-Terre in the south to organize the resistance, under the leadership of officers Louis Delgrès, Joseph Ignace, and Palerme, all of whom had fought with distinction under the banner of the Republic to defend emancipation during the 1790s. Delgrès was mixed-race, and Ignace and Palerme black. Their revolt had some support among local white supporters of emancipation, especially a creole white officer named Monnereau, who helped Delgrès compose his blistering proclamation, addressed to 'the entire universe', denouncing the return of the 'chains of slavery'.[47]

Inspired by the proclamation, the anti-slavery fighters soon swelled to number around 12,000 combatants, around 3,000 of whom were soldiers armed with rifles; the rest were labourers bearing pikes and machetes.[48] As in Saint-Domingue, the resistance forces included many women, who took part in military encounters and further assisted by acting as messengers, transporting ammunition and supplies, caring for the wounded, and raising spirits by singing revolutionary chants, including the *Marseillaise*.[49] Few of the names of these exceptional women fighters have been recorded for posterity, except for Solitude, who fought the French at the battle of Dolé, and was later captured and executed.[50] Marthe-Rose, the companion of Delgrès, who was present at his side throughout the rebellion, was accused of inciting the killing of whites and hanged.[51] These insurgent groups fought heroically but lacked the overwhelming popular support that the anti-Napoleonic campaign in Saint-Domingue enjoyed; after years of being subjected to coercive labour, Guadeloupe's plantation workers did not fully trust the local military, and the loyalties of mixed-race elites were divided: one of their senior commanders, Magloire Pélage, supported the French restoration of slavery. The last group of five hundred fighters under Delgrès' command were eventually pinned back by the French forces in the Danglemont plantation on the heights of Matouba in late May 1802.

Determined to live by their slogan of 'live free or die', the rebels lined up the approaches to the plantation and their fortified defences with gunpowder, and lit the fuses when the enemy forces came through; the insurgents all died in the explosion, which also killed four hundred French soldiers. The brutal repression that followed the restoration of slavery was overseen by specially appointed military commissions; 3,000 rebels were deported to France or sold into slavery in America, among them all the surviving soldiers and officers who had fought with the resistance.[52] A further 7,000 men and women died in combat or in the summary executions and killings that followed the defeat of Delgrès, and in many instances their decapitated heads were exposed in public, and their bodies left hanging for twenty-four hours – a grim return to the mass terrorizing practices common in times of slavery.[53]

Guadeloupe's return to slavery was thus consummated in a bloodbath. There were further rebellions in October 1802, when a small group of insurgents became maroons and continued to cause problems for the French authorities until the middle of the decade.[54] During their last stand, Delgrès and his fighters had symbolically ripped out the white element from the tricolour flag, leaving only the blue and red, a gesture of defiance against Bonaparte that would soon be repeated by the Haitians after they won their independence from the French two years later.[55] In one of his early proclamations after Haitian independence, Jean-Jacques Dessalines paid tribute to the 'brave and immortal Delgrès, plucked by the wind rather than living in chains'.[56]

A closer look at events in Guyana after the restoration of slavery reveals an equally vigorous pattern of resistance from local black populations, here principally through marronage. As we have seen, Victor Hugues came to the colony to implement Bonaparte's December 1802 proclamation. With effect from April 1803 around 14,000 former emancipated citizens, including those who had become smallholding *propriétaires*, were re-enslaved; only a few hundred were able to buy their freedom.[57] There were immediate revolts in the capital Cayenne and across the territory, and scores of labourers fled into the colony's dense forest hinterlands, where they set up maroon communities. The scale of these desertions is difficult to track, as Hugues and his administrators were publicly at pains to stress that the return to slavery had occurred 'without the shedding of blood'. They even extravagantly claimed that the captives had gone back to their former owners 'with pleasure'.[58] In his private correspondence, however, Hugues acknowledged widespread flights from plantations by the now re-enslaved agricultural workers, and he set up a militia whose primary purpose was to hunt down the runaways and destroy their settlements.

Later published in France, the recollections of one of the militia's members, Sévère Hérault, charted the increasingly precarious position of the

French authorities as they attempted to manage this mass maroon resistance. The runaways he tried to track were organized in a group of camps, approximately three leagues from each other, and linked with concealed paths that were barely detectable. The huts in each community were designed with multiple exits to facilitate escape. Many of the maroons forged links with plantation captives, allowing them regular access to food supplies and tools. Some of the camp leaders became famous figures, among them Pompée, Old Simon, Charlemagne, Frossard, and Paulin. They drew on traditions of marronage among fugitives in the region to preside over well-ordered communities that sustained themselves through hunting and fishing, and by growing a wide array of crops, including manioc, bananas, sugar cane, and potatoes.[59] Pompée, who became a runaway in 1801, had a companion named Gertrude, and he remained in the bush for around twenty years. He was only captured in 1822, after eluding repeated attempts by the authorities to seize him. Like many maroons his shooting skills were outstanding.[60] Another charismatic maroon leader named Linval stayed out of reach of French slavers until 1824.[61]

Hérault's account of his time in the Guyana jungle confirms the pattern we saw repeatedly in chapter 2: the near impossibility for slavers and their militias to achieve a complete military victory over organized, inventive, and mobile maroon groups. Despite the success of these militias in capturing some maroon leaders and burning their encampments, the runaways often anticipated their arrival and quietly withdrew ahead of them. French militias were thus unable to destroy the runaway communities, and Hérault conceded that over time they grew in number.[62] The interrogation of Télémaque and Catherine, two runaways captured in 1808, showed that the maroons were unbowed and indeed eager to avenge the killings of their comrades. After his seizure, Frossard was hacked to death, decapitated, and his head exposed in Cayenne.[63] The slavers' militias were constantly vulnerable to ambushes, with runaways exploiting their superior knowledge of the terrain to inflict lethal attacks on the French forces. Hérault reported that the runaway leader Charlemagne was personally responsible for the deaths of a dozen of his men during one single attack. After each such encounter, the maroons would 'flee into the thick bush shouting cries of joy'.[64]

Sniper ambushes were common, with the French being unable to respond in any effective way, as Hérault conceded: 'We returned fire, but upon whom? We could see no one!'[65] By 1808, the overall situation had become so desperate that Hugues began to recruit enslaved Africans into his militia, but when they reached the jungle many of them deserted and joined the runaways. In early 1809 Hugues and his officials fled to Guadeloupe after capitulating to the British and Portuguese forces that invaded the colony. This incursion prompted an insurrection of the enslaved, initiated by an uprising of three hundred armed agricultural labourers led by a captive named Apollo.[66]

The fall of Guyana into British and Portuguese hands was thus a direct consequence of Bonaparte's bungled and chaotic reimposition of slavery. Unlike Saint-Domingue, this loss was not permanent. But even after the colony's return to France in 1817, at the end of the Napoleonic Wars, enslaved resistance continued to flourish there in the 1820s and 1830s, mostly through marronage.[67] Indeed, runaways proliferated across French colonies during the first half of the nineteenth century. The extent of their success can be seen in the updated version of the *Code Noir* produced by the Ministry for Naval and Colonial Affairs in 1829. The text stressed the importance of addressing and containing the problem, while offering no new solutions. Registers of runaways kept in local colonial archives show that captives continued to escape in small but consistent numbers until 1848.[68]

Overall resistance to the French slave order after 1802 took different forms. When speaking among themselves, captives derided the plantation system and its enforcers. For example, in their everyday language, and in their sharp and pithy proverbs, they associated all negative human characteristics – laziness, bad faith, violence, and incompetence – with white people. This dark humour was expressed in slave songs performed on weekends, or during special gatherings of associations that met regularly for festive, religious, and funereal purposes in Martinique and Guadeloupe. Their members broke their isolation by establishing links across plantations and in town *quartiers*.[69]

In Guadeloupe two of these organizations were known as the *Grenats* and *Violettes*, and they provided support and medical assistance to those in need. Their solidarity activities often raised suspicion among white settlers, but they were tolerated by the authorities.[70] Sometimes these organizations acted as fronts for more militant collective movements. Obeah-inspired poisoning plots dominated Martinique in the early nineteenth century and particularly for much of the 1820s, as we saw in chapter 3. These conspiracies were thought to be grounded in a 'sect of poisoners' whose networks operated across the island. Even though their members were never apprehended or identified, many individual captives were convicted and severely punished. For example, a man named Joséphat was sentenced to be flogged, branded, and sent to a penal colony in Senegal.[71] The constant fear of poisoning provoked a collective psychosis among settlers.[72]

In French-controlled territories in the Indian Ocean, the Revolutionary and Napoleonic periods witnessed considerable resistance activity, partly resulting from the fierce opposition of local settlers to any alteration to the slavery regime after the Revolution, as we saw earlier. In Mauritius (then known as Ile de France) there were around 50,000 captives in the late eighteenth century. The Colonial Assembly's rejection of the 1794 emancipation decree led to a sharp increase in marronage, which was already well established in the island's interior regions by that point. Two years later the enraged *colons* chased away French republican officials who had arrived in the colony.[73] Some captives responded by openly embracing French revolutionary language and symbols. For example, an armed maroon named Pierre, who had previously escaped on several occasions, was captured again in May 1801. As a symbol of his self-emancipation he wore a hat with a tricolour cockade that he had manufactured from old pieces of cloth.

Reports from Ile de France around the time of Bonaparte's formal restoration of slavery highlight an upsurge in violent acts of opposition by the enslaved, as well as an increase in the number of attempted flights by sea.[74] Charismatic maroon leaders such as Bellaca and Tatamaka became widely known during this period and enjoyed a considerable appeal among resistance communities.[75] Faced with this revolutionary situation, the island's Colonial Assembly decreed in 1801 that anyone convicted of these crimes – already punishable by the death penalty – would henceforth be burnt alive (for poisoning) and broken alive (for assassinations).[76] In December 1802, following a spate of arson attacks on settler properties and cane fields by maroons, a special judicial commission was established. It was empowered to sentence those found guilty of this crime also to be burnt alive.

As in neighbouring Bourbon Island, the militias formed to hunt down runaways on Ile de France were reinforced. Over a thousand fugitives were captured by its nine detachments in 1805, although the numbers declined in subsequent years.[77] The taking of Ile de France by the British in 1810 was not directly connected to the restoration of slavery. But as in Guyana it was plain that the fierce repression of black protest and resistance, as well as the restrictions imposed on free people of colour under the governorship of Charles Decaen, weakened French control of the island during the final years of the Napoleonic era and facilitated the British victory. In 1809 Decaen attempted to shore up the island's defences by recruiting a battalion of 650 captives, but he was forced to abandon the project after protests from the local *colons*.[78] By this point the trade in African captives had been banned in Britain, so some of the enslaved in

Ile de France entertained the hope (of which they were rapidly disabused) that they would be emancipated by their new British conquerors.[79]

Along with Ile de France, in 1810 the British took over neighbouring Bourbon Island, where there had been slave uprisings across the eighteenth century, and especially in 1705, 1730, and 1779. Maroon traditions had similarly developed, mainly in the mountainous hinterlands and among the island's Malagasy captives, whose first major leader Anchain created a 'kingdom of the interior' where they governed themselves in accordance with autonomous maroon practices. They gave empowering names to their settlements, such as 'Cimandef', which signifies 'he who does not yield'.[80] As in Ile de France, white settlers in Bourbon had rejected the 1794 emancipation, effectively rebelling against French authority until Bonaparte's restoration of slavery in 1802, which they welcomed enthusiastically. Bolstered by the events in Saint-Domingue and by Haitian independence a few years later, maroons continued to dream of emancipation. One of many expressions of militancy on their part was the regular organization of secret military training exercises on plantations, as revealed by a fugitive captured in 1799.[81]

The defeat of the French by the British created an opportunity for the enslaved in Bourbon Island to mobilize for their rights. It was against this backdrop that an insurrection unfolded in November 1811 at Saint-Leu, one of the few places on the island where the ratio of captives to settlers was quite high.[82] It had been planned for several months, and involved around five hundred people of different origins: Africans in the majority, as well as Malagasy people, creole natives, and a small number of Indians from the subcontinent. Many had met and become maroons earlier that year while conscripted to gather timber for repairing a British ship. Among them were the rebellion's two principal leaders, Elie and Gilles. The conspirators met regularly at a natural pond where captives from the neighbourhood were sent to gather water. This meeting point allowed them to increase their recruits while planning their strategy. Their aim was to take over the large plantations in the area, and then rally support from their brethren across the island, with a view to pushing the British to abolish slavery. As in Louisiana that same year, the Saint-Leu insurgency was rapidly defeated, and the main conspirators were publicly executed after a summary trial.[83] However, the organization of this Indian Ocean rebellion – the only major uprising in the island's history – again brought home the determination of captives across French colonies to resist Bonaparte's reimposition of slavery.

In neighbouring Mauritius, there was no large-scale rebellion or plot, with the possible exception of the 1822 conspiracy attributed to

Ratsitatanina, a Malagasy prince accused of fomenting a slave revolt against the colony's white population, who was executed along with two of his alleged accomplices. The affair remains murky and the voluminous trial records are difficult to penetrate, not least because many of the insurgents were subsequently coerced into testifying against the Malagasy rebel.[84] Recent scholarship has expressed scepticism as to Ratsitatanina's involvement in any plot; it is more likely that the prince was trying to emulate many of his countrymen and organize an escape by sea to return to his homeland.[85] However, this did not mean that the enslaved in Mauritius were passive. As we saw in chapter 2, marronage was a constant issue faced by both the French and after 1810 the British, until abolition. The enslaved resisted by a range of other means, such as theft, sabotage, clandestine meetings, and verbal confrontations. In 1832 a captive named Bagnon was accused of singing a 'subversive song', whose refrain gleefully affirmed that 'we young people must not rely on white people, we must instead depend on enslaved people like ourselves, who know how effectively to grind the roots in order to kill the sergeants'.[86]

In the French Caribbean, the violence and trauma inflicted by Bonaparte's restoration of human bondage in 1802 were followed by a return to the most brutal practices of the *ancien régime*. In 1819 in Guadeloupe one planter had eighteen enslaved persons burnt alive in a single day.[87] Yet records show that the captives refused to acquiesce in their subjugation and continued to struggle for their autonomy during the early decades of the nineteenth century. Conspiracies and revolts were frequent and remained the authorities' greatest fear.[88] A plot uncovered in Martinique in September 1811 targeted the town of Saint-Pierre, where there was a large captive population of over 8,000, who moved with relative freedom and interacted with the significant number of runaways in the surrounding areas. The insurgents' plan was to set fire to the town, seize weapons from the gendarmerie, and kill the local white settlers before spreading the movement across the island. A decade later, in October 1822, in the rural areas around Saint-Pierre, a group of armed captives from Carbet rebelled under the slogan of 'Liberty or Death'. They aimed to provoke a collective uprising; dozens of rebels were arrested and twenty-one were executed.

Seven months after the July 1830 Revolution in France, there were further slave revolts in Martinique, in February 1831 (in plantations around Saint-Pierre, again) and 1833 (Grand'Anse), while in Guadeloupe similar plots and uprisings were put down in 1830, and once more in 1831.[89] These movements were sometimes blamed by the authorities on external groups with abolitionist sympathies. In the aftermath of the 1822 events

in Martinique, a repressive campaign against advocates of racial equality
was conducted, and a mixed-race man named Cyrille Bissette was arrested
for defending the rights of his people. Bissette was tried on trumped-
up charges, sentenced to life as a galley slave in 1824, and branded on
the shoulder. *L'Affaire Bissette* caused an uproar in France and in 1827
the sentence was reduced to deportation by an appellate court in Guadeloupe, following a review ordered by the Court of Cassation in Paris.
Bissette was eventually pardoned and became one of France's leading
abolitionist campaigners, founding the country's first black anti-slavery
organization, the Société des Hommes de Couleur.[90]

In all these instances of slave rebellion, myriad Haitian echoes, connections, and associations again surfaced and were mobilized by the rebels.
This belief in the contagious effect of the Haitian revolution was widely
shared among Martinique's planters.[91] For the *colon* Pierre Dessalles its
influence was particularly conveyed through the free black population,
who gave 'bad advice' to the captives.[92] In their moments of lucidity the
French authorities understood the inspirational impact of the Haitian
revolution on enslaved populations in French colonies, whether or not
they had previously been emancipated due to the Revolution. These points
were specifically highlighted in a briefing note to the incoming governor
of Martinique in 1815.[93] The appeal of Haiti to free black communities
in Martinique and Guadeloupe was powerful, and many families emigrated to the land of freedom between 1804 and 1848.[94] But there were
population movements from Haiti to the French colonies as well. One of
the Martinique insurgents in 1811 was a free black man named Edmond
Thétis, who was born in Saint-Domingue and had served in Henri Christophe's army. Examples of this kind led French colonial authorities to call
for constant vigilance against 'agents' of the revolutionary state. Martinique's slaves were fascinated by the Haitian example, because they had
not been emancipated during the Revolutionary era.[95]

In the Carbet uprising of 1822, the leaders of the conspiracy galvanized
their recruits with the promise of a landing of Haitian troops, causing the
Martinique authorities to denounce the 'destructive volcano originating
from Saint-Domingue', and to recognize that thanks to the existence of
the Haitian state 'all black slaves now aspire to freedom'.[96] Among the
Guadeloupe plots of 1830, one was planned in the area of Saint-Anne,
and was explicitly intended to 'create a new Haiti'.[97] This objective was
shared by one of the leaders of the 1831 uprising, a man named Chéry. He
had taught himself to read and was seen shortly before the insurrection
with a book in his hand, commenting that in the near future his brethren would be freed and 'serve as officers in the army' – one of the classic

martial images associated with Haitian sovereignty. Many of those who were captured after the rebellion shouted 'we will follow Saint-Domingue' before their execution.[98]

One of the banners boldly hoisted on a local church tower during the February 1831 revolt in Saint-Pierre echoed the 'Freedom or Death' slogan of the Guadeloupe resistance in 1802, adding 'The Answer in Three Days'.[99] Liberty was longer in coming, and this emancipatory yearning continued during the years of the July Monarchy in the 1830s and 1840s, right up to the proclamation of the second abolition by the Republic in 1848. Speaking of the captives in French colonies, the poet and republican statesman Alphonse de Lamartine observed in a speech to parliament in 1835 that 'the impatience for freedom is driving them, they are expecting it, they are conspiring for it, and they are deserting their plantations in great numbers'.[100]

Largely due to the increased French military presence in the colonies, there were no more revolts. This abjuration of violence was perhaps also connected to the British abolition of slavery, which may have raised collective expectations of a similar outcome in the French colonies. However, the main French resistance effect of British abolition was to boost maritime marronage, with an increase in attempted flights from French to British-controlled territories by sea. In a letter to the French statesman Victor de Broglie in February 1842, Thomas Clarkson observed that 'great numbers of slaves belonging to Martinique and Guadeloupe have attempted to make their escape from thence to the British islands in the neighbourhood, and many of these have accomplished their purchase'.[101] There is clear evidence of runaway escapes to coastal regions, systematic boat thefts, and canoe fabrication during this period, enabling successive waves of departures from French colonies – especially between 1833 and 1838, and again in the mid-1840s. Up to 5,000 refugees found their way to British territories such as Saint Lucia, Demerara, Trinidad, and Antigua.[102] After the abolition of slavery, some returned to the French islands where they had been held in captivity, and where they most likely had friends and family members.[103]

Yet if French captives had hoped that their continued resistance might spark a greater awareness of the imperative of emancipation among metropolitan political and intellectual leaders, they were disappointed. The activities of the principal abolitionist organization of the Restoration era, the Société de la Morale Chrétienne, showed the persistence of the intellectual gap between the aspirations of the enslaved in the colonies and the preoccupations of French abolitionists themselves. Founded in late 1821 by moderate opponents of the ruling conservative monarchists, the Société was a philanthropic association that counted among its members some past heroes of the revolutionary period such as Lafayette and Grégoire. It was mainly a cocoon for France's most prominent liberal intellectuals, including Jean Charles de Sismondi, François Guizot, Charles de Rémusat, Auguste de Staël, and Victor de Broglie; many of these men would become leading government figures under the July Monarchy between 1830 and 1848.

Like the Société des Amis des Noirs in the late 1780s and early 1790s, the Société de la Morale Chrétienne took its main cue not from an analysis of the situation in French colonies, but from the British abolitionist movement, with which it was closely affiliated, materially, philosophically, and religiously (most of the Société's elites were Protestant). The bulk of its publications by the mid-1820s were translations of British pamphlets.[104] At the behest of its British patrons, the Société thus remained exclusively focused on the abolition of the slave trade, which France had formally signed up to in 1815, and had been further confirmed by royal decrees in 1817 and 1818. But the trade still continued through the participation of French ships from Nantes and Bordeaux in the illegal traffic of African captives.[105] Also in alignment with British abolitionists, the organization's position on emancipation remained strictly gradualist. As de Broglie put it in a speech to the French parliament in 1822: 'slavery is an ill for which freedom is not the immediate cure'. This was exactly what Wilberforce and Clarkson were saying at the time in London.[106]

The social and political influence of the Société de la Morale Chrétienne was limited. But one of its contributions was to promote a more constructive public conversation in France about the Haitian revolution. French colons and their conservative royalist allies remained bitterly resentful of the loss of Saint-Domingue after 1815; they denounced the collapse of order in the former colony, which they claimed had become a 'new Guinea', a 'nest of pirates and brigands, and a source of insurrection';[107] in addition Haitian independence was seen as one of the (many) perverse consequences of the French Revolution.[108] As part of their wider efforts to rehabilitate the Revolutionary heritage, French liberals responded with a raft of positive appreciations of the Haitian revolution, adding their voices to that of Grégoire, who up to that point had been its principal champion in France. Charles de Rémusat compared the revolution of 1791 with the popular uprising that overthrew the ancien régime in 1789, and extolled the Toussaint Louverture years of 'order and discipline' as 'the beautiful moment of Saint-Domingue'.[109] The remarkable growth of Haiti's population since the end of the eighteenth century led Auguste

Billiard, another member of the Société, to affirm that the new state had taken its people to an unprecedented degree of prosperity, while Sismondi celebrated Haitian self-determination as evidence of the capacities of the black race: 'it is here that the sons of Africa have proven that they are humans, that they deserved to be free, that they know how to appreciate enlightenment and virtue'.[110] The same point was made by Lafayette in a letter to his friend Clarkson, noting the success of the 'Republic of Haiti' where 'the sons of Africa will, one hopes, attain an advanced degree of civilization and prosperity'.[111]

While positive, these assessments nonetheless revealed ongoing French liberal hesitations about black sovereignty and empowerment. Initiating an interpretation among progressives that proved enduring (and remains common in France to this day), the Haitian revolution was presented not as an autonomous struggle of enslaved captives, but as a by-product of the 1789 Revolution. One of the main liberal newspapers, *Le Globe*, celebrated Saint-Domingue's overthrow of colonial slavery and the advent of racial equality as triumphs of French Revolutionary ideals.[112] Haiti also provided a racialized narrative about regeneration that rested on French cultural superiority, preparing the ground for the myth of the French civilizing mission in the colonies. In this context liberals depicted Haiti's Francophile mixed-race elites under Pétion and Boyer as symbols of how African-born former captives could turn away from their 'primitive' conditions and embrace European enlightenment. This was the basis of the distinction made by Sophie Doin, another member of the Société de la Morale Chrétienne, between the miserable 'Negro of Africa' and the happy 'Negro of Haiti'.[113]

The event that captured the liberals' divergence from the real interests of enslaved and emancipated black communities in the Atlantic was France's diplomatic recognition of Haiti in 1825. Negotiated by the naval officer Armand de Mackau, this agreement was essentially imposed on the Boyer government of Haiti at gunpoint, with French warships waiting on the shores of Port-au-Prince armed with over five hundred cannons. The royal proclamation that followed in April 1825 was a monument of French colonial arrogance and bad faith: its three articles referred to Haiti as 'the French part of Saint-Domingue', and 'granted' its inhabitants their independence – which the Haitian people had of course seized for themselves two decades earlier.[114] Alongside its lofty language, the agreement forced Haiti to offer commercial privileges to French merchants (a 50 per cent reduction in customs duties levied on their goods), and to pay an indemnity of 150 million francs for the 'dispossessions' incurred by French *colons* for the 'loss' of their slaves. In order to raise this astronomical sum, the Haitian government had to borrow from leading French banks at high interest rates. The ruinous provisions of this double debt (the principal and the interest payments) fatally damaged its economy: in 1826 the state's expenditure was twice the size of its income.[115] The social and political effects of the debt ravaged Haiti during the ensuing decades, and destabilized it well into the twentieth century.[116]

French liberals fully supported the agreement and its reparations clause, applauding its 'dignity' as well as the show of force that had made it possible. It was not coincidental that the Laffitte banking consortium which benefited massively from the agreement was largely controlled by French liberal interests.[117] If we might wonder how Christian morality, which was meant to be inspiring the Société's thinking, could justify former captives paying their former masters for their emancipation, the answer could be seen through liberal proposals for emancipation at the time. Some French gradualist pamphleteers, such as Charles Coquerel, argued that it would be appropriate for captives to contribute to their own liberation by working three days a week for their masters.[118] This form of indentured emancipation demonstrated that, like their British counterparts, French metropolitan abolitionists had no moral qualms about making the enslaved pay for their freedom.

Given their already narrow and self-interested vision of emancipation, there was not much to be hoped of French liberals when they came to power through the July 1830 Revolution. They managed to disappoint even these low expectations. In April 1833 a law gave free people of colour in the colonies the same civil and political rights as whites. At the same time another law basically took away their political entitlements, as it set an income bar for the right to vote that was impossible for most black citizens to meet.[119] Faced with uprisings in Martinique and Guadeloupe, and mindful of the powerful revolts in Jamaica (1831–2) and Brazil (1835), the main response of the July Monarchy was significantly to increase its troop presence in its colonies, from around 4,000 in 1836 to 6,000 in 1838, and then 9,000 by 1845. This was in addition to colonial militia forces, which numbered over 10,000. Such a massive display of force demonstrated that the principal preoccupation of liberals was to protect the slave order by violent and coercive means.[120]

After the British ending of slavery, French abolitionists created a new organization in 1834, the Société Française pour l'Abolition de l'Esclavage. Like its predecessor, it was dominated by gradualist liberals (Tocqueville, Guizot, Rémusat, Broglie) and remained closely tied to the British movement, in particular through Zachary Macaulay, who played a key role in founding the organization and was appointed its honorary president.[121]

Broglie, the Société's president, chaired a parliamentary commission on slavery that worked for three years (1840–43) and recommended gradual abolition over a period of twenty years. The idea of asking captives to contribute financially to their emancipation through unpaid indentured labour was revived, even though this practice had visibly failed in the British colonies.[122]

In July 1845, Armand de Mackau, now the French Minister of Colonies – the same man who had negotiated the harsh agreement with Haiti twenty years earlier – came up with legislative proposals in the wake of the Broglie commission's report. They consisted of minor reforms to improve the treatment of slaves and their working conditions (for example, the number of whip lashes was to be limited to fifteen). Even as a distant horizon, emancipation was not on the agenda, although by this point slavery had been abolished in Britain. When the Société Française pour l'Abolition de l'Esclavage attempted to organize mass meetings in order to mobilize wider support for the anti-slavery cause in 1842, they were banned by the government, which curtailed the Société's activities.[123] French liberals were now in open and public contradiction with their professed beliefs, as the head of the government at the time was none other than the former abolitionist François Guizot.

By the early 1840s the French liberal gradualist approach to emancipation was clearly floundering. This was apparent even to its despairing British friends, who had been in a similar impasse two decades earlier. This failure symbolized the July Monarchy's wider shortcomings as a reformist movement, which would lead to its overthrow by the February 1848 Revolution, which brought in a republican government committed to the Revolutionary principles of liberty, equality, and fraternity. One of the first acts of the new regime, on 4 March, was to proclaim the immediate abolition of enslavement for France's 200,000 captives. Affirming that human bondage was an 'attack on human dignity', and a 'blatant violation of the republican principles of Liberty, Equality, and Fraternity', the subsequent decree of 27 April 1848 stipulated that slavery would be completely abolished in all French colonies two months after its publication, and that in the meantime all physical punishments as well as sales of human persons were banned.[124]

In its unequivocal and universal character, and its association with a new revolutionary republican order, the abolition of 1848 carried echoes of the early 1790s. But it was different too. Unlike the debacle with the Société des Amis des Noirs, republican intellectuals in Paris and across France were this time in step with full abolition, and they made every effort to present the second abolition as consensual and non-violent. Indeed, references to 1794 were generally avoided: no mention was made of the Revolutionary precedent in the 1848 emancipation decrees. Its intellectual genesis was the product of a realization among metropolitan republican thinkers during the 1840s that any form of enslavement was incompatible with their basic values and ideals, particularly in the aftermath of British abolition.

But just as in the Revolutionary years there were major prompts from the colonies: from the struggles of the enslaved, as well as from those who were able to make their voices heard in Paris. Among the pioneers in adopting and promoting immediate emancipation was Martinique's anti-slavery campaigner Cyril Bissette, who remained in France after his appeal and then founded the *Revue des Colonies*. Its first issue in 1834 urged all progressives to embrace immediate emancipation as logically entailed by the 1789 Declaration of the Rights of Man. Bissette campaigned vigorously for abolition and argued that compensation was owed to the enslaved, rather than to the *colons*.[125] In the 1840s this message was progressively embraced by leading thinkers across the republican ideological spectrum, from Lamartine, François Arago, Jules Michelet, Edgar Quinet, Louis Blanc, and Alexandre Ledru-Rollin to Victor Considérant, all of whom signed petitions calling for an end to slavery.

Between 1844 and 1847 republicans took their campaigns to the public through parliamentary petitions, which gathered thousands of signatures, in particular from working-class communities across France. Petitions demanding abolition were sent to Paris by local anti-slavery committees, departmental councils, and Protestant and women's groups, although not all favoured an immediate end to slavery.[126] But in a sense the very distinction between gradual and immediate abolition was being undermined by events on the ground. Although still a gradualist the republican parliamentarian Hippolyte Carnot observed in an article in 1845 that if the colonial settlers resisted emancipation, 'the black populations will know how to seize freedom for themselves'.[127] This sense of democratic self-empowerment was confirmed in 1848. When news of the abolition decree reached Guadeloupe and Martinique, and fearing that some diehard *colons* might try some form of rearguard action, captives revolted and forced local colonial authorities to proclaim emancipation in late May, well ahead of the two-month deadline. As Aimé Césaire later observed, black populations were driven by the active democratic sentiment that 'freedom does not fall from the sky, and it is never completely granted, but taken and conquered'.[128]

Thus 1848 did not occur in isolation. The push for immediate abolition was prompted by evolutions in the colonies, which provoked an inexor-able decomposition of the slave order. From the early 1840s, anti-slavery positions were adopted by some Masonic lodges in Guadeloupe and Mar-tinique, accompanied by campaigns directed at plantations; one lodge was closed in 1846 for its abolitionist propaganda.[129] Although there was nothing comparable to the scale of the Saint-Domingue revolution, local acts of enslaved resistance in French colonies increased, particularly in the development of collective refusals to work.[130] These phenomena can further be glimpsed in judicial records of the period, as with the trials of two Martinique *colons* accused of mistreating their captives. Testimonies revealed consistent patterns of enslaved defiance, including high levels of marronage, verbal and physical acts of resistance, and regular instances of what was described as 'insolence'. Taken together these expressions of dissent pointed to a clear breakdown of slaver authority, even if its phys-ical and coercive power was still manifest.[131]

The more realistic settlers acknowledged that enslaved resistance had taken its toll in the French Caribbean, and moreover that the geographical closeness of British colonies made the preservation of slavery unten-able. The General Council of Guadeloupe, dominated by white *colons*, declared at the end of 1838 that 'emancipation is now an inevitable fact, not only because of the efforts of abolitionists, but also as a topographical consequence of the position of our islands and their proximity to British territories'.[132] In 1847 the same Council officially wrote to King Louis-Philippe endorsing the 'path to emancipation'.[133] One of the petitions received by the French parliament in 1847 was from French slaveholding settlers on the island of Saint-Martin, who demanded immediate aboli-tion for their 3,000 captives as most of their able workers were escaping to neighbouring British islands, and they were being left with 'old people, children, disabled people, and the indolent'.[134]

In the story of the individual figures who shaped and enacted the second French abolition, one person towers above all others: Victor Schoelcher, the author of the emancipation decree of April 1848 (see Plate 14). As Under-Secretary of State for Colonial Affairs and president of the Repub-lic's abolition commission, he oversaw the process that finally ended human bondage in France. Born into a wealthy merchant family, Schoel-cher developed an ardent interest in emancipation from the early 1830s, after a first trip to the Americas in 1829–30. Upon his return to France he joined the liberal Société Française pour l'Abolition de l'Esclavage, which as we saw earlier was committed to gradualism. The Haitian revolution, about which he collected an enormous body of material, played a pivotal role in the maturation of Schoelcher's political thought, enabling him to confront standard slaver and gradualist arguments about disorder, black incapacity, and African backwardness.[135]

In *De l'esclavage des noirs* (1833) Schoelcher countered traditional stereotypes against black people with a glowing tribute to the 'valour, spiritual resources, and genius' of the Haitian revolution.[136] In *Abolition de l'esclavage* (1840) he celebrated the Haitian revolution as an expression of Revolutionary patriotism, and a right of oppressed people to fight for their freedom.[137] It was after an extensive trip to the Caribbean in 1840–41 (including Haiti) that Schoelcher broke emphatically with gradualism, with most of his fellow republicans in France following his lead. They often quoted his writings directly thereafter. In 1842 he published *Des colonies françaises*, whose subtitle was *Abolition immédiate de l'esclavage*. He concluded that captives in French colonies had an 'unassailable desire for emancipation', which they expressed in revolts that would only increase in intensity over time.[138]

Des colonies françaises departed from conservative and mainstream progressive thinking in France at the time by dwelling on African scientific, technical, and cultural achievements. This was a time when Africans were still widely represented as living in a 'state of near savagery'.[139] This publication was followed a year later by *Colonies étrangères et Haïti*, whose second volume further broke the mould by giving the principal credit for the Haitian revolution not to the French Revolution but to the black masses in Saint-Domingue. Schoelcher heaped praise on the 'genius' of Toussaint Louverture, 'one of the most extraordinary men of his times', remarkable for his military prowess, administrative genius, and political astuteness.[140]

At the same time, Schoelcher did not hesitate to criticize the 'tyrannical' Haitian regime after his 1841 visit, lamenting the wide gap between the elites and the people, the lack of investment in education and infrastructure, and the exclusion of the black majority from power.[141] He blamed these failings on the mixed-race administration of President Boyer – a controversial position that caused a rift with his fellow abolitionist Bissette, who believed Schoelcher had disparaged Haiti's *gens de couleur*.[142] Schoelcher's impatience with Haiti's lack of progress since independence was tinged with a certain nostalgia for the glory days of colonial Saint-Domingue. He did take note of the ongoing economic impact of the compensation payments agreed with France, imposing a crippling burden on the national budget, one-third of which was consumed with repayments to France.[143] Forced to raise taxes, the Boyer government struggled to keep up with repayments and in 1838 the debt was renegotiated and the overall sum brought down to 60 million francs. The negative impact on Haitian public resources remained significant, and the highly unpopular debt was one of the factors that brought down the Boyer regime in 1843.

Championing the ideals of emancipation, autonomy, and racial equality, the anti-slavery traditions that unfolded in French colonial territories in the early decades of the nineteenth century were inventive and resilient.[144] Except during the uprisings that episodically challenged slavers, their activities occurred mostly underground or at the interstices of the official slave system and were often not documented. This was because French authorities made a determined effort to suppress all information about slave dissent, even destroying the records of interrogations.

However, as we have seen throughout this chapter, the captives' opposition to Bonaparte's restoration of slavery was widespread in Atlantic and Indian Ocean colonies, coalescing around popular memories of resistance in Saint-Domingue and Guadeloupe and the patterns of *grand marronnage* that developed thereafter. It was further expressed in ongoing confrontations with the plantation order, in particular through arson attacks, continuous forms of labour unrest, and poisoning conspiracies, particularly those driven by practitioners of Obeah in Martinique. Captives also found refuge in self-help societies and associations that kept African cultural traditions and rituals alive. In the aftermath of emancipation, there was a strong urge among the *affranchis* (newly emancipated) to reconnect with their African roots, as shown in the names they chose when recording their new status in civil registry offices.[145] These constant acts of self-affirmation and defiance kept alive the dream of emancipation, while challenging French colonial slavery, and helping bring about its demise by damaging its self-confidence and legitimacy.

Seen in a *longue durée*, French metropolitan abolitionism was consistent too, mostly in its similarities with its British counterpart. Given the close ties between the two anti-slavery movements from the late eighteenth century onwards – and indeed, the British material and intellectual influence over the Société des Amis des Noirs, and later French liberal movements – this is unsurprising. One of the main historians of French abolitionism concluded that 'up until 1848 British support probably impeded as much as it advanced the French struggle against slavery'.[146] But if we take the struggle against slavery to include emancipation, and not just the fight against the slave trade, British influence was clearly counter-productive, being based on a shared preference for giving priority to white-settler interests over the plight of the enslaved. The only French abolitionist who consistently avoided this moral quagmire was Grégoire.

But he was a singular figure, even among republicans, and his influence on Restoration abolitionism was limited, as he was marginalized by the dominant liberals.

Like the British, French liberals approached abolition from a vantage point of entrenched cultural superiority. None of them went to Haiti after 1804, even though they wrote extensively about its revolution. Schoelcher's visit in 1841 was the first by a leading French public figure. French liberals did not have the excuse of facing a formidable adversary: unlike in Britain, where pro-slavery views were embedded in the country's public institutions, organized colonial interests in France became progressively weaker after the loss of Saint-Domingue, and the fall of sugar and coffee prices after 1815. Even when the British became committed to full and immediate abolition after 1833 and demonstrated the benefits of emancipation for British colonial planters, their friends in the July Monarchy remained impervious – a paradox for a regime that prided itself on its rationalism.[147]

In this context, unlike in Britain and the United States, no autobiographical black narratives were published in France by anti-slavery campaigners, either before or after the second abolition; the voices of the captive resistance were thus silenced in metropolitan France. This absence has sometimes been attributed to the close relationship between the slave-narrative literary genre and the Protestant ideal of salvation through personal religious redemption, which was one of the standard features of Anglo-American writings. It has been suggested that such an intellectual approach could not thrive in a French setting dominated by republican and Catholic cultures.[148] This is an interesting hypothesis, although, as we have noted earlier, many of the leading French anti-slavery campaigners were Protestant. The real source of the erasure was political, not religious: French liberal campaigners against slavery were not committed to immediate abolition and therefore had little interest in publicizing the voices of the enslaved.

Victor Schoelcher is sometimes portrayed as the French Wilberforce – a comparison that flatters the British abolitionist, who unlike Schoelcher was never able to move away from his racial elitism and his gradualist dogma. The simple difference between the two men, which reveals the main contrast between the British and French cases, was Schoelcher's republicanism: it furnished him with the intellectual resources to break free from these prejudices. Although laced with elements of paternalism (especially in his belief in assimilation and France's civilizing influence), his was a creative republicanism, forged through his recognition of the remarkable contributions of black revolutionaries to their emancipation since the early 1790s, and his belief in racial equality. It was no coincidence that Schoelcher later wrote the most impressive biography of Toussaint Louverture to be published in the nineteenth century.[149] But, contrary to the conventional grand narrative of French republican abolitionism, the 1848 emancipation was not achieved solely by French metropolitan intervention. Given the multiple influences of the Haitian revolution on Schoelcher's thinking, and the decades of captive resistance after 1802, we can see that 1848 was the culmination of the long heritage of popular mobilizations across French colonies by the enslaved people themselves.

The year 1848 marked the formal end of slavery. It represented the beginning of another struggle for the *affranchis*: the recognition of their full citizenship, and recovery of their economic and social rights. That complex story cannot be told here. But it is sobering to see how quickly the egalitarian and democratic promises of republican abolition were reversed – or, as one historian put it vividly, liberty was assassinated.[150] In his proclamation that promised the end of slavery shortly after the 1848 Revolution, Martinique's colonial administrator warned against 'idleness' and 'disorder', asserting that such behaviour had 'forced the Republic to bring back slavery in Guadeloupe in 1802' – an astonishing statement, both for its threat and its rewriting of history.[151] By the late 1840s, under the combined pressures of local settlers, a reactionary colonial administration, and a conservative government in Paris after parliamentary elections and Louis-Napoléon Bonaparte's accession to the presidency, the political freedoms of the colony's new citizens were severely curtailed. Associations, for example, were banned, while their economic liberty was similarly restricted by labour codes adopted in the early and mid-1850s in Guadeloupe and Martinique.[152]

In a letter to his editor Louis-Antoine Pagnerre, Schoelcher confessed his frustration: 'in truth I had not anticipated how difficult it would be to kill off slavery under the Republic'.[153] Yet he exacerbated the problem by endorsing the French government's decision to compensate only the slavers, which set aside the sum of 126 million francs for this purpose in 1849. Despite his earlier commitment to providing equal financial reparation to the former captives, in the end Schoelcher sided with the slavers. He even declared that this one-sided compensation was 'truly worthy of the Republic'.[154]

8

To End this Empire of Tyranny

In April 1812 Cuban authorities were on high alert, after a series of insur-rections were initiated or planned in several provincial towns. During their investigations they arrested José Antonio Aponte, a literate free black artist and craftsman who lived on the outskirts of Havana. Aponte was a seasoned campaigner, who had fought in the American Revolution and travelled around the Caribbean. He was a captain in the local militia, and it was rumoured that he was the leader of a Yoruba fraternal society (*cabildo*) dedicated to the African deity of lightning and thunder, Shango. His extensive network included other militia members, artisans, and black captives, whom he sought to recruit to the revolutionary cause; many attended clandestine meetings in his house. Aponte was also a member of a Catholic brotherhood established by the carpenters' guild and dedicated to Saint Joseph. Many militia members were active in this brotherhood, and several of them were part of the 1812 conspiracy.[1]

The plot was one of the first in Cuba to reach across all key social and political lines. It was preceded by interconnected political mobiliza-tions in Puerto Príncipe (Camagüey), Bayamo, and Holguín in the early months of 1812, followed by a massive uprising on a plantation on the outskirts of Havana. The rebellion sought to establish links across the island, particularly between urban and rural communities, and included secular as well as religious affiliates; free as well as enslaved black con-spirators; black, mixed-race, and white people, and also captives from different parts of Africa. Its aim was written in a document dictated by Aponte and nailed to the house of the Cuban captain-general, the Mar-quis of Someruelos. The goal was to declare the island's independence from Spanish rule, and build an independent free state, as the Haitians had done – but following a path dictated by the needs of Cuban society. As the proclamation warned: 'at the sound of a drum and a trumpet you will find us ready and fearless to end this empire of tyranny and vanquish the arrogance of our enemies'.[2]

Aponte and his associates planned to draw the enslaved into the insurgency with the hope of securing a general emancipation. As we have seen in many other such instances, part of their strategy relied on the promise of Haitian military support: they told their recruits that 5,000 armed soldiers from the revolutionary state were waiting on the hills outside Havana to join their insurrection. Intended to galvanize the enslaved into joining the movement, these prospects were entirely fabricated, although there was almost certainly some Haitian involvement in the conspiracy. One of the rebels who was arrested was a free black man named Juan Barbier, who spoke French and presented himself as a Saint-Domingue veteran. Barbier sometimes impersonated the former rebel leader Jean-François, who was well known in Cuba; Barbier had spent time in South Carolina as well, another theatre of enslaved revolutionary activity.[3] The plotters played on the rumour that the Spanish monarch had granted the captives freedom but that local settlers would not implement the decree. This was a variant of the emancipation legends that had been circulating across the Atlantic since the early 1790s, but which received a fresh impetus in the aftermath of the abolition of the slave trade (but not slavery itself) by Britain and the United States in 1807.

When Aponte's house was searched, a blue army jacket was discovered among his effects; he probably used it to lend credence to the tale of massive Haitian military involvement. His intellectual sophistication was shown by an item found in his home library: a book of paintings (as the authorities called it), consisting of more than sixty drawings of biblical episodes and distinguished international heroes, mingled with scenes depicting black soldiers defeating white troops. Aponte had been using these visual aids during his meetings with enslaved and free black people to recruit support for his revolutionary goals. The portraits included Greek and Roman deities, Abyssinian kings, and George Washington. There were several images of Haitian heroes, including Toussaint Louverture and Dessalines, as well as Henri Christophe, the king of northern Haiti. This was the freshly crowned monarch who was allegedly sending the military force necessary to help the rebels in 1812.[4]

One of the most forceful pictures in Aponte's book was an image with two ships in the background, and a group of secular and religious men gathered around a black monarch holding a sabre in his right hand and pointing with his left hand. One of the conspirators testified that this was a representation of Christophe, with the caption below reading: 'Carry out what has been ordered'.[5] In their celebration of different symbols of black empowerment, these portraits confirmed the richness of the internationalism that drove Aponte's anti-slavery activities. More generally, the 1812 rebellion in Cuba again highlighted the ways in which the Haitian example could creatively mobilize African, European, American, and Caribbean traditions of resistance and emancipation.[6]

Anti-slavery resistance in the Spanish Americas was widespread in the Age of Revolutions and the decades that followed. All such struggles need to be seen in their local contexts, and especially in the challenges they posed to colonial power. In this respect the 1812 rebellion's rejection of European rule was part of the wider Spanish American wars of independence, as well as the opening salvo in a long battle in Cuba, which culminated in self-government in the late nineteenth century. Cuba was singular, too, in the duration of the institution of slavery, which was formally abolished only in 1886. Also distinctive was the important role played by free people of colour like Aponte in the early phases of the anti-slavery struggle, and the large numbers of African captives forcibly brought to the island in the wake of Saint-Domingue's elimination as a slave-based sugar-producing colony. These characteristics help explain the scale of the revolts and conspiracies that developed in Cuba, both in urban and in rural settings, until the early 1840s. But Cuba was also typical of wider patterns of dissent across the Spanish Americas, especially the broad range of ideological and cultural inspirations for anti-slavery revolts, the significant role of maroons and African-born captives, and the yearning for dignity, autonomy, and self-determination characteristic of Cuban resistance movements.

In the immediate aftermath of the insurrection in Saint-Domingue, and the abolition of slavery in French colonies in 1794, there were enslaved rebellions across Spanish possessions in Central America, New Granada, the Guyanas, through to Uruguay. There in 1803 a group of African-born captives escaped from Montevideo with their families and possessions and established an independent settlement on a small island in the river Yi, proclaiming their adhesion to the 'French system' of liberty, equality, and fraternity. The settlement was attacked, and the rebels were eventually defeated.[7] In Venezuela, revolts broke out in Coro, Cumaná, Carúpano, Cariaco, Río Caribe, Maracaibo, and Cartagena. They were all suppressed by the authorities, but their frequency and complexity highlighted the growth of Saint-Domingue-inspired black internationalism as well as early ideas about independence from Spanish rule and federal governance.

In Puerto Rico enslaved resistance grew from the mid-1790s thanks in part to an influx of French settler refugees from Saint-Domingue, many of whom came with their captives. Once in Puerto Rico, however, many of these men and women did not accept their enslaved status and challenged it in court, claiming that they had been emancipated in Saint-Domingue and could not therefore be re-enslaved. They spread this spirit of dissent to local Spanish captives.[8] Puerto Rico witnessed several attempted uprisings, some spearheaded by African-born *bozales*. There were further Haitian inspirations here, both in the plans of rebels to escape to Hispaniola, and in at least one instance in 1805 through the presence of an alleged Haitian 'emissary' named Chaulette. His role remained mysterious, although the Puerto Rican authorities believed that he was involved in a wider conspiracy against slavery in the Americas. In several of these territories, as in colonial Saint-Domingue, traditions of resistance were deeply embedded over many generations and even centuries: in Puerto Rico the first major captive revolt had occurred back in 1527.[9]

The complexities of some of these revolts have only recently become apparent. For example, the 1795 Coro insurrection in Venezuela involved around three hundred enslaved black sugar-cane workers and mixed-race people (*pardos*), and was led by two free black men, José Leonardo Chirino and Josef Caridad Gonzales. Chirino was a farmer of mixed African and Amerindian heritage. He had been a regular visitor to Saint-Domingue in the previous years and had built close contacts with revolutionaries in the French colony, as well as with refugees from Curaçao, where a large captive uprising would occur in the same year. The stated aim of the Coro insurgents was to create a political system based on the republican principle of popular sovereignty and to eliminate the slaver white aristocracy (about whom the rebels sang raucously menacing songs). They sought to emancipate all captives and abolish servitude, in keeping with what they called 'the French law' (the 1794 abolition of slavery), and abrogate all punitive taxes against the poor – particularly the *demora* levied on local native Americans.[10] African egalitarian and communalist ideas were the principal ideological inspirations for the Coro rebels, most of whom hailed from the Guinean Gold Coast and Loango Coast of west-central Africa.[11] As elsewhere in the Atlantic, anti-slavery struggles in the Spanish Americas were steeped in African influences.

Later in the 1790s, as the Louverturean revolution was consolidated, enslaved rebels in Venezuela drew explicit inspiration from it. In April 1799 an abortive uprising in Cartagena was led by enslaved groups from Saint-Domingue and other French colonies. On this occasion they joined forces with African-born captives and mixed-race recruits from the local militia. They planned to seize the two main forts in Cartagena and launch a general insurrection against white slaver rule from there, killing the Spanish governor, taking control of the city's assets, and eliminating the settlers. When another conspiracy in the coastal town of Maracaibo was suppressed a month later, the Spanish authorities discovered that its prime movers were locally based black captives originating from Saint-Domingue. They had enlisted sympathizers of various other ethnic origins, with the aim of introducing 'the same system of freedom and equality' as in the French colony.[12] Events in Saint-Domingue were followed with fascinated enthusiasm by enslaved communities in Venezuela, and the conquest of Spanish Santo Domingo by Toussaint's army in 1801 was greeted with delight by captives in Coro (some of whom were no doubt involved in the 1795 revolt). Louverture, known as 'Tusen' in the Spanish Americas, was nicknamed 'the firebrand' by his Coro supporters; they warned local Spanish authorities to 'watch out', as they would be next in line.[13]

As the wars of independence unfolded in the Spanish Americas in the early nineteenth century, enslaved captives enlisted on both royalist and patriot sides in exchange for their freedom. Thus in Venezuela, New Granada, Peru, and the River Plate colonies, revolutionary war effectively crippled slavery, even though the institution itself formally survived until the middle of the century.[14] Anti-slavery was a significant component of the Mexican war of independence from Spain, which was achieved in 1821; slavery was formally abolished in Mexico in 1829 by President Vincente Guerrero, who was committed to racial equality and was himself of African, Amerindian, and Spanish descent.[15]

Along with its colony in Puerto Rico, Spain retained its colonial presence in Cuba. Indeed, this Spanish Caribbean colony became the principal alternative centre of sugar production in the Atlantic in the wake of the 'loss' of Saint-Domingue, and the most active site of anti-slavery revolutionary activity in the Americas. The geographical proximity of Saint-Domingue to Cuba and the regular naval connections between the two territories ensured that news about the revolution in Saint-Domingue travelled rapidly to the Spanish colony throughout the 1790s. Information came through newspapers, private letters exchanged between French and Spanish settlers, and eyewitness accounts by French plantation owners (many of whom became refugees in Cuba), as well as Spanish soldiers who fought in Saint-Domingue. Another major source of news was the gossip circulated by sailors and dock workers in ports such as Havana, where free people of colour, captives, and urban workers constantly mingled.

Immediately after the start of the 1791 insurrection in Saint-Domingue, the Havana city council reported that sacrificial offerings were being made by black people in honour of the insurgents.[16] Within a year there were uprisings on plantations around Havana, Puerto Príncipe, and Trinidad. They were easily suppressed. But a few years later a revolt initiated by the black freedman Nicolás Morales in Bayamo spread rapidly across the entire eastern part of the island. Forging an alliance with progressive whites, the rebels' demands included equality, the abolition of taxes, and a redistribution of land. This was not an overtly abolitionist movement, but it represented an implicit challenge to slavery with its call for a greater recognition of the role of free labour in the system of economic production.[17]

These early Cuban revolts shared many characteristics of the 1791 uprising in Saint-Domingue, with similar economic demands and a combination of French Revolutionary and Makandalist slogans about liberty, equality, and the elimination of white settlers. In some Cuban towns such as Puerto Príncipe, the leaders of the rebellions were former black captives from Saint-Domingue, who had been brought to Cuba with French settlers fleeing the colony in various waves after 1791. As in Puerto Rico, many of them were ardent sympathizers of the revolution, and in Puerto Príncipe some were arrested and punished for their role in promoting ideas of liberty, equality, and justice.[18] A report by the Cuban governor in 1798 observed that the plans of rebels were directly inspired by Louverture's military and political operations.[19]

Between 1795 and the 1812 Aponte rebellion no fewer than nineteen significant insurrections and conspiracies took place in Cuba, even though in 1796 the authorities took the drastic step of banning the import of all enslaved people from neighbouring French and British colonies, and expelling all those who had arrived from Saint-Domingue since 1790. Nonetheless, between 1796 and 1798 there were uprisings in Trinidad and Puerto Príncipe (again), and Santa Cruz del Sur. In Puerto Príncipe, a plantation owner rushed back to his property to be greeted by one of his captives, named Romualdo, who waved a machete at him and insulted him. Romualdo affirmed that black and white people were now equal, and that 'nobody here has a master anymore, we are all free'.[20]

Cuban captives and freemen became mesmerized by Saint-Domingue: one local newspaper observed that they knew all the main events of the Haitian revolution 'as if from memory'.[21] The court testimonies of Cuban rebels confirmed this fascination, many of them noting that the exploits of Louverture, Dessalines, and other Haitian revolutionaries featured regularly in their conversations. Some conspirators confessed that they used the names of these Haitian heroes as a means of recruiting fellow rebels. The fact that this tactic worked is further evidence of the shared collective understanding of the Haitian revolution among Cubans of African origin.[22]

Saint-Domingue under Louverture thus represented the fulfilment of an ideal cherished by many captives in the Spanish colonies (and the wider Atlantic): the military rout of their oppressors. News of the humiliating expulsion of the British from the colony in 1798 was greeted with a mixture of joy and admiration among enslaved communities in Cuba, and it produced a flood of martial rumours about Toussaint's plans to send further military expeditions against Atlantic slavers. Possible targets were thought to include Cuba, Puerto Rico, and Mexico, as well as Jamaica, Saint Lucia, Tobago, and even the United States.[23]

Louverture had no such expansionary ambitions, and indeed went out of his way to foil a French-led conspiracy against British control in Jamaica in 1799. However, this was as much about the idealized vision of black internationalism as its reality. Cuban authorities were particularly concerned about the defences on the eastern side of the island in the event of an invasion by Toussaint's forces. Around this time, a Cuban captive urged one of his friends to take up arms by telling him that they should not be cowards, and 'be men, and follow the lead given by Tusen [sic], who has taken away their lands from the French'.[24] These emancipatory visions and imaginings had no geographical limits: one story that reached Cuba in 1800 even suggested Toussaint had set his sights on 'the whole globe'.[25]

The 1806 conspiracy in the region of Güines, an area of intensive sugar cultivation south-east of Havana where the slave regime was particularly brutal, showed the variety of ways in which enslaved Cubans could be mobilized by events in Saint-Domingue and later Haiti. The plot's three ringleaders were Mariano Congo, an African-born person; Francisco Fuertes, a creole from Cuba, and Estanislao, a 'French' captive who was a veteran of the Haitian revolution. The plot was carefully elaborated, and it was drawn up with the complicity of older groups of enslaved persons based in Havana. It would start in the surrounding plantations, with the killing of all white planters and their families, as well as the overseers. After gathering momentum, it would lead on to Havana, where the San Carlos fortress would be captured as a prelude to a general insurrection leading to a seizure of power. The conspiracy's political ideas combined African, European, and Caribbean elements, including republicanism and royalism, as well as ritual dances and religious sacrifices. But the common thread uniting the conspirators was Haiti, whose hardy rebels were admired for having had the 'balls' to take their destiny into their own hands. When he went to rouse a group of plantation captives, Fuertes gave an extensive account of the Haitian revolution and its accomplishments. He extolled the martial qualities of its leaders, which had enabled them to become the 'absolute masters' of their country.[26]

Saint-Domingue captives and free persons of colour were involved in even larger numbers in the social unrest that accompanied the expulsion of French refugees from Cuba in 1809, whose consequences we discussed in chapter 5. Around 6,000 black and mixed-race people, mostly enslaved, were expelled to Louisiana with their white French masters in the aftermath of the Napoleonic invasion of Spain. Some of them ended up becoming involved in the 1811 uprising led by Charles Deslondes, as we have seen. We can now add that these 'French' captives were already highly mobilized before their arrival in the American South. They had participated heavily in the riots that broke out in the coffee plantations east and south of Havana in March 1809, which belonged overwhelmingly to white French Saint-Domingue settlers.

Beginning as a nationalist and anti-French protest, encouraged by the Cuban authorities, this movement rapidly took a diametrically different ideological orientation and assumed an overtly anti-slavery character. Soon the protests began to be directed at Cuban-Hispanic plantation owners, many of whose properties were ransacked and burnt across the island's western regions; the Saint-Domingue captives who participated in these riots professed violent slogans against human bondage and urged their fellow Cuban captives to embrace them. In the end the unrest was contained and the episode ended with the expulsion of all the French refugees, both captives and their masters. These events nonetheless confirmed the Cuban authorities' repeatedly expressed fears about the contagious effects of the Haitian revolution – as would become further apparent in the Aponte rebellion a few years later.[27]

Alongside urban-based plots and insurrections and plantation insurgencies, the slave order in Cuba faced stiff resistance from maroons. This was not a new problem; the Havana municipality had discussed the best ways of keeping marronage under control as early as 1599–1603.[28] The sheer volume of documentation on maroons for the first half of the nineteenth century, held in public archival collections in Cuba, attests to the scale of marronage from the authorities' viewpoint.[29]

In many respects Cuba's runaways had much in common with *grand marronnage* across the Atlantic world. Maroon communities were predominantly masculine, and organized hierarchically in *palenques*, whose membership could rise to several hundred people (smaller settlements were called *rancherías*), based in mountains, caves, and mangroves. During the first half of the nineteenth century these communities continued to grow in number, despite the authorities' repeated and largely ineffective attempts to reduce them through the use of militias and slave hunters. Maroon encampments were viewed as a menace by the settlers, so much so that the leading historian of Cuban maroons has described their conflict with the authorities as a 'long war'.[30] Their communities were ubiquitous, developing in the west of Cuba, in the central regions around Trinidad and Puerto Príncipe, and especially in the eastern parts of the island. The Cuban east is where some of the most complex settlements were based, such as El Frijol, which existed formally until 1816, and had its own sugar mill, beehives, pig farms, and tobacco, cane, and banana plantations. There was in addition a metal workshop in which javelins and arrows were manufactured, no doubt using skills honed by fugitives before their capture and enslavement in west Africa.[31]

The growth of slavery in Cuba during the first half of the nineteenth century cannot be seen in isolation from wider developments across Atlantic slavery capitalism. Haitian independence and British abolition did not bring about an immediate decline of slavery, but instead it shifted the supply of commodity production elsewhere, thus enabling the 'second slavery' wave in the Americas, particularly in Cuba, Brazil, and the southern United States.[32] The development of maroon communities in eastern Cuba was a direct consequence of this wider trend. The regions around Santiago de Cuba and north of Guantánamo Bay were transformed by the arrival of French settler refugees, who developed coffee plantations and considerably expanded the forced labour used in the area from the early nineteenth century. This in turn led to the flight of a greater number of captives. In some parts of the east, for example in the Sierra Maestra, these runaways joined existing settlements, while in others they created new ones. There is some evidence of maritime marronage, unsurprisingly given the physical proximity of eastern Cuba to Haiti.[33] Maroons thus posed a direct challenge to the institution of slavery: in their rejection of the plantation system, in the provision of sanctuaries to their fellow runaways, in the ways they accommodated a range of religious and spiritual practices, in their embodiment of the possibility of an alternative society based on principles of dignity and respect, in their economic disruption of the colonial system, and in the military threats they periodically posed to Spanish rule in Cuba.

The power of this resistance was expressed through strong leaders, many of whom became legendary figures, and were spoken of with fascination among captive and even settler communities across Cuba. The authority these captains wielded was despotic. But it was a despotism largely based on consent, as they were trusted because of their superior knowledge of the local terrain, technical expertise and tactical acumen, and physical bravery, often mentioned in reports from slave hunters. Runaway captains held their communities together, sometimes with the support of military and spiritual assistants; they organized combat training and the provision of weapons. Among the best known of these maroon leaders were Ventura Sanchez and Manuel Griñán (known by their respective nicknames of Coba and Gallo), two of the most recognized captains in eastern Cuba, with whom the authorities attempted to reach a settlement. The female companions of settlement captains, such as the elusive 'Madre Melchora', were often venerated in their own right.[34]

There was an important intellectual dimension to this leadership. The fact that these maroon commanders were based in remote areas did not mean they were cut off from other resistance groups. One of the leaders of the El Frijol settlement, a captive named Sebastian, originated from Havana, a hub of Atlantic anti-slavery ideas and practices, and he was no doubt associated with the numerous revolutionary networks operating in the area. He was believed to be Aponte's lieutenant in eastern Cuba and would have played a major 'national' role if the 1812 rebellion had succeeded.[35] Black internationalist ideas and values were nurtured in runaway settlements: around 1815 another captain of a large maroon band based in the east of the island, named Manuel, originated from Saint-Domingue. He had come to Cuba with his French enslaver, a refugee from the revolution, and then escaped into marronage; there was little doubt that the Haitian revolution featured prominently in his political vocabulary, practice, and symbolic repertoire.[36] In the 1840s the maroon captains' hall of fame included José Dolores, upon whom his followers bestowed the commanding title of *mayimbe*, an African term reserved for the most senior and respected members of a community. His reputation even extended to local Spanish settlers, one of whom wrote of him as an 'extraordinary being', a sort of Cuban version of Makandal.[37]

Despite the voluminous records on Cuban maroons, the voices of these fugitive men and women have not come through to us directly, as they were not transcribed by the administrative and military authorities who tracked their activities. But the information gathered further attests to the dynamism of Cuban maroon settlements. Their communities were made up of African-born *bozales*, across the full range of ethnic groups; as well as creoles, mixed-race people – and whites. These European maroons were a distinctive but heterogeneous group consisting of men who refused to serve in the militia, together with army deserters or dissidents; their training enabled them to play important roles in the defence of maroon communities. There were also thieves, smugglers, and fugitives from the law, without forgetting strangers on enigmatic missions. A report on a maroon settlement from 1816 mentioned the presence of 'a European woman who is believed to be of high rank and who has come from Havana'.[38] These white maroons were all interesting in different ways, but perhaps the most remarkable were the handful of clergymen who volunteered to officiate in the Catholic churches that were founded in runaway settlements. At El Frijol there were two white priests, both of them Spanish missionaries who had chosen to bring the word of Christ to the fugitives. They appeared to have had a considerable following. Many larger settlements had buildings designated as churches, as for example the Todos Tenemos *palenque*, where there was a rudimentary altar on which a figure representing Christ had been mounted.[39]

As in the syncretic tradition exemplified by Palmares in Brazil and so many others across the Atlantic, this fugitive Christianity was not a fixed doctrine, but a faith practised alongside African religious rituals of protection, healing, divination, and empowerment. These spiritual combinations were not uncommon on Cuban plantations (one report complained of a French refugee planter who allowed his captives to practise a fusion of Methodism and *vodun*), and runaways took these practices with them when they escaped. Most settlements had at least one person who bore the title of high priest, and sometimes there were several. Other reports about El Frijol, written around the same time as the presence of the Catholic missionaries was noted, refer to divination ceremonies being carried out by two African priests (called 'sorcerers' by the slave hunters), in the aftermath of the execution of a militia member who had participated in an attack against the settlement. Conversely, a number of the runaways killed in combat were carrying religious items. Many such objects, generally sculpted from wood, were found at abandoned or destroyed settlements. In 1837 a report following the capture of a fugitive site in Santa Cruz de los Pinos in central Cuba indicated the discovery of a dozen leather pouches filled with ritual objects, including statues, pieces of glass, and feathers.[40]

How did the maroons prosecute their war against Cuban slavers? Like their African and Atlantic comrades, Cuban runaways combined both defensive and offensive techniques. Throughout the first half of the nineteenth century they fought a war of attrition against the slave order, raiding plantations, and operating in the vicinity of small and even large towns. For example, bands of fugitives carried out attacks on the outskirts of Santiago de Cuba in 1815, where the local municipality put out a proclamation declaring the community was in peril.[41] Although these armed groups were never very large, there were many similar expressions of anxiety about the threats posed by these Cuban maroons to individuals, local settler communities, and military officials.

These forms of runaway violence were typically described by Cuban authorities as acts of banditry. But they were much more than that, being rooted in a wider pattern of anti-slavery beliefs; the authorities tacitly acknowledged this when they blamed maroon actions against plantations on the 'bad example' of Haiti. Some of the attacks were aimed at securing the release of former runaways who had been recaptured and returned to enslavement at their plantations. Many incursions were accompanied by acts of sabotage such as the burning down of buildings, factories, and cane fields, to disrupt the production system. Fugitives inflicted symbolic punishments against key upholders of the plantation order: 'loyal' slaves, white foremen, and in many instances landowners and their families, some of whom were killed. More frequently, fugitives chose to use the same instruments of torture that were deployed against themselves. Many plantation owners and foremen were whipped, and in some cases their ears were cut off. This was the typical sanction used by the settlers against those who ran away repeatedly, and maroon hunters would cut off the ears of fugitives they killed in order to claim their reward.[42]

These sorts of raids against the plantation system occurred regularly, and were generally conducted at lightning speed, thus maximizing the chances of success while minimizing the risks of detection and reaction from local military authorities. Maroons preferred wherever possible to avoid conflict. Concealment or withdrawal were the ideal tactics, and physical remoteness was exploited to the full. El Frijol was situated near the source of the river Jagua, in an almost inaccessible mountainous region surrounded by thick forests, and several days' march away from the nearest town. Countless reports from militia officials and slave hunters described their vain efforts to track down settlements that turned out to be mirages, disappearing when approached. Even when a *palenque* was found and then overrun, it was almost invariably reconstructed at a nearby site. The retreat of fugitive communities in advance of any incursion was facilitated by elaborate early-warning systems, including sentinels posted in strategic places. These were mostly operated by humans but in at least once instance included domesticated agoutis. The high-pitched squeaks of these carefully trained rodents would alert settlement residents to any approaching intruders.[43]

Boldly highlighted in the Cuban code of rules relating to maroons and slave-hunting, lethal plant- and herb-based poisons were mixed in with provisions and left in prominent areas for supply-starved militias.[44] More common were land traps: many larger settlements were surrounded by ditches, often containing sharp stakes. These were found in the wooded territories controlled by fugitives. In 1830 a militia member from the village of Arroyo Seco, by the Mayarí river, went in pursuit of a runaway band that had been systematically attacking his locality. As he was advancing into the woods, he fell into a concealed pit studded with sharp wooden pikes, which injured him in three separate places. He then looked up to find fifty machete-bearing runaways surrounding the pit. Such was their confidence in their tactical superiority that they brought him into one of their refuges, and later released him. The local military commander admitted that he was 'powerless' to deal with these skilled maroons.[45] Right across rebel territories, these sorts of concealed defences were common, and known only to fugitive guides. As a landowner acknowledged, 'every road is a deadly trap for anyone who is not familiar with the terrain'.[46]

When faced with attack, fugitives engaged militarily with their assailants. These defensive operations often succeeded because of the maroons' superior knowledge of the terrain as well as their remarkable capacity to gather intelligence about enemy movements. Not only did they know of approaching militias thanks to their sentinels, but they often found out about these operations through networks of town- and plantation-based informants. This was one of the many ways in which the world of marronage remained closely connected with Cuban colonial society. These encounters allowed maroons to display their panoply of guerrilla techniques, as a military force discovered when it tried to attack the El Frijol settlement in November 1815. After a four-day march, the forty men reached a wooded area where they fell upon three gunnysacks filled with bananas, which they took as evidence that the settlement they were looking for was close by. Soon they captured a fugitive, who initially resisted but then proceeded to give them precise information about the position of the *palenque*, claiming it was protected by just twenty-five men armed with five rifles.

Led by their captive, the force plunged deeper into the woods, where they were ambushed by a first group of fugitives. During this brief but intense battle, the colonial militia lost one man, with three others being seriously wounded. The first group of runaway combatants then retreated towards their settlement, with the militia in pursuit. As his men finally reached the *palenque*, the militia commander was faced with a terrifying vision of warfare: 'three divisions of fugitive combatants were making their way towards us, marching at the sound of drums, while shouts mingled with war chants could be heard from the inside the camp, announcing the charge of two hundred additional men'.[47] He hastily withdrew, and this first military expedition against El Frijol thus ended in a complete fiasco.

Sometimes these combat engagements were simply a means of better executing a collective tactical retreat. When a maroon settlement in the Sierra de Linares was attacked by a colonial militia in March 1820, the runaways' first line of defenders, perched on the heights of a mountain, greeted the approaching forces with gunfire. They also rolled large rocks down the slope, pinning the enemy back. After three hours, the runaways suddenly stopped firing and swiftly withdrew into the nearby woods. When the militia finally managed to reach their *palenque*, they realized that while they were being kept at bay all the inhabitants had escaped into the forest, following what was no doubt a carefully designed drill. Not a single maroon was captured, while the commander of the colonial militia was killed by two shots. These rebels were not only well equipped but had excellent marksmen. There was a widespread (albeit unsubstantiated) belief among Cuban officials that the eastern rebels were being armed by the Haitians.[48]

Military operations against maroon settlements did have some successes, but these were very relative. The capture and dissolution of El Frijol in 1816, after a second military expedition, simply led to a retreat and regrouping of its inhabitants, who joined forces to form an effective confederation of *palenques* around the towns of Tiguabos, Guantánamo, Baracoa, and Sagua under the combined leadership of Coba and Gallo.[49] In 1819, as they came under increased pressure, the authorities tried the classic colonial tactic of appeasement, offering runaways a cessation of hostilities in exchange for their submission.[50] Although the terms offered were far from generous, they managed to divide the two main rebel leaders from each other. Whereas Gallo and his men refused any compromise, Coba continued to negotiate with the authorities and seemed to have been willing to reach a settlement. The rebels nevertheless held on to their anti-slavery and fugitive principles, demanding to retain control of their territories and unconditional freedom for all their followers.[51]

In any event, the Spanish authorities broke the truce in September 1819, launching a full-scale attack on the eastern *palenques*. They claimed that the rebels were using the discussions to extend their operations against local plantations. Coba was cornered and committed suicide, but Gallo escaped, and the short-lived episode destroyed any possible agreement between the runaways and the colonists. In the end, it was all for nothing:

maroons continued to escape and head east, and those who were already
in the eastern area regrouped. El Frijol eventually re-emerged in the same
remote area in 1832.[52]

Throughout the 1820s eastern runaway settlements on Cuba continued
to grow in number and sophistication, forcing the authorities to recruit
more slave hunters. Although these mercenaries were able to destroy
some *palenques*, they rarely succeeded in capturing fugitives in any significant numbers.[53] During the following decade, the runaways of the
east continued to disrupt the plantation order, particularly those settlements clustered on the mountains around the towns of Mayarí, Tiguabos,
and Baracoa. Their bold behaviour and repeated attacks elicited further
concerns from regional and central officials that the fugitives were being
supplied by Haiti. No evidence of this revolutionary connection has been
found, but the fears were themselves symptomatic of the Cuban authorities'
sense of helplessness, and the continuing force of the St Domingo myth.[54]

Meanwhile, another major front opened up in western Cuba. Despite
Spain's agreement with Britain in 1817 to end the slave trade, the traffic continued illegally, with the support of Spanish metropolitan officials,
merchants, creole planters, and Cuban officials who were bribed to look
the other way. Thanks to this thriving trade and the effective transfer
of the advanced technologies of sugar production from Saint-Domingue,
Cuba became the world's largest producer of sugar by the 1820s. This
transformation was made possible by the exponential rise in the number
of enslaved Africans: according to the Transatlantic Slave Trade Database,
643,935 slaves were forcibly embarked to Cuba from various African
ports between 1817 and 1866, of whom 561,656 arrived on the island,
and were mostly put to work on its sugar and coffee plantations.[55] The
largest African ethnic groups were the Kongos, the Carabalis, the Gangas,
and the Lucumis, who came respectively from west-central Africa, the
Bight of Biafra, Sierra Leone, and the Bight of Benin. While some of these
Africa-born men and women escaped into marronage, others became
involved in conspiracies and revolts. This insurgent pattern, which lasted
for two decades, was distinct both from the fugitive wars we just reviewed
and the previous cycle of insurrections culminating in the 1812 Aponte
rebellion. These were mainly the work of creoles and free black people.
Here, African-born captives were the movement's principal drivers.

The opening shot in this new cycle of radical anti-slavery resistance
was fired in 1825 in the region of Matanzas, the site of Cuba's second-
largest city. Its surrounding area had witnessed considerable economic
growth in previous years through the development of coffee plantations

and the arrival of new cohorts of white settlers from Europe, the United States, and the former Saint-Domingue, who were attracted by a dedicated campaign by the Cuban authorities to develop the plantation system in the western part of the island. The labour for this growth came from recently imported African-born captives, most of whom were put to work on coffee plantations, which dominated the region's economy in the 1820s, before sugar took over in the following decade. The majority of those involved in the 1825 rebellion were based in these coffee plantations.[56]

Planned over the first half of the year, and co-ordinated across several estates in the district of Guamacaro, the 1825 uprising began on 15 June at two plantations, El Solitario and El Sabanazo. It rapidly spread to neighbouring areas, with rebels attacking settler properties and setting them on fire, killing around fifteen whites and injuring several more. The insurgents collected rifles and ammunition as they progressed, destroying more than twenty sugar and coffee estates. They were eventually defeated by a combined force of local settlers and dragoons sent from the city of Matanzas. The rebels retreated and dispersed into smaller groups, heading into forests and mountains, where they likely joined the numerous runaway bands in the region. Over the course of the next month the insurgents caused further damage to plantations in the area. Many were hunted down and killed, while others were arrested and later tried. At its peak over two hundred captives (around 20 per cent of the 973 people officially listed in the Guamacaro district) took part in the uprising.[57]

A second conspiracy was uncovered in the same district in August, again centred around a group of coffee plantations. When interrogated, these rebels declared that they hoped to kill the white slavers on these estates and then join forces with the remaining groups of insurgents from the June insurrection, whose actions had inspired them. They praised these men for 'cutting off many white heads'. The Guamacaro conspiracy in August was fuelled by stories that work had ceased on the two coffee plantations where the June uprising had taken place. This provides an interesting insight into the role of rumours, as well as evidence that many captives were convinced that military resistance could be an effective weapon against the slavers.[58]

Although the Cuban authorities initially believed the Matanzas rebellion may have been fomented by anti-Spanish revolutionary nationalists from Colombia or Mexico, they eventually came to the conclusion that it was an all-Cuban affair. Indeed, it was purely local, and the conspirators were predominantly African-born captives; only a handful of free black people were involved. Over two-thirds of the rebels were of Carabali, Mandinga, and Ganga origin. The solidarity that united the insurgents rested on multiple connections. A core group belonged to the estates where the rebellion was planned and initiated, and some of them shared family ties. Federico Carabali, one of the three main leaders, had kinship links with captives in several other plantations. Most importantly, many rebels had known each other in Africa and had been grouped together before being transported in the same vessels across the Atlantic to reach Cuba. These 'shipmate' affinities, which we have encountered in many other Atlantic revolutionary settings, played a crucial role in strengthening their group cohesiveness.[59]

The spiritual experiences, rituals, and beliefs of the insurgents further attested to these African ways of being. On Sundays the enslaved on the main plantations were allowed to organize traditional drumming and dancing parties, and these occasions were used by Federico Carabali to finalize the plot with Pablo Gangá, another key conspirator. Gangá was a coach driver who moved around a great deal in the region, enabling him to build contacts across plantations, as we have observed in so many other instances.[60] Above all, the insurgents understood themselves as soldiers: many referred to the events of June 1825 as a 'war'. The slave Pio testified that he had been promised 'weapons and gunpowder for the day of the war', while José Luis stated he had been recruited by a black man who told him that 'it was necessary to make war' against the whites.[61]

Their understanding of this conflict echoed patterns of warfare seen in early nineteenth-century west Africa. Although he did not come from the predominant ethnic communities, the military command was entrusted to Lorenzo, a Lucumi slave with extensive combat experience who had recently arrived in Cuba after being sold as a prisoner of war in Africa. Lorenzo was at one point seen wearing a black jacket with gold buttons, and a small hat with cock feathers, and his choice as their commander highlighted the rebels' strategic capacity to organize themselves. Their martial conduct during the uprising further reflected their African military traditions: they danced and leapt, and they marched to the beat of drums; they used threat and coercion to recruit recalcitrant followers on plantations; and they ruthlessly targeted and killed their white enemies, whom they despatched with machetes, spears, and clubs. Their overarching aim was to achieve freedom through the destruction of the region's plantation settlers who had enslaved them.[62]

In the planning and execution of their scheme they practised what the authorities called 'sorcery', in which we can see African religious beliefs and rituals, used for protection, healing, divination, and empowerment.[63] As in Africa, there was a close connection across the military, political, and spiritual realms. Carabali was reputed to be a priest, and Gangá was implicated in a later conspiracy and accused by the authorities of practis-ing 'witchcraft'; he was undoubtedly a holy man.[64] And when the rebellion was defeated, many insurgents preferred to commit suicide rather than be forcibly returned into slavery. This expressed both a traditional African reaction to the dishonour of military defeat and a widespread belief in the transmigration of the soul, where death would hasten their eastward journey back to their homeland.[65]

Alongside the Matanzas-style military rebellions, urban anti-slavery movements continued to develop in Cuba among free black communities and people of colour. By the late 1820s there was a growing educated and literate population in cities such as Havana and Matanzas, many of whose inhabitants were members of military, religious, and cultural associations, and who embraced radical ideas about freedom and equality that came from Europe, Haiti, the newly independent postcolonial states of South America – and even further afield.

In 1827, for example, in an echo of the Aponte case, the authorities arrested a mixed-race tailor named Domingo Santaya in Havana. He was accused of holding clandestine meetings in his house, and among his books and papers was a volume entitled *Sultan of Mecca*, and a drawing of a black man in a high-ranking military uniform.[66] In 1830, Francisco Trujillo, a person of colour who regularly travelled across the Matan-zas countryside, was arrested for making various incendiary statements, notably that Cuba 'belongs to the Indians, and the Spaniards, foreigners and other Europeans should leave'.[67] In 1831 a group of free black men and women were reported to have toasted the memory of the Liber-ator, Simón Bolívar.[68] In the city of Matanzas, police searching the house of a free mixed-race carpenter named Bernardo Sevillán found a volume entitled *Dictionary or New Philosophical Democratic Vocabulary, Indis-pensable for All Those Who Wish to Understand the New Revolutionary Language*. There was little doubt where his sympathies lay, and he was promptly arrested.

Many literate free black and mixed-race people became involved in con-spiracies in Cuba during the later 1830s and 1840s. Indeed, the Matanzas uprising of 1825 was the first of a series of around sixty plots, revolts, and insurrections spanning a period of two decades. This sequence rocked the foundations of the Cuban slave order until the mid-1840s. These conspiracies and revolts unfolded almost every year between 1826 and 1844, and in many cases several times a year. Although some uprisings occurred in urban areas, as in Pinar del Río in September 1826, Trinidad in April 1838, and Havana in 1840 and 1841, most still took place on sugar and coffee plantations and refineries. Participant numbers could vary from a small handful (the six captives who assassinated their master and overseer in Catalina de Güines in September 1827 using bows and arrows) to the full complement of enslaved men and women on a plantation or in a factory. In Banes in August 1833 over three hundred captives rose up collectively, and in 1838 more than eight hundred were involved in a conspiracy in central Cuba.[69] Many revolts, as in Ceiba Mocha in December 1837, were executed with the support of maroon communities, while others led to successful escapes into marronage. For example, in June 1843 more than three hundred captives escaped from a refinery in Guamacaro.

There were rare instances of creole captive involvement, such as in Trinidad in 1838. Almost everywhere else these movements were led by African-born people, often newly arrived in Cuba in the preceding months. They sometimes consisted of a combination of different ethnic groups, as in July 1830 on a coffee plantation in Matanzas, where the rebels were Ganga, Mina, Carabali, Lucumi, and Kongo; in such instances, it is likely that most of the captives would have been multilingual. Quite often it was a single ethnic group that was preponderant, and in such instances they tended to be Lucumis, who developed a reputation for fierceness and intractability. The number, scale, and intensity of the revolts increased over time. There were three each in 1837 and 1838, six in 1840, five in 1841–2, and seven in 1843. This wave culminated in the La Escalera conspiracies, the last major collection of Cuban revolts that involved thousands of captives and free people of colour, both urban and rural, as we will see below.[70]

As with the 1825 Matanzas rebellion, these conflicts all bore the hallmarks of African military traditions. Contrary to widespread views of these episodes as spontaneous actions, undertaken on the spur of the moment, these movements were based on careful planning. In several cases they had specific leaders, chosen for their political, religious, and military skills. In the 1833 uprising in Banes, two of the commanders, Joaquín and Fierabrás, rode horses and carried red umbrellas as they led their men into battle. These were generally symbols of military authority wielded by Yoruba kings, which suggested that these men had prior military experience in Africa.[71] In this instance, the underlying ideology of the revolt was royalist. In others the leadership was based on kinship or more personal factors, such as loyalty to a charismatic individual. The Catalina de Güines revolt in September 1827 was commandeered by a captive called Tomás, who was described by one of the other rebels as their 'captain from Africa' – a remarkable example of the resilience of the military solidarities produced by nineteenth-century west African wars.[72] Women acted as military commanders in at least one instance. They actively participated in several operations, for example on the Favorito coffee plantation in Matanzas in May 1824, in the July 1835 uprising at Havana, and the May 1843 rebellion on the Perseverancia coffee plantation.[73]

Even when such specific leaders did not emerge, these movements took a collective form, with clear preparation and an overarching set of goals. In June 1837 at the sugar plantation La Sonora in Matanzas, a group of thirty-four newly arrived Lucumis attacked the plantation overseer and other white employees. It emerged that they had started planning this initiative five months earlier, when one of them had been abused by the white slavers. From that moment, the enslaved began to make clubs and spears that they hid in the bush in preparation for the assault.[74] Planning also involved building momentum behind the revolt by bringing in new recruits as they advanced from one area to the other, and rallying them to their final destination. For the seventeen captives at the sugar estate in the Havana province of Güira de Melena in September 1832 the objective was manifestly to reclaim their freedom by reaching the nearby mountains.[75]

The insurgents' battle practices provided further evidence of the depth of their knowledge and experience. Attacks were often carried out by highly trained men, who followed tactical drills that had clearly been rehearsed. In the September 1832 operation the insurgents advanced towards the white plantation employees using a typically African method, approaching in small groups while denying their opponents the possibility of striking back. One of these estate workers testified that the captives 'did not attack him frontally; instead they were always jumping, dancing, and attacking him with their machetes'. Every time he tried to confront one of his assailants, two or three others would come at him from behind. This disorienting technique was enhanced by high-pitched screams, bodily contortions, and rallying cries chanted in African languages – all standard elements of the west African military repertoire. Nor did the rebels flinch when faced with firearms. At the La Arratia estate in Matanzas in July 1842 they confidently dealt with armed plantation workers. When fired upon the rebels fell to the ground to dodge the bullets and then stood up again to resume their charge. The estate overseer had little doubt that he was facing soldiers who had once been part of a regular army.[76]

There were no firearms in the insurgents' arsenal. Most plots involved attempts to lay their hands at an early stage on such weapons, generally kept secure by plantation employees. These efforts were sometimes successful, as in the attacks that took place in November 1843, where some captives were seen carrying pistols taken from an estate store. But the combatants were able to draw on a broad array of African instruments of war. Swords and machetes were their preferred weapons, and they were widely used by maroons, as we saw earlier. These weapons were often wielded with great expertise, using hand-to-hand combat tactics that left their enemies perplexed. Bows and arrows were occasionally used, with lethal effects. Alongside these conventional war instruments, the rebels repurposed their work tools, especially knives, sickles, and hatchets. They also made clubs specifically for these military operations. In some battles, captives were seen with spears, another traditional piece of African hardware. They went to considerable lengths to produce these lances, slowly sharpening the ends with fire so that they would eventually become as hard as iron.[77] And when all else failed, the insurgents relied on stones and rocks, which they again manipulated with considerable skill. Numerous reports from the 1830s and early 1840s mention the use of these natural weapons, both for defence and attack. In July 1840, for example, a group of rebels killed their master and overseer with rocks, and then used them to confront the colonial militia that had tried to intervene against them.[78]

As with the 1825 rebellion, and as seen throughout this narrative, military resistance was embedded in the Cuban captives' broader moral and spiritual frameworks. During their interrogations, insurgents often justified their actions with reference to their own gods. Moreover, fighting bravely in battle was a matter of honour, and indeed one of the highest accolades that could be earned in the African combatants' scheme of virtues. Divination was constantly relied on, particularly around the planning and execution of military operations, and fighters wore protective religious amulets to keep themselves from harm. One of the best documented uprisings, the 1833 rebellion on the Salvador estate in Banes, was accompanied by animal sacrifices, which were carried out as the rebellion began. These rituals and beliefs help explain the frequently heard injunctions of rebel leaders to their followers that they could not be hurt by the settlers. As one of the insurgents put it, 'What can white men do to us? Let us go and fight them.'[79]

In the end, death was not seen as the end of existence, but as an opportunity for the transmigration of the soul. This was part of the rationale for the group suicides that sometimes followed the insurgents' defeats, when combatants would drown or hang themselves.[80] But it would be wrong to infer that captive military revolts were acts of despair: in overall terms, combat was an act of self-affirmation. This was reflected in the care taken by many insurgents to wear military uniforms, and to sport specific flags

and banners whose colours were associated with particular African figures of authority, both secular and spiritual, as with the red umbrellas at
Banes. During the 1825 Matanzas rebellion some participants wore green
hats, the shade being linked to Ogun, the African god of iron, warfare,
and hunting.[81]

This cycle of revolts culminated in the Bemba and Triunvirato insurrections of March and November 1843 in the Matanzas region, which saw
the burning of several plantations and the participation of hundreds of
captives. The authorities then discovered that these actions were connected
to a wider conspiracy which had been brewing from the early 1840s. This
plot embraced much of the western countryside, major urban centres,
and some of Cuba's most prominent free blacks and people of colour, as
well as some white intellectuals such as the writer Domingo del Monte.
In the fierce repression that ensued during 1844, captives from over two
hundred plantations were arrested, thousands of people were tortured,
banished, and executed, and many more disappeared without trace. The
plot was named 'La Escalera' after the ladders on which detained suspects
were tied, whipped, and coerced into confessing their involvement and
naming their accomplices.

In their obsessive search for plot leaders the authorities fastened on
well-known figures in the mixed-race community such as the poet Plácido,
an ardent supporter of Cuban independence and racial equality. He was
definitely involved in the movement, although he denied being its leader.
He was tried and executed in June 1844, with the court sentence describing how he headed a conspiracy of enslaved and free people of colour
who sought to eliminate whites and become masters of the island, with
the help of Britain and Haiti.[82] Among Plácido's contacts was the mysterious Luis Gigaut, a Haitian-born artisan based in Havana who seems
to have been connected to the British consul David Turnbull, who was
actively involved in promoting abolitionist views among Cuban elites
in the early 1840s. Gigaut was reported to be one of the intermediaries
between urban and rural conspirators. Sentenced to death *in absentia*, he
was never found by the authorities, having probably escaped from the
island after the plot was uncovered.[83]

Although the movement was shaped by such urban and international
influences, its main drivers were again the African-born men and women
fighting for their liberty on Cuba's sugar and coffee estates. Already
primed by the revolts of the previous decade and a half, their revolutionary activity was spurred by the frenzied expansion of the sugar industry
in Matanzas between the late 1830s and the early 1840s. The number

of sugar mills rose from 145 to around 350 in a matter of a few years, confirming the region's status as the largest sugar producer in the Atlantic world. Working under brutal conditions, the African-born enslaved labourers who built and operated these estates constituted the bedrock of the 1843–4 revolutionary movement. Their court testimonies provide further insights into the character of this rural anti-slavery activity, confirming the patterns identified in the previous sections but adding further detail and nuance to the picture. Particularly significant was the co-ordination of revolutionary endeavours across estates and the role played by urban organizers such as the free black José María Mondejar, who was sent to rural Matanzas by Plácido to rally slaves to the rebellion. Mondejar was initially sceptical, but the poet convinced him by telling him that what would happen in Cuba would echo the revolution in St Domingo, where 'everyone was black ... [and] they were the ones who governed'.[84]

There was no single leader of the movement in the countryside, but rather a group of around a hundred local commanders, each controlling their respective networks. They mostly came from the enslaved elite we have encountered so often: drivers, coachmen, domestics, and artisans. By virtue of their greater mobility, these captains were able to travel across the Matanzas region, building connections with each other, and heading regularly to urban centres to meet with free black and mixed-race urban conspirators such as Mondejar, and designing plans for the forthcoming uprising. These estate rebels held clandestine meetings in their dwellings, when the white plantation owners and managers were sleeping, or in discreet places on the edge of plantations. Thus at the Nueva Esperanza sugar mill, the local captain Román Macúa brought a group of captives together at a clearing between the woods and the cane fields, and told them 'not to be faint of heart about the uprising'.[85] The plans were carefully thought out: the rebellions would typically start with the killing of prominent white slavers on the estates, followed by the torching of buildings. In some instances, local captives from the estate were told to await the arrival of an armed group, who would come to ignite the rebellion there. The violence was targeted; only the white enforcers of the violent slave plantation system (owners, managers, overseers, accountants) were generally designated to be killed.[86]

One of the fascinating aspects of these mobilizations was the support they received from maroon bands. As we saw earlier in this chapter, one of the most celebrated Cuban runaway leaders in the early 1840s was José Dolores, whose group of around twenty fugitives operated in the eastern Matanzas region. These men and women usually entered plantations after dark to steal animals and food, or to engage in trade with black residents.

Dolores was a master of maroon warfare, training his fighters in the art of guerrilla movements, and building extensive contacts across plantations, where he was idolized by the enslaved.[87] It seems he forged contacts with local rebel organizers in 1843, and attempted to help them free some insurgents who had been detained in the aftermath of the uprisings. He also had links to members of the wider 1844 conspiracy.[88] Despite frantic attempts by the local authorities to apprehend Dolores, the fugitive leader and his highly mobile followers remained out of reach. They were not captured even during the fierce repression that followed the uncovering of the 1844 plot, or in the intensified search for runaways in the 1840s. In all likelihood they retreated into the swampy zones south of Matanzas, a territory that remained an inviolable maroon sanctuary.[89]

The events of 1843–4 brought into sharper focus the revolutionary roles of women. Among the principal captains of the November 1843 uprising were Carlota and Fermina Lucumí. Carlota wielded a machete and personally attacked the daughter of the slave estate overseer, and was heard repeatedly urging her fellow insurgents to confront and cut down the enemy. She travelled with them as they moved from one plantation to another, then was killed in a battle between the insurgents and local militias; her body was discovered the next day. Fermina, who had been held in shackles for her insurgent activities in the months preceding the November uprising, led the rebels to the homes of the estate owners and their managers. When she came across one of the most brutal overseers, she exclaimed to her comrades: 'grab that fat white man and hit him with your machete, for he is the one who puts us in shackles'. She used a hammer to liberate those captives who were chained on the estate.[90] Although she denied any involvement in these actions, Fermina was arrested, tried, and later executed.

Many other women emerged as active participants in the 1843–4 movements: like Carlota and Fermina they encouraged their fellow rebels to join the movement and attack the white slavers.[91] Others attended secret planning meetings, where they provided key information and intelligence that they had overheard from conversations among plantation elites.[92] Adapting a convention from African *cabildos*, many rebel captains were given the titles of 'kings' by their followers, and their wives were often crowned 'queens'. These were not symbolic appointments: a number of these female figures participated in the planning of the movements locally, and sometimes were designated to play key parts in their execution. For example, Simona Criolla, a mixed-race captive on the Macutivo estate in Matanzas, was offered the position of queen in exchange for opening the doors to the slavers' home, so that they could be killed and their weapons seized.[93] Another domestic servant, Rosa, was crowned as a queen and asked to poison the estate overseer.[94]

The 1843–4 revolts confirmed the Lucumis' reputation for military prowess, an extension of the warlike qualities attributed to the Yorubas in Africa. Local captains in rural Matanzas were predominantly Lucumis, as were both Carlota and Fermina.[95] More precise information about the religious and spiritual underpinnings of the insurgency emerged during the 1844 trials. It was clear that African sacred beliefs and objects were highly valued among rural captives in Matanzas, and were already part of their everyday lives. Naturally, this was reflected in their preparations for warfare, which included spiritual consultations, protective ceremonies, and rituals involving fetishes and amulets. One group of fighters wore specially treated leather pouches on their chests. It was widely believed that if the fighters were fired upon, the bullets would slide off their bodies and fall to the ground.[96] So central were these practices to the rebels' revolutionary culture that their clandestine planning meetings would typically begin with a religious ceremony (or the sale of protective amulets), and would only then turn to practical and organizational matters.[97]

In the decades following Haitian independence in 1804, Cuba was often spoken of as the next potential site of a revolution against slavery, as much by those who feared this eventuality as by those who wished it. The conditions seemed similarly propitious, with an arrogant, greedy, and brutal slaveholding plantocracy that prided itself as much on its racial supremacy as on its success in supplanting Saint-Domingue as the world's largest sugar producer. Cuba was tied to a weak European metropole, unwilling to impose any effective controls on what by then had become the illegal slave trade, and leaning heavily towards the interests of the slavers. Cuba also had a massive captive population, which became as large as Saint-Domingue's in the late eighteenth century.

As in the former French colony, this enslaved population harboured powerful yearnings to break free from their shackles, and they created complex social institutions in towns and rural areas to further their revolutionary goals. Just as in Saint-Domingue, many African-born Cubans had considerable military experience. In the end, however, despite the intensification of revolt patterns from the late 1790s through to the mid-1840s, Cuba did not become a second Saint-Domingue. After the mid-1840s there were no more mass uprisings, and maroon communities declined after a final round of militia attacks. The import of enslaved Africans was officially stopped in 1867, after the abolition of slavery in the United States.

American emancipation was a turning point for Cuba, prompting a process of reform that culminated in the abolition of slavery in 1886, just over a decade before the achievement of independence from Spanish rule in 1898.[98]

Compared to elsewhere in the Atlantic, one obvious difference was the absence of anything in Spain resembling the revolutionary traditions that developed in France and the United States. Despite some brief reformist moments, nineteenth-century Spain experienced none of the social mobilizations and political upheavals which created the civic spaces that made abolitions possible in France and Britain. Spanish liberalism lacked the capacity to nurture the kind of mass movement that pushed forward the abolitionist cause in Britain; the Spanish Abolitionist Society was founded only in December 1864, towards the end of the American Civil War, long after the revolutionary waves in Cuba had peaked.[99]

The fierceness of the official responses to anti-slavery and anticolonial movements was a further important inhibiting factor. The colonial state in Cuba was much more brutal and repressive than its French counterpart had been in Saint-Domingue, and it was obsessed with preventing a mass insurrection of the captives. To this extent, the Haitian precedent was a constraint, as it made Cuban colonial powers and settlers realize the potential force that captives could wield (not that any further confirmation was needed, but the Baptist revolt in Jamaica in 1831–2 brought the point home forcefully). Cuban anti-slavery movements were also fragmented. Although by the early 1840s there was evidence of a rapprochement among its three main constituencies (urban free black and mixed-race militants, maroons, and plantation-based African captives), these groups did not have enough time to work together to build the broad, durable, and effective social coalition that made the Saint-Domingue insurrection successful – a process which came to fruition in the French colony only after several decades.

At the same time, the radical anti-slavery ideas and practices of the first half of the nineteenth century were significant in shaping the Cuban movement for national self-determination, which gathered momentum from the 1860s. In December 1868, two months after launching his appeal for independence, the white creole landowner and republican lawyer Carlos Manuel de Céspedes freed his own enslaved workers and supported the abolition of human bondage in Cuba (see Plate 14). He thus connected the anti-slavery cause with that of national freedom, as Aponte's rebellion had done in 1812. In the ensuing Ten Years War (1868–78), the first of the three conflicts that finally ended Spanish rule in Cuba, many enslaved people joined the rebel army. Still, the independence movement did not unequivocally support immediate abolition, because it needed the support of slaveholding landowners, so it settled instead on a gradual-ist compromise.[100] Nonetheless the end of human bondage was endorsed by prominent republican advocates of Cuban independence such as José Martí, as well as soldiers and military leaders of the rebel army, many of whom were of African descent.[101] Among these was Antonio Maceo, a mixed-race officer who became one of the leading commanders in the Cuban war of independence. His political consciousness had been shaped in his youth by stories he heard from his mother about the history of Cuban enslaved resistance, especially in the years 1843–4.[102]

Cuban anti-slavery movements were significant both in their own terms and as remarkable and creative manifestations of the Atlantic resistance movements we have discussed throughout this book. Studies of the Cuban case sometimes approach its different manifestations of resistance – free black and captive; creole and African-born; urban, plantation-based, and marronage – separately and in isolation from each other, thus poten-tially pitting European, Haitian, and South American revolutionary styles against African ones. There were clearly singularities in these respective approaches, for example in the African resistance cultures, decisively shaped by the military and 'shipmate' experiences of the captives, as well as their African religious and spiritual values.

What transpires from our account are not only commonalities but synergies and reciprocal influences. White people became maroons; African-born men and women learned to wage war not only in the ways they had known in their homelands, but by organizing underground resistance networks, and creating links with black radicals from Havana and Matanzas. Urban-based figures such as Aponte heard and shared epic stories about Toussaint Louverture, Dessalines, and Christophe while celebrating African histories, and engaging in African spiritual ritu-als. Maroons established contacts with other types of rebels and worked with them to challenge and bring down the system. And of course these fugitives were often intimately familiar with Haiti, and not just as an ideal: they could see the coastline of the land of liberty from the far east-ern end of Cuba, and some of them took to the seas to find refuge from slavery there.

Moreover, Cuban anti-slavery movements all came to see their strug-gles as a war. They waged this conflict implacably and despite facing overwhelming material disadvantages, which they countered by drawing on their intellectual, technical, and spiritual resources. Across western Cuba black creole and African-born communities held religious services and exchanged sacred items to protect themselves and help forge new destinies.[103] There was clarity, too, in the understanding that this war was directed against slavery as a system, in all its essential aspects: the slave trade, the plantocracy and its surrogates, and the colonial power that stood behind it. Revolts that were driven by African-born captives were in this respect not different from urban-based actions and conspiracies.

Indeed, what emerged over time in Cuba was a common awareness across anti-slavery movements of the emancipatory ends of resistance, centred around the ideal of autonomy. This could mean reclaiming territorial spaces within and around slave plantations from settler control, recognizing civil and political equality for all, ending the tyrannical domination of white overseers, separating from colonial society through marronage, gaining the freedom to possess and cultivate one's own land, challenging patriarchy, securing independence from Spanish imperial domination, and even returning to the indigenous social arrangements existing on the island before the arrival of the Europeans – and sometimes, in a sweeping vision of possibility, all of these things at once.

9

White and Black Spirits
Engaged in Battle

On the evening of 21 August 1831 in Southampton County, rural south-eastern Virginia, six enslaved black men came together to launch a crusade against human bondage. The last to arrive was their leader, a carpenter and Baptist lay preacher named Nat Turner. At two o'clock in the morning – it was now 22 August, the date mattered – he took his companions to the property of his enslaver Joseph Travis, who was the first to die along with his family. During the next twenty-four hours Turner's band covered around twenty miles, recruiting more captives as they advanced, and attacking the white-owned slave plantations in the area. A few miles out from the village of Jerusalem (now called Sebrell), the county seat, where they hoped to find a significant store of weapons, the insurgents were confronted by a militia, and most of them dispersed. By this point around fifty-five white people had been killed, and a wave of panic was spreading across the state. In the violent repression that ensued well over a hundred black men were massacred in Southampton, many of whom had no connection to the revolt. Turner managed to escape, remaining in hiding until he was caught at the end of October, carrying an old sword. Charged with conspiracy and 'making insurrection', the man who had led the most consequential enslaved rebellion in the history of the United States was tried and hanged on 11 November.[1]

Turner had been born in 1800, the same year as Gabriel planned his conspiracy in Richmond, and Denmark Vesey bought his freedom in South Carolina. He kept the surname of his first enslaver, Benjamin Turner, although he probably did not use it much during his later life. In the white slaver world, where captives had no surnames, he was just known as 'Nat'. His religious audiences saw him as 'Prophet Nat', and his revolutionary followers called him 'General Nat' or 'Captain Nat'.[2] He lived an ascetic life, consuming no alcohol or tobacco, and preaching on Sundays at Baptist gatherings. People travelled from neighbouring states to hear his apocalyptic sermons.[3] According to the reward notice circulated after his escape in late August, he had a rather bright complexion, thin hair, wide shoulders, large eyes, and broad, flat feet, and moved in a 'brisk and active' way.[4]

In early November, as he was awaiting trial, Turner was interviewed by the attorney Thomas Gray and offered his account of the rebellion. Published immediately, Gray's *Confessions of Nat Turner* was intended as a 'faithful record' of their conversations. The text provides authentic insights into Turner's way of thinking. But it was also Gray's manuscript, written for a white readership. For example, Gray has the prisoner describing the rebels' actions as 'murder' throughout the text, a term that Turner is unlikely to have used – especially as he expressed no remorse about the rebellion, and when confronted about his actions at one point he replied by comparing his martyrdom to that of Christ.[5]

The *Confessions* were constructed as a singular tale of revolutionary predestination. Turner recalled that from early childhood he was believed to possess special skills. He learned to read and write 'with the most perfect of ease' and was known for carrying out physical and chemical experiments (Gray acknowledged his 'uncommon intelligence').[6] The young Nat spent a lot of his time in prayer, under the guidance of his devout grandmother Bridget – he believed that the Almighty had 'intended him for some purpose'.[7] The nature of this calling long remained unclear. At one point he even ran away from his plantation, just as his father had done. But he returned after a month because his Spirit told him that God had a much grander mission for him than the realization of his personal freedom.[8]

In 1825 he had a mystical vision of 'white spirits and black spirits engaged in battle, and the sun was darkened' (see Plate 24). While working in the fields he claimed to have found drops of Christ's blood on the corn, hieroglyphic characters and numbers on leaves, and the forms of men portrayed in blood. Three years later the message became more precise. He was to take on the fight of Jesus against 'the Serpent' and await a sign from the heavens to 'arise and prepare myself, and slay my enemies with their own weapons'.[9] It was now clear to him that he had been chosen to break the rule of the slave-masters in Virginia. In February 1831 the awaited celestial portent appeared in the form of a solar eclipse. He then (for the first time) shared his plans with four of his closest associates, Henry Porter, Hark Travis, Nelson Williams, and Sam Edwards. They resolved to strike on Independence Day, the symbolic national anniversary of 4 July. However, Turner became ill and the uprising had to be postponed until he received another heavenly sign, which came on 13 August, when the sky took on a 'greenish blue' colour.[10]

Turner shrouded his preparations for the 1831 rebellion in evangelical mysticism, framing the entire episode around his personal journey towards the Kingdom of Heaven.[11] Gray was one of many contemporaries who dismissed his actions as those of a 'gloomy fanatic'.[12] This view was echoed by many subsequent commentators, some of whom criticized Turner's lack of planning, and the choice of such a remote rural area for his uprising.[13] But this apparent isolation was misleading. Reports of discontent among enslaved populations in the South were widespread in the early 1830s. A federal military report in 1831, issued before the outbreak of the Southampton uprising, noted that two infantry companies had been despatched to Louisiana following rumours of an impending slave insurrection there. There were accounts of 'disorderly conduct' among captives in Delaware, Maryland, the Carolinas, and Virginia (during his conversation with Gray, Turner denied any involvement in the unrest in North Carolina).[14] Moreover, Turner's millenarianism fitted very comfortably within the traditions of resistance we have encountered thus far. His evangelical quest for redemption was in the tradition of the black narratives we discussed in chapter 6, while his Baptist revolutionism was similar to the outlooks of Gabriel and Denmark Vesey, Quamina in Demerara, and Sam Sharpe in Jamaica (whose uprising was to follow just a few months later). Enslaved revolts that unfolded in Brazil and Cuba in the 1830s and 1840s, as we have seen, were steeped in spiritual beliefs derived from Catholicism, Islam, and traditional African religions. In short, there was nothing singular about Nat Turner's revolutionary profile: quite the opposite. Indeed, it is possible to trace west African religious resonances in some of his visions and practices.[15]

The charge of disorganization needs to be examined more closely. Like all such insurgencies, the gathering of intelligence about intended targets was crucial, and depended on an effective support network. Many of these agents were enslaved domestic women in Southampton such as Esther, Charlotte, Cynthia, and Venus, who provided critical information. Once the rebellion had begun, they met the rebels at the farms where they laboured and undertook to provide them with supplies; one enslaved woman, Lucy, was prosecuted and executed for conspiracy.[16] At the same time, given the well-established tendency for enslaved conspiracies in the United States to be betrayed, Turner prudently opted to keep his original circle as small as possible. This was the strategy adopted by Charles in Louisiana in 1811, and the Demerara rebels in 1823. In this sense, Turner's rebellion unfolded according to plan. He began with six men, then multiplied his numbers by at least eight. Insurgents were still being recruited on Sunday 14 August, at a large religious gathering close to the North Carolina border where Turner spoke, asking those who were willing to join his rebellion to sport red bandanas around their necks.[17] His overall objectives remain mysterious, but had he succeeded in taking the village of Jerusalem – and he came close – there would have been several options available to him, including travelling to the nearby Dismal Swamp and setting up a maroon colony.

The clearest sign of Turner's wider revolutionary affiliations was the date he chose for the insurrection's starting point: 22 August marked the fortieth anniversary of the launching of the Saint-Domingue revolt in 1791. What exactly Turner understood about the Haitian revolution is not known for certain. However, it was reported that he mentioned the land of liberty during his recruiting conversations, and particularly the possibility of African Americans establishing 'a government of their own', like their 'brethren' in Haiti.[18] Moreover, Southampton County was not very far from the coastal port of Norfolk, which he would have been able to visit regularly, and where many of the mariners were black and provided intelligence about revolutionary activities in the Atlantic. It is likely that Turner would have heard stories about Haiti from these sources.[19] This black emancipatory commemorative landmark was plainly significant for a man so deeply attached to the symbolic order of things. The start of the Atlantic world's most successful enslaved revolution was an auspicious moment, especially as its leader Dutty Boukman was a religious leader, like Turner.

By picking this date Nat Turner also transcended his initial choice of 4 July. The national anniversary, as Frederick Douglass would remark in his speech two decades later, looked very different from an enslaved perspective: it was a 'thin veil to cover up the crimes' of American slavery.[20] What better response to the American Revolution's failure to bring emancipation to its captive population than the memory of Saint-Domingue's formidable insurrection? There was furthermore something of the early 1790s' Makandalist vision in Turner's visceral abomination of the 'white spirits', and his singular determination to visit the 'work of death' upon them.[21] It is not too much of a stretch to think of the mystical ensemble of spiritual communications, celestial signs, and African natural revelations as Prophet Nat's very own version of the Bois-Caïman ceremony.

In earlier chapters, we saw the emergence of powerful traditions of resistance to slavery in colonial America, as expressed through revolts, conspiracies, and marronage. However, the institution of slavery remained entrenched, and the system of violent control of captives was reinforced. African-American resistance received little support from the American Revolution. The Founding Fathers shelved the issue of slavery

by agreeing that it should be primarily regulated at state level, which
suited Southern states adamantly opposed to abolition. The Constitution
did not mention slavery, even though captives were included in taxation
calculations to finance the federal government; the dishonourable compromise reached here was that a slave was deemed to be 'three-fifths'
of a person. In the four decades that followed the Revolution, a tacit
territorial division emerged in the United States between slave states (in
the South) and free states (in the North), where human bondage was in
principle prohibited. As we will see, this distinction was not as clear-cut
as it seemed. But even though the United States banned the slave trade in
1807, domestic American abolitionism made little headway in the early
decades of the nineteenth century. The status quo between slave states and
free states served the interests of both sides, and it was clear that for the
federal government the civil rights of liberty and equality applied only to
white people.[22]

The three and a half decades between Turner's insurrection and the abolition of slavery in the United States marked the second wave of American
abolitionism. This period witnessed a growth of anti-slavery movements
in the North, and an intensification of black resistance, culminating in
the democratic revolution of Emancipation. Shortly after Turner's rebellion the governor of Virginia received a letter signed 'Nero', predicting
the outbreak of another revolt under a leader who had been enslaved in
Virginia and had escaped to Haiti, where 'his noble soul became warmed
by the spirit of freedom, and where he imbibed a righteous indignation,
and an unqualified hatred for the oppressors of his race'. Nero warned
the state official of an 'approaching carnage'.[23] Neither the author nor the
future liberator was ever identified; perhaps they were the same person.
But with its robust language, confident assertion of black rights and
dignity, and notice of an impending confrontation of racial slavery, the
missive demonstrated that African Americans were becoming increasingly
bold in their demands for universal freedom. The letter was significant too
for its reassertion, through the 1831 revolt, of the powerful connections
between American struggles for emancipation and the Haitian revolution.

The Haitian example of freedom and self-emancipation was one of the
recurrent themes in African-American thinking throughout this era, and
among the principal ways in which the intellectual argument for black
freedom was advanced and justified. This nexus can be illustrated in the
New York-based *Freedom's Journal*, the United States' first black newspaper, founded in 1827 by John Russwurm and Samuel Cornish, two
freeborn African Americans. During its two-year existence, it was distributed to black and white readers in the North, and some parts of the South,

as well as in Canada, Britain, and Haiti. Its aims were to celebrate black achievements, campaign for the rights of enslaved and free black people, and develop a sense of shared purpose among African-American communities. The revolution in Saint-Domingue played a pivotal role in this enterprise: as the editors observed in the first issue, Haiti's hard-fought independence was a remarkable example of black strength, achieved 'in the face of the universe'.[24]

The point of the Haitian example in moral terms was to demonstrate to the readers of *Freedom's Journal* that patience was not a virtue in the face of absolute oppression, and that 'people of colour had not deserved the name of men, had they tamely submitted'.[25] This resistance was presented as part of a divine plan, which would see the realization of a wider pan-African destiny. One article singled out the distinctiveness of the Haitian revolution, when compared to the American and French, for its embodiment of African ideals.[26] Another presented the existence of Haiti as proof that 'the descendants of Africa are capable of self-government'.[27] Another again saw the present moment as an opportunity for African Americans, under the eye of the 'God of Heaven', to take a leadership role in advancing the cause of 'the African nation'.[28]

Freedom's Journal completed this account of black destiny by offering its readers a three-part series on its principal Haitian embodiment: Toussaint Louverture. Taken from a British publication, the pieces celebrated the military victories of the Black Spartacus during the 1790s, and his administrative qualities as a governor, where he displayed a sense of integrity and dedication to the common good. It was (approvingly) pointed out that, while he was regarded as a 'guardian angel' by the black people of Saint-Domingue, Toussaint was also a 'favourite of the whites', whom he invited to his social gatherings. His emphasis on discipline and order was praised, too, as was his attachment to piety and sexual morality (Toussaint's numerous mistresses were quietly erased).[29] Louverture's leadership was an exemplar of black masculinity, but the newspaper provided space for feminine heroism, too. A four-part fictional narrative entitled 'Theresa – A Haytien Tale' was published in *Freedom's Journal* in 1828. It depicted the courageous engagement of a young black woman at the time of the Napoleonic invasion of the colony in the early nineteenth century. Overhearing crucial information about a planned military attack against Toussaint's position, the dauntless young woman risks her life (and that of her family) to travel to the governor's camp to pass on the intelligence, enabling Toussaint to avoid the danger.[30]

Among the radical anti-slavery contributors to *Freedom's Journal* was the freeborn abolitionist David Walker, one of the leading campaigners for emancipation in Boston. In 1829 Walker published his *Appeal in Four Articles, Together with a Preamble, to the Coloured Citizens of the World*. The pamphlet's revolutionary nature was apparent in the full title. Unlike much abolitionist writing, which was aimed at converting white audiences, and therefore trod carefully around their sensitivities, it was written 'very expressly' for black people, vigorously calling upon them to take an active part in their emancipation.[31] Central to this message was Walker's sweeping underlying conception of freedom, which was nourished by the ideals of autonomy and self-determination, as symbolized by the frontispiece of the *Appeal*'s 1830 edition. It showed a self-emancipated black man in a white tunic, standing on top of a rock and holding his hands up to the sky, on which the words 'liberty' and 'justice' are emblazoned (see Plate 19). For Walker, the fight against slavery was a 'heavenly cause'.[32]

In order to realize this promise of black citizenship, Walker uncovered the different dimensions of the 'wretchedness' that had been visited upon African Americans since the Revolution. These included exclusions from the right to vote, jury service and office-holding, systematic and ongoing racial discrimination, and of course the continuation of slavery. This unparalleled violence and human degradation amounted to the real American exceptionalism. Walker did not spare the Founding Fathers, lambasting Thomas Jefferson for claiming in 1785 that 'the blacks, whether originally a race, or made distinct by time and circumstances, are inferior to the whites in the endowments both of body and mind'.[33] Emphatically rejecting this assertion, as well as any legal or moral justification for enslavement, Walker reaffirmed the universal equality and dignity of all human beings in the eyes of God: 'we are men as well as [the slavers]; they have no more right to hold us in slavery than we have to hold them',[34] adding that whites were the 'natural enemies' of the black people, their murderers and oppressors.

Walker devoted much attention to exposing false sentiments and beliefs, such as the 'colonization' plans for African-American resettlement in Africa, the religious submissiveness preached by white Churches, the empathy felt by some captives towards their masters, and the complicity of some free black people with the wider system of enslavement. These sorts of attitudes, he argued, rested on a toxic combination of power, ignorance, and narrow self-interest, and were major obstacles to the creation of collective solidarity among black communities. Walker did not shy away from confronting the question of violence, invoking the spectre of Haiti, 'the glory of the blacks and the terror of tyrants'.[35] His vision combined a robust nationalism ('America is more our country than it is the whites'')[36] with an internationalist aspiration for 'the entire emancipation' of enslaved people across the world.[37] He openly endorsed the killing of white slavers as a form of self-defence: 'there is no more harm for you to kill a man, who is trying to kill you, than it is for you to take a drink of water when thirsty; in fact the man who will stand still and let another murder him is worse than an infidel.'[38]

Walker was a second-hand clothes dealer, and copies of the *Appeal* were smuggled in garments intended for enslaved labourers in the South, and there were reports of the pamphlet being seen in Georgia, Louisiana, and North Carolina in 1830.[39] The text was received with especial consternation by Southern planters, who offered a $3,000 bounty for Walker's head and $10,000 for his capture.[40] In fact, even though we can only speculate whether Turner read Walker's pamphlet,[41] we can now see that these African-American emancipatory texts and the 1831 rebellion were closely linked, expressing a radical turn in African-American resistance from the early 1830s.[42] When Nat Turner chose 22 August as the date for his insurrection, he was appealing to well-established collective understandings of the Haitian revolution among African Americans, as confirmed by the multiple references to Saint-Domingue in *Freedom Journal* and in Walker's pamphlet.

Moreover, Walker and Turner both saw the fight against slavery as a holy war, which black people could win because of their superior military valour, as demonstrated by the Haitian example. A statement from the *Appeal* could have been adopted by Turner as his motto: 'let twelve black men get well armed for battle, and they will kill and put to flight fifty whites'.[43] And likewise, as Theresa risks her life to pass on critical information to Louverture in the 'Haytien Tale', she anticipates the boldness of the women domestics from Southampton County who provided intelligence to Turner in the months leading up to his insurrection. There was also the fiery Charity Bowery, an enslaved woman from North Carolina, who later remembered the early 1830s as a time when 'the best and brightest' among the captives would meet in secret places, sending slavers into fits of panic. Her imagination was entranced by the uprising of 'Prophet Nat', around which all the other events in her life were framed.[44] Charity would no doubt have heard the popular song that did the rounds in the American South after 1831, and relished its opening lines:

> You mought be rich as cream
> And drive you coach and four-horse team,
> But you can't keep de world from moverin' round
> Nor Nat Turner from gainin' ground.[45]

*

The year 1831 marked the last large-scale revolutionary effort to overturn slavery in the South until the Civil War. Revolts in towns and individual acts of rebellion continued, by men as well as women. Pauline Howell remembered her aunt killing and castrating two overseers, the punishment for those who violently molested enslaved women on the estate.[46] We can also interpret the poisoning of a Fourth of July celebration on a South Carolina plantation in 1832 in similar terms, although the female domestic who spiked the slavers' food at the behest of her co-conspirator denied any knowledge of his intentions.[47] Evidence from newspaper and court records from the eighteenth century all the way to Emancipation further shows that large numbers of captive women conspired to murder their slavers. They used a variety of methods, including poisoning, arson, drowning, and physical attack.[48]

Resistance continued in other forms. One of the most significant elements here was the retention of African cultures by the enslaved, for example through the 'ring shout', a synthesis of central African (Bakongo) and west African (Dahomey) cultures mentioned in chapter 3. Its performance was widespread across black America, especially in Southern plantations, and as captives moved round an ecstatic circle they appealed to their cosmological community of ancestors and rejected their status as enslaved people.[49] In the words of one witness, these ceremonies brought the captives 'to the gate of heaven'.[50] The ring shout was one of the main ways in which enslaved Africans brought to the United States resisted their cultural destruction by preserving their connection with their homeland. They practised this ritual away from the gaze of their enslavers in their quarters, their churches, or in nearby wooded areas.[51] In the American North they infused it into their Christian worship, embedding these multiple African sounds and meanings into their religious expressions. These adaptations allowed their spiritual beliefs to survive in a form that would not be seen as threatening by their enslavers. African ethnicity was thus one of the foundations of black unification in antebellum America.[52]

There were other acts of dissent, distinct from the classic patterns expressed through fugitive escape to the North, joining maroon settlements, or hiding in free black communities. As elsewhere in the Atlantic, many African-American captives challenged the oppressive slave order through mockery, derision, and defiant gestures. These more circumscribed actions included not following orders, meeting in secret to pray (many African places of worship were destroyed after the Nat Turner insurrection), refusing to show emotion when punished, or as in the case of a captive named Hal Hutson, disobeying his master to listen in on the teaching of his enslaver's son in order to learn the alphabet and arithmetic.[53] This dissent was expressed, too, by women seeking limited escapes from the tight physical controls imposed upon their bodies and their mobility through the system of tickets, passes, and patrols.

Short-term absences (*petit marronnage*) were the most common and characteristic form of plantation dissent by women. Enslaved women ran away for brief periods of time to avoid the harvest periods in the plantation cycle. They took off to escape punishment from violent enslavers, or the attentions of sexually predatory foremen. They disappeared to find herbs and roots needed to prepare healing medicines, or to visit friends and relatives, who were often not nearby. Sometimes they just removed themselves because of the overwhelming nature of the institution of slavery. As the repeat absentee Sallie Smith later recalled about her place of enslavement: 'I tell you, I could not stay there.' From time to time she simply had to escape out of range: 'I'd go so afar off the plantation I could not hear the cows low or the rooster crow.' But in the end she always returned, even though she was severely punished.[54]

How Sallie was able to survive during these periods of short-term flight sheds light on why she chose to come back. During her absences, she regularly received supplies from other enslaved plantation workers who passed on food to her when the overseer was not looking, or sought her out on the edge of the woods.[55] In other words, she was part of a community to which she felt a sense of belonging, and whose solidarity both legitimized her individual protest and made it practically possible – both by not betraying her whereabouts and helping her materially. These occasional escapes enabled Sallie first to separate herself from the control of those who had power over her, and then to reconnect with the world. In a system that sought complete coercive domination over her body and spirit, these moments of autonomy were eminently political acts.

Illicit nocturnal group activities could reinforce this sense of freedom. In the 1840s South Carolina planters formed the Savannah River Association to counter the rise of alcohol sales to captives, which they believed was leading to an increase in drinking, as well as trading and stealing. They also claimed that 'hundreds' of enslaved people were 'prowling about the country every night and at all hours of the night' without permission to attend meetings of various kinds.[56] Among the most common of these were unauthorized social gatherings, typically held in outbuildings, woods, and swamps. These were occasions of great merriment, with singing, dancing, games, and the performance of African music on fiddles, tambourines, and banjos. Later in her life, as she recalled the hushed excitement of these events away from the Virginia plantation where she was held in bondage, Nancy Williams dwelled on the effort she took in preparing herself for these festivities. She adorned her dress with special yellow dye and had matching yellow shoes. Even though her clothes were ill-fitting, and the clogs hurt her feet, she had fond memories of these occasions, where she could dance, drink, and flirt with men. These parties were thus not just welcome moments of respite from the harshness of plantation life, but also opportunities for the enslaved to recapture a sense of dignity and self-worth.[57] Some of the dances performed on these occasions were religious and spiritual in nature.[58]

Like Nancy Williams, many women took pride in their appearance, making buttons and animal-based ornaments for their dresses, wearing hand-crafted necklaces and earrings, and perfuming themselves with rose and honeysuckle flowers. Some wore elaborate headwraps, while others removed their scarves to reveal a distinctive range of hairstyles.[59] As in many other, similar Atlantic settings, these were occasions to deride the plantation world. Women imitated the dances they saw in the homes of their masters, but in a mocking way.[60] Their songs celebrated the illicit events they had organized, their ability to circumvent slave patrols, and their spirit of defiance, as with this Mississippi ditty remembered by Mollie Williams: 'Run tell Coleman, Run tell everbody Dat de niggers is arisin'!'[61] Again, these apparently innocuous private pursuits had wider political ramifications, which were not lost on slave planters. The Savannah River Association observed that by allowing enslaved Africans an independent social life, these nightly 'prowling' activities were eroding the hierarchical order they were trying to preserve, while encouraging enslaved people to see their masters as their 'natural enemies'[62] – the very expression used in David Walker's 1829 pamphlet.

How often and with what effects these expressions of autonomy were translated into fuller forms of resistance in this period is something for which we lack systematic records. Significant patterns will emerge during the Civil War years, as we shall see later. However, a fascinating further piece of evidence about these connections comes from a letter written by a plantation manager in Mississippi in 1847. After complaining about the general indiscipline of his labour force, he then turned to a captive woman named California, who 'has an idea that she is free. Comes & goes & does as she pleases, infuses a good deal of these feelings and notions in her childrens heads.' It emerged that one of the sources of California's beliefs was a collection of outlawed anti-slavery prints in her possession, which she had put up on the walls of her cabin.[63]

We know of many instances, in the United States and elsewhere in the Atlantic, of captive homes being used as meeting places for the planning of rebellions, and the holding of prayers and religious ceremonies. But this was something more remarkable: an enslaved person's cabin openly adorned with anti-slavery propaganda. The letter did not reveal how California had come by these prints. However, we know that from the 1830s abolitionist associations such as William Lloyd Garrison's American Anti-Slavery Society were mass-producing anti-slavery material of this kind. Two years after its founding in 1833, the Society carried out a sustained postal campaign, sending out a million printed items (tracts, flyers, prayer books, catechisms), a large number of which reached cities, towns, and rural areas across the South.[64] Many states then issued bans against such material, including Mississippi, where the extreme penalty for an enslaved person found in possession of such texts and prints was death. California's example shows not only that these materials still got through, but that the enslaved were willing to take high risks to receive and display them, and promote their contents among their families and friends.[65]

Black narratives were another significant instrument for promoting abolitionist ideas across the United States. Before 1865, around sixty-five titles written by former African-American captives were published, introducing prominent black voices into the discussions about slavery, and offering perspectives about liberty, citizenship, and democratic action. These testimonies were written to affirm the humanity and dignity of black people. They were direct refutations of the reactionary accounts of Southern slavers, which depicted the plantation as a family, and maintained the myths of the benign treatment and well-being of captives, and the godliness of their enslavers. Moreover, black narratives placed a deliberate emphasis on detailed facts, sometimes supplemented with documents – again as a counter to the enslavers' claims that abolitionists were exaggerating the evils of human bondage. Intended for white audiences, these works typically followed settled conventions of structure and content. As with the works produced in Britain in the late eighteenth century, they were tales of individual redemption, which began with graphic descriptions of the harrowing experiences of enslavement in the South (Africa and the Middle Passage were rarely evoked in any detail). The texts had a narrative arc beginning with awakening, then moving on to self-consciousness, and ending with freedom secured through fugitive escape to a free state.

Flight from slavery was never easy, as with the case of Moses Roper, who tried to escape sixteen times from his various captors before finally succeeding in fleeing out of Savannah in Georgia. He eventually reached England, where he was educated at London University and published his autobiographical *Narrative of the Adventures and Escape of Moses*

Roper in 1838. It was a dramatic tale, which exposed the cruelty and violence of Southern slavery. The book became one of the early successes of the genre, selling over 30,000 copies. The titles of these works often summed up their entire prospectus, as with *The Narrative of the Sufferings of Lewis Clarke, during a Captivity of More than Twenty-Five Years, among the Algerines of Kentucky, One of the So-Called Christian States of America*, which appeared in 1845. Many books ended with an explicit call for immediate and comprehensive abolition: Clarke urged 'all the people of the civilized world' to curse slavery ' ... till the sun of a FREE DAY sends a beam of light and joy into every cabin'.[66] These calls were typically cast in the form of moral appeals to the religious sensibilities of white Americans. Self-liberation by black people, particularly by violent or insurrectionary means, was not a feature of the genre. These writings rarely dwelled on, let alone mentioned, the Haitian revolution, even when their authors were familiar with it.

This narrative tradition was exemplified by Frederick Douglass, the most eminent and influential African-American abolitionist of the era. Born of a white father whose identity he never established, Douglass was enslaved in Maryland, escaping to the North in September 1838, when he was around twenty years of age. Three years later, he was hired as a paid speaker for the Anti-Slavery Society, and he became known for his spellbinding oratory. Based on a synthesis of his early lectures, his *Narrative of the Life of Frederick Douglass* became an instant success on its publication in 1845, selling 11,000 copies in the United States by 1848, and going through nine editions in England; two years later the book had sold 30,000 copies.[67] In this, the first of his three autobiographies, Douglass started with the classic features of the slave narrative but turned the text into a tale of self-emancipation. From the opening pages, where he mentions the nightly visits of his mother, an enslaved woman who could only come to see him by stealth, and who dies when he is seven years old, he vividly captures the humiliation and inhumanity of enslavement. He is not allowed to pay her a final visit or attend her burial.[68] The 'savage barbarity' of the white slave overseer, who casually kills the slave Demby for refusing to yield to him, and the whipping of his Aunt Hester in the kitchen, which Douglass witnesses, are among the most horrifying early scenes of the book.[69]

Slavery is also denounced for the ways in which it corrupts the slavers themselves, as revealed through his portrait of his cruel masters, various depraved Southern clergymen, and the 'snake' Edward Covey, a vicious slave-breaker who whips Douglass regularly and emerges as one of the *Narrative*'s most insidious villains.[70] At the same time, Douglass dwells on his personal resistance. Although deeply pious, his awakening comes not from religious salvation but through his dogged pursuit of literacy. This painstaking journey to self-enlightenment through education, which he follows for a decade, is his 'pathway from slavery to freedom'.[71] He later becomes a Sunday-school teacher for a group of forty enslaved men and women, and he feels his soul uplifted.[72] Liberty is depicted very much in terms of rational self-mastery, in line with classical Enlightenment thinking. Douglass is at pains to distinguish this 'virtuous' freedom from the alcoholic licentiousness that slavers granted their workers during their holidays.[73]

He appears to have little time for the African religious rituals of his comrade Sandy Jenkins, a 'clever soul' whose protective totem he rather brusquely dismisses as 'ignorant superstition', although it clearly helped him in his struggle against Covey.[74] Yet upon closer inspection his autobiographical writings dwell on various elements of African cultural retention among captives, including spoken dialects, dancing rituals, work skills, and dreams, as well as a sense of community.[75] At several points Douglass underscores the solidarity he experienced among his fellow captives, which creates a powerful affective and political bond, as well as a highly valued sense of collective autonomy. One of the climaxes of the book comes when Douglass physically confronts Covey and after a two-hour fight forces him to stop using the whip against him. He describes this act of resistance as a 'turning-point' in his enslavement, rekindling his sense of freedom and his manhood.[76]

Douglass thus accentuated one of the central themes of these narratives: achieving freedom was an intense struggle, but it was worth pursuing at all costs. This was not only for personal reasons, but because it was an essential condition of democratic citizenship. As they made the case for their emancipation, these African-American texts appealed to broader collective beliefs from the revolutionary era about American fortitude and valour. Patrick Henry's celebrated motto ('Give me liberty or give me death!') was often alluded to when fugitives evoked their love of freedom, and the risks they had to take to secure it.[77] Harriet Jacobs, about whom we will hear more shortly, summed up her personal motto by repeating the exact formula.[78] Describing his flight to freedom, Samuel Ringgold Ward proclaimed that he would never 'seek or accept peace at the expense of liberty',[79] while the escapee Henry Brown would opt only for 'victory or death'.[80] Death could be inflicted upon the enemy: chased by a slaver, John Anderson had to stab and kill him before making his escape from Missouri.[81]

Many fugitives recounted the terrible physical and mental hardships

they experienced during their long journeys to freedom. On his way to
Canada, Henry Bibb walked for two days without stopping, thinly clad
and pelted by snow, and terrified of slave-hunting dogs. His shoes were
worn through and his feet froze.[82] After reaching free territory, William
Wells Brown observed that 'none but a slave could place such an appreciation upon liberty as I did at that time, because few had earned liberty
at such a great price'.[83] Some captives displayed considerable ingenuity in
making their escapes. William and Ellen Craft got away from their Georgian plantation by having Ellen, who was light-complexioned, pose as an
invalid white gentleman travelling with her black servant (see Plate 22).
She covered her right hand and face with a poultice to avoid signing her
name in hotel registers.[84] The most original act of self-emancipation was
accomplished by Henry Brown, who earned his nickname 'Box' after he
successfully mailed himself out of the South in a chest three feet long and
two feet wide. At one point during the journey from Virginia, the con-
tainer was tilted and he found himself upside down. Still, Brown made
it to Washington alive, 'sustained . . . by the thoughts of sweet liberty'.[85]

These fugitive journeys were undertaken across large swathes of
American territory, generally requiring group solidarity in the form of
information gathering, planning, and systems of support. Douglass
escaped with the help of his future wife Anna Murray, who provided
clothing and part of her savings, which she augmented by selling one
of her beds. Free African Americans, aided by white abolitionists (often
Quakers), established local networks of assistance to enable runaways to
flee to the North. This Underground Railroad, as it came to be known,
was based in parts of Ohio, the eastern port towns of New Bedford and
Boston, south-central Pennsylvania and Philadelphia, Detroit, western
Illinois, Upstate New York and New York City, and the area around the
District of Columbia.[86] By 1860 there were 226,000 free people of colour
in the North, and just under 500,000 in the Union as a whole. They were
active participants in this anti-slavery network. In 1838 black women
in Philadelphia established a Vigilance Committee to support the Underground Railroad, raising funds and providing shelter for maroons on their
way to Canada.[87] Free black rural communities played a key facilitating
role, especially in Indiana, Illinois, and Ohio.[88] The forging of false documentation to enable escapees to flee from the South became widespread
in Northern black urban settings.[89]

The Underground Railroad was a social movement without a central
leadership, but with well-established collective practices and norms. This
was reflected in the coded language used by its operatives, borrowed
largely from railway terminology. The entire network was called the

'Freedom Train', organizers were 'agents', and those responsible for moving fugitives from one place to another, 'conductors'. Safe houses were 'stations' and supporters who donated food and clothing, 'stock-holders'. In some instances, organized group escapes led to pitched battles between fugitives and their supporters on one side, and law enforcement authorities and slavers and their agents on the other.[90] Passed by Congress in 1850, the Fugitive Slave Act criminalized material support for runaways in the North, and required officials from free states to help capture and return escapees to the South. Underground Railroad organizers defied the law to help thousands reach Canada, which was the primary destination of maroons until the Civil War. Many successful fugitives now became targets of slave hunters, like the Crafts, who had to be hidden by Boston abolitionists before fleeing to Britain via Nova Scotia. This time Ellen Craft disguised herself as a white woman.[91]

During the 1850s some two hundred captives were sent back to the South, but the numbers who managed to escape enslavement and find refuge outside the United States ran into the thousands. Most runaways from the South were men, but it was a woman who became the emblematic embodiment of the Underground Railroad movement. Harriet Tubman (see Plate 17) escaped enslavement from Maryland in 1849 with the help of local abolitionists, and until 1860 she made repeated journeys back to lead her family members and others to freedom. In 1856 Maryland authorities offered a reward of $12,000 for her capture, which only increased her determination. By the eve of the Civil War, with the active help of abolitionist networks, Tubman had made at least thirteen clandestine trips and brought out around seventy captives, escorting many of them personally to the Canadian frontier.[92] In 1860 she happened to be in the town of Troy in New York State as the escaped maroon Charles Nalle was detained to be sent back to his enslaver in Virginia. Tubman led a crowd that managed to grab him from law-enforcement officials and ferry him across the Hudson river to West Troy. However, as soon as Nalle reached the other bank he was re-arrested. Tubman again came to the rescue, commandeering a flotilla of boats with several hundred supporters. After another pitched battle with the police, Nalle was seized once more by his abolitionist liberators and spirited away. The local newspaper commented that most of his rescuers were African Americans.[93]

Black narratives had a profound impact on American literature, none more so than via the publication in 1852 of *Uncle Tom's Cabin*, a sentimental anti-slavery novel that became an international bestseller, with a vigorous concluding condemnation of slavery as 'unChristian'. Its author Harriet

Beecher Stowe based her work on recently published fugitive accounts (notably those of Josiah Henson, Lewis Clarke, and Henry Bibb). Other episodes were inspired by real Underground Railroad incidents, such as the escape from slavery by the maid Eliza Harris and her son Harry, and their dramatic leap across the frozen ice on the Ohio river during their journey to safety in Canada.[94] However, even as it was praised by Frederick Douglass as an 'efficient agent of change', Stowe's novel was problematic for many radical abolitionists, particularly in its racially stereotypical portrait of Tom as a Christ-like martyr who refused to resist his enslavement, its endorsement of African-American resettlement out of the United States, and its contempt for the 'worn-out, effeminate' Haitian republic.[95] Published in 1856, Stowe's second novel *Dred* was more forthright about enslaved resistance, casting its main character as Nat Turner's fugitive son, who is an active participant in the 1831 rebellion. The unbowed Dred lives in the Dismal Swamps, and his continuing anti-slavery militancy threatens plantation society.[96]

At times controversial too, but in very different ways, were the contributions of black women to the enslaved autobiographical genre. Published in 1850, the *Narrative of Sojourner Truth*, one of the few accounts of enslavement in the North, confirmed Truth's prominence as one of the leading black women abolitionists. Stowe wrote in her preface to the 1853 edition that the author had 'a mind of no common energy & power'. Born in 1798 in Upstate New York as Isabella Baumfree, she grew up in a milieu exposed to Dutch, African, and Caribbean cultures, before embracing Methodism.[97] Isabella escaped with her baby daughter from the farm where she was enslaved in October 1826, before New York's abolition law was adopted a year later. After a decade of Christian preaching she joined the anti-slavery movement in the 1840s, changing her name to Sojourner Truth and becoming a feminist orator against human bondage. Speaking at a Women's Rights Convention in Ohio in 1851, she captivated the audience with her affirmation of equality, declaring: 'I have as much muscle as any man, and can do as much work as any man.' Her speeches were full of wit: noting that men seemed to be in a state of 'confusion', she declared 'I am a woman's rights', and told men that if they recognized these rights they would 'feel better'.[98]

The *Narrative* was unconventional in that abolitionist writings typically depicted enslaved women as exploited for both their labour and their sexuality. Truth, however, chose not to dwell on her own sexual history or the violence against women more generally, taking pride in her work ethic as a farm labourer under her last enslaver John Dumont, a man she respected – even though he sometimes used the whip on her. She

14. (Left to right, above to below) Antislavery campaigners from nineteenth-century France, Cuba and Britain: Henri Grégoire, revolutionary priest, abolitionist and ardent champion of Haitian rights and racial equality; Victor Schoelcher, the intellectual driving force behind the second French abolition of 1848; Carlos Manuel de Céspedes, Cuban plantation owner and revolutionary statesman who freed his slaves; and Elizabeth Heyrick, campaigner for the immediate abolition of slavery; this silhouette is the only known portrait of her.

15. The two French abolitions of slavery: the ending of human bondage by the Jacobin Convention in 1794 (above), and (below) an idealized portrayal of the proclamation of the 1848 abolition by an official envoy of the Second Republic (holding the decree in his hand) in the French colonies.

16. José Aponte was the best-known figure of the 1812 revolt in Cuba. This artwork (*Jubilo de Aponte*, 2017) by the Cuban artist José Bedia pays homage to him and highlights the qualities of the conspirators: the marching figures represent their collective determination, while the hands, feet and ears symbolize the boldness of their underground revolutionary activities. The bottom row has horsemen galloping towards freedom, inspired by various religious and spiritual ideals, while the top tier depicts anti-slavery heroes (Toussaint Louverture's silhouette is on the left).

17. (Left to right, above to below) Anti-slavery campaigners and combatants from the United States and Saint-Domingue's war of independence: early twentieth- and nineteenth-century photographs of Harriet Tubman and Frederick Douglass; a period drawing of Martin Delany in military uniform, and a portrait of the Saint-Domingue revolutionary fighter Sanité Belair, by the contemporary Haitian artist François Cauvin.

THE GREAT PLEA FOR FREEDOM.

READ IT AND YOU CANNOT RESIST IT.

MY BONDAGE AND MY FREEDOM.

BY FREDERICK DOUGLASS.

One Vol. 12mo. 464 pp. Illustrated, Price 7s 6d.

IT WILL BE READ WITH AVIDITY.

It cannot fail to be read with avidity, as one of the most striking illustrations of American Slavery, which either fact or fiction has presented to the public.—*N. Y. Tribune.*

A WORK OF INTRINSIC MERIT.

It is a work of intrinsic merit, and speaks volumes in praise of the man, his intellect and culture. The incidents of his life, woven up in the web of narrative by his polished and classical mind, and graceful pen, are full of interest.—*Buffalo Express.*

A MASTER AUTHOR AND ORATOR.

Frederick Douglass is a remarkable man. As a writer and speaker, he ranks with the most effective and natural—after our master authors and orators.—*Utica Herald.*

TRUE, AND OF ABSORBING INTEREST.

The story of Frederick Douglass' life as detailed in this volume, possesses an interest which is really absorbing. The truthfulness of the narrative which he gives of his bondage will be generally conceded, and certainly realises the truth of the old adage—"truth is strange—stranger than fiction."—*Boston Journal.*

EXPOSES THE BANE OF THE REPUBLIC.

It reveals the miseries of servile life with an intense vividness and impressiveness, that can but fasten its facts and arguments upon the reader's mind as with a pen of iron and with the point of a diamond.—*Vt. Journal.*

NO ROMANCE MORE EXCITING.

No romance can be more exciting to the reader than this truthful narrative. The work is having a wide circulation.—*Yates Co. Whig.*

IT STIRS THE FEELINGS.

We have not read a work which has stirred our feelings to a greater extent for some years, and we are glad that Mr Slosson intends to keep a good stock on hand. We think he will need it. The book is a powerful, vivid picture of a slave's life, and effectually removes the gloss which pro-slavery men attempt to throw over the beatitudes of this aid to the "highest state of human existence !"—*Oswego Times.*

A SELF-MADE MAN.

This volume, besides its many moving and thrilling details, affords evidence of a most remarkable man. Mr Douglass has emphatically made himself. As a writer and speaker, he has but few equals in the country. His book is readable and interesting.—*Christian Advocate.*

AN INTERESTING AND REMARKABLE WORK.

The book is one of the most interesting and remarkable ever published—a well written work on Slavery, by one who was born and bred a slave.—*Vt. Watchman.*

NERVOUS, CLEAR, AND TELLING.

It presents a clear and graphic picture of his slave-life from his earliest recollections : his escape and his life since, including his experiences in this country and Europe. No one will deny Mr Douglass the possession of genius and character of a high order. He writes in a nervous, clear and most telling manner, clothing his narrative with intense interest, and conveying his moral impressions with a vividness that leaves the reader scarcely any escape. The subject is deeply tragic, and, in his masterly handling possesses an engrossing interest.—*N. Y. Evangelist.*

WORTH A HUNDRED VOLUMES OF ROMANCE.

We recommend the book as worth a hundred volumes of the trashy literature of the day.—*Pittsburg Herald.*

HOW IT DIFFERS FROM OTHER WORKS.

We have before listened to the homely tale of the liberated slave, but it did not impress us as does this narrative of Douglass, for the reason that we were left to supply the commentary which is here pressed upon us by one who has both seen and felt what he relates. The story bears throughout the impress of truth, and the manner in which it is told stamps the writer as a man of genius, and a high order of talent.—*Ohio State Journal.*

CIRCULATE IT WIDELY

The encroachments and usurpations of Slavery are becoming more flagrant every day, and a work animating the public mind enlightening it upon this bane of the American Republic, and from the high source whence this emanates, ought to be very extensively read in the Free States.—*Whitehall Chronicle.*

HOW WRITTEN—ITS CHARACTER.

The book is written with the happiest descriptive power, with nerve and vigour of expression, and with richness of style. It has an ample resource in phrase, great perspicuity, and a musical, resonating, and half rhythmatic style, which reminds the reader of the author's origin, and of the native melodies of his race. The book manifests a high, and, to us, unexpected polish. The interest aroused and kept up by a perusal of this book is of a high order, and rarely degenerates.—*Detroit Daily Advertiser.*

IT IS PECULIARLY ATTRACTIVE.

We need not say that the volume possesses extraordinary attractions. The life of such a man cannot fail to excite an interest in the public mind seldom equalled, even in this book-making age.—*Christian Ambassador.*

THE AUTHOR POPULAR—HIS BOOK IN DEMAND.

This is a splendid work. The personal worth of the author, the deserved popularity he has secured throughout this nation, and the universal desire that prevails to have a memento of one of nature's noblemen, will conspire to create an unprecedented demand for this book.—*Wesleyan.*

THE EVILS OF SLAVERY CALMLY UNFOLDED.

There are no lines of ranting madness here. Calmly, dispassionately he unfolds to us all the evils of the bondage system in its varies aspects, and must thus commend his disclosures to all true Americans, south as well as north. The entire work is of a high intellectual order, and intensely interesting from its beginning to its close.—*American Spectator.*

THOUGHT AND REASON IN WHAT HE SAYS.

Mr Douglass is a spirited and pointed writer, and his oratory will bear favourable comparison with any of our public speakers. There is thought and reason in all he says, and though his language is sometimes bitter, it is usually calm, dignified, and earnest.—*Buffalo Courier.*

WE WONDER HOW HE DID IT.

As an orator, the public here and elsewhere have had abundant opportunity to judge ; and we suppose that none have ever listened to his graceful elocution, his cutting satire, and his frequent bursts of eloquence, without wonder that a man who emerged from the dense darkness of slavery, after reaching his manhood, who in fact learned his alphabet after coming to maturity, could deservedly rank among the first orators of the day.—*Roch. American.*

☞ For sale by all Booksellers and News-Agents.

☞ Single copies sent by mail post paid, on receipt of price.

MILLER, ORTON & MULLIGAN,

Publishers, 25 Park Row, New York, and 107 Genesee St., Auburn.

Glasgow : GEORGE GALLIE ; Edinburgh : A. & C. BLACK ;

18. Scottish flysheet for Frederick Douglass's second autobiography, *My Bondage and My Freedom* (1855). Douglass was the greatest and best-known anti-slavery campaigner in the USA. He visited Britain twice in the mid-nineteenth century, going on lengthy speaking tours to promote his writings and encourage solidarity with the abolitionist cause.

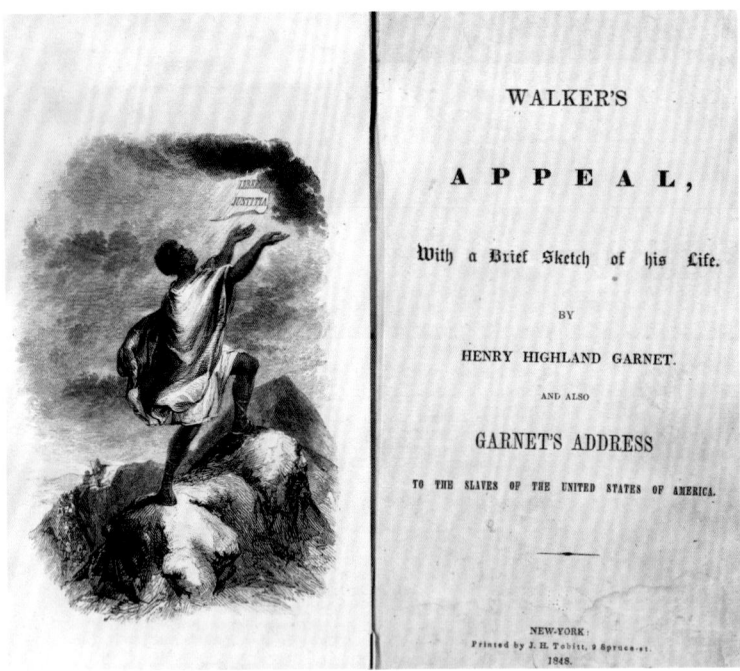

WALKER'S

APPEAL,

With a Brief Sketch of his Life.

BY

HENRY HIGHLAND GARNET.

AND ALSO

GARNET'S ADDRESS

TO THE SLAVES OF THE UNITED STATES OF AMERICA.

NEW-YORK:
Printed by J. H. Tobitt, 9 Spruce-st.
1848.

19. Inside illustration and title page of David Walker's *Appeal* (1829), one of the first texts written specifically for black people in the United States, urging them to stand up to enslavement and rally in support for the struggle for emancipation.

20. Celebration of the abolition of slavery in Washington D.C., 1866. On 19 April, around 5,000 African-American citizens from D.C. marked emancipation by marching to the White House, preceded by two black regiments; at the rally there were religious services and speeches by prominent abolitionist political figures and campaigners.

21. Soldiers from the 54th Massachusetts regiment photographed in front of the Robert Gould Shaw memorial. Unveiled in 1897, this was the first sculpture to pay public homage to the heroism of African-American combatants during the Civil War.

22. The antislavery campaigner Ellen Craft, who escaped servitude in Georgia with her husband William by disguising herself as an invalid white gentleman travelling with her black servant.

23. (Left) Marcus Garvey, the most influential and creative champion of black emancipation and empowerment in the early decades of the twentieth century, and (right) Aimé Césaire, the political and intellectual leader from Martinique, who campaigned for black civil and political rights during the anticolonial era. Both men were fervent admirers of Toussaint Louverture.

24. Nat Turner was a black preacher and anti-slavery campaigner from Virginia who led a rebellion against servitude in 1831; his political thinking was also shaped by the Haitian revolution. This quilt artwork (*The Revelation*, 2019), by the American artist Stephen Towns, represents one of Turner's mystical visions from six years earlier, when 'white spirits and black spirits were engaged in battle, and the sun was darkened – the thunder rolled in the Heavens and blood flowed in the streams'.

25. The French film *Ni chaînes ni maîtres* (2024), features Mati (Anna Thiandoum) and her father Massamba (Ibrahima Mbaye Thié), two African-born runaways who escape from their brutal plantation in eighteenth-century Ile de France (Mauritius).

believed her work deserved not only economic but also civic recognition. This sense of personal accomplishment did not conform with standard autobiographical accounts, where the workplace was merely an arena of coercion, violence, and humiliation. The *Narrative* made for uncomfortable reading for white abolitionists for a further reason, as it highlighted the North's complicity in slavery and the demands of free black people for full citizenship. Truth was scathing about the North's system of 'free' labour, which she regarded as barely different from enslavement, and part of a generalized system of worker exploitation. As she put it, 'the rich rob the poor, and the poor rob each other'.[99]

Other narratives confronted the complex sexual issues facing women captives, as with Louisa Picquet's account, transcribed in conversation form by the white abolitionist clergyman Hiram Mattison and published as *Louisa Picquet, the Octoroon: Or, Inside Views of Southern Domestic Life*. Despite Mattison's rather sensationalized editing, Picquet's powerful defence of her integrity as a mixed-race woman and mother shines through, particularly as she navigates her way around the predatory sexual behaviour she faces. In Georgia she manages to avoid being raped by her second enslaver Mr Cook, despite enduring a severe whipping from him. Cook impregnates her mother Elizabeth Ramsey several times, but Louisa succeeds in protecting her own body from violation through her own resistance as well as the support of Mrs Bachelor, who runs the boarding house where they are staying. Louisa regards this lady as her 'best friend . . . in the world' – a rare example of gender solidarity trumping the divisions created by enslavement and race.[100]

Louisa is eventually sold again after Cook is jailed (for his debts). Now separated from her mother, she becomes the concubine of her final enslaver John Williams in New Orleans. During these six years, as Williams fathers her children, she continues to push back against her condition, dealing with his fits of jealousy and threats of violence. He vows to kill her if she tries to escape, and she prays that he might die; Louisa is racked with guilt for the life she is forced to lead.[101] When Williams passes away in 1847, she does not mourn him, and manages to secure her emancipation, eventually moving north to Cincinnati with her children. She eventually tracks down Elizabeth in Texas and publishes her book to complement the fundraising operation to buy her mother's freedom. She is reunited with her in 1860, just as the book is nearing publication. Louisa Picquet's narrative thus overcomes her status as a 'fallen woman' by celebrating her humanity and her dedication to her family, and excoriating the moral corruption of white Southern enslavers.[102]

The year 1861 also saw the publication of Harriet Jacobs' *Incidents in the Life of a Slave Girl*, which became the best-known woman's enslaved narrative text of its time and has since become a classic. Composed between 1853 and 1858 (the subtitle proudly announced 'Written by Herself'), but with the names of all living characters changed (Jacobs appears as 'Linda Brent'), it powerfully combines standard abolitionist themes with appeals to feminine sentimentality and solidarity. Jacobs recounts the intense anti-black violence that followed Nat Turner's revolt, ironically noting that in its aftermath 'the slaveholders came to the conclusion that it would be well to give the slaves enough of religious instruction to keep them from murdering their masters'. She brings to life the sham Christianity of the South with vivid examples, as with the Methodist class leader who serves as the local police officer, and performs the 'Christian office' of whipping slaves for fifty cents.[103] In an even more forthright way than Frederick Douglass, Jacobs evokes the importance of African religion in the lives of the enslaved, especially through her evocation of ring-shout ceremonies and the sacredness of burial grounds, where release from oppression can be felt, and 'the servant is free from the master'.[104]

The centrepiece of the book, as with Picquet, are Jacobs' struggles as a woman and mother. She asserts that 'slavery is terrible for men; but it is far more terrible for women'. Jacobs must fight a long battle to save herself from rape at the hands of her master James Norcom, a white physician from North Carolina. She manages this by using her sexuality as a defence, entering into a liaison with another white man, 'Mr Sands' (Samuel Sawyer), with whom she has two children. Still persecuted and threatened by Norcom, Jacobs decides to run away. Her flight from enslavement begins in 1835, and symbolizes her extraordinary tenaciousness. She hides in a tiny space in her grandmother's roof for nearly seven years, during which she reads the Bible and newspapers, finally escaping to New York in 1842. But instead of presenting her experience with Sawyer as an example of loss of virtue, Jacobs transforms the narrative into a tale of triumphant feminist motherhood, in which she succeeds in saving and rescuing her children from Norcom's clutches. She celebrates her challenge to convention by addressing the reader on a footing of equality rather than contrition, declaring 'my story ends with freedom; not in the usual way, with marriage.'[105]

Powerful women's voices emerged in the North, entering the abolitionist arena and making a strong case for women's equality as part of the anti-slavery argument, as with the white abolitionist Sarah Grimké's *Letters on the Equality of the Sexes* (1838).[106] Another sign of the radical turn in African-American abolitionism was the increasing emphasis on pan-African and cosmopolitan ideals, often discussed through evocations of Haiti and its revolution in anti-slavery speeches and literature. Earlier in the nineteenth century, Haiti was typically celebrated on its own terms, and as a remarkable but singular event, almost outside the realm of history. There was now a growing tendency to compare it with the American Revolution, and to demonstrate the superiority of the Haitian accomplishment, as well as the possibilities it presented for redemptive political action in the United States. Thus in 1841 an author who signed as 'R' (probably the black abolitionist journalist Charles Ray) hailed Haiti as an inspiration for black resistance, asserting that its successful challenge to 'aristocratic and cruel oppression' was proof to African Americans 'that as a race *we cannot be crushed*'. 'R' was sharply critical of the American government's failure formally to recognize Haitian independence, despite the growth in the trade relationship between the two nations.[107]

That same year in Manhattan, the physician and community leader James McCune Smith delivered a passionate lecture on the Haitian revolution, which was subsequently published as a pamphlet. His aim was both to counter the racist depictions of Haiti among white American slavers and conservatives, and to honour the revolution's 'presiding genius', Toussaint Louverture, widely idolized by African Americans of his generation. Smith spoke lyrically about Toussaint's abilities as an administrator and military leader, as well as his Christian moral qualities of forgiveness and sobriety. Toussaint's emergence out of enslavement was evidence that the black 'race' was 'entirely capable of achieving liberty and of self-government'.[108] Defending Saint-Domingue's war of national liberation against the French, Smith cast Jean-Jacques Dessalines as the 'Robespierre of Haiti', adding that his violence was directed only at those who were attempting to re-enslave his people. In his lecture on Haiti, the pan-African preacher James Theodore Holly, who supported African-American emigration (being among the 3,000 of his compatriots who settled in Haiti in the early 1860s), was more guarded in his praise for Dessalines. He recognized that his 'sanguinary deeds' during the war against Napoleonic forces were necessary but ultimately provoked by 'the treachery of the whites', which had led to the betrayal, capture, and imprisonment of Louverture.[109]

The abolitionist William Wells Brown made the unfavourable contrast between Haiti and the United States even more explicit in his December 1854 lecture (also published as a pamphlet), where he too heaped praise on Toussaint Louverture, the revolution's foremost hero. Comparing him as a 'Christian, statesman, and general' to George Washington, Brown observed that both men succeeded in overcoming colonial oppression and creating a new political order against great odds. However, here their paths diverged. Whereas Louverture was a great emancipator, Washington was an enslaver, who 'enacted laws by which chains were fastened upon the limbs of millions of people'.[110]

Brown contemplated the possibility of a Haitian-type insurrection in the American South: 'the day is not far distant when the revolution of St. Domingo will be re-enacted in South Carolina and Louisiana' (a thinly veiled reference to the earlier conspiracies of Denmark Vesey and Charles). At that moment, he added, the 'God of Justice' would be on the side of the oppressed black people, and the 'exasperated genius of Africa would rise from the depths of the ocean'. Only when this transformation was completed could the American Revolution truly realize its founding ideals.[111] In anticipation of the event, some Southern African-American communities in Arkansas, Maryland, Missouri, North Carolina, and Virginia would give themselves the name 'Haiti'.[112] A growing number of African Americans in the North endorsed the use of violence as a means of self-protection and resistance against enslavement. For example, in 1851 the Lancaster Black Self-Protection Society, led by former slave William Parker, confronted a US marshal who had come to his neighbourhood in Christiana, Pennsylvania, to search for four fugitive captives. The slave hunters were routed, and the event became known as the 'Christiana Resistance'.[113]

Abolitionist internationalism was further developed through the cultivation of privileged links with Britain, and particularly with the British people. After the publication of his book in 1838, Moses Roper extensively toured the British Isles, both to promote his writing and to use the examples from his autobiography to make the case for ending slavery in the United States. He delivered over 2,000 lectures in churches and town halls, often attracting large crowds. He brought whips, chains, and manacles with him to demonstrate the different ways in which he and his fellow captives were tortured. In August 1845, facing the threat of recapture after the publication of his *Narrative*, Frederick Douglass was forced to flee the United States, travelling to Britain, where he completed a twenty-one-month speaking tour. He gave at least eight talks in Manchester and the surrounding area, where he was directly confronted by the entrenchment of slavery in Britain's economic life: one of the houses he stayed in (22 St Ann's Square) was sandwiched between the Cotton Exchange, where textiles manufactured by enslaved people were sold, and Heywood's Bank, financed by profits from the slave trade.[114] His lectures attracted considerable interest, thanks to his remarkable qualities as a performer and an ability to dramatize key episodes from his *Narrative*, such as the horrifying beating of his Aunt Hester.[115] He was consummately political in his approach, celebrating Britain's abolitionist history and praising its liberal heroes such as William Wilberforce and Thomas Clarkson, while showing a subtle capacity to tailor his speeches to the local sensitivities of his audiences in England, Scotland, and Ireland. In Dublin he was captivated by an anti-slavery speech given by the veteran Irish nationalist Daniel O'Connell, who invited Douglass to address the audience.[116]

At the same time, Douglass was implacable when it came to exposing the links between religion and slavery in the United States. Even though these parts of his speeches sometimes drew criticism, he succeeded in highlighting the clear implication of Christian churches in the South associated with the institution of human bondage, particularly in this forensic demonstration during a speech in Liverpool: 'Ministers of religion defend slavery from the Bible – ministers of religion own any number of slaves – bishops trade in human flesh – churches may be said literally to be built up in human skulls, and their very walls cemented in human blood – women are sold at the public block to support a minister, to support a church – human beings sold to buy sacramental services, and all of course with the sanction of the religion of the land.'[117]

During his British tour, Douglass also experienced racial abuse, particularly in the characterizations of his physical appearance in the press. Overall, however, he received overwhelming public support, and some of this solidarity was personally invaluable. His *Narrative* was praised by reviewers, one of whom wrote that it was a book which 'every Englishman should read'. A group of his British admirers raised the $700 needed to buy his freedom in December 1846. Upon his return to the United States in 1847 he used the bulk of the funds raised by British and Irish friends to purchase a printing press, with which he started his newspaper *Northern Star*.[118] In a blazing article published in 1849, Douglass blamed America's refusal to recognize the Haitian state on their desire to appease the Southern slave lobby, 'the colorphobia of a few fanatics'.[119] During his lectures, Douglass made frequent references to Toussaint Louverture, a man who 'towered among the tallest of his times'.[120] His own vivid and engaging style evoked the Saint-Domingue revolutionary in the minds of his audiences. A journalist from the *Liberator* who listened to Douglass at a meeting in Concord, New Hampshire, wrote: '[Douglass] reminded me of Toussaint among the plantations of Haiti . . . an insurgent slave, taking hold on the right of speech, and charging on his tyrants the bondage of his race'.[121]

These manifestations of radical black anti-slavery thinking fleshed out the growing rifts between white and black abolitionists in the United

States. Again, Douglass was an excellent example of this divergence. As a remunerated speaker in William Lloyd Garrison's Anti-Slavery Society, his role was appreciated, but Douglass's pay was less than that of his white colleagues, and he was constantly treated in a patronizing manner. During Douglass's British tour, Garrison and his associates tried to control his engagements and financial rewards, and they objected to Douglass agreeing to the payment of his manumission, as they believed such transactions legitimized and reinforced the institution of slavery. More generally, they found it difficult to accept his growing stature within the abolitionist movement, and in particular his independence.[122] Garrison believed in moral suasion as a means of bringing about the end of slavery, and he was stridently opposed to collective political action. He believed the American system of government to be irreparably corrupt, referring to the Constitution as a 'covenant with death and an agreement with hell'.[123]

Douglass's views on these issues shifted decisively between the late 1840s and the mid-1850s. He had by now rejected Garrison's doctrines, become firmly committed to political action and government intervention to end slavery, and was more confident in his own intellectual abilities. Douglass signalled this move in an 1848 speech in which he endorsed the right of the enslaved to revolt. In 1853 he published his novella *The Heroic Slave*. This work was loosely based around Madison Washington's shipboard rebellion on the brig *Creole* in 1841, in which the ship travelling from Virginia to New Orleans was seized by its 128 captives and steered to freedom in the British-controlled Bahamas.[124] Douglass consummated his rupture with white paternalism in his second memoir, *My Bondage and My Freedom* (1855), its preface written by a black abolitionist, his friend James McCune Smith. Douglass asserted his philosophical autonomy by his resolute focus on politics and national regeneration, and his willingness to take on difficult subjects for white abolitionists, such as racial discrimination in the North. He made a passionate plea for the universality of the struggle against slavery, which was 'a crime against God, and all members of the human family, and it belongs to the whole human family to seek its suppression' (see Plate 18).[125]

President Abraham Lincoln issued the Emancipation Proclamation on 1 January 1863, at the height of the Civil War between Northern and Southern states. Lincoln had been elected in 1860 as the candidate of the Republican Party, carrying all the free states outright except New Jersey. Many of his voters were ardently opposed to slavery, but his own platform was moderate and gradualist, promising not to interfere with Southern slavery and to uphold the 1850 Fugitive Slave Act. Lincoln declared in 1860 that he did not believe in racial equality, and many abolitionists were critical of his prudent constitutionalism. In the characteristically blunt evaluation of Frederick Douglass, Lincoln was 'pre-eminently the white man's president' at the time of his entry into the White House, and he was 'ready and willing at any time during the first years of his administration to deny, postpone and sacrifice the rights of humanity in the coloured people to promote the welfare of the white people'.[126]

But secession and war changed everything. Prior to Lincoln's inauguration, seven Southern states had broken away from the Union, choosing a president and vice-president of their own, and adding a clause to their Constitution protecting the right to own enslaved people. The Confederacy then went to war in April 1861 by attacking and capturing Fort Sumter on the South Carolina coast. Lincoln initially hoped to prosecute the conflict by relying on Northern patriotism, and until the end of 1861 clung on to the hope that he might reach some sort of compromise with the rebels. Throughout the following the year the pressures from abolitionists on his side began to accumulate, soon turning the Civil War into a conflict between supporters and opponents of slavery. Congress banned slavery in the District of Columbia in April 1862, and the United States finally recognized Haiti in July. Lincoln issued the preliminary Emancipation Proclamation in September; it announced that from 1 January 1863, all persons held as slaves would become free. In November 1863 Lincoln's Gettysburg Address redefined the war as heralding a 'new birth of freedom', effectively making immediate emancipation its central feature. In December 1865, eight months after the end of the Civil War, the Thirteenth Amendment was duly ratified, ending slavery across the United States, and fully emancipating the nation's four million captives. Lincoln did not live to witness this abolitionist climax, as he was assassinated in April, merely a week after the capitulation of the South. But his actions had irrevocably sealed his reputation as the Great Emancipator, although he was the first to admit that he was simply the instrument of the dynamic forces pushing for abolition.[127]

The defeat of the South was not the product of Northern political and military agency alone. Enslaved men and women in the South made significant contributions to their own emancipation. Indeed, they did not await the start of the Civil War to resist actively, and they spread the message of revolutionary abolitionism. Runaway slaves who reached the North were integrated into networks of anti-slavery resistance, and through their interactions with militant activists (especially those operating in Vigilance Committees) played a significant role in shaping the radicalization of American abolitionism in the decades leading up to the Civil War.[128] Throughout the 1850s there were widespread reports of enslaved dissent in Southern states, as well as numerous specific cases of conspiracy and revolt in Virginia, Mississippi, Louisiana, Texas, the Carolinas, and Maryland. Some of these plots, as with the one uncovered in Tennessee in November 1856, had connections across several states. Arms were seized from enslaved people in Tennessee, Kentucky, and Texas, and preparations for blowing up bridges were found. In many of these instances white abolitionists were involved, and some of them were executed.[129]

The best-known revolt of this period was carried out by John Brown, a white farmer who believed he was appointed by God to free enslaved people, and whose supporters included veterans of fugitive rebellions. Brown's anti-slavery philosophy was strongly shaped by black resistance traditions.[130] Assisted by twenty-three black and white men, he launched an attack on an American military armoury at Harpers Ferry, Virginia, in October 1859. Brown hoped that its capture would initiate a wider uprising against Southern slavery. The movement failed and Brown was captured and hanged in December. But his actions were praised by Northern abolitionist leaders, including those like Garrison who did not believe in violence. Enslaved people in the South spread the news of his insurrection.[131] Brown had asked Frederick Douglass to join the rebellion but he declined, believing the uprising would not succeed. Harriet Tubman and Martin Delany were more supportive, but they too stayed away.[132] Douglass nonetheless wrote a warm tribute to his friend in November, praising his heroism, love of liberty, and hatred of tyranny, and predicting that his rebellion would be seen by posterity as 'the first effectual blow' against American slavery.[133]

The contributions of African-American soldiers proved critical to the victory of the North. Around 200,000 black men enlisted in the Union Army, fighting with distinction in over four hundred engagements. This included forty major battles, most significantly at Port Hudson, Milliken's Bend, and Fort Wagner.[134] These soldiers helped turn the tide of the war, as was acknowledged by Lincoln himself: 'without the military help of black freedmen, the war in the South could not have been won'.[135] Black soldiers later recalled their engagements with pride. Cornelius Garner, who took part in the battle of Richmond, Virginia, in April 1865, stressed that his regiment was the first to enter the town and plant the Union flag on the capitol.[136] Black abolitionists played a significant role in recruiting these soldiers by generating a sense of revolutionary patriotic fervour among African Americans. Frederick Douglass called on his black compatriots to join the Union Army so that they could claim America as their country,

while appealing to the emancipatory ideals of American anti-slavery figures such as Denmark Vesey and Nat Turner.[137]

The potent force of the myths and memories of the Haitian revolution in
mid-nineteenth-century America provided an invaluable resource for these
appeals, again mainly centring around the figure of Toussaint Louverture.
Writing in the *Weekly Anglo-African*, 'Bob Logic' urged his fellow black
citizens to enlist, and not to ask themselves why they should take up arms:
'Did Toussaint L'Ouverture stop to ask the question? Did his followers
stop to ask that question? No, no, not all. They rose up with all their
strength and struck blow after blow for freedom.'[138] Another incentive for
the military service of these 'black Toussaints', as another publicist called
them, was that it would be the prelude to full citizenship for black people
in the United States, and the emergence of an African-American military
and political elite – as had happened in Haiti after independence.[139]

Among the many admirers of the Haitian revolution who were active
in recruiting black soldiers was the pan-African nationalist campaigner
Martin Delany. He was committed to black emigration from the United
States before the Civil War, and, following a widely practised tradition
among African Americans, he named one of his sons Toussaint Louverture.
In 1865 he met Lincoln, who was highly impressed by his energy. Delany
was commissioned in the Union Army as a major, serving in the 104th
Regiment of the Colored Infantry, and he rose to become the highest-
ranking African-American officer in the Civil War (see Plate 17). This
Haitian-inspired valour came to life in the military record of the 54th
Massachusetts Regiment, which had a thousand black soldiers, a quarter
of whom were former captives; just thirty-seven came from the South.

One of the regiment's companies that particularly distinguished itself
(in particular by storming the battery at Fort Wagner, South Carolina,
in July 1863) went by the name of 'Toussaint's Guards'. Black officers
distributed copies of the *Weekly Anglo-African*, in which the exploits of
Haitian revolutionaries were regularly celebrated. Among these men were
two of Frederick Douglass's sons, Lewis and Charles, as well as Toussaint
Louverture Delany.[140] Northern abolitionist newspapers made regular
connections between African-American military valour and the fighting traditions of the Haitian revolutionaries, sometimes comparing their
actions with specific episodes in Saint-Domingue's war of national liberation, such as the siege of Crête-à-Pierrot in 1802, where the insurgents
inflicted severe losses on French forces despite their numerical inferiority and tactical disadvantage.[141] A Union chaplain stationed in the South
testified to the popularity of Toussaint Louverture among local black
recruits, inspiring their 'love of liberty'; he observed that Louverture's

name 'has been passed from mouth to mouth until it has become a secret household word'.[142]

John Brown's failure at Harpers Ferry was interpreted by some of his contemporary critics as evidence of the passivity of Southern captives. But this was not the case, as shown by the patterns of enslaved dissent in the 1850s, as well as the mass flight of captives from Southern plantations towards Union-controlled territories from the early 1860s. This marronage is generally acknowledged as a key feature of the Civil War. By mid-1864 nearly 500,000 people – around 10 per cent of the entire enslaved population in the South – had escaped from their places of bondage. These escapes were initially portrayed as uncoordinated and spontaneous responses to the advances of the Union Army. But starting with W. E. B. Du Bois, historians have made a compelling case that they constituted a social movement that was part of a general strategy of self-emancipation. Du Bois specifically argued that this autonomous movement of men and women was effectively a general strike, which saw the enslaved abandoning their workplaces as a deliberate means of joining the war effort against slavery. He argued that this flight from bondage was America's 'largest and most successful slave revolt', and that it caused the defeat of the South.[143]

There is much evidence that Southern captives were in open rebellion from 1861. The language used by planters about those escaping their farms typically included such terms as 'revolts', 'disturbances', 'mutinies', 'strikes', and 'states of insurrection'. And far from being unconnected incidents, these movements relied on collective understandings, resistance tactics, and networks of communication and solidarity among enslaved and fugitive captives that had developed over years and even decades; we discussed some of these patterns earlier in the chapter.[144] Captives later recalled that they secretly listened to conversations among white Southerners, gathering information among themselves about troop movements and the proximity of Union lines in order to be able to plan their escapes.[145] Maroon bands, sometimes operating with guerrilla groups consisting of fugitives from the Confederate Army, posed a substantial threat throughout the Civil War. In 1862 six Florida counties were put under martial law to contain these activities. Similar reports were filed from South Carolina, Virginia, and Alabama.[146] In North Carolina the authorities reported the existence of a community of five to six hundred black fugitives, who were not connected to the Union Army; they were described as 'lead[ing] the lives of banditti, roving the country with fire and committing all sorts of horrible crimes'.[147]

Captives who remained on Southern plantations were portrayed as being rebellious in numerous letters, reports, and newspaper articles, and many conspiracies were uncovered. One in Mississippi was led by a black enslaved person named Orange, who was in contact with local maroons, and was assisted by a white man who painted his face black. Thirty-six captives and a white preacher were hanged in Arkansas for attempted insurrection in May 1861.[148] In addition, many acts of sabotage and arson were reported, including a fire that blazed through Charleston, South Carolina, in December 1862, destroying six hundred buildings. Incendiary attacks were one of the main weapons of a group of rebel insurgents in Yazoo City, Mississippi.[149] Unrest among enslaved workers at an iron plant in Richmond, Virginia, led to the punishment of its leaders in 1863, and a year later detachments of the Confederate Army had to be used to suppress planned rebellions in Florida and South Carolina, whose aim was to enable mass escapes to Union-controlled territories.[150]

Enslaved women often assumed leadership roles in these plantation challenges. Discussing the revolts on his estate, one South Carolina overseer lamented that he could see 'a great deal of obstinacy in some of the people, Mostly among the Woman [sic]'.[151] Women fugitives could not be recruited into the Union Army, but they waged their own war against their Southern enslavers. They sabotaged the Confederate war effort by refusing their labour, damaging and destroying buildings and factories, and helping provide intelligence about Confederate military movements. When Robert E. Lee, commander of the Confederate Army, discussed a planned attack during a visit to a friend in Virginia, the enslaved women working in the house relayed the information to nearby Union forces; the messenger was a former captive.[152] News of the Emancipation Proclamation was likewise carried across slaver plantations by groups of women who developed a secret code using 'knocks, signs and passwords'. There was little doubt that during the Civil War slave plantations became places of resistance.[153] In June 1863 Harriet Tubman went to South Carolina to carry out one of her most famous operations, the Combahee River Raid, in which 150 formerly enslaved soldiers were freed, along with more than 756 freedmen and women trapped in plantations.[154]

Women deserted and moved away from their plantations in large numbers; in one census of 24,000 'contraband' captives in Virginia, nearly half were women.[155] The careful planning of entire family escapes was often organized by matriarchs. Young Amanda Tellis later recalled being told to pretend that she had a cold, and to repair to their home cabin. When she got there, she found that her mother had arranged a pillow slip for each member of the family, filled with clothing and provisions, which they carried with them as they took flight.[156] These women faced particularly challenging conditions in Union-controlled territories, living in military-sponsored camps, working hard to produce food for Yankee combatants, and often experiencing emancipation 'in slow motion'.[157] Nonetheless their resistance on plantations and escapes disrupted the Southern economy and played an important role in the unravelling of Confederate slavery. By 1863 Confederate armies faced acute food shortages, largely as a result of mass desertions from plantations and farm workers reducing their output to subsistence levels. When asked after the war what they felt about their freedom, Southern black women typically answered with pride that it had not been a gift from on high: they had earned it.[158]

On 14 April 1865 – the day of President Lincoln's assassination – a ceremony was held in Fort Sumter, where the first military salvo of the Civil War had been fired. The conflict had ended a week earlier, on 9 April, and the Union general Robert Anderson was returning to raise the now-tattered star-spangled banner that he had lowered four years earlier when surrendering to Confederate forces. The event was held in the presence of distinguished guests, among them leading abolitionists William Lloyd Garrison and Henry Ward Beecher, who delivered the main oration. Also among the speakers was the former captive Robert Smalls, who audaciously emancipated himself by making off with a Confederate gunboat from Charleston harbour in 1862 and delivering it to Union forces. Smalls became a naval officer and was later elected to Congress. Another hero in attendance was Major Martin Delany, who had actively recruited black Charlestonians into the Union Army during the final stages of the war. Between 2,000 and 3,000 African Americans came to the ceremony, perhaps the most arresting of whom was Robert Vesey, the son of Denmark, who was twenty-two at the time of his father's conspiracy. His presence closed the magic circle, symbolically uniting all the different strands of the abolitionist coalition – white and black, free and enslaved, civilian and military, urban and rural, moderate and revolutionary, Northern and Southern – who banded together during the Civil War to defeat the Southern rebellion, and in the process end American slavery.

   The American fight against slavery had its singularities. Perhaps most intriguing here was the figure of Lincoln, the reluctant emancipator. For much of his political life, the struggle against human bondage was not Lincoln's defining priority, as it was for Louverture and Schoelcher. But at the pivotal moment he assumed the anti-slavery mantle and became a resolute champion of the abolitionist cause. Lincoln symbolized the ultimate power of American abolitionism, and its grounding (also very American) in lofty moralist rhetoric. He reflected its contradictions as well – especially its improvised character during the Civil War, and its limited conception of racial equality. This was no doubt because, as a democratic politician, the President had to try and appeal to conservative electorates across the country. Hence another curious feature of antebellum America: the territorial division, within the same sovereign country, of one entity in which human bondage was progressively abolished, and another where it was maintained – although even this line was not as clear-cut as it first appeared. It was blurred (to the advantage of the enslavers) by the 1850 Fugitive Slave Act, by the widespread incidence of racial discrimination and prejudice in the North, and by the 1857 Dred Scott Supreme Court ruling entrenching the idea that African Americans, whether free or enslaved, had 'no rights which the white man was bound to respect' and could therefore never become full citizens of the United States. This racially exclusive view of American citizenship was further underscored by the belief among many Northern political leaders that African Americans had no long-term future in the United States. Even though his position eventually evolved, this was a view long held by Lincoln himself, and he bluntly expressed it to an African-American delegation in August 1862.[159]

At the same time, there were important Atlantic commonalities in the American story. As in Cuba, although the insurrectionary road to ending slavery in the United States failed, it was essential to putting an end to human bondage overall. This was highlighted by the rich rebellious culture among anti-slavery rebels, which was strongly shaped by the legends and memories of Saint-Domingue. From Gabriel and Charles through Denmark Vesey and Nat Turner, all the way to John Brown, American insurgents against human bondage shared the view that the only way slavery could be brought down was by force. American abolitionism was a broad social coalition, which became increasingly radical in its final decades, mirroring the trajectory followed in Britain. In the end, it achieved its objective through a revolutionary war, as in Saint-Domingue. Above all, like everywhere else, the resistance of the enslaved in the United States was grounded in pan-African values, ideas, and spiritual precepts. Finally, as in Britain and France, the end of slavery did not bring about equal citizenship for black people, and the gains of emancipation were rapidly clawed back. The year 1865 was in this sense only the first stage in the long struggle for African-American equality and dignity.

We can see from the material gathered here and in previous chapters that anti-slavery resistance in the United States was not fundamentally different from all other cases of Atlantic slavery. Opposition to human bondage remained widespread among the enslaved and was manifested across the full spectrum of their activities, thoughts, and plans. There is also a view that American abolitionism was not very original, and that it added little to anti-slavery thought.[160] On the contrary, from an intellectual perspective, three groups of contributions stand out. First, the proliferation of black narratives, which provided great depth to the popularization of the ideal of emancipation. Next, the widespread appeal of the Haitian revolution: this generated a black internationalism that inspired conservatives and revolutionaries alike, helped draw out the failings of American post-revolutionary citizenship for black people, and acted as a bridge across all the different expressions of African-American nationalism in early to mid-nineteenth-century America. Finally, there was the emphasis on the ideal of autonomy, the common principle that was shared by all the black Americans who emigrated (or tried to escape) to Haiti, or just cherished a sense of transnational identity that included Africa.

This sense of autonomy was expressed in many other ways: in David Walker's fierce rallying call to his brethren to take their fates into their own hands, and Frederick Douglass's efforts to free himself of white paternalism. It surfaced in Harriet Jacobs' emphasis on the distinctiveness of the issues faced by women captives, and her reminder that masculine valour was not the only measure of resistance. It took shape in the web of local solidarities and forms of democratic inventiveness that made the Underground Railroad possible, and in the antebellum defensive mobilizations of black militias, which prepared the ground for African-American participation in the Civil War. It came to life in the independent struggles of Southern men and women – particularly women – against their oppressors. These oppositions culminated in the transformation of plantations into places of resistance during the Civil War, thus enabling the large-scale population movements to Union-controlled territories. Autonomy was manifested, too, in the ways in which the enslaved mapped their African-derived cosmologies onto their biblical and church practices to create a singular form of anti-slavery black Christianity in the United States.[161]

When we look together at Civil War resistance, flight, and marronage, and the long tradition of enslaved conspiracies and rebellions, there is no doubt that they were interconnected, further attesting to the decisive shaping of American emancipation by captive men and women. These manifestations of solidarity and active citizenship should be seen as creative forms of political action in the sense that they were nurtured and flourished outside mainstream American political culture, and gave African-American black nationalism its distinctive shape. A parallel emerges here with the early years of the insurrection in Saint-Domingue, where the general revolt that overthrew slavery began as a series of localized insurgencies in the northern plain, in which women played a significant part. These mobilizations then interacted and merged with broader political and military contests involving standing armies.[162]

This black internationalism was very much in the minds of African-American militia members and soldiers, as we saw earlier, and its spirit was also present across the plantations of the South. When 10,000 fugitive men and women refugees from North Carolina plantations came together at Newbern in 1863 and founded a free colony, they named it 'New Hayti'.[163] These synergies provide a fuller context to the observation of John Brown junior (John Brown's eldest son) about Southern slaves, when he declared that Toussaint Louverture's 'soul' visited their cabins at night, 'proclaiming that the despots of America shall yet know the strength of the toiler's arm, and that they who would be free must themselves strike the first blow'.[164]

10

Taking Their Cause into
Their Own Hands

Martin Delany's novel *Blake* offered a sweeping portrayal of black Atlantic resistance to enslavement in the mid-nineteenth century. Henry Holland Blake, the novel's main character, is a captive from a Mississippi plantation whose wife Maggie is sold to a Cuban slaver for refusing her master's sexual advances. Henry then escapes and becomes a maroon, adopting the classic resistance motto of 'freedom or the grave'.[1] After travelling across the American South, he ends up in Canada with a group of fellow fugitives, and formulates a grand design to rescue Maggie by instigating a general slave insurrection. It emerges that Henry is himself of Cuban origin, and that he had been kidnapped and sold into slavery in the South. When he goes to the island to purchase Maggie's freedom, he discovers that he is a cousin of the rebel anti-slavery poet Plácido. As we saw in chapter 8, Plácido was executed for his role in the 1844 La Escalera conspiracy.

In the novel (set in the early 1850s), Delany creates an alternative reality, allowing Henry to find a still-living Plácido in Cuba. Henry joins the rebels' secret society dedicated to the overthrow of Spanish colonial rule and securing freedom. The end of the novel has been lost and so the dénouement is unknown. In 1849 Delany had urged Cubans to imitate the Haitians and 'take their cause in their own hands'.[2] It is also possible that the rebels set sail for Africa and create a free settlement there. Henry is an enthusiastic pan-African hero, who like the Haitian revolutionaries seeks to recover American lands for indigenous peoples and African-born captives, while ridding the territories of all white slavers, 'those devils'.[3]

Delany's novel neatly captures the different facets of enslaved resistance we have encountered across the book. In his fugitive journeys Henry encounters other maroons, sees the force of African culture, is anointed priest in the order of High Conjurors, and hears stories about Gabriel, Denmark Vesey, and Nat Turner, whose names are 'held in sacred reverence'.[4] A providential God and the Haitian revolution lurk in the background, and through the character of Madame Bonselle, a fervent French republican, we glimpse the abolition of slavery in France in 1848.[5] Henry witnesses or is involved in multiple conspiracies: there are at least twenty in the novel. He travels on the Underground Railroad and across the Black Atlantic, rallying support for his international revolutionary crusade against human bondage and colonialism. He embraces a universal ideal of freedom that is underpinned by racial equality and an attachment to his African heritage.

Blake foregrounds the captives' quest for an autonomous space of liberty with the term 'Afraka'. This could be the physical continent of Henry's origins as well as an imaginary world of possibility beyond the reach of white slavers (Delany is credited with coining the slogan 'Africa for Africans' in 1861).[6] Just as importantly – and this is an often-overlooked facet of the novel because of Delany's own Civil War military heroism – *Blake* celebrates the resistance of women captives in the South. The tactically effective disguises of characters such as Mammy Judy, Ailcey, and Rachel enable the maroons to escape while providing misleading information to the plantation slavers, and turning the tables against their predatory sexual behaviour. Mammy Judy pretends to be loyal and submissive but back in her cabin she emerges as a powerful trickster figure who helps subvert the plantation's patriarchal slave order.[7]

Blake was published in serialized form in the late 1850s and early 1860s in two short-lived American periodicals, and it only appeared as a book for the first time in 1970. As a work of fiction it never found a proper audience in Delany's lifetime. We should treat it as an active intervention, and as a symbol of the expansive imagination of black Atlantic anti-slavery radicals. The novel opens a window into the ways in which enslaved and free black people actively considered their circumstances and the prospects of emancipation. They thought about its hopes and promises; the tragedies, sufferings, and myriad forms of solidarity that made emancipation possible; and the ways in which they strove to be true to themselves and to their ideals once it had been achieved. They remained proud and defiant, still refusing the paternalistic and self-serving narratives that their white slaver overlords tried to impose upon them even after the formal end of slavery as an institution.

As we have seen, Haiti was the pre-eminent land of freedom in the Atlantic anti-slavery imagination. What did independence mean to the Haitian people after 1804, and how did they commemorate it? Jean-Jacques Dessalines, the state's first ruler, picked 1 January as the date for officially celebrating its founding. He chose it both to symbolize the new dawn and to mark some continuity with the country's slavery past: New Year's Day was traditionally a holiday on the slave plantation.[8]

Dessalines was assassinated by his rivals in 1806 and the political history of nineteenth-century Haiti was thereafter turbulent. However, its founding date remains a fixture to this day. In the early decades, official ceremonies typically included a reading of the Declaration of Independence, military parades, and oaths of allegiance to the Constitution – and during the years of Christophe's northern kingdom, to the sovereign. After the French diplomatic recognition of Haiti in 1825, the strongly anti-French Declaration was no longer read out at these events.[9] The Haitian public memorialization of independence thus centred around sovereignty. However, as we saw in chapter 5, Haiti's robust opposition to the slave trade and its official welcome to escaped captives and black migrants from the Atlantic made resistance to enslavement an integral part of its collective self-image. It also gave the nation an internationalist and pan-African character from the outset.[10]

This rich melange of patriotism and pan-Africanism can be heard in the many songs generated by Haiti's popular *vodou* religion from the nineteenth century on, which provide additional glimpses of how ordinary men and women made sense of the revolutionary era. *Vodou* was not a centralized spiritual system but it was the de facto national religion in Haiti, observed by most of the population. Its musical compositions, performed during *vodou* rituals, often contained specific historical allusions to the times of enslavement and the war of independence, reflecting collective popular understandings about the Haitian revolutionary past. For example, one song from the Artibonite area expressed an important aspect of the struggle for sovereignty: 'This land is not for the whites / It's the land of the Africans / Let's go!' Another song mentioned Makandal, who was captured and executed in 1758, pointing out that he was warned but 'did not listen' and was killed by the French slavers – a fate which befell many other leaders, including Toussaint Louverture. The song was a warning about the importance of collective vigilance, especially for a young nation dealing with a world dominated by pro-slavery empires.[11]

Toussaint Louverture was held in 'the highest esteem' by Haitians, according to a local American merchant, who compared him to the 'Washington of the Negro Empire'.[12] In the *vodou* repertoire, however, the revolutionary figure who towered above all others was Dessalines. Long before his official rehabilitation by the Haitian state in the early twentieth century, the independence leader was lionized in popular religious rituals. He is the 'Bull of Haiti', protecting his people from genocide. In another song, he 'fires the cannon' against the nation's enemies, and 'holds the temple keys' in his hands. He thus symbolizes the warrior, the saviour, and the priest (*houngan*). Dessalines was the only revolutionary leader who became a *vodou* 'lwa' (spirit), in the form of Ogou Desalin,[13] a name associated with the African god of iron, blacksmiths, and war.[14]

Haitian commemorations of abolition were different from those in Britain, France, and the United States in one key respect. For the black revolutionary state, the final defeat of French slavers in 1804 coincided with national independence, a moment of collective unity, mobilization, and sacrifice. While there were inevitably some differences between public and popular memorializations of the event, there was a broadly shared understanding of what 1 January signified. This remains the case today despite the growing social divide in nineteenth-century Haiti between ruling elites and the peasantry.[15] In Britain this (relative) consensus only applied to the metropole. The abolition of slavery was immediately appropriated by the authorities as a symbol of the nation's humanity and grandeur. The role of the British Dessalines, so to speak, was assigned to William Wilberforce. On his death in 1833 his remains were interred with great ceremony at Westminster Abbey, and two years later an imposing statue of the great man, modelled on Nelson's Column, was inaugurated in Hull, his birthplace. The centenary of his birth (1859) and golden jubilee anniversary of his death (1883) were occasions for collective self-congratulation, which were seamlessly folded into the conquering narrative of Victorian imperialism. The Whig historian W. E. H. Lecky described British abolition as 'one of the three or four perfectly virtuous pages comprised in the history of nations'.[16] There was little more to add after such hyperbole, and it is not surprising that there were few further public monuments dedicated to abolition in Britain, even in the twentieth century.[17] Such an exemplary narrative left no room for the enslaved, except as grateful recipients of British benevolence. In a similar spirit, official celebrations were organized in the immediate aftermath of emancipation in Atlantic colonies by local authorities and missionaries. Generally aimed at containing any unrest, these gatherings were held in places of worship on 1 August (the anniversary of the Abolition Act coming into effect). They stressed the importance of order, sobriety, and deference, exhorting the former captives to be 'worthy of the high boon which God had conferred upon them'.[18]

The newly freed men and women, however, did not recognize themselves in this kind of subservient language. They sought instead to use these occasions to reclaim their freedom in their own terms. In Trinidad black Afro-Creole men formed the Auxiliary Anti-Slavery Society in 1838, which met regularly in the 1840s and 1850s on 1 August. Their interventions celebrated the benefits of liberty, and they challenged white elites by criticizing the continuing discriminations experienced by black people in the colony.[19] A traditional pre-Lenten carnival was adapted by former slaves both to honour their freedom and to reclaim their African heritage. People painted themselves black, or with the kind of body mutilations they suffered during enslavement, and they carried whips and torches. This was a commemoration with more than a hint of defiance.[20]

Likewise, in Jamaica former captives subverted the 1 August anniversary by holding Jonkunnu costume festivals on the day. These celebrations normally occurred at Christmas, but they were brought forward by the newly freed to circumvent official commemorations, impose their own style upon them, and as in Trinidad to voice economic and social demands. These were cheerful occasions, with drumming, fifing, and dancing influenced by Afro-Caribbean traditions. As from the 1840s independent black preachers played an increasingly important role.[21] In effect, 1 August was appropriated by the former Jamaican enslaved to assert their autonomy, enabling them to 'observe their day of freedom as they wished'.[22] In both Trinidad and Jamaica, accordingly, the newly emancipated added an independent pan-African character to the commemorations, contrary to the desires of the local authorities.

Like the British, the French approached their emancipations in paternalistic terms. Alphonse de Lamartine, who had been part of the abolitionist revolutionary government in 1848, wrote a play about Toussaint Louverture in 1850. The drama was an ode to European cultural and aesthetic superiority. It had little to say about black resistance and their struggle for freedom in Saint-Domingue, sticking instead to the conventional republican mantra that the 1794 abolition had been entirely the work of the Paris revolutionaries – a view which Lamartine applied to the 1848 emancipation. Louverture was depicted as an ugly man, who loathed his own body, and was obsessed with the French, the acme of all the military and political qualities he admired.[23] This condescending colonial vision was most compellingly represented in François-Auguste Biard's painting, *L'Abolition de l'esclavage dans les colonies françaises en 1848* (1849) (see Plate 15). It shows a French republican parliamentarian solemnly saluting the emancipated slaves, most of whom are kneeling in front of him. In another corner, a liberated enslaved woman – on her knees too – tearfully expresses her gratitude to her former mistresses, who look upon her with benevolence. As the historian Françoise Vergès puts it, this is a portrait of 'white freedom liberating black servitude'.[24]

As in British colonies, events unfolded very differently on the ground. The first anniversary of the 1848 abolition was publicly marked in French colonial territories with the planting of trees of liberty, the traditional symbol of republican civic regeneration. But there was no shared narrative between the authorities and the formerly enslaved. As we saw in chapter 7, the final months of slavery had been marked by numerous acts of resistance by the captives, with a general uprising in Martinique in May 1848, during which French plantation slavers were killed. It was this insurrection, and the fear that it would be repeated in Guadeloupe, which had made abolition inevitable. Moreover, hopes of compensation for the enslaved, which had been floated in the run-up to abolition, were rapidly dashed: as in Britain, only the enslavers received public funds, which allowed them to consolidate their social, political, and economic dominance. This led to an enormous sense of injustice among the new citizens (*affranchis*). To stifle these sentiments, both about how emancipation was handled and the historic sufferings they endured, conservative republicans rapidly moved to sweep the entire 1848 episode under the carpet. The concept of *oubli* ('forgetting') – in effect, erasure – was given a euphemistic gloss through the language of 'reconciliation' between the *affranchis* and their former enslavers. The former mixed-race anti-slavery campaigner Cyril Bissette, who became a bitter adversary of Victor Schoelcher after emancipation, rallied to this notion in 1849, declaring that 'the past should remain forever buried under the stone of oblivion'.[25]

This effectively became the motto of the French authorities in the decades that followed, as we will see later. The burial of the past was vigorously contested by the *affranchis*, whose cause was championed in Guadeloupe by Léonard Sénécal, a mixed-race republican and Freemason. He decided to enter the political fray and challenge his island's conservative turn in the late 1840s. Initially a supporter of Schoelcher's inclusive republicanism, Sénécal soon realized that the conservative officials sent from Paris were actively working against it. He then began to campaign for a different approach: the sharing of state financial compensation with the colony's recently emancipated citizens, the distribution of land to peasants, and the creation of a sovereign state along Haitian lines. He spread this revolutionary message through public meetings and two newspapers, *La Canaille* and *Le Brigand*; their ironic titles mocked the pejorative terms used by white settlers and colonial authorities when referring to the *affranchis*. The papers were distributed across the island and read aloud in *kreyol* to black plantation workers.[26]

Sénécal established strong ties with these men and women, urging them to stand up for their rights, and not to be intimidated by the *békés* (white settlers). He built a large following among them, and they turned out to cheer the man they called their 'general'. One of his key themes was that emancipation had been a pyrrhic victory, with the gains immediately reclaimed by dominant white settlers. Sénécal and his anti-slavery follow-ers also subverted official abolitionist celebrations. In May 1849, shortly before the first anniversary of emancipation in Guadeloupe, Sénécal stole the tree of liberty that was to be planted during the official ceremony, and held a parallel event instead, in which he championed the rights of the *affranchis*. As in Trinidad and Jamaica, this counter-festival was a power-ful assertion of black revolutionary autonomy.

By the early 1850s, local officials were describing Sénécal as 'more powerful than the colonial governor', and his festive subversions were seen as a menace to the interests of the local *colons* and their mixed-race political allies. With the help of colonial prosecutors, a case against him and his followers was fabricated. More than four hundred advo-cates of self-determination in Guadeloupe were arrested and prosecuted for 'waging war against colonial society' in 1850 and 1851. And even though he never committed or advocated any violent act, Sénécal himself was convicted of 'promoting civil war' and sentenced to deportation in Guyana, from where he was released in May 1862.[27] Banned from enter-ing France and the colonial territories, he chose to settle in Haiti, joining the long line of Atlantic exiles who had made their final home in the land of liberty.[28]

The victorious post-slavery alliance between mixed-race and white elites dominated local politics thereafter, and helped forge the French 'family romance' of colonialism, in which the Republic replaced the enslavers as the figure of Enlightenment and protection. The citizenship of former captives was understood not as a product of their active strug-gles, nor even their conscious choice: it was bestowed as a gift, and their allegiance was expected as a duty.[29]

In the United States, African Americans began to mobilize collectively for freedom long before the Civil War. However, their mere presence in a public space – even if they were free persons – was fiercely contested in the North, as at the July 4th celebrations. In the early nineteenth century they were not allowed to participate in New York's Independence Day festiv-ities, and in Boston a group of black spectators were driven away from the main square.[30] In Philadelphia black Freemasons were permitted to join a procession to mark George Washington's birthday, but were placed firmly at the rear.[31]

In response, African Americans created their own liberty rituals. July 5th became their own 'Freedom Day', observed by religious, civic, and mutual-aid associations. In New York the first celebration was essentially a copy of the previous day's Independence commemoration. Beginning in 1808, they began regularly to mark the anniversary of the slave trade's abolition by Britain and the United States, on 1 January. These occasions too could end in confrontation: facing a club-hurling white mob in Boston, festive participants chose to stand their ground, led by a black veteran officer from the Revolutionary period who rallied them to 'resist to the last'.[32] When New York formally abolished slavery in 1827, African Americans across the state again celebrated on July 5th, calling it 'Black Independence Day'. The black minister Nathaniel Paul delivered a speech in Albany looking forward to the advent of universal emancipation, while alluding to the remarkable transfer of power that had occurred in Haiti.[33] In New York City, James McCune Smith recalled a spectacular celebration with black people in attendance 'shouting for joy and marching through the crowded streets with feet jubilant to songs of freedom'. He observed the presence of men and women from West Indies and Africa, noting that there was a collective embrace of their transatlantic heritage: 'the people of those days rejoiced in their nationality, and hesitated not to call each other "Africans" or "descendants of Africa"'.[34]

Given the challenges they faced merely to occupy public space, these early African-American celebrations generally avoided explicit references to Haiti; there were no overt commemorations of Saint-Domingue's independence on 1 January. Nevertheless, it was clear that the Haitian epic was very much in African-American minds as they organized and observed their alternative rituals, and they sometimes made the connection openly. In 1823, at a celebration of the abolition of the slave trade – whose anniversary of course coincided with Haiti's national day – the young black Philadelphian Jeremiah Gloucester lauded the 'brilliant exploits' of the Haitians in securing their freedom and proclaiming the 'imprescribable rights of man' in their country.[35] The British abolition of slavery in 1834 provided African Americans with a much more usable anniversary. It was widely marked as 'West India' day in the antebellum North: in abolitionist strongholds like New York and Massachusetts, and cities with large black populations such as Philadelphia.[36] These were initially sober occasions, typically held in churches, meeting houses, and educational institutions. Even when participants ventured outdoors, as in the aftermath of a women's literary society commemorative event in Philadelphia in 1836, the 'sumptuous dinner' was washed down with 'good cool water and fine pure lemonade'. This temperance meshed very well with the appreciation of British abolition held by most white American reformers because, unlike Haiti, it was not the product of a revolution.[37]

In the 1840s, anniversaries on 1 August became more settled in style and content. There were formal gatherings and speeches by leading abolitionists, as well as open-air social events such as picnics, boat rides, games, music, and even dances. One of the organizers of the revelries stressed that these Freedom Days should be 'joyful' occasions. The general message from orators such as the leading white abolitionists Wendell Phillips and William Lloyd Garrison was that British emancipation was a great success, and one worthy of emulation in the United States.[38] None of this was to the liking of white anti-abolitionists, who provoked a three-day riot in Philadelphia in 1842, causing huge destruction in black districts of the city. Some of the aggressors claimed to have been incited by a banner celebrating the Haitian revolution, although when produced in court this emblem turned out to be a typical British image of a kneeling slave breaking his chains. The incident nonetheless highlighted the racial and class tensions within the city, while demonstrating the still-explosive nature of the Saint Domingo myth in the United States nearly four decades on.[39]

But the momentum for the celebrations was not broken, as shown by a massive event on 1 August held in Hingham, Massachusetts, in 1844, for the tenth anniversary of British emancipation. About 8,000 people turned out, both black and white, and heard Ralph Waldo Emerson applaud the 'good order and decorum' of West Indian emancipation. The attendees processed in public carrying banners with abolitionist images and slogans; one showed the American eagle trampling an enslaved man, with a message ironically stating 'This is American Liberty'.[40] Some orators praised the Underground Railroad, and in 1845 a collection was held in Massachusetts for the white abolitionist Jonathan Walker, who had been arrested the previous year for attempting to sail with a group of runaways to the British Caribbean; Walker's hand had been branded with the initials 'SS' (slave stealer).[41]

The speakers on these occasions were mostly male. But women's voices were sometimes heard, none more forcefully than the feminist, atheist, and utopian socialist Ernestine Rose. During a speech delivered in 1853 at Flushing, New York, she compared the enslavement in the South to the oppression of women, and called for the human rights of all people to be championed with equal strength.[42]

As from the 1840s, events of 1 August became more radical in the format as well as the tone of abolitionist speeches. Black voices grew in confidence. Speaking in Cleveland, Ohio, in 1850, the pan-African abolitionist Hezekiah Ford Douglas claimed to be a descendant of the 'Ethiopian race' that had been one of the dominant powers in the ancient world, and that had shaped Greek civilization through its influence on

Egypt. The emphasis on a British-style peaceful transition was challenged by the appearance of black militia companies that performed drills, adding a distinctively martial air to the festive occasions. Orators now openly spoke about radical forms of resistance, paying tribute to outlaws in America and Atlantic revolutionaries such as Toussaint Louverture.[43] Some of the organizations that celebrated West India Day bore his name.[44]

In the same spirit, at a speech in Rochester, New York, in 1848, Frederick Douglass hailed Nat Turner as a man of 'noble courage' whose 'strike for liberty' had been the work of God.[45] Some intellectuals such as James McCune Smith made the same point differently, criticizing the tameness of the 1 August celebrations, and calling his African-American brethren to adopt a much more militant approach, and to take inspiration from earlier rebellions in the United States and elsewhere. Douglass, as we just saw, did not disagree, but he replied by reminding his friend that enslaved men and women in British colonies had violently rebelled against their oppressors, and their resistance had played an important role in their eventual achievement of freedom. In celebrating British abolition, Douglass argued, African Americans were honouring these insurrectionary struggles.[46]

With ratification of the Thirteenth Amendment in December 1865, abolitionists across the United States were finally able to commemorate their own achievement, and march alongside the black men and women who had been freed from the institution of slavery (see Plate 20). The celebrations in the South at the end of the Civil War were especially festive, and they brought crowds of enthusiastic people into the streets. Later in his life Albert Brooks, who had been born into slavery, remembered a ceremony in his home town that was attended by local inhabitants as well as African Americans who had travelled from surrounding rural areas. They joined the massive parade that included white missionaries and teachers, and Brooks recalled his stepfather climbing to the top of the church and raising the Stars and Stripes. He attended many Freedom Day ceremonies in the decades that followed. But this first one remained for ever engraved in his memory.[47]

Emancipation was celebrated on different days by communities in the North and South. Some chose dates to mark Lincoln's preliminary 1862 Proclamation on 22 September or his final one on 1 January 1863, which came to be known as 'Freedom Day'. Others picked 9 April, when Robert E. Lee had surrendered to the Northern commander, Ulysses Grant.[48] In Hampton, Virginia, 1 January was celebrated in 1866 by a turnout of over 4,000 freed people. The event was held in a local school and preceded by a band-led procession from the local Black Baptist church. Among the benevolent societies that took part were The Rising Sons, The Morning Stars, Good Samaritans, Sons of Bethel, Sons of Abraham, and Sons of Zion.[49] Behind their charitable appearances many of these organizations championed black rights, and they featured high levels of participation by black women.[50]

In Texas the anniversary that took pride of place was June 19th, marking the date in 1865 when Union troops in Galveston Bay proclaimed the emancipation of 250,000 enslaved people from that state. These 'Juneteenth' commemorations, as they came to be known in the late nineteenth century, became a fixture until the First World War. They took place in large cities in Texas such as Galveston, Houston, and San Antonio, as well as in smaller towns and rural communities. The events brought together the traditional commemorative and festive rituals associated with national celebrations, and they became so popular that several 'emancipation parks' were dedicated for their purpose. In 1870 some African Americans in Austin floated the idea that emancipation should be celebrated on July 4th rather than June 19th, and a meeting was called by community leaders to discuss the matter. The result was an overwhelming majority choosing 'Juneteenth'. Reporting the outcome, a local newspaper concluded that African Americans believed that 'the fourth of July was a very good liberty day for the white man, but it never brought their freedom'.[51]

As in Britain and France, this distinction between white and black approaches to emancipation was a sign of things to come. After a brief period until the late 1870s, which saw continued efforts to make post-Civil War America a more democratic and inclusive society, the so-called Reconstruction period came to an end, and was followed by a conservative turn across the United States. In the South, white supremacist visions re-emerged powerfully, celebrating the Confederacy as a 'Lost Cause', and as a gallant attempt to preserve state rights and Southern values. The American collective memory of the Civil War pivoted to an emphasis on national reconciliation between Northern and Southern whites, reinterpreting the conflict as a struggle to preserve the Union.[52] Against this backdrop, the abolitionist narrative that viewed the Civil War as a conflict about slavery was gradually marginalized, and the contributions of African Americans to the emancipation process were erased.

These intellectual shifts had a significant impact on post-bellum commemorations. Emancipation Day celebrations continued, but primarily in African-American neighbourhoods. When they reported on these events, articles in the Northern press tended to emphasize the coming together of former Civil War belligerents.[53] Reunions of war veterans likewise were dominated by the so-called 'Blue-Grey' gatherings between surviving white Unionist and Confederate soldiers. Black soldiers were sometimes invited but they were confined to separate camps, and the subject of slavery was avoided: the general theme was reconciliation. African-American veterans held their own reunions but they were more sparsely attended, and former black soldiers lacked the resources to meet on a regular basis.[54]

This erosion of abolitionist and black resistance memories was most pronounced with respect to monuments and war memorials, where there was a 'failure at all levels to relinquish the hold of white supremacy'.[55] Plinths in the South, placed in prominent places from the mid-1880s, glorified Confederate combatants and very rarely referred to enslaved populations – except to praise their alleged 'faithfulness' to the rebel cause. In the North the majority of monuments reproduced the unity narrative: the war had been about 'saving the Union'.[56] African-American soldiers were generally not honoured in these public shrines, and sometimes consciously omitted: an 1887 Civil War monument in Brattleboro, Vermont, did not include the names of the town's five black veterans, depicting a Confederate and Union soldier shaking hands, while the latter passes down a copy of the Emancipation Proclamation to a supplicant black captive, without looking at him.[57]

There were more affirmative public memorializations, such as the late nineteenth-century Boston bronze sculpture featuring black soldiers of the 54th Massachusetts Regiment (see Plate 21). It was designed for its commanding officer Robert Gould Shaw, who is featured riding on horseback in the foreground, with a group of black infantrymen around him. The inscription praises the military valour of these African-American soldiers, and hails them for coming to the rescue of the Union.[58] However, the regressive vision of the enslaved remained widespread, and its most emphatic symbol was the Emancipation Memorial erected in Washington D.C. in 1876. Paid for by black veterans and formerly enslaved men and women, it shows President Lincoln holding a copy of his Emancipation Proclamation, with a kneeling captive in front of him, having just broken his shackles. Frederick Douglass, who spoke at the inauguration ceremony, publicly criticized the statue in a letter to the *National Republican* newspaper a few days later. He deplored the prostrate position of the black figure, expressing the hope that he might live to see the day when an African-American would be shown 'erect on his feet like a man'.[59]

It fell to Douglass, the most brilliant abolitionist writer of his age, to provide the overall conclusions about emancipation commemorations in the early 1890s. By this point, he had visited Britain several times, as well as France, where he had met Victor Schoelcher and written an introduction for a projected American translation of his biography of Toussaint

Louverture.[60] Douglass had remained close to Haiti and later in his life served as its resident American consul between 1889 and 1891. He was then appointed by the Haitian government to act as the commissioner for its pavilion at the World's Columbian Exposition held in Chicago in 1893. For its inauguration, Douglass spoke about Haiti's glorious contributions to world history, acting as a pioneer for emancipation and the cause of universal liberty. He paid a glowing tribute to Toussaint Louverture, as a unique figure who inspired his soldiers and conveyed the universal moral imperative of abolition to the Christian world. Moreover, the Haitian revolutionaries were not just working for themselves, Douglass argued: 'interlinked with their race, and striking for their freedom, they struck for the freedom of every black man in the world'.[61]

Yet, despite these remarkable accomplishments, Douglass observed, the standards by which international revolutions were judged were still strongly influenced by race, and there was a notable absence of 'monuments of marble' to commemorate black revolutionaries. In his mind there was little doubt as to why this erasure had taken place: in considering the history of emancipation, 'colour and race' made 'all the difference'.[62] This was illustrated by the fact that the only black representation at the World's Columbian Exposition was a village from Dahomey in west Africa. As Douglass noted, slavery may have been abolished in America, but 'its asserted spirit' remained alive and well.[63]

By the late nineteenth century a popular Black Atlantic tradition of freedom from enslavement had taken shape, entirely distinct from the self-congratulatory and paternalistic official narratives of white abolitionists in Britain, France, and the United States. It was radical and spiritual, national and transnational, highlighting the autonomous agency of the enslaved, and their embrace of Haitian-type self-determination as well as internationalist pan-Africanism. It was also forward-looking in that it viewed emancipation not as an end point, but rather as the start of a deeper empowerment of black people.

The man who forged this composite tradition into a new revolutionary synthesis was the Jamaican-born Marcus Garvey, one of the most creative black thinkers and political leaders of the twentieth century (see Plate 23). Garvey believed that the accommodation and promise of civic integration championed by figures such as Frederick Douglass had failed, a view reinforced in his mind after the American race riots of 1917 and 1919. Moreover, Garvey was keenly aware that emancipation had done nothing to alter the international racial balance of power. Even though they were damaged by the First World War, white empires still dominated the international system, using their resources to subjugate black communities materially and spiritually, and deny them civil and political rights as well as access to education – an essential feature of freedom for Garvey. This brutal re-assertion of control over colonial and postcolonial peoples was symbolized in July 1915 by the American invasion and military occupation of Haiti. The United States seized control of Haitian finances, and imposed a pro-American president on the nation, crushing the sovereignty of the world's first black state.[64]

In response, Garvey created the Universal Negro Improvement Asso-ciation (UNIA). He founded this movement in Jamaica on 1 August 1914 – the eightieth anniversary of British Emancipation – and moved its offices to New York in 1916. Two years later, he launched his global campaign to raise the spirits of black people, so that they could be proud of their race, self-reliant, and united in their common African heritage. He sought to protect them from violence and exploitation, and ultimately be free from the white world's 'mental slavery' – words echoed decades later in Bob Marley's 'Redemption Song'. At the height of its influence in the 1920s, the UNIA had over a million members (and several million more sympathizers), grouped in over eight hundred chapters spread across four continents. It communicated with them through its newspaper, *The Negro World*, published in English, French, and Spanish.

As a young boy Garvey had trained as an apprentice printer, and he was a gifted propagandist who understood the power of rhetoric. With its central organization in Harlem the UNIA developed the trappings of a sovereign black political community, with Garvey as its president, a bureaucracy, a court system, paramilitary units, a shipping company (the Black Star Line), an economic co-operative system, and its own red, black, and green flag, beneath which members sang the organization's anthem, 'Ethiopia, Land of Our Fathers'. The ultimate goal of this movement was the return of the diaspora to a free and independent Africa.[65] The repeated invocation of Ethiopia was part of a long-established pan-African biblical tradition, which took its source from Psalm 68:31: 'Princes shall come out of Egypt; Ethiopia shall soon stretch out her hands to God.' Garvey's 1923 *Philosophy and Opinions* ends with a paraphrase of these lines, and his admirers often referred to him as the 'Black Moses'.[66]

The wide appeal of Garvey's philosophy lay in its capacity to strad-dle nationalist and internationalist visions of black empowerment. He operated comfortably in both dimensions and indeed his vision of sover-eignty cut across territorial boundaries.[67] Garvey reconciled the two main strands of black emancipation thinking that emerged from the Age of Revolutions. He embraced the religious approach, which was grounded in

Christianity, and the revolutionary one, which centred around the Haitian insurrection. In practice, as we saw in the previous chapter, both elements came together in the nineteenth century, for example in the writings of David Walker and the insurrections of Nat Turner and Sam Sharpe, and the American Civil War.[68] Both were key features of the Black Atlantic commemorative tradition.

Garvey repeatedly invoked the heroism of Toussaint Louverture, 'the greatest Negro ever to come out of the West', even adjusting the historical record to credit him with establishing an 'independent republic'. In his writings and speeches the UNIA leader clearly identified personally with Louverture's struggle, and saw himself as his modern emulator.[69] Garvey's roots in the anti-slavery tradition were reflected in the strong conceptual connection he established between human bondage and modern imperialism. The UNIA's *Declaration of the Rights of the Negro Peoples of the World* (1920) denounced the colonization of Africa, which had led to its native peoples being treated 'like slaves'. It challenged the limitations on citizenship in the United States and European colonies, which were 'but a modified form of slavery'. Garvey's quest to transcend this enduring post-emancipation bondage underpinned his advocacy of universal freedom and equality for black people.[70] At the same time he looked resolutely to the future. Alongside his fascination with the Haitian revolution, the UNIA leader understood the immense anti-imperial potential of movements fighting for colonial emancipation. As he put it humorously in a speech in 1918, two years after the Easter Rising in Dublin, he supported the self-determination of all black people, including the 'Irish negro'. At the first UNIA conference two years later, he saluted Éamon de Valera as the symbol of a 'free Ireland'.[71] And when the British authorities arrested the Indian nationalist leader Mahatma Gandhi in 1922, Garvey sent a telegram to King George V asking for his immediate release in the name of 'four hundred million negroes'.[72]

Garvey was by no means always a consensual figure. He provoked hostility within progressive ranks, especially among communists (who were dismayed by the large swathes of support for the UNIA among black workers) and the African-American intellectual establishment (who objected to his rejection of integration, belief in racial purity, and contempt for light-skinned black people). More generally, his hierarchical and Social-Darwinist conceptions of politics were controversial and caused tensions within UNIA ranks, while his long-term plan to gather the black people of the Western hemisphere and march them back to a 'free and redeemed Africa' was tinged with its own form of paternalism.[73] But Garvey's emphasis on power was an important source of strength

too. He argued that in the Age of Empire, black people could not ener-
gize themselves by appealing to white liberal sentimentality or relying on
biblical morality alone. Overwhelming force was needed: hence his calls
for 'an African army second to none and a navy second to none', so that
an attack on black communities anywhere in the world could unleash the
destructive response of their 'battleships'.[74]

In his efforts to kindle a sense of black pride, Garvey reclaimed
antiquity for the black race, extolling the rule of Ethiopian kings, and
celebrating the majesty and sophistication of Egypt and Timbuctu.[75] He
praised the valour of Zulu warriors, observing that the next global conflict would be a race war, in which black people would be victoriously led
by a 'new Toussaint Louverture'.[76] Garvey was sensitive to the symbolic
dimensions of authority, and the public performances of freedom through
rituals – hence his gold-tasselled turban and his military uniforms with
their flowing robes of scarlet, and the smart outfits worn by his African Legion during UNIA parades, fashioning a sense of collective black
grandeur.[77]

The United States had more UNIA divisions than any other country, most of them based in the deep South, in small towns, villages, and
rural areas, where they had remarkable success.[78] In Arkansas the typical
member of the UNIA was a black cotton farmer in his early forties, who
was married and leased rather than owned his land but was able to send
his children to school. In other words, this was a movement that appealed
to the descendants of those former captives who had enjoyed some economic success in the post-slavery era, and believed in self-improvement
and opportunity.[79]

The correspondence of these Southern chapters reveals that among the
most popular parts of Garvey's programme were his advocacy of armed
self-defence, especially to protect women; his opposition to interracial
marriages; and his vision of 'reclaiming' Africa.[80] But the movement also
tapped into the attachment of the black post-slavery South to autonomous
self-governance. This was shown by the efforts of newly freed people to
reconstitute their kinship groups, and to pool resources to acquire land
and mobilize paramilitary organizations. When possible, they migrated,
establishing black towns and settlements so they could better insulate
themselves from white violence.[81] In this sense these African-American
communities managed, in their own ways, to create localized versions of
Martin Delany's 'Afraka' ideal from his novel *Blake*.

The UNIA declined in the United States after the mid-1920s due to
its internal contradictions and its racist hounding by the American government, which prosecuted and jailed Garvey on spurious charges, finally

deporting him to Jamaica in 1927. However, as a source of collective empowerment and a way of thinking about black emancipation Garveyism enjoyed fruitful extensions in both space and time. The richness of its influences ranged from black workers in American industrial heartlands from across the Caribbean to Australia, where it shaped Aboriginal politics. In South Africa the African National Congress was nurtured by Garveyism in its formative years, and the Rastafarian movement shared significant intellectual commonalities with Garveyism, especially in the redemptive vision of Ethiopia and the decolonization of the Greek-centred vision of antiquity.[82] Garveyism contributed to progressive politics in other important ways. Although the movement was dominated by a masculine ethos at its centre, it also drew in and strengthened women organizers at grassroots levels.[83]

Just as importantly, Garvey's critique of empire played a foundational role in anticolonial challenges to the white-dominated international racial order. As we have seen, two of the key elements of the UNIA's denunciation of the post-1919 international system were the imperial subjugation of Africans by Europeans and the denial of full citizenship to African Americans, both of which were explicitly compared to slavery in the UNIA's 1920 *Declaration*. Anticolonial thinkers developed this 'empire as enslavement' argument between the 1920s and the 1960s, even as they moved away from Garvey's internationalism and embraced more nationalist visions of freedom. In their publications on the history of enslavement W. E. B. Du Bois, C. L. R. James, and Eric Williams made strong connections between slavery and the modern struggles against colonialism and racism, while Aimé Césaire's *Cahier d'un retour au pays natal*, one of the founding texts of Negritude, defined colonial oppression through the poignant 'white death' suffered by Toussaint Louverture in his prison cell in the Jura Mountains.[84]

After the United Nations failed to address colonial emancipation at its formation in 1945, critics such as the Nigerian nationalist Nnamdi Azikiwe deplored the continuation of 'colonialism and economic enslavement of the Negro'.[85] This battle continued in the United Nations General Assembly, where advocates of the right of self-determination argued that colonial subjugation was 'little better than slavery'.[86] George Padmore, who eventually became one of the leading pan-African disciples of Garvey, likewise argued that colonial labour practices amounted to slavery by another name – the very language used in the UNIA's 1920 *Declaration*.[87] In December 1960 the United Nations General Assembly Resolution 1514 finally adopted the principle of self-determination for all peoples, and specifically declared any colonial subjugation as a denial of individual and collective human rights.[88] There was another important connection with the anti-slavery tradition in this document, as the

Resolution rejected any attempt to deny colonial independence on the grounds of 'political, economic, social, or educational preparedness'.[89] This was the classic argument used by slavers and so-called gradual abolitionists for delaying emancipation indefinitely over the nineteenth century.

Pan-Africanism was the driving force in this international mobilization for colonial emancipation, and here too Garvey's ideas were prominent. The Fifth Pan-African Congress that met in Manchester in 1945 called for 'autonomy and independence' for black Africa, while Padmore picked up Garvey's key message in calling for a 'united states of Africa' in 1953.[90] Among the commanding figures in the movement was the Ghanaian leader Kwame Nkrumah, who led his country to independence in 1957. His ideas were shaped by a range of ideologies, including nationalism and Marxism. But Nkrumah credited Garvey above all with firing his enthusiasm for the broader internationalist cause of African unity, and for understanding the historical significance of slavery as the progenitor of racism.[91] In 1958, with Padmore at his side, Nkrumah hosted the All-African People's Conference, which was attended by black revolutionaries such as Frantz Fanon, Amilcar Cabral, and Patrice Lumumba, and sought to accelerate the eradication of white-settler colonialism in Africa. Nkrumah hailed the pioneering role of Garvey, who 'fought for African national and racial equality'.[92]

The 1960s witnessed the culmination of the African-American struggle for civil rights, and here too Garvey was lionized by its principal leaders. When he visited Jamaica in 1965, Martin Luther King praised the UNIA leader as 'the first man on a mass scale and level to give millions of Negroes a sense of dignity and destiny'.[93] Garvey became one of the models of the Black Power movement, which called for a 'second emancipation' to complete the social and economic liberation of black people. For example, he influenced the thought of Stokely Carmichael, as well as the feminist Obi Egbuna, who reprised Garvey's celebration of black feminine beauty.[94] Malcolm X, whose parents Earl and Louise Little were both Garveyites (they met at a UNIA Convention in Montreal), was perhaps the most iconic embodiment of this pan-African revolutionism. Shortly before his assassination in February 1965, Malcolm X created the Organization of Afro-American Unity, which followed in the footsteps of the UNIA in seeking to bring together African Americans with the people of the African continent. This Garveyite lineage and its wider anti-slavery roots were crisply celebrated by the poet Albert Haynes: 'statues of saints and heroes / Malcolm! Garvey! / Into fading mottled statues of saints and heroes / Nat Turner, Denmark Vesey'.[95]

*

Frederick Douglass had deplored the lack of 'monuments of marble' to commemorate black revolutionaries in the late nineteenth century. He would no doubt have been pleased that this void would eventually be filled – and often by himself. Douglass has emerged as the most memorialized African-American former captive in the United States, with statues in Rochester (where he lived for twenty-five years and is buried), New York, Washington D.C., Michigan, Pennsylvania, and Maryland.

As part of a wider movement to recognize African-American struggles for equality and dignity from the 1990s, numerous memorials to slavery have been erected in the United States, with many honouring specific resistance figures.[96] A bronze replica of the crate in which Henry 'Box' Brown shipped himself to freedom stands in Richmond, Virginia, to memorialize his daring escape. Sojourner Truth has a bust in the Washington Capitol, and statues in Esopus in New York State (where she was born), Sacramento and San Diego in California, Florence in Massachusetts, and Battle Creek in Michigan. Equally impressive is Harriet Tubman's record, with statues and monuments in Arizona, Georgia, Michigan, New York, New Jersey (where she replaced Christopher Columbus), Halifax, North Carolina, and Boston in Massachusetts, where her memorial is situated on a park also named after her. Since 2021 'Juneteenth' has become a Federal public holiday.

Interestingly, a few of these monuments pay homage to the most combative forms of resistance. Thus the *Amistad* sculpture in New Haven, Connecticut, built on the site of the jail where the African rebels were held before their trial, powerfully represents three moments in the life of its leader, Joseph Cinqué (Sengbe Pieh). Since 2014, Charleston in South Carolina has a statue to honour Denmark Vesey (see Plate 13), and in 2021 an Emancipation monument was inaugurated in Richmond. Funded by the state of Virginia, it features bronze statues of a man and woman who have just been freed from enslavement, and below the monument are plaques with brief stories of a group of Virginians who fought against human bondage. They include the revolutionary rebels Gabriel and Nat Turner, as well as William Carney, who served in the 54th Regiment during the Civil War, and Mary Jane Richards Bowser, who provided vital intelligence to the Union forces during the conflict. Since the late twentieth century there has been a memorial in Washington D.C. dedicated to African-American soldiers who fought in the Civil War. It carries an 1863 quote from Frederick Douglass: 'who would be free themselves must strike the blow; better even die free than to live slaves'.[97]

The story of how enslaved resistance finally entered Atlantic public space in modern times begins in the 1960s. It was a movement that owed a great deal to the dynamic force of Garveyism, and the anticolonial and anti-imperialist campaigns for the self-determination of black peoples. The main impetus for this process came not from the United States, but from indigenous political organizations that had been fighting for their freedom for decades and came to power as European colonial empires in the Atlantic world came to an end. As they assumed control of their respective states, these indigenous movements sought to make a clean break with colonialism by affirming their pan-African historical lineage, celebrating both the historical opposition of their peoples to white rule and the fight of their ancestors against enslavement. This connection between sovereignty and resistance was made visible through the erection of statues and monuments as well as the celebration of particular slave insurgent figures, who became national public icons. A good example of the mobilization of this 'usable past' was independent Jamaica, where Paul Bogle and Marcus Garvey were anointed as official heroes in 1969, followed in the early 1980s by Queen Nanny and Samuel Sharpe. More recently, 8 April has been declared 'Chief Takyi Day' in honour of Tacky, the principal leader of the 1760 rebellion.[98] In Sengbe Pieh's African birthplace in Sierra Leone, the face of the *Amistad* hero appeared on a national banknote.

This symbolic connection between slave insurgency and postcolonial independence was reinforced by the dedication of resistance monuments to specific rebel leaders, all of whom we have encountered in earlier chapters. In 1975, when the equatorial island of São Tomé gained its independence from Portugal, Amador, who had led the 1595 rebellion against Portuguese slavers, was made into a national hero, and a statue in his honour was later inaugurated. Likewise in Guyana, a monument to Cuffy, one of the initial Akan leaders of the 1763 Berbice insurrection, was unveiled in 1976 to mark the tenth anniversary of independence; among the faces represented on his body are Quamina, the leader of the 1823 Demerara revolt. In Antigua the 1736 rebellion was memorialized with a statue to its leader Prince Klass, an African Coromantee slave, to mark twelve years of independence from Britain. Klass is depicted blowing a conch shell to rally the island's captives. In Barbados the monument to emancipation was first inaugurated in 1985 as a general homage to the enslaved, and was later associated specifically with Bussa, the African-born leader of the 1816 insurrection, who was made a Barbadian national hero in the late twentieth century. Likewise in Curaçao, the *Desenkadená* (unchained) monument, which depicts three bronze figures freeing themselves from their shackles, was commissioned to honour the bicentenary of the 1795 uprising. The sculpture is commonly known as the 'Tula monument', after the captive who led the insurgency. The date of his execution (March 10th) is inscribed on a plaque.[99]

Newly independent postcolonial states were soon joined in this celebration of their long history of enslaved resistance by progressive national and local authorities in Latin America. In 1976 a statue of the maroon leader Nyanga was inaugurated in Mexico, in the town that now bore his name. In the same spirit the free settlement of San Basilio in Colombia commissioned a statue in honour of its founder, the rebel captive commander Benkos Biohó.[100] In Cuba, where as we saw earlier Carlota was celebrated as a revolutionary icon, a monument was erected in honour of the Matanzas insurrection in which she participated. It depicts three captives in postures of revolt, with Carlota in the middle, her machete raised. The memory of slavery played a significant role in Cuba's late Cold War African policies, especially its military intervention in Angola and support for the fight against Apartheid in South Africa. This war was cast by the Castro regime as a contemporary reprise of the battle between the enslaved and their imperial masters. When Nelson Mandela visited Cuba in 1991, shortly after his release from imprisonment, he gave a speech at the Matanzas monument in which he linked his people's struggle against racial oppression with the historic fight for freedom in Cuba.[101]

This pan-African insurgent spirit remains present on both sides of the Atlantic. It was immortalized in the Ecuadorean capital Quito in 2015 in a public square renamed 'Haiti 1804', where statues of Dessalines and Pétion were unveiled. With the active military support of Haiti, Bolívar's capture of Quito had been a crucial moment in his drive to liberate Spanish South America. On 1 January 2024, for the 220th anniversary of Haitian independence, a bronze bust of Dessalines was inaugurated in Benin, west Africa, and placed in Ogoun Dessalines, a *vodun* space north of Cotonou.[102] Cuba's anti-slavery resistance was honoured in a 2018 exhibition curated by the historian Ada Ferrer and the painter Edouard Duval-Carrié, which brought together fourteen artists to commemorate José Antonio Aponte's book of paintings. The different works reimagined Aponte's revolutionary drawings for the contemporary present, and they reflected on the connection between art and social change (see Plate 16).[103]

Without doubt the most celebrated Latin American figure from the slavery period is Zumbi, the charismatic warrior and leader of the Palmares *quilombo*. In contemporary Brazil the Serra da Barriga in Alagoas, one of the main locations of the settlement founded by Zumbi after his refusal to compromise with the Portuguese, has become a national heritage site. Zumbi has emerged as a Brazilian national hero, with monuments and memorials in his honour in different cities across the country; since 2011,

November 20th has become the official National Day of Zumbi and Black Awareness. At the same time – fittingly – the memory of slavery and resistance is still contested in Brazil. The Zumbi monument in Rio has become a major rallying point for ceremonies to celebrate Afro-Brazilian culture, and for demonstrations demanding greater social, economic, and racial justice for Brazil's black citizens.[104]

The Brazilian case is in this respect not isolated. As it has entered mainstream political conversations in the Atlantic world, the memorialization of slavery and enslaved resistance continues to generate discussion and sometimes controversy. These divisions relate both to how the past should be remembered and to how ongoing legacies of enslavement should be addressed in the contemporary era. In the United States, where more than 2,000 monuments to the Confederacy still exist, over a hundred and fifty have been removed over the past decade, generally by state and local governments, but these actions have at times been a source of bitter contention locally.[105] In Spain and Portugal, in contrast, these conversations are only in their infancy. The 'Africanity' of Spain, in terms of both the historic presence of a black population and the violence of colonial conquest, is beginning to be discussed both by political leaders and scholars.[106] In 2023 the Portuguese President Marcelo Rebelo de Sousa declared that it was time for the nation to acknowledge its role in the history of the Atlantic slave trade, apologize for it, and make financial reparations. However, the government rejected the proposal.[107] A monument to commemorate Portuguese slavery has yet to materialize on the Lisbon quayside, even though the project was approved in 2017. Designed by the Angolan conceptual artist Kiluanji Kia Henda, *Plantation* is to consist of 540 blackened metal sugar canes. These are intended to evoke the oppressive nature of plantation labour as well as the resistance of the enslaved, who would often set fire to the crops during their revolts or escapes.[108]

The early wave of monuments commissioned by postcolonial states did not face this sort of problem. Those who conceived them were agreed on their broad purposes: to serve as powerful acts of pan-African recovery, while providing an important corrective to European paternalistic accounts of emancipation. But other difficulties emerged over time. The focus on single rebel leaders tended to emphasize the masculine and martial dimensions of resistance, and to underplay the role of women. Carlota and Queen Nanny, two of the most prominent women memorialized, fitted comfortably within this heroic framework. Moreover, the prominence given to individual insurgent leaders somewhat obscured the collective dimensions of resistance, and the key fact which has been illustrated throughout this book, namely that all rebellions were grounded in acts of co-operation and solidarity among the enslaved; even an individual act of flight was underpinned by networks of community support.[109] The commemoration of the 1816 revolt in Barbados generated a fierce debate between Hilary Beckles and the anthropologist Jerome Handler over Bussa's African identity and the prominent role ascribed to him in national resistance narratives in preference to other figures such as the mixed-race rebel Joseph Pitt Washington Francklyn. Such disagreements illustrate the wider tensions that can simmer within these contemporary resistance memories over issues of race, gender, and agency.[110]

In these postcolonial contexts, a division between metropolitan and postcolonial memories of Atlantic slave abolition and slave resistance remains identifiable. In Britain there are no state-commissioned monuments remembering captive revolts, and the nation's nineteenth-century memorials are all dedicated to white abolitionists (mostly MPs or members of abolitionist societies). Of the ninety-four such structures identified in a recent survey, none incorporate or refer meaningfully to the experiences of enslaved Africans. Even the Demerara martyr John Smith, much discussed in his time, has no monument in his honour.[111] Official celebrations of abolitionist anniversaries have tended to steer well clear of resistance. The 2007 bicentenary of the British abolition of the slave trade was a good recent case in point. It produced some rich and striking exhibitions in London, Bristol, Liverpool, and Hull, drawing on the best international scholarship, and an effort was made not only to integrate the experiences of the enslaved, but to show how these men and women were agents of their own liberation.[112]

This dynamic message was lost on the British authorities, who used the bicentenary mainly to reprise the well-known refrain about the pioneering roles of white abolitionists such as Wilberforce and Clarkson, and their embodiment of the British values of humanity, kindness, and compassion. Of the six commemorative stamps issued, only two featured black figures (Olaudah Equiano and Ignatius Sancho), while calls for the British state and the monarchy to apologize for their roles in the slave trade were dismissed.[113] This reluctance to portray black resistance can be illustrated by locally commissioned artefacts. In 2008 a sculpture sponsored by Black British Heritage and the City of London to mark the 1807 bicentenary was unveiled in Fen Court, London. Entitled *Gilt of Cain*, created by the sculptor Michael Visocchi and the poet Lemn Sissay, the monument consists of seventeen carved granite columns clustered around the podium. The artists intended it to suggest a group of people gathering to listen to an abolitionist speaker such as Wilberforce or the cleric John Newton. In its classic representation of white abolitionist didacticism, the sculpture broadly maintained the traditional British commemorative approach.[114]

In the Caribbean, the 2007 anniversary was seen not as a cause for celebration. It was rather a reminder that (if we include the period of so-called 'apprenticeship') slavery endured in the British Empire for three further decades after 1807. Caribbean nations that were formerly British colonies have generally gone back to marking the anniversary of emancipation on 1 August, which is a public holiday on many of the islands. This local tradition (as mentioned earlier) began in the late 1830s, after the complete abolition of slavery. Since the late twentieth century, Caribbean remembrance events and ceremonies have dwelled on the importance of enslaved agency and collective sacrifice in the fight for freedom, and the demands for reparative justice. In Barbados, for example, 1 August is observed as a day of 'resistance, struggle and solidarity'.[115] From an official British perspective, in contrast, resistance has remained an uncomfortable topic, and anything that detracts from the 'self-congratulatory and defensive' celebration of white abolitionism has been seen as problematic.[116]

When the (first-ever) black local government in the British Overseas Territory of Bermuda decided to mark the island's 400th anniversary of British settlement, in 2009, it commissioned a statue of Sally Bassett, the enslaved black woman executed in 1730 for allegedly attempting to poison her enslavers, as we saw in chapter 3. This choice reflected a widespread view among Bermudians of African descent that Bassett had been a freedom fighter, and that the struggles of their enslaved forebears should be honoured. However, the statue was loudly denounced by local white settlers, who claimed that Bassett's actions had been 'criminal' and were not deserving of public memorialization. At the unveiling of the monument, which shows Bassett gazing defiantly at the sky, the British governor caused further bemusement by comparing Bassett to the Confederate leader Robert E. Lee – even though Lee dedicated his life to defending slavery whereas Bassett gave hers to challenge it.[117]

Afro-Caribbean communities in Britain have been pushing for more inclusive and comprehensive commemorations of abolition. They have generated a growing body of artistic work that is capturing public attention, and is featured in slavery exhibitions such as the Fitzwilliam Museum's 'Black Atlantic: Power, People, Resistance' (2023). It included works highlighting the resilience of the enslaved by modern black artists Barbara Walker, Donald Locke, Alberta Whittle, and Keith Piper. The National Trust and other cultural and educational institutions have begun to take steps to reveal the links between their heritage sites and the slave trade.[118] This movement has found further expression in public calls for the creation of counter-monuments in major national places of remembrance such as Trafalgar Square, and mobilizations against public statues honouring British slavers. After the emergence of the Black Lives Matter movement in 2015, more than twenty such monuments have been removed or modified, for example the statue of Edward Colston in Bristol in 2020. While they have generated attention and stimulated public discussion, these acts of 'strategic vandalism' have so far provoked little overall change in the institutional policies of the British government.[119]

Dissonances between metropole and periphery concerning the memories of abolition and enslaved resistance are also heard in France. As we saw earlier, the Republic's approach to the aftermath of the 1848 emancipation centred around three key principles: forgetting what happened under slavery; emphasizing national reconciliation through the paternalistic intercession of the Republic; and promoting Victor Schoelcher as its single architect. There were no public commemorations of the 1848 abolition under the Third Republic (1870–1940), and the centenary of abolition in 1948 was entirely fixated on Schoelcher, whose remains were moved into the Panthéon at this juncture. This individual focus was confirmed with François Mitterrand's solemn tribute to the French abolitionist in the Panthéon in 1981, shortly after his election to the Presidency. In 1998 the 150th anniversary of abolition essentially replicated this classic vision. The authorities reproduced the paternalistic paintings of the late 1840s, mostly avoiding any reference to enslaved suffering or self-emancipation. Abolition was officially presented as a triumph for the 'French republican model' of integration, enabling a 'creative expression of identity' that had erased all social and cultural antagonisms.[120]

From the 1990s this self-satisfied posture was increasingly challenged by French academics and pressure groups, who campaigned effectively to enable the passing of the 2001 Taubira Law, which named slavery and the slave trade as crimes against humanity; since 2006, May 10th has become a national slavery commemorative day. Thanks to these French legislative acts, and ongoing campaigns by national and local groups, the French public conversation about the history of slavery has become much more diverse and inclusive. Plaques honouring Toussaint Louverture and Louis Delgrès were installed in the Panthéon. Furthermore, a major slavery memorial was erected in Nantes in 2012, while Bordeaux installed a bust of Toussaint Louverture in 2005, and also in 2019 a statue of Modeste Testas, a captive woman in Saint-Domingue who was enslaved by two sugar plantation owners from Bordeaux. As we saw in the Introduction, Paris now has a statue of Solitude, the enslaved female resistance figure from Guadeloupe. And since 2015 a major city in Guadeloupe,

Pointe-à-Pitre, has been hosting the Mémorial ACTe, an ambitious archi-
tectural monument that serves both as an international slavery museum and
a cultural centre dedicated to the history of slavery and the slave trade.[121]

There remains an official tendency to present abolition as a majestic
gift of the French Republic, and to idolize Schoelcher. However, organizations such as the Fondation pour la Mémoire de l'Esclavage, headed by
former Prime Minister Jean-Marc Ayrault, have played a significant role
in emphasizing the importance of resistance as an integral feature of the
history of the fight against enslavement. The Fondation was one of the
principal organizers of the 'Oser la Liberté – We Could Be Heroes' exhibitions, held on the ground floor and crypt of the Panthéon in late 2023 and
early 2024, and entirely dedicated to the struggle against slavery in France
and the wider Atlantic world. For the first time in a publicly sponsored
event of this type in Paris, the active resistance of the enslaved featured
prominently in the artistic and documentary displays, as well as in the
exhibition's accounts of the abolitions of 1794 and 1848.[122]

The resistance of the enslaved has been more openly and creatively
memorialized in French overseas territories, through symbolic and substantive challenges to the Republic's grand narrative, the celebration of
local rebellions and insurgent figures, and the search for alternative commemorative styles. The anticolonial progressive intellectual Aimé Césaire
was one of the pioneers of this movement. In 1971, as Mayor of Fort-de-
France in his native Martinique, he commissioned a remarkable statue of
a female maroon figure. This was no doubt a direct response to one of the
most colonialist Schoelcher statues in Fort-de-France, dating from the early
twentieth century, which has the emancipator benevolently looking down
upon a grateful young woman. Produced by the local artist Khokho René-
Corail, the 1971 work features a bronze statue of an enslaved woman
embedded in a white stone background; she wields a weapon in one hand
and protects a wounded child with the other. It was a revolutionary piece
of art, as Césaire pointed out in his speech at the statue's inauguration on
22 May 1971: for its depiction of a black captive, a woman, and a citizen who was not gratefully receiving freedom but 'seizing it'.[123] Césaire
questioned the primacy accorded to Schoelcher in the French republican
emancipation canon: he had been an important figure, undoubtedly, but
there was no doubt for Césaire that the enslaved themselves had been the
principal architects of the 1848 emancipation in the Caribbean.

This constant challenge to the Republic's official Schoelcher myth has
played out in many ways across French overseas territories. Maroon
statues, such as the *Neg Mawon* memorials in Diamant (1998) and Saint-
Esprit (2000) in Martinique, continued the tradition initiated by Césaire

and René-Corail by depicting figures in positions of self-emancipation. The Diamant sculpture is that of an enslaved man, head held high and looking confident and resolute, while the Saint-Esprit structure has a maroon standing on a drum and blowing a conch shell, calling to others in a purposeful and determined pose. In French Guyana, the *Marrons de la Liberté* statue (2008) shows a man breaking his chains and a woman releasing a bird. In Abymes, in Guadeloupe, the local authorities marked the 150th anniversary of abolition by erecting a statue in honour of Solitude in 1999. In Saint-Anne a maroon memorial inaugurated in 2002 further challenged the official heroic conventions by representing a disembodied female figure, alongside several objects of resistance. The point here was to highlight both the dynamism of captive revolts and the extreme violence perpetrated against its agents.[124] In Lamentin, Martinique, the maroon memorial avoids the human body altogether and instead is shaped as an imposing *Tree of Liberty* to symbolize the closeness of fugitives to nature and the importance of spiritual traditions in African religions.[125]

More conventional representations of enslaved resistance figures have continued to appear, as with the statue of Delgrès inaugurated in his native town of Saint-Pierre in Martinique in 2022. The most dramatic challenge to the Schoelcher myth was the vandalization of several of his statues in 2020. At Basse-Terre in Guadeloupe a bust of the great man was hacked off, and a statue pulled down in Cayenne, French Guyana. In Martinique two Schoelcher statues were brought down: the one in Fort-de-France with the paternalistic pose, and another in a town that bears his name. A year later yet another bust in his honour was decapitated in Diamant; it had been erected in 1998. The anticolonial activists responsible demanded more memorializations of black resistance figures and declared that 'Schoelcher is not our saviour'. Some recalled that he had supported the indemnity given to French slavers. Echoing these criticisms, the municipal council of Lamentin voted to remove its bust of Schoelcher in May 2021. These decapitations of the French abolitionist leader were not so much directed at Schoelcher's person as at the French metropolitan authority he had come to symbolize in these territories – an arrogant white paternalism that cloaked its neocolonial mentalities in lofty republican rhetoric.

In 1997 UNESCO established August 23rd – the start of the Saint-Domingue slave insurrection in 1791 – as the International Day for the Remembrance of the Slave Trade and its Abolition. This anniversary is widely observed across the Atlantic, by public institutions, museums, and civil society organizations. The occasion is also an opportunity for intellectuals to lobby governments that are still dragging their feet on the issue, such as the British, to take steps to institute a proper national commemoration.[126]

In the Indian Ocean, the abolition of slavery is marked with public holidays in Réunion and Mauritius, on 20 December and 1 February respectively. The resistance of the enslaved is specifically commemorated in public monuments. An imposing cenotaph was inaugurated in 2011 in Réunion to mark the centenary of the Saint-Leu insurrection. It depicts the heads of ten of the captives sentenced to death for their participation in the uprising. A bust of Toussaint Louverture was unveiled in the town of Saint-André in 2019. Likewise in neighbouring Mauritius, in 2008 the Morne mountain on the southwest coast of the island was recognized as a UNESCO World Heritage Site. It served as one of the principal refuges for runaways during the eighteenth and early nineteenth centuries (so much so that it became known as a 'maroon republic'). A year later a monument was unveiled at the foot of the mountain, as part of the International Slave Route project. Following the recommendations of the 2011 Truth and Justice Commission, which examined the legacies of slavery in Mauritius, an Intercontinental Slavery Museum was established in Port Louis in 2023. Set in Mauritius under French colonial rule, the film *Ni chaînes ni maîtres* (2024), directed by Simon Moutaïrou, centres on the escape of two runaways, Massamba and Mati, from the plantation of their captivity in 1759. Massamba's determination to challenge the slave order is summed up by his exhortation: 'we must fight' (see Plate 25).

Thanks to the efforts of black communities and creative artists in the Caribbean and Europe, the history of enslaved resistance has now entered mainstream public space in the Atlantic and Indian Ocean, offering varied and empowered representations of the enslaved's struggles for freedom – in films, plays, poems, novels, and paintings. One of the significant features here has been the depiction of female figures, none more haunting than Sethe, the protagonist in Toni Morrison's great novel *Beloved*, who kills her own child because she believes death to be preferable to slavery.[127] More such examples would include Andrea Levy's novel *The Long Song*, set in Jamaica at the time of the Baptist uprising, and centring around July, an enslaved girl with a powerful spirit (the novel was adapted by the BBC in 2018). The Haitian artist François Cauvin's remarkable paintings of Haitian revolutionaries include several women such as Sanité Belair (see Plate 17) and Marie-Jeanne Lamartinière. Also significant is the dedication of a 2019 Hollywood movie to Harriet Tubman, in which she is described as 'one of America's greatest heroes'. (Tubman is a prominent presence in Ta-Nehisi Coates' surrealist novel *The Water Dancer*, in which she has the magical power of 'conduction', moving people through great distances.) In a similar vein, Rebecca Hall's acclaimed graphic novel and memoir *Wake* (2021) is devoted to the 'hidden history' of women-led captive revolts. Through the portrait of its main character Rachel, Eleanor Shearer's *River Sing Me Home* powerfully recounts a maroon mother's journey in search of her lost children in British Guyana, Trinidad and Barbados in 1834-5.[128]

Marronage has also become a political and literary term. Neil Roberts' *Freedom as Marronage* thus argues that the experiences of runaways underscore freedom's historically unstable character.[129] He finds ongoing patterns of marronage in the modern world in the ways people remove themselves (physically and mentally) from conditions of oppression and create dynamic forms of freedom.[130] In a related vein, Sean Gerrity has reinterpreted Martin Delany's *Blake* as a novel about freedom as marronage. Gerrity shows that its key features all engage with the ideal: from Henry's absolute rejection of enslavement and the unfinished character of his revolt to the narrative's emphasis on black self-reliance, ambiguity (Henry is always creating confusion in the minds of the adversary) and constant movement across the black landscape.[131] Likewise, marronage underpins Lawrie Balfour's exploration of freedom in Toni Morrison's novels. Quoting her proposition that 'modern life begins with slavery', Balfour sees Morrison's novels as reflecting on how black people engaged with freedom before and after slavery. In these senses freedom cannot be properly understood without appreciating its impact on those suffering from domination – or, to use Balfour's maroon metaphor, without 'the experiences of the hunted'.[132]

In this entrenchment of enslaved resistance in our collective imagination, pride of place is occupied by memorials to Toussaint Louverture, which have proliferated since the early twenty-first century. In addition to the tributes honouring him in his native Haiti (in Port-au-Prince, Haut-du-Cap, and Ennery), busts or statues of him have appeared in Benin, Canada, the United States, Cuba, and Réunion. His most spectacular restoration has come in France, where in addition to his plaque in the Panthéon in Paris, there are statues commemorating Louverture in Massy and La Rochelle, and busts in the Fort de Joux – where he died – and Bordeaux. In 2023 President Macron gave a major speech hailing Louverture as a French national hero and embracing his motto of 'doucement allé loin'.[133] Through this presence in Africa, the Caribbean, North America, and Europe, Louverture has thus come to personify the principle of enslaved resistance, as well as the globalization of the Haitian revolution in our contemporary imagination. It is no accident that the son of the late king T'Challa, who makes a welcome appearance at the end of the blockbuster movie *Black Panther: Wakanda Forever* (2022), is named Toussaint. The extraordinary resilience of enslaved resistance in Atlantic collective memory is reflected in the epic verses of a Haitian *vodou* song dedicated to Toussaint's great inspiration, Makandal:

> Since I left Africa, people have been testing me
> I am the root
> Since I left Africa, people have been testing me
> I am a great rock
> I came from under the water, I fly up into the sky
> When they thought they captured me
> I turned to smoke.

Conclusion
Honouring Our Debts

Daring to be Free has aimed to identify consistent patterns of enslaved resistance in the Atlantic world, from the early moments of European colonization of the New World to the revolutionary and abolitionist eras in the late eighteenth and nineteenth centuries. Viewing the period as a whole has helped to restore forgotten stories, heroic figures, and collective achievements. Drawing on what a scholar has rightly called 'the spectacularly boisterous archive of slavery'[1] has allowed me to highlight the historical depth of opposition to enslavement, and to make comparisons across time, geographical areas, and colonial regimes. I have sought to trace links among types of opposition often treated as distinct categories, such as kinship and transnational networks, maroon activities, spiritual beliefs and practices, anti-slavery pamphlets and narratives, urban revolts, and slave-plantation uprisings. The cumulative evidence demonstrates, I hope, that at all times the enslaved made major contributions to their freedom, and that emancipation cannot be understood without appreciating their critical agency in all these domains.

The key connection among these forms of resistance is the concept of solidarity, which brought men and women together across the Atlantic world in their struggles against enslavement. Solidarity united them through networks based on African-originating factors such as ethnicity, membership of military groups or secret societies, and religious affiliations. These links were reinforced during the Middle Passage 'shipmate' bonding, and they were further consolidated through shared resistance experiences in the New World. Those included conspiratorial co-ordination, sacred rituals and oath-taking, runaway escapes (by land and sea) and maroon settlements, along with ideological and affective connections forged in the places where men and women were held in bondage. These sophisticated affiliations were empowering, operating for the most part in a clandestine manner, or under cover of apparently innocuous religious or cultural activities. Their existence was typically unsuspected by the

slavers, or came to their attention only in more public moments of revolutionary activity. Even when these solidarity networks did not lead to
open confrontation with their oppressors, they were a source of moral
force and practical assistance to the enslaved. They enabled both women
and men to work together and nurture strong friendships.[2] Summing
up his personal experience of this special bond among fellow enslaved
people, Frederick Douglass observed: 'I believe we would have died for
each other. We never undertook to do anything, of any importance, without a mutual consultation.'[3]

Our focus on these commonalities across enslaved and black communities has downplayed the significance of divisions traditionally invoked
to view African-originating groups separately from one another. The
point is not to minimize such differences, which were real and sometimes
consequential. When it came to the issue of liberty, however, captives were
plainly driven by the same key requirements. This was the case whether
they were brought to the colonies in the 1500s or the 1800s; African-
born or creole; plantation or town-based captives; hinterland or coastal
maroons; enslaved or freeborn persons; upholders of Christianity, Obeah,
or Islam (or any combination of these); men or women. In the latter
respect, the book has portrayed women as bold and resourceful agents in
the struggle against slavery. This was exemplified in their various roles as
priestesses and healers, their active engagements in political and military
mobilizations, their provision of networks of familial support, and their
effective functions as intelligence providers across the Atlantic, from slave
ships to plantation settings. They performed these roles while confronting
and often subverting masculine hierarchies.

Africa emerges as a key pillar of resistance practices: practically,
through the development of marronage on the continent itself; militarily,
in the combat experiences of many rebels; politically, by the organization
of clandestine movements and networks; and morally, by generating
spiritual beliefs that provided a refuge from oppression and a spring-
board for opposition. This African influence also operated ideologically,
through the design of radical anti-slavery ideals from the very early stages
of European colonization, as with the case taken to the Vatican by the
African abolitionist Lourenço da Silva Mendonça in the late seventeenth
century. Africa was furthermore one of the main sources of maritime marronage. And as a myth of origins and focus for sacred repatriation, the
continent furnished complementary and sometimes alternative visions of
emancipation.[4] Through the later development of pan-African ideas and
movements this anti-slavery tradition was a major force in modern efforts
to promote anticolonial liberation and racial equality. As summed up by

two scholars of this black internationalism, the resistance of the enslaved was 'blithely oblivious to established political boundaries'.[5]

Traditions of resistance to slavery could operate in short and long time spans within the same area. They could reverberate more widely across regions through oral and symbolic transmissions – as illustrated by the successive examples of Kisama, São Tomé, Bayano, Palmares, the Jamaican maroons, and of course the Haitian revolution. The Haitian achievement of territorial sovereignty became a defining episode in the nineteenth-century Atlantic: positively for those fighting to achieve emancipation, and negatively for those trying to contain it. The aura of the Haitian revolution reached back to Africa, as shown in the remarkable example of the October 1808 revolt that began in the Cape Town hinterland. Over three hundred captives launched an insurrection, overran dozens of slave farms, and then marched towards Cape Town, where they sought to 'fight themselves free' until they were defeated by superior firepower. One of their main leaders was Louis van Mauritius, an enslaved native of that Indian Ocean island, who was forcibly transported to the Cape Colony as a young boy. Louis became dedicated to fighting for freedom after he heard about Atlantic anti-slavery uprisings and the abolition of the slave trade from two Irish sailors who had arrived at the African port. But the strongest influence on his thinking was the Haitian revolution. This could be gauged by the outfit he wore during the insurrection – a blue jacket, white linen trousers, gold and silver epaulettes, and a hat with feathers. This was exactly how Toussaint Louverture was depicted in one of his most widely circulated prints from the early nineteenth-century Atlantic.[6]

Haiti was an exemplar for Louis van Mauritius and so many others like him because its revolution combined the main features of enslaved resistance, and it took each of them to its highest plane. This was true of Africanism, marronage, military skills, slave-plantation mobilization, charismatic leadership, co-operation across social and ethnic lines, and creative religious systems. Saint-Domingue's *vodou* was essentially a syncretic religion of the enslaved, arising through and defined by its opposition to human bondage. In terms of revolutionary tactics from the Makandal era onwards, Saint-Domingue optimized the conditions of a battle in which power was asymmetrically held by the oppressors. This entailed, among other things, operating well away from the limelight, while adopting strategies that were deliberately invisible to the slavers. This approach relied on improvisation as well, and it sought solutions that were hybrid in character both in their form and in the range of groups associated with the enterprise. Louverture borrowed from Makandal's maroon tactics in all these respects, to which he added constant movement and a sense of closeness to nature, expressed in his extensive knowledge of Saint-Domingue's topography. These key aspects of Louverture's maroon sensibility allowed him to create his own parallel system of movement and communication, an instance of what Stephanie Camp (following Edward Said) would later describe as a 'rival geography'.[7]

However, this singularity was consistent with another important feature: Haiti was an admired exemplar for black Atlantic communities but not a model. Its force resided in its role as a symbol of black martial valour and capacity for self-government, rather than a template for complete emulation. It provided a general but flexible inspiration for anti-slavery mobilizations against the Spanish, British, and French empires, all of whom the Haitians defeated. These qualities were invoked and then adapted to local needs, objectives, and practices, which varied considerably across the Atlantic. After 1804, Haiti provided a refuge for all those (both enslaved and free) seeking to escape to a place where black sovereignty was recognized as a constitutional right. In other words, Haiti represented the ideal that united the different strands of resistance: the principle of autonomy. Contrary to a widely held view among scholars until relatively recently, the fight for freedom by the enslaved was not driven by the quest for individual rights as defined by the Enlightenment and Western liberalism, although captives did at times draw on these common languages. In fact, it has become abundantly clear that neither the *philosophes* nor British, French, and American abolitionists could imagine Africans as fully human subjects capable of agency and self-determination.

For enslaved people fighting against their oppression, in contrast, autonomy was a defining quality. It was an ideal more broadly connected to the creation of intermediate spaces of freedom that were under black control, and beyond the reach of white slavers and reformers. In practical terms, autonomy could be achieved on different scales. At the smallest, it was a matter of containing the tyranny of the brutal overseer or securing the freedom to cultivate one's own land. It could involve the kind of small-scale liberties allowed by *petit marronnage*, such as temporary absences to visit family or friends or attending clandestine social or cultural gatherings. More boldly, it could mean joining the congregation of a black church or going through the motions of white-led Christian worship while continuing to engage with African-based spiritual beliefs and rituals (which could include their own, African-derived, Christian motifs). Most radically, it could precipitate a separation from colonial society. This could take different forms: carving out self-sufficient territorial enclaves (as in Palmares), establishing a self-governing community while remaining part of a European colonial empire (the Toussaint Louverture formula in Saint-Domingue), or ultimately achieving complete independence, as the Haitians did from 1804. Autonomy is the thread that unites all these different endeavours. It also shows that marronage, local self-governance, and independent sovereign statehood were not at all philosophically dissonant; they were simply different means of achieving the same end.

This takes us to the wider intellectual and moral implications of this story. Slavery and the constant resistance it provoked among captives were defining parts of our modernity, shaping the history of human bondage as well as the general movement for freedom and equality in the contemporary world. This is already recognized in terms of the study of slavery and emancipation, and it is thanks to the major scholarly advances in these fields over the past decades that a book such as this one could be written. But this is only the beginning. The real challenge remains to integrate these important insights into broader analyses of the constitutive elements of our modern order. Within the political realm, this would involve revisiting how we understand freedom, as well as such 'mainstream' concepts as nation-building, citizenship, self-determination, the rule of law, capitalism, justice, and democracy.

The concept of democracy is a good illustration. In the standard ways in which its emergence in the modern world is narrated, the focus is generally directed at Enlightenment ideas of rationalism, individualism, self-determination, the public good, and efficient institutional governance. The history of slavery and the resistance of the enslaved do not typically feature in this West-centred story, even in agonistic accounts that stress the importance of dissent in democratic traditions. Yet this book has revealed powerful connections between the ideals and practices of democracy and the resistance of the enslaved. The push for abolition and emancipation in the later eighteenth and nineteenth century was an integral part of wider social movements for mass empowerment and social justice, in which (for example) women, young people, workers, sailors, soldiers, and free black people played significant roles. Many of these groups identified with the enslaved and compared their own predicaments to the captives' fight for freedom. The Underground Railroad in the United States illustrates how this support could be translated into inventive forms of democratic mobilization, appealing to the disenfranchised, creating local networks of solidarity, and challenging unjust laws. In the aftermath of Emancipation, during the Reconstruction era, liberated black communities in the American South developed a range of organizations to push for their social, economic, and civic rights. In forging this regional 'Emancipation Circuit' they drew on their experiences as maroons during the Civil War, as well as earlier traditions of collective resistance of enslaved people in black churches, runaway movements, and secret societies; this was America's first mass Black democratic movement.[8] The 'foundational tool' for building these organizations were mass meetings, which were convened across the South. They were open to all, appealed to expertise as well as experience, and decisions were taken by consensus, as during the times of enslavement.[9]

More fundamentally, the enslaved themselves were pioneers, as their aspirations for freedom and ownership of their bodies conveyed core values of self-expression and self-determination. Frederick Douglass can thus be seen as a democratic theorist in his emphasis on the revolutionary and unsettled character of modern politics, and the right of citizens to interpret the law in a democracy.[10] More generally, anti-slavery arguments advanced by captives rested on claims that their subjugation was based on coercion rather than free choice, and that their freedom stemmed from their right to full membership of the societies in which they lived – essential democratic principles. In their battles against the slavers, moreover, captives practised multiple forms of democracy among themselves – in their collective deliberations about confronting their oppressors, from strike action to going to war; in how they chose their leaders (where they often inventively combined republican and monarchical forms); in the governance of maroon settlements; in the running of their civic and cultural associations; and of course in their revolutionary organizations, which combined underground operations with network-building and covert consultations across communities. The paradigm of democratic inclusion during the Age of Revolutions was neither America nor France, but Saint-Domingue, where both the revolution that overthrew slavery in the early 1790s and the war of national liberation leading to Haitian independence were driven by the power of the *demos*. As we saw in chapter 4, popular movements practised democracy in revolutionary Saint-Domingue through collective discussions, mass mobilizations, public interventions (speeches, meetings, signatures of petitions), as well as vigorous challenges to their own leadership.

Enslaved resistance was equally pioneering in the emergence of modern anticolonialism. The fight for emancipation from Western colonial rule was grounded in universal principles sketched out and practised by the captives in their fight against the slavers, which began right from the first acts of opposition to European settlers in Africa and in the Americas: the illegitimacy of white-settler rule; the condemnation of the barbaric treatment of local and indigenous populations; the equal dignity of all peoples, irrespective of their race or religion; and the formulation of alternative political arrangements based on the ideal of self-determination. This rich genealogy of anticolonialism further highlights the significance of decolonial and postcolonial approaches, which have already started to make fruitful inroads in revisiting our core political concepts, and there is much more to look forward to from these sources.[11] The story of enslaved resistance also opens a window into black imagination. Achille Mbembe's *Critique of Black Reason* offers a sweeping reflection on how slavery and colonialism created the exclusions that continue to define our contemporary global order, as well as the racialized foundations on which Western understandings of the world have long rested. At the same time, Mbembe shows how it is impossible to separate the history of Africa and blackness from the modern conception of the self that emerged in Europe; the two are completely enmeshed. *Critique of Black Reason* argues that black figures constantly stood up to this hegemony, both theoretically and through their practices, and went about conceiving different possible worlds. Mbembe pays a particular tribute to the enslaved, 'the fertilizers of history', who in the midst of extreme barbarity were able to devise their own idioms, forms of thinking, literatures, music, and ways of celebrating the divine. By their inventiveness these insurgent men and women were able to transform blackness, a badge of non-humanity in the eyes of the white world, into 'a symbol of beauty and pride' and 'a sign of radical defiance'. He suggests that recovering these achievements can open up possibilities for redemptive thought and action in contemporary politics.[12] In a related but different context, Ta Nehisi Coates' *The Message* draws on the rich tradition of African-American emancipatory writing to reflect on the commonalities in the experiences of 'the enslaved, the colonized, and the conquered' in the contemporary world, and in particular the racism and dispossession experienced by the Palestinian people since 1948.[13]

Giving this history the prominence it deserves is a matter of proper dissemination and more comprehensive memorialization: thus in 2023 the Mayor of London, Sadiq Khan, agreed to fund a project to honour the victims of slavery in London's Docklands, with the final design by the American artist Khaleb Brooks being announced in August 2024.[14] One of the essential ways in which this story can become more widely appreciated is through education. There have been advances in the teaching of the history of slavery and enslaved resistance in schools. In Britain, for example, the focus is essentially on the celebratory narrative of abolition. In the United States the tendency likewise is to hone in on key individuals (Frederick Douglass, Harriet Tubman), whereas the more active forms of black resistance are avoided. This phenomenon is accentuated by the highly decentralized education system and the resurgence of a conservative white nationalism that seeks systematically to downplay the significance of slavery. In many widely used American textbooks, especially in private schools in the South, the Civil War is portrayed as a conflict about states' rights, and enslaved people have even been described as 'immigrants'.[15] Moreover, plantation museums in the South generally continue to present the antebellum period in rosy terms.[16]

In France there have been significant advances since the early twenty-first century: for example, under the impetus of the archivist and art curator Florence Alexis an annual competition entitled 'La Flamme de l'Égalité' is organized across secondary schools to encourage artistic, literary, and audiovisual projects around the theme of slavery and slave resistance. The winners are announced each year in May.[17] However, even though Toussaint Louverture has become a national hero in France, the history of the Haitian revolution is not taught in secondary schools in the *métropole*; only students in overseas departments and territories are given the option of learning about it. The story of abolition remains focused around 1848, and classically framed as a vindication of triumphant French republicanism.[18] In terms of public monuments in France, the absence of any national memorial to enslavement in Paris has long been discussed. In an initiative announced in 2023, French authorities have unveiled plans for the construction of a memorial to the victims of slavery in the Trocadéro Gardens. One of its aims is to list the names of the 200,000 enslaved people in French colonies who were freed in 1848.[19]

The most urgent issue surrounding the legacy of slavery is reparations. As we saw in earlier chapters, state financial compensation in the aftermath of emancipation was afforded to British and French slavers in the 1830s and 1840s. Both of these arrangements were publicly funded, and former French settlers from Saint-Domingue also received a settlement extorted from the Haitian government in 1825.[20] It bears repeating that this was the only time in modern history when former captives directly compensated slavers. Despite various promises, in particular General Sherman's 'Forty Acres and a Mule' order to allocate Southern land to former captives in 1865, and the short-lived Freedmen's Bureau, a Federal agency that handed out relief in the South from 1865 to 1872, the enslaved themselves received no proper restitution from public authorities, even though there was support among leading nineteenth-century abolitionists for the idea of compensating them. However, these setbacks did not inhibit their demands for justice. One of the important but little-known facts is that although reparations are much discussed in contemporary times, such claims in the context of Atlantic chattel slavery are not recent.

Drawing on French, Portuguese, Spanish, and English sources, Ana Lucia Araujo has shown that petitions for financial and material reparations have been consistently made by formerly enslaved people and their descendants for well over two centuries. They expressed their claims in correspondence, speeches, pamphlets, enslaved narratives, and legal cases, and through powerful intellectual advocacy. As we saw earlier in the book, during the initial phases of the British abolitionist movement, Ottobah Cugoano was calling for 'adequate reparation' for the harm inflicted upon the enslaved. Cyril Bissette made the same argument in France, and Marcus Garvey was among the vocal supporters of slave reparations in the early twentieth century.[21] One of the earliest petitions of this kind to be successful was a claim by Ghanaian-born Belinda Sutton in the United States. She received an annual pension in late eighteenth-century Massachusetts from the proceeds of her enslaver's estate, after she had been held in bondage there for fifty years; she had to make several claims before finally receiving her due.[22] Such perseverance was shown by former captives all the way through to the end of their lives in the twentieth century. The last known survivor of the transatlantic slave trade in the United States was Matilda McCrear, who died in 1940. She was captured from Dahomey in west Africa and brought to Alabama in 1860; in 1931, when in her seventies, she unsuccessfully filed a claim for reparations at the Dallas County Courthouse.[23]

This book's contribution to the case for reparations is to add more context to the debate's historical and theoretical elements. There is little doubt that from the very outset, captives experienced a profound sense of injustice at their enslavement. They did not consent to their forcible seizure and they regarded it as illegitimate from the moment they became bonded. This deprivation of their freedom was among the principal causes of their ongoing resistance; the wars fought against their enslavers were in this sense underpinned by a powerful search for reparatory justice. Moreover, as we saw in the second half of the book, emancipation did not bring complete freedom and in many respects the former captives experienced continued forms of civic, social, political, and economic discrimination long after formal emancipation.[24]

In this sense, the history of captive resistance is an exercise in what David Scott calls 'reparatory history', a reconstruction of the 'evil pasts' of enslavement 'in ways that potentially enable us to rethink the moral responsibility that the present owes in respect of them'.[25] It is important to bear in mind that reparations are not only, or even essentially, about monetary compensation: this is fundamentally an ethical issue. We can further suggest strong connections between claims for reparations and the concept of freedom as marronage, discussed in the previous chapter. Both see a proper understanding of past wrongs as a necessary precondition for understanding modern liberty. Both express ideals of justice that are inspired by oppressed groups and animated by international solidarity. Both are best thought of not as finished programmes but as inclusive conversations among different communities and movements. And both are achieved not through the realization of a single ideal but as a deliberative process that moves forward through the collective search for a democratic consensus involving both beneficiaries and victims of historic injustices.

Atlantic slavery cast a long shadow over black communities in both Africa and the West. Contemporary claims for redress rest on past injustices as well as their structural effects across time, for postcolonial nations as well as populations descending from enslaved people. Indeed, the public conversation about the issue of reparations now extends well beyond the question of the institution of slavery to include discussions about historical wrongs arising from colonialism, mass killings, and war crimes. And these claims are not purely theoretical. Recent examples of settlements (although studiously avoiding the term 'reparation') include the British government's decision to pay £19.9 million to compensate over 5,000 surviving Kenyans who suffered torture in British-run colonial prison camps during the Mau Mau uprisings in Kenya in the 1950s. This arrangement was concluded in the wake of a High Court action initiated by a group of Kenyan victims. Also significant is Germany's agreement to disburse 1.1 billion Euros through aid payments to Namibia to atone for the colonial genocide against the Herero and Nama peoples in South-West Africa in the early twentieth century. Such examples, and what they might entail in terms of good-faith reparations settlements, have been the subject of wide-ranging exchanges among political philosophers as well as campaigners for reparative justice.[26]

It is against this wider backdrop of international awareness of historic injustices that demands for slavery reparations have resurfaced with increasing intensity since the late twentieth century, both through grass-roots movements and state-led initiatives. One of the major landmarks in this revival was the First Pan-African Conference on Reparations held in Nigeria in 1993, which ended with the proclamation of the Abuja Declaration. Noting the 'unique and unprecedented moral debt owed to the African peoples' on the grounds of their enslavement over four centuries, this seminal document called for the pursuit of slavery reparations claims as well as debt cancellation. The Declaration drew explicitly on international precedents of reparations given to Jewish victims of the Holocaust and Japanese-American victims of internment during the Second World War.[27]

At the 2001 Durban World Conference against Racism, Atlantic slavery was presented as a crime against humanity; the meeting called on 'concerned states' to consider mitigating the long-term social and economic impacts of human bondage through reparations. Haitian president Jean-Bertrand Aristide followed up with a powerful speech in 2003 demanding 'reparation' from France; he was toppled in a Western-backed coup a year later. The Caribbean Community (CARICOM) addressed a ten-point plan for reparatory justice to European governments historically involved in the slave trade in 2013. Among the key demands were a full apology, debt cancellation, and investment in education and health systems;[28] the declaration stressed that the African-descended population in the Caribbean had the highest incidence in the world in terms of chronic diseases such as hypertension and Type 2 diabetes.[29] In 2023 this alliance was joined by the fifty-five members of the African Union, overcoming the initial opposition to reparations from some African states, and establishing a united global front to lobby European states to pay for their 'historical crimes' of Atlantic slavery.[30]

There has been some movement in response. In the United States, Congress formally apologized for the 'enslavement and racial segregation of African Americans' in 2008, and between 2007 and 2016 nine of the eighteen states that had held slaves prior to 1865 issued official apologies for slavery. The debate about reparations was further relaunched by a seminal article published by Ta-Nehisi Coates in the *Atlantic* in 2014, the *New York Times*' 1619 Project, and the adoption of reparations by campaigning organizations such as Black Lives Matter. Largely due to pressure from students and Faculty members, several American universities have investigated their historic links with slavery and proposed reparatory measures. Thus Georgetown University in Washington D.C., which sold 272 enslaved people to two Louisiana planters in 1838 in order to finance the university's expansion, has set up an annual fund to offer financial support to the descendants of those who were enslaved on Jesuit plantations in Maryland.[31] Harvard University announced in 2022 that it was setting aside $100 million to help close the educational and economic gaps that have emerged through the legacies of slavery and racism. Harvard Law School was established with significant financial support from an Antigua-based enslaver family, and before 1865 enslaved Africans carried the books and bags of students attending classes.[32] The first black students at Harvard faced intense hostility: one of them was Martin Delany. Before becoming the author of *Blake*, Delany had been a talented freshman at Harvard Medical School. He was expelled in 1850, less than two terms into his first semester, because white students refused to accept his presence.

Meanwhile in Europe, the closest any British government has come to public acknowledgement of the nation's historic role in slavery was Tony Blair's expression of 'deep sorrow' in 2006. Dutch King Willem-Alexander and his Prime Minister Mark Rutte apologized for their nation's role in the slave trade in late 2022 (the first European government to do so), and pledged £200 million towards restoration work in former Dutch colonies. Other governments have yet to follow their lead. As in the United States, academics, students, research institutions, and civil-society groups have been campaigning and raising awareness about the issue, and their pressure has started to have some impact. In recent years some institutions once owned by slavers or that have benefited from the proceeds of enslavement have begun actively to engage with their past, researching their links with enslavement, and taking steps to make this information more clearly visible to the public. Examples from the United States and Britain include, respectively, Thomas Jefferson's Monticello plantation and the buildings owned by the National Trust, which commissioned an interim report on the ninety-three sites connected with British colonialism and the slave trade.[33]

In a few cases public apologies have been forthcoming and funds set aside for reparatory purposes. Notable British examples would include the pledges of *The Guardian* newspaper, Glasgow University, the global insurer Lloyd's, and the Church of England of £10 million, £20 million, £40 million, and £100 million respectively, to make amends for their historical links to the transatlantic slave trade. The Church of England's commitment has been widely commented upon, and internal discussions are still ongoing within the institution. In March 2024 an independent oversight group chaired by Bishop Rosemarie Mallett produced another report stating that the £100-million pledge was insufficient, and calling for the sum to be raised to at least £1 billion.[34] On a related but separate track, the economist Thomas Piketty calculated in 2020 that the Haitians are owed $28 billion by the French government as restitution for the debts incurred for their independence payments. Marking the bicentenary of the agreement between France and Haiti in April 2025, President Emmanuel Macron acknowledged Haiti's debt as a manifestation of the 'unjust force of history', and set up a Commission further to investigate the issue and make recommendations.[35] It remains unclear whether the French will eventually offer financial reparations. But as the enslaved resisters have shown us throughout this book, and as pertinently summarized by Frederick Douglass: 'power concedes nothing without a demand.'[36]

Notes

INTRODUCTION: RECOVERING A VAST TRADITION

1. Louis Delgrès, 'A l'univers entier' (10 May 1802). Aix-en-Provence: Archives Nationales d'Outre-Mer (ANOM), COLC7 A 57.
2. Auguste Lacour, *Histoire de la Guadeloupe*, Guadeloupe: Basse-Terre, 1858, vol. III, p. 311.
3. Maryse Condé, *I, Tituba, Black Witch of Salem*, Charlottesville, VA: University of Virginia Press, 1992, p. 179.
4. See Laurent Dubois, 'Solitude's Statue: Confronting the Past in the French Caribbean', *Outre-Mers*, 93:350–51 (2006), pp. 27–38.
5. 'Trans-Atlantic Slave Trade – Estimates', SlaveVoyages.org: https://www.slavevoyages.org/assessment/estimates
6. For the full text, see Appendix in Julia Gaffield (ed.), *The Haitian Declaration of Independence*, Charlottesville, VA: University of Virginia Press, 2016, pp. 239–48. On Dessalines, see also the biography by Julia Gaffield, *I Have Avenged America: Jean-Jacques Dessalines and Haiti's Fight for Freedom*, New Haven and London, Yale University Press, 2025.
7. James C. Scott, *Domination and the Arts of Resistance: Hidden Transcripts*, New Haven, CT: Yale University Press, 1990.
8. I am grateful to Quentin Skinner for this insight; see Quentin Skinner, *Liberty as Independence: The Making and Unmaking of a Political Ideal*, Cambridge: Cambridge University Press, 2025.
9. For further discussion of the imagery of the enslaved, see Jeffrey R. Kerr-Ritchie, 'Slaves Supplicant and Slaves Triumphant: The Middle Passage of an Abolitionist Icon', in A. L. Araujo (ed.), *Paths of the Atlantic Slave Trade: Interactions, Identities, and Images*, Amherst, MA: Cambria Press, 2011, pp. 327–58.
10. Gabriel Debien, *Les esclaves aux Antilles françaises (XVIIe–XVIIIe siècles)*, Société d'Histoire de la Guadeloupe, Guadeloupe: Basse-Terre, 1974, p. 393.
11. On this theme see Sarah Churchwell, *The Wrath to Come: Gone with the Wind and the Lies America Tells*, London: Apollo, 2022.
12. Ples Sterling Stuckey, 'Through the Prism of Folklore: The Black Ethos in Slavery', *Massachusetts Review*, 9:3 (Summer 1968), p. 6.

13. Herbert Aptheker, *American Negro Slave Revolts*, New York: Columbia University Press, 1943, p. 374.

14. C. L. R. James, *The Black Jacobins*, London: Penguin Classics, 2022; Aimé Césaire, *Toussaint Louverture, la Révolution française et le problème colonial*, Paris: Présence Africaine, 2000 (an English translation has been published by Polity Press in 2024: *Toussaint Louverture: The French Revolution and the Colonial Problem*, trans. Kate Nash).

15. Eugene Genovese, *From Rebellion to Revolution: Afro-American Slave Revolts in the Making of the Modern World*, Baton Rouge, LA: Louisiana State University Press, 1992, p. xxiii.

16. For interesting recent samples of this archaeological approach, see A. L. Araujo, K. Boyer-Rossol, and M. Cottias (eds.), *Esclavages: Représentations visuelles et cultures matérielles*, Paris: CNRS Éditions, 2024.

17. See Maxine Berg and Pat Hudson, *Slavery, Capitalism and the Industrial Revolution*, London: Polity Press, 2023.

18. Robin Blackburn, *The Reckoning: From the Second Slavery to Abolition, 1776–1888*, London: Verso, 2024.

19. Carolyn Fick, *The Making of Haiti*, Knoxville, TN: University of Tennessee Press, 1990; Manuel Barcia, *West African Warfare in Bahia and Cuba*, Oxford: Oxford University Press, 2014; Vincent Brown, *Tacky's Revolt*, Cambridge, MA: Harvard University Press, 2020; Marjoleine Kars, *Blood on the River*, New York: New Press, 2020.

20. See for example Johnhenry Gonzalez, *Maroon Nation: A History of Revolutionary Haiti*, New Haven, CT: Yale University Press, 2019, and Jean-Marc Pruit, 'Black Atlantic Republicans and the Limits of the Plantation', *Journal of Haitian Studies*, 28:1 (2022), pp. 39–59.

21. See Laurent Dubois, 'An Enslaved Enlightenment: Rethinking the Intellectual History of the French Atlantic', *Social History*, 31:1 (February 2006), pp. 1–14.

22. For a general assessment of the field, see Manuel Barcia, 'Into the Future: A Historiographical Overview of Atlantic History in the Twenty First Century', *Atlantic Studies*, 19:2 (2022), pp. 181–99.

23. See Wendy Wilson-Fall, *Memories of Madagascar and Slavery in the Black Atlantic*, Athens, OH: Ohio University Press, 2015.

24. Amédée Nagapen, *Le marronnage à l'Isle de France – Ile Maurice*, Port Louis, Mauritius: Centre Culturel Africain, 1999, pp. 373–4.

25. Richard Allen, 'Licentious and Unbridled Proceedings: The Illegal Slave Trade to Mauritius and the Seychelles during the Early Nineteenth Century', *Journal of African History*, 42:1 (2001), pp. 91–116.

26. David Eltis estimates that around 400,000 enslaved people were transported to the United States; see his article 'The Volume and Structure of the Transatlantic Slave Trade: A Reassessment', *William and Mary Quarterly*, 58:1 (January 2001), p. 37.

27. For an excellent analysis of this tendency, and particularly the absence of a comparative perspective in American slavery studies, see Jeffrey R. Kerr-Ritchie,

Freedom's Seekers: Essays on Comparative Emancipation, Baton Rouge, LA: Louisiana State University Press, 2013.

28. Saidiya Hartman, *Scenes of Subjection*, Oxford: Oxford University Press, 1997, p. 6.

29. See Vincent Carretta, *Equiano the African: Biography of a Self-Made Man*, Atlanta, GA: University of Georgia Press, 2005; on Makandal, see John Garrigus, *A Secret among the Blacks*, Cambridge, MA: Harvard University Press, 2023; Michael P. Johnson, 'Denmark Vesey and His Co-Conspirators', *William and Mary Quarterly*, 58:4 (October 2001).

30. Aviva Ben-Ur, 'Bound Together? Reassessing the "Slave Community" and "Resistance" Paradigms', *Journal of Global Slavery*, 3:3 (2018), pp. 195–210.

31. Frédéric Régent, 'Résistances serviles en Guadeloupe à la fin du XVIIIe siècle', *Bulletin de la Société d'Histoire de la Guadeloupe*, 140 (2005), pp. 15–16.

32. David Scott, *Conscripts of Modernity: The Tragedy of Colonial Enlightenment*, Durham, NC: Duke University Press, 2004.

33. Marisa Fuentes, *Dispossessed Lives: Enslaved Women, Violence and the Archive*, Philadelphia, PA: University of Pennsylvania Press, 2016, p. 10.

34. Aisha Finch, *Rethinking Slave Rebellion in Cuba*, Chapel Hill, NC: University of North Carolina Press, 2015, p. 142.

35. Vincent Brown, 'Social Death and Political Life in the Study of Slavery', *American Historical Review*, 114:5 (December 2009), p. 1,235.

36. Frank Wilderson III, *Afropessimism*, New York: Liveright, 2020, p. 39.

37. For a critique of the 'antipolitics' of Afropessimism, see Kevin Ochieng Okoth, *Red Africa: Reclaiming Black Revolutionary Politics*, London: Verso, 2023, pp. 24–38; see also Annie Olaloku-Teriba, 'Afro-Pessimism and the (Un)Logic of Anti-Blackness', *Historical Materialism*, 26:2 (July 2018), pp. 96–122.

38. Aline Helg, *Slave No More: Self-Liberation before Abolitionism in the Americas*, tr. Lara Vergnaud, Chapel Hill, NC: University of North Carolina Press, 2019.

39. Hilary Beckles, 'Caribbean Anti-Slavery: The Self-Liberation Ethos of Enslaved Blacks', *Journal of Caribbean History*, 22:1 (January 1988).

40. Walter Johnson, 'On Agency', in Gad Heuman and Trevor Burnard (eds.), *Slavery: Critical Concepts in Historical Studies*, vol. IV, London: Routledge, 2014, p. 219.

41. On this point, see the Introduction in Paul Lovejoy, *Jihad in West Africa during the Age of Revolutions*, Athens, OH: Ohio University Press, 2016.

42. *Dahoméens déportés en esclavage* database: https://symbole-amitie.com/bases-de-donnees/base-de-donnees-2/

43. See in particular the seminal article by Barbara Bush, 'Defiance or Submission? The Role of the Slave Woman in Slave Resistance in the British Caribbean', *Immigrants & Minorities*, 1:1 (1982), pp. 16–38.

44. Heather Rachelle White, 'Between the Devil and the Inquisition: African Slaves and the Witchcraft Trials in Cartagena de Indies', *The North Star: A Journal of African-American Religious History*, 8:2 (Spring 2005), pp. 1–2.

45. December 1830 report, quoted in Gordon Gill, 'Enslavement, Emotions and Oppositional Insolence in the Slave Society of British Guiana', *Slavery & Abolition*, 45:1 (2024), p. 145.

46. Satyendra Peerthum, '"Daughters of Bondage": The Struggle of the Mauritian Maroon Women in the early 19th Century', *Mauritius Times* (30 January 2014).

47. Jean Casimir, *The Haitians: A Decolonial History*, tr. Laurent Dubois, Chapel Hill, NC: University of North Carolina Press, 2020, p. 3.

48. See notably Leslie Alexander, *Fear of a Black Republic: Haiti and the Birth of Black Internationalism in the United States*, Urbana, IL: University of Illinois Press, 2023.

49. For an analysis of the Stono rebellion from this perspective, see John Thornton, 'African Dimensions of the Stono Rebellion', *American Historical Review*, 96:4 (1991), pp. 1,101–13.

50. On the 1814 plot, see Stuart Schwartz, 'Cantos and Quilombos: A Hausa Rebellion in Bahia, 1814', in Gad Heuman and Trevor Burnard (eds.), *Slavery: Critical Concepts in Historical Studies*, vol. III, London: Routledge, 2014, pp. 291–308.

51. See Walter Hawthorne, '"Being now, as it were, one family": Shipmate Bonding on the Slave Vessel *Emilia*, in Rio de Janeiro and throughout the Atlantic World', *Luso-Brazilian Review*, 45:1 (2008), pp. 53–77.

52. Governor report, Basse-Terre, 11 September 1845, in René Bélénus (ed.), *Les abolitions de l'esclavage aux Antilles et en Guyane Française, 1794–1848*, Martinique: Éditions Exbrayat, 2022, pp. 145–6.

53. Julius Scott, *The Common Wind*, London: Verso, 2018.

54. Genovese, *From Rebellion to Revolution*.

55. See the collection edited by Charles Stewart, *Creolization: History, Ethnography, Theory*, Abingdon: Routledge, 2016. For a brilliant case study, see Megan Vaughan, *Creating the Creole Island: Slavery in Eighteenth-Century Mauritius*, Durham, NC: Duke University Press, 2005.

56. https://www.slavevoyages.org/voyage/database

57. For an illuminating exploration of this point, see Jennifer Morgan, *Reckoning with Slavery: Gender, Kinship and Capitalism in the Early Black Atlantic*, Durham, NC: Duke University Press, 2021.

58. Baron de Vastey, *The Colonial System Unveiled*, tr. Chris Bongie, Liverpool: Liverpool University Press, 2014.

59. See notably Marlene Daut, *Baron de Vastey and the Origins of Black Atlantic Humanism*, New York: Palgrave, 2017. See also Daut's more recent work, *Awakening the Ashes: An Intellectual History of the Haitian Revolution*, Chapel Hill, NC: University of North Carolina Press, 2023.

60. On Cuba see Manuel Barcia, 'Fighting with the Enemy's Weapons: The Usage of the Colonial Legal Framework by 19th Century Cuban Slaves', *Atlantic Studies*, 3:2 (2006), pp. 159–81.

61. See for example F. Régent et al. (eds.), *Libres et sans fers*, Paris: Fayard, 2015.

62. Sophie White, *Voices of the Enslaved*, Chapel Hill, NC: University of North Carolina Press, 2021.

63. John Ernest (ed.), 'Introduction', *The Oxford Handbook of the African American Slave Narrative*, Oxford: Oxford University Press, 2014, p. 4; see also the chapter on WPA narratives by Marie Jenkins Schwartz.

64. The seminal work here is Ples Sterling Stuckey, *Slave Culture: Nationalist Theory and the Foundations of Black America*, Oxford: Oxford University Press, 2013.

65. Michel-Rolph Trouillot, *Silencing the Past: Power and the Production of History*, Boston, M A: Beacon Press, 1995.

66. *The Memoir of General Toussaint Louverture*, tr. and ed. Philippe R. Girard, Oxford: Oxford University Press, 2014.

67. On the Atlantic circulation of the writings of Toussaint Louverture and Dessalines, see Deborah Jenson, *Beyond the Slave Narrative*, Liverpool: Liverpool University Press, 2012, chs. 1 and 2.

68. For a more general discussion of these writings in the British Caribbean, Cuba, and Brazil, see Winfried Siemerling, 'Slave Narratives and Hemispheric Studies', in Ernest (ed.), *The Oxford Handbook*, pp. 344, 361.

69. Laurent Estève, *Montesquieu, Rousseau, Diderot*, Paris: Editions UNESCO, 2002, p. 218.

70. For an illuminating discussion, see Adom Getachew, 'Universalism after the Post-Colonial Turn: Interpreting the Haitian Revolution', *Political Theory*, 44:6 (2016), pp. 821–45.

71. Louis Sala-Molins, *Dark Side of the Light: Slavery and the French Enlightenment*, Minneapolis, MN: University of Minnesota Press, 2006.

72. Halik Kochanski, *Resistance: The Underground War in Europe 1939–1945*, London: Penguin, 2023.

73. Frederick Douglass, 'What to the Slave is the Fourth of July?', in J. Stauffer and H. L. Gates Jr (eds.), *The Portable Frederick Douglass*, New York: Penguin, 2016, p. 207.

74. Barcia, *West African Warfare*, pp. 99–100.

75. Robin Kelley, 'Introduction', in Matt Callahan et al. (eds.), *Songs of Slavery and Emancipation*, Jackson, MS: University Press of Mississippi, 2022, pp. 3–4.

76. André Schwarz-Bart, *La mulâtresse Solitude*, Paris: Seuil, 1972, pp. 151–2.

1: THE AFRICAN FOUNDATIONS OF RESISTANCE

1. 'des êtres sans aucune volonté de réagir ou de se rebeller'. For a broader study see Robin Law, *Ouidah: The Social History of a West African Slaving Port*, Athens, OH: Ohio University Press, 2004.

2. For a discussion based on contemporary oral interviews, see Anne C. Bailey, *African Voices of the Atlantic Slave Trade: Beyond the Silence and the Shame*, Kingston, Jamaica: Ian Randle, 2007.

3. See notably the two edited volumes by Alice Bellagamba et al., *African Voices on Slavery and the Slave Trade*, Cambridge: Cambridge University Press, 2013 (vol. 1) and 2016 (vol. 2).

4. Quoted in José Lingna Nafafé, *Lourenço da Silva Mendonça and the Black Atlantic Abolitionist Movement in the Seventeenth Century*, Cambridge: Cambridge University Press, 2022, p. 372.

5. James Searing, *West African Slavery and Atlantic Commerce*, Cambridge: Cambridge University Press, 1993, pp. 2–3.

6. See Saidiya Hartman, *Lose Your Mother: A Journey along the Atlantic Slave Route*, London: Profile Books, 2021, pp. 230–31.

7. See Sean Stilwell, *Slavery and Slaving in African History*, Cambridge: Cambridge University Press, 2014, pp. 32–3, 48–50.

8. Richard Reid, *Warfare in African History*, Cambridge: Cambridge University Press, 2012, p. 80.

9. On the key role of slave traders in Africa, and the system they created with the support of African middlemen, see Chapter 1 in Nicholas Radburn, *Traders in Men: Merchants and the Transformation of the Transatlantic Slave Trade*, New Haven, CT: Yale University Press, 2023.

10. See Akosua Adoma Perbi, *A History of Indigenous Slavery in Ghana*, Accra: Sub-Saharan Publishers, 2004.

11. Stilwell, *Slavery and Slaving in African History*, pp. 4 and 20.

12. Joseph Inikori, 'The Struggle against the Transatlantic Slave Trade', in Sylviane Diouf (ed.), *Fighting the Slave Trade*, Athens, OH: Ohio University Press, 2003, pp. 186–7.

13. Walter Rodney, 'Jihad and Social Revolution in Futa Djalon in the Eighteenth Century', *Journal of the Historical Society of Nigeria*, 4:2 (June 1968), p. 282.

14. See Linda Heywood, 'Slavery and its Transformation in the Kingdom of Kongo 1491–1800', *Journal of African History*, 50:1 (March 2009), pp. 1–22.

15. Toby Green, *A Fistful of Shells*, London: Allen Lane, 2019, p. 268.

16. See for example Felton Perry, 'Kidnapping: An Underreported Aspect of African Agency during the Slave Trade Era', *Ufahamu, A Journal of African Studies*, 35:2 (2009).

17. Ottobah Cugoano, *Thoughts and Sentiments on the Evil and Wicked Traffic of the Slavery and Commerce of the Human Species*, London, 1787, pp. 6–7.

18. Winston McGowan, 'African Resistance to the Atlantic Slave Trade in West Africa', *Slavery & Abolition*, 11:1 (1990), p. 13.

19. John Thornton, 'Early Kongo-Portuguese Relations: A New Interpretation', *History in Africa*, 8 (1981), p. 197.

20. McGowan, 'African Resistance', pp. 13–14.

21. Ibid, pp. 10, 12–13.

22. Catherine Coquery-Vidrovitch and Éric Mesnard, *Être esclave*, Paris: La Découverte, 2019, p. 162.

23. Howard French, *Born in Blackness: Africa, Africans and the Making of the Modern World*, New York: Liveright, 2022, pp. 132–3.

24. See Gerhard Seibert, 'São Tomé's Great Slave Revolt of 1595', *Portuguese Studies Review*, 18:2 (2011), 29–50.

25. Quoted in Richard Rathbone, 'Some Thoughts on Resistance to Enslavement in West Africa', *Slavery & Abolition*, 6:3 (1985), p. 12.

26. Quoted in Searing, *West African Slavery and Atlantic Commerce*, p. 2.

27. Martin Klein, 'The Slave Trade and Decentralized Societies', *Journal of African History*, 42 (2001), pp. 55–6.

28. Olaudah Equiano, *The Interesting Narrative and Other Writings*, London: Penguin, 2003, p. 25.

29. John Oriji, 'Igboland, Slavery and the Drums of War and Heroism', in Diouf (ed.), *Fighting the Slave Trade*, pp. 122–5.

30. Ibid, pp. 125 and 128.

31. Bernard Dossa, 'Dahomey: résistance à l'esclavage et à l'arrachement', *Symbole de l'Amitié* (11 August 2021); https://symbole-amitie.com/dahomey-resistance-a-lesclavage-et-a-larrachement

32. Martin Klein, 'Defensive Strategies: Wasulu, Masina and the Slave Trade', in Diouf (ed.), *Fighting the Slave Trade*, p. 69.

33. Oriji, 'Igboland, Slavery', p. 125.

34. Ibid, p. 127.

35. Allison Howell, '"Showers of Arrows": The Reactions and Resistance of the Kasena to Slave Raids in the 18th and 19th Centuries', in J. K. Anquandah, N. J. Opoku-Agyemang, and M. Doortmont (eds.), *The Transatlantic Slave Trade: Landmarks, Legacies, Expectations*, Accra: Sub-Saharan Publishers, 2007, pp. 189–207.

36. Klein, 'Defensive Strategies', pp. 66–7.

37. Elisée Soumonni, 'Lacustrine Villages in South Benin as Refuges from the Slave Trade', in Diouf (ed.), *Fighting the Slave Trade*, pp. 7–8 and 10.

38. Samuel Ntewusu, 'Arrows of Power: The Builsa *Feok* Festival of Slave Resistance and Abolition in Ghana', in James O'Neil Spady (ed.), *Fugitive Movements*, Columbia, SC: University of South Carolina Press, 2022, p. 163.

39. Walter Hawthorne, 'Strategies of the Decentralized: Defending Communities from Slave Raiders in Coastal Guinea-Bissau, 1450–1815', in Diouf (ed.), *Fighting the Slave Trade*, p. 158.

40. Ibid.

41. Ibid, p. 159.

42. Klein, 'Defensive Strategies', p. 65.

43. Equiano, *Interesting Narrative*, p. 48.

44. Ntewusu, 'Arrows of Power', p. 163.

45. Adama Guèye, 'The Impact of the Slave Trade on Cayor and Baol', in Diouf (ed.), *Fighting the Slave Trade*, p. 56.

46. Klein, 'Defensive Strategies', p. 65.

47. Soumonni, 'Lacustrine Villages', p. 9.

48. McGowan, 'African Resistance', p. 16.

49. Hawthorne, 'Defending Communities', p. 156.

50. Thierno Mouctar Bah, 'Slave-Raiding and Defensive Systems South of Lake Chad from the Sixteenth to the Nineteenth Century', in Diouf (ed.), *Fighting the Slave Trade*, p. 17.

51. Ibid, pp. 18–20.

52. Naana Jane Opoku-Agyemang, *Where There Is No Silence: Articulations*

of Resistance to Enslavement, Accra: Sub-Saharan Publishers, 2008, pp. 24 and 26.

53. Emmanuel Saboro, *Wounds of Our Past*, Leiden: Brill, 2021, p. 143.
54. Dennis Cordell, 'The Myth of Inevitability and Invincibility', in Diouf (ed.), *Fighting the Slave Trade*, p. 41.
55. Bah, 'Slave-Raiding', p. 21.
56. Klein, 'Defensive Strategies', p. 66.
57. Nafafé, *Lourenço da Silva Mendonça*, p. 163.
58. Rathbone, 'Some Thoughts on Resistance', p. 19; Roquinaldo Ferreira, 'Slave Flights and Runaway Communities in Angola', *Anos 90*, 21:40 (December 2014), pp. 68 and 79.
59. Ismail Rashid, 'Escape, Revolt, and Marronage in Eighteenth and Nineteenth Century Sierra Leone Hinterland', *Canadian Journal of African Studies*, 34:3 (2000), p. 665.
60. Ferreira, 'Slave Flights', pp. 69 and 70.
61. Rathbone, 'Some Thoughts on Resistance', p. 12.
62. Ibid, p. 19.
63. Alexander Gordon Laing, *Travels in the Timannee, Kooranko and Soolima Countries in Western Africa*, London: John Murray, 1825, p. 405.
64. F. W. H. Migeod, *A View of Sierra Leone*, London: Kegan Paul, Trench, Trubner and Co., 1926, pp. 49–50.
65. Rashid, 'Escape, Revolt and Marronage', p. 666.
66. Rathbone, 'Some Thoughts on Resistance', p. 19.
67. Rashid, 'Escape, Revolt and Marronage', p. 668.
68. The classic study is by Bronislaw Nowak, 'The Mandingo Slave Revolt of 1785–1796', *Hemispheres*, 3 (1986), pp. 150–69.
69. Bruce Mouser, 'Rebellion, Marronage and *Jihād*: Strategies of Resistance to Slavery on the Sierra Leone Coast, *c*. 1783–1796', *Journal of African History*, 48 (2007), p. 44.
70. Rashid, 'Escape, Revolt and Marronage', p. 669.
71. Jessica Krug, *Fugitive Modernities*, Durham, NC: Duke University Press, 2018, pp. 49 and 59.
72. Ferreira, 'Slave Flights', p. 68.
73. Ibid, p. 79.
74. Ibid, p. 78.
75. Ibid, pp. 81–2.
76. Ismail Rashid, 'Patterns of Rural Protest: Chiefs, Slaves and Peasants in Northwestern Sierra Leone, 1896–1956', PhD thesis, Department of History, McGill University, 1998, p. 33.
77. Frederick William Butt-Thompson, *Sierra Leone in History and Tradition*, London: H. F. and G. Witherby, 1926, pp. 57–8.
78. Mouser, 'Rebellion, Marronage and *Jihād*', p. 44.
79. See William Piersen, 'White Cannibals, Black Martyrs: Fear, Depression, and Religious Faith as Causes of Suicide among New Slaves', *Journal of Negro History*, 62:2 (April 1977), pp. 147–59.

80. McGowan, 'African Resistance', p. 24.

81. Ibid.

82. Nafafé, *Lourenço da Silva Mendonça*, p. 135.

83. See Nathan Marvin, 'Gender, Family and Social Control: The Catholic Clergy and Slavery in the Eighteenth-Century Mascarenes', in S. Sénèque and V. Teelock (eds.), *Women in the Making of Mauritian Society*, Port Louis: Éditions de l'Océan Indien, 2024.

84. Coquery-Vidrovitch and Mesnard, *Être esclave*, p. 164.

85. Guèye, 'The Impact of the Slave Trade', p. 43.

86. For further discussion, see Roquinaldo Ferreira, *Cross-Cultural Exchange in the Atlantic World*, Cambridge: Cambridge University Press, 2012, pp. 177–88.

87. Joachim Jack Agamba, 'Beyond Elmina: The Slave Trade in Northern Ghana', *Ufahamu* 32:1/2 (Fall 2005/Winter 2006), pp. 46 and 51.

88. Soumonni, 'Lacustrine Villages', p. 8.

89. See Brent Sinclair-Thomson and Sam Challis, 'Runaway Slaves, Rock Art and Resistance in the Cape Colony, South Africa', *Azania*, 55:4 (2020), pp. 475–91.

90. For a full exposition, see John Thornton, 'African Traditional Religion and Christianity in the Formation of *Vodun*', *Slavery & Abolition*, 43:4 (July 2022), pp. 730–57.

91. Cécile Fromont, 'Paper, Ink, Vodun, and the Inquisition: Tracing Power, Slavery, and Witchcraft in the Early Modern Portuguese Atlantic', *Journal of the American Academy of Religion*, 88:2 (June 2020), pp. 461–2.

92. Oriji, 'Igboland, Slavery', p. 128.

93. Dossa, 'Dahomey: résistance à l'esclavage'.

94. Krug, *Fugitive Modernities*, p. 42.

95. Ismail Rashid, '"A Devotion to the Idea of Liberty at Any Price": Rebellion and Antislavery in the Upper Guinea Coast in the Eighteenth and Nineteenth Centuries', in Diouf (ed.), *Fighting the Slave Trade*, pp. 140–42.

96. James Sweet, *Recreating Africa*, Chapel Hill, NC: University of North Carolina Press, 2003, p. 163.

97. Quoted in McGowan, 'African Resistance', p. 17.

98. Ferreira, 'Slave Flights', p. 80.

99. Ntewusu, 'Arrows of Power', p. 169.

100. Oriji, 'Igboland, Slavery', pp. 124–5.

101. See Marcus Rediker, *The Slave Ship: A Human History*, London: Penguin, 2008.

102. On *Misericordia*, see Coquery-Vidrovitch and Mesnard, *Être esclave*, p. 168; on *Gato*, see slavevoyages.org.

103. John Atkins, *A Voyage to Guinea, Brasil, and the West-Indies*, London, 1735, in Elizabeth Donnan (ed.), *Documents Illustrative of the History of the Slave Trade to America*, vol. II, Washington D.C.: Carnegie Institution, 1931, pp. 265–6.

104. https://www.slavevoyages.org/voyage/database

105. Eric Robert Taylor, *If We Must Die: Shipboard Insurrections in the Era of the Atlantic Slave Trade*, Baton Rouge, LO: Louisiana State University Press, 2006.

106. John Newton, *The Journal of a Slave Trader*, London:Epworth Press, 1962, p. 56.

107. Log of Captain Robert Norris, June 1770, Liverpool Maritime Museum, D/Earle/1/4.

108. Jerome Handler, 'Survivors of the Middle Passage', *Slavery & Abolition*, 23:1 (April 2002), p. 34.

109. Newton, *Journal*, p. 87; entry for 2 December 1753.

110. Rathbone, 'Some Thoughts on Resistance', p. 17.

111. Many ships were damaged during these insurrections, and insurers received claims to cover the repair costs and the captives killed; some insurance policies had a specific slave-insurrection clause. For a more general analysis, see Robin Pearson and David Richardson, 'Insuring the Transatlantic Slave Trade', *Journal of Economic History*, 79:2 (June 2019).

112. Donnan (ed.), *Documents*, II, p. 409; and III, pp. 1 and 42.

113. Ibid, III, pp. 54–6.

114. Nagapen, *Le marronnage à l'Isle de France – l'Ile Maurice*, pp. 343–4.

115. Newton, 'Thoughts upon the African Slave Trade', in *Journal*, pp. 103–4.

116. Taylor, *If We Must Die*, pp. 78–9.

117. Mariana Candido, 'Different Slave Journeys: Enslaved African Seamen on Board of Portuguese Ships, *c.* 1760–1820s', *Slavery & Abolition* 31:3 (2020), pp. 397–8.

118. Taylor, *If We Must Die*, pp. 67–8.

119. Ibid, p. 96.

120. 1733 letter, Donnan (ed.), *Documents*, III, p. 41.

121. 'The Voyage of the *Little George*', Donnan (ed.), *Documents*, III, pp. 118–21.

122. Marcus Rediker, *The Amistad Rebellion*, London: Verso, 2013, pp. 92–3.

123. Ibid, pp. 73–4.

124. Ibid, p. 75.

125. Ibid, pp. 78–9, 80.

126. Ibid, pp. 84–5.

127. Ibid, p. 98.

128. Green, *A Fistful of Shells*, p. 302.

129. Rediker, *The Amistad Rebellion*, p. 73.

130. Dianne M. Stewart, *Three Eyes for the Journey: African Dimensions of the Jamaican Religious Experience*, New York: Oxford University Press, 2005, p. 18.

131. Issa Asgarally, 'Systèmes esclavagistes et abolitions dans les colonies de l'océan Indien (1723 à 1860)', in Edmond Maestri (ed.), *Esclavage et abolitions dans l'Océan Indien*, Paris: L'Harmattan, 2002, pp. 178–9.

132. Barcia, *West African Warfare*, p. 99.

133. Taylor, *If We Must Die*, pp. 127–33.

134. Hawthorne, 'Defending Communities', p. 165.

135. On the significance of these alterations to slave ships, see Radburn, *Traders in Men*, pp. 99–103.

136. See Anita Rupprecht, '"Inherent vice": Marine Insurance, Slave Ship Rebellion and the Law', *Race & Class*, 57:3 (2016), pp. 31–44.

137. David Richardson, 'Shipboard Revolts, African Authority, and the Atlantic Slave Trade', *William and Mary Quarterly*, 58:1 (January 2001), pp. 66–7.

2: 'THE MOST NATURAL DESIRE OF THE HUMAN HEART'

1. Pitta, quoted in Nafafé, *Lourenço da Silva Mendonça*, p. 241.
2. Francisco de Brito Freire, governor of Pernambuco, quoted in Glenn Alan Cheney, *Quilombo dos Palmares: Brazil's Lost Nation of Fugitive Slaves*, Hanover, CT: New London Librarium, 2016, pp. 95–6.
3. See Silvia Hunold Lara, *Palmares & Cucaú. O aprendizado da dominação*, São Paulo: Edusp Editora, 2021.
4. Chronicle of Governor Pedro de Almeida, cited in Robert Nelson Anderson, 'The *Quilombo* of Palmares: A New Overview of a Maroon State in Seventeenth-Century Brazil', *Journal of Latin American Studies*, 28:3 (1996), p. 560.
5. Quoted in Cheney, *Quilombo dos Palmares*, p. 41; on the São Tomé rebellion, see chapter 1.
6. Nafafé, *Lourenço da Silva Mendonça*, pp. 242–3 and n. 193.
7. See chapter 5 in Krug, *Fugitive Modernities*.
8. Bantu languages were predominant in the Kongo and Angola regions.
9. Cheney, *Quilombo dos Palmares*, p. 109.
10. Nafafé, *Lourenço da Silva Mendonça*, pp. 257–60, and p. 273.
11. Ibid, pp. 246–8.
12. Anderson, 'The Quilombo of Palmares', p. 556.
13. Nafafé, *Lourenço da Silva Mendonça*, p. 199.
14. Ibid, pp. 260–61.
15. Cheney, *Quilombo dos Palmares*, p. 147; Anderson, 'The Quilombo of Palmares', p. 560.
16. For a general discussion of the types of marronage, see Alvin Thompson, *Flight to Freedom: African Runaways and Maroons in the Americas*, Kingston, Jamaica: University of the West Indies Press, 2006, pp. 53–88.
17. Jean-Pierre Tardieu, 'Cimarrón-Maroon-Marron, note épistémologique', *Outre-Mers*, 93:350–51 (2006).
18. Helg, *Slave No More*, p. 44.
19. Quoted in Margaret Olsen, 'African Reinscription of Body and Space in New Granada', in S. Arias and M. Meléndez (eds.), *Mapping Colonial Spanish America*, Lewisburg, PA: Bucknell University Press, 2002, p. 60.
20. Olsen, 'African Reinscription of Body and Space', pp. 58–60.
21. Ruth Pike, 'Black Rebels: The Cimarrons of Sixteenth-Century Panama', *The Americas*, 64:2 (October 2007), pp. 244–5.
22. Ibid, pp. 246–50.
23. 'Concession of Liberty', May 1579, in Robert Schwaller (ed.), *African Maroons in Sixteenth-Century Panama: A History in Documents*, Norman, OK: University of Oklahoma Press, 2021, p. 188.
24. 'Account of the Foundation of Santa Cruz', in Schwaller (ed.), *African Maroons*, pp. 234–7.
25. Pike, 'Black Rebels', p. 265.
26. June 1579 declaration, in Schwaller (ed.), *African Maroons*, p. 189.
27. Treasurer report, February 1581, in ibid, p. 212.

28. Account of Captain Salcedo, September 1579, in ibid, p. 202.

29. Census of the residents of Santiago del Príncipe, 1580, in ibid, pp. 205–11.

30. Ibid, p. 258.

31. Edgar Love, 'Negro Resistance to Spanish Rule in Colonial Mexico', *Journal of Negro History*, 52:2 (April 1967), pp. 96–7.

32. Ibid, p. 94.

33. Charles Henry Rowell, 'The First Liberator of the Americas', *Callaloo*, 33:1 (Winter 2008), pp. 6–7.

34. Omar Ali, 'Benkos Biohó: African Maroon Leadership in New Granada', in J. Fortin and M. Meuwese (eds.), *Atlantic Biographies*, Leiden: Brill, 2013, pp. 276–8.

35. John Thornton, *Africa and the Africans in the Making of the Atlantic World*, Cambridge: Cambridge University Press, 2012, pp. 294–5.

36. Omar Ali, 'Benkos Biohó', pp. 281–2.

37. Olsen, 'African Reinscription of Body and Space', p. 63.

38. Stuart Schwartz, 'The "Mocambo": Slave Resistance in Colonial Bahia', *Journal of Social History*, 3:4 (Summer 1970), p. 321.

39. Helg, *Slave No More*, p. 52.

40. Almeida report, 20 April 1719; cited in José Alípio Goulart, *Da fuga ao suicídio (Aspectos de rebeldia dos escravos no Brasil)*, Rio de Janeiro: Conquista, 1972, pp. 284–6.

41. Paul Lokken, 'A Maroon Moment: Rebel Slaves in Early Seventeenth-Century Guatemala', *Slavery & Abolition*, 25:3 (2004), pp. 47 and 49.

42. Lucien-René Abénon, 'La révolte avortée de 1736 et la répression du marronage à la Guadeloupe', *Bulletin de la Société d'Histoire de la Guadeloupe*, 55 (1983).

43. Régent, 'Résistances serviles en Guadeloupe', pp. 30 and 31.

44. Ibid, pp. 31–2.

45. Patrick Carroll, 'Mandinga: The Evolution of a Mexican Runaway Slave Community', *Comparative Studies in Society and History*, 19:4 (October 1977).

46. Kenneth Bilby, *True-Born Maroons*, Gainesville, FL: University Press of Florida, 2006, pp. 130 and 136.

47. Philip Wright, 'War and Peace with the Maroons 1730–1793', *Caribbean Quarterly*, 16:1 (1970), p. 23.

48. Kenneth Bilby, 'Swearing by the Past, Swearing to the Future: Sacred Oaths, Alliances and Treaties among the Guianese and Jamaican Maroons', *Ethnohistory*, 44:4 (Fall 1997).

49. Richard Price, *Alabi's World*, Baltimore, MD: Johns Hopkins University Press, 1990, p. 297.

50. Gabino La Rosa Corzo, *Runaway Slave Settlements in Cuba*, Chapel Hill, NC: University of North Carolina Press, 2003, p. 23.

51. Sylviane Diouf, *Slavery's Exiles: The Story of the American Maroons*, New York: NYU Press, 2014, pp. 10–11.

52. Corzo, *Runaway Slave Settlements*, p. 246.

53. Schwaller (ed.), *African Maroons*, p. 66.

54. Richard Price, *Maroon Societies: Rebel Slave Communities in the Americas*, Baltimore, MD: Johns Hopkins University Press, 1996, p. 6.

55. Thompson, *Flight to Freedom*, pp. 139–40.

56. Schwartz, 'The "Mocambo"', pp. 328–31.

57. David Alston, 'The Guyana Maroons 1796–1834: Persistent and Resilient until the End of Slavery', *Slavery & Abolition*, 44:2 (2023), p. 301.

58. Rowell, 'The First Liberator of the Americas', p. 6.

59. Corzo, *Runaway Slave Settlements*, p. 182.

60. Spy report from the late 1670s, quoted in Cheney, *Quilombo dos Palmares*, p. 39.

61. Thompson, *Flight to Freedom*, pp. 250–51.

62. Barbara Klamon Kopytoff, 'The Early Political Development of Jamaican Maroons', *William and Mary Quarterly*, 35:2 (April 1978), p. 296.

63. Schwartz, 'The "Mocambo"', p. 332.

64. Jean-Pierre Tardieu, 'Le substrat africain dans la résistance des rois marrons', *Journal des Africanistes*, 86:2 (2016), pp. 7–8.

65. Thornton, *African and the Africans*, pp. 294–5.

66. Thompson, *Flight to Freedom*, p. 184.

67. Aguado, *Historia de Venezuela*, in Schwaller (ed.), *African Maroons*, p. 66.

68. Thompson, *Flight to Freedom*, p. 200.

69. Tardieu, 'Le substrat africain', p. 3.

70. Thompson, *Flight to Freedom*, p. 194.

71. Flávio dos Santos Gomes and H. Sabrina Gledhill, 'A "Safe Haven": Runaway Slaves, Mocambos, and Borders in Colonial Amazonia, Brazil', *Hispanic American Historical Review*, 3 (2002), pp. 488–9.

72. R. K. Kent, 'Palmares: An African State in Brazil', *Journal of African History*, 6:2 (1965), p. 180.

73. Kopytoff, 'The Early Political Development of Jamaican Maroons', p. 298.

74. 'Account of the Foundation of Santa Cruz la Real', January–February 1582, in Schwaller (ed.), *African Maroons*, p. 234.

75. Corzo, *Runaway Slave Settlements*, p. 158.

76. On this fusion, see Sweet, *Recreating Africa*, pp. 172–86.

77. Jane Landers, 'Maroon Women in Colonial Spanish America', in D. B. Gaspar and D. C. Hine (eds.), *Beyond Bondage: Free Women of Color in the Americas*, Urbana and Chicago: University of Illinois Press, 2004, p. 10.

78. Alston, 'Guyana Maroons', p. 308.

79. Hilary Beckles, 'From Land to Sea: Runaway Barbados Slaves and Servants', *Slavery & Abolition*, 6:3 (1985), p. 91.

80. Quoted in David Barry Gaspar, 'From "The Sense of Their Slavery": Slave Women and Resistance in Antigua, 1632–1763', in D. B. Gaspar and D. C. Hine (eds.), *More Than Chattel: Black Women and Slavery in the Americas*, Bloomington, IN: Indiana University Press, 1996, p. 224.

81. Landers, 'Maroon Women', pp. 8–10.

82. Corzo, *Runaway Slave Settlements*, pp. 53–8.

83. Ibid, p. 161.

84. Schwartz, 'The "Mocambo"', p. 332.

85. Silvia de Groot, 'Maroon Women as Ancestors, Priests and Mediums in Suri-nam', *Slavery & Abolition*, 7:2 (1986), pp. 164–6.

86. Jean-Pierre Tardieu, 'Des amazones noires chez les marrons de Carthagène des Indes vers 1586–1587: un héritage africain', *Nouveaux Mondes Nou-veaux* (2020), pp. 7–10.

87. Roger Bastide, 'The Other *Quilombos*', in Price, *Maroon Societies*, p. 197.

88. Alston, 'Guyana Maroons', p. 309.

89. João José Reis, 'Slave Resistance in Brazil', *Luso-Brazilian Review*, 25:1 (1988), pp. 122–3.

90. Jean-Baptiste Labat, quoted in Beckles, 'From Land to Sea', p. 89.

91. Ibid, p. 90.

92. Jane Landers, *Black Society in Spanish Florida*, Champaign, IL: University of Illinois Press, 1999.

93. Elena Schneider, 'A Narrative of Escape: Self-Liberation by Sea and the Mental Worlds of the Enslaved', *Slavery & Abolition*, 42:3 (2021), p. 485.

94. Ibid, p. 488.

95. Jorge Chinea, 'A Quest for Freedom: The Immigration of Maritime Maroons into Puerto Rico, 1656–1800', *Journal of Caribbean History*, 31:1–2 (1997), p. 57.

96. Edward Alpers, 'Flight to Freedom: Escape from Slavery among Bonded Afri-cans in the Indian Ocean World', *Slavery & Abolition*, 24:2 (2003), p. 63.

97. Nagapen, *Le marronnage à l'Isle de France – Ile Maurice*, p. 332.

98. Ibid, p. 326.

99. Beckles, 'From Land to Sea', p. 87.

100. Kevin Dawson, 'A Sea of Caribbean Islands: Maritime Maroons in the Greater Caribbean', *Slavery & Abolition*, 42:3 (2021), p. 441.

101. Ibid.

102. Rediker, *Slave Ship*, p. 304.

103. Dawson, 'Sea of Caribbean Islands', p. 435.

104. Ibid, p. 433.

105. Philip Morgan, 'Colonial South Carolina Runaways', in Gad Heuman (ed.), *Out of the House of Bondage*, London: Frank Cass, 1986, p. 69.

106. Dawson, 'Sea of Caribbean Islands', p. 436.

107. Diouf, *Slavery's Exiles*, p. 19.

108. Ibid, pp. 39–40.

109. Ibid, p. 51.

110. Ibid, pp. 98–106.

111. Ibid, pp. 243–52.

112. For a full account, see Brent Morris, *Dismal Freedom: A History of the Maroons of the Great Dismal Swamp*, Chapel Hill, NC: University of North Carolina Press, 2022.

113. Damian Pargas, *Freedom Seekers*, Cambridge: Cambridge University Press, 2021, p. 19.

114. Diouf, *Slavery's Exiles*, p. 217.

115. Esteban Montejo, *The Autobiography of a Runaway Slave*, New York: Pantheon, 1968.

116. Diouf, *Slavery's Exiles*, pp. 256–85.

117. See Timothy Walker (ed.), *Sailing to Freedom: Maritime Dimensions of the Underground Railroad*, Amherst, MA: University of Massachusetts Press, 2021.

118. Patrick Chamoiseau, *The Old Slave and Mastiff*, London: Dialogue Books, 2018, p. 56.

119. Thompson, *Flight to Freedom*, p. 130. The case of Hispaniola will be discussed separately in chapter 4.

120. P. J. Moree, *A Concise History of Dutch Mauritius 1598–1710*, Leiden and Amsterdam: Kegan Paul, 1998, p. 31.

121. Richard Allen, 'Marronage and the Maintenance of Public Order in Mauritius', *Slavery & Abolition*, 4:3 (1983).

122. Richard Allen, 'Maroonage and its Legacy in Mauritius', *Outre-Mers* (2002), pp. 132–3.

123. Satteeanund Peerthum and Satyendra Peerthum, 'Shattering the Shackles of Slavery', in V. Teelock (ed.), *Maroonage and the Maroon Heritage in Mauritius*, Réduit: University of Mauritius, 2005, pp. 77–86; see also Satyendra Peerthum and Stephan Karghoo, *Our First Freedom Fighters*, Mauritius: Nelson Mandela Centre for African Culture, 2011.

124. Rev. T. H. Adams, 'Washington's Runaway Slave, and How Portsmouth Freed Her', *The Granite Freeman* (22 May 1845). For a full account of Ona Judge's story, see Erica Armstrong Dunbar, *Never Caught: The Washingtons' Relentless Pursuit of Their Runaway Slave, Ona Judge*, New York: 37 INK/Simon & Schuster, 2017.

3: NOT TO BE HURT BY THE WHITE MEN

1. Orlando Patterson, *Slavery and Social Death: A Comparative Study*, Cambridge, MA: Harvard University Press, 1982, p. 13.

2. Walter Rucker, *Gold Coast Diasporas: Identity, Culture, and Power*, Bloomington, IN: Indiana University Press, 2015, p. 6.

3. See João José Reis, 'Candomblé and Slave Resistance in Nineteenth-Century Bahia', in Luis Nicolau Parés and Roger Sansi (eds.), *Sorcery in the Black Atlantic*, Chicago, IL: University of Chicago Press, 2011, pp. 55–74.

4. Edward Long, *The History of Jamaica*, London: T. Lowndes, 1774, vol. II, p. 451.

5. For further discussion see Kwasi Konadu, *The Akan Diaspora in the Americas*, Oxford: Oxford University Press, 2010, pp. 139–40, 146–7.

6. Jerome Handler and Kenneth Bilby, 'On the Early Use and Origin of the Term "Obeah" in Barbados and the Anglophone Caribbean', *Slavery & Abolition*, 22:2 (2001), pp. 87–100.

7. See Randy Browne, 'Spiritual Power and the Bad Business of Obeah', in Randy Browne, *Surviving Slavery in the British Caribbean*, Philadelphia, PA: University of Pennsylvania Press, 2017, pp. 23–4.

8. See chapter 1 in Stewart, *Three Eyes for the Journey*.

9. Walter Rucker, 'Conjure, Magic and Power: The Influence of Afro-Atlantic Religious Practices on Slave Resistance and Rebellion', *Journal of Black Studies*, 32:1 (September 2001), pp. 89–91.

10. Kofi Boukman Karima, 'Cutting across Space and Time: Obeah's Service to Jamaica's Freedom Struggle', *Africology: The Journal of Pan-African Studies*, 9:4 (July 2016), pp. 17–19.

11. Kelly Wisecup, 'Obeah, Slave Revolt, and Plantation Medicine in the British West Indies', in *Medical Encounters: Knowledge and Identity in Early American Literatures*, Amherst, MA: University of Massachusetts Press, 2013, p. 138.

12. Quoted in John Savage, 'Slave Poison/Slave Medicine: The Persistence of Obeah in Early Nineteenth-Century Martinique', in Diana Paton and Maarit Forde (eds.), *Obeah and Other Powers*, Durham, NC: Duke University Press, 2012, p. 165.

13. William Wells Brown, *My Southern Home*, quoted in Rucker, 'Conjure, Magic and Power', pp. 98–9.

14. *Narrative of the Life of Frederick Douglass*, in Stauffer and Gates (eds.), *The Portable Frederick Douglass*, pp. 62 and 69n.

15. John Blassingame, *The Slave Community: Plantation Life in the Antebellum South*, New York: Oxford University Press, 1972, p. 110.

16. Matthew Lewis, *Journal of a West India Proprietor*, London: John Murray, 1834, pp. 82–3.

17. Wisecup, 'Obeah, Slave Revolt, and Plantation Medicine', p. 140.

18. For a detailed account of one such incident, see Browne, 'Spiritual Power and the Bad Business of Obeah'.

19. Sasha Turner Bryson, 'The Art of Power: Poison and Obeah Accusations and the Struggle for Dominance and Survival in Jamaica's Slave Society', *Caribbean Studies*, 41:2 (July–December 2013), p. 80.

20. Kars, *Blood on the River*, p. 84.

21. Kenneth Bilby and Jerome Handler, 'Obeah: Healing and Protection in West Indian Slave Life', *Journal of Caribbean History*, 38:2 (2004), pp. 153–83.

22. Clarence Maxwell, 'The Horrid Villainy: Sarah Bassett and the Poisoning Conspiracies in Bermuda', *Slavery & Abolition*, 21:3 (2000), pp. 48–74.

23. Quoted in Michael Mullin, *Africa in America*, Chicago, IL: University of Illinois Press, 1992, p. 177.

24. Bryson, 'The Art of Power', pp. 81–2.

25. Garrigus, *Secret among the Blacks*, pp. 34–5.

26. Bryson, 'The Art of Power', pp. 70–71.

27. These two revolts will be discussed more fully in chapter 5.

28. Jerome Handler, 'Slave Medicine and Obeah in Barbados', *New West Indian Guide*, 74:1–2 (2000), p. 64.

29. Rucker, 'Conjure, Magic and Power', pp. 86–9.

30. Walter Rucker, *The River Flows On: Black Resistance, Culture and Identity Formation in Early America*, Baton Rouge, LO: Louisiana State University Press, 2006, pp. 35–6.

31. Walter Rucker, '"Only draw in your countrymen": Akan Culture and

Community in Early New York City', *Afro-Americans in New York Life and History*, 34:2 (2010), p. 103.

32. David Barry Gaspar, 'The Antigua Slave Conspiracy of 1736', *William & Mary Quarterly*, 35 (1978), pp. 308–23.

33. Rucker, '"Only draw in your countrymen"', pp. 78–9.

34. Ibid, pp. 102–8.

35. John Savage, '"Black Magic" and White Terror: Slave Poisoning and Colonial Society in Early 19th Century Martinique', *Journal of Social History*, 40:3 (2007), 635–62.

36. Quoted in Savage, 'Slave Poison/Slave Medicine', p. 156.

37. Bryson, 'The Art of Power', pp. 64–5.

38. Jenny Sharpe, *Ghosts of Slavery*, Minneapolis, MN: University of Minnesota Press, 2003, p. 3.

39. Ibid, p. 7.

40. Karla Gottlieb, *The Mother of Us All*, Trenton, NJ: Africa World Press, 2000, p. 95.

41. Brown, *Tacky's Revolt*, p. 77.

42. Bryan Edwards, *The History, Civil and Commercial, of the British Colonies in the West Indies*, vol. 2, Dublin: Luke White, 1793, p. 88.

43. Rucker, 'Conjure, Magic and Power', p. 87.

44. Edwards, *The History, Civil and Commercial*, vol. 2, p. 92.

45. Helg, *Slave No More*, p. 103.

46. Michael Craton, *Testing the Chains: Resistance to Slavery in the British West Indies*, Ithaca, NY: Cornell University Press, 1983, pp. 138–9.

47. See 'Judicial Proceedings Relative to the Trial and Punishment of Rebels, or Alleged Rebels, in the Island of Jamaica', in *Papers Relating to the Manumission, Government, and Population of Slaves in the West Indies; 1822–1824*, London, 1825, esp. pp. 91, 93, 96, 99–100, 105, and 106.

48. Rediker, *Amistad Rebellion*, p. 24.

49. Mustafa Amin Farooq, 'Legal Representations of Muslim Slaves by American Courts and Legislative Bodies 1650–1861', *Journal of Muslim Minority Affairs*, 37:1 (2017), p. 24.

50. Sylviane Diouf, *Servants of Allah*, New York: NYU Press, 1998, pp. 9 and 22.

51. Alonso Sandoval, quoted in John Tofik Karam, 'African Rebellion and Refuge on the Edge of Empire', in María del Mar Logroño Narbona et al. (eds.), *Crescent Over Another Horizon*, Austin, TX: University of Texas Press, 2015, p. 49.

52. Diouf, *Servants of Allah*, p. 25.

53. Ibid, pp. 60–61.

54. Michael Gomez, 'Muslims in Early America', *Journal of Southern History*, 60:4 (November 1994), pp. 689 and 693; on Bilali's recollections of Massina, see Philip Curtin (ed.), *Africa Remembered: Narratives by West Africans from the Era of the Slave Trade*, Madison, WI: University of Wisconsin Press, 1967, pp. 147–51.

55. Charles Malenfant, *Des colonies, et particulièrement celle de Saint-Domingue*, Paris, 1814, p. 215.

56. Rev. Jean-Baptiste Labat, quoted in Diouf, *Servants of Allah*, p. 74.

57. *The Biography of Mahommah Gardo Baquaqua*, ed. R. Law and P. Lovejoy, Princeton, NJ: Markus Wiener Publishers, 2007, p. 158.

58. Diouf, *Servants of Allah*, pp. 76–7.

59. For further discussion see Mbaye Lo and Carl W. Ernst, *I Cannot Write My Life: Islam, Arabic and Slavery in Omar ibn Said's America*, Chapel Hill, NC: University of North Carolina Press, 2023.

60. Jeffry Halverson, 'West African Islam in Colonial and Antebellum South Carolina', *Journal of Muslim Minority Affairs*, 36:3 (2016), p. 420.

61. Diouf, *Servants of Allah*, pp. 164–5.

62. Charles Ball, *Slavery in the United States*, New York: John S. Taylor, 1837, p. 165.

63. Craton, *Testing the Chains*, p. 48.

64. Diouf, *Servants of Allah*, pp. 94–5.

65. Ibid, pp. 96–7.

66. Halverson, 'West African Islam', pp. 421–2. The shout's wider significance in the American setting will be discussed more fully in chapter 9.

67. The name of a landlocked West African confederation whose subjects were among the principal source of enslaved labour for the Portuguese and Spanish.

68. Erin Woodruff Stone, 'America's First Slave Revolt', *Ethnohistory*, 60:2 (Spring 2013), pp. 195–217.

69. 1532 decree, quoted in Karam, 'African Rebellion and Refuge on the Edge of Empire', p. 48.

70. Taylor, *If We Must Die*, p. 63.

71. Manuel Barcia, 'West African Islam in Colonial Cuba', *Slavery & Abolition*, 35:2 (2014), p. 294.

72. *Affiches Américaines* (22 January 1766), p. 26.

73. Farooq, 'Legal Representations'.

74. Diouf, *Servants of Allah*, p. 113.

75. Gomez, 'Muslims in Early America', p. 684.

76. Ibid, p. 685.

77. Philip Morgan, 'Colonial South Carolina Runaways', in Heuman (ed.), *Out of the House of Bondage*, p. 60.

78. Gomez, 'Muslims in Early America', pp. 687–8.

79. Ibid, p. 688.

80. Fromont, 'Paper, Ink, Vodun', p. 465.

81. Diouf, *Servants of Allah*, pp. 183–4.

82. João José Reis et al., *The Story of Rufino: Slavery, Freedom, and Islam in the Black Atlantic*, New York: Oxford University Press, 2020, p. 209.

83. Walter Hawthorne, *From Africa to Brazil*, New York: Cambridge University Press, 2010, p. 209.

84. Diouf, *Servants of Allah*, pp. 184–6.

85. Dominique Lamiral, *L'Affrique et le peuple Affriquain*, Paris: Dessenne, 1789, pp. 254–5.

86. Manuel Barcia, '"An Islamic Atlantic Revolution": Dan Fodio's *Jihād* and Slave Rebellion in Bahia and Cuba, 1804–1844', *Journal of African Diaspora Archaeology and Heritage*, 2:1 (2013), p. 11.

87. Daniel Domingues da Silva et al., 'The Transatlantic Muslim Diaspora to Latin America in the Nineteenth Century', *Colonial Latin American Review*, 26:4 (2017), p. 533.

88. Corzo, *Runaway Slave Settlements*, pp. 49–62.

89. For a full chronology of these Cuban rebellions from 1798 to 1844, see Appendix 2 in Barcia, *West African Warfare*, pp. 161–5.

90. Barcia, 'West African Islam in Colonial Cuba', p. 300.

91. Barcia, *West African Warfare*, p. 130.

92. Barcia, 'An Islamic Atlantic Revolution', p. 14.

93. Barcia, *West African Warfare*, p. 148. These Cuban insurrections will be discussed more fully in chapter 8.

94. Nikolay Dobronravin, 'Literacy among Muslims in Nineteenth-Century Trinidad and Brazil', in B. A. Mirzai et al. (eds.), *Slavery, Islam and Diaspora*, Trenton, NJ: Africa World Press, 2009, pp. 217–36.

95. João José Reis, *Slave Rebellion in Brazil*, Baltimore, MD: Johns Hopkins Press, 1993, p. 43.

96. Ibid, pp. 66–7.

97. Ibid, pp. 57–8.

98. Barcia, *West African Warfare*, pp. 113, 122, and 130.

99. Diouf, *Servants of Allah*, pp. 222–3.

100. Reis, *Slave Rebellion*, pp. 73–92.

101. Ibid, p. 134.

102. Barcia, *West African Warfare*, p. 101.

103. Diouf, *Servants of Allah*, p. 174.

104. Ibid, p. 186.

105. Ibid.

106. Reis, *Slave Rebellion*, pp. 127–8.

107. Dale Graden, 'An Act "even of public security": Slave Resistance, Social Tensions and the End of the International Slave Trade to Brazil, 1835–1856', *Hispanic American Historical Review*, 76:2 (1996), p. 262.

108. Reis et al., *The Story of Rufino*, pp. 212, 215, and 242.

109. Savage, '"Black Magic" and White Terror', pp. 649–50.

110. Stewart, *Three Eyes for the Journey*, p. 68.

111. Vincent Brown, 'Spiritual Terror and Sacred Authority: The Power of the Supernatural in Jamaican Slave Society', in E. Baptist and S. Camp (eds.), *New Studies in the History of American Slavery*, Athens, GA: University of Georgia Press, 2006, p. 192.

112. [Cynric Williams], *Hamel, the Obeah Man*, London: Hunt and Clarke, 1827, vol. I, p. 29.

113. Ibid, p. 30.

114. [Williams], *Hamel*, vol. II, p. 323.

4: FULL OF RESOLVE AND DETERMINATION

1. Thomas Madiou, *Histoire d'Haïti*, Port-au-Prince: J. Courtois, 1847, vol. I, p. 23. An alternative claim is that Makandal originated from the Kongo region, but this is unlikely, as there was very little Islamic culture in the area.

2. 'Makandal, histoire véritable', *Mercure de France* (September 1787), pp. 102-14.

3. Melvil Bloncourt, 'La colonie française de Saint-Domingue avant la révolution: épisode du Prophète Makandal', *Revue du Monde Colonial, Asiatique et Américain* (July 1864), p. 449.

4. 'Le Mémoire du Juge Courtin' (20 January 1758), ANOM, F/3/88; see also Pierre Pluchon (ed.), *Vaudou, sorciers, empoisonneurs*, Paris: Éditions Karthala, 1987, pp. 215-16.

5. Ibid, pp. 209-10.

6. *Relation d'une conspiration tramée par les nègres dans l'Isle de Saint-Domingue*, Paris, 1758, p. 5.

7. See for example Christina Mobley, 'The Kongolese Atlantic', PhD thesis, Duke University, 2015, which argues that Makandal was a Kongolese spiritual healer and not a political or military leader; see also Garrigus, *Secret among the Blacks*.

8. 'Le Mémoire du Juge Courtin', in Pluchon (ed.), *Vaudou, sorciers, empoisonneurs*, p. 210.

9. Marquis de Rouvray, *Mémoire*, quoted in Mobley, 'The Kongolese Atlantic', p. 297.

10. Fick, *The Making of Haiti*, p. 59.

11. Rachel Beauvoir-Dominique, *Investigations autour du site historique du Bois-Caïman*, Cap-Haïtien: Ministry of Culture, Government of Haiti, 2000, pp. 14 and 51.

12. Robert Schwaller, 'Contested Conquests: African Maroons and the Incomplete Conquest of Hispaniola', *The Americas*, 74:4 (2018), p. 634.

13. Jean Fouchard, *Les marrons de la liberté*, Paris: Éditions de l'École, 1972.

14. Gabriel de Avilez Rocha, 'Maroons in the *Montes*: Toward a Political Ecology of Marronage in the Sixteenth-Century Caribbean', in C. Smith et al. (eds.), *Early Modern Black Diaspora Studies*, London: Palgrave, 2018, p. 19.

15. Crystal Nicole Eddins, *Rituals, Runaways and the Haitian Revolution*, Cambridge: Cambridge University Press, 2022, p. 74.

16. Landers, 'Maroon Women', p. 5.

17. Schwaller, 'Contested Conquests', p. 637.

18. Eddins, *Rituals, Runaways and the Haitian Revolution*, p. 40.

19. Ibid, pp. 44-5.

20. Ibid, p. 58.

21. Ibid, p. 124.

22. Ibid, p. 125.

23. Ibid, pp. 153-162.

24. Fick, *The Making of Haiti*, p. 52.

25. Kofi Barima, 'Militancy and Spirituality: Haiti's Revolutionary Impact on Jamaica's Africans and Afro-Creoles, 1740–1824', *Wadabagei*, 14:1–2 (2013), pp. 85–6.

26. Eddins, *Rituals, Runaways and the Haitian Revolution*, pp. 225–6.

27. Ibid, p. 215.

28. Fick, *The Making of Haiti*, p. 53.

29. Eddins, *Rituals, Runaways and the Haitian Revolution*, p. 263.

30. Ibid, p. 220.

31. See D. Geggus (ed.), *The Haitian Revolution: A Documentary History*, Indianapolis, IN: Hackett, 2014, pp. 22–5.

32. Eddins, *Rituals, Runaways and the Haitian Revolution*, p. 128.

33. Tanguy de la Boissière, *Réflexions impartiales d'un citoyen sur les affaires de Saint-Domingue*, Port-au-Prince, 1789.

34. Fick, *The Making of Haiti*, p. 95.

35. See Robbie Shilliam, 'Race and Revolution at Bwa Kayiman', *Millenium* 45:3 (2017).

36. Fick, *The Making of Haiti*, p. 93.

37. See for example David Geggus, 'Marronage, Voodoo, and the Saint-Domingue Slave Revolt of 1791', *Proceedings of the Meeting of the French Colonial Historical Society*, 15 (1992), pp. 22–35.

38. Franklin Midy, 'Vers l'indépendance des colonies à esclaves d'Amérique: l'exception haïtienne', *Outre-Mers. Revue d'Histoire*, 340–41 (2003), pp. 126–7.

39. Laënnec Hurbon, *Les mystères du vaudou*, Paris: Gallimard, 1993, p. 39.

40. 'A Saint-Domingue seule, le vodou s'est recrée comme la religion de la masse esclave': Midy, 'Vers l'indépendance des colonies', p. 133.

41. Eddins, *Rituals, Runaways and the Haitian Revolution*, p. 295.

42. Fick, *The Making of Haiti,* pp. 105–7.

43. Ibid, p. 100.

44. Madiou, *Histoire d'Haïti*, vol. I, p. 181.

45. See Terry Rey, *The Priest and the Prophetess: Abbé Ouvière, Romaine Rivière, and the Revolutionary Atlantic World*, New York: Oxford University Press, 2017.

46. Gérard Barthélémy, 'Le rôle des Bossales dans l'émergence d'une culture de marronnage en Haïti', *Cahiers d'Études Africaines*, 148 (1997), p. 848.

47. *Affiches Américaines*, Port-au-Prince, no. 91.

48. On the role of women in the Haitian revolution, see Sabine Manigat, 'Les femmes au cours de la période révolutionnaire (1790–1804)', *Revue de la Société Haïtienne d'Histoire et de Géographie*, 210 (2002).

49. Journal of La Phalange Paramilitaries, Léogane, quoted in Geggus (ed.), *Haitian Revolution*, p. 96.

50. 'An End to the Whites', in Fick, *The Making of Haiti*, p. 116.

51. 'Skinny Stick'.

52. December 1785 register, cited in Jean-Louis Donnadieu, 'Nouveaux documents sur la vie de Toussaint Louverture', in *Bulletin de la Société d'Histoire de la Guadeloupe*, 166:7 (2013), p. 133.

53. 'Né dans l'esclavage, mais ayant reçu de la nature l'âme d'un homme libre': Toussaint Louverture report to Directory, 4 September 1797, Archives Nationales (AN), Paris, AFIII 210.

54. On this important point, see Shilliam, 'Race and Revolution at Bwa Kayiman', p. 276.

55. As the French official Kerversau wrote in a report in 1801, Louverture was venerated by his followers 'like some kind of Macanda [*sic*]': 22 March 1801, ANOM, CC9B 23.

56. Geggus (ed.), *Haitian Revolution*, p. 125.

57. Quoted in Sudhir Hazareesingh, *Black Spartacus: The Epic Life of Toussaint Louverture*, London: Allen Lane, 2020, p. 43.

58. Henry Louis Gates, Jr, *The Signifying Monkey*, New York: Oxford University Press, 1988, p. 6.

59. Toussaint Louverture, Camp Turel proclamation, 29 August 1793. AN, AA 53.

60. Toussaint Louverture, letter to Laveaux, 23 May 1797, BNF, NAF 12104.

61. Toussaint Louverture, proclamation, 25 April 1796, cited in Victor Schoelcher, *Vie de Toussaint Louverture*, Paris: Éditions Karthala, 1982, p. 175.

62. Toussaint Louverture, letter to the French Minister of the Navy, 13 April 1799, quoted in *Testament politique de Toussaint Louverture*, Paris, 1855, p. 5.

63. Toussaint's remarks about Jamaica, cited in French report, 22 March 1801, ANOM, CC9B 23; quoted in Geggus (ed.), *Haitian Revolution*, p. 147.

64. Toussaint Louverture, *Réfutation de quelques assertions d'un discours prononcé au Corps Législatif*, Cap-Français, 1797, p. 32.

65. *Constitution Républicaine*, Port-Républicain, 1801.

66. See Judith Kafka, 'Action, Reaction and Interaction: Slave Women in Resistance in the South of Saint-Domingue', *Slavery & Abolition* 18:2 (1997), pp. 48–72.

67. Philippe Roume, 'Moyens proposés au gouvernement français par son agent à Saint-Domingue pour la réorganisation de cette colonie', 11 June 1800, ANOM, CC9 B2.

68. Proclamation of the municipality of Petite-Rivière, 29 October 1798, AN, AFIII 210.

69. See Miriam Franchina, 'Beyond the (Holy) Shroud: A Glimpse into Afro-Catholicism during the Haitian Revolution', *Atlantic Studies*, 21:3 (May 2023), pp. 16–17.

70. Toussaint Louverture, *Réfutation*, pp. 28–9.

71. Michel Laguerre, *Voodoo and Politics in Haiti*, London: Palgrave, 1989, p. 65.

72. For further discussion, see John Thornton, '"I am the subject of the King of Congo": African Ideology in the Haitian Revolution', *Journal of World History*, 4:2 (1993), pp. 181–214.

73. Hazareesingh, *Black Spartacus*, p. 310.

74. *Procès-verbal de l'expédition du Général Toussaint Louverture sur le Mirebalais, 9 Avril 1797*. Archives Départementales de la Gironde, Collection Marcel Chatillon, 61 J 18.

75. Toussaint Louverture, 'Adresse aux officiers, sous-officiers et soldats composant l'armée en marche', 23 January 1798, ANOM, CC9A 19.

76. 'You (whites) cannot wage war successfully against black people': cited in Charles Malenfant, 'Observations sur Saint-Domingue', 11 February 1798, ANOM, CC9A 19.

77. Quoted in Guillaume-Thomas Dufresne, 'Considérations politiques sur la révolution des colonies françaises' (1805), BNF, NAF 4372, f. 291.

78. Jean-Baptiste Mirambeau, 'Victoria', Le Document, 2 (February 1940), p. 107.

79. Philippe Girard, 'Rebelles with a Cause: Women in the Haitian War of Independence', Gender & History, 21:1 (April 2009), p. 69.

80. Ibid, p. 71.

81. Madiou, Histoire d'Haïti, vol. II, p. 222.

82. Leclerc letter to Napoleon Bonaparte, 7 October 1802, in Lettres du Général Leclerc, Paris: Ernest Leroux, 1937, p. 256.

83. Claude Auguste, 'L'Affaire Moïse', Revue de la Société Haïtienne d'Histoire et de Géographie (July–August 1994), pp. 7–55.

84. Geggus (ed.), Haitian Revolution, p. 182.

85. Deborah Jenson, 'Jean-Jacques Dessalines and the African Character of the Haitian Revolution', William and Mary Quarterly, 69:3 (July 2012), pp. 615–38.

86. M. E. Descourtilz, Voyages d'un naturaliste, Paris: Dufart, 1809, Vol. 3, p. 254.

87. Ibid, pp. 208–9.

88. Laurent Dubois, 'Dessalines, Toro d'Haïti', William and Mary Quarterly, 69:3 (July 2012), pp. 547–8.

89. On this theme, see more generally Scott, Common Wind.

90. Geggus (ed.), Haitian Revolution, p. 186.

91. James Sidbury, 'Saint-Domingue in Virginia', Journal of Southern History (1997), p. 541.

92. John Balfour to Henry Dundas, Tobago, 15 February 1794. Correspondence of Henry Dundas, Bodleian Library, Oxford, MSS W.Ind. S8.

93. Quoted in Christer Petley, White Fury: A Jamaican Slave-Holder and the Age of Revolution, Oxford: Oxford University Press, 2018, pp. 176–7.

94. Cited in Scott, Common Wind, p. 180.

95. 'Rebeldia na Bandabou', in Callahan et al. (eds.), Songs of Slavery and Emancipation, pp. 84–5.

96. Quoted in Hazareesingh, Black Spartacus, pp. 327–8.

97. Quoted in Laurent Dubois, 'The Promise of Revolution: Saint-Domingue and the Struggle for Autonomy in Guadeloupe', in D. Geggus (ed.), The Impact of the Haitian Revolution, Columbia, SC: University of South Carolina Press, 2001, pp. 113, 116 and 117.

98. Quoted in Sue Peabody, '"Free upon higher ground"', in D. Geggus and N. Fiering (eds.), The World of the Haitian Revolution, Bloomington, IN: Indiana University Press, 2009, p. 268.

99. Quoted in Donald Hickey, 'America's Response to the Slave Revolt in Haiti', Journal of the Early Republic, 2:4 (Winter 1982), p. 368.

100. Ashil White, *Encountering Revolution: Haiti and the Making of the Early Republic*, Baltimore, MD: Johns Hopkins University Press, 2012, p. 145.

101. Aptheker, *American Negro Slave Revolts*, p. 98.

102. White, *Encountering Revolution*, pp. 146–7.

103. Laveaux letter, 9 September 1795, in Girard Papers, American Philosophical Society, Philadelphia, quoted in ibid, p. 148.

104. Ibid, pp. 144–5.

105. Quoted in Rucker, *The River Flows On*, p. 155.

106. Quoted in Peabody, '"Free upon higher ground"', p. 272.

107. 'Uncle Gabriel, the Negro General', in Callahan et al. (eds.), *Songs of Slavery and Emancipation*, p. 86.

108. Rucker, *The River Flows On*, pp. 141–3.

109. Douglas Egerton, *Gabriel's Rebellion: The Virginia Slave Conspiracies of 1800 and 1802*, Chapel Hill, NC: University of North Carolina Press, 1993, p. 46.

5: LAND OF LIBERTY

1. Quoted in Claudius Fergus, 'The Bicentennial Commemorations: The Dilemma of Abolitionism in the Shadow of the Haitian Revolution', *Caribbean Quarterly*, 56:1–2 (2010), p. 154.

2. Ibid, p. 142.

3. David Eltis, 'The British Contribution to the Nineteenth-Century Transatlantic Slave Trade', *Economic History Review*, 32:2 (1979), p. 211.

4. Report of Martinique captain-general, Fort de France, 10 February 1806, ANOM, COL C8 A112.

5. For an analysis of thirty-one such cases, see Peabody, '"Free upon higher ground"'.

6. Ada Ferrer, 'Haiti, Free Soil, and Antislavery in the Revolutionary Atlantic', *American Historical Review*, 117:1 (February 2012), p. 56.

7. Ibid, p. 62.

8. Ibid, p. 57.

9. Ibid, p. 43.

10. Ibid, p. 63.

11. For an illuminating exploration of this theme from the perspective of Haiti's relations with the Vatican, see Julia Gaffield, 'The Racialization of International Law after the Haitian Revolution', *American Historical Review* (June 2020).

12. Sara Fanning, 'The Roots of Early Black Nationalism', *Slavery & Abolition* 28:1 (April 2007), pp. 61–85.

13. Alexander, *Fear of a Black Republic*, p. 17.

14. Ada Ferrer, 'Speaking of Haiti', in Geggus and Fiering (eds.), *The World of the Haitian Revolution*, p. 240.

15. Hazareesingh, *Black Spartacus*, pp. 329–30.

16. Petition of merchants, April 1814, cited in João José Reis and Flávio dos Santos Gomes, 'Repercussions of the Haitian Revolution in Brazil 1791–1850', in Geggus and Fiering (eds.), *The World of the Haitian Revolution*, p. 288.

17. Quoted in Jeffrey Kerr-Ritchie, 'Slave Revolt across Borders', *Journal of African Diaspora Archaeology and Heritage*, 2:1 (2013), p. 68.

18. Reis and Gomes, 'Repercussions of the Haitian Revolution in Brazil', p. 284.

19. 'The bread we have eaten / Is the white man's flesh / The wine we have drunk / Is the white man's blood': quoted in Kerr-Ritchie, 'Slave Revolt across Borders', p. 67.

20. Quoted in Barima, 'Militancy and Spirituality', p. 79.

21. Ibid, p. 89.

22. 'Judicial Proceedings Relative to the Trial and Punishment of Rebels, or Alleged Rebels, in Jamaica', pp. 89 and 93.

23. Ibid, p. 109.

24. Robert Paquette, 'A Horde of Brigands? The Great Louisiana Slave Revolt of 1811 Reconsidered', *Historical Reflections*, 35:1 (March 2009), pp. 81–2.

25. Nathan Buman, 'To Kill Whites: The 1811 Louisiana Slave Insurrection', Master of Arts thesis, Department of History, Louisiana State University, 2008, p. 63.

26. Quoted in Alexander, *Fear of a Black Republic*, p. 32.

27. Buman, 'To Kill Whites', pp. 56–7.

28. Ibid, p. 71.

29. Paquette, 'A Horde of Brigands?', p. 78.

30. Buman, 'To Kill Whites', p. 71.

31. Alexander, *Fear of a Black Republic*, p. 32.

32. Buman, 'To Kill Whites', p. 85.

33. Ignace Marion, *Expédition de Bolivar*, Port-au-Prince, 1849, p. 30.

34. Sibylle Fischer, 'Bolívar in Haiti: Republicanism in the Revolutionary Atlantic', in Carla Calargé et al. (eds.), *Haiti and the Americas*, Jackson, MS: University Press of Mississippi, 2013, pp. 38–41.

35. Ibid, p. 43.

36. Quoted in Geggus (ed.), *Haitian Revolution*, p. 197.

37. Thomas Madiou, quoted in Sibylle Fischer, 'Specters of the Republic: The Case of Manuel Piar', *Journal of Latin American Cultural Studies*, 27:3 (2018), p. 306.

38. Ferrer, 'Haiti, Free Soil, and Antislavery', p. 61.

39. Letter cited in Paul Grunebaum-Ballin, *Henri Grégoire, l'ami des hommes de toutes les couleurs*, Paris, 1948, p. 243.

40. Civique de Gastine (pseudonym for Eustache Toulotte), *Lettre au Roi sur l'indépendance de la République d'Haïti*, Paris, 1821, p. 4.

41. James O'Neil Spady, 'Denmark Vesey and the 1822 Charleston Antislavery Uprising: New Themes and New Methods', in Spady (ed.), *Fugitive Movements*, pp. 39–40.

42. Bernard Powers Jr, 'Denmark Vesey, South Carolina and Haiti', in Spady (ed.), *Fugitive Movements*, p. 20.

43. The documents around the conspiracy have been gathered in the collection edited by Douglas Egerton and Robert Paquette, *The Denmark Vesey Affair: A Documentary History*, Gainesville, FL: University Press of Florida, 2017.

44. Rucker, *The River Flows On*, pp. 169–76.

45. His third wife Susan was free.

46. Spady, 'Denmark Vesey', pp. 42–5.

47. Jeremy Schipper, *Denmark Vesey's Bible*, Princeton, NJ: Princeton University Press, 2022.

48. Spady, 'Denmark Vesey', p. 40.

49. Quoted in Rucker, *The River Flows On*, p. 164.

50. Quoted in Powers, 'Denmark Vesey, South Carolina and Haiti', p. 27.

51. Rucker, *The River Flows On*, p. 169.

52. David Robertson, *Denmark Vesey*, New York: Vintage, 2000, p. 51.

53. Powers, 'Denmark Vesey, South Carolina and Haiti', p. 28.

54. Ibid.

55. Ibid.

56. Quoted in Alexander, *Fear of a Black Republic*, pp. 38–9.

57. Powers, 'Denmark Vesey, South Carolina and Haiti', p. 30.

58. Stuckey, *Slave Culture*, pp. 47–8.

59. Powers, 'Denmark Vesey, South Carolina and Haiti', p. 31.

60. Quoted in Spady, 'Denmark Vesey', p. 46.

61. Neil Vaz, 'Maroon Emancipationists: Dominica's Africans and Igbos in the Age of Revolution', *Journal of Caribbean History*, 53:1 (2019), pp. 35–6.

62. Lennox Honychurch, *In the Forests of Freedom: The Fighting Maroons of Dominica*, Jackson, MS: University Press of Mississippi, 2019, pp. 74–82.

63. Vaz, 'Maroon Emancipationists', pp. 43 and 47.

64. Honychurch, *In the Forests of Freedom*, pp. 84–5.

65. Vaz, 'Maroon Emancipationists', pp. 34–5.

66. Ibid, p. 33.

67. Honychurch, *In the Forests of Freedom*, p. 142.

68. Ibid, p. 158.

69. Ibid, p. 162.

70. Ibid, p. 143.

71. Quoted in Vaz, 'Maroon Emancipationists', p. 45.

72. Ibid, pp. 29–30.

73. Honychurch, *In the Forests of Freedom*, p. 94.

74. Hilary Beckles, 'The Slave-Drivers' War: Bussa and the 1816 Barbados Slave Rebellion', *Boletín de Estudios Latinoamericanos y del Caribe*, 39 (December 1985), p. 86.

75. Ibid, p. 106.

76. Ibid, pp. 91–2.

77. Hilary Beckles, *Natural Rebels*, NJ: Rutgers University Press, 1989, pp. 171–2.

78. Beckles, 'The Slave-Drivers' War', p. 90.

79. Ibid, p. 91.

80. Ibid, p. 92.

81. Hilary Beckles, *Bussa: The 1816 Revolution in Barbados*, Cave Hill, Barbados: University of the West Indies, 1998, pp. 20–21.

82. Lilian McNaught, 'The Barbados Slave Revolt', Masters by Research in History thesis, University of Exeter, 2017, p. 15.
83. Ibid, p. 21.
84. Hilary Beckles, *Black Rebellion in Barbados: The Struggle against Slavery, 1627–1838*, Bridgetown: Carib Research and Publications, 1987, p. 97.
85. Craton, *Testing the Chains*, p. 258.
86. Barbados Select Committee Report, 1818, p. 26.
87. Patrick Taylor, 'The Mobility of the Haitian Revolution', *The Black Scholar*, 51:2 (2021), p. 17.
88. Examination of slave Daniel, in the Barbados Select Committee Report, 1818, quoted in Beckles, *Bussa*, p. 54.
89. Barbados Select Committee Report, 1818, p. 27.
90. Beckles, 'The Slave-Drivers' War', p. 104.
91. Ibid, p. 109.
92. Ibid, pp. 99–100.
93. Quoted in Taylor, 'The Mobility of the Haitian Revolution', p. 11.
94. Barbados Select Committee Report, 1818, p. 29.
95. Ibid, p. 34.
96. Ibid, p. 28.
97. B. W. Higman, *Slave Populations of the British Caribbean*, Baltimore, MD: Johns Hopkins University Press, 1984, p. 116.
98. The Jamaican uprising will be examined in chapter 6.
99. Emilia Viotti da Costa, *Crowns of Glory, Tears of Blood: The Demerara Slave Rebellion of 1823*, New York: Oxford University Press, 1994, pp. 196–7.
100. Ibid, p. 222.
101. Ibid, p. 240.
102. Ibid, pp. 180–82.
103. Ibid, pp. 171–2, 196–7.
104. Ibid, p. 193.
105. See chapter 3 in Konadu, *The Akan Diaspora in the Americas*.
106. Da Costa, *Crowns of Glory, Tears of Blood*, p. 113.
107. Ashli White, *Revolutionary Things: Material Culture and Politics in the Late Eighteenth-Century Atlantic World*, New Haven, CT: Yale University Press, 2023.
108. 'Recognition March of the Independence of Hayti', in Callahan et al. (eds.), *Songs of Slavery and Emancipation*, p. 91.
109. Craton, *Testing the Chains*, p. 261.
110. Da Costa, *Crowns of Glory, Tears of Blood*, p. 226.
111. Buman, 'To Kill Whites', pp. 8–9.
112. Honychurch, *In the Forests of Freedom*, pp. 161–2.
113. Genovese, *From Rebellion to Revolution*.
114. Getachew, 'Universalism after the Post-Colonial Turn'.
115. Spady, 'Denmark Vesey', p. 48.
116. Quoted from Archie Epps, 'A Negro Separatist Movement', *Harvard Review*, IV:1 (Summer–Fall 1956), p. 75.

6: MAN AND BROTHER

1. Trial of Samuel Sharpe, testimony of Robert Rose, 19 April 1832, National Archives, Kew, London, CO 137/182, folio 373.

2. Tom Zoellner, *Island on Fire: The Revolt that Ended Slavery in the British Empire*, Cambridge, MA: Harvard University Press, 2020, p. 231.

3. William A. Green, *British Slave Emancipation*, Oxford: Oxford University Press, 1991, p. 115.

4. The beneficiaries are listed on the database curated by the Centre for the Study of the Legacies of British Slavery at University College London: https://www.ucl.ac.uk/lbs/project/details

5. Berg and Hudson, *Slavery, Capitalism and the Industrial Revolution*, p. 10.

6. Green, *British Slave Emancipation*.

7. See for example Theodore Foulks, *Eighteen Months in Jamaica: With Recollections of the Late Rebellion*, London and Bristol, 1833.

8. Rebecca Schneider, 'Black Literacy and Resistance in Jamaica', *Social and Economic Studies*, 67:1 (2018), p. 57.

9. Abigail Bakan, *Ideology and Class Conflict in Jamaica*, Montreal: McGill University Press, 1990, pp. 55–6.

10. Stewart, *Three Eyes for the Journey*, p. 106.

11. Ibid, pp. 104, 105, and 129.

12. Henry Bleby, *Death Struggles of Slavery*, London, 1853, p. 8.

13. Ibid, p. 111.

14. Quoted in Mary Reckord, 'The Jamaica Slave Rebellion of 1831', *Past and Present*, 40 (July 1968), p. 115.

15. Bleby, *Death Struggles of Slavery*, p. 112.

16. Craton, *Testing the Chains*, p. 301.

17. Bleby, *Death Struggles of Slavery*, p. 116.

18. Quoted in Zoellner, *Island on Fire*, p. 85.

19. For further discussion, see Simon Newman, *Freedom Seekers: Escaping from Slavery in Restoration London*, London: University of London Press, 2022.

20. See more generally William Pettigrew, *Freedom's Debt: The Royal African Company and the Politics of the Atlantic Slave Trade*, Chapel Hill, NC: University of North Carolina Press, 2013.

21. Paula Dumas, *Proslavery Britain: Fighting for Slavery in an Era of Abolition*, Houndmills: Palgrave, 2016, p. 25.

22. James Walvin, *The Zong: A Massacre, the Law and the End of Slavery*, New Haven, CT: Yale University Press, 2011.

23. See for example *Select Parts of the Holy Bible, For the Use of the Negro Slaves in the British West-India Islands*, London, 1807.

24. Jerome Handler, 'Escaping Slavery in a Caribbean Plantation Society: Marronage in Barbados, 1650s–1830s', *New West Indian Guide*, 71:3/4 (1997), p. 187.

25. Berg and Hudson, *Slavery, Capitalism and the Industrial Revolution*, pp. 222–8.

26. See for example William Fox, *An Address to the People of Great Britain on the Propriety of Abstaining from West India Sugar and Rum*, 10th edition, London, 1791; and *No Rum, No Sugar! Or The Voice of Blood*, London, 1792.
27. Dumas, *Proslavery Britain*, p. 35.
28. Ibid, p. 42.
29. Ibid, p. 20.
30. See notably the pamphlet *Truth: Addressed to the People at large, containing Some Strictures on the English Jacobins, and the Evidence of Lord McCartney and Others, before the House of Lords, respecting the Slave Trade*, London, 1792.
31. Dumas, *Proslavery Britain*, p. 23.
32. Ibid, p. 31.
33. Quoted in ibid, p. 47.
34. See Michael Taylor, *The Interest: How the British Establishment Resisted the Abolition of Slavery*, London: Bodley Head, 2020.
35. Dexter Gabriel, *Jubilee's Experiment: The British West Indies and American Abolitionism*, Cambridge: Cambridge University Press, 2023, p. 23.
36. Dumas, *Proslavery Britain*, pp. 149–50.
37. Ibid, p. 121.
38. *The Speech of the Right Honourable William Pitt, on a Motion for the Abolition of the Slave Trade, in the House of Commons, on Monday the Second of April, 1792*, London, 1792, p. 3.
39. Charles Crawford, *Observations upon Slavery*, Tunbridge Wells, n.d. [1785], p. 1.
40. William Roscoe, *A General View of the African Slave-Trade, demonstrating its Injustice and Impolicy*, London, 1788.
41. J. R. Oldfield, 'Antislavery Sentiment in Children's Literature, 1750–1850', *Slavery & Abolition*, 10:1 (1989), pp. 44–59.
42. See Srividhya Swaminathan, *Debating the Slave Trade: Rhetoric of British National Identity, 1759–1815*, Farnham: Ashgate, 2009.
43. See more generally Michael E. Woods, 'A Theory of Moral Outrage: Indignation and Eighteenth-Century British Abolitionism', *Slavery & Abolition*, 36:4 (2015), pp. 662–83.
44. William Wilberforce, *A Letter on the Abolition of the Slave Trade*, London, 1807, p. 259.
45. Ibid.
46. Quoted in Gabriel, *Jubilee's Experiment*, p. 19.
47. David Hume, 'Of National Characters', in *Essays, Moral, Political and Literary*, ed. E. Miller, Indianapolis: Liberty Fund, 1985, p. 208, n. 10; Immanuel Kant, 'Observations on the Feeling of the Beautiful and Sublime', in G. Zöller and R. B. Louden (eds.), *Anthropology, History and Education*, Cambridge and New York: Cambridge University Press, 2007, p. 59.
48. Long, *History of Jamaica*, vol. 3, p. 353. For a comprehensive discussion of Long's views of slavery, see Catherine Hall, *Lucky Valley: Edward Long and the History of Racial Capitalism*, Cambridge: Cambridge University Press, 2024.

49. Quoted in Gabriel, *Jubilee's Experiment*, p. 28.

50. Thomas Clarkson, *The Substance of the Evidence of Sundry Persons*, London, 1788; see also Leonora Warren, 'Insurrection at Sea: Violence, the Slave Trade and the Rhetoric of Abolition', *Atlantic Studies*, 10:2 (2013), pp. 197–210.

51. Dumas, *Proslavery Britain*, p. 43.

52. Kris Manjapra, *Black Ghost of Empire*, London: Allen Lane, 2022, p. 81.

53. Zoellner, *Island on Fire*, pp. 29–30.

54. Thomas Clarkson, *An Essay on the Impolicy of the African Slave Trade*, London, 1788, p. 115.

55. See Wayne Ackerson, *The African Institution (1807–1827) and the Antislavery Movement in Great Britain*, Lewiston, NY: E. Mellen Press, 2005.

56. Wilberforce, *Letter*, p. 328.

57. Thomas Clarkson, *The True State of the Case, respecting the Insurrection at St. Domingo*, Ipswich, 1792.

58. Paul Clammer, *Black Crown: Henri Christophe, the Haitian Revolution and the Caribbean's Forgotten Kingdom*, London: Hurst, 2023, pp. 250–53.

59. *The Correspondence of William Wilberforce*, London: John Murray, 1840, vol. 1, pp. 363, 375, and 384–5.

60. Ibid, p. 387.

61. David Geggus, 'Haiti and the Abolitionists', in D. Richardson (ed.), *Abolition and its Aftermath: The Historical Context, 1790–1916*, London: Frank Cass, 1985, p. 123.

62. See Joseph la Hausse de Lalouvière, 'A Business Archive of the French Illegal Slave Trade in the Nineteenth Century', *Past and Present*, 252:1 (August 2021), pp. 139–77.

63. Seymour Drescher, *The Mighty Experiment*, Oxford: Oxford University Press, 2002, pp. 117–21.

64. Clarkson letter to Christophe, 26 August 1818, in E. Griggs and C. Prator (eds.), *Henry Christophe and Thomas Clarkson: A Correspondence*, Berkeley, CA: University of California Press, 1952, p. 113.

65. Wilberforce, *Correspondence*, vol. 1, p. 382.

66. Letter to Lord Holland, 11 December 1820, quoted in Ackerson, *African Institution*, p. 256.

67. Clarkson letter to Christophe, 7 September 1819, in Griggs and Prator (eds.), *Henry Christophe and Thomas Clarkson*, pp. 154–5.

68. See Clarkson's letter to his French friend Baron Turckheim in March 1820, quoted in Marlene Daut, *First and Last King of Haiti: The Rise and Fall of Henry Christophe*, New York: Alfred Knopf, 2025, p. 459.

69. Manjapra, *Black Ghost of Empire*, p. 76.

70. On Sancho's life, see Peter Fryer, *Staying Power: The History of Black People in Britain*, London: Pluto Press, pp. 93–8.

71. Ryan Hanley, 'Calvinism, Proslavery and James Albert Ukawsaw Gronniosaw', *Slavery & Abolition*, 36:2 (2015), p. 375.

72. James Albert Ukawsaw Gronniosaw, *A Narrative of the Most Remarkable Particulars in the Life of James Albert Ukawsaw Gronniosaw, an African Prince, as Related by Himself*, Bath: W. Gye, 1791, p. 9.

73. Hanley, 'Calvinism', p. 366.

74. Gronniosaw, *Narrative*, pp. 8.

75. Ibid, p. 14.

76. Hanley, 'Calvinism', p. 374.

77. James Oldfield, *Popular Politics and British Anti-Slavery*, London: Routledge, 1998, p. 125.

78. On this theme see Bryan C. Williams, 'Olaudah Equiano's Enchantments', *Early American Literature*, 58:2 (2023), pp. 337–62.

79. Equiano, *Interesting Narrative*, p. 234.

80. Ibid, pp. 234–5.

81. Vincent Caretta, 'Olaudah Equiano, Phillis Wheatley Peters, and the Black Evangelical Experience', in J. Yeager (ed.), *The Oxford Handbook of Early Evangelicalism*, Oxford: Oxford University Press, 2022, pp. 611–12.

82. Equiano, *Interesting Narrative*, p. 190.

83. Ibid, pp. 190–91.

84. Vincent Caretta, *Equiano the African: Biography of a Self-Made Man*, Atlanta, GA: The University of Georgia Press, 2005.

85. Hakim Adi, *African and Caribbean People*, London: Allen Lane, 2022, p. 93.

86. See for example his letter to Thomas Hardy, Edinburgh, 28 May 1792, in Fryer, *Staying Power*, Appendix A.

87. Equiano, *Interesting Narrative*, p. 34.

88. Ibid, p. 42.

89. Ibid, p. 45.

90. A shortened version of the text, with some additional material, was published in 1791.

91. Cugoano, *Thoughts and Sentiments*, pp. 30–31.

92. Ibid, p. 13.

93. Ibid, pp. 64, 130, 129.

94. Ibid., p. 84.

95. Ibid, p. 31.

96. Ibid., pp. 30–31.

97. Schneider, 'Black Literacy and Resistance in Jamaica', p. 57.

98. Cugoano, *Thoughts and Sentiments*, p. 137.

99. Ibid, pp. 26–8.

100. Ibid, pp. 12 and 138.

101. Ibid, pp. 148, 119, 76, 143, 133.

102. Fryer, *Staying Power*, pp. 106 and 108.

103. Ibid, p. 108.

104. Cugoano, *Thoughts and Sentiments*, p. 132.

105. Fryer, *Staying Power*, p. 101.

106. William Wilberforce, *An Appeal to the Religion, Justice and Humanity of the Inhabitants of the British Empire, in Behalf of the Negro Slaves in the West Indies*, London, 1823, p. 1.

107. See Simon Schama, *Rough Crossings: Britain, the Slaves and the American Revolution*, London: BBC Books, 2005, p. 376.

108. On the West Africa Squadron, see Mary Wills, *Envoys of Abolition: British Naval Officers and the Campaign against the Slave Trade in West Africa*, Liverpool: Liverpool University Press, 2019.

109. See Padraic Scanlan, *Freedom's Debtors: British Antislavery in Sierra Leone in the Age of Revolution*, New Haven, CT: Yale University Press, 2017.

110. Manjapra, *Black Ghost of Empire*, pp. 160–61.

111. Thomas Clarkson, *Thoughts on the Necessity of Improving the Condition of the Slaves in the British Colonies, with a View to Their Ultimate Emancipation*, London, 1823, p. 32.

112. Wilberforce, *An Appeal*, pp. 35–6.

113. Taylor, *The Interest*, p. 113.

114. Quoted in Gabriel, *Jubilee's Experiment*, p. 25.

115. Dumas, *Proslavery Britain*, p. 11.

116. Clarkson, *Thoughts*, p. 26.

117. Ibid, p. 31.

118. Ibid, p. 27.

119. Ibid, p. 31.

120. Ibid, p. 29.

121. Vijaya Teelock, *Mauritian History: From its Beginnings to Modern Times*, Moka: Mahatma Gandhi Institute, 2009, p. 183.

122. Tyler Yank, 'Slave Protection and Resistance in Colonial Mauritius', 1829–1830, in *Slaving Zones: Cultural Identities, Ideologies, and Institutions in the Evolution of Global Slavery*, Studies in Global Slavery 4, ed. Jeff Fynn-Paul and Damian Alan Pargas, Leiden: Brill, 2018, pp. 227–8; on the limits of the recourse offered by the Protector over the 1832–5 period, see Vijaya Teelock, *Bitter Sugar: Sugar and Slavery in 19th-Century Mauritius*, Moka: Mahatma Gandhi Institute, 1998, pp. 224–5.

123. *The London Missionary Society's Report of the Proceedings against the Late Rev. J. Smith*, London, 1824, p. vii.

124. Charlotte Sussman, 'Women and the Politics of Sugar', *Representations*, 48 (Autumn 1994), p. 60.

125. [Elizabeth Heyrick], *Immediate, Not Gradual Abolition . . .*, London, 1824, p. 6.

126. Ibid, pp. 3–4.

127. Ibid, pp. 6 and 11.

128. Ibid, pp. 8, 13, and 14.

129. Ibid, p. 11.

130. Ibid, pp. 16 and 21.

131. Ibid, pp. 5 and 7.

132. Ibid, p. 15.

133. Ibid, p. 19.

134. Ibid.

135. Julie Holcomb, *Moral Commerce: Quakers and the Transatlantic Boycott of the Slave Labor Economy*, Ithaca, NY: Cornell University Press, 2016, p. 90.

136. Clare Midgley, *Women against Slavery: The British Campaigns, 1780–1870*, London: Routledge, 1992, p. 202.

137. Holcomb, *Moral Commerce*, p. 100.

138. Gabriel, *Jubilee's Experiment*, p. 31.

139. Marika Sherwood, *After Abolition: Britain and the Slave Trade since 1807*, London: I.B. Tauris, 2007, pp. 147 and 149.

140. Alexander McDonnell, quoted in Dumas, *Proslavery Britain*, p. 60.

141. See Richard Huzzey, *Freedom Burning: Anti-Slavery and Empire in Victorian Britain*, Ithaca, NY, and London: Cornell University Press, 2012.

142. Eric Williams, *Capitalism and Slavery*, Chapel Hill, NC: University of North Carolina Press, 1994.

143. Ibid, pp. 126–7. The only exception here was the United States, where slavers received nothing.

144. Richard B. Allen, 'Marronage and the Maintenance of Public Order in Mauritius', *Slavery & Abolition*, 4:3 (1983), p. 216.

145. Taylor, *The Interest*, p. 301.

146. Julie Saville, 'Rites and Power: Reflections on Slavery, Freedom and Political Ritual', *Slavery & Abolition*, 20:1 (1999), pp. 84–5.

147. Petition of rebel leaders, 10 October 1865, National Archives, Kew, London, CO 137/394, folios 482–8.

148. For a contemporary journalist's view of the 1865 rebellion, see Stephen Russell, 'Slavery Dies Hard: A Radical Perspective on the Morant Bay Rebellion in Jamaica', *Slavery & Abolition*, 43:1 (2022), pp. 185–204.

149. Seymour Drescher, *Abolitionism: A History of Slavery and Antislavery*, New York: Cambridge University Press, 2009, p. 254.

150. For a local study focused on abolitionism in Plymouth, see Richard Huzzey, 'A Microhistory of British Antislavery Petitioning', *Social Science History*, 43 (Fall 2019), pp. 599–623.

151. On this point, see Wilberforce, *An Appeal, passim*.

152. 1813 speech in Parliament, quoted in Andrea Major, *Slavery, Abolitionism and Empire in India*, Liverpool: Liverpool University Press, 2012, p. 257.

153. Quoted in Geggus, 'Haiti and the Abolitionists', p. 131.

154. Manjapra, *Black Ghost of Empire*, p. 93.

155. [Heyrick], *Immediate, Not Gradual Abolition*, p. 5.

7: THE RIGHTS OF MAN ARE INALIENABLE

1. Jeremy Popkin, 'The French Revolution's Other Island', in Geggus and Fiering (eds.), *The World of the Haitian Revolution*, p. 207.

2. See chapter 4.

3. See Bernard Gainot, 'Le général Laveaux, gouverneur de Saint-Domingue, député néo-jacobin', *Annales Historiques de la Révolution Française*, 278 (1989), pp. 433–54.

4. Christian Schneider, 'Le colonel Vincent, officier du génie à Saint-Domingue', *Annales Historiques de la Révolution Française*, 329 (July–September 2002), pp. 101–22.

5. Laurent Dubois, 'The Price of Liberty: Victor Hugues and the Administration of Freedom in Guadeloupe', *William and Mary Quarterly*, 56:2 (April 1999), p. 389.

6. Bernard Moitt, 'Slave Resistance in Guadeloupe and Martinique', *Journal of Caribbean History*, 25:2 (January 1991), p. 143.

7. Quoted in François de Kerversau, report to French government, 22 March 1801, ANOM, CC9B 23.

8. Report to Directory, 27 January 1798, AN, AFIII 210.

9. Letter to Minister of the Navy, Paris, 8 December 1799, ANOM, CC9A 23.

10. Burnel report, 7 Germinal an VII, quoted in Yves Bénot, *La Guyane sous la Révolution*, Kourou: Ibis Rouge Éditions, 1997, p. 165.

11. *Discours prononcé par Laveaux sur l'anniversaire du 16 Pluviôse an II*, Corps Législatif, séance du 16 Pluviôse an VII, Paris, 1799, p. 2.

12. Hazareesingh, *Black Spartacus*, p. 175.

13. Marcel Dorigny and Bernard Gainot, *La Société des Amis des Noirs*, Paris: UNESCO, 1998, pp. 43 and 45.

14. *Règlements de la Société des Amis des Noirs*, Paris, 1789, pp. 2 and 6.

15. Ibid, pp. 8–9.

16. Minutes of 8 April 1788 meeting, quoted in Jean-Pierre Barlier, *La Société des Amis des Noirs 1788–1791*, Paris: L'Amandier, 2010, p. 94.

17. Condorcet, *Réflexions sur l'esclavage des nègres*, first published in 1781, and republished in 1788, quoted in Sala-Molins, *Dark Side of the Light*, p. 18.

18. See Françoise Thésée, 'Autour de la Société des Amis des Noirs: Clarkson, Mirabeau et l'abolition de la traite', *Présence Africaine*, 125 (1983), pp. 3–82.

19. Lawrence Jennings, 'The Interaction of French and British Antislavery, 1789–1848', *Proceedings of the Meeting of the French Colonial Historical Society*, 15 (1992), pp. 82–3.

20. Marcel Dorigny, 'La Société des Amis des Noirs et les projets de colonisation en Afrique', *Annales Historiques de la Révolution Française*, 293–4 (July–December 1993), p. 425.

21. François Barbé de Marbois report, 10 October 1789, quoted in Geggus (ed.), *Haitian Revolution*, p. 76.

22. Frédéric Régent, *La France et ses esclaves*, Paris: Grasset, 2007, pp. 233–4.

23. Moitt, 'Slave Resistance in Guadeloupe and Martinique', p. 140.

24. Ibid.

25. Régent, *La France et ses esclaves*, pp. 233–4.

26. Henri-Baptiste Grégoire, *Lettre aux citoyens de couleur et nègres libres*, Paris, 1791, p. 12.

27. *Adresse à l'Assemblée Nationale pour l'abolition de la traite des noirs, par la Société des Amis des Noirs*. Paris, February 1790, pp. 2–4.

28. *Adresse de la Société des Amis des Noirs à l'Assemblée Nationale*, Paris, March 1791, p. 76.

29. Sala-Molins, *Dark Side of the Light*, p. 128.

30. Dorigny and Gainot, *La Société des Amis des Noirs*, p. 14.

31. Brissot, *Discours sur un project de décret relatif à la révolte des noirs*, Paris, October 1791, pp. 8 and 12.

32. Ibid, pp. 16–17.

33. Décret de la Convention Nationale, 1794, in Geggus (ed.), *Haitian Revolution*, p. 112.

34. [François Barbé de Marbois], *Réflexions sur la colonie de Saint-Domingue*, vol. II, Paris, 1796, p. 99.

35. Étienne Laveaux, *Réponse aux calomnies de Viénot Vaublanc, colon à Saint-Domingue*, Paris, 1797, p. 27.

36. For a full analysis, see Hazareesingh, *Black Spartacus*, pp. 122–3.

37. Gainot, 'Le général Laveaux', p. 451.

38. Quoted in Antoine-Clair Thibaudeau, *Mémoires sur le Consulat*, Paris, 1827, pp. 120–21.

39. See Yves Bénot and Marcel Dorigny (eds.), *Rétablissement de l'esclavage dans les colonies françaises*, Paris, 2003.

40. Dorigny and Gainot, *La Société des Amis des Noirs*, p. 311.

41. Ibid, pp. 344–5, n. 50.

42. Dubois, 'The Price of Liberty', p. 391.

43. Dorigny and Gainot, *La Société des Amis des Noirs*, pp. 319 and 326.

44. *Compte-rendu de la cérémonie commémorative du décret d'abolition, organisée le 16 pluviôse an VII*, quoted in Dorigny and Gainot, *La Société des Amis des Noirs*, p. 393.

45. Abbé Grégoire, *De la noblesse de peau*, Paris, 1826, p. 69.

46. Régent, *La France et ses esclaves*, p. 314.

47. Quoted in Laurent Dubois, *A Colony of Citizens: Revolution and Slave Emancipation in the French Caribbean 1787–1804*, Chapel Hill, NC: University of North Carolina Press, 2004, p. 392.

48. Dubois, 'The Promise of Revolution', p. 127.

49. See Oruno Lara, *La Guadeloupe dans l'histoire*, Paris: L'Harmattan, 1979, pp. 137–8.

50. Moitt, 'Slave Resistance in Guadeloupe and Martinique', pp. 144–5. Solitude's life and struggle were presented in the Introduction.

51. Ibid, p. 149.

52. Régent, *La France et ses esclaves*, p. 267.

53. Moitt, 'Slave Resistance in Guadeloupe and Martinique', pp. 148–9; on the use of criminal courts (both ordinary and special) to prosecute enslaved men and women accused of 'rebellion' between 1802 and 1806, see Elyssa Gage, 'The Re-Enslavement of Guadeloupe: Criminal Courts in the Re-Establishment of Slavery, 1802–1806', *Slavery & Abolition* (2024), pp. 303–24.

54. Jacques Adélaïde-Merlande, 'Lendemains de Baimbridge et Matouba', in Michel Martin and Alain Yacou (eds.), *Mourir pour les Antilles*, Paris: Éditions Caribéennes, 1991, p. 206.

55. Dubois, 'The Promise of Revolution', p. 128.

56. Dessalines proclamation, 28 April 1804.

57. Monique Pouliquen, 'L'esclavage subi, aboli, rétabli en Guyane de 1789 à 1809', in Philippe Hrodĕj (ed.), *L'esclave et les plantations*, Rennes: Presses Universitaires de Rennes, 2019, pp. 241–60.

58. Hugues memorandum, 8 December 1803, cited in Françoise Thésée, 'Un mémoire inédit de Victor Hugues sur la Guyane', *Revue Française d'Histoire d'Outre-Mer*, 209 (1970), p. 472.

59. Gabriel Debien (ed.), *Trois documents d'histoire Antillaise: Un Nantais à la chasse des marrons en Guyane*, Nantes, 1971, pp. 168–9.

60. Eugène Epailly, *Esclavage et résistance en Guyane française*, Cayenne: L'Harmattan, 2005, pp. 56–7.

61. Serge Mam Lam Fouck, 'La résistance au rétablissement de l'esclavage en Guyane française', in Bénot and Dorigny (eds.), *Rétablissement de l'esclavage dans les Antilles françaises*, pp. 261 and 265.

62. Debien (ed.), *Trois documents*, pp. 168–9.

63. 'Interrogatoire de Télémaque dit Congo Rouge' and 'Interrogatoire de Catherine', in Dominique Rogers (ed.), *Voix d'esclaves*, Paris, 2021, p. 122.

64. Debien (ed.), *Trois documents*, pp. 171–2.

65. Ibid.

66. Régent, *La France et ses esclaves*, p. 276.

67. Pouliquen, 'L'esclavage subi', p. 263.

68. For an example from Guadeloupe, see *Cahier de Marronnage du Moule (1845–1848)*, Basse-Terre: Société d'Histoire de la Guadeloupe, 1996.

69. On Martinique, see Albanie Burand, *L'esclave avait-il une âme? La fête servile à la Martinique dans la première moitié du XIXe siècle*, Matoury: Ibis Rouge Éditions, 2009.

70. Casimir Dugoujon, *Lettres sur l'esclavage dans les colonies françaises*, Paris: Pagnerre, 1845, pp. 94–6.

71. On the slave testimonies gathered during the trial of Joséphat, see 'Joséphat, empoisonneur à l'arsenic', in Rogers (ed.), *Voix d'esclaves*, pp. 127–43.

72. For a more detailed analysis, see Geneviève Leti, 'L'empoisonnement aux Antilles françaises à l'époque de l'esclavage (1724–1848)', in Hrodĕj (ed.), *L'esclave et les plantations*, pp. 209–27.

73. See Nagapen, *Le marronnage à l'Isle de France – Ile Maurice*, pp. 105–46.

74. Ibid, p. 205.

75. Ibid, p. 207.

76. Ibid, p. 206.

77. Ibid, p. 209.

78. Bernard Gainot, 'Une construction impériale: le Code Decaen à l'Île de France (1803–1810)', in F. Régent et al. (eds.), *Les colonies, la Révolution française, la loi*, Rennes: Presses Universitaires de Rennes, 2014, p. 182.

79. Deryck Scarr, *Slaving and Slavery in the Indian Ocean*, Houndmills: Macmillan, 1998, p. 76.

80. See Gilles Pignon and Jean-François Rebeyrotte (eds.), *Esclavage et marron-ages. Refuser la condition servile à Bourbon (île de la Réunion) au XVIIIe siècle*, Paris: Riveneuve, 2022, pp. 57–9 and 65.

81. Ibid, p. 58.

82. Sudel Fuma, 'Le procès d'une insurrection d'esclaves en 1811 à La Réunion', in Régent et al. (eds.), *Les colonies, la Révolution française, la loi*, p. 219.

83. Ibid, p. 227.

84. Trial of Madagascar Slaves, National Archives, Kew, London, CO 167/64.

85. See Pier Larson, 'The Vernacular Life of the Street: Ratsitatanina and Indian Ocean *Créolité*', *Slavery & Abolition*, 29:3 (2008), pp. 336 and 340.

86. Quoted in Asgarally, 'Systèmes esclavagistes et abolitions dans les colonies de l'océan Indien', p. 175; the expression 'grinding the roots' ('râper les racines') was no doubt a reference to poison.

87. Inspector report, 1819, in Josette Fallope, *Esclaves et citoyens: Les noirs à la Guadeloupe au XIXe siècle dans les processus de resistance et d'intégration: 1802–1910*, Basse-Terre: Société d'histoire de la Guadeloupe, 1992, p. 187. On the punishments inflicted on slaves in the first half of the nineteenth century, see the testimony of a former French colonial administrator, J.-B. Rouvellat de Cussac, *Situation des esclaves dans les colonies françaises*, Paris: Pagnerre, 1845. See also Régent et al. (eds.), *Libres et sans fers*, pp. 67–103.

88. Silyane Larcher, *L'autre citoyen*, Paris: Armand Colin, 2014, pp. 118–19.

89. Nelly Schmidt, 'Les luttes contre l'esclavage dans les Caraïbes françaises au 19e siècle', in O. Ette and G. Müller (eds.), *Caleidoscopios coloniales* (2010), pp. 160–61.

90. Lawrence Jennings, 'Cyrille Charles Auguste Bissette', in F. W. Knight and H. L. Gates Jr (eds.), *Dictionary of Caribbean and Afro-Latin American Biography*, Oxford: Oxford University Press, 2016.

91. Rebecca Hartkopf Schloss, *Sweet Liberty: The Final Days of Slavery in Martinique*, Philadelphia, PA: University of Pennsylvania Press, 2009, p. 96.

92. Letter of 18 February 1825, in Pierre Dessalles, *La vie d'un colon à la Martinique*, Fort-de-France: H. de Frémont, 1980, p. 143.

93. 'Mémoire', 4 September 1815, quoted in Schmidt, 'Les luttes contre l'esclavage', p. 158.

94. Oruno D. Lara, 'L'influence de la révolution Haïtienne dans son environne-ment caraïbe', *Présence Africaine*, 169 (2004), p. 99.

95. Moitt, 'Slave Resistance in Guadeloupe and Martinique', p. 149.

96. Letter to Martinique's governor Donzelot, 28 December 1822, quoted in Fran-çoise Thésée, 'La révolte des esclaves du Carbet', *Revue Française d'Histoire d'Outre-Mer*, 80:301 (1993), p. 576.

97. Fallope, *Esclaves et citoyens*, p. 202.

98. Georges Mauvois, *Un complot d'esclaves: Martinique 1831*, Bordeaux: Librairie Mollat, 1999, pp. 88–9.

99. Schmidt, 'Les luttes contre l'esclavage', p. 161.

100. Lamartine speech to French parliament, 23 April 1835, in Nelly Schmidt, *Abolitionnistes de l'esclavage et réformateurs des colonies*, Paris: Éditions Karthala, 2000, p. 560.

101. 'purchase' here means 'goal'. Clarkson letter, 7 February 1842, quoted in ibid, p. 496.

102. Georges Mauvois, *Les marrons de la mer*, Paris: Éditions Karthala, 2018, p. 106.

103. Fallope, *Esclaves et citoyens*, p. 322.

104. See chapter 13 in Alan Forrest, *The Death of the French Atlantic*, Oxford: Oxford University Press, 2020.

105. On the French illegal trade see Lalouvière, 'A Business Archive of the French Illegal Slave Trade in the Nineteenth Century'.

106. *Discours prononcé par M. le Duc de Broglie sur la traite des nègres*, Paris, 1822, p. 7.

107. De la Martinière, *Des moyens de la restauration de la colonie de Saint-Domingue*, Paris, 1814.

108. Yun Kyoung Kwon, 'Ending Slavery, Narrating Emancipation: Revolutionary Legacies in the French Antislavery Debate', PhD thesis, Department of History, University of Chicago, 2012, pp. 324–5.

109. Kwon, 'Ending Slavery, Narrating Emancipation', p. 321.

110. Ibid, pp. 324 and 326.

111. Lafayette letter to Clarkson, 11 May 1823, quoted in Étienne Taillemite, 'La Fayette et l'abolition de l'esclavage', in Hrodêj (ed.), *L'esclave et les plantations*, p. 236.

112. Kwon, 'Ending Slavery, Narrating Emancipation', p. 321.

113. Ibid, p. 326.

114. Ordonnance de Sa Majesté le Roi, 17 April 1825, in M. Dorigny et al. (eds.), *Haïti-France, les chaînes de la dette*, Paris: Hémisphères Éditions, 2021, pp. 194–5.

115. Alexander, *Fear of a Black Republic*, p. 74.

116. See Gusti-Klara Gaillard-Pourchet, 'Dette de l'indépendance d'Haïti [1825]. Canonnière et huis-clos pour une rançon néo-coloniale', in *Haïti-France*, pp. 71–123.

117. Narcisse-Achille de Salvandy, *De l'émancipation de Saint-Domingue*, Paris, 1825, pp. 56–8.

118. Bernard Gainot, 'Bref aperçu concernant l'histoire du mouvement abolitionniste français', *La Révolution Française*, 16 (2019), p. 10.

119. Frédéric Régent, *Les maîtres de la Guadeloupe*, Paris: Tallandier, 2019, p. 349.

120. Lawrence Jennings, 'Le second mouvement pour l'abolition de l'esclavage colonial', *Outre-Mers*, 89:336–7, (2002), p. 180.

121. Patricia Motylewski, *La Société française pour l'abolition de l'esclavage*, Paris: L'Harmattan, 1998, pp. 50–51.

122. Gainot, 'Bref aperçu', p. 11.

123. Jennings, 'Interaction', p. 88.

124. Decree of 27 April 1848, in Myriam Cottias (ed.), *D'une abolition, l'autre*, Marseille: Persée, 1998, p. 17.

125. Schmidt, *Abolitionnistes de l'esclavage*, pp. 254–7.

126. Ibid, pp. 286–92.

127. Hippolyte Carnot, 'Esclavage', in *Revue Indépendante* (1845), quoted in Schmidt, *Abolitionnistes de l'esclavage*, p. 270.

128. Aimé Césaire, 'Victor Schoelcher et l'abolition de l'esclavage' [1948]. Quoted in Larcher, *L'autre citoyen*, p. 171.

129. Léo Ursulet, 'Les francs-maçons et l'abolition de l'esclavage aux Antilles françaises', *Humanisme*, 310 (2016), p. 89.

130. Dale Tomich, *Slavery in the Circuit of Sugar: Martinique and the World-Economy*, Albany, NY: State University of New York Press, 2016, pp. 356–66; Fallope, *Esclaves et citoyens*, p. 322.

131. See Caroline Oudin-Bastide, *Maîtres accusés, esclaves accusateurs*, Mont-Saint-Aignan: Presses Universitaires de Rouen et du Havre, 2015.

132. Declaration of 26 December 1838, quoted in Louis Blanc, 'De l'abolition de l'esclavage aux colonies', *Revue du Progrès* (1840), pp. 8–9.

133. 'Adresse au Roi, 10 Juillet 1847', in René Bélénus, *10 Juillet 1847*, Martinique: Éditions Exbrayat, 2022, p. 37.

134. Schmidt, *Abolitionnistes de l'esclavage*, p. 287.

135. Some of this material can be found in Schoelcher's papers at BNF, NAF 3633.

136. Victor Schoelcher, *De l'esclavage des noirs* (1833), in *idem, Esclavage et colonisation*, Paris: Presses Universitaires de France, 2002, pp. 97–8.

137. Victor Schoelcher, *Abolition de l'esclavage*, Paris: Pagnerre, 1840, pp. 107–11.

138. Victor Schoelcher, *Des colonies françaises*, Paris: Pagnerre, 1842, pp. 375–6.

139. See for example the anti-abolitionist pamphlet by Charles Levasseur, *Esclavage de la race noire aux colonies françaises*, Paris, 1840, p. 66.

140. Victor Schoelcher, *Colonies étrangères et Haïti*, Paris, 1843, vol. II, p. 135.

141. Ibid, pp. 181, 199–200.

142. See Léo Ursulet, *Parcours contrastés des abolitionnistes Cyrille Bissette & Victor Schoelcher*, Paris: Éditions Orphie, 2022.

143. Schoelcher, *Colonies étrangères et Haïti*, p. 279.

144. Moitt, 'Slave Resistance in Guadeloupe and Martinique', p. 155.

145. For examples from Guadeloupe, see Fallope, *Esclaves et citoyens*, pp. 620–21.

146. Jennings, 'Interaction', p. 91.

147. See for example Clarkson's letter to Guizot, 18 January 1841, quoted in Schmidt, *Abolitionistes de l'esclavage*, pp. 514–15; see also Yun Kyoung Kwon, 'When Parisian Liberals Spoke for Haiti: French Antislavery Discourses on Haiti under the Restoration', *Atlantic Studies*, 8:3 (2011), pp. 317–41.

148. For further discussion see White, *Voices of the Enslaved*, p. 6 and note 7 (p. 228).

149. Schoelcher, *Vie de Toussaint Louverture*.

150. Oruno Lara, *La liberté assassinée: Guadeloupe, Guyane, Martinique et la Réunion en 1848–1856*, Paris: L'Harmattan, 2005.

151. Proclamation of Louis Husson, Saint-Pierre, 31 March 1848, in Cottias (ed.), *D'une abolition, l'autre*, p. 177.

152. Nelly Schmidt, '1848 dans les colonies françaises des Caraïbes: Ambitions républicaines et ordre colonial', *Revue Française d'Histoire d'Outre-Mer*, 85:320 (1998), p. 52.

153. Ibid.

154. Victor Schoelcher, *La vérité aux ouvriers et cultivateurs de la Martinique*, Paris, 1849, p. 260. In an earlier work, he had declared: 'if France owes an indemnity for this social condition which she has tolerated, and which she then suppresses, she owes it without doubt to those who have suffered from it as much as to those who have profited from it': Schoelcher, *Esclavage et colonisation*, p. 25.

8: TO END THIS EMPIRE OF TYRANNY

1. Jane Landers, 'Catholic Conspirators? Religious Rebels in Nineteenth-Century Cuba', in Jane Landers (ed.), *Slavery and Abolition in the Atlantic World*, London: Routledge, 2017, pp. 502–4; there is some dispute about Aponte's membership of the Yoruba *cabildo*.

2. Matt Childs, *The 1812 Aponte Rebellion in Cuba and the Struggle against Atlantic Slavery*, Chapel Hill, NC: University of North Carolina Press, 2006, pp. 156–7.

3. Ibid, pp. 21–2.

4. Ada Ferrer, *Freedom's Mirror: Cuba and Haiti in the Age of Revolution*, New York: Cambridge University Press, 2014, p. 288.

5. Sibylle Fischer, *Modernity Disavowed: Haiti and the Cultures of Slavery in the Age of Revolution*, Durham, NC: Duke University Press, 2004, p. 46.

6. Childs, *The 1812 Aponte Rebellion in Cuba*, pp. 3–4, 168–9.

7. Lara, 'L'influence de la révolution Haïtienne', p. 98.

8. 1796 document, in Geggus (ed.), *Haitian Revolution*, p. 187.

9. The classic work on Puerto Rico is Guillermo Baralt, *Slave Revolts in Puerto Rico: Conspiracies and Uprisings, 1795–1873*, Princeton, NJ: Markus Wiener, 2007.

10. Lara, 'L'influence de la révolution Haïtienne', pp. 96–7.

11. See Enrique Salvador Rivera, 'The Political Economy of Anti-Slavery Resistance: An Atlantic History of the 1795 Insurrection at Coro, Venezuela', PhD thesis, University of California, 2019.

12. Aline Helg, 'A Fragmented Majority', in Geggus (ed.), *The Impact of the Haitian Revolution*, p. 159.

13. Ibid.

14. Christopher Schmidt-Nowara, 'Anti-Slavery in Spain and its Colonies, 1808–86', in W. Mulligan and M. Bric (eds.), *A Global History of Anti-Slavery Politics in the Nineteenth Century*, London: Macmillan, 2013, p. 137.

15. See Theodore Vincent, *The Legacy of Vicente Guerrero, Mexico's First Black Indian President*, Gainesville, FL: University Press of Florida, 2001.

16. Eric Paul, 'The Circulation of Transatlantic Ideas and People in Cuban Slave Society, 1791–1844', PhD thesis, University of California, 2009, p. 49.

17. Lara, 'L'influence de la révolution Haïtienne', p. 93.
18. Alain Yacou, 'Les rébellions nègres à Cuba dans la première moitié du XIXe siècle', *Bulletin de la Société d'Histoire de la Guadeloupe*, 59 (1984), p. 81.
19. Ibid.
20. Manuel Barcia, *The Great African Slave Revolt of 1825*, Baton Rouge, LA: Louisiana State University Press, 2012, p. 51.
21. See Ferrer, 'Speaking of Haiti', p. 224.
22. Ibid.
23. Consuelo Naranjo Orovio, 'Le fantasme d'Haïti: l'élaboration intéressée d'une grande peur', in A. Yacou (ed.), *Saint-Domingue espagnol et la révolution nègre d'Haïti* (1790–1822), Paris: Éditions Karthala, 2007, p. 639.
24. Cited in Alejandro Gomez, 'Le syndrome de Saint-Domingue. Perceptions et représentations de la Révolution haïtienne dans le Monde Atlantique, 1790–1886'. PhD thesis, EHESS, Paris 2010, p. 189.
25. June 1800 report, cited in Ferrer, *Freedom's Mirror*, p. 152.
26. Ada Ferrer, 'La société esclavagiste cubaine et la révolution haïtienne', *Annales. Histoire, Sciences Sociales*, 2 (2003), pp. 352–5.
27. Yacou, 'Les rébellions nègres à Cuba', pp. 83–4.
28. Barcia, *Great African Slave Revolt*, pp. 43–4.
29. Alain Yacou, *La longue guerre des nègres marrons de Cuba*, Paris: CERC/Éditions Karthala, 2009, p. 23.
30. Ibid, p. 93.
31. Ibid, pp. 181 and 183.
32. Ada Ferrer, 'Cuban Slavery and Atlantic Antislavery', in J. M. Fradera and C. Schmidt-Nowara (eds.), *Slavery and Antislavery in Spain's Atlantic Empire*, New York: Berghahn Books, 2013, p. 136.
33. Ferrer, *Freedom's Mirror*, p. 224.
34. Yacou, *La longue guerre*, p. 171.
35. César Leante, *Los guerrilleros negros*, Havana: Unión de Escritores y Artistas de Cuba, 1976, p. 142.
36. Yacou, *La longue guerre*, p. 172.
37. Ibid, p. 171.
38. Ibid, p. 157, n. 42.
39. Ibid, p. 152.
40. Ibid, p. 151.
41. 14 February 1815 declaration, in ibid, p. 226, n. 61.
42. Yacou, *La longue guerre*, pp. 216–19.
43. 24 February 1845 report, in ibid, p. 166.
44. First produced in December 1796.
45. 26 June 1830 report, in Yacou, *La longue guerre*, p. 141.
46. 8 February 1840 report, in ibid, p. 162.
47. December 1815 report, in ibid, p. 407.
48. 24 March 1820 report, in ibid, p. 373.
49. Yacou, *La longue guerre*, p. 414.
50. For a full analysis, see ibid, pp. 414–24.

51. Ferrer, *Freedom's Mirror*, p. 233.
52. Yacou, *La longue guerre*, p. 143.
53. Corzo, *Runaway Slave Settlements*, p. 126.
54. Ibid, p. 138.
55. See Appendix 1 in Barcia, *Great African Slave Revolt*.
56. Ibid, pp. 81–2.
57. Ibid, p. 132.
58. Ibid, p. 135.
59. Ibid.
60. Ibid, p. 101.
61. Quoted in Barcia, *West African Warfare*, p. 97.
62. Barcia, *Great African Slave Revolt*, pp. 107 and 119.
63. Ibid, p. 141.
64. Ibid, pp. 146 and 150.
65. Ibid, p. 151.
66. Paul, 'The Circulation of Transatlantic Ideas', pp. 95–6.
67. Ibid, p. 122.
68. Landers, 'Catholic Conspirators?', p. 506.
69. Paul, 'The Circulation of Transatlantic Ideas', p. 130.
70. 'Chronology of Slave Movements in Cuba, 1798–1844', in Barcia, *West African Warfare*, Appendix 2, pp. 161–5.
71. Ibid, p. 117.
72. Ibid, p. 118.
73. Ibid, pp. 119 and 129.
74. Ibid, p. 114.
75. Ibid.
76. Ibid, p. 126.
77. Ibid, pp. 136–9.
78. Ibid, pp. 127 and 143.
79. June 1837 testimony of Valentin Lucumi, quoted in Barcia, *West African Warfare*, p. 122.
80. Ibid, pp. 128–9.
81. Ibid, p. 151.
82. Fischer, *Modernity Disavowed*, p. 79.
83. Finch, *Rethinking Slave Rebellion in Cuba*, p. 121.
84. Quoted in ibid, p. 134.
85. Quoted in ibid, p. 63.
86. Ibid, pp. 185–6.
87. Yacou, *La longue guerre*, p. 212, n. 4.
88. Manuel Barcia, *Seeds of Insurrection: Domination and Resistance on Western Cuban Plantations, 1808–1848*, Baton Rouge, LA: Louisiana State University Press, 2008, p. 70.
89. Yacou, *La longue guerre*, p. 113.
90. Finch, *Rethinking Slave Rebellion in Cuba*, p. 147.

91. William Van Norman Jr, *Shade-Grown Slavery: The Lives of Slaves on Coffee Plantations in Cuba*, Nashville, TN: Vanderbilt University Press, 2013, p. 136.

92. Finch, *Rethinking Slave Rebellion in Cuba*, pp. 154–7, 176–7.

93. Ibid, p. 164.

94. Ibid, pp. 165–6.

95. Ibid, p. 180.

96. Ibid, p. 212.

97. Ibid, p. 213.

98. See Samantha Payne, '"A general insurrection in the countries with slaves": The US Civil War and the Origins of an Atlantic Revolution, 1861–1866', *Past and Present*, 257 (November 2022), pp. 248–79.

99. Schmidt-Nowara, 'Anti-Slavery in Spain and its Colonies', p. 143.

100. See Ada Ferrer, 'Armed Slaves and Anticolonial Insurgency in Late Nineteenth-Century Cuba', in Christopher Brown and Philip Morgan (eds.), *Arming Slaves: From Classical Times to the Modern Age*, New Haven, CT: Yale University Press, 2006, 304–29.

101. Matt Childs and Manuel Barcia, 'Cuba', in Robert Paquette and Mark Smith (eds.), *The Oxford Handbook of Slavery in the Americas*, Oxford: Oxford University Press, 2010, p. 104.

102. Finch, *Rethinking Slave Rebellion in Cuba*, p. 221.

103. Ibid, p. 200.

9: WHITE AND BLACK SPIRITS ENGAGED IN BATTLE

1. Herbert Aptheker, 'The Event', in Kenneth Greenberg (ed.), *Nat Turner: A Slave Rebellion in History and Memory*, New York: Oxford University Press, 2003, pp. 52–4.

2. Kenneth Greenberg, 'Name, Face, Body', in Greenberg (ed.), *Nat Turner*, p. 7.

3. Douglas Egerton, 'Nat Turner in a Hemispheric Context', in Greenberg (ed.), *Nat Turner*, p. 136.

4. Aptheker, 'The Event', p. 46.

5. Thomas R. Gray, *The Confessions of Nat Turner*, Baltimore, 1831, p. 12.

6. Ibid, p. 18.

7. Ibid, pp. 7–8 and 9.

8. Ibid, p. 9.

9. Ibid, p. 11.

10. Aptheker, 'The Event', p. 51.

11. This interpretation of Turner as a Black Methodist 'holy warrior' is fully developed in Anthony E. Kaye, with Gregory P. Downs, *Nat Turner, Black Prophet*, New York: FSG, 2024.

12. Gray, *Confessions of Nat Turner*, pp. 4 and 18.

13. See for example Genovese, *From Rebellion to Revolution*, pp. 48–9.

14. Gray, *Confessions of Nat Turner*, p. 18.

15. Kaye, *Nat Turner, Black Prophet*, pp. 30–31.

16. For an examination of the active role of women in the 1831 rebellion, see Vanessa Holden, *Surviving Southampton: African American Women and Resistance in Nat Turner's Community*, Champaign, IL: University of Illinois Press, 2021, pp. 26–38.

17. Egerton, 'Nat Turner in a Hemispheric Context', p. 143.

18. Quoted in Alexander, *Fear of a Black Republic*, p. 93.

19. I am grateful to Oliver St Clair Franklin for bringing this point to my attention.

20. Douglass, 'What to the Slave is the Fourth of July?', p. 208.

21. Gray, *Confessions of Nat Turner*, p. 11.

22. Drescher, *Abolitionism*, pp. 131–40.

23. Quoted in Maurice Jackson and Jacqueline Bacon, 'Fever and Fret: The Haitian Revolution and African American Responses', in Maurice Jackson and Jacqueline Bacon (eds.), *African Americans and the Haitian Revolution*, New York: Routledge, 2010, p. 14.

24. Quoted in Jacqueline Bacon, '"A revolution unexampled in the history of man": The Haitian Revolution in *Freedom's Journal*, 1827–1829', in Jackson and Bacon (eds.), *African Americans and the Haitian Revolution*, p. 85.

25. Ibid.

26. Ibid, p. 84.

27. Ibid, p. 89.

28. Ibid, p. 88.

29. Ibid, pp. 85–6.

30. Ibid, p. 86.

31. David Walker, *Appeal in Four Articles, Together with a Preamble, to the Coloured Citizens of the World, but in Particular, and Very Expressly, to Those of the United States of America*, Boston, 1829.

32. Walker, *Appeal*, 1830, p. 15.

33. Ibid, p. 31.

34. Ibid, p. 14.

35. Ibid, p. 24.

36. Ibid, p. 73.

37. Ibid, p. 34.

38. Ibid, p. 30.

39. Aptheker, *American Negro Slave Revolts*, p. 288.

40. Alex Zamalin, *Struggle on their Minds: The Political Thought of African-American Resistance*, New York: Columbia University Press, 2017, p. 26.

41. For further discussion, see Peter Hinks, *To Awaken My Afflicted Brethren: David Walker and the Problem of Antebellum Slave Resistance*, Philadelphia, PA: Pennsylvania State University Press, 1997, pp. 167–9.

42. For further discussion of Walker's intellectual influence, see Marcy J. Dinius, *The Textual Effects of David Walker's Appeal*, Philadelphia, PA: Philadelphia, University of Pennsylvania Press, 2022.

43. Walker, *Appeal*, p. 29.

44. Blassingame, *Slave Community*, p. 267.

45. Quoted in Sterling Stuckey, 'Through the Prism of Folklore: The Black Ethos in Slavery', *Massachusetts Review*, 9:3 (Summer 1968), p. 428.

46. George Rawick (ed.), *The American Slave: A Composite Autobiography*, vol. 9, Westport, CT: Greenwood, 1972, p. 342.

47. Matthew J. Clavin, *Symbols of Freedom: Slavery and Resistance before the Civil War*, New York: NYU Press, 2023, p. 101.

48. For an account of several such cases from Massachusetts, Texas, North Carolina, Virginia, Pennsylvania, and New York, see Nikki M. Taylor, *Brooding over Bloody Revenge: Enslaved Women's Lethal Resistance*, New York: Cambridge University Press, 2023. On violent resistance by enslaved women in Virginia specifically, see Tamika Nunley, *The Demands of Justice: Enslaved Women, Capital Crime and Clemency in Early Virginia*, Chapel Hill, NC: University of North Carolina Press, 2023.

49. See Stuckey, *Slave Culture*.

50. Harriet Jacobs, quoted in Jermaine O. Archer, *Antebellum Slave Narratives*, New York: Routledge, 2009, p. 59.

51. Stuckey, *Slave Culture*, p. 25.

52. Ibid, p. 38 and n. 53.

53. George Rawick (ed.), *The American Slave: A Composite Autobiography*, vol. 7, Westport, CT: Greenwood, 1972, p. 145.

54. Stephanie Camp, *Closer to Freedom: Enslaved Women and Everyday Resistance in the Plantation South*, Chapel Hill, NC: University of North Carolina Press, 2004, pp. 35 and 40.

55. Ibid, p. 50.

56. Ibid, p. 90.

57. Ibid, pp. 60–61.

58. Stuckey, *Slave Culture*, pp. 72–3.

59. Camp, *Closer to Freedom*, p. 84.

60. Ibid, p. 76.

61. Quoted in ibid, p. 75.

62. Ibid, p. 91.

63. Ibid, pp. 97–8.

64. Ibid, p. 101.

65. Ibid, p. 104.

66. Lewis Clarke, Narrative of the sufferings of Lewis Clarke, during a captivity of more than twenty-five years, among the Algerines of Kentucky, one of the so-called Christian states of North America, dictated by himself, Boston, 1845, pp. 62–3.

67. John Stauffer, 'Frederick Douglass's Self-Fashioning and the Making of a Representative American Man', in A. Fisch (ed.), *The Cambridge Companion to the African American Slave Narrative*, New York: Cambridge University Press, 2007, p. 204.

68. Douglass, *Narrative*, p. 16.

69. Ibid, pp. 19, 29–30.

70. Ibid, p. 55.

71. Ibid, p. 37.

72. Ibid, p. 69.

73. Ibid, p. 65.

74. Ibid, p. 69, fn.

75. For further discussion, see the chapter on Douglass in Archer, *Antebellum Slave Narratives*, pp. 1–20.

76. Douglass, *Narrative*, p. 63.

77. For further discussion and illustrations, see Clavin, *Symbols of Freedom*.

78. Harriet Jacobs, *Incidents in the Life of a Slave Girl*, Boston, 1861, p. 151.

79. Samuel Ringgold Ward, *Autobiography of a Fugitive Negro* (1855), New York, 1968, p. 12.

80. Henry Brown, *Narrative of Henry Box Brown*, Boston, 1849, p. 61.

81. Harper Twelvetrees, from *The Story of the Life of John Anderson, the Fugitive Slave* (1863), in M. Commander (ed.), *Unsung: Unheralded Narratives of American Slavery & Abolition*, New York: Penguin, 2021, p. 295.

82. Henry Bibb, *Narrative of the Life and Adventures of Henry Bibb, an American Slave, Written by Himself*, New York, 1849, p. 52.

83. William Wells Brown, *Narrative*, in P. Jefferson (ed.), *The Travels of William Wells Brown*, New York, 1991, p. 65.

84. William Craft, from *Running a Thousand Miles for Freedom* (1860), in Commander (ed.), *Unsung*, pp. 268–77. For an outstanding account of the Crofts' escape, see Ilyon Woo, *Master Slave Husband Wife: An Epic Journey from Slavery to Freedom*, New York: 37 INK/Simon & Schuster, 2024.

85. Brown, *Narrative of Henry Box Brown*, p. 61.

86. See Eric Foner, *Gateway to Freedom: The Hidden History of the Underground Railroad*, New York: W. W. Norton, 2015.

87. Julie Winch, '"You have talents – only cultivate them": Philadelphia's Black Female Literary Societies and the Abolitionist Crusade', in J. Yellin and J. Van Horne (eds.), *The Abolitionist Sisterhood*, Ithaca, NY: Cornell University Press, 1994, p. 115.

88. See Cheryl Janifer LaRoche, *Free Black Communities and the Underground Railroad*, Champaign, IL: University of Illinois Press, 2013.

89. Damian Alan Pargas, *Freedom Seekers: Fugitive Slaves in North America, 1800–1860*, Cambridge: Cambridge University Press, 2022, pp. 104–5.

90. Manisha Sinha, *The Slave's Cause: A History of Abolition*, New Haven, CT: Yale University Press, 2016, p. 399.

91. Ibid, p. 438.

92. Milton Sernett, *Harriet Tubman*, Durham, NC: Duke University Press, 2007, p. 55.

93. Sinha, *The Slave's Cause*, pp. 534–5.

94. Ibid, p. 441.

95. Ibid, pp. 442–3 and 444.

96. Ibid, p. 451.

97. See the chapter on Truth in Mary Grace Albanese, *Black Women and Energies of Resistance in Nineteenth-Century Haitian and American Literature*, New York: Cambridge University Press, 2023.

98. 'Sojourner Truth', *Anti-Slavery Bugle* (21 June 1851), p. 160.

99. Quoted in Xiomara Santamarina, 'Black Womanhood in North American Women's Slave Narratives', in Fisch (ed.), *Cambridge Companion to the African American Slave Narrative*, p. 237.

100. *Louisa Picquet, the Octoroon: Or, Inside Views of Southern Domestic Life*, New York, 1861, p. 11.

101. Ibid, p. 20.

102. Ibid, pp. 50–51.

103. Jacobs, *Incidents in the life of a Slave Girl*, pp. 105, 108.

104. Quoted in Archer, *Antebellum Slave Narratives*, p. 59.

105. Jacobs, *Incidents in the life of a slave girl*, p. 302.

106. Yellin and Van Horne (eds.), *The Abolitionist Sisterhood*, p. 15.

107. Quoted in Sinha, *The Slave's Cause*, p. 454; emphasis in text; for further analysis see Alexander, *Fear of a Black Republic*.

108. James McCune Smith, 'A Lecture on the Haytien Revolutions', in Jackson and Bacon (eds.), *African Americans and the Haitian Revolution*, pp. 180 and 181.

109. James Theodore Holly, 'A Vindication of the Capacity of the Negro Race for Self-Government', in ibid, pp. 192–3.

110. William Wells Brown, 'St. Domingo: Its Revolution and its Patriots', in ibid, p. 188.

111. Ibid, p. 189.

112. Matthew J. Clavin, 'American Toussaints', in ibid, p. 116.

113. For further examples and a wider account of the embrace of force by black anti-slavery groups in antebellum America, see Kellie Carter Jackson, *Force and Freedom: Black Abolitionists and the Politics of Violence*, Philadelphia, PA: University of Pennsylvania Press, 2019.

114. William Douch, 'Frederick Douglass in Manchester', *Global Threads*, https://globalthreadsmcr.org/douglass-in-manchester/. I am very grateful to Matt Stallard for providing me with this information and the link to the platform.

115. Hannah-Rose Murray and John R. McKivigan (eds.), *Frederick Douglass in Britain and Ireland, 1845–1895*, Edinburgh: Edinburgh University Press, 2023, pp. 49–50.

116. Ibid, p. 52.

117. Ibid, p. 46.

118. Ibid, pp. 30, 67, and 87.

119. 5 January 1849, quoted in Leslie Alexander, '"The Black Republic"', in Jackson and Bacon (eds.), *African Americans and the Haitian Revolution*, p. 68.

120. Clavin, 'American Toussaints', p. 109.

121. Quoted in Marion W. Starling, *The Slave Narrative: Its Place in American History*, Boston, MA: G. K. Hall, 1981, pp. 250–51.

122. Murray and McKivigan (eds.), *Frederick Douglass in Britain and Ireland*, p. 64.

123. Quoted in Sinha, *The Slave's Cause*, p. 471.

124. For an excellent study, see Jeffrey R. Kerr-Ritchie, *Rebellious Passage: The Creole Revolt and America's Coastal Slave Trade*, Cambridge: Cambridge University Press, 2019.

125. *My Bondage*, quoted in Commander (ed.), *Unsung*, p. 131.

126. Quoted in David Blight, *Frederick Douglass: Prophet of Freedom*, New York: Simon and Schuster, 2018, p. 6.

127. Sinha, *The Slave's Cause*, pp. 584–5.

128. See Jesse Olsavsky, *The Most Absolute Abolition: Runaways, Vigilance Committees and the Rise of Revolutionary Abolitionism 1835–1861*, Baton Rouge, LA: Louisiana State University Press, 2022.

129. Aptheker, *American Negro Slave Revolts*, pp. 346–9.

130. Carter Jackson, *Force and Freedom*.

131. Thavolia Glymph, *The Women's Fight: The Civil War's Battles for Home, Freedom, and Nation*, Chapel Hill, NC: University of North Carolina Press, 2020, p. 91.

132. Clavin, *Symbols of Freedom*, p. 191.

133. 'Capt. John Brown Not Insane', in Stauffer and Gates (eds.), *The Portable Frederick Douglass*, p. 447.

134. See Douglas Egerton, *Thunder at the Gates: The Black Civil War Regiments that Redeemed America*, New York: Basic Books, 2016.

135. Quoted in Errol A. Henderson, 'Slave Religion, Slave Hiring, and the Incipient Proletarianization of Black Labor: Developing Du Bois' Thesis on Black Participation in the Civil War as a Revolution', *Journal of African American Studies*, 19 (2015), p. 198.

136. S.-M. Grant, '"Dere never wuz a war like dis war": The WPA Narratives and the Emotional Echoes of the Civil War', *Slavery & Abolition*, 43:1 (2022), p. 175.

137. Clavin, 'American Toussaints', p. 109.

138. 1 August 1863, quoted in ibid, p. 107.

139. Ibid, p. 110.

140. Ibid, pp. 111–12.

141. Ibid, p. 113.

142. Ibid, p. 115.

143. Quoted in Henderson, 'Slave Religion, Slave Hiring', p. 193.

144. Steven Hahn, 'But What Did Slaves Think of Lincoln?', in W. A. Blair and K. F. Younger (eds.), *Lincoln's Proclamation: Emancipation Reconsidered*, Chapel Hill, NC: University of North Carolina Press, 2009, pp. 112–13.

145. Grant, '"Dere never wuz a war like dis war"', p. 170.

146. Aptheker, *American Negro Slave Revolts*, pp. 360–61.

147. Ibid, pp. 361–2.

148. Glymph, *The Women's Fight*, p. 91.

149. Aptheker, *American Negro Slave Revolts*, pp. 365–6.

150. Ibid, pp. 366–7.
151. Stephanie McCurry, 'War, Gender, and Emancipation in the Civil War South', in Blair and Younger (eds.), *Lincoln's Proclamation*, p. 143.
152. Glymph, *The Women's Fight*, p. 105.
153. Ibid, p. 98.
154. Thulani Davis, *The Emancipation Circuit*, Durham, NC: Duke University Press, 2022, p. 139.
155. McCurry, 'War, Gender, and Emancipation', p. 129.
156. Grant, '"Dere never wuz a war like dis war"', p. 173.
157. Amy Murrell Taylor, *Embattled Freedom*, Chapel Hill, NC: University of North Carolina Press, 2018, p. 8.
158. McCurry, 'War, Gender, and Emancipation', pp. 144–5.
159. Mark Neely, 'Colonization and the Myth that Lincoln Prepared the People for Emancipation', in Blair and Younger (eds.), *Lincoln's Proclamation*, p. 45.
160. Blackburn, *The Reckoning*, p. 251.
161. Stuckey, *Slave Culture*, p. 38.
162. Hahn, 'But What Did Slaves Think of Lincoln?', p. 114.
163. Clavin, 'American Toussaints', p. 116.
164. Quoted in ibid.

10: TAKING THEIR CAUSE INTO THEIR OWN HANDS

1. Martin Delany, *Blake, or The Huts of America*, Cambridge, MA: Harvard University Press, 2017, p. 45.
2. Sinha, *The Slave's Cause*, p. 455.
3. Delany, *Blake*, p. 313.
4. Ibid, p. 114.
5. Ibid, p. 170.
6. Jerome McGann, 'Introduction', in Delany, *Blake*, p. xxv.
7. Andy Doolen, 'When Mammy Lies: The Everyday Resistance of Slave Women in Martin Delany's *Blake*', *Studies in American Fiction*, 45:1 (2018), pp. 9–13.
8. Erin Zavitz, 'Revolutionary Commemorations: Jean-Jacques Dessalines and Haitian Independence Day, 1804–1904', in Gaffield (ed.), *The Haitian Declaration of Independence*, p. 221.
9. Ibid, p. 226.
10. Ibid, p. 222.
11. Laurent Dubois, 'Thinking Haitian Independence in Haitian Vodou', in Gaffield (ed.), *The Haitian Declaration of Independence*, p. 208.
12. 'Notes of Information Relative to the Island of St Domingo', n.d., in *Papiers de l'Abbé Henri Grégoire*, Bibliothèque de l'Arsenal, Paris, Ms.6339, f. 87.
13. Dubois, 'Thinking Haitian Independence', pp. 206 and 209.
14. Zavitz, 'Revolutionary Commemorations', p. 225.
15. See Mimi Sheller, 'The Army of Sufferers: Peasant Democracy in the Early Republic of Haiti', *New West Indian Guide* 74:1/2 (2000), pp. 33–55.
16. W. E. H. Lecky, *History of European Morals*, London, 1884, vol. 1, p. 153.

17. Gavin Grindon, Jennie Williams and Duncan Hay, 'Mapping British Public Monuments Related to Slavery', *Slavery & Abolition*, 45:2 (2024), pp. 384–407.

18. Quoted in Gabriel, *Jubilee's Experiment*, p. 286.

19. Ibid, p. 287.

20. Selwyn Cudjoe, *Beyond Boundaries: The Intellectual Tradition of Trinidad and Tobago in the Nineteenth Century*, Wellesley, MA: Calaloux Publications, 2003, pp. 89–93.

21. J. R. Kerr-Ritchie, *Rites of August First: Emancipation Day in the Black Atlantic World*, Baton Rouge, LA: Louisiana State University Press, 2007, p. 42.

22. Errol Hill, *The Jamaican Stage 1655–1900: Profile of a Colonial Theatre*, Amherst, MA: University of Massachusetts Press, 1992, p. 253.

23. Hazareesingh, *Black Spartacus*, p. 361.

24. Françoise Vergès, 'Exposer l'esclavage', *Africultures*, 91 (2013), pp. 8–19.

25. Quoted in Doris Garraway, 'Memory as Reparation? The Politics of Remembering Slavery in France from Abolition to the Loi Taubira (2001)', *International Journal of Francophone Studies*, 11:3 (November 2008), p. 376.

26. Fallope, *Esclaves et citoyens*, p. 388.

27. ANOM, Aix, COL H 233, dossier Marie Léonard Sénécal.

28. See Oruno Lara, *Léonard Sénécal, le rebelle écartelé*, Paris: L'Harmattan, 2013.

29. See Françoise Vergès, *Monsters and Revolutionaries: Colonial Family Romance and Métissage*, Durham, NC: Duke University Press, 1999, pp. 6–7 and 14–15.

30. See David Waldstreicher, *In the Midst of Perpetual Fêtes*, Chapel Hill, NC: University of North Carolina Press, 1997.

31. Gabriel, *Jubilee's Experiment*, p. 294.

32. Ibid, p. 298.

33. Ibid, p. 296.

34. James McCune Smith, 'Introduction', in *A Memorial Discourse by Reverend Henry Highland Garnet*, Philadelphia, 1865, p. 24.

35. Quoted in Mitch Kachun, 'Antebellum African Americans, Public Commemoration, and the Haitian Revolution', in Jackson and Bacon (eds.), *African Americans and the Haitian Revolution*, p. 95.

36. Kerr-Ritchie, *Rites of August First*, pp. 83–5.

37. Gabriel, *Jubilee's Experiment*, pp. 304–5.

38. Ibid, pp. 309 and 312.

39. Ibid, p. 313.

40. Ibid, p. 315.

41. Ibid, p. 319.

42. Ibid, p. 317.

43. Davis, *The Emancipation Circuit*, p. 248.

44. Kerr-Ritchie, *Rites of August First*, p. 228.

45. Gabriel, *Jubilee's Experiment*, p. 320.

46. Ibid, p. 322.

47. Kathleen Ann Clark, *Defining Moments: African American Commemoration and Political Culture in the South*, Chapel Hill, NC: University of North Carolina Press, 2005, p. 1.

48. Mitch Kachun, *Festivals of Freedom: Memory and Meaning in African American Emancipation Celebrations*, Amherst, MA: University of Massachusetts Press, 2003.

49. Davis, *The Emancipation Circuit*, p. 93.

50. Ibid, pp. 64–6.

51. Edward Cotham, *Juneteenth*, College Station, TX: Texas A&M University Press, 2021, pp. 241–2.

52. David Blight, *Race and Reunion: The Civil War in American Memory*, Cambridge, MA: Harvard University Press, 2001, p. 2.

53. Kachun, *Festivals of Freedom*, p. 179.

54. Paul Shackel, *Memory in Black and White: Race, Commemoration and the Post-Bellum Landscape*, Walnut Creek, CA: Altamira Press, 2003, pp. 29 and 33.

55. Kirk Savage, *Standing Soldiers, Kneeling Slaves*, Princeton, NJ: Princeton University Press, 2018, p. x.

56. Blight, *Race and Reunion*, p. 288.

57. Erin Thompson, 'The Social Messages of Civil War Monuments', *History Compass*, 20:2 (February 2022), p. 6.

58. Shackel, *Memory in Black and White*, p. 129.

59. For the full text of this (recently recovered) letter, see Jonathan White and Scott Sandage, 'What Frederick Douglass Had to Say about Monuments', *Smithsonian Magazine* (30 June 2020).

60. For the full text, written around 1891, see Stauffer and Gates (eds.), *The Portable Frederick Douglass*, pp. 527–37.

61. Frederick Douglass, *Lecture on Haiti*, Chicago, 1893, p. 205.

62. Quoted in Hazareesingh, *Black Spartacus*, p. 346.

63. 'Introduction to *The Reason Why the Colored American Is Not in the World's Columbian Exposition*', in Stauffer and Gates (eds.), *The Portable Frederick Douglass*, p. 519.

64. See Yveline Alexis, *Haiti Fights Back*, New Brunswick, NJ: Rutgers University Press, 2021.

65. Robbie Shilliam, 'What about Marcus Garvey? Race and the Transformation of Sovereignty Debate', *Review of International Studies*, 32 (2006), pp. 379–80.

66. Quoted in Michael West, 'Garveyism Root and Branch: From the Age of Revolution to the Onset of Black Power', in R. J. Stephens and A. Ewing (eds.), *Global Garveyism*, Gainesville, FL: University Press of Florida, 2019, pp. 30 and 32.

67. Charles Carnegie, 'Garvey and the Black Transnation', *Small Axe*, 5 (March 1999), pp. 48–71.

68. West, 'Garveyism Root and Branch', pp. 18–19.

69. Ibid, pp. 25–6.

70. *Declaration of the Rights of the Negro Peoples of the World.*

71. Miriam Nyhan Grey, '"Ireland should be free, even as Africa shall be free": Marcus Garvey's Irish Influences', in P. Mannion and F. McGarry (eds.), *The Irish Revolution: A Global History*, New York: NYU Press, 2022, pp. 341 and 348.

72. Robbie Shilliam, '"Ethiopia shall stretch forth her hands unto God": Garveyism, Rastafari, and Antiquity', in D. Orrells et al. (eds.), *African Athena: New Agendas*, Oxford: Oxford University Press, 2011, p. 113.

73. Shilliam, 'What about Marcus Garvey?', pp. 397–8.

74. Quoted in Steven Hahn, *The Political Worlds of Slavery and Freedom*, Cambridge, MA: Harvard University Press, 2009, p. 134.

75. See Shilliam, '"Ethiopia shall stretch forth her hands unto God"'.

76. Garvey speech at UNIA meeting, New York, March 1920, in R. Hill (ed.), *The Marcus Garvey and Universal Negro Improvement Association Papers*, Berkeley, CA: University of California Press, 1983, vol. 2, p. 255.

77. Leslie R. James, 'Caribbean Icons in Uniform: A Comparative Analysis of Toussaint L'Ouverture, Marcus Garvey, and Fidel Castro', *Black Theology*, 16:2 (2018), pp. 119–20.

78. Hahn, *The Political Worlds of Slavery and Freedom*, p. 125.

79. See Mary G. Rolinson, *Grassroots Garveyism: The Universal Negro Improvement Association in the Rural South*, Chapel Hill, NC: University of North Carolina Press, 2007.

80. Ibid, pp. 150–54.

81. Hahn, *The Political Worlds of Slavery and Freedom*, pp. 142–5.

82. Shilliam, '"Ethiopia shall stretch forth her hands unto God"'.

83. See the chapters by Blain, Vinson, and Bourbonnais in Stephens and Ewing (eds.), *Global Garveyism*; see also Rodney Worrell, 'Women in the Barbadian Garveyite Movement', in V. A. Shepherd et al. (eds.), *Interrogating Injustices: Essays in Honour of Hilary McD. Beckles*, Kingston: Ian Randle, 2023, pp. 275–98. On the empowerment of black women in Canada, see Melissa Shaw, '"Who used to run the UNIA Hall?" Black Canadian Women's Leadership of Toronto Division 21, 1919–1939', *Journal of African American History*, 109:2 (Spring 2024), pp. 200–230.

84. Quoted in Hazareesingh, *Black Spartacus*, p. 354.

85. Adom Getachew, *Worldmaking after Empire: The Rise and Fall of Self-Determination*, Princeton, NJ: Princeton University Press, 2019, p. 72.

86. Ibid, p. 89.

87. Ibid, p. 83.

88. Ibid, p. 73.

89. Resolution adopted by the United Nations General Assembly: 1514 (XV), 'Declaration on the Granting of Independence to Colonial Countries and Peoples', 14 December 1960. http://www.un-documents.net/a15r1514.htm.

90. Getachew, *Worldmaking after Empire*, p. 78.

91. Ibid, p. 80.

92. Michael West, 'Decolonization, Desegregation, and Black Power: Garveyism in Another Era', in Stephens and Ewing (eds.), *Global Garveyism*, p. 271.

93. Ibid, p. 277.

94. Ibid, pp. 275 and 280.

95. Quoted in ibid, p. 281.

96. http://www.slaverymonuments.org/items/browse

97. https://www.nps.gov/places/000/african-american-civil-war-memorial-the-spirit-of-freedom.htm

98. Desmond Allen, 'GG [Governor General] Declares April 8 as National Chief Takyi Day', *Jamaica Observer* (7 April 2022).

99. Roberto Conduru, 'Transnational Counter-Monuments: Anti-Slavery and Pro-Freedom Memorials', *ReVista*, 20:3 (Spring–Summer 2021).

100. Ibid.

101. Myra Ann Houser, 'Avenging Carlota in Africa: Angola and the Memory of Cuban Slavery', *Atlantic Studies* 12:1 (2015), p. 62.

102. *Haitian Times* (4 January 2024).

103. 'Visionary Aponte: Art and Black Freedom', NYU (February–May 2018). The works featured can be seen in the exhibition catalogue: https://aponte.hosting.nyu.edu/wp-content/uploads/2019/09/Visionary-Aponte-Brochure-NYU.pdf

104. Conduru, 'Transnational Counter-Monuments'.

105. See Karen L. Cox, *No Common Ground: Confederate Monuments and the Ongoing Fight for Racial Justice*, Chapel Hill, NC: University of North Carolina Press, 2021.

106. Tamar Herzog, 'How Did Early-Modern Slaves in Spain Disappear? The Antecedents', *Republics of Letters*, 1 (September 2012), pp. 6–7.

107. Sam Jones and Ashifa Kassam, 'Portuguese Government Rejects President's Suggestion of Slavery Reparations', *The Guardian* (28 April 2024).

108. 'We Need to Tell People Everything', *The Guardian* (5 October 2023), pp. 93–116.

109. Laurence Brown, 'Monuments to Freedom, Monuments to Nation: The Politics of Emancipation and Remembrance in the Eastern Caribbean', *Slavery & Abolition*, 23:3 (2002), p. 109.

110. Ibid, p. 107.

111. Grindon et al., 'Mapping British Public Monuments', p. 390.

112. Beth Kowaleski Wallace, 'Uncomfortable Commemorations', *History Workshop Journal*, 68:1 (Autumn 2009), pp. 228–9.

113. J. R. Kerr-Ritchie, 'Reflections on the Bicentennial of the Abolition of the British Slave Trade', *Journal of African American History*, 93:4 (Fall 2008), pp. 532–42.

114. http://www.slaverymonuments.org/items/show/1165

115. Shamar Blunt, 'Barbados Celebrates Emancipation Day', *Barbados To-Day* (1 August 2024), https://barbadostoday.bb/2024/08/01/440765

116. Madge Dresser, 'Set in Stone?', *History Workshop Journal*, 61:1 (2007), p. 164.

117. For further discussion see Quito Swan, 'Smoldering Memories and Burning Questions: The Politics of Remembering Sally Bassett and Slavery in

Bermuda', in A. L. Araujo (ed.), *Politics of Memory: Making Slavery Visible in the Public Space*, London: Routledge, 2016, pp. 71–91.

118. https://www.nationaltrust.org.uk/who-we-are/research/addressing-our-histories-of-colonialism-and-historic-slavery

119. Grindon et al., 'Mapping British Public Monuments', p. 403.

120. Nelly Schmidt, 'Commémoration, histoire et historiographie: A propos du 150e anniversaire de l'abolition de l'esclavage', *Ethnologie Française*, 29:3 (July–September 1999), p. 455.

121. https://memorial-acte.fr

122. See Jean-Marie Théodat, 'Oser la Liberté – *We Could Be Heroes*', *Suds*, 288:2 (2023), pp. 225–31.

123. Quoted in Laura McGinnis, 'Memorialising Masculinity? Gendering the Iconography of French Colonialism and Anticolonial Resistance in Martinique and Guadeloupe', *Interventions*, 24:7 (2022), p. 1,080.

124. Ibid, pp. 1,082–3.

125. Ibid, pp. 1,084–5.

126. See for example Olivette Otele, 'To-day We Remember', *The Guardian* (23 August 2022).

127. Toni Morrison, *Beloved*, New York: Penguin, 1987.

128. Eleanor Shearer, *River Sing Me Home*, London, Headline, 2023.

129. Neil Roberts, *Freedom as Marronnage*, Chicago, IL: University of Chicago Press, 2015, pp. 11 and 27.

130. Ibid, pp. 116–17.

131. Sean Gerrity, 'Freedom on the Move: Marronage in Martin Delany's *Blake*', *Melus*, 43:3 (Fall 2018), p. 7.

132. Lawrie Balfour, *Toni Morrison: Imagining Freedom*, Oxford: Oxford University Press, 2023, pp. 22–3.

133. Speech at Fort de Joux, 27 April 2023, on the occasion of the 175th anniversary of the abolition of slavery; https://www.vie-publique.fr/discours/289309-emmanuel-macron-27042023-abolition-de-lesclavage-en-france

CONCLUSION: HONOURING OUR DEBTS

1. Thavolia Glymph, 'Paper Tracings in the Spectacularly Boisterous Archive of Slavery', *American Historical Review*, 130: 1 (2025), pp. 1–18.

2. See Sergio Lussana, *My Brother Slaves: Friendship, Masculinity, and Resistance in the Antebellum South*, Lexington, KY: University Press of Kentucky, 2016.

3. Douglass, *Narrative*, p. 70.

4. Stewart, *Three Eyes for the Journey*, pp. 33 and 60.

5. Michael O. West and William G. Martin, 'Haiti, I'm Sorry: The Haitian Revolution and the Forging of the Black International', in M. O. West, W. G. Martin, and F. C. Wilkins (eds.), *From Toussaint to Tupac: The Black International since the Age of Revolution*, Chapel Hill, NC: University of North Carolina Press, 2009, p. 82.

6. Nigel Worden, 'How a Slave from Mauritius Led a Rebellion in Cape Town', *GroundUp* (30 March 2016).

7. Camp, *Closer to Freedom*, pp. 6–7.

8. See Davis, *The Emancipation Circuit*.

9. Ibid, pp. 48–9.

10. Juliet Hooker, '"A black sister to Massachusetts": Latin America and the Fugitive Democratic Ethos of Frederick Douglass', *American Political Science Review*, 109:4 (2015), p. 691.

11. See Robbie Shilliam, *Decolonizing Politics: An Introduction*, Cambridge: Polity, 2021.

12. Achille Mbembe, *Critique of Black Reason*, Durham, NC: Duke University Press, 2017, pp. 28–9, 47 and 48.

13. Ta-Nehisi Coates, *The Message*, London: Penguin, 2025, p. 16.

14. Lanre Bakare, 'Cowrie Shell Sculpture Chosen as Slavery Memorial for London', *The Guardian* (23 August 2024). For a full discussion of London's memorializations of slavery over the past decade, see Katie Donington, '(In)human Capital: London and the Legacies of Transatlantic Slavery', *The London Journal*, 50:1 (Spring 2025), pp. 72–92.

15. Rebecca Klein, 'The Right-Wing US Textbooks that Teach Slavery as "Black Immigration"', *The Guardian* (12 August 2021).

16. For a comparative study of the memorializations of slavery in American plantation museums and British country houses, see Jessica Moody and Stephen Small, 'Slavery and Public History at the Big House: Remembering and Forgetting at American Plantation Museums and British Country Houses', *Journal of Global Slavery*, 4:1 (2019), pp. 34–68.

17. https://www.laflammedelegalite.org/le-concours/presentation

18. Françoise Vergès, 'The Slave Trade, Slavery, and Abolitionism: The Unfinished Debate in France', in Mulligan and Bric (eds.), *A Global History of Anti-Slavery Politics*, pp. 198–213.

19. 'Un Mémorial national des victimes de l'esclavage sera érigé aux Jardins du Trocadéro', *Le Monde* (22 September 2023).

20. The beneficiaries of the British and (both) French compensation schemes can be viewed at Legacies of Slavery: https://www.ucl.ac.uk/lbs/ and CNRS websites https://esclavage-indemnites.fr/public

21. Robert Allen, 'Past Due: The African American Quest for Reparations', *The Black Scholar*, 28:2 (1998), pp. 7–8.

22. Ana Lucia Araujo, *Reparations for Slavery and the Slave Trade: A Transnational and Comparative History*, London: Bloomsbury, 2017, p. 50.

23. For further details, see Hannah Durkin, *Survivors: The Lost Stories of the Last Captives of the Atlantic Slave Trade*, London: William Collins (2024), pp. 247–9.

24. On this theme, see Manjapra, *Black Ghost of Empire*.

25. David Scott, 'Evil Beyond Repair', *Small Axe*, 22:1 (March 2018), p. viii; see also his more recent *Irreparable Evil: An Essay in Moral and Reparatory History*, New York: Columbia University Press, 2024.

26. See Daniel Butt, 'Settling Claims for Reparations', *Journal of Race, Gender, and Ethnicity*, 11:1 (2022), pp. 60–79. For a 'constructive' defence of reparations more generally, see Olúfémi Táíwò, *Reconsidering Reparations*, New York: Oxford University Press, 2022.

27. Declaration of the first Abuja Pan-African Conference on Reparations for African Enslavement, Colonization and Neo-Colonization, sponsored by the Organization of African Unity, April 1993.

28. Hilary Beckles, 'The Reparation Movement: Greatest Political Tide of the Twenty-First Century', *Social and Economic Studies*, 68:3/4 (2019), pp. 11–30.

29. 'Public Health Crisis', in 'Ten Point Action Plan: Caribbean Community Reparations Commission', *Africology: The Journal of Pan African Studies*, 9:5 (August 2016), p. 118.

30. Amelia Gentleman, 'African and Caribbean Nations Agree on Move to Seek Reparations for Slavery', *The Guardian* (17 November 2023).

31. Rachel Swarns, *The 272: The Families Who Were Enslaved and Sold to Build the American Catholic Church*, New York: Random House, 2023.

32. Beckles, 'The Reparation Movement', p. 22.

33. https://www.nationaltrust.org.uk/who-we-are/research/addressing-our-histories-of-colonialism-and-historic-slavery

34. Nathan Standley, 'Church Fund "Not Enough" to Right Slavery Wrongs', BBC News (4 March 2024), https://www.bbc.com/news/articles/cjrjv9r1jyko

35. 'Déclaration du Président de la République sur la relation entre la France et Haïti', Paris, 17 April 2025, https://www.elysee.fr/emmanuel-macron/2025/04/17/declaration-du-president-de-la-republique-sur-la-relation-entre-la-france-et-haiti.

36. 'The Significance of Emancipation in the West Indies', speech given in New York, May 1857, in Stauffer and Gates (eds.), *The Portable Frederick Douglass*, p. 288.

Glossary

abolitionist	person who believes slavery should be outlawed (see also **emancipation** and **self-emancipation**)
affranchi	newly emancipated person in French colonies (see also *nouveau libre*)
Age of Revolutions	mass-driven political challenges to European empires and slavery in the Atlantic world from the 1760s to 1848
Amerindian	original native population of Americas (see also **Taino**)
amulet	sacred object worn on the body for protection and healing (see also *bolsas de mandinga* and *gris-gris*)
Arawak	Amerindian language spoken by Taino people
Baptist insurrection	revolt of enslaved people in Jamaica (1831–2)
béké	white settler in French Caribbean colonies
bolsas de mandinga	sacred pouches used for bodily protection and spiritual well-being in Angola and colonial Brazil (see also **amulet** and *gris-gris*)
Bourbon Island	French colonial name for Réunion Island until 1848
bozale, bossale	African-born enslaved person in the Americas
bukra	white settler in British Caribbean colonies and the American South
cabildo	African fraternal association in Cuba and the Spanish Americas
captain	maroon military commander responsible for training combatants and organizing attacks against settlers
captive	enslaved person
cimarrón	original Spanish slaver term for maroon
Code Noir	French rule book first published in 1685 codifying treatment of the enslaved

colon	white settler in French colonies
conjuror	person recognized for their Obeah skills in the United States
creole	black, mixed-race or white person born in the Atlantic colonies, as opposed to Europe or Africa (see also *kreyol*)
diaspora (black)	African peoples forcibly separated from their place of birth through enslavement in Europe, the Americas, or the Indian Ocean
divination	art of foretelling the future and communicating with spirits
doctor	title used as a sign of respect for Obeah-men and women in the Americas
dugout	canoe used by maroons for maritime escapes
emancipation	collective freeing of enslaved people through official abolition of human bondage
erasure	amnesia or deliberate concealment of past events about slavery and enslaved resistance
free black people	black populations in slave societies who are not enslaved
free community	settlement of former enslaved people granted emancipation by local colonial authorities
free state	state in the USA where slavery was prohibited before the 1865 Emancipation
French negro	white-slaver term across the English-speaking Americas referring to a black person from Saint-Domingue
fugitive	person who has escaped from their enslaver
gradualist	abolitionist who believed slavery should be ended in stages rather than immediately
gris-gris	small cloth pouch worn in Africa and in the Americas for bodily protection and spiritual well-being (see also **amulet,** *bolsas de mandinga*)
Hispaniola	original Spanish name for the second-largest Caribbean island, today divided between Haiti and the Dominican Republic
houngan	*vodou* priest in Saint-Domingue and Haiti
human bondage	slavery
Ile de France	French colonial name for Mauritius until 1810
jihad	Islamic holy war
kalinda	African-originating dance performed by black communities in the Caribbean

king, queen	titles of authority given to maroon leaders in fugitive settlements
kreyol	languages that developed in Atlantic and Indian Ocean colonies through mixing between European and non-European languages
ladino	black person born in Spain or Portugal (or living there for some time), and familiar with Iberian culture and Christian religion
lwa	*vodou* spirit
macandal	type of fetish named after Saint-Domingue maroon leader
Makandalism	revolutionary anti-slavery doctrine asserting that black emancipation required the elimination of colonial white settlers
Malagasy	person from the Indian Ocean island of Madagascar
Mama Wata	female water spirit worshipped for protection on both sides of the Atlantic
manumission	legal freeing of an individual enslaved person from bondage, typically through death or financial compensation of the slaver, or military service
marabout	Islamic cleric and learned man
maroon	runaway enslaved person (in French, *marron*)
marronage	flight by enslaved person or people (in French, *marronnage*); sometimes distinguished between a short-term absence (*petit marronnage*) and a lengthier escape (*grand marronnage*)
Middle Passage	forcible transportation of captives in slave ships from west Africa to the Americas
mocambo	Portuguese term for runaway settlement
nouveau libre	newly emancipated enslaved person in French colonies (see also *affranchi*)
oath	pledge sworn by enslaved people to affirm group loyalty and shared purpose
Obeah	African-originating spiritual system appealing to natural and supernatural forces for healing, poisoning, protection, and divination
Obeah-man, -woman	person with recognized Obeah skills
Ogun	west African spirit of warfare, iron, and hunting
oubli	French term for historical amnesia or erasure of enslaved resistance

palenque	Spanish term for runaway settlement
pardo	mixed-race person in Spanish colonies
petro	fiery variant of Saint-Domingue *vodou* created by Dom Pedro
philosophe	major writer and thinker in the French Enlightenment era
priest, priestess	intermediary between humans and the spiritual world in traditional African and enslaved religious systems in the Americas
quilombo	central-African originating term for runaway slave settlement in Portuguese colonies
Qur'an	central religious text of Islam
ring shout	spiritual dance around a sacred object in the American South and the Caribbean
runaway	person who has escaped from their enslaver
Saint-Domingue	French part of island of Hispaniola before Haitian independence
Santo Domingo	Spanish part of island of Hispaniola before advent of Dominican Republic
self-emancipation	liberation of enslaved person through their own agency or group action
settler	white colonist
shipmates	expression used by enslaved captives who travelled together on the same slave ship during Middle Passage
slave narrative	published autobiographical account of experiences of enslavement
soba	local military and spiritual leader in pre-colonial Africa
syncretic	quality of a spiritual or religious system combining elements from different cultural traditions and geographical areas (see also *vodou* and ***vodun***)
Taino	historic indigenous people of the Caribbean
trader	person engaging in the commerce of enslaved African people
West India interest	principal lobby in Britain defending slavery
vodou	religion from west Africa, developed among black communities in Saint-Domingue and Haiti, combining Taino, Caribbean, Christian, and African spiritual elements
vodun	west African religious and spiritual systems centering on spirit worship, divination, healing, and the cult of ancestors

Timeline of Enslaved Resistance

1503	ongoing maroon activity reported by Spanish governor in Hispaniola
1519	African and Taino maroons based in the Baoruco Mountains launch rebellion against Spanish rule in Hispaniola
1521	Wolof Christmas-day uprising against Spanish settlers in Hispaniola
1523	first of extended series of anti-slavery insurrections in Mexico, including 1537 plot to 'kill all Spaniards and seize their land'
1526	Kongo King Nzinga Mbemba writes to Portuguese king protesting against slave traders' operations on his territory
1527	first captive insurrection against Spanish slavers in Puerto Rico
1530s	maroon revolts against Spanish slavers in Panama, leading to emergence of leader Bayano
1532	captive revolt on Portuguese slave ship *Misericordia*, one of the first recorded insurrections during the Middle Passage
1552	Miguel initiates rebellion against Spanish settlers in Venezuela, South America
1570s	Nyanga revolt in Mexico, eventually leading to recognition of free community of San Lorenzo in 1618
1580	treaty between Spanish authorities in Panama and maroon rebels leads to free settlement of Santiago del Príncipe (followed in 1582 by settlement of Santa Cruz la Real)
1594	Kafuxi Ambari defeats Portuguese colonial forces and establishes enduring anti-slavery haven in Angolan province of Kisama, Africa

1595	major uprising against Portuguese in São Tomé island, off the coast of West Africa, led by Amador
1599	Benkos Biohó initiates revolt against Spanish rule in Cartagena, South America
1605	Palmares free communities emerge in colonial Brazil, eventually joining forces under ruler Gana Zumba to resist European slaver attacks
1612	plot to poison Spanish slavers' food and water in Mexico City
1620	priestess Leonor vows to 'kill, maim and dismember' Spanish settler population at Cartagena Inquisition Tribunal
1638	captive rebellion on Caribbean island of Providence
1642	Dutch forcibly transport 142 captives to Mauritius, more than half of whom immediately escape
1680	Zumbi becomes Palmares leader after rejecting agreement signed by Gana Zumba with Portuguese, and fights on until defeat in 1694
1684	Angolan prince Lourenço da Silva Mendonça presents anti-slavery petition to Pope in Vatican City
1685	first publication of Code Noir, French rule book codifying treatment of the enslaved
1687	maroon insurrection against British slavers in Antigua, part of wider pattern of rebellion in 1685–1700 period
1692	intensification of maroon attacks against plantations around Camamú in Bahia, Brazil; large-scale conspiracy in Barbados
1695	maroon insurgents destroy Dutch fort in Mauritius
1712	rebellion by African and Amerindian captives in New York
1719	plot by maroons in Minas Gerais province, Brazil
1719	maroons on Saint Vincent island (eastern Caribbean) defeat French military expedition
1724	maroons attack French fort in Mauritius (and again in 1732)
1730	Sarah Bassett sentenced to death in Bermuda for attempted poisoning of white slavers
1733	captive rebellion on Saint John, Danish Virgin Islands
1735	Mandinga maroons establish settlement in Oaxacan mountains in Mexico, eventually recognized as free community in 1769

1737	maroon plot in Guadeloupe to kill settlers and liberate island
1739	Stono rebellion in South Carolina (September)
1739–40	First Maroon War in Jamaica ends with treaties between British authorities and Jamaican maroons
1740	maroon leader Makandal begins his anti-slavery campaign in Saint Domingue's northern province
1741	arson revolt of enslaved people in New York
1743	*Jolly Batchelor* slave ship attacked in Sierra Leone, captives freed
1756	captive rebellion in Futa Jallon leads to creation of fortified free town of Kondeah
1758	Makandal captured and executed after trial in Saint-Domingue
1760	series of revolts against British slave order in Jamaica
1760, 1762, 1767	major treaties between Dutch authorities and maroons in Surinam
1763	revolt in Berbice (Guyana) under leadership of Atta and Cuffy
1765	Islamic revolt against slave trade in Senegambia
1770	captive revolt on slave ship *Unity*
1772	publication of James Albert Ukawsaw Gronniosaw's *Narrative*
1775	revolt by Malagasy captives on slave ship *Flore*
1784–5	First Maroon War in Dominica (conflicts continue until 1814)
1785	launching of Yangiakuri rebellion in Upper Guinea
1787	creation of Society for the Abolition of the Slave Trade in London; publication of Ottobah Cugoano's *Thoughts and Sentiments*
1788	creation of Société des Amis des Noirs in Paris (February)
1789	French Revolution proclaims Rights of Man (July); publication of Olaudah Equiano's *Interesting Narrative*
1791	enslaved uprising begins in Saint-Domingue (August)
1793	republican decree abolishing slavery in Saint-Domingue (August)
1794	general abolition of slavery by French Convention (February)
1795	enslaved uprising in the Dutch colony of Curaçao, and in Coro (Venezuela); Second Maroon War in Jamaica

1795–8	series of anti-slavery arsonist conspiracies in Charleston, South Carolina
1796	slave ship *Young Tom* attacked from African shores, captives liberated
1797	publication of Toussaint Louverture's *Réfutation*
1798	British defeat in Saint-Domingue by Toussaint Louverture's army
1799	anti-slavery uprising in Cartagena, South America (April)
1800	Gabriel planned conspiracy in Richmond, Virginia
1801	Toussaint Louverture constitution in Saint-Domingue
1802	Napoleon restores slavery in French colonies, provoking republican insurrection led by Louis Delgrès in Guadeloupe (May)
1803	French army defeated by Saint-Domingue insurgents at battle of Vertières (November)
1804	proclamation of Haitian independence (January); launching of Usman dan Fodio *jihad* against Sultan of Gobir in West Africa
1806	first of series of revolts in Bahia (Brazil), running until mid-1830s; conspiracy uncovered in Güines (Cuba)
1807	abolition of Atlantic slave trade by Britain and United States
1808	Cape Town captive revolt, led by Louis van Mauritius
1809	rebellion of African-born captives in St Mary's parish, Jamaica
1811	Louisiana revolt led by Charles Deslondes (January); Saint-Leu uprising in Réunion island (November)
1812	Aponte rebellion uncovered by Cuban authorities (April)
1816	Barbados anti-slavery rebellion (April); Simón Bolívar expeditions to liberate South America from Spanish rule assisted by Haitians (March, December)
1818	ruler of Futa Jallon, Abdulkadur, decrees transatlantic slave trade is incompatible with Islamic teaching
1820s	Obeah conspiracies in Martinique meet with fierce repression by French authorities
1822	uncovering of Charleston anti-slavery plot led by Denmark Vesey (June); Carbet uprising in Martinique (October)
1823	Demerera anti-slavery revolt (August); Boxing Day rebellion uncovered in Jamaica (December)

1824	publication of Elizabeth Heyrick's *Immediate Not Gradual Abolition*
1825	Sierra Leone captive revolt leads to creation of free community of Tambakka; Matanzas rebellion in Cuba
1826	maroon uprising in Urubu *quilombo* in Bahia, with Zeferina among its leaders
1827	publication of New York-based *Freedom's Journal*, first African-American newspaper (March)
1829	formal abolition of slavery in Mexico by President Vincente Guerrero (September); publication of David Walker's *Appeal to the coloured citizens of the world*
1830–31	captive revolts in Martinique and Guadeloupe
1831	Nat Turner rebellion in Virginia (August); Baptist insurrection in Jamaica (December)
1833	Abolition Act adopted by British Parliament (May), in the wake of Jamaican insurrection
1833	Banes rebellion in Cuba (August)
1835	major anti-slavery uprising in San Salvador, Bahia (January)
1838	West African revolt by abolitionist leader Bilali leads to creation of free community of Laminyah; Moses Roper publishes *Narrative of the Adventures and Escape of Moses Roper*
1839	*Amistad* slave-ship revolt (July); after trial in USA surviving captives return to Sierra Leone in 1841
1842	publication of Victor Schoelcher's *Des colonies françaises: abolition immédiate de l'esclavage*
1843–4	La Escalera revolts and conspiracies in Cuba
1845	publication of *Narrative of the Life of Frederick Douglass*, the first of his three autobiographical works
1848	abolition of slavery by French Second Republic (March)
1852	publication of Harriet Beecher Stowe's *Uncle Tom's Cabin*, followed in 1856 by *Dred*
1853	publication of Frederick Douglass's novel *The Heroic Slave*, followed in 1855 by his second memoir, *My Bondage and My Freedom*
1859	John Brown anti-slavery revolt at Harpers Ferry, Virginia (October)
1861	publication of Harriet Jacobs' *Incidents in the Life of a Slave Girl*

1863	Lincoln Emancipation Proclamation (January); Harriet Tubman carries out Combahee River raid in South Carolina, rescuing hundreds of black men and women from servitude (June)
1865	Morant Bay rebellion in Jamaica (October); Thirteenth Amendment ratified, ending slavery across the USA (December)
1876	inauguration of emancipation memorial in Washington DC, with speech by Frederick Douglass (April)
1886	abolition of slavery in Cuba (October)
1888	abolition of slavery in Brazil (May)
1914	Marcus Garvey creates Universal Negro Improvement Association (UNIA) (August)
1920	UNIA issues *Declaration of The Rights of the Negro Peoples of the World* (August)
1945	Fifth Pan-African Congress calls for 'autonomy and independence' of black Africa (October)
1958	Kwame Nkrumah hosts All-African People's Conference, calls for immediate decolonization of Africa (December)
1960	United Nations General Assembly Resolution 1514 adopts the principle of self-determination for all peoples (December)
1965	Malcolm X creates Organization of Afro-American Unity (June)
1971	Aimé Césaire inaugurates monument to enslaved woman by Khokho René-Corail in Fort-de-France (Martinique)
1975	Fidel Castro names Cuban anti-imperialist intervention in Angola 'Operation Carlota' (November)
1993	First Pan-African Conference on Reparations issues Abuja Declaration (April)
1997	UNESCO establishes 23 August (the start of Saint-Domingue's slave insurrection in 1791) as the International Day for the Remembrance of the Slave Trade and its Abolition
1998	Bussa honoured as one of the national heroes of Barbados, after statue erected in 1985
2001	French Taubira law recognizes slave trade and slavery as crimes against humanity (May); Durban World Conference against Racism declares slavery to be a crime against humanity (September)

2006	President Jacques Chirac adopts 10 May as French national memorial day of commemoration of slavery and its abolitions
2009	unveiling of Sally Bassett statue in Bermuda, celebrating her sacrifice for racial equality (February)
2011	Brazil makes 20 November the official National Day of Zumbi and Black Awareness
2013	Caribbean Community (CARICOM) sets up Reparations Commission, whose ten-point plan for reparatory justice is endorsed by heads of government in March 2014
2014	Denmark Vesey monument inaugurated in Charleston, South Carolina (February)
2021	Juneteenth (June 19th) becomes federal holiday in US to commemorate ending of slavery
2022	inauguration of statue of Solitude in Paris, the first dedicated to a black woman (May)
2023	official opening of Intercontinental Slavery Museum in Port Louis, Mauritius (September); African Union Accra summit adopts declaration calling for slavery reparations (November)
2024	*Oser La Liberté* exhibition in Panthéon, Paris (November 2023–February 2024)

Acknowledgements

This book could not have been written without the friendship and generosity of all those who encouraged me to undertake this project and accompanied me throughout its execution. In the beginning there was Marisa Fuentes, whom I first met when she came to Balliol College, Oxford, as an Oliver Smithies Visiting Fellow in 2019–20. Marisa's ground-breaking scholarship on slavery was an inspiration, as was her determination critically to reflect on the sources that underpin its history; her resolute support and timely feedback were invaluable as I was completing my book proposal. Laurent Dubois took in the manuscript at an early stage, combining insightful comments with fertile suggestions; his enthusiasm was wonderfully reassuring. Robbie Shilliam carefully went through my entire draft, and shared his immense knowledge of the histories of Atlantic slavery, colonialism, and religious movements with his characteristic analytical rigour and fraternal warmth. I learned a lot from my exchanges with these distinguished colleagues and this book is much improved in light of their observations.

My exploration of enslaved resistance in Cuba was guided by Manuel Barcia's expertise, notably on the Afro-Cuban anti-slavery connections that his scholarship has done so much to recover; Manuel also made effective suggestions about the book's conceptual framework. Maxine Berg, whose recently published volume (co-authored with Pat Hudson) on slavery and capitalism has been a landmark, likewise supplied excellent recommendations for my chapter on British abolitionism. Des King has been marvellously supportive of my endeavours over the years, and his close reading of my American chapter was tremendously helpful. I am also grateful to Phaidra Buchanan for her comments on this chapter, and particularly for her emphasis on the importance of solidarity as a crucial underpinning of enslaved resistance; her insights from her experiences of learning about and teaching slavery in American high schools were illuminating. Phaidra represents the best of Balliol's PPE traditions of scholarship, internationalism, and social responsibility, and it was a pleasure to have her with us in Oxford.

Colleagues from political theory helped me work through some key issues surrounding the intellectual aspects of resistance. Adom Getachew's reconstruction of the Haitian revolution's universalism helped me foreground its ideal of autonomy as one of this book's overarching themes; her comments on my section on Marcus Garvey and Garveyism were much appreciated. My Balliol colleague Daniel Butt shared his vast knowledge of contemporary discussions around historical injustices and international mobilizations for reparations. I would like to express my thanks to Lawrie Balfour, who spent a memorable year with us as a Winant Visiting Fellow in 2023; her superb book on Toni Morrison helped me reflect on the complexities of freedom as seen from the perspective of the enslaved. It is also a pleasure to record my gratitude to Quentin Skinner for his ever-generous support, and for his stimulating observations on the intellectual limitations of Anglo-American abolitionist thinking.

The book was enriched by contributions from colleagues on a range of specific questions. Toby Green and Ricardo Soares de Oliveira pointed me in the right directions as I was beginning my research on the history of slavery in Africa. Robin Kelley helped me navigate my way around the complex issues surrounding shifting linguistic conventions about enslavement. Gusti Gaillard Pourchet talked me through the histories of Haitian debt and *vodou*, and suggested fruitful avenues for tapping into the collective memory of the revolution in post-independence Haiti. Tony Crowley drew on his colossal literary knowledge to assist my search for creative portrayals of captive resistance in modern novels. Ahmed Ziat translated a passage written in Arabic from a notebook found on an anti-slavery rebel in Bahia in 1835, and helped me establish its religious significance; and my huge thanks to John-Paul Ghobrial as well for generously sharing his expertise in Islamic writings and transnational history. Marina Ristuccia's accounts of her trips to Brazil and Mexico helped me make sense of the contrasting commemorations of enslaved rebellions in the Americas, while Diana Berruezo-Sánchez shone a light on the complexities of public discussions of Atlantic slavery in Spain. In Mauritius, Nikhita Obeegadoo made stimulating comparative observations about slave narratives, and Issa Asgarally kindly shared his research on the history of enslaved resistance. I would also like to pay tribute to Vijaya Teelock's remarkable scholarship, which has enabled me to appreciate both the historical significance of slavery on the island and the weight of its legacies. I was fortunate to be invited to present some of my research at the recently inaugurated Intercontinental Slavery Museum in Port Louis, and am grateful to Vijaya Teelock and Jimmy Harmon for their welcome, and to all those who attended the seminar for their questions and comments. Robbie Shilliam led an enriching conversation with me at a webinar hosted by the School of the Sacrament Rastafari University, and it was a great blessing to exchange ideas with all the brothers and sisters present.

A serendipitous moment as I was finishing the book was my visit to the 'Oser la Liberté' exhibition in Paris in late 2023, dedicated to the history of enslaved resistance in France and the Atlantic world. In the imposing crypt of the Panthéon, where the great French abolitionist Victor Schoelcher is buried, and plaques commemorate the anti-slavery struggles of Toussaint Louverture and Louis Delgrès, many of the episodes, themes, and figures I had been writing about came to life through evocative visual displays of paintings, sculptures, and manuscripts. One of the main sponsors of the exhibition was the Fondation pour la Mémoire de l'Esclavage, which under the leadership of Jean-Marc Ayrault and Pierre-Yves Bocquet has done so much to promote a fuller understanding of the history of slavery in France. I was subsequently privileged to meet the exhibition's brilliant curator Florence Alexis, who personifies the humanism of the Haitian revolutionary tradition. Florence introduced me to a rich collection of online sources about slavery and generously shared with me her extensive knowledge of the iconography of enslaved resistance.

This book has enjoyed the patronage of a pair of magnificent editors, Stuart Proffitt at Allen Lane and Alex Star at Farrar, Straus & Giroux. It has been a privilege to work with these two dedicated professionals, who have such a profound understanding of the importance of this subject. I thank them both for their continuing confidence in me, for their unwavering encouragement, and for their insightful comments on the manuscript, delivered with typical promptness in both cases. At Penguin I also thank Vartika Rastogi for reading through an early draft of the manuscript and offering excellent advice and suggestions, Richard Duguid for steering the book through its production phase with his usual dexterity, Richard Mason for his wonderfully smooth and sharp-eyed copy-editing, Stephen Ryan for his extraordinarily thorough and dedicated proofreading, and Mark Wells for the remarkable and exquisitely crafted index. I am also grateful to Amanda Russell for her brilliant work with sourcing and licensing the images.

At Oxford it is a pleasure to acknowledge the institutional support provided by Balliol College and the Department of Politics and International

Relations, which furnished me with research grants as well as a two-term sabbatical in autumn 2023 and spring 2024, during which most of this book's first draft was written. At Balliol I warmly thank the Senior Tutor Nicky Trott for her unstinting support, as well as my PPE colleagues who covered for me during my absence. I also salute the Master of Balliol Helen Ghosh for creating the 'Balliol and Empire' programme which included a significant strand about the history of slavery. Among its most significant outputs was the 'Slavery in the Age of Revolution' exhibition in 2021, which was organized by the Balliol Library. I here record my appreciation to our librarians Naomi Tiley, Aishah Olubaji, and Nigel Buckley for all their fantastic work, and their practical help with my research.

I would like to offer a special tribute to my dear friend and colleague Oliver St Clair Franklin, CBE, Honorary British Consul for Greater Philadelphia and Honorary Fellow of Balliol. Oliver has generously deployed his ambassadorial skills to promote my work in the United States, and has been a constant source of encouragement for this project, from its tentative early moments all the way through to its final stages, and his energy and dedication in nurturing a wider public understanding of Atlantic slavery are much appreciated. He read my last two chapters and I am grateful for his perceptive comments and insights, as well as his enthusiastic support – all the more of an honour for me as Oliver's lineage descends from the indomitable Nat Turner. Oliver also helped organize a seminar at Temple University, Philadelphia, in 2022 during which I presented some of my initial findings, and it was a privilege to have the opportunity to exchange ideas with colleagues from Temple's Departments of History, Africology and African-American Studies, and Biology; I am especially indebted to Diane Turner, Seema Freer and Molefi Kete Asante for their encouragement.

'Special' is also the apposite term for my fabulous agent James Gill, who has resolutely stood by me over the past decades and has been a purveyor of excellent suggestions, wise advice, and good cheer. He has been a steadfast friend and working with him is an absolute delight. I am especially thrilled that he has now brought his outstanding talents over to Felicity Bryan Associates, and is thus only a few hundred yards down the road from me in Oxford. Thank you Jim for all the practical and moral support, and I look forward to many more fruitful collaborations in the years to come.

The best is always left for the end. Karma Nabulsi has been my loyal accomplice throughout this epic journey, and I could not have completed it without her love and intellectual companionship. As with all my previous projects, she was always there by my side, listening to my anecdotes, asking all the pertinent questions, and assisting me in making sense of the material by teasing out its complexities. Karma combed through my draft with consummate deftness, wielding her editorial magic on my stylistic imperfections and helping me see the world through the eyes of the enslaved resisters, and portray their courage, humanity, and vision. Her scholarship is magnificently authoritative on the subject of resistance to colonial and imperial domination, and I have drawn upon her knowledge, insights, and wisdom throughout this book.

S.H.
Calodyne
December 2024

Index

Abdulkadur (ruler of Futa Jallon), 25
abolitionism in Britain: African Institution, 184; anti-slavery petitions, 182, 198, 200; anti-slavery views in children's literature, 182; British Anti-Slavery Society, 195–6, 199–200, 203; and compensating of slave-owners, 186, 200, 202, 334; deference to/overlap with slaver views, 174, 180, 183, 184, 186, 188, 192–3, 195–6, 198–9, 202–3, 233; doctrine of gradualism, 173–6, 181, 182–3, 184, 194, 195–6, 202–3, 234; failure to imagine Africans as fully human subjects, 4, 174, 183–4, 194, 196, 203–4, 227, 330; and Haitian revolution, 145, 184–6, 196–7; Jacobin and anti-British labels, 180, 181, 202; momentum towards immediate abolition in 1820s, 175, 177, 182, 198–200, 202, 203; parliamentary bill on registration (1815), 164–5; parliamentary bills in 1790s, 182; Quaker involvement, 198; racialized view of African captives, 183–5, 188, 192–3,

195, 196–7, 202, 203–4, 213–14, 215–16, 227; radical voices in 1820s/30s, 198–200, 204; settlers blame for revolts, 164–5, 166, 181, 185; and Sierra Leone, 194–5; and slave narratives, 188–93, 194, 335; John Smith as martyr for cause, 167, 198, 318; Society for Effecting the Abolition of the Slave Trade, 182, 209; sugar boycotts, 179, 182, 198, 199; vantage point of cultural/racial superiority, 182–7, 234; Wedgwood's clay medallion, 184, 199; and *Zong* atrocity (1781), 179; *see also* Clarkson, Thomas; Wilberforce, William
abolitionism in France: and black empowerment/self-determination, 207, 208, 210–11, 214, 227, 235, 330; British material/intellectual influence over, 209–10, 211, 226, 228–9, 233–4; and compensating of slave-owners, 235, 322, 334; doctrine of gradualism, 209–11, 226, 228–9, 230, 231–2; and Haitian revolution, 154–5, 181, 206–7, 208, 215, 226–8,

232–3, 234, 235; under July Monarchy, 228–9, 230–34; and Laveaux, 142, 206, 208, 213, 214, 215; liberal support for indemnity on Haiti (1825), 227–8, 234; republican break with gradualism (1840s), 229–32; Restoration era, 225–7, 233–4; *Revue des Colonies*, 230; Société de la Morale Chrétienne, 225–7; Société des Amis des Noirs (Society of the Friends of the Blacks), 208–12, 214–16; Société des Hommes de Couleur, 224; Société Française pour l'Abolition de l'Esclavage, 228–9, 231–2; Sonthonax's revisionist account of history of, 215–16; vantage point of cultural/racial superiority, 16–17, 207, 211–12, 227, 234, 300, 302; weak and contradictory nature of, 214
abolitionism in USA: American Anti-Slavery Society, 275, 276, 286; black narratives, 275–8, 279–82, 284–5, 294; John Brown's revolt, 288, 290; Civil War narrative marginalized, 306; contradictions,